Preface

Software engineering is an ever-evolving discipline at the heart of the technological revolution that has transformed our world. In an era where software powers our daily lives, from the devices in our pockets to the systems that drive global enterprises, understanding the principles and practices of software engineering is more critical than ever before. This book aims to serve as a comprehensive guide to the field of software engineering, offering both beginners and experienced professionals a thorough understanding of the fundamental concepts, methodologies, and best practices that underpin the creation of high-quality software. Our journey through the world of software engineering begins with a deep dive into its fundamentals. We explore the nature of software, debunk myths that surround it, and introduce various software process models that have shaped the way we develop software. Maintenance, often an underestimated aspect of software engineering, is examined in detail, emphasizing the importance of keeping software systems healthy and up-to-date. In a world increasingly shaped by object-oriented thinking, we introduce you to the Unified Modeling Language (UML) and object-oriented principles. It serves as both a comprehensive foundation and a springboard for exploring advanced topics, emerging trends, and evolving best practices.

Key Features

Extensive Theoretical Content: The book covers the full spectrum of deep learning topics, from fundamental concepts to advanced techniques. Each chapter is designed to build on the previous one, ensuring a logical progression and deep comprehension of the subject matter.

Online Test Papers: To reinforce your learning, we provide a series of online test papers that mimic real-world scenarios and challenges. These tests are designed to evaluate your understanding and help you identify areas that need further study.

Video Tutorials: Understanding deep learning concepts can sometimes be challenging through text alone. Our book includes links to a series of video tutorials that provide visual and auditory explanations of complex topics. These videos are created by experts and are intended to complement the written material, offering a more immersive learning experience.

Practical Applications: Each chapter includes real-world examples and case studies that illustrate how deep learning is applied across different industries. These examples help bridge the gap between theory and practice, demonstrating the practical relevance of deep learning skills.

Self-Assessment Tools: At the end of each chapter, self-assessment questions and exercises allow you to test your understanding and track your progress. These tools are invaluable in helping you gauge your readiness and build confidence as you move forward.

Our goal is to empower you to become a proficient software engineer, capable of tackling complex challenges, creating innovative solutions, and contributing to the advancement of technology. We invite you to embark on this journey through the fascinating world of software engineering.

Contents

Chapter 1: Introduction to Software Engineering

1.1 Definition and Scope of Software Engineering

What is Software Engineering?

The term software engineering is the product of two words, software, and engineering.

The software is a collection of integrated programs.

Software subsists of carefully-organized instructions and code written by developers on any of various particular computer languages.

Computer programs and related documentation such as requirements, design models and user manuals.

Engineering is the application of scientific and practical knowledge to invent, design, build, maintain, and improve frameworks, processes, etc.

Software Engineering is an engineering branch related to the evolution of software product using well-defined scientific principles, techniques, and procedures. The result of software engineering is an effective and reliable software product.

Why is Software Engineering required?

Software Engineering is required due to the following reasons:

1. To manage large software
2. For more Scalability
3. Cost Management
4. To manage the dynamic nature of software
5. For better quality Management

Need of Software Engineering

The necessity of software engineering appears because of a higher rate of progress in user requirements and the environment on which the program is working.

Huge Programming: It is simpler to manufacture a wall than to a house or building, similarly, as the measure of programming become extensive engineering has to step to give it a scientific process.

Adaptability: If the software procedure were not based on scientific and engineering ideas, it would be simpler to re-create new software than to scale an existing one.

Cost: As the hardware industry has demonstrated its skills and huge manufacturing has let down the cost of computer and electronic hardware. But the cost of programming remains high if the proper process is not adapted.
Dynamic Nature: The continually growing and adapting nature of programming hugely depends upon the environment in which the client works. If the quality of the software is continually changing, new upgrades need to be done in the existing one.
Quality Management: Better procedure of software development provides a better and quality software product.
Characteristics of a good software engineer

The features that good software engineers should possess are as follows
Exposure to systematic methods, i.e., familiarity with software engineering principles.
Good technical knowledge of the project range (Domain knowledge).
Good programming abilities.
Good communication skills. These skills comprise of oral, written, and interpersonal skills.
High motivation.
Sound knowledge of fundamentals of computer science.
Intelligence.
Ability to work in a team
Discipline, etc.

Main Attributes of Software Engineering
Software Engineering is a systematic, disciplined, quantifiable study and approach to the design, development, operation, and maintenance of a software system. There are Four main Attributes of Software Engineering.
Efficiency
Reliability
Robustness
Maintainability

Scope of Software Engineering
The field of software engineering offers a wide scope with numerous opportunities and challenges. Here are some key points highlighting the scope of software engineering:
Vast Demand: The demand for software engineers continues to grow as software plays an increasingly critical role in various industries.
Diverse Career Paths: Software engineering offers a broad range of career options, including software developer, software architect, quality assurance engineer, data scientist, and more.
Cross-Industry Relevance: Software is ubiquitous across industries, including healthcare, finance, entertainment, and transportation, creating opportunities in various sectors.
Innovation Hub: Software engineers drive innovation, working on cutting-edge technologies like artificial intelligence, machine learning, blockchain, and more.
Job Security: The need for software maintenance ensures long-term job security for engineers.
High Earning Potential: Software engineers often enjoy competitive salaries, especially those with specialized skills.
Global Opportunities: The field is global, providing opportunities to work and collaborate with international teams and clients.
Freelancing and Entrepreneurship: Software engineers can work as freelancers or start their own tech companies, creating innovative solutions.
Remote Work: Many software engineering roles offer remote work options, increasing work flexibility.
Continuous Learning: The fast pace of technological change keeps the field dynamic, requiring ongoing learning and skill development.
Teamwork: Software development often involves collaboration with multidisciplinary teams, enhancing interpersonal and communication skills.
Quality Assurance: Software testing and quality assurance roles are critical for ensuring the reliability and security of software products.
Project Management: Opportunities exist in software project management, guiding teams to successful project completion.
Open Source Contributions: Many software engineers participate in open-source projects, making valuable contributions to the community.

Startups and Innovation: Software engineering is at the heart of many startups, contributing to groundbreaking innovations.
Ethical Considerations: The field encompasses ethical dimensions, such as data privacy, security, and responsible AI development.
Education and Academia: There is a demand for software engineering educators, offering a fulfilling career in academia.
Consulting: Software engineers can work as consultants, offering expertise to various organizations.
Specialization: Engineers can specialize in areas like mobile app development, web development, cybersecurity, or data science.

1.2 Importance of Software Engineering

Importance of Software Engineering

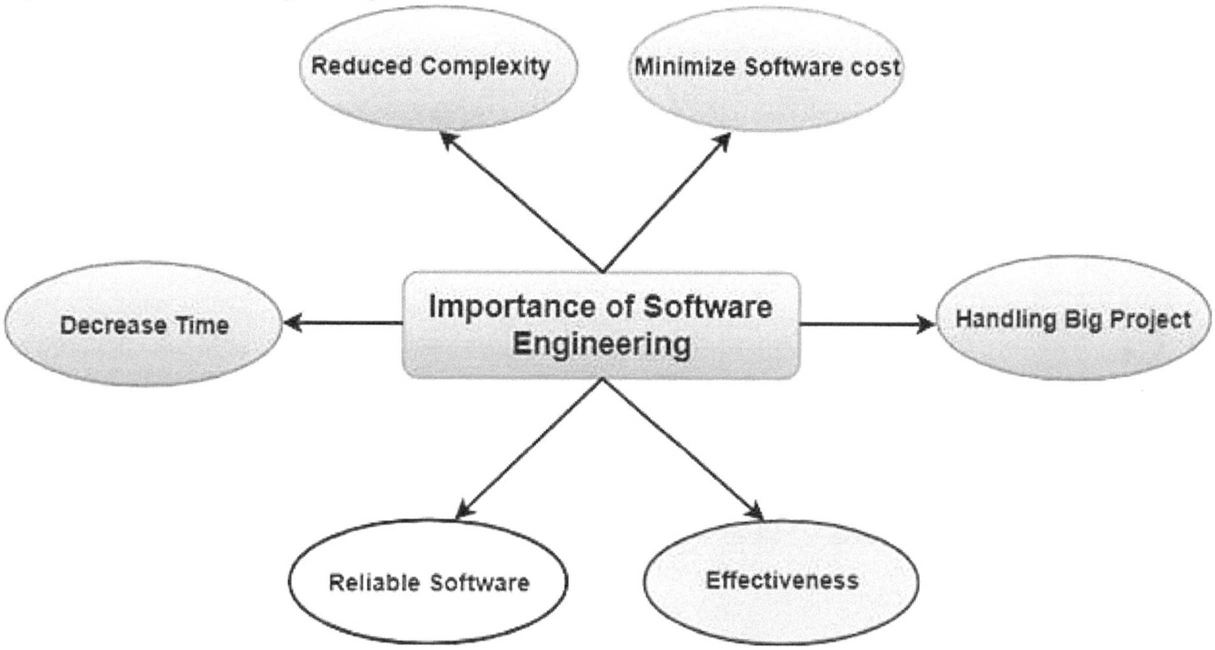

The importance of Software engineering is as follows

Reduces complexity: Big software is always complicated and challenging to progress. Software engineering has a great solution to reduce the complication of any project. Software engineering divides big problems into various small issues. And then start solving each small issue one by one. All these small problems are solved independently to each other.
To minimize software cost: Software needs a lot of hardwork and software engineers are highly paid experts. A lot of manpower is required to develop software with a large number of codes. But in software engineering, programmers project everything and decrease all those things that are not needed. In turn, the cost for software productions becomes less as compared to any software that does not use software engineering method.
To decrease time: Anything that is not made according to the project always wastes time. And if you are making great software, then you may need to run many codes to get the definitive running code. This is a very time-consuming procedure, and if it is not well handled, then this can take a lot of time. So if you are making your software according to the software engineering method, then it will decrease a lot of time.
Handling big projects: Big projects are not done in a couple of days, and they need lots of patience, planning, and management. And to invest six and seven months of any company, it requires heaps of planning, direction, testing, and maintenance. No one can say that he has given four months of a company to the task, and the project is still in its first stage. Because the company has provided many resources to the plan and it should be completed. So to handle a big project without any problem, the company has to go for a software engineering method.
Reliable software: Software should be secure, means if you have delivered the software, then it should work for at least its given time or subscription. And if any bugs come in the software, the company is responsible for solving all these bugs. Because in software engineering, testing and maintenance are given, so there is no worry of its reliability.

Effectiveness: Effectiveness comes if anything has made according to the standards. Software standards are the big target of companies to make it more effective. So Software becomes more effective in the act with the help of software engineering.

1.3 Software Engineering Layers

Software engineering is a fully layered technology, to develop software we need to go from one layer to another. All the layers are connected and each layer demands the fulfillment of the previous layer.

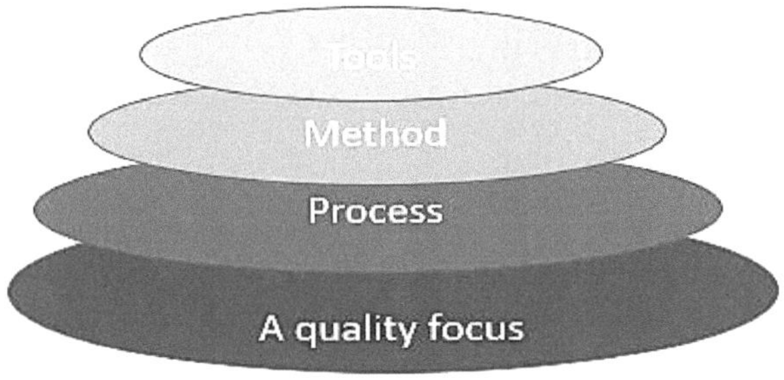

Fig: The diagram shows the layers of software development

Layered technology is divided into four parts

1. A quality focus: It defines the continuous process improvement principles of software. It provides integrity that means providing security to the software so that data can be accessed by only an authorized person, no outsider can access the data. It also focuses on maintainability and usability.
2. Process: It is the foundation or base layer of software engineering. It is key that binds all the layers together which enables the development of software before the deadline or on time. Process defines a framework that must be established for the effective delivery of software engineering technology. The software process covers all the activities, actions, and tasks required to be carried out for software development.

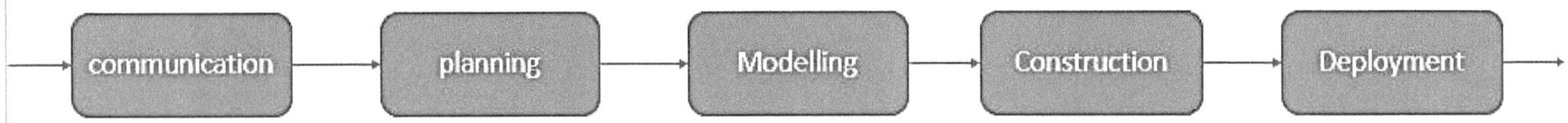

Process activities are listed below: -

Communication: It is the first and foremost thing for the development of software. Communication is necessary to know the actual demand of the client.

Planning: It basically means drawing a map for reduced the complication of development.

Modeling: In this process, a model is created according to the client for better understanding.

Construction: It includes the coding and testing of the problem.

Deployment: - It includes the delivery of software to the client for evaluation and feedback.

3. Method: During the process of software development the answers to all "how-to-do" questions are given by method. It has the information of all the tasks which includes communication, requirement analysis, design modeling, program construction, testing, and support.
4. Tools: Software engineering tools provide a self-operating system for processes and methods. Tools are integrated which means information created by one tool can be used by another.

1.4 Paradigms in Software Engineering

Software paradigms refer to the methods and steps, which are taken while designing the software. There are many methods proposed and are in work today, but we need to see where in the software engineering these paradigms stand. These can be combined into various categories, though each of them is contained in one another:

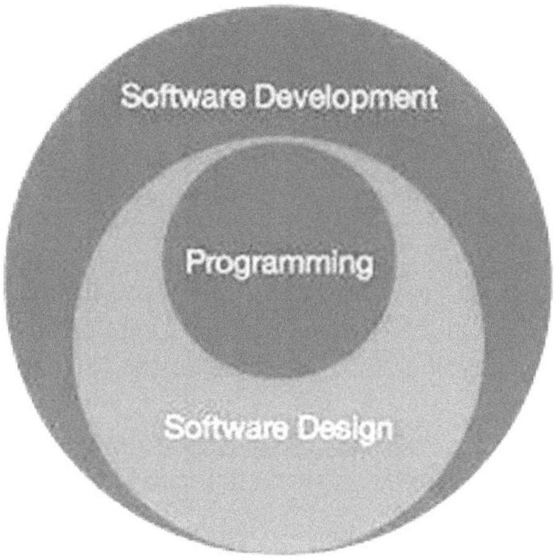

Programming paradigm is a subset of Software design paradigm which is further a subset of Software development paradigm.

Here's an overview of some common software paradigms in detail:

Imperative Paradigm

Description: The imperative paradigm is one of the oldest and most widely used paradigms. It focuses on describing a sequence of steps to achieve a desired outcome. It is also known as procedural programming.

Key Concepts: Variables, assignments, loops, and control structures (e.g., if-else, switch).

Example Languages: C, Pascal, and Fortran.

Strengths: Simple, efficient, and suitable for low-level programming.

Object-Oriented Paradigm

Description: In this paradigm, software is organized into objects, which are instances of classes. It promotes modularity, reusability, and encapsulation.

Key Concepts: Classes, objects, inheritance, encapsulation, and polymorphism.

Example Languages: Java, C++, and Python.

Strengths: Reusability, maintainability, and scalability.

Functional Paradigm

Description: Functional programming focuses on treating computation as the evaluation of mathematical functions. It emphasizes immutability and avoids changing state.

Key Concepts: Higher-order functions, pure functions, immutability, and recursion.

Example Languages: Haskell, Lisp, and Erlang.

Strengths: Concurrency support, ease of reasoning about code, and mathematical precision.

Event-Driven Paradigm

Description: Event-driven programming revolves around reacting to events or signals. It is commonly used in graphical user interfaces and real-time systems.

Key Concepts: Events, event handlers, callbacks, and listeners.

Example Languages: JavaScript, C#, and Visual Basic.

Strengths: Responsiveness, user interface development, and real-time systems.

Logical Paradigm (or Declarative Paradigm)

Description: Logical programming focuses on specifying what should be achieved, rather than how it should be achieved. It's based on formal logic and rule-based reasoning.

Key Concepts: Facts, rules, and queries.

Example Languages: Prolog and Mercury.

Strengths: Expert systems, knowledge representation, and theorem proving.

Component-Based Paradigm

Description: In this paradigm, software is constructed by assembling pre-built, reusable components or modules. It promotes rapid development and maintainability.

Key Concepts: Components, interfaces, and component composition.
Example Frameworks: .NET, Java EE (Enterprise Edition), and OSGi.
Strengths: Reusability, scalability, and ease of maintenance.

Agile Paradigm
Description: Agile is more of a methodology than a programming paradigm. It emphasizes collaboration, customer feedback, and iterative development.
Key Concepts: Iterative development, continuous feedback, and collaboration.
Example Methodologies: Scrum, Kanban, and Extreme Programming (XP).
Strengths: Flexibility, customer-centric development, and adaptability to changing requirements.

Concurrent and Parallel Paradigm
Description: This paradigm focuses on developing software that can execute multiple tasks concurrently or in parallel to make the most of multi-core processors.
Key Concepts: Threads, synchronization, and parallelism.
Example Languages: Go, Rust, and concurrent features in Java and Python.
Strengths: Improved performance on modern hardware.
Software development often involves a combination of these paradigms, depending on the specific requirements and constraints of a project. Choosing the right paradigm or combination of paradigms is crucial for the success of a software project.

1.5 Classification of Software

Classification of Software
The software can be classified based on various criteria, including:
Purpose: Software can be classified as system software (e.g. operating systems, device drivers) or application software (e.g. word processors, games).
Platform: Software can be classified as native software (designed for a specific operating system) or cross-platform software (designed to run on multiple operating systems).
Deployment: Software can be classified as installed software (installed on the user's device) or cloud-based software (hosted on remote servers and accessed via the internet).
License: Software can be classified as proprietary software (owned by a single entity) or open-source software (available for free with the source code accessible to the public).
Development Model: Software can be classified as traditional software (developed using a waterfall model) or agile software (developed using an iterative and adaptive approach).
Size: Software can be classified as small-scale software (designed for a single user or small group) or enterprise software (designed for large organizations).
User Interface: Software can be classified as Graphical User Interface (GUI) software or Command-Line Interface (CLI) software.
These classifications are important for understanding the characteristics and limitations of different types of software, and for selecting the best software for a particular need.

Types of Software
The software is used extensively in several domains including hospitals, banks, schools, defense, finance, stock markets, and so on. It can be categorized into different types:
Based on Application
Based on Copyright

Based on Application
The software can be classified on the basis of the application. These are to be done on this basis.
1. System Software: System Software is necessary to manage computer resources and support the execution of application programs. Software like operating systems, compilers, editors and drivers, etc., come under this category. A computer cannot function without the presence of these. Operating systems are needed to link the machine-dependent needs of a program with the capabilities of the machine on which it runs. Compilers translate programs from high-level language to machine language.
2. Application Software: Application software is designed to fulfill the user's requirement by interacting with the user directly. It could be classified into two major categories: - generic or customized. Generic Software is software that is

open to all and behaves the same for all of its users. Its function is limited and not customized as per the user's changing requirements. However, on the other hand, Customized software is the software products designed per the client's requirement, and are not available for all.
3. Networking and Web Applications Software: Networking Software provides the required support necessary for computers to interact with each other and with data storage facilities. Networking software is also used when software is running on a network of computers (such as the World Wide Web). It includes all network management software, server software, security and encryption software, and software to develop web-based applications like HTML, PHP, XML, etc.
4. Embedded Software: This type of software is embedded into the hardware normally in the Read-Only Memory (ROM) as a part of a large system and is used to support certain functionality under the control conditions. Examples are software used in instrumentation and control applications like washing machines, satellites, microwaves, etc.
5. Reservation Software: A Reservation system is primarily used to store and retrieve information and perform transactions related to air travel, car rental, hotels, or other activities. They also provide access to bus and railway reservations, although these are not always integrated with the main system. These are also used to relay computerized information for users in the hotel industry, making a reservation and ensuring that the hotel is not overbooked.
6. Business Software: This category of software is used to support business applications and is the most widely used category of software. Examples are software for inventory management, accounts, banking, hospitals, schools, stock markets, etc.
7. Entertainment Software: Education and Entertainment software provides a powerful tool for educational agencies, especially those that deal with educating young children. There is a wide range of entertainment software such as computer games, educational games, translation software, mapping software, etc.
8. Artificial Intelligence Software: Software like expert systems, decision support systems, pattern recognition software, artificial neural networks, etc. come under this category. They involve complex problems which are not affected by complex computations using non-numerical algorithms.
9. Scientific Software: Scientific and engineering software satisfies the needs of a scientific or engineering user to perform enterprise-specific tasks. Such software is written for specific applications using principles, techniques, and formulae particular to that field. Examples are software like MATLAB, AUTOCAD, PSPICE, ORCAD, etc.
10. Utility Software: The programs coming under this category perform specific tasks and are different from other software in terms of size, cost, and complexity. Examples are anti-virus software, voice recognition software, compression programs, etc.
11. Document Management Software: Document Management Software is used to track, manage, and store documents to reduce the paperwork. Such systems are capable of keeping a record of the various versions created and modified by different users (history tracking). They commonly provide storage, versioning, metadata, security, as well as indexing and retrieval capabilities.

Based on Copyright

Classification of Software can be done based on copyright. These are stated as follows:
1. Commercial Software: It represents the majority of software that we purchase from software companies, commercial computer stores, etc. In this case, when a user buys software, they acquire a license key to use it. Users are not allowed to make copies of the software. The company owns the copyright of the program.
2. Shareware Software: Shareware software is also covered under copyright but the purchasers are allowed to make and distribute copies with the condition that after testing the software, if the purchaser adopts it for use, then they must pay for it. In both of the above types of software, changes to the software are not allowed.
3. Freeware Software: In general, according to freeware software licenses, copies of the software can be made both for archival and distribution purposes but here, distribution cannot be for making a profit. Derivative works and modifications to the software are allowed and encouraged. Decompiling of the program code is also allowed without the explicit permission of the copyright holder.
4. Public Domain Software: In the case of public domain software, the original copyright holder explicitly relinquishes all rights to the software. Hence software copies can be made both for archival and distribution purposes with no restrictions on distribution. Modifications to the software and reverse engineering are also allowed.

1.6 Software Development Life Cycle

SDLC stands for software development life cycle. It is a process followed for software building within a software organization. SDLC consists of a precise plan that describes how to develop, maintain, replace, and enhance specific software. The life cycle defines a method for improving the quality of software and the all-around development process.

Need of SDLC

The development team must determine a suitable life cycle model for a particular plan and then observe to it.

Without using an exact life cycle model, the development of a software product would not be in a systematic and disciplined manner. When a team is developing a software product, there must be a clear understanding among team representative about when and what to do. Otherwise, it would point to chaos and project failure. This problem can be defined by using an example. Suppose a software development issue is divided into various parts and the parts are assigned to the team members. From then on, suppose the team representative is allowed the freedom to develop the roles assigned to them in whatever way they like. It is possible that one representative might start writing the code for his part, another might choose to prepare the test documents first, and some other engineer might begin with the design phase of the roles assigned to him. This would be one of the perfect methods for project failure.

A software life cycle model describes entry and exit criteria for each phase. A phase can begin only if its stage-entry criteria have been fulfilled. So without a software life cycle model, the entry and exit criteria for a stage cannot be recognized. Without software life cycle models, it becomes tough for software project managers to monitor the progress of the project.

SDLC Cycle

SDLC Cycle represents the process of developing software. SDLC framework includes the following steps:

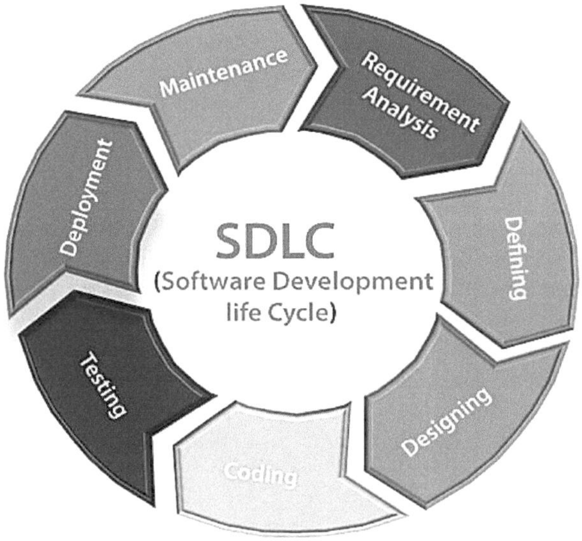

The stages of SDLC are as follows

Stage 1: Planning and requirement analysis

Requirement Analysis is the most important and necessary stage in SDLC.

The senior members of the team perform it with inputs from all the stakeholders and domain experts or SMEs in the industry.

Planning for the quality assurance requirements and identifications of the risks associated with the projects is also done at this stage.

Business analyst and Project organizer set up a meeting with the client to gather all the data like what the customer wants to build, who will be the end user, what is the objective of the product. Before creating a product, a core understanding or knowledge of the product is very necessary.

For Example, A client wants to have an application which concerns money transactions. In this method, the requirement has to be precise like what kind of operations will be done, how it will be done, in which currency it will be done, etc.

Once the required function is done, an analysis is complete with auditing the feasibility of the growth of a product. In case of any ambiguity, a signal is set up for further discussion.

Once the requirement is understood, the SRS (Software Requirement Specification) document is created. The developers should thoroughly follow this document and also should be reviewed by the customer for future reference.

Stage 2: Defining Requirements

Once the requirement analysis is done, the next stage is to certainly represent and document the software requirements and get them accepted from the project stakeholders.

This is accomplished through "SRS"- Software Requirement Specification document which contains all the product requirements to be constructed and developed during the project life cycle.

Stage 3: Designing the Software

The next phase is about to bring down all the knowledge of requirements, analysis, and design of the software project. This phase is the product of the last two, like inputs from the customer and requirement gathering.

Stage 4: Developing the project

In this phase of SDLC, the actual development begins, and the programming is built. The implementation of design begins concerning writing code. Developers have to follow the coding guidelines described by their management and programming tools like compilers, interpreters, debuggers, etc. are used to develop and implement the code.

Stage 5: Testing

After the code is generated, it is tested against the requirements to make sure that the products are solving the needs addressed and gathered during the requirements stage.

During this stage, unit testing, integration testing, system testing, acceptance testing are done.

Stage 6: Deployment

Once the software is certified, and no bugs or errors are stated, then it is deployed.

Then based on the assessment, the software may be released as it is or with suggested enhancement in the object segment.

After the software is deployed, then its maintenance begins.

Stage 7: Maintenance

Once when the client starts using the developed systems, then the real issues come up and requirements to be solved from time to time.

This procedure where the care is taken for the developed product is known as maintenance.

Exercise

Exercise 1 – MCQ

Q 1. What is the primary goal of software engineering?

A. Developing software without documentation
B. Delivering software as quickly as possible
C. Developing high-quality software efficiently
D. Writing as much code as possible

Q 2. What is the purpose of software requirements analysis?

A. To design the user interface
B. To develop test cases
C. To gather and document software requirements
D. To manage project schedules

Exercise 2 – True/ False

Q 1. Software engineering primarily focuses on developing high-quality software efficiently.

Q 2. The implementation phase of the Software Development Life Cycle (SDLC) involves coding.

Exercise 3 – Fill in the blanks

Q 1. Software engineering primarily focuses on developing high-quality software ___________.

Q 2. The primary goal of software quality assurance (SQA) is to ensure that software meets ___________ standards.

Exercise 4 – Match case

1. Requirements Analysis
2. Design
3. Implementation
4. Testing
5. Deployment

A. Creating a blueprint for the software system.
B. Writing code and building the software.
C. Identifying and documenting user and system requirements.
D. Releasing the software to end-users.
E. Evaluating the software to ensure it works correctly.

Exercise 5 – One word answer

Q 1. What is the primary output of the Software Development Life Cycle (SDLC)?

Q 2. What do you call a systematic and structured approach to software development?

Exercise 6 – Small answer

Q 1. What is software engineering?

Q 2. What are software requirements?

Exercise 7 – Long answer

Q 1. What is software engineering, and why is it important in the field of computer science and IT?

Q 2. Can you explain the Software Development Life Cycle (SDLC) and its phases in detail?

Answers

Exercise 1 – Ans: 1 C, 2 C
Exercise 2 – Ans: 1 True, 2 True
Exercise 3 – Ans: 1 efficiently, 2 quality
Exercise 4 – Ans: 1 C, 2 A, 3 B, 4 E, 5 D
Exercise 5 – Ans: 1 Software, 2 Software Engineering

Online Resources

Online Exam Paper:
Link: https://forms.gle/yygCEzdaQS9UQ8XQ6
QR Code:

Chapter 1 Videos Playlist:
Link: https://www.youtube.com/playlist?list=PLzlh_31VWEFrDf4zXXgAioMA65U29k8HO

QR Code:

Previous Years Solved Questions

Q1. Suggest a suitable life-cycle model for a software product which an organization has undertaken on behalf of a specific customer who is likely to change his requirements. justify your answer. [R.T.U.2018]

Ans 1: In the context of developing a software product for a customer whose requirements are prone to change, the most suitable software development life-cycle model is the Agile methodology, specifically the Scrum framework. This choice is justified by several key considerations:

Customer-Centric Approach: Scrum places a strong emphasis on customer collaboration. By involving the customer as a product owner in the Scrum team, the organization can actively engage with the customer to gather and prioritize evolving requirements. This iterative approach ensures that the software product aligns with the customer's changing needs.

Iterative and Incremental Development: Scrum divides the project into small, time-boxed iterations known as sprints. Each sprint typically lasts two to four weeks, during which a potentially shippable product increment is developed. This iterative and incremental nature allows the team to quickly adapt to changing requirements, as adjustments can be incorporated at the beginning of each sprint.

Frequent Feedback and Adaptability: Scrum encourages regular reviews and feedback from the customer. Sprint reviews provide the customer with the opportunity to evaluate the software and request adjustments or new features as needed. This feedback loop ensures that the product remains aligned with the customer's evolving expectations.

Flexibility in Prioritization: The product backlog in Scrum is a dynamic list of requirements. The product owner can frequently re-prioritize items based on changing needs, allowing the organization to focus on the most critical features in response to evolving customer requirements.

Transparency and Collaboration: Scrum ceremonies, such as daily stand-up meetings and sprint reviews, promote transparency and collaboration. The organization can maintain a clear line of communication with the customer, keeping them informed of project progress and the implications of changing requirements.

Risk Mitigation: The iterative nature of Scrum allows the organization to identify and address risks early in the project. By delivering functional increments, risks can be identified, and necessary adjustments made promptly.

Empowered and Self-Organizing Teams: Scrum empowers cross-functional teams to make decisions and adapt to changes. This self-organizing approach is essential in addressing evolving requirements as the team collectively responds to new challenges.

Scrum is a well-suited choice for a project with a customer who is likely to change requirements. It offers a flexible, customer-centric, and adaptive approach to software development, ensuring that the organization can efficiently respond to evolving customer needs while maintaining transparency and delivering a high-quality software product.

Q 2. List the requirement analysis tasks. [R.T.U. 2018]

Ans 2: Requirement analysis is a crucial phase in the software development process, where the primary objective is to understand and document the needs and constraints of the software system to be developed. The tasks involved in requirement analysis typically include:

Requirement Elicitation:

Identify and gather requirements from various sources, including stakeholders, users, and existing documentation.

Conduct interviews, surveys, workshops, and brainstorming sessions to capture requirements.

Requirement Documentation:

Record and document the collected requirements in a structured format, such as requirement specifications, user stories, or use cases.

Use clear and unambiguous language to describe the requirements.

Requirement Prioritization:

Prioritize requirements to determine their relative importance and criticality to the project.

Use techniques like MoSCoW (Must-haves, Should-haves, Could-haves, and Won't-haves) or other prioritization methods.

Requirement Analysis and Modeling:

Analyze requirements to understand their implications on the system's design, functionality, and scope.

Create models or diagrams (e.g., data flow diagrams, use case diagrams) to represent the requirements visually.

Requirement Validation:

Review and validate requirements with stakeholders to ensure they are complete, consistent, accurate, and feasible.
Use techniques like inspections, reviews, and walkthroughs to identify and resolve issues.

Requirement Traceability:
Establish and maintain traceability links to connect requirements to design elements, test cases, and other project artifacts.
Ensure that each requirement is addressed and validated through the development process.

Requirement Change Management:
Implement a change control process to manage and document changes to requirements.
Assess the impact of changes on the project timeline, budget, and scope.

Requirement Specification:
Develop detailed, unambiguous, and well-structured requirement specifications that serve as a basis for design and development.
Include functional and non-functional requirements, constraints, and acceptance criteria.

Requirement Communication:
Communicate requirements effectively to all project stakeholders, including developers, testers, project managers, and users.
Use clear and understandable language, visual aids, and documentation to facilitate communication.

Risk Assessment:
Identify and assess risks associated with the requirements, including potential conflicts, ambiguities, and gaps.
Develop strategies to mitigate and manage these risks.

User Acceptance Testing (UAT) Planning:
Plan for UAT by defining test cases, test scenarios, and acceptance criteria based on the requirements.
Ensure that UAT aligns with the documented requirements.

Requirement Sign-off:
Obtain formal approval and sign-off from key stakeholders, indicating their acceptance of the documented requirements.
Sign-off establishes a baseline for the project's scope.

Requirements Review and Feedback:
Engage stakeholders in regular reviews of the requirements to collect feedback and refine the documentation.
Address any concerns or issues raised during the review process.

Requirement Change Control:
Establish a formal process to control and manage changes to requirements, ensuring that changes are properly evaluated, documented, and communicated.

Requirements Management Tool Usage:
Utilize requirements management tools to store, track, and manage requirements throughout the project's lifecycle.
These tools help with version control, traceability, and collaboration among team members.

Q 3. Elaborate all requirement analysis principles. [RTU 2013]

Ans 3: Requirement analysis principles in software engineering are fundamental guidelines and best practices that shape the process of gathering, understanding, and documenting software requirements. They are essential to ensure that the software system meets the needs and expectations of stakeholders. Here, we'll elaborate on the key requirement analysis principles:

User-Centered Focus:
Principle: Prioritize the needs and perspectives of end-users and stakeholders. Understand the "voice of the customer."
Elaboration: Put users at the center of requirement analysis to ensure that the software system addresses their requirements and expectations. This involves conducting user interviews, surveys, and usability studies to gather insights.

Clear and Unambiguous Language:
Principle: Use clear, precise, and unambiguous language in requirement documentation.
Elaboration: Ensure that requirements are written in a way that leaves no room for misinterpretation or confusion. Avoid technical jargon or vague terms.

Completeness and Consistency:
Principle: Requirements should be comprehensive, covering all aspects of the system, and they should be free from conflicts or contradictions.
Elaboration: Verify that the requirements address all functional and non-functional aspects of the software. Check for consistency within and across requirements documents.

Feasibility and Achievability:
Principle: Ensure that the identified requirements are feasible within the project's constraints (e.g., budget, timeline, resources).
Elaboration: Assess whether it is technically and economically possible to implement the requirements. Consider potential risks and challenges.
Traceability:
Principle: Establish and maintain traceability links to connect requirements to design elements, test cases, and other project artifacts.
Elaboration: Create a traceability matrix to track how each requirement is addressed in the design and testing phases. This ensures that nothing is overlooked.
Change Management:
Principle: Implement a change control process to manage and document changes to requirements.
Elaboration: Define a process for requesting, evaluating, and approving requirement changes. Assess the impact of changes on project scope, schedule, and budget.
Stakeholder Collaboration:
Principle: Involve stakeholders from diverse roles and backgrounds in the requirement analysis process.
Elaboration: Engage in active collaboration with users, business analysts, developers, testers, and other relevant parties to collect a comprehensive set of requirements.
Testability:
Principle: Ensure that requirements are testable, meaning that it is possible to verify whether they have been met.
Elaboration: Include acceptance criteria and define how each requirement will be tested. This facilitates validation and verification during the development process.
Modularity and Decomposition:
Principle: Divide complex requirements into smaller, more manageable components or modules.
Elaboration: Break down large, complex requirements into smaller, independent parts. This promotes clarity and makes it easier to manage and develop the system.
Documentation and Transparency:
Principle: Document requirements in a structured and organized manner, making them accessible and understandable to all stakeholders.
Elaboration: Create clear, well-structured requirement documents, diagrams, and use cases. Maintain transparency by sharing these documents with the entire project team.
Validation and Verification:
Principle: Implement methods for validating that the requirements capture the true needs of stakeholders and verifying that they are correctly implemented in the software.
Elaboration: Employ techniques like inspections, reviews, walkthroughs, and testing to validate and verify requirements at various stages of the project.
Risk Management:
Principle: Identify and assess risks associated with the requirements, including potential conflicts, ambiguities, and gaps.
Elaboration: Develop strategies to mitigate and manage these risks to ensure that the requirements do not become sources of problems later in the project.
Evolution and Adaptability:
Principle: Acknowledge that requirements can change and evolve throughout the project.
Elaboration: Create a flexible and adaptive requirement analysis process that can accommodate changing needs and priorities as the project progresses.

Q 4. Write a note on resources required for software development. [R.T.U.2018]
Ans 4: resources are fundamental to the successful development of software projects. In software engineering, these resources span various categories and are essential for the planning, execution, and completion of projects. Here's a comprehensive note on the resources required for software development:
1. Human Resources:
Software Developers: Skilled programmers who write code, design, and develop the software.
Project Managers: Individuals responsible for planning, organizing, and overseeing the entire project.
Business Analysts: Professionals who gather, analyze, and document user requirements.
Quality Assurance/Testers: Experts responsible for testing the software for defects and ensuring its quality.
Designers: Graphic and user experience (UX/UI) designers who create the software's visual and interactive elements.

Domain Experts: Specialists with domain-specific knowledge to guide requirements gathering and development in specialized industries.

2. Infrastructure and Hardware:

Computers and Servers: Adequate hardware for development, testing, and production environments.

Networking Infrastructure: Reliable network connectivity for collaboration and data exchange.

Software Tools: Development environments, integrated development tools (IDEs), and version control systems (e.g., Git).

3. Financial Resources:

Funding: Adequate budget allocation for personnel, infrastructure, software licenses, and other project-related costs.

Cost Estimation and Tracking: Tools and processes for accurate cost estimation and financial tracking throughout the project.

4. Time:

Project Schedules: Well-defined project schedules, timelines, and milestones to manage time effectively.

5. Information and Data:

Requirements Documentation: Clear, comprehensive, and well-documented requirements to guide the development process.

Data and Content: Access to relevant data sources and content, especially in data-intensive software, often requiring databases, APIs, or external services.

6. Legal and Regulatory Compliance:

Legal Expertise: Legal professionals who ensure the software complies with intellectual property rights, licensing, and privacy regulations.

7. Knowledge and Expertise:

Domain Expertise: Subject matter experts who provide insights into specific industries or fields.

Technical Knowledge: Continuous learning and expertise in the latest technologies and best practices.

8. Collaboration and Communication Tools:

Tools such as email, project management software, collaboration platforms, and communication channels to facilitate team interaction, information sharing, and project coordination.

9. Training and Skill Development:

Resources for ongoing training and skill development to keep the team updated on the latest technologies and methodologies in software engineering.

10. Security Resources:

Security experts, tools, and protocols to ensure the software is protected against vulnerabilities and threats.

Effective resource management is essential for delivering software that meets user needs, is of high quality, and is completed within the expected timeframe and budget. Software development projects require the harmonious orchestration of these resources to achieve success.

Previous Years Unsolved Questions

Q 1. Discuss the phases of Software Development Life Cycle with the help of an example project. [IGNOU, June, 2018] [Kota university 2021]
Q 2. What are the activities that are performed as part of "Design" phase of process of software development? [IGNOU, December, 2016]
Q 3. Define "Software Engineering". Illustrate various phases of Life cycle of Software Development. [IGNOU, June, 2016]
Q 4. How is software development for mobile devices different from PCs? [IGNOU, June, 2016]
Q 5. How is Software Configuration Management done in Software Development Process? Explain. [IGNOU, June, 2016]
Q 6. Define Software Engineering. [Anna University 2022]
Q 7. How does engineering from Software engineering? Also write brief notes on computer-based system and system
engineering hierarchy. [Kota University 2021]
Q 8. Explain the structure of software requirements document? [Kota University 2021]
Q 9. Explain about software Engineering paradigm in detail. [RGPV June 2020]
Q 10. What are the attributes of good software. [VTU 2021]

Chapter 2: Requirements Analysis and Specification

2.1 Software Prototyping

The Software Prototyping refers to building software application prototypes which display the functionality of the product under development but may not actually hold the exact logic of the original software. Software prototyping is becoming very popular as a software development model, as it enables to understand customer requirements at an early stage of development. It helps get valuable feedback from the customer and helps software designers and developers understand about what exactly is expected from the product under development.

2.1.1 Introduction to Software Prototyping

1. Prototype is a working model of software with some limited functionality.
2. The prototype does not always hold the exact logic used in the actual software application and is an extra effort to be considered under effort estimation.
3. Prototyping is used to allow the users evaluate developer proposals and try them out before implementation.
4. It also helps understand the requirements which are user specific and may not have been considered by the developer during product design.

Following is the stepwise approach to design a software prototype:

Basic Requirement Identification: This step involves understanding the very basics product requirements especially in terms of user interface. The more intricate details of the internal design and external aspects like performance and security can be ignored at this stage.

Developing the initial Prototype: The initial Prototype is developed in this stage, where the very basic requirements are showcased and user interfaces are provided. These features may not exactly work in the same manner internally in the actual software developed and the workarounds are used to give the same look and feel to the customer in the prototype developed. **Review of the Prototype:** The prototype developed is then presented to the customer and the other important stakeholders in the project. The feedback is collected in an organized manner and used for further enhancements in the product under development.

Revise and enhance the Prototype: The feedback and the review comments are discussed during this stage and some negotiations happen with the customer based on factors like , time and budget constraints and technical feasibility of actual implementation. The changes accepted are again incorporated in the new Prototype developed and the cycle repeats until customer expectations are met.

Prototypes can have horizontal or vertical dimensions. Horizontal prototype displays the user interface for the product and gives a broader view of the entire system, without concentrating on internal functions. A vertical prototype on the other side is a detailed elaboration of a specific function or a sub system in the product.

The purpose of both horizontal and vertical prototype is different. Horizontal prototypes are used to get more information on the user interface level and the business requirements. It can even be presented in the sales demos to get business in the market. Vertical prototypes are technical in nature and are used to get details of the exact functioning of the sub systems. For example, database requirements, interaction and data processing loads in a given sub system.

2.1.2 Prototyping Types (Throwaway, Evolutionary)

There are different types of software prototypes used in the industry. Following are the major software prototyping types used widely:

1. Throwaway/Rapid Prototyping: Throwaway prototyping is also called as rapid or close ended prototyping. This type of prototyping uses very little efforts with minimum requirement analysis to build a prototype. Once the actual requirements are understood, the prototype is discarded and the actual system is developed with a much clear understanding of user requirements.

2. **Evolutionary Prototyping:** Evolutionary prototyping also called as breadboard prototyping is based on building actual functional prototypes with minimal functionality in the beginning. The prototype developed forms the heart of the future prototypes on top of which the entire system is built. Using evolutionary prototyping only well understood requirements are included in the prototype and the requirements are added as and when they are understood.

3. Incremental Prototyping: Incremental prototyping refers to building multiple functional prototypes of the various sub systems and then integrating all the available prototypes to form a complete system.

4. Extreme Prototyping: Extreme prototyping is used in the web development domain. It consists of three sequential phases. First, a basic prototype with all the existing pages is presented in the html format. Then the data processing is simulated using a prototype services layer. Finally, the services are implemented and integrated to the final prototype. This process is called Extreme Prototyping used to draw attention to the second phase of the process, where a fully functional UI is developed with very little regard to the actual services.

2.1.3 Pros and Cons of Software Prototyping

Pros	Cons
• Increased user involvement in the product even before implementation. • Since a working model of the system is displayed, the users get a better understanding of the system being developed. • Reduces time and cost as the defects can be detected much earlier. • Quicker user feedback is available leading to better solutions. • Confusing or difficult functions can be identified.	• Risk of insufficient requirement analysis owing to too much dependency on prototype. • Users may get confused in the prototypes and actual systems. • Practically, this methodology may increase the complexity of the system as scope of the system may expand beyond original plans. • Developers may try to reuse the existing prototypes to build the actual system, even when its not technically feasible. • The effort invested in building prototypes may be too much if not monitored properly.

2.2 Software Requirements Specification (SRS)

The production of the requirements stage of the software development process is Software Requirements Specifications (SRS) (also called a requirements document). This report lays a foundation for software engineering activities and is constructing when entire requirements are elicited and analyzed. SRS is a formal report, which acts as a representation of software that enables the customers to review whether it (SRS) is according to their requirements. Also, it comprises user requirements for a system as well as detailed specifications of the system requirements.

The SRS is a specification for a specific software product, program, or set of applications that perform particular functions in a specific environment. It serves several goals depending on who is writing it. First, the SRS could be written by the client of a system. Second, the SRS could be written by a developer of the system. The two methods create entirely various situations and establish different purposes for the document altogether. The first case, SRS, is used to define the needs and expectation of the users. The second case, SRS, is written for various purposes and serves as a contract document between customer and developer.

2.2.1 Software Requirement Specification format

In order to form a good SRS, here you will see some points that can be used and should be considered to form a structure of good Software Requirements Specification (SRS). These are below mentioned in the table of contents and are well explained below.

Table of Content

1. Introduction
2. General description
3. Functional Requirements
4. Interface Requirements
5. Performance Requirements
6. Design Constraints
7. Non-Functional Attributes
8. Preliminary Schedule and Budget
9. Appendices
10. Uses of SRS document
11. FAQs on SRS Format
12. Conclusion

Software Requirement Specification (SRS) Format as the name suggests, is a complete specification and description of requirements of the software that need to be fulfilled for the successful development of the software system. These requirements can be functional as well as non-functional depending upon the type of requirement. The interaction between different customers and contractors is done because it is necessary to fully understand the needs of customers. Depending upon information gathered after interaction, SRS is developed which describes requirements of software that may include changes and modifications that is needed to be done to increase quality of product and to satisfy customer's demand.

1. Introduction

Purpose of this Document – At first, main aim of why this document is necessary and what's purpose of document is explained and described.

Scope of this document – In this, overall working and main objective of document and what value it will provide to customer is described and explained. It also includes a description of development cost and time required.

Overview – In this, description of product is explained. It's simply summary or overall review of product.

2. General description

In this, general functions of product which includes objective of user, a user characteristic, features, benefits, about why its importance is mentioned. It also describes features of user community.

3. Functional Requirements

In this, possible outcome of software system which includes effects due to operation of program is fully explained. All functional requirements which may include calculations, data processing, etc. are placed in a ranked order. Functional requirements specify the expected behavior of the system-which outputs should be produced from the given inputs. They describe the relationship between the input and output of the system. For each functional requirement, detailed description all the data inputs and their source, the units of measure, and the range of valid inputs must be specified.

4. Interface Requirements

In this, software interfaces which mean how software program communicates with each other or users either in form of any language, code, or message are fully described and explained. Examples can be shared memory, data streams, etc.

5. Performance Requirements

In this, how a software system performs desired functions under specific condition is explained. It also explains required time, required memory, maximum error rate, etc. The performance requirements part of an SRS specifies the performance constraints on the software system. All the requirements relating to the performance characteristics of the system must be clearly specified. There are two types of performance requirements: static and dynamic. Static requirements are those that do not impose constraint on the execution characteristics of the system. Dynamic requirements specify constraints on the execution behaviour of the system.

6. Design Constraints

In this, constraints which simply means limitation or restriction are specified and explained for design team. Examples may include use of a particular algorithm, hardware and software limitations, etc. There are a number of factors in the client's environment that may restrict the choices of a designer leading to design constraints such factors include standards that must be followed resource limits, operating environment, reliability and security requirements and policies that may have an impact on the design of the system. An SRS should identify and specify all such constraints.

7. Non-Functional Attributes

In this, non-functional attributes are explained that are required by software system for better performance. An example may include Security, Portability, Reliability, Reusability, Application compatibility, Data integrity, Scalability capacity, etc.

8. Preliminary Schedule and Budget

In this, initial version and budget of project plan are explained which include overall time duration required and overall cost required for development of project.

9. Appendices

In this, additional information like references from where information is gathered, definitions of some specific terms, acronyms, abbreviations, etc. are given and explained.

Uses of SRS document

1. Development team require it for developing product according to the need.
2. Test plans are generated by testing group based on the describe external behaviour.
3. Maintenance and support staff need it to understand what the software product is supposed to do.
4. Project manager base their plans and estimates of schedule, effort and resources on it.
5. customer rely on it to know that product they can expect.
6. As a contract between developer and customer.
7. in documentation purpose.

2.2.2 Purpose and Importance of SRS

Purpose of SRS

A Software Requirements Specification (SRS) is a crucial document in the software development process. It serves as a foundation for the entire project and plays several important roles:

Communication and Understanding: The primary purpose of an SRS is to establish a clear and common understanding of the software project's scope, objectives, and requirements among all stakeholders. It acts as a bridge between the client or end-users and the development team.

Documentation of Requirements: The SRS provides a formal and structured document that captures all the functional and non-functional requirements of the software. It details what the software should and should not do, including user interactions, system behavior, and performance expectations.

Basis for Agreement: It acts as a contract or agreement between the client and the development team. By documenting the agreed-upon requirements in the SRS, both parties have a reference point to ensure that the final software product meets the specified criteria.

Scope Management: An SRS helps define the boundaries of the project. It outlines the features and functionalities to be included in the software and sets limits on what is out of scope. This prevents "scope creep," where additional features are added without proper documentation or approval.

Risk Management: By detailing requirements in the SRS, potential risks and challenges can be identified early in the project. This allows for better risk management planning and mitigation strategies.

Basis for Estimation: Software development teams use the SRS to estimate the project's cost, time, and resources accurately. It helps in determining the effort required for each requirement and task.

Design and Development Guidance: The SRS provides a blueprint for software architects and developers. It guides them in designing the software's architecture, database structure, and coding. Developers can use the SRS as a reference during implementation.

Testing and Validation: Testers use the SRS to develop test cases and verify that the software meets the specified requirements. Without clear requirements, testing becomes challenging, and it's harder to determine whether the software functions correctly.

Documentation for Maintenance: Once the software is in production, the SRS continues to be a valuable reference for maintenance and updates. It ensures that any changes or enhancements align with the original requirements.

Legal and Regulatory Compliance: In some industries, especially those with strict regulatory requirements (e.g., healthcare, finance), an SRS helps demonstrate compliance with regulations. It provides a record of how the software meets legal and industry standards.

Traceability: The SRS often includes a traceability matrix, linking each requirement to the corresponding design elements, code, and test cases. This ensures that all requirements are adequately addressed throughout the software development lifecycle.

Quality Assurance: The SRS serves as a basis for quality assurance and quality control processes. It helps define the criteria for a successful software product and sets the standard for quality.

Importance of SRS

1. The users and the client get a brief idea about the software while in the initial stages.
2. The purposes and the intentions as well as the expected results are properly defined. It hence lays the outline for software design.
3. The desired goals are defined thereby easing off the efforts of the developers in terms of time and cost.
4. It forms a basis for the agreement between the client and the developer.
5. It becomes easier while transferring and using the solution elsewhere or with new customers as the basis of functioning of the software is mentioned.
6. It acts as a material for reference at a later stage.
7. It acts as the basis for reviews.

2.2.3 Parts of SRS

The important parts of the Software Requirements Specification (SRS) document are:

1. Functional requirements of the system
2. Non-functional requirements of the system, and
3. Goals of implementation

These are explained as following below.

1. Functional Requirements:

The purposeful requirements part discusses the functionalities needed from the system, The system is taken into account to perform a group of high- level functions Fi. The functional view of the system is shown in below diagram Each function F*i* of the system can be considered as a transformation of a set of input data Ii to the corresponding set of output knowledge Oi.

The user will get some purposeful piece of labor done employing a high-level operate.

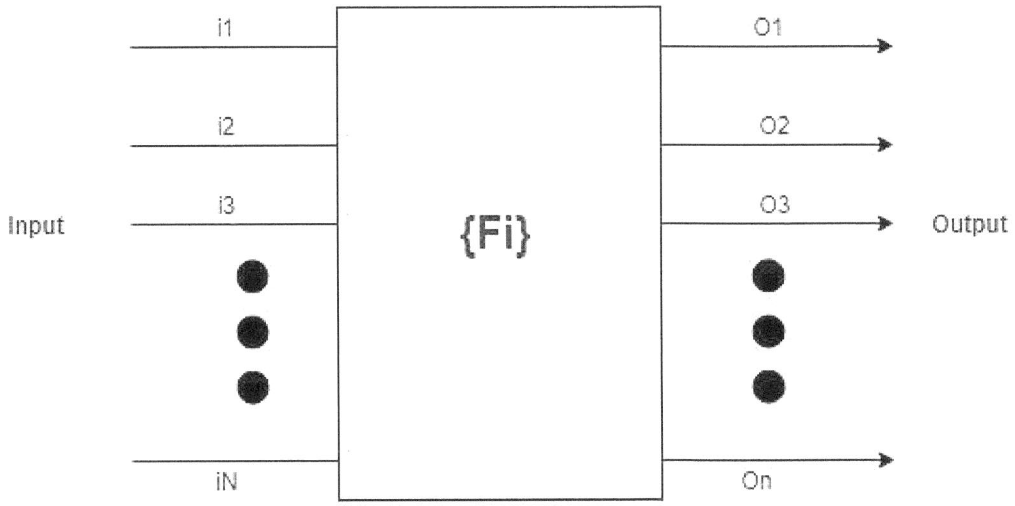

View of a system performing a set of functions

2. Non-functional Requirements:

Non-functional necessities accommodate the characteristics of the system which may not be expressed as functions – like the maintainability of the system, movability of the system, the usability of the system, etc. Non-functional requirements may include:

1. Reliability issues
2. Accuracy of results
3. Human-computer interface issues
4. Constraints on the system implementation, etc.

3. Goals of Implementation:

The goals of implementation part documents some general suggestions relating to development. These suggestions guide trade-off among style goals. The goals of the implementation section would possibly document problems like revisions to the system functionalities that will be needed within the future, new devices to be supported within the future, reusability problems, etc. These are the things that the developers would possibly detain their mind throughout development in order that the developed system may meet some aspects that don't seem to be needed straightaway.

2.2.4 Classification of Software Requirement

According to IEEE standard 729, a requirement is defined as follows:

1. A condition or capability needed by a user to solve a problem or achieve an objective
2. A condition or capability that must be met or possessed by a system or system component to satisfy a contract, standard, specification or other formally imposed documents
3. A documented representation of a condition or capability as in 1 and 2.

Main types of software requirement can be of 3 types:

1. Functional requirements
2. Non-functional requirements
3. Domain requirements

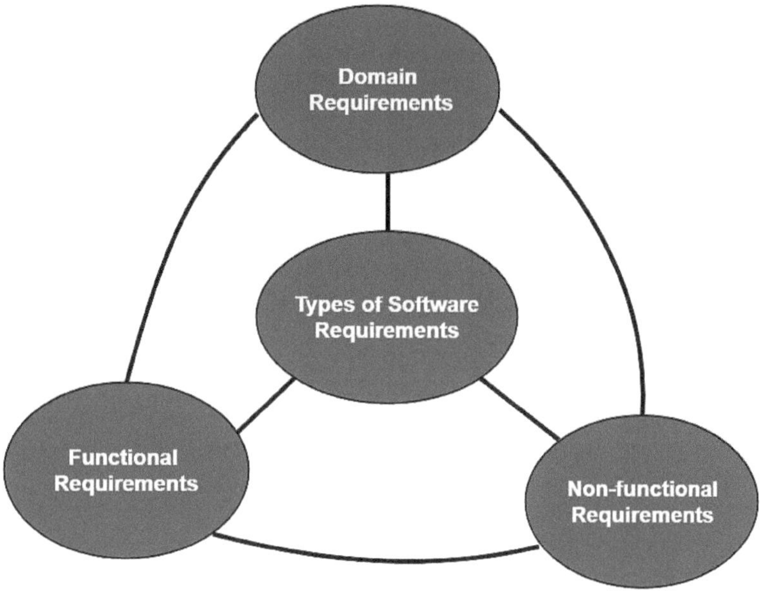

Functional Requirements:

1. These are the requirements that the end user specifically demands as basic facilities that the system should offer. It can be a calculation, data manipulation, business process, user interaction, or any other specific functionality which defines what function a system is likely to perform.
2. All these functionalities need to be necessarily incorporated into the system as a part of the contract. These are represented or stated in the form of input to be given to the system, the operation performed and the output expected. They are basically the requirements stated by the user which one can see directly in the final product, unlike the non-functional requirements.

For example, in a hospital management system, a doctor should be able to retrieve the information of his patients. Each high-level functional requirement may involve several interactions or dialogues between the system and the outside world. In order to accurately describe the functional requirements, all scenarios must be enumerated. There are many ways of expressing functional requirements e.g., natural language, a structured or formatted language with no rigorous syntax and formal specification language with proper syntax. Functional Requirements in Software Engineering are also called Functional Specification.

Non-functional requirements:

These are basically the quality constraints that the system must satisfy according to the project contract. Nonfunctional requirements, not related to the system functionality, rather define how the system should perform The priority or extent to which these factors are implemented varies from one project to other. They are also called non-behavioral requirements.

They basically deal with issues like:

Portability
Security
Maintainability
Reliability
Scalability
Performance
Reusability
Flexibility

NFR's are classified into following types:

Interface constraints
Performance constraints: response time, security, storage space, etc.
Operating constraints
Life cycle constraints: maintainability, portability, etc.
Economic constraints

The process of specifying non-functional requirements requires the knowledge of the functionality of the system, as well as the knowledge of the context within which the system will operate.

They are divided into two main categories:

1. Execution qualities like security and usability, which are observable at run time.
2. Evolution qualities like testability, maintainability, extensibility, and scalability that embodied in the static structure of the software system.

Domain requirements:

Domain requirements are the requirements which are characteristic of a particular category or domain of projects. Domain requirements can be functional or nonfunctional.

Domain requirements engineering is a continuous process of proactively defining the requirements for all foreseeable applications to be developed in the software product line.

The basic functions that a system of a specific domain must necessarily exhibit come under this category.

For instance, in an academic software that maintains records of a school or college, the functionality of being able to access the list of faculty and list of students of each grade is a domain requirement. These requirements are therefore identified from that domain model and are not user specific.

Other common classifications of software requirements can be:

User requirements: These requirements describe what the end-user wants from the software system. User requirements are usually expressed in natural language and are typically gathered through interviews, surveys, or user feedback.

System requirements: These requirements specify the technical characteristics of the software system, such as its architecture, hardware requirements, software components, and interfaces. System requirements are typically expressed in technical terms and are often used as a basis for system design.

Business requirements: These requirements describe the business goals and objectives that the software system is expected to achieve. Business requirements are usually expressed in terms of revenue, market share, customer satisfaction, or other business metrics.

Regulatory requirements: These requirements specify the legal or regulatory standards that the software system must meet. Regulatory requirements may include data privacy, security, accessibility, or other legal compliance requirements.

Interface requirements: These requirements specify the interactions between the software system and external systems or components, such as databases, web services, or other software applications.

Design requirements: These requirements describe the technical design of the software system. They include information about the software architecture, data structures, algorithms, and other technical aspects of the software.

2.2.5 Quality characteristics of a good SRS

Quality characteristics of a good Software Requirements Specification (SRS) document include:

Complete: The SRS should include all the requirements for the software system, including both functional and non-functional requirements.

Consistent: The SRS should be consistent in its use of terminology and formatting, and should be free of contradictions.

Unambiguous: The SRS should be clear and specific, and should avoid using vague or imprecise language.

Traceable: The SRS should be traceable to other documents and artifacts, such as use cases and user stories, to ensure that all requirements are being met.

Verifiable: The SRS should be verifiable, which means that the requirements can be tested and validated to ensure that they are being met.

Modifiable: The SRS should be modifiable, so that it can be updated and changed as the software development process progresses.

Prioritized: The SRS should prioritize requirements, so that the most important requirements are addressed first.

Testable: The SRS should be written in a way that allows the requirements to be tested and validated.

High-level and low-level: The SRS should provide both high-level requirements (such as overall system objectives) and low-level requirements (such as detailed functional requirements).

Relevant: The SRS should be relevant to the software system that is being developed, and should not include unnecessary or irrelevant information.

Human-readable: The SRS should be written in a way that is easy for non-technical stakeholders to understand and review.

Aligned with business goals: The SRS should be aligned with the overall business goals and objectives of the organization, so that the software system meets the needs of the business.

Agile methodologies: Agile methodologies, such as Scrum and Kanban, provide an iterative approach to requirements capturing and validation, where requirements are captured and validated in small chunks of functionality and feedback is gathered from the customer.

By keeping these quality characteristics in mind, developers and stakeholders can ensure that the SRS document is clear, complete, and accurate, which in turn can help to ensure that the final software system meets the needs of the business and its users.

Following are the characteristics of a good SRS document:

Correctness:

User review is used to ensure the correctness of requirements stated in the SRS. SRS is said to be correct if it covers all the requirements that are actually expected from the system.

Completeness:

Completeness of SRS indicates every sense of completion including the numbering of all the pages, resolving the to be determined parts to as much extent as possible as well as covering all the functional and non-functional requirements properly.

Consistency:

Requirements in SRS are said to be consistent if there are no conflicts between any set of requirements. Examples of conflict include differences in terminologies used at separate places, logical conflicts like time period of report generation, etc.

Unambiguousness:

A SRS is said to be unambiguous if all the requirements stated have only 1 interpretation. Some of the ways to prevent unambiguousness include the use of modelling techniques like ER diagrams, proper reviews and buddy checks, etc.

Ranking for importance and stability:

There should a criterion to classify the requirements as less or more important or more specifically as desirable or essential. An identifier mark can be used with every requirement to indicate its rank or stability.

Modifiability:

SRS should be made as modifiable as possible and should be capable of easily accepting changes to the system to some extent. Modifications should be properly indexed and cross-referenced.

Verifiability:

A SRS is verifiable if there exists a specific technique to quantifiably measure the extent to which every requirement is met by the system. For example, a requirement starting that the system must be user-friendly is not verifiable and listing such requirements should be avoided.

Traceability:

One should be able to trace a requirement to design component and then to code segment in the program. Similarly, one should be able to trace a requirement to the corresponding test cases.

Design Independence:

There should be an option to choose from multiple design alternatives for the final system. More specifically, the SRS should not include any implementation details.

Testability:

A SRS should be written in such a way that it is easy to generate test cases and test plans from the document.

Understandable by the customer:

An end user maybe an expert in his/her specific domain but might not be an expert in computer science. Hence, the use of formal notations and symbols should be avoided to as much extent as possible. The language should be kept easy and clear.

Right level of abstraction:

If the SRS is written for the requirements phase, the details should be explained explicitly. Whereas, for a feasibility study, fewer details can be used. Hence, the level of abstraction varies according to the purpose of the SRS.

Exercise

Exercise 1 – MCQ

Q 1. **Which of the following is a non-functional requirement?**

A. User authentication
B. Response time for a search operation
C. Database schema
D. Use case diagram

Q 2. Which of the following is a characteristic of a well-written requirement?

A. Ambiguity
B. Unverifiability
C. Testability
D. Complexity

Exercise 2 – True/ False

Q 1. Non-functional requirements describe what the system should do.

Q 2. Requirements analysis should occur after coding and design work begins.

Exercise 3 – Fill in the blanks

Q 1. The ____________ requirements define what the system should do under specific conditions.

Q 2. A well-written requirement is clear, concise, ____________, and testable.

Exercise 4 – Match case

1. Functional Requirements	A. Describe the quality attributes of the system.
2. Non-Functional Requirements	B. Provide details on what the software system should do.
3. Software Requirement Specification (SRS)	C. A formal document that captures software requirements.
4. Use Case Diagrams	D. A technique to capture user interactions with the system.
5. Quality Attributes	E. Constraints, such as platform or environment specifications.

Exercise 5 – One word answer

Q 1. What is an SRS?

Q 2. Name one type of requirement.

Exercise 6 – Small answer

Q 1. What is the key difference between functional and non-functional requirements?

Q 2. Why is it essential to document software requirements?

Exercise 7 – Long answer

Q 1. Explain the concept of functional and non-functional requirements in software engineering. Provide examples of each and discuss their importance in the software development process.

Q 2. Describe the various stages of the requirements analysis process. How does it contribute to successful software development projects?

Answers

Exercise 1 – MCQ

Ans: 1 B, 2 C

Exercise 2 – True/ False

Ans: 1 False, 2 False

Exercise 3 – Fill in the blanks

Ans: 1 Functional, 2 Unambiguous

Exercise 4 – Match case

Ans: 1 B, 2 A, 3 C, 4 D, 5 E

Exercise 5 – One word answer

Ans: 1 Document, 2 Functional

Online Resources

Online Exam Paper:
Link: https://forms.gle/h9MW49zYb2z3Yaho8
QR Code:

Chapter 2 Videos Playlist:

Link: https://www.youtube.com/playlist?list=PLzlh_31VWEFrDf4zXXgAioMA65U29k8HO
QR Code:

Previous Years Solved Questions

Q 1. Explain the components of Software Requirement Specification (SRS). Write the IEEE recommended structure of SRS. [R.T.U.2018]

Ans 1: Ans. Software Requirement Specification (SRS) document forms. the basis for agreement between customers and the
suppliers on what the software product should do. There is not standard way of writing requirements specification document, but the following steps should be followed.

1. Creating SRS Outline : An SRS outline contains the following details

(a) Purpose of software
(b) Scope of software
(c) System overview
(d) References
(e) Definitions
(f) Definitions
(g) Functional Requirements
(h) Non-Functional Requirements.

2. Choosing SRS Writer : The SRS writer is a person or group of persons who understand the specifications of the software to present clear and unambiguous requirement from customer.

3. Provide only Relevant Information.: The document should be proper and must be represented legibly in graphical or tabular form.

4. Keep updating the SRS : As the task progresses, SRS is updated in order to signify the changes that have been made.

The users related to SRS are :
(1) Client
(2) SRS writer
(3) Designer / Developer
(4) Tester.

The table listing the users and use of SRS with respect to that user has been shown in table.

S. No.	User	Use of SRS with respect to user
1.	Client	Specify the requirements to be met by the software.
2.	SRS Writer	Documents the requirements specified by the user in clear and unambiguous manner in form of SRS.
1.	Developer/ Designer	Uses SRS to translate the requirements in form of software by design implementing it.
2.	Tester	Tests the software progress with SRS and mark revisions as per need.

SRS Documentation, following IEEE std. 830:

1. Introduction: This section sets the stage by outlining the purpose and scope of the document, defining key terms, referencing external sources, and providing an overview of the content.

2. Overall Description: This section offers a comprehensive view of the software, including its place within a broader context, its functions and features, user characteristics, constraints, assumptions, and dependencies.

3. Specific Requirements: The heart of the SRS, this section breaks down the requirements into several sub-sections:

3.1 External Interface Requirements: Details about the software's interactions with external systems.

3.2 Product Functions: A comprehensive list of functions and features the software should provide, often illustrated through use cases or diagrams.

3.3 User Characteristics: A clear definition of the intended users, specifying their roles and characteristics.

3.4 Constraints: Any limitations or restrictions that might affect the software's design or development.

3.5 Assumptions and Dependencies: Documenting the assumptions made during the requirement analysis and dependencies on external factors.
3.6-3.10: Further sub-sections dive into more detailed requirements, including external interfaces, functional requirements, non-functional requirements, system attributes, and any additional, specific requirements not covered elsewhere.
4. Appendices: This section can include supplementary information such as a glossary, analysis models (diagrams and visuals), user manuals, or any other relevant materials that enhance the understanding of the SRS.
5. Index: An index, if included, helps users navigate the document efficiently.
6. Change History: This section logs any revisions, updates, and versions of the SRS document, providing a historical record of changes.
Following IEEE Std. 830 is essential for standardizing the process of documenting software requirements, ensuring that stakeholders are on the same page, and facilitating effective communication among developers, testers, project managers, and clients. It also enhances the chances of a successful software development project by providing clear and unambiguous requirements that guide the entire development process.

Q 2. Describe how to prepare a Software Requirement specification (SRS) document. List possible Users and Use of SRS for each User. [RTU 2014]
Ans 2: Preparing a Software Requirements Specification (SRS) document is a critical step in the software development process. An SRS serves as a blueprint that outlines the software system's functionality, performance, constraints, and other essential details. Here's a guide on how to prepare an SRS document, along with a list of possible users and their uses for the SRS:
How to Prepare an SRS Document:
Define the Purpose and Scope:
Clearly articulate the purpose of the SRS and the scope of the software system.
Identify the software's primary objectives and the problems it aims to solve.
Gather and Analyze Requirements:
Conduct interviews, surveys, and workshops with stakeholders to gather requirements.
Analyze and prioritize requirements, distinguishing between functional and non-functional ones.
Document Requirements:
Use a structured format to document requirements. You can follow a template or use a specific standard, like IEEE Std. 830.
Describe each requirement in detail, providing a unique identifier, a clear description, and any associated constraints.
Create Use Cases and Diagrams:
Illustrate software functionality using use cases, flowcharts, or data flow diagrams.
Visual aids make complex requirements easier to understand.
Define User Profiles:
Identify potential users and their roles within the software system.
Define the responsibilities, permissions, and access levels for each user group.
Specify System Behavior:
Describe how the software should behave under different conditions or scenarios.
Define the expected response to various inputs and actions.
Non-Functional Requirements:
Document non-functional requirements, including performance, security, scalability, and usability.
Specify constraints related to technology, standards, and compliance.
Validation and Verification Criteria:
Define criteria for validating and verifying each requirement.
Establish acceptance criteria and testing guidelines.
Dependencies and Assumptions:
Document any dependencies on external systems or components.
List assumptions made during the requirements analysis.
Traceability Matrix:
Create a traceability matrix to map requirements to design elements and test cases.
This ensures that each requirement is addressed and tested.
Review and Approve:
Conduct a thorough review of the SRS document with stakeholders, including users, business analysts, and development teams.

Obtain formal approval and sign-off from key stakeholders.

Possible Users and Their Use of the SRS:

Development Team:

Use: Developers use the SRS as a blueprint for coding and designing the software.

Benefit: It provides clear instructions on what to build and guides the development process.

Testing Team:

Use: Testers refer to the SRS to create test cases and ensure that the software meets the specified requirements.

Benefit: It serves as the foundation for quality assurance and validation.

Project Managers:

Use: Project managers use the SRS to create project plans, schedules, and allocate resources.

Benefit: It helps in project planning and ensures alignment with the client's requirements.

Client or Product Owner:

Use: The client uses the SRS to verify that the software aligns with their needs and expectations.

Benefit: It ensures that the final product meets the client's vision.

Stakeholders and Regulators:

Use: External stakeholders and regulatory bodies may use the SRS to assess compliance and functionality.

Benefit: It aids in ensuring that the software complies with industry or legal standards.

Designers and UX/UI Specialists:

Use: Designers refer to the SRS to understand the functionality and user requirements, allowing them to create a user-friendly interface.

Benefit: It guides the creation of a user experience that aligns with the software's purpose.

Q 3. Write short note on Control and Process Specification. [R.T.U.2017]

Ans 3: In software engineering, "Control and Process Specification" is a critical aspect of software development methodology that focuses on defining and managing the processes and control mechanisms used throughout the software development lifecycle. This ensures that the development process is well-organized, controlled, and adheres to established standards and best practices. Here's a short note on this concept:

Process Definition:

Definition: Process specification involves clearly defining the step-by-step procedures, methods, and activities to be followed during software development.

Purpose: It helps in achieving consistency and predictability in the development process, making it easier to manage, measure, and improve.

Quality Assurance:

Definition: Process specifications include quality assurance measures, such as testing, reviews, and inspections, to ensure that the software meets defined quality standards.

Purpose: Quality assurance helps identify and rectify defects early in the development cycle, reducing the likelihood of costly issues in later stages.

Process Control:

Definition: Process control involves monitoring, measuring, and controlling the development process to ensure that it adheres to defined standards and goals.

Purpose: Process control enables project managers and stakeholders to track progress, identify deviations, and take corrective actions when necessary to keep the project on course.

Change Management:

Definition: Process specifications often include change management procedures, outlining how changes to the software or project scope are requested, evaluated, and approved.

Purpose: Effective change management ensures that modifications to the software or project are thoroughly assessed for their impact on the development process, cost, and timeline.

Configuration Management:

Definition: Process specifications also cover configuration management, detailing how software components, versions, and configurations are managed and documented.

Purpose: Configuration management helps maintain a clear record of software changes, ensuring that the right version of the software is being developed and delivered.

Compliance and Standards:

Definition: Process specifications often address compliance with industry standards, methodologies, and best practices, such as ISO 9001 or specific software development frameworks like Agile or Scrum.

Purpose: Adherence to established standards ensures that the development process is efficient, reliable, and meets recognized quality benchmarks.

Documentation and Training:

Definition: Process specifications include documentation of procedures and training materials to ensure that team members understand and follow the defined processes.

Purpose: Proper documentation and training support knowledge transfer and consistent application of processes across the development team.

Q 4. What is requirement specification in Software Engineering? Describe in detail along with importance in software development. [R.T.U. 2017]

Ans 4: Requirement specification in software engineering refers to the process of clearly and comprehensively defining what a software system is expected to do, how it should behave, and the constraints it must adhere to. It is a fundamental phase in software development that transforms the needs and desires of stakeholders into precise and unambiguous requirements that serve as the foundation for designing, building, and testing the software. This specification typically includes both functional and non-functional requirements and is crucial for a successful software development process.

Importance of Requirement Specification in Software Development:

Clear Understanding: Requirement specification ensures that all stakeholders, including developers, testers, project managers, and clients, have a shared and unambiguous understanding of what the software is supposed to achieve. This clarity is essential for effective communication and collaboration.

Alignment with User Needs: It helps align the software with the needs and expectations of end-users and clients, making sure that it addresses the problems or opportunities that led to the development project in the first place.

Scope Control: Requirement specification defines the scope of the project, outlining what is and isn't within the boundaries of the software system. This prevents "scope creep" and helps manage project constraints, such as time and budget.

Design Guidance: It provides essential guidance for designing the software. Once the requirements are specified, the design phase can be based on these requirements, ensuring that the design meets the functional and non-functional criteria.

Quality Assurance: Well-defined requirements serve as the basis for quality assurance activities. Testing teams use them to create test cases, ensuring that the software meets the specified criteria.

Risk Mitigation: Requirement specification can help identify potential risks and challenges early in the project. It allows for risk assessment and mitigation planning, reducing the chances of costly issues later in development.

Change Management: When changes to the software or project scope are needed, a well-documented requirement specification provides a basis for evaluating and managing these changes effectively.

Stakeholder Involvement: The requirement specification process often involves stakeholders, including end-users, clients, and subject matter experts. This engagement ensures that the software truly addresses user needs.

Documentation: A well-documented requirement specification serves as a reference for all phases of the software development lifecycle. It provides a historical record of the software's intended functionality.

Contractual Agreement: In many cases, the requirement specification serves as a contractual agreement between the development team and the client or organization. It outlines what will be delivered and under what conditions.

Compliance and Regulations: In industries subject to regulations and standards (e.g., healthcare or finance), requirement specification helps ensure compliance with legal and industry requirements.

Client Satisfaction: Meeting the specified requirements is essential for client satisfaction. A well-specified software product is more likely to meet or exceed client expectations.

Q 5. Write a short note on Software Requirement Specification. [R.T.U.2016]

Ans: A Software Requirement Specification (SRS) is a critical document in the field of software engineering. It serves as the foundation for any software development project, defining what the software should do, how it should behave, and any constraints it must adhere to. The SRS document outlines the software's functional and non-functional requirements in a clear, precise, and unambiguous manner. Here's a concise overview of the SRS:

Key Components of an SRS:

Introduction: The document begins with an introduction that provides an overview of the software, its purpose, and scope.

Functional Requirements: This section defines what the software is expected to do, such as specific features, interactions, and functionality.

Non-Functional Requirements: It outlines requirements related to non-functional aspects, including performance, security, usability, and compliance.
User Interfaces: Details about the user interface, including design elements, user interactions, and user experience considerations.
Data Requirements: Describes data sources, data flow, and data processing requirements, specifying how the software handles information.
System Architecture: High-level system architecture, components, and interactions between modules are outlined.
Testing and Validation Requirements: Criteria for testing and validation, including expected results and acceptance criteria.
Dependencies: Identifies external systems, hardware, or software the software relies on.
Constraints: Any limitations or restrictions affecting the design and development process.
Assumptions: Any assumptions made during the requirements gathering process.
Change Management: Procedures for requesting and managing changes to the requirements.
Importance of an SRS:
Clear Communication: The SRS ensures a common and clear understanding among all stakeholders, including developers, testers, project managers, and clients.
Scope Control: It defines the project's boundaries, preventing scope creep and ensuring the project stays on track.
Quality Assurance: SRS serves as the basis for quality assurance activities, helping ensure that the software meets specified criteria.
Design Guidance: The design phase is based on the SRS, ensuring alignment with user needs and expectations.
Risk Mitigation: Identifying potential risks and challenges early and allowing for risk assessment and mitigation planning.
Change Management: Managing changes effectively by evaluating them against the documented requirements.
Client Satisfaction: Meeting the specified requirements is essential for client satisfaction, as it ensures that the software addresses their needs.

Q 6. Explain the requirement management phase of the requirement engineering. [R.T.U.2016]
Ans 6: The Requirement Management phase is a crucial component of the requirement engineering process in software engineering. Requirement management involves the systematic and controlled management of software requirements throughout the software development lifecycle. It encompasses several key activities and plays a critical role in ensuring that the project remains on track, requirements are properly handled, and changes are managed effectively. Here's an explanation of the Requirement Management phase:
Key Activities in Requirement Management:
Requirement Identification and Capture:
In this phase, stakeholders identify and capture requirements. This includes gathering input from end-users, clients, business analysts, and subject matter experts. The aim is to create a comprehensive list of requirements.
Documentation and Specification:
Once requirements are identified, they need to be documented and specified in a clear and unambiguous manner. This involves using standardized formats and templates to create detailed Requirement Specification documents, such as Software Requirement Specifications (SRS).
Change Control:
Change control mechanisms are established to manage changes to requirements effectively. This involves documenting change requests, evaluating their impact on the project, and making informed decisions about whether to accept or reject them.
Traceability:
Traceability ensures that requirements are linked to design elements, test cases, and other project artifacts. It allows project teams to track how each requirement is addressed throughout the development process, ensuring nothing is overlooked.
Version Control:
Version control is crucial for maintaining a history of requirements. As changes occur, each version is documented and preserved, ensuring transparency and the ability to track changes over time.
Validation and Verification:
Validation confirms that the requirements meet the actual needs of stakeholders. Verification ensures that the requirements have been correctly implemented in the software. This involves reviews, inspections, testing, and validation against acceptance criteria.
Bi-directional Communication:

Effective communication with stakeholders is essential. Requirements should be communicated both to the development team and to the stakeholders to ensure mutual understanding and alignment with project goals.

Requirement Prioritization and Scheduling:

Requirements should be prioritized based on their importance and dependencies. A schedule is established for when each requirement will be addressed during the development process.

Importance of Requirement Management:

Scope Control: Requirement management helps manage scope by preventing scope creep, ensuring that changes are documented and evaluated before implementation.

Change Management: It provides a systematic process for handling requirement changes, which are inevitable in most software projects.

Risk Management: Effective management of requirements helps identify and mitigate risks early in the project.

Quality Assurance: Requirement management ensures that the software meets the specified requirements and quality standards.

Traceability: Traceability ensures that every requirement is addressed, enhancing project transparency.

Client Satisfaction: A well-managed requirement process helps ensure that the software aligns with client needs and expectations.

Efficiency: It improves the efficiency of the development process by providing a clear roadmap for design and testing.

Q 7. What is requirement analysis. Explain the requirement analysis tusks and principles. [RTU2015]

Ans 7: Requirement analysis is a critical phase in software engineering that involves the systematic gathering, identification, clarification, and validation of requirements for a software system. It is the process of understanding and defining what a software system needs to do, how it should behave, and what constraints it must adhere to. Effective requirement analysis is foundational to the success of a software project, as it serves as the basis for all subsequent development activities.

Tasks in Requirement Analysis:

Elicitation: This task involves collecting requirements from various stakeholders, including end-users, clients, business analysts, and subject matter experts. Techniques like interviews, surveys, workshops, and observations are used to elicit requirements.

Documentation: Once requirements are gathered, they need to be documented in a structured and clear manner. This typically involves creating documents such as Software Requirement Specifications (SRS) that outline each requirement with its description, source, priority, and dependencies.

Analysis and Prioritization: Requirements are analyzed to ensure they are complete, unambiguous, and consistent. They are also prioritized based on their importance and criticality to the software's success.

Validation and Verification: Requirements are subject to validation to ensure they align with stakeholders' needs. Verification is the process of checking that requirements are correctly implemented in the software design and development.

Modeling: Requirement analysis often involves creating models and diagrams to represent the system's structure and behavior. These may include data flow diagrams, use cases, entity-relationship diagrams, and more.

Conflict Resolution: Conflicts or inconsistencies in requirements are resolved through negotiation and communication with stakeholders. The goal is to reach a consensus on how to handle conflicts.

Change Management: Requirements are dynamic and may change over the course of the project. Requirement analysts must establish a process for managing changes, including documenting change requests and evaluating their impact.

Principles of Requirement Analysis:

Clarity: Requirements should be clear, concise, and unambiguous. Avoiding vague language and ensuring that all stakeholders understand the requirements is crucial.

Completeness: All necessary requirements must be identified and included. There should be no critical functionality or constraints missing.

Consistency: Requirements should not conflict with each other. They should be consistent with the software's overall goals.

Correctness: Requirements should accurately reflect stakeholders' needs and expectations. They must be factually correct.

Feasibility: Requirements should be feasible within the given project constraints, including budget, time, and available technology.

Relevance: Requirements should be relevant to the software's goals and user needs. Avoid including superfluous or unnecessary features.

Traceability: There should be traceability from requirements to design elements and test cases, ensuring that each requirement is addressed throughout the development process.
Change Management: Establish a clear process for handling requirement changes, ensuring that they are documented, evaluated, and communicated to all stakeholders.
Validation: Validate requirements to ensure they meet the actual needs of stakeholders. Validation may include user reviews, inspections, and prototype testing.
Priority and Dependency Management: Prioritize requirements based on their importance and dependencies, allowing for an organized development schedule.

Q 8. What is prototyping? How it is useful for the development of requirement specification? [R.T.U.2015]
Ans 8: **Prototyping** in the context of software development is a technique used to visualize and validate the requirements and functionalities of a software system. It involves creating a simplified, working model or prototype of the software to help stakeholders better understand how the final product will look and function. Here's how prototyping is useful for the development of requirement specifications:

Improved Communication:
Prototypes provide a tangible and visual representation of the software. This aids in bridging the gap between stakeholders with varying levels of technical expertise, such as developers, business analysts, and end-users. It's often easier for non-technical stakeholders to understand and provide feedback on a prototype rather than abstract textual requirements.

Requirement Validation:
Prototypes allow stakeholders to interact with a basic version of the software early in the development process. This hands-on experience helps identify potential gaps, inconsistencies, and misunderstandings in the initial requirement specification. Stakeholders can verify whether the prototype aligns with their actual needs and expectations.

Early Problem Identification:
By using a prototype, issues and challenges that may not have been evident through static documentation can be identified and resolved early. This prevents costly and time-consuming changes later in the development process.

Requirement Refinement:
Prototyping often leads to valuable feedback and suggestions for improving requirements. As stakeholders interact with the prototype, they may realize additional features or changes that should be incorporated into the final product.

Reduced Misunderstandings:
The visual and interactive nature of prototypes reduces the potential for misunderstandings. Stakeholders can see and experience the software, making it easier to convey their expectations and requirements.

User Involvement:
Prototypes promote user involvement and collaboration in the requirement specification process. Users can actively participate in refining and shaping the software by providing feedback on the prototype, increasing their sense of ownership.

Iterative Development:
Prototyping often follows an iterative approach. As feedback is collected from stakeholders and changes are made to the prototype, it leads to an iterative refinement of the requirement specification. This agile process ensures that requirements are continually improved and aligned with evolving needs.

Risk Mitigation:
By addressing potential issues early, prototyping helps mitigate risks associated with misunderstandings or changing requirements, reducing the likelihood of costly rework.

Visualization of Complex Functionality:
For complex software systems, especially those with intricate user interfaces or unique features, prototypes offer a clear way to visualize and experiment with how these elements will function.

Cost Savings:
Detecting and resolving requirement issues during the early stages of development is considerably less expensive than doing so later in the process. Prototyping helps in cost savings by avoiding rework and delays.

Q 9. Define software requirement engineering. [R.T.U.2014]
Ans9: Software Requirement Engineering, often referred to as Requirement Engineering, is a systematic and disciplined approach to the elicitation, documentation, analysis, and management of software requirements. It serves as a foundational phase in the software development process, dedicated to comprehending and defining what a software system should achieve, how it should operate, and the limitations it must adhere to. Requirement engineering involves a structured workflow, starting with the collection of requirements from various stakeholders,

including clients, end-users, and experts, followed by meticulous documentation and rigorous analysis. Prioritization of requirements, validation, and verification processes ensure the quality and relevance of the requirements. Moreover, modeling techniques aid in visualizing the system's structure and behavior. An integral part of the process is the management of changes, given that requirements are subject to evolution throughout the project. Effective communication is maintained with stakeholders to ensure mutual understanding and alignment with project objectives. Ultimately, requirement engineering is pivotal for software development, as it establishes the groundwork upon which the entire project is built, ensuring the delivery of software that fulfills user needs and complies with project constraints.

Q 10. What are functional and non-functional software system requirements? [RTU 2014]

Ans 10: Functional and Non-Functional Requirements are two distinct categories of software system requirements that collectively define the behavior, features, and constraints of a software application or system:

Functional Requirements:

Definition: Functional requirements describe the specific functions, capabilities, and interactions a software system should perform. They outline what the system is expected to do and how it should respond to different inputs or user actions.

Examples:

User authentication and login functionality.

Order processing and payment handling in an e-commerce system.

Inventory management and tracking of items in a warehouse management system.

Search and filtering options in a search engine.

Generation of reports or documents in a document management system.

Characteristics:

They are task-oriented, focusing on what the system accomplishes.

Functional requirements can often be validated through testing or by observing the software in action.

They are typically represented through use cases, user stories, flowcharts, and other modeling techniques.

Non-Functional Requirements:

Definition: Non-functional requirements define the attributes or qualities of a software system rather than its specific functionality. They describe how the system should perform in terms of speed, security, scalability, reliability, and user experience.

Examples:

Response time: Specifies how quickly the system should respond to user requests.

Security: Outlines the security measures, access control, and encryption requirements.

Scalability: Describes how the system should handle increased workloads or user loads.

Availability: Specifies the system's uptime and reliability expectations.

Usability: Defines the user interface and user experience requirements.

Characteristics:

Non-functional requirements focus on the quality aspects of the system.

They may not always be directly testable but are essential for the overall success of the system.

Non-functional requirements can significantly impact the user's perception of the software.

Previous Years Unsolved Questions

Q 1. How can formal methods be used to specify the aspects of a system other than the functionality? Also list some of the areas where the formal specifications can be applied. [IGNOU, June, 2018]

Q 2. Write the top-level structure of SRS. [IGNOU, December, 2015]

Q 3. Write a short note on software prototyping. [IGNOU, December, 2016]

Q 4. Discuss in detail about the problems in SRS. [IGNOU, June, 2017]

Q 5. Define Prototyping. Explain throw-away prototype and evolutionary prototype and describe for which kind of projects can one use these types of prototypes. What are advantages and disadvantages? [IGNOU, December, 2017, 2011]

Q 6. S/w Requirements Specification (SRS) is 10 generated as the o/p of Requirement Analysis." Explain the properties and the outlines of the SRS. Also mention various features which makes the requirements analysis difficult. [IGNOU, December, 2011]
Q 7. Differentiate between functional and non - functional requirements. [IGNOU, December, 2012] [Kota university 2021]
Q 8. State and explain the requirement 10 Engineering process. [IGNOU, December, 2012]
Q 9. Give two examples for functional and non-functional requirements. [Anna University 2022]
Q 10. With examples state the difference between user requirements and system requirements. [Anna University 2022]
Q 11. What are Software Requirements Specifications (SRS)? How do you prepare this? [MCU 2019] [VTU 2022]
Q 12. What do you understand by software quality control and SQA activities. [MCU 2019]
Q 13. Explain in detail of evolutionary process model. [Kota University 2021]
Q 14. Explain the different type of non- functional requirement? [VTU 2021]
Q 15. Explain the steps involved in Requirements engineering process. [VTU 2021]

Chapter 3: Software Measurement and metrics

3.1 Introduction of Software Measurement and Metrics

Software Measurement: A measurement is a manifestation of the size, quantity, amount, or dimension of a particular attribute of a product or process. Software measurement is a titrate impute of a characteristic of a software product or the software process. It is an authority within software engineering. The software measurement process is defined and governed by ISO Standard.

Software Measurement Principles:

The software measurement process can be characterized by five activities-

Formulation: The derivation of software measures and metrics appropriate for the representation of the software that is being considered.

Collection: The mechanism used to accumulate data required to derive the formulated metrics.

Analysis: The computation of metrics and the application of mathematical tools.

Interpretation: The evaluation of metrics resulting in insight into the quality of the representation.

Feedback: Recommendation derived from the interpretation of product metrics transmitted to the software team.

Need for Software Measurement:

Software is measured to:

Create the quality of the current product or process.

Anticipate future qualities of the product or process.

Enhance the quality of a product or process.

Regulate the state of the project in relation to budget and schedule.

Enable data-driven decision-making in project planning and control.

Identify bottlenecks and areas for improvement to drive process improvement activities.

Ensure that industry standards and regulations are followed.

Give software products and processes a quantitative basis for evaluation.

Enable the ongoing improvement of software development practices.

Classification of Software Measurement:

There are 2 types of software measurement:

Direct Measurement: In direct measurement, the product, process, or thing is measured directly using a standard scale.

Indirect Measurement: In indirect measurement, the quantity or quality to be measured is measured using related parameters i.e. by use of reference.

Metrics:

A metric is a measurement of the level at which any impute belongs to a system product or process.

Software metrics will be useful only if they are characterized effectively and validated so that their worth is proven.

There are 4 functions related to software metrics:

Planning

Organizing

Controlling

Improving

Characteristics of software Metrics:

Quantitative: Metrics must possess quantitative nature. It means metrics can be expressed in values.

Understandable: Metric computation should be easily understood, and the method of computing metrics should be clearly defined.

Applicability: Metrics should be applicable in the initial phases of the development of the software.

Repeatable: The metric values should be the same when measured repeatedly and consistent in nature.

Economical: The computation of metrics should be economical.

Language Independent: Metrics should not depend on any programming language.

Classification of Software Metrics:

There are 3 types of software metrics:

Product Metrics: Product metrics are used to evaluate the state of the product, tracing risks and undercover prospective problem areas. The ability of the team to control quality is evaluated. Examples include lines of code, cyclomatic complexity, code coverage, defect density, and code maintainability index.

Process Metrics: Process metrics pay particular attention to enhancing the long-term process of the team or organization. Examples include effort variance, schedule variance, defect injection rate, and lead time.

Project Metrics: The project matrix describes the project characteristic and execution process. Examples include effort estimation accuracy, schedule deviation, cost variance, and productivity.

Number of software developer

Staffing patterns over the life cycle of software

Cost and schedule

Productivity

Advantages of Software Metrics :

Reduction in cost or budget.

It helps to identify the particular area for improvising.

It helps to increase the product quality.

Managing the workloads and teams.

Reduction in overall time to produce the product,.

It helps to determine the complexity of the code and to test the code with resources.

It helps in providing effective planning, controlling and managing of the entire product.

Disadvantages of Software Metrics :

It is expensive and difficult to implement the metrics in some cases.

Performance of the entire team or an individual from the team can't be determined. Only the performance of the product is determined.

Sometimes the quality of the product is not met with the expectation.

It leads to measure the unwanted data which is wastage of time.

Measuring the incorrect data leads to make wrong decision making.

3.2 People Metrics and Process Metrics

People Metrics

People metrics play an important role in software project management. These are also called personnel metrics. Some authors view resource metrics to include personnel metrics, software metrics, and hardware metrics but most of the authors mainly view resource metrics to consist of personnel metrics only. In the present context, we also assume resource metrics to include mainly personnel metrics.

People metrics quantify useful attributes of those generating the products using the available processes, methods, and tools. These metrics tell you about the attributes like turnover rates, productivity, and absenteeism.

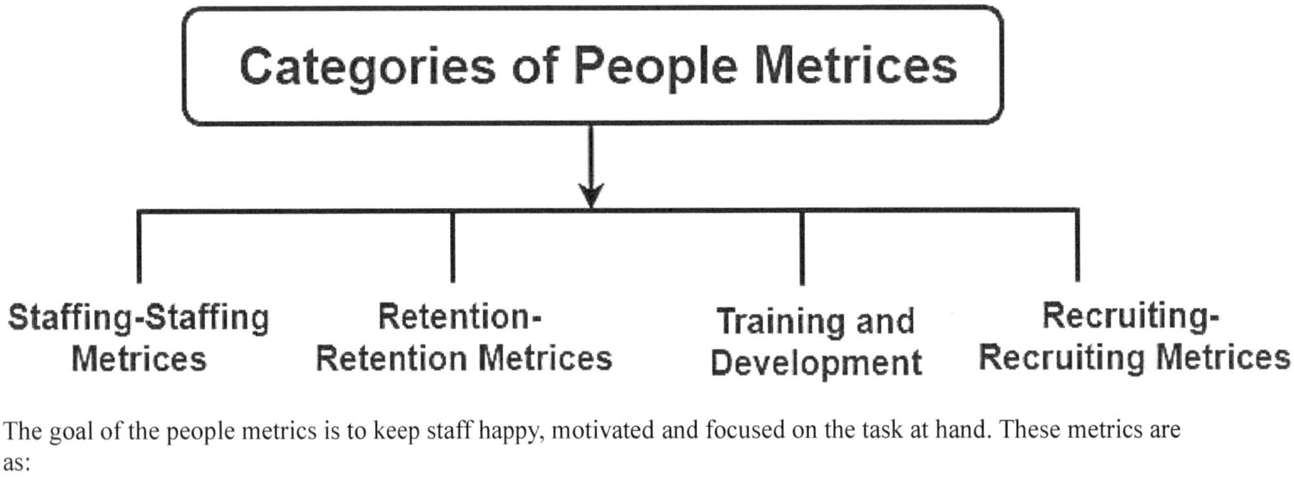

The goal of the people metrics is to keep staff happy, motivated and focused on the task at hand. These metrics are as:

Programming Experience Metrics

Programming language experience

Development methods experience

Management experience

Communication Level Metrics

Teamwork experience

Communication hardware software level.

Personal availability.
Productivity Metrics
Size productivity
Productivity statistics
Quality vs. Productivity
Team Structure Metrics
Hierarchy metrics.
Team stability metrics
People metrics are very helpful in assisting the appropriate allocation of resources amongst various software project activities.
Process Metrics
Process Metrics are the measures of the development process that creates a body of software. A common example of a process metric is the length of time that the process of software creation tasks.
Based on the assumption that the quality of the product is a direct function of the process, process metrics can be used to estimate, monitor, and improve the reliability and quality of software. ISO- 9000 certification, or "Quality Management Standards", is the generic reference for a family of standards developed by the International Standard Organization (ISO).
Often, Process Metrics are tools of management in their attempt to gain insight into the creation of a product that is intangible. Since the software is abstract, there is no visible, traceable artifact from software projects. Objectively tracking progress becomes extremely difficult. Management is interested in measuring progress and productivity and being able to make predictions concerning both.
Process metrics are often collected as part of a model of software development. Models such as Boehm's COCOMO (Constructive Cost Model) make cost estimations for software projects. The boat's COPMO makes predictions about the need for additional effort on large projects.
Although valuable management tools, process metrics are not directly relevant to program understanding. They are more useful in measuring and predicting such things as resource usage and schedule.
Types of Process Metrics
Static Process Metrics: Static Process Metrics are directly related to the defined process. For example, the number of types of roles, types of artifacts, etc.
Dynamic Process Metrics: Dynamic Process Metrics are simply related to the properties of process performance. For example, how many activities are performed, how many artifacts are created, etc.)
Process Evolution Metrics: Process Evolution Metrics are related to the process of making changes over a period of time. For example, how many iterations are there within the process)

3.3 Halstead's Software Metrics

Halstead's Software metrics are a set of measures proposed by Maurice Halstead to evaluate the complexity of a software program. These metrics are based on the number of distinct operators and operands in the program and are used to estimate the effort required to develop and maintain the program.
Field of Halstead Metrics
Program length (N): This is the total number of operator and operand occurrences in the program.
Vocabulary size (n): This is the total number of distinct operators and operands in the program.
Program volume (V): This is the product of program length (N) and the logarithm of vocabulary size (n), i.e., V = N*log2(n).
Program level (L): This is the ratio of the number of operator occurrences to the number of operand occurrences in the program, i.e., L = n1/n2, where n1 is the number of operator occurrences and n2 is the number of operand occurrences.
Program difficulty (D): This is the ratio of the number of unique operators to the total number of operators in the program, i.e., D = (n1/2) * (N2/n2).
Program effort (E): This is the product of program volume (V) and program difficulty (D), i.e., E = V*D.
Time to implement (T): This is the estimated time required to implement the program, based on the program effort (E) and a constant value that depends on the programming language and development environment.
Halstead's software metrics can be used to estimate the size, complexity, and effort required to develop and maintain a software program. However, they have some limitations, such as the assumption that all operators and operands are equally important, and the assumption that the same set of metrics can be used for different programming languages and development environments.

Overall, Halstead's software metrics can be a useful tool for software developers and project managers to estimate the effort required to develop and maintain software programs.
n1 = Number of distinct operators.
n2 = Number of distinct operands.
N1 = Total number of occurrences of operators.
N2 = Total number of occurrences of operands.

Halstead Metrics

Halstead metrics are:

Halstead Program Length: The total number of operator occurrences and the total number of operand occurrences.
N = N1 + N2
And estimated program length is, N^ = n1log2n1 + n2log2n2
The following alternate expressions have been published to estimate program length:
NJ = log2(n1!) + log2(n2!)
NB = n1 * log2n2 + n2 * log2n1
NC = n1 * sqrt(n1) + n2 * sqrt(n2)
NS = (n * log2n) / 2

Halstead Vocabulary: The total number of unique operators and unique operand occurrences.
n = n1 + n2

Program Volume: Proportional to program size, represents the size, in bits, of space necessary for storing the program. This parameter is dependent on specific algorithm implementation. The properties V, N, and the number of lines in the code are shown to be linearly connected and equally valid for measuring relative program size.
V = Size * (log2 vocabulary) = N * log2(n)
The unit of measurement of volume is the common unit for size "bits". It is the actual size of a program if a uniform binary encoding for the vocabulary is used. And error = Volume / 3000

Potential Minimum Volume: The potential minimum volume V* is defined as the volume of the most succinct program in which a problem can be coded.
V* = (2 + n2*) * log2(2 + n2*)
Here, n2* is the count of unique input and output parameters

Program Level: To rank the programming languages, the level of abstraction provided by the programming language, Program Level (L) is considered. The higher the level of a language, the less effort it takes to develop a program using that language.
L = V* / V
The value of L ranges between zero and one, with L=1 representing a program written at the highest possible level (i.e., with minimum size).
And estimated program level is L^ =2 * (n2) / (n1)(N2)

Program Difficulty: This parameter shows how difficult to handle the program is.
D = (n1 / 2) * (N2 / n2)
D = 1 / L
As the volume of the implementation of a program increases, the program level decreases and the difficulty increases. Thus, programming practices such as redundant usage of operands, or the failure to use higher-level control constructs will tend to increase the volume as well as the difficulty.

Programming Effort: Measures the amount of mental activity needed to translate the existing algorithm into implementation in the specified program language.
E = V / L = D * V = Difficulty * Volume

Language Level: Shows the algorithm implementation program language level. The same algorithm demands additional effort if it is written in a low-level program language. For example, it is easier to program in Pascal than in Assembler.
L' = V / D / D
lambda = L * V* = L2 * V

Intelligence Content: Determines the amount of intelligence presented (stated) in the program This parameter provides a measurement of program complexity, independently of the programming language in which it was implemented.
I = V / D

Programming Time: Shows time (in minutes) needed to translate the existing algorithm into implementation in the specified program language.
T = E / (f * S)

The concept of the processing rate of the human brain, developed by psychologist John Stroud, is also used. Stoud defined a moment as the time required by the human brain requires to carry out the most elementary decision. The Stoud number S is therefore Stoud's moments per second with:
5 <= S <= 20. Halstead uses 18. The value of S has been empirically developed from psychological reasoning, and its recommended value for programming applications is 18.
Stroud number S = 18 moments / second seconds-to-minutes factor f = 60

Counting Rules for C Language

Comments are not considered.
The identifier and function declarations are not considered
All the variables and constants are considered operands.
Global variables used in different modules of the same program are counted as multiple occurrences of the same variable.
Local variables with the same name in different functions are counted as unique operands.
Functions calls are considered operators.
All looping statements e.g., do {…} while ( ), while ( ) {…}, for ( ) {…}, all control statements e.g., if ( ) {…}, if ( ) {…} else {…}, etc. are considered as operators.
In control construct switch ( ) {case:…}, switch as well as all the case statements are considered as operators.
The reserve words like return, default, continue, break, size, etc., are considered operators.
All the brackets, commas, and terminators are considered operators.
GOTO is counted as an operator and the label is counted as an operand.
The unary and binary occurrences of "+" and "-" are dealt with separately. Similarly "*" (multiplication operator) is dealt with separately.
In the array variables such as "array-name [index]" "array-name" and "index" are considered as operands and [ ] is considered as operator.
In the structure variables such as "struct-name, member-name" or "struct-name -> member-name", struct-name, and member-name are taken as operands, and '.', '->' are taken as operators. Some names of member elements in different structure variables are counted as unique operands.
All the hash directives are ignored.

Example – List out the operators and operands and also calculate the values of software science measures like

```
int sort (int x[ ], int n)
{
  int i, j, save, im1;
  /*This function sorts array x in ascending order */
  If (n< 2) return 1;
  for (i=2; i< =n; i++)
  {
    im1=i-1;
    for (j=1; j< =im1; j++)
      if (x[i] < x[j])
      {
        Save = x[i];
        x[i] = x[j];
        x[j] = save;
      }
  }
  return 0;
}
```

Explanation

Operators	Occurrences	Operands	Occurrences
int	4	sort	1
()	5	x	7
,	4	n	3
[]	7	i	8
if	2	j	7

<	2	save	3
;	11	im1	3
for	2	2	2
=	6	1	3
–	1	0	1
<=	2	–	–
++	2	–	–
return	2	–	–
{}	3	–	–
n1=14	N1=53	n2=10	N2=38

Therefore,
N = 91
n = 24
V = 417.23 bits
N^ = 86.51
n2* = 3 (x:array holding integer to be sorted. This is used both as input and output)
V* = 11.6
L = 0.027
D = 37.03
L^ = 0.038
T = 610 seconds

3.4 Cyclomatic Complexity

The cyclomatic complexity of a code section is the quantitative measure of the number of linearly independent paths in it. It is a software metric used to indicate the complexity of a program. It is computed using the Control Flow Graph of the program. The nodes in the graph indicate the smallest group of commands of a program, and a directed edge in it connects the two nodes i.e. if the second command might immediately follow the first command.

For example, if the source code contains no control flow statement then its cyclomatic complexity will be 1, and the source code contains a single path in it. Similarly, if the source code contains one if condition then cyclomatic complexity will be 2 because there will be two paths one for true and the other for false.

Mathematically, for a structured program, the directed graph inside the control flow is the edge joining two basic blocks of the program as control may pass from first to second.

So, cyclomatic complexity M would be defined as,
M = E – N + 2P where E = the number of edges in the control flow graph
N = the number of nodes in the control flow graph
P = the number of connected components

In case, when exit point is directly connected back to the entry point. Here, the graph is strongly connected, and cyclometric complexity is defined as

$M = E - N + P$

where
E = the number of edges in the control flow graph
N = the number of nodes in the control flow graph
P = the number of connected components

In the case of a single method, P is equal to 1. So, for a single subroutine, the formula can be defined as

$M = E - N + 2$

where
E = the number of edges in the control flow graph
N = the number of nodes in the control flow graph
P = the number of connected components

How to Calculate Cyclomatic Complexity?

Steps that should be followed in calculating cyclomatic complexity and test cases design are:
Construction of graph with nodes and edges from code.
Identification of independent paths.
Cyclomatic Complexity Calculation
Design of Test Cases
Let a section of code as such:

```
A = 10
  IF B > C THEN
    A = B
  ELSE
    A = C
  ENDIF
Print A
Print B
Print C
```

Control Flow Graph of the above code

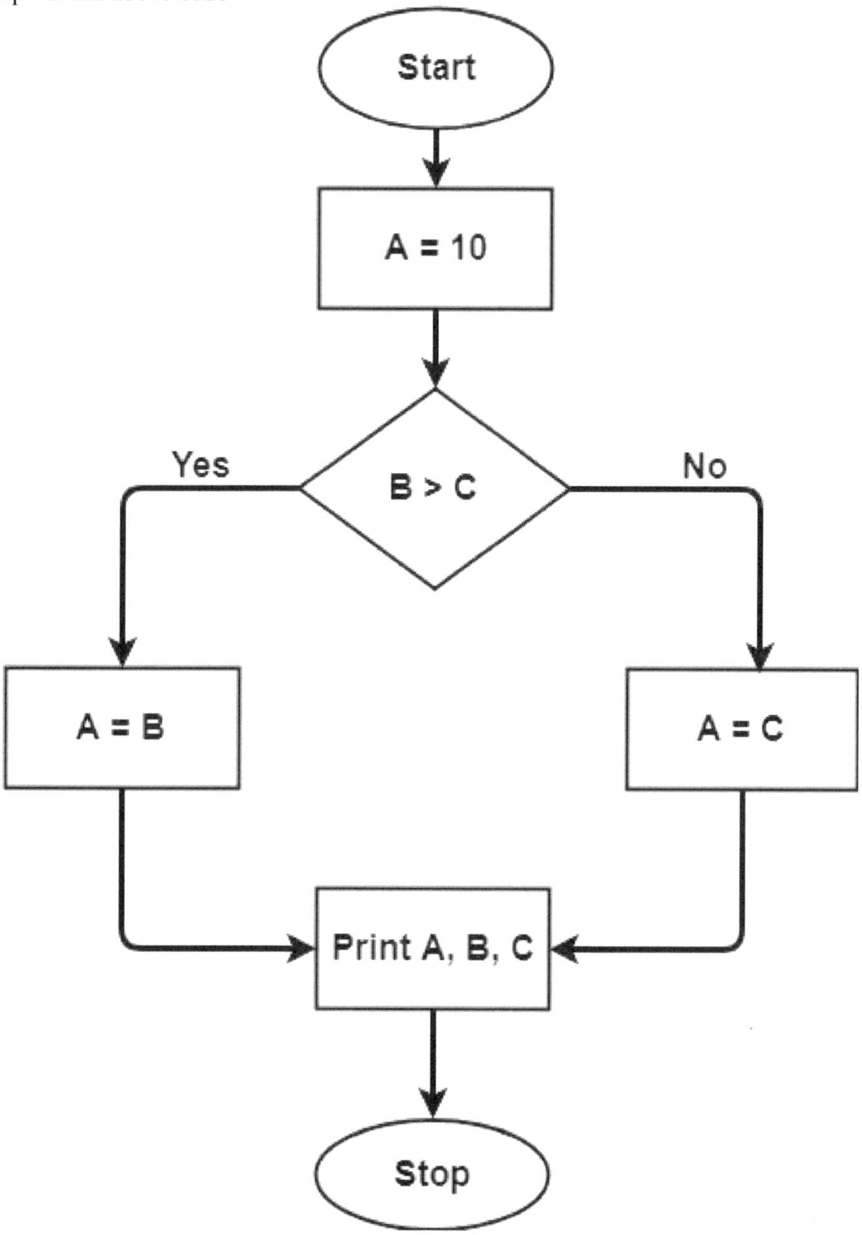

Cyclomatic Complexity

The cyclomatic complexity calculated for the above code will be from the control flow graph. The graph shows seven shapes(nodes), and seven lines(edges), hence cyclomatic complexity is 7-7+2 = 2.

Use of Cyclomatic Complexity

Determining the independent path executions thus proven to be very helpful for Developers and Testers.

It can make sure that every path has been tested at least once.

Thus help to focus more on uncovered paths.

Code coverage can be improved.

Risks associated with the program can be evaluated.

These metrics being used earlier in the program help in reducing the risks.

3.5 Functional Point Analysis

Function Point Analysis was initially developed by Allan J. Albrecht in 1979 at IBM and it has been further modified by the International Function Point Users Group (IFPUG). The initial definition is given by Allan J. Albrecht.

Functional Point Analysis gives a dimensionless number defined in function points which we have found to be an effective relative measure of function value delivered to our customer.

Objectives of Functional Point Analysis

The objective of FPA is to measure the functionality that the user requests and receives.

The objective of FPA is to measure software development and maintenance independently of the technology used for implementation.

It should be simple enough to minimize the overhead of the measurement process.

It should be a consistent measure among various projects and organizations.

Types of Functional Point Analysis

There are basically two types of Functional Point Analysis, that are listed below.

Transactional Functional Type

Data Functional Type

Transactional Functional Type

External Input (EI): EI processes data or control information that comes from outside the application's boundary. The EI is an elementary process.

External Output (EO): EO is an elementary process that generates data or control information sent outside the application's boundary.

External Inquiries (EQ): EQ is an elementary process made up of an input-output combination that results in data retrieval.

Data Functional Type

Internal Logical File (ILF): A user-identifiable group of logically related data or control information maintained within the boundary of the application.

External Interface File (EIF): A group of users recognizable logically related data allusion to the software but maintained within the boundary of another software.

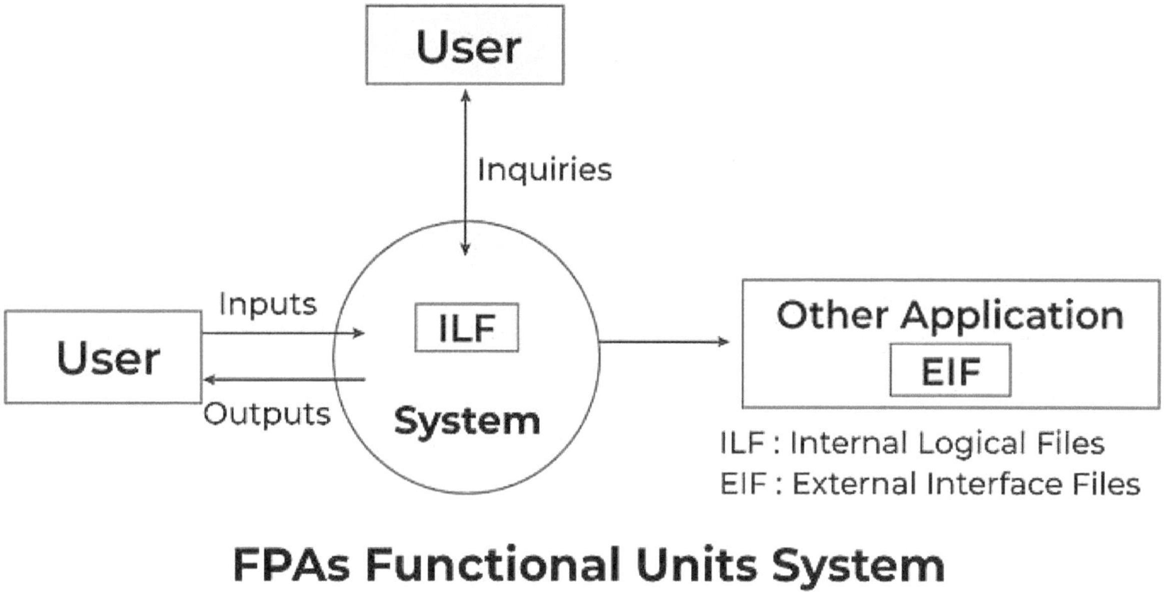

Functional Point Analysis

Benefits of Functional Point Analysis

FPA is a tool to determine the size of a purchased application package by counting all the functions included in the package.

It is a tool to help users discover the benefit of an application package to their organization by counting functions that specifically match their requirements.

It is a tool to measure the units of a software product to support quality and productivity analysis.

It is a vehicle to estimate the cost and resources required for software development and maintenance.

It is a normalization factor for software comparison.

Characteristics of Functional Point Analysis

We calculate the functional point with the help of the number of functions and types of functions used in applications. These are classified into five types.

Measurement Parameters	**Examples**
Number of External Inputs (EI)	Input screen and tables
Number of External Output (EO)	Output screens and reports
Number of external inquiries (EQ)	Prompts and interrupts
Number of internal files (ILF)	Databases and directories
Number of external interfaces (EIF)	Shared databases and shared routines

Functional Point helps in describing system complexity and also shows project timelines. It is majorly used for business systems like information systems.

Weights of 5 Functional Point Attributes

Measurement Parameter	**Low**	**Average**	**High**
Number of external inputs (EI)	3	4	6
Number of external outputs (EO)	4	5	7
Number of external inquiries (EQ)	3	4	6

Number of internal files (ILF)	7	10	15
Number of External Interfaces (EIF)	5	7	10

Functional Complexities help us in finding the corresponding weights, which results in finding the Unadjusted Functional point (UFp) of the Subsystem. Consider the complexity as average for all cases. Below mentioned is the way how to compute FP.

Measurement Parameter	**Count**		**Weighing Factor**		
		Total Count	**Simple**	**Average**	**Complex**
Number of external inputs (EI)	32	32*4=128	3	4	6
Number of external outputs (EO)	60	60*5=300	4	5	7
Number of external inquiries (EQ)	24	24*4=96	3	4	6
Number of internal files (ILF)	8	8*10=80	7	10	15
Number of external interfaces (EIF)	2	2*7=14	5	7	10
Algorithms used Count total →		618			

From the above tables, Functional Point is calculated with the following formula

FP = Count-Total * [0.65 + 0.01 * ∑(fi)]

= Count * CAF

Here, the count-total is taken from the chart.

CAF = [0.65 + 0.01 * ∑(fi)]

∑(fi) = sum of all 14 questions and it also shows the complexity factor – CAF.

CAF varies from 0.65 to 1.35 and ∑(fi) ranges from 0 to 70.

When ∑(fi) = 0, CAF = 0.65 and when ∑(fi) = 70, CAF = 0.65 + (0.01*70) = 0.65 + 0.7 = 1.35

3.6 Line of code (LOC)

A line of code (LOC) is any line of text in a code that is not a comment or blank line, and also header lines, in any case of the number of statements or fragments of statements on the line. LOC clearly consists of all lines containing the declaration of any variable, and executable and non-executable statements. As Lines of Code (LOC) only counts the volume of code, you can only use it to compare or estimate projects that use the same language and are coded using the same coding standards.

Features:

Variations such as "source lines of code", are used to set out a codebase.

LOC is frequently used in some kinds of arguments.

They are used in assessing a project's performance or efficiency.

Advantages:

Most used metric in cost estimation.

Its alternates have many problems as compared to this metric.

It is very easy in estimating the efforts.

Disadvantages:

Very difficult to estimate the LOC of the final program from the problem specification.

It correlates poorly with quality and efficiency of code.

It doesn't consider complexity.

Research has shown a rough correlation between LOC and the overall cost and length of developing a project/ product in Software Development, and between LOC and the number of defects. This means the lower your LOC measurement is, the better off you probably are in the development of your product.

Let's take an example and check how does the Line of code work in the simple sorting program given below:

```
void selSort(int x[], int n) {
  //Below function sorts an array in ascending order
  int i, j, min, temp;
  for (i = 0; i < n - 1; i++) {
    min = i;
    for (j = i + 1; j < n; j++)
    if (x[j] < x[min])
    min = j;
    temp = x[i];
    x[i] = x[min];
    x[min] = temp;
  }
}
```

So, now If LOC is simply a count of the number of lines, then the above function shown contains 13 lines of code (LOC). But when comments and blank lines are ignored, the function shown above contains 12 lines of code (LOC).

Let's take another example and check how does the Line of code work the given below:

```
void main ()
{
   int fN, sN, tN;
   cout << "Enter the 2 integers: ";
   cin >> fN >> sN;
   // sum of two numbers in stored in variable sum
   sum = fN + sN;
   // Prints sum
   cout << fN << " + " << sN << " = " << sum;
   return 0;
}
```

Here also, If LOC is simply a count of the numbers of lines then the above function shown contains 11 lines of code (LOC). But when comments and blank lines are ignored, the function shown above contains 9 lines of code (LOC).

Exercise

Exercise 1 – MCQ

Q 1. Which of the following is an example of a process metric in software measurement?

A. Lines of code (LOC)
B. Defect density
C. Cyclomatic complexity
D. Effort estimation

Q 2. What is the main goal of software measurement in software engineering?

A. Identifying bugs
B. Project management
C. Code optimization
D. Process improvement

Exercise 2 – True/ False

Q 1. Software metrics are primarily used for identifying and fixing defects in software.

Q 2. A product metric measures aspects related to the software development process.

Exercise 3 – Match case

1. Function Points	A. Measures the number of defects per unit of code.
2. Cyclomatic Complexity	B. Quantifies the size of a software product.
3. Lines of Code	C. Evaluates the complexity of control flow in code.
4. Defect Density	D. Counts the actual lines of code in a program.
5. Product Metrics	E. Focuses on assessing the quality of the software product.

Exercise 4 – One word answer

Q 1. What is a quantifiable measure of software characteristics?

Q 2. What metric measures the size of a software product's source code?

Exercise 5 – Small answer

Q 1. What does the term "LOC" stand for in software measurement?

Q 2. What is the purpose of using function points (FP) as a metric in software development?

Exercise 6 – Long answer

Q 1. Explain the importance of software measurement and metrics in the context of software engineering. How do software metrics contribute to the overall software development process?

Q 2. Discuss the concept of "function points" as a software metric. How are function points calculated, and what insights do they provide about software size and complexity?

Answers

Exercise 1 – MCQ

Ans: 1 D, 2 D

Exercise 2 – True/ False

Ans: 1 False, 2 False

Exercise 3 – Match case

Ans: 1 B, 2 C, 3 D, 4 A, 5 E

Exercise 4 – One word answer

Ans: 1 Metric, 2 LOC (Lines of code)

Online Resources

Online Exam Paper:
Link: https://forms.gle/qVRfeXmNHJ8Ajtst8
QR Code:

Chapter 3 Videos Playlist:
Link: https://www.youtube.com/playlist?list=PLzlh_31VWEFq6abfB2vbz8ywNTiJHYlT-
QR Code:

Previous Years Solved Questions

Q 1. Write any two major differences between LOC and FP estimation techniques. [R.T.U. 2018]
Ans 1:

Aspect	Lines of Code (LOC)	Function Point (FP)
Measurement Unit	LOC measures the size of the codebase in terms of the number of lines or statements written in a programming language. It's a physical measure.	FP measures the functional size of the software based on the number of functionalities and their complexities. It's a functional measure.
Focus	LOC primarily focuses on the code's size, making it more about quantifying the volume of code. It does not consider the functionality.	FP focuses on the functionality provided by the software and how complex or intricate these functions are, thus offering a better representation of the software's real value.

Q 2. Write advantages and disadvantages of function points. [R.T.U.2018]
Ans 2: **Advantages of Function Points in Software Engineering:**
Agile and User-Centric: Function points are a user-centric metric, focusing on the functionality provided by the software from an end-user perspective. This approach aligns well with modern agile development methodologies, where customer needs and user stories are essential.
Technology and Language Independent: Function points are independent of the technology or programming language used, making them applicable across various software development projects. This allows for comparisons and benchmarking between different systems.
Improved Estimation Accuracy: Function points provide a more accurate measure of software size than lines of code, as they account for both internal and external functionalities. This leads to better project estimation and planning.
Resource Allocation: They help in efficient resource allocation by quantifying the functionality, making it easier to allocate the right level of effort for various project components.
Objective Measurement: Function points offer a more objective and standardized way of measuring software, reducing subjectivity in size estimation and making it easier to communicate project requirements.
Project Performance Benchmarking: Function points allow organizations to benchmark their project performance, helping them identify areas for improvement and best practices.

Disadvantages of Function Points in Software Engineering:
Complexity: Calculating function points can be complex and time-consuming, especially for large and intricate software systems. It requires a detailed understanding of the system's functionality.
Learning Curve: Function point analysis requires training and expertise. Teams need to invest in learning the methodology to use it effectively.
Subjectivity: While it aims to be objective, there is some subjectivity involved in determining the complexity of function point components, which can lead to variations in estimations.

Inaccuracy in Early Phases: Estimating function points accurately in the early stages of a project can be challenging when the system's functionality is not well-defined.
Not Suitable for All Projects: Function points may not be suitable for very small or very large projects. They work best for medium to large systems with well-defined functionality.
Documentation Overhead: Proper documentation of function point analysis can be burdensome, requiring additional time and effort.

Q 3. Explain line of code and function point estimation techniques. [R.T.U.2018]
Ans 3: **Line of Code (LOC) Estimation Technique:**
Definition: LOC estimation is a software size estimation technique that measures the size of a software project based on the number of lines of code or statements written in a programming language. It's a simple and widely used method for estimating the size of a software system.
Process:
Counting Lines: The first step is to count the lines of code in the source code files. This can include all lines, including code lines, comments, and blank lines.
Adjustment: Adjustments can be made for different languages and coding practices. For example, some languages are more verbose, so additional lines may be added to the count.
Calculating Size: Once the lines are counted and adjustments made, the size of the software in lines of code is calculated. This is often used as a basis for effort estimation, cost estimation, and productivity measurement.
Advantages of LOC Estimation:
Simplicity and ease of use.
Well-suited for small to medium-sized projects.
Provides a direct correlation between size and effort.
Disadvantages of LOC Estimation:
Not language-independent; different languages may have varying levels of verbosity.
Ignores the complexity of the code or the functionality delivered.
Prone to inaccuracies due to variations in coding styles and practices.
Function Point (FP) Estimation Technique:
Definition: Function points are a software size estimation technique that measures the functional aspects of a software system based on the number and complexity of functionalities provided to the end-users. It's a more abstract and comprehensive method for estimating software size.
Process:
Identifying Functions: Functions provided by the software are identified. These can be inputs, outputs, inquiries, or internal logical files.
Assigning Complexity: Each function is assigned a complexity rating (low, average, or high) based on specific criteria, such as data elements, processing logic, and user interactions.
Calculating Function Points: Function points are calculated by applying a weighted count of the identified functions. The formula typically involves summing the complexity-weighted functions.
Estimating Effort: Once the function points are determined, they are used as a basis for estimating effort, cost, and other project metrics.
Advantages of FP Estimation:
Language-independent; works for projects developed in various programming languages.
Focuses on the functionality delivered to end-users.
More comprehensive and abstract than LOC, considering both external and internal functionality.
Disadvantages of FP Estimation:
Requires a detailed understanding of the software's functionality.
Can be complex and time-consuming, particularly for large projects.
Subjectivity can influence complexity ratings.
When to Use Each Technique:
LOC estimation is often used for smaller projects where a quick and simple estimate is needed.
FP estimation is preferred for medium to large projects with well-defined functionality, as it provides a more comprehensive and objective measure of software size. It aligns well with user-centric, functional specifications.

Q 4. Explain data flow and control flow diagrams with suitable example. [RTU2014, 2010]

Ans 4: A Data Flow Diagram (DFD) is a traditional visual representation of the information flows within a system. A neat and clear DFD can depict the right amount of the system requirement graphically. It can be manual, automated, or a combination of both.

It shows how data enters and leaves the system, what changes the information, and where data is stored.

The objective of a DFD is to show the scope and boundaries of a system as a whole. It may be used as a communication tool between a system analyst and any person who plays a part in the order that acts as a starting point for redesigning a system. The DFD is also called as a data flow graph or bubble chart.

The following observations about DFDs are essential:

All names should be unique. This makes it easier to refer to elements in the DFD.

Remember that DFD is not a flow chart. Arrows is a flow chart that represents the order of events; arrows in DFD represents flowing data. A DFD does not involve any order of events.

Suppress logical decisions. If we ever have the urge to draw a diamond-shaped box in a DFD, suppress that urge! A diamond-shaped box is used in flow charts to represents decision points with multiple exists paths of which the only one is taken. This implies an ordering of events, which makes no sense in a DFD.

Do not become bogged down with details. Defer error conditions and error handling until the end of the analysis.

Standard symbols for DFDs are derived from the electric circuit diagram analysis and are shown in fig:

Symbol	Name	Function
	Data flow	Used to Connect Processes to each , other , to sources or Sinks; te arrow head indicates direction of data flow.
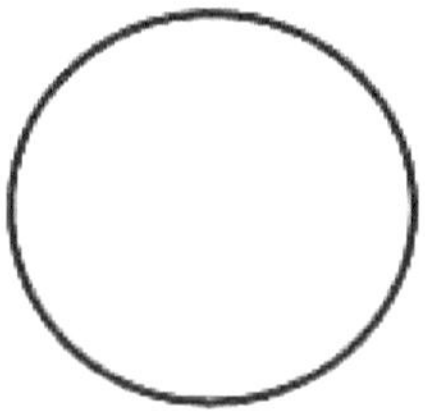	Process	Perfroms Some transformation of Input data to yield output data.
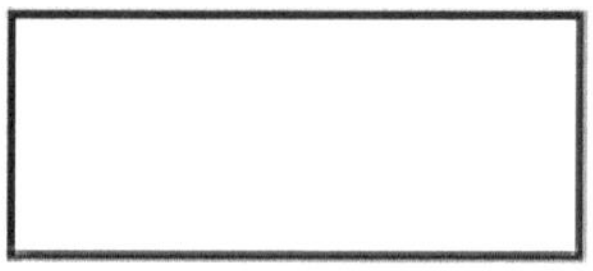	Source of Sink (External Entity)	A Source of System inputs or Sink of System outputs.
	Data Store	A repository of data; the arrow heads indicate net inputs and net outputs to store.

Symbols for Data Flow Diagrams

Circle: A circle (bubble) shows a process that transforms data inputs into data outputs.

Data Flow: A curved line shows the flow of data into or out of a process or data store.

Data Store: A set of parallel lines shows a place for the collection of data items. A data store indicates that the data is stored which can be used at a later stage or by the other processes in a different order. The data store can have an element or group of elements.

Source or Sink: Source or Sink is an external entity and acts as a source of system inputs or sink of system outputs.

Control Flow Diagrams are used to model the flow of control or the sequence of execution in a program or a system. They emphasize the flow of commands, decision points, loops, and other control structures that dictate how a program or system functions.

Elements in a CFD:

Start and End Points: Represent the beginning and end of a program or a particular process.

Control Structures: Include decision points (if statements), loops (for, while), branching, and sequential execution of commands.

Commands: Represent specific actions or operations executed within the program or system.

Example of a Control Flow Diagram:

Consider a simple program for calculating the sum of numbers from 1 to N:

Start Point: Indicates the beginning of the program.

Command: Set Sum = 0 initializes the variable Sum to zero.

Control Structure (Loop): For i = 1 to N represents a loop that iterates from 1 to N.

Inside the loop:

Command: Add i to Sum accumulates the sum of numbers.

Control Structure (End of Loop)

Command: Display Sum is a command to show the result.

End Point: Represents the end of the program.

Previous Years Unsolved Questions

Q 1. Define Software Metrics. List and explain the parameters for software measurement. [IGNOU June,2018] [Kota University 2021]
Q 2. What is Cyclomatic Complexity? How is it computed? Calculate Cyclomatic Complexity for the program to find the smallest of three numbers. [IGNOU, December, 2015]
Q 3. List and explain the features to be considered for function point analysis. [IGNOU, December, 2016]
Q 4. Write a short note on Cyclomatic Complexity. [IGNOU, June,2016]
Q 5. List and explain the two categories of project metrics along with the help of an example for each. [IGNOU, June,2017]
Q 6. What are the various Core metrics to be 10 measured and analyses for the web - applications? Explain them briefly. [IGNOU, December, 2011]
Q 7. Differentiate process and product. [Anna university 2022]
Q 8. Brief out the impact of LOC and FP in cost estimation. [Anna University 2022]
Q 9. Describe Function Oriented Matrices and Extended Function Point Matrices in detail. [MCU 2019]
Q 10. Explain the limitations of LOC over FP as defined by IFPUG. [Kota University 2021]

Chapter 4: Software Development Models

4.1 Classical Waterfall Model

The classical waterfall model is the basic software development life cycle model. It is very simple but idealistic. Earlier this model was very popular but nowadays it is not used. But it is very important because all the other software development life cycle models are based on the classical waterfall model.

Why Do We Use the Waterfall Model?

The waterfall model is a software development model used in the context of large, complex projects, typically in the field of information technology. It is characterized by a structured, sequential approach to project management and software development.

The waterfall model is useful in situations where the project requirements are well-defined and the project goals are clear. It is often used for large-scale projects with long timelines, where there is little room for error and the project stakeholders need to have a high level of confidence in the outcome.

Features of the Waterfall Model

Sequential Approach: The waterfall model involves a sequential approach to software development, where each phase of the project is completed before moving on to the next one.

Document-Driven: The waterfall model relies heavily on documentation to ensure that the project is well-defined and the project team is working towards a clear set of goals.

Quality Control: The waterfall model places a high emphasis on quality control and testing at each phase of the project, to ensure that the final product meets the requirements and expectations of the stakeholders.

Rigorous Planning: The waterfall model involves a rigorous planning process, where the project scope, timelines, and deliverables are carefully defined and monitored throughout the project lifecycle.

Overall, the waterfall model is used in situations where there is a need for a highly structured and systematic approach to software development. It can be effective in ensuring that large, complex projects are completed on time and within budget, with a high level of quality and customer satisfaction.

Phases of Classical Waterfall Model

Waterfall Model is a classical software development methodology that was first introduced by Winston W. Royce in 1970. It is a linear and sequential approach to software development that consists of several phases that must be completed in a specific order. The phases include:

Requirements Gathering and Analysis: The first phase involves gathering requirements from stakeholders and analyzing them to understand the scope and objectives of the project.

Design: Once the requirements are understood, the design phase begins. This involves creating a detailed design document that outlines the software architecture, user interface, and system components.

Implementation: The implementation phase involves coding the software based on the design specifications. This phase also includes unit testing to ensure that each component of the software is working as expected.

Testing: In the testing phase, the software is tested as a whole to ensure that it meets the requirements and is free from defects.

Deployment: Once the software has been tested and approved, it is deployed to the production environment.

Maintenance: The final phase of the Waterfall Model is maintenance, which involves fixing any issues that arise after the software has been deployed and ensuring that it continues to meet the requirements over time.

The classical waterfall model divides the life cycle into a set of phases. This model considers that one phase can be started after the completion of the previous phase. That is the output of one phase will be the input to the next phase. Thus the development process can be considered as a sequential flow in the waterfall. Here the phases do not overlap with each other. The different sequential phases of the classical waterfall model are shown in the below figure.

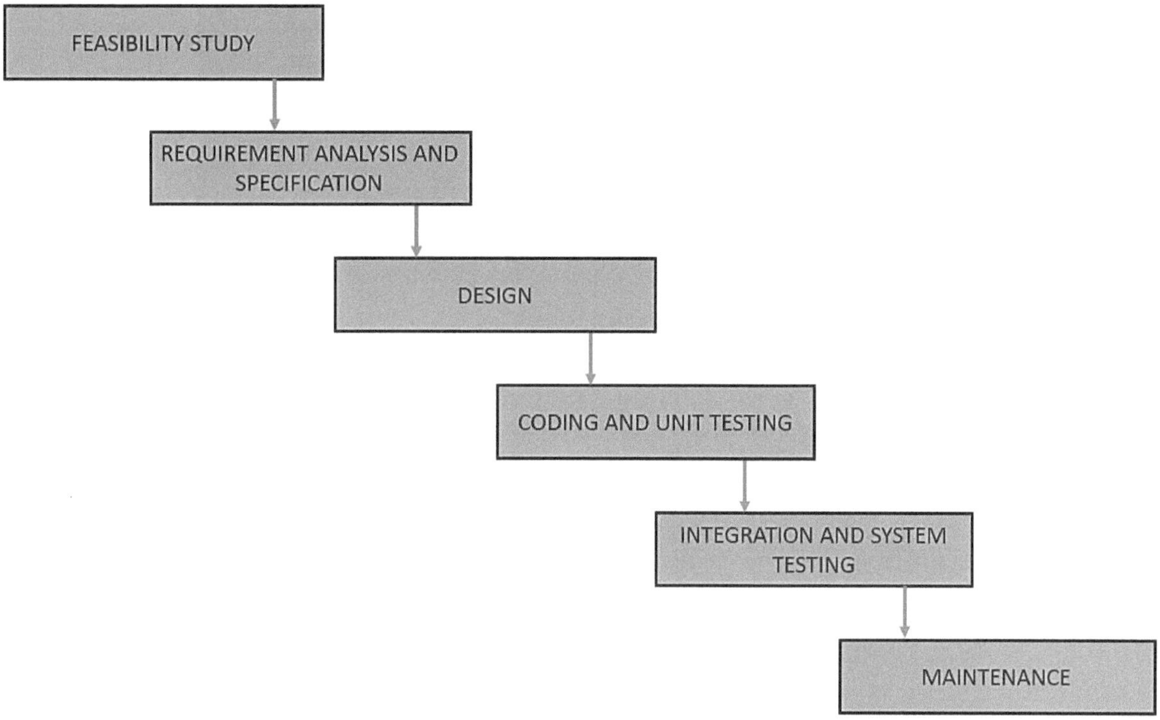

Phases of Classical Waterfall Model

Let us now learn about each of these phases in detail.

1. Feasibility Study

The main goal of this phase is to determine whether it would be financially and technically feasible to develop the software.

The feasibility study involves understanding the problem and then determining the various possible strategies to solve the problem. These different identified solutions are analyzed based on their benefits and drawbacks, The best solution is chosen and all the other phases are carried out as per this solution strategy.

2. Requirements Analysis and Specification

The aim of the requirement analysis and specification phase is to understand the exact requirements of the customer and document them properly. This phase consists of two different activities.

Requirement gathering and analysis: Firstly all the requirements regarding the software are gathered from the customer and then the gathered requirements are analyzed. The goal of the analysis part is to remove incompleteness (an incomplete requirement is one in which some parts of the actual requirements have been omitted) and inconsistencies (an inconsistent requirement is one in which some part of the requirement contradicts some other part).

Requirement specification: These analyzed requirements are documented in a software requirement specification (SRS) document. SRS document serves as a contract between the development team and customers. Any future dispute between the customers and the developers can be settled by examining the SRS document.

3. Design

The goal of this phase is to convert the requirements acquired in the SRS into a format that can be coded in a programming language. It includes high-level and detailed design as well as the overall software architecture. A Software Design Document is used to document all of this effort (SDD)

4. Coding and Unit Testing

In the coding phase software design is translated into source code using any suitable programming language. Thus each designed module is coded. The aim of the unit testing phase is to check whether each module is working properly or not.

5. Integration and System testing

Integration of different modules is undertaken soon after they have been coded and unit tested. Integration of various modules is carried out incrementally over a number of steps. During each integration step, previously planned modules are added to the partially integrated system and the resultant system is tested. Finally, after all the modules have been successfully integrated and tested, the full working system is obtained and system testing is carried out on this. System testing consists of three different kinds of testing activities as described below.

Alpha testing: Alpha testing is the system testing performed by the development team.

Beta testing: Beta testing is the system testing performed by a friendly set of customers.

Acceptance testing: After the software has been delivered, the customer performed acceptance testing to determine whether to accept the delivered software or reject it.

6. Maintenance

Maintenance is the most important phase of a software life cycle. The effort spent on maintenance is 60% of the total effort spent to develop a full software. There are basically three types of maintenance.

Corrective Maintenance: This type of maintenance is carried out to correct errors that were not discovered during the product development phase.

Perfective Maintenance: This type of maintenance is carried out to enhance the functionalities of the system based on the customer's request.

Adaptive Maintenance: Adaptive maintenance is usually required for porting the software to work in a new environment such as working on a new computer platform or with a new operating system.

4.2 Iterative waterfall Model

In this Model, you can start with some of the software specifications and develop the first version of the software. After the first version if there is a need to change the software, then a new version of the software is created with a new iteration. Every release of the Iterative Model finishes in an exact and fixed period that is called iteration.

The Iterative Model allows the accessing earlier phases, in which the variations made respectively. The final output of the project renewed at the end of the Software Development Life Cycle (SDLC) process.

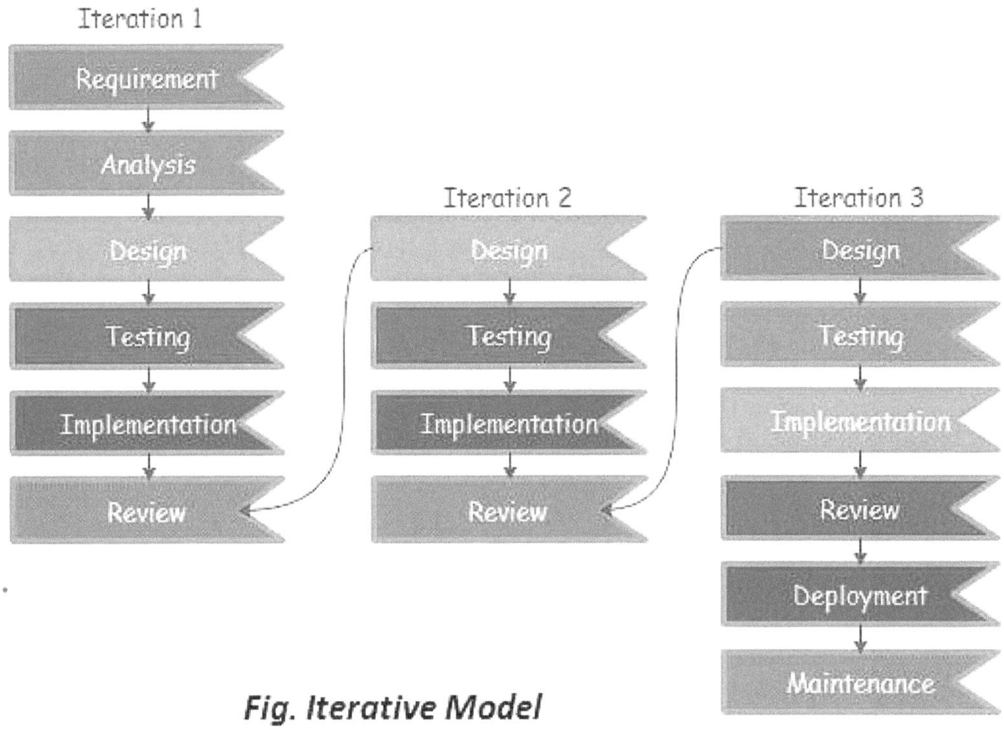

Fig. Iterative Model

The various phases of Iterative model are as follows:

1. Requirement gathering & analysis: In this phase, requirements are gathered from customers and check by an analyst whether requirements will fulfil or not. Analyst checks that need will achieve within budget or not. After all of this, the software team skips to the next phase.

2. Design: In the design phase, team design the software by the different diagrams like Data Flow diagram, activity diagram, class diagram, state transition diagram, etc.

3. Implementation: In the implementation, requirements are written in the coding language and transformed into computer programmes which are called Software.
4. Testing: After completing the coding phase, software testing starts using different test methods. There are many test methods, but the most common are white box, black box, and grey box test methods.
5. Deployment: After completing all the phases, software is deployed to its work environment.
6. Review: In this phase, after the product deployment, review phase is performed to check the behaviour and validity of the developed product. And if there are any error found then the process starts again from the requirement gathering.
7. Maintenance: In the maintenance phase, after deployment of the software in the working environment there may be some bugs, some errors or new updates are required. Maintenance involves debugging and new addition options.

When to use the Iterative Model?

When requirements are defined clearly and easy to understand.
When the software application is large.
When there is a requirement of changes in future.

Advantage(Pros) of Iterative Model:

Testing and debugging during smaller iteration is easy.
A Parallel development can plan.
It is easily acceptable to ever-changing needs of the project.
Risks are identified and resolved during iteration.
Limited time spent on documentation and extra time on designing.

Disadvantage(Cons) of Iterative Model:

It is not suitable for smaller projects.
More Resources may be required.
Design can be changed again and again because of imperfect requirements.
Requirement changes can cause over budget.
Project completion date not confirmed because of changing requirements.

4.3 Spiral Model

The spiral model, initially proposed by Boehm, is an evolutionary software process model that couples the iterative feature of prototyping with the controlled and systematic aspects of the linear sequential model.
The Spiral Model is a Software Development Life Cycle (SDLC) model that provides a systematic and iterative approach to software development. It is based on the idea of a spiral, with each iteration of the spiral representing a complete software development cycle, from requirements gathering and analysis to design, implementation, testing, and maintenance.

The Spiral Model is shown in fig:

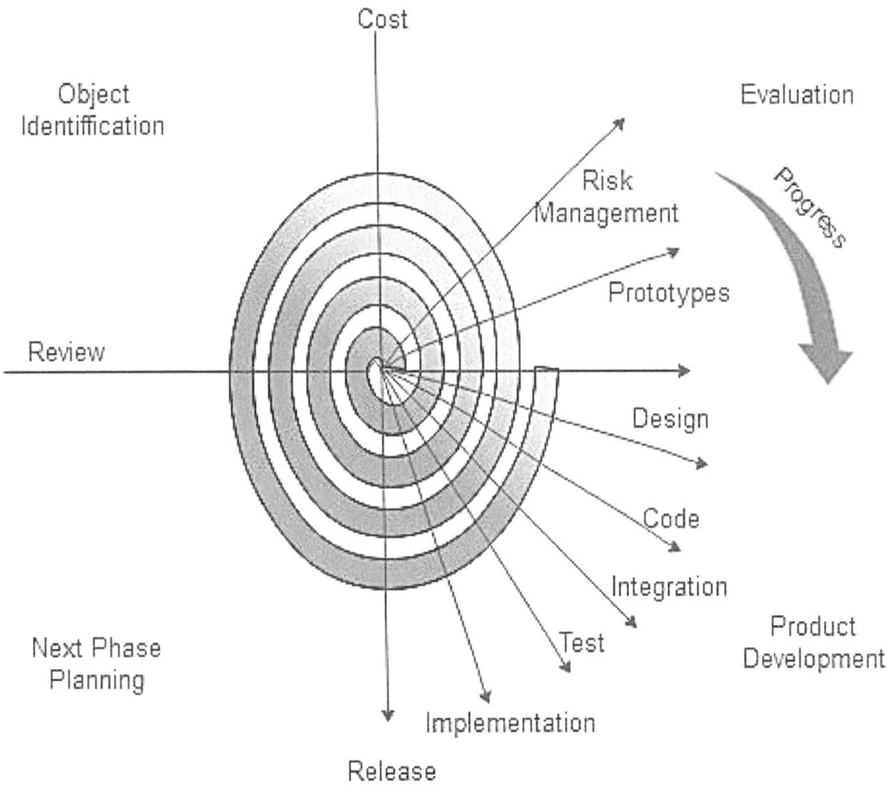

Fig. Spiral Model

Each cycle in the spiral is divided into four parts:

Objective setting: Each cycle in the spiral starts with the identification of purpose for that cycle, the various alternatives that are possible for achieving the targets, and the constraints that exists.

Backward Skip 10sPlay VideoForward Skip 10s

Risk Assessment and reduction: The next phase in the cycle is to calculate these various alternatives based on the goals and constraints. The focus of evaluation in this stage is located on the risk perception for the project.

Development and validation: The next phase is to develop strategies that resolve uncertainties and risks. This process may include activities such as benchmarking, simulation, and prototyping.

Planning: Finally, the next step is planned. The project is reviewed, and a choice made whether to continue with a further period of the spiral. If it is determined to keep, plans are drawn up for the next step of the project.

The development phase depends on the remaining risks. For example, if performance or user-interface risks are treated more essential than the program development risks, the next phase may be an evolutionary development that includes developing a more detailed prototype for solving the risks.

The risk-driven feature of the spiral model allows it to accommodate any mixture of a specification-oriented, prototype-oriented, simulation-oriented, or another type of approach. An essential element of the model is that each period of the spiral is completed by a review that includes all the products developed during that cycle, including plans for the next cycle. The spiral model works for development as well as enhancement projects.

When to use Spiral Model?

When deliverance is required to be frequent.

When the project is large

When requirements are unclear and complex

When changes may require at any time

Large and high budget projects

Advantages

High amount of risk analysis

Useful for large and mission-critical projects.

Disadvantages

Can be a costly model to use.
Risk analysis needed highly particular expertise
Doesn't work well for smaller projects.

4.4 Prototyping Model

The Prototyping Model is one of the most popularly used Software Development Life Cycle Models (SDLC models). This model is used when the customers do not know the exact project requirements beforehand. In this model, a prototype of the end product is first developed, tested, and refined as per customer feedback repeatedly till a final acceptable prototype is achieved which forms the basis for developing the final product.

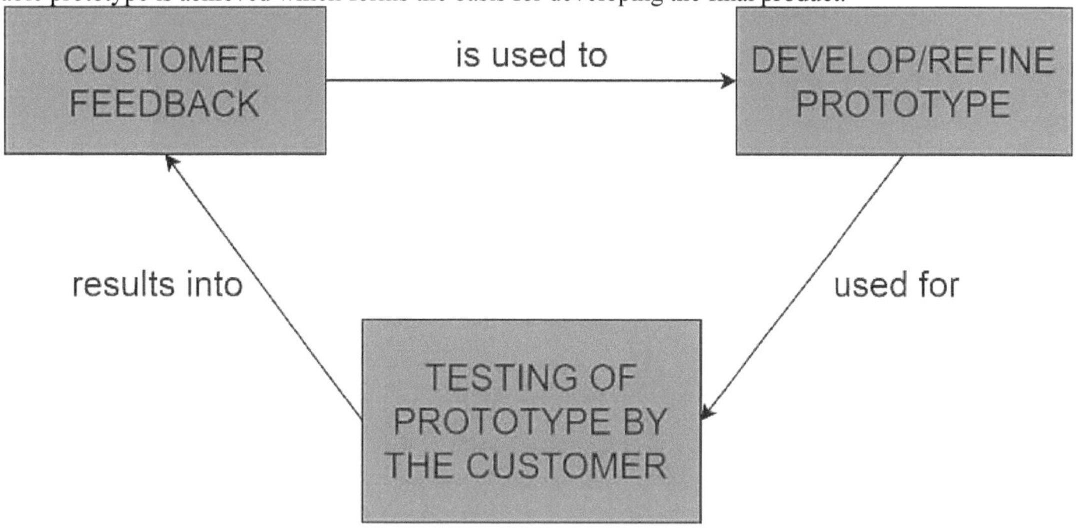

Prototyping Concept

In this process model, the system is partially implemented before or during the analysis phase thereby giving the customers an opportunity to see the product early in the life cycle. The process starts by interviewing the customers and developing the incomplete high-level paper model. This document is used to build the initial prototype supporting only the basic functionality as desired by the customer. Once the customer figures out the problems, the prototype is further refined to eliminate them. The process continues until the user approves the prototype and finds the working model to be satisfactory.

Steps Prototyping Model

Step 1: Requirement Gathering and Analysis: This is the initial step in designing a prototype model. In this phase, users are asked about what they expect or what they want from the system.

Step 2: Quick Design: This is the second step in Prototyping Model. This model covers the basic design of the requirement through which a quick overview can be easily described.

Step 3: Build a Prototype: This step helps in building an actual prototype from the knowledge gained from prototype design.

Step 4: Initial User Evaluation: This step describes the preliminary testing where the investigation of the performance model occurs, as the customer will tell the strength and weaknesses of the design, which was sent to the developer.

Step 5: Refining Prototype: If any feedback is given by the user, then improving the client's response to feedback and suggestions, the final system is approved.

Step 6: Implement Product and Maintain: This is the final step in the phase of the Prototyping Model where the final system is tested and distributed to production, here program is run regularly to prevent failures.

For more, you can refer to Software Prototyping Model Phases.

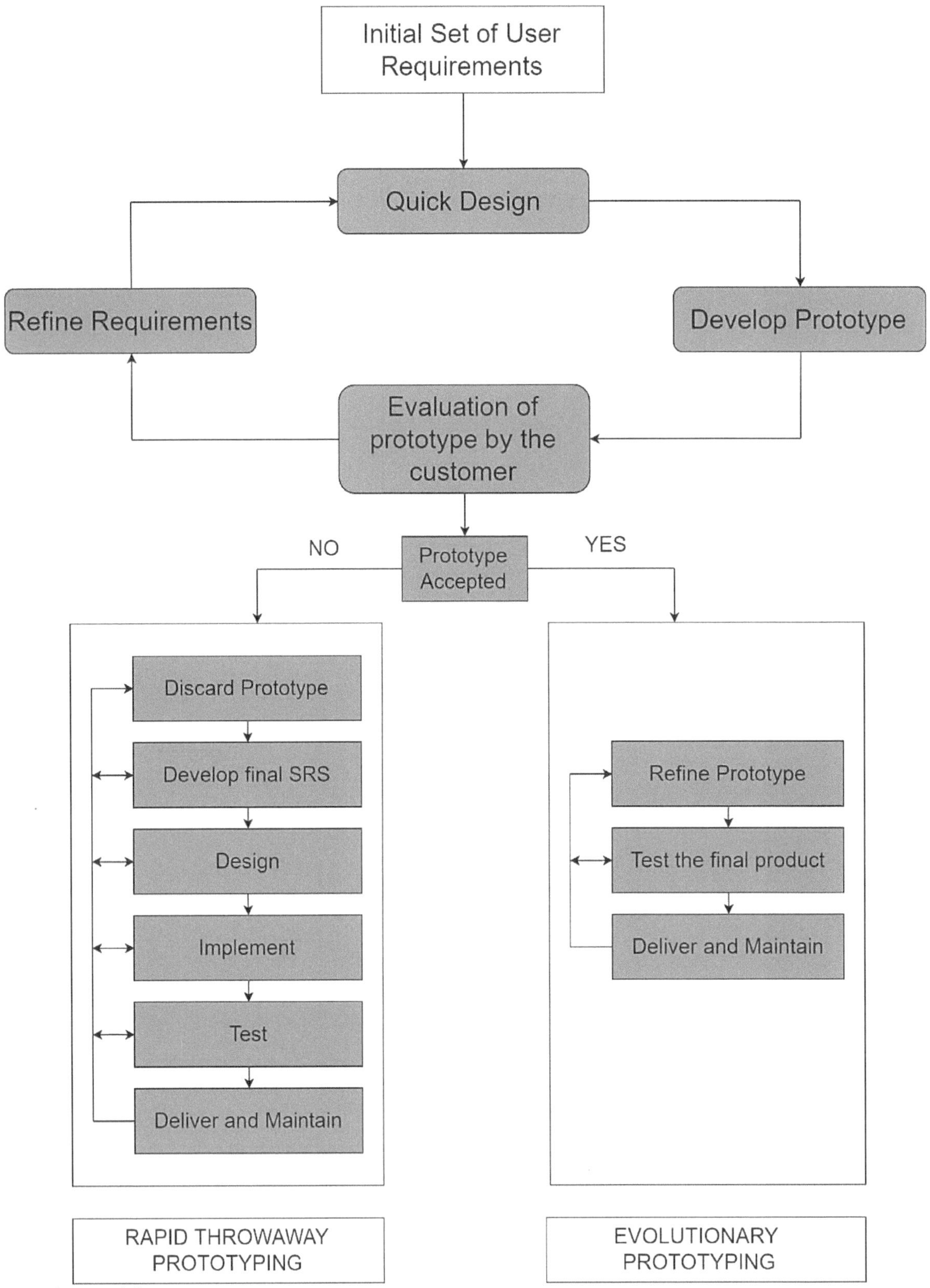

Prototyping Models

4.5 Incremental Process Model

Advantage of Prototype Model
Reduce the risk of incorrect user requirement
Good where requirement are changing/uncommitted
Regular visible process aids management
Support early product marketing
Reduce Maintenance cost.
Errors can be detected much earlier as the system is made side by side.
Disadvantage of Prototype Model
An unstable/badly implemented prototype often becomes the final product.
Require extensive customer collaboration
Costs customer money
Needs committed customer
Difficult to finish if customer withdraw
May be too customer specific, no broad market
Difficult to know how long the project will last.
Easy to fall back into the code and fix without proper requirement analysis, design, customer evaluation, and feedback.
Prototyping tools are expensive.
Special tools & techniques are required to build a prototype.
It is a time-consuming process.

4.6 Rapid Application Development Model (RAD)

RAD is a linear sequential software development process model that emphasizes a concise development cycle using an element based construction approach. If the requirements are well understood and described, and the project scope is a constraint, the RAD process enables a development team to create a fully functional system within a concise time period.

RAD (Rapid Application Development) is a concept that products can be developed faster and of higher quality through:
Gathering requirements using workshops or focus groups
Prototyping and early, reiterative user testing of designs
The re-use of software components
A rigidly paced schedule that refers design improvements to the next product version
Less formality in reviews and other team communication

Fig: RAD Model

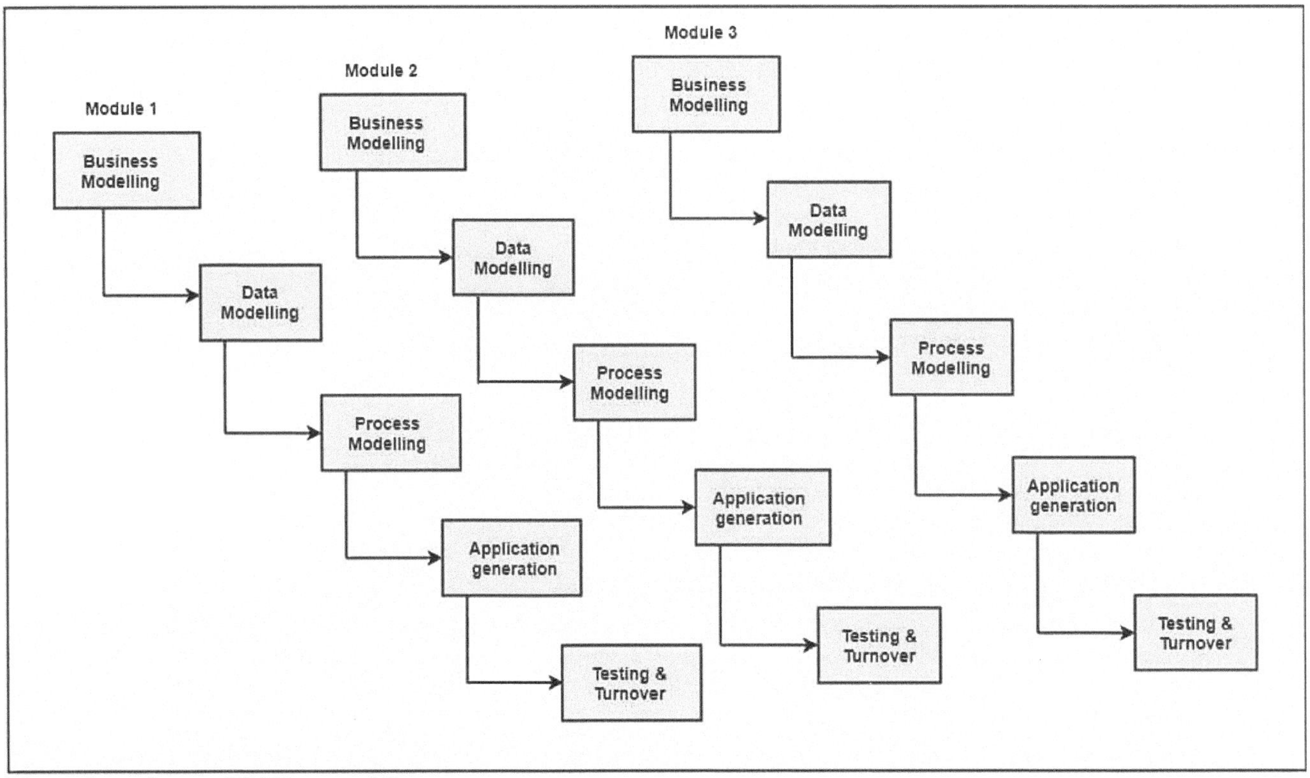

The various phases of RAD are as follows:

1.Business Modelling: The information flow among business functions is defined by answering questions like what data drives the business process, what data is generated, who generates it, where does the information go, who process it and so on.

2. Data Modelling: The data collected from business modeling is refined into a set of data objects (entities) that are needed to support the business. The attributes (character of each entity) are identified, and the relation between these data objects (entities) is defined.

Backward Skip 10sPlay VideoForward Skip 10s

3. Process Modelling: The information object defined in the data modeling phase are transformed to achieve the data flow necessary to implement a business function. Processing descriptions are created for adding, modifying, deleting, or retrieving a data object.

4. Application Generation: Automated tools are used to facilitate construction of the software; even they use the 4th GL techniques.

5. Testing & Turnover: Many of the programming components have already been tested since RAD emphasis reuse. This reduces the overall testing time. But the new part must be tested, and all interfaces must be fully exercised.

When to use RAD Model?

When the system should need to create the project that modularizes in a short span time (2-3 months).

When the requirements are well-known.

When the technical risk is limited.

When there's a necessity to make a system, which modularized in 2-3 months of period.

It should be used only if the budget allows the use of automatic code generating tools.

Advantage of RAD Model

This model is flexible for change.

In this model, changes are adoptable.

Each phase in RAD brings highest priority functionality to the customer.

It reduced development time.

It increases the reusability of features.

Disadvantage of RAD Model

It required highly skilled designers.

All application is not compatible with RAD.
For smaller projects, we cannot use the RAD model.
On the high technical risk, it's not suitable.
Required user involvement.

4.7 V-Model

V-Model also referred to as the Verification and Validation Model. In this, each phase of SDLC must complete before the next phase starts. It follows a sequential design process same as the waterfall model. Testing of the device is planned in parallel with a corresponding stage of development.

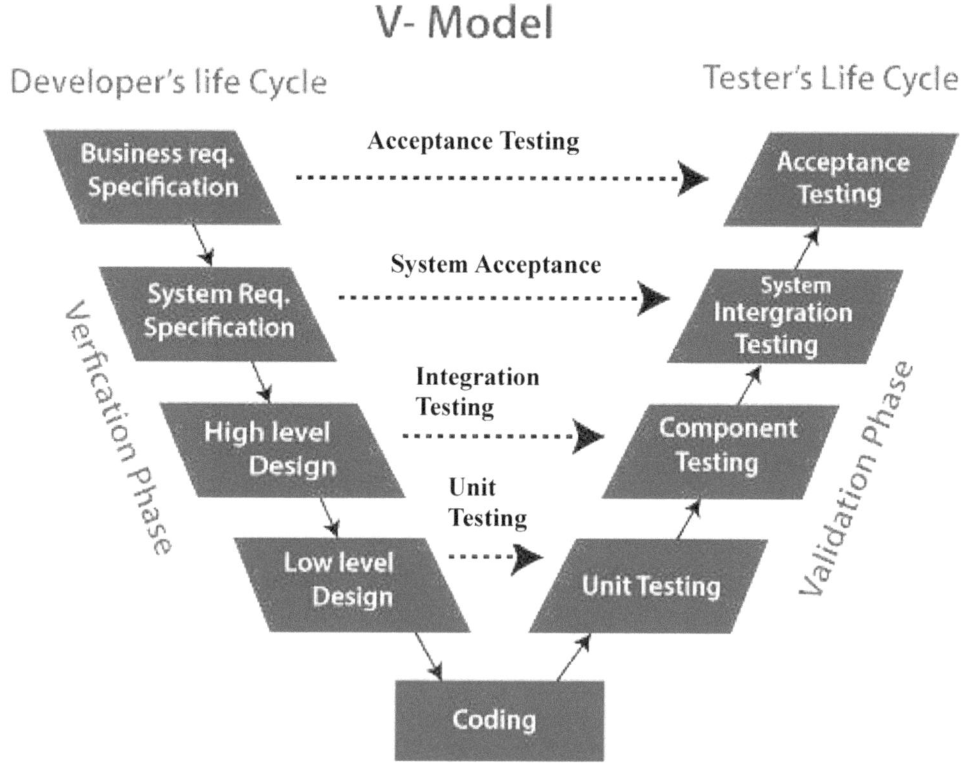

Verification: It involves a static analysis method (review) done without executing code. It is the process of evaluation of the product development process to find whether specified requirements meet.
Validation: It involves dynamic analysis method (functional, non-functional), testing is done by executing code. Validation is the process to classify the software after the completion of the development process to determine whether the software meets the customer expectations and requirements.
So V-Model contains Verification phases on one side of the Validation phases on the other side. Verification and Validation process is joined by coding phase in V-shape. Thus it is known as V-Model.
There are the various phases of Verification Phase of V-model:
Business requirement analysis: This is the first step where product requirements understood from the customer's side. This phase contains detailed communication to understand customer's expectations and exact requirements.
System Design: In this stage system engineers analyze and interpret the business of the proposed system by studying the user requirements document.
Architecture Design: The baseline in selecting the architecture is that it should understand all which typically consists of the list of modules, brief functionality of each module, their interface relationships, dependencies, database tables, architecture diagrams, technology detail, etc. The integration testing model is carried out in a particular phase.
Module Design: In the module design phase, the system breaks down into small modules. The detailed design of the modules is specified, which is known as Low-Level Design
Coding Phase: After designing, the coding phase is started. Based on the requirements, a suitable programming language is decided. There are some guidelines and standards for coding. Before checking in the repository, the final build is optimized for better performance, and the code goes through many code reviews to check the performance.
There are the various phases of Validation Phase of V-model:

Unit Testing: In the V-Model, Unit Test Plans (UTPs) are developed during the module design phase. These UTPs are executed to eliminate errors at code level or unit level. A unit is the smallest entity which can independently exist, e.g., a program module. Unit testing verifies that the smallest entity can function correctly when isolated from the rest of the codes/ units.
Integration Testing: Integration Test Plans are developed during the Architectural Design Phase. These tests verify that groups created and tested independently can coexist and communicate among themselves.
System Testing: System Tests Plans are developed during System Design Phase. Unlike Unit and Integration Test Plans, System Tests Plans are composed by the client?s business team. System Test ensures that expectations from an application developer are met.
Acceptance Testing: Acceptance testing is related to the business requirement analysis part. It includes testing the software product in user atmosphere. Acceptance tests reveal the compatibility problems with the different systems, which is available within the user atmosphere. It conjointly discovers the non-functional problems like load and performance defects within the real user atmosphere.
When to use V-Model?
When the requirement is well defined and not ambiguous.
The V-shaped model should be used for small to medium-sized projects where requirements are clearly defined and fixed.
The V-shaped model should be chosen when sample technical resources are available with essential technical expertise.
Advantage (Pros) of V-Model:
Easy to Understand.
Testing Methods like planning, test designing happens well before coding.
This saves a lot of time. Hence a higher chance of success over the waterfall model.
Avoids the downward flow of the defects.
Works well for small plans where requirements are easily understood.
Disadvantage (Cons) of V-Model:
Very rigid and least flexible.
Not a good for a complex project.
Software is developed during the implementation stage, so no early prototypes of the software are produced.
If any changes happen in the midway, then the test documents along with the required documents, has to be updated.

4.8 Behavioral Model

Behavioral Model is specially designed to make us understand behavior and factors that influence behavior of a System. Behavior of a system is explained and represented with the help of a diagram. This diagram is known as State Transition Diagram. It is a collection of states and events. It usually describes overall states that a system can have and events which are responsible for a change in state of a system.
Example:
Consider an Elevator. This elevator is for n number of floors and has n number of buttons one for each floor. Elevator's working can be explained as follows:
Elevator buttons are type of set of buttons which is there on elevator. For reaching a particular floor you want to visit, "elevator buttons" for that particular floor is pressed. Pressing, will cause illumination and elevator will start moving towards that particular floor for which you pressed "elevator buttons". As soon as elevator reaches that particular floor, illumination gets canceled.
Floor buttons are another type of set of buttons on elevator. If a person is on a particular floor and he wants to go on another floor, then elevator button for that floor is pressed. Then, process will be same as given above. Pressing, will cause illumination and elevator to start moving, and when it reaches on desired floor, illumination gets canceled.
When there is no request for elevator, it remains closed on current floor.
State Transition Diagram for an elevator system is shown below –

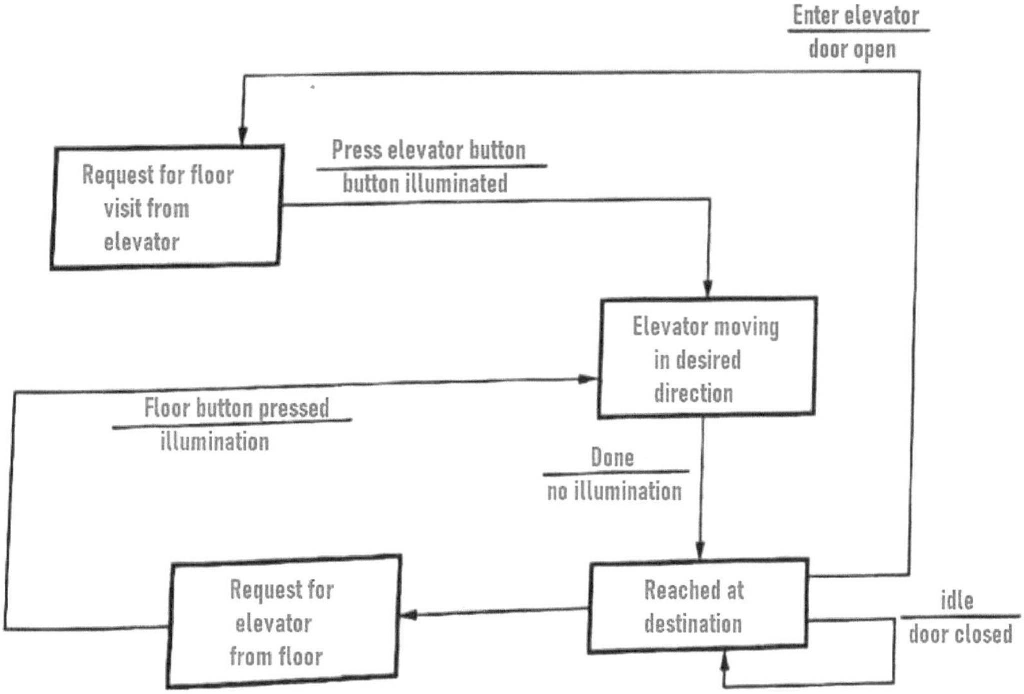

STATE TRANSITION DIAGRAM

Exercise

Exercise 1 – MCQ

Q 1. Which software development model is also known as the "waterfall model"?

A. Agile Model B. V-Model
C. Iterative Model D. Sequential Model

Q2. In the Agile development model, what is the primary focus?

A. Comprehensive documentation B. Extensive planning
C. Customer collaboration D. Sequential phases

Exercise 2 – True/ False

Q 1. The Waterfall model is an iterative and incremental software development approach.

Q 2. Agile development models prioritize extensive documentation and planning.

Exercise 3 – Fill in the blanks

Q 1. The ______________ model focuses on managing risks by breaking down the project into smaller, more manageable cycles.

Q 2. In the Iterative model, the software is developed in ________________ cycles, with each cycle refining and adding to the previous version.

Exercise 4 – Match case

1. Waterfall Model	A. Highly adaptable to changing requirements and customer feedback.
2. Agile Model	B. Suitable for projects where high predictability is essential.
3. V-Model	C. Divides the project into stages, with each stage dependent on previous one.
4. Spiral Model	D. Emphasizes early identification of risks and working software.
5. Iterative Model	E. Prioritizes customer collaboration and flexible responses to change.

Exercise 5 – One word answer

Q 1. Which model divides the project into phases, with each phase dependent on the previous one?

Q 2. Which model is known for its high predictability and validation at each stage?

Exercise 6 – Small answer

Q 1. What is the main principle of the Waterfall model?

Q 2. What's the primary goal of the Iterative model?

Exercise 7 – Long answer

Q 1. What are the advantages and disadvantages of the Waterfall model in software development?

Q 2. Describe the V-Model in software development and its advantages.

Answers

Exercise 1 – MCQ

Ans: 1 B, 2 C

Exercise 2 – True/ False

Ans: 1 False, 2 False

Exercise 3 – Fill in the blanks

Ans: 1 Spiral, 2 Iterations

Exercise 4 – Match case

Ans 1 C, 2 E, 3 B, 4 D, 5 A

Exercise 5 – One word answer

Ans: 1 Waterfall, 2 V-Model

Online Resources

Online Exam Paper:

Link: https://forms.gle/LoFn4GhSW8rHXhq18

QR Code:

Chapter 4 Videos Playlist:

Link: https://www.youtube.com/playlist?list=PLzlh_31VWEFqbzHlzjwusOUsKqmd--N_y

QR Code:

Previous Years Solved Questions

Q 1. Write advantages and disadvantages of waterfall model. [R.T.U. 2018, 2015]

Ans 1: **1. It uses a clear structure.**

The waterfall model uses a clear and defined set of steps to follow when compared with other methodologies. Its structure is simple because every project must go through the same sequence of events. That includes gathering requirements and documentation, system design, implementation, testing, delivery, and maintenance. A team must complete the entire step before moving to the next one, causing any roadblocks in the way to get identified immediately.

Half-finished projects are less likely to get set aside when using the waterfall model because of the need to progress through each set of steps. You're more likely to receive a polished and complete work at the end of the experience.

2. The progression of the waterfall model is intuitive.

Unlike other methodologies that get used for development, the waterfall model doesn't require specific training or certifications for employees or project managers. You can jump right into the system without needing to go through a steep learning curve that could slow down individual progress. That makes it one of the most intuitive systems that's available to use today, especially since the structures promote consistency within the team.

3. The waterfall model determines the end goal early.

One of the defining advantages of using the waterfall model is that it commits to the end goal, product, or deliverable from the beginning of the process. Teams are encouraged to avoid deviation from that commitment. When you have small projects with clear goals, then this benefit allows everyone to be aware of what the intended outcome is supposed to be from the beginning of the project. That means there is less potential for getting lost in the details of daily activities as each step moves forward.

The focus of the waterfall model is always on the final goal. When your team has a concrete definition of what it hopes to accomplish with a specific deadline in mind, then this approach eliminates the risk of getting bogged down.

1. It transfers information in superior ways when compared to other methodologies.

The waterfall model's approach is highly methodical. It emphasizes a clean transfer of information at each step to ensure that the transitions are smooth and effective. When this benefit gets applied in non-traditional settings like software development, then a new group of people are entering into the project. Documenting the lifecycle of the project at each step will ensure that everyone has a better chance of staying on the same page.

When you use the waterfall model, then the priority is to have information access that is as clean and accurate as possible. That makes it easier for new additions to the team to get caught up quickly.

2. The waterfall model keeps a project to a specific timescale.

The phased development cycles in the waterfall model enforce discipline for the work a project requires. Every phase provides a clearly defined starting point and a conclusion for teams to follow. That makes it easier for leaders to manage the progress of each step to ensure everything proceeds as expected. This benefit works to reduce any slippage that can happen in other methodologies from the agreed-upon timescales.

3. There are fewer financial surprises with the waterfall method.

Because the waterfall model requires a specific outline of each phase, the financial expectations of every task have more accuracy. Teams can estimate the time, labor, and monetary costs of each task with greater specification once everyone has defined the requirements of the project at each step. This level of detail makes the needs and outcomes of the project clear to everyone, even if some teams don't enter until the latter 50% of the work because of their roles in this methodology.

4. It reinforces good testing habits.

Since the waterfall model uses an outlined approach in each phase, the testing steps receive prior planning before implementation. This benefit allows a team to structure their best practices into the solution before any of the work every occurs. It creates an organized, disciplined approach to a step that reinforces good habits because every task must get completed before the project can proceed. Although, some deadlines and milestones can be unpredictable during the testing phase, teams do have more structures with which to work. That means it tends to be easier to root out the issues that could be holding a project back.

5. The phases of the waterfall model are predictable and don't overlap.

The waterfall model stays the same for every team in any industry. You go from requirement gathering and analysis to system design. Then you move to implementation before going to the testing step. At that stage, you will proceed to the deployment of the system. The final step is always the maintenance phase. Because each step gets processed and completed on its own, the phases will never overlap when using this approach to complete a project.

That means the requirements remain clearly defined at each phase. There is a complete understanding throughout the team about the expectations involved.

List of the Disadvantages of the Waterfall Model

1. The waterfall model doesn't support making changes.

The waterfall model follows a set of steps that always keep a team moving forward. When you use the traditional methodology of this approach, then there is almost no room for change if something unexpected occurs during a project. A team can loyally follow each step until almost the end of the project but then encounter an unplanned obstacle. If a change in the goals or the scope of the work is necessary, then it can be virtually impossible to make the necessary pivot to keep moving forward.

2. It can invalidate the work you've previously accomplished.

When you need to make a pivot after completing some or most of a project, then the waterfall model isn't going to let you proceed. The only way to get around this disadvantage is to find a way to complete the work at the current step where the difficulties occurred. If that outcome isn't possible, then you're stuck going back to the beginning of the process to start over with the new information.

That means a project that is unpredictable or involves frequent change needs room in each step for revision or reflection to avoid invalidating the previous work. If you use the traditional methodology, your team might find that it wasted a lot of time and energy.

3. This method excludes end-users and clients.

The waterfall model focuses on the internal processes of the work instead of looking at the client or end-user who gets involved with the project. Its main purpose is to create efficiencies within the internal systems so that internal teams can efficiently move through the different phases of a project. That means there isn't much room available for someone to share ideas or opinions because the outlines become part of the planning stages.

4. It delays testing until after the completion of the project.

The waterfall model saves the testing phase of each project until the final half of the work is necessary. The traditional method makes it the fourth step out of six. Since the project is likely taken a considerable amount of time to complete at this stage, any adverse results could trigger the need for a significant revision. Ignoring the empirical data from the proposed value proposition until you start thinking about reaching the marketplace can result in significant user issues to manage.
This disadvantage is the specific reason why agile methodologies got developed. There is a lot of room for problems to remain unnoticed until you begin to reach the completion stages of the project.

5. The waterfall model can promote longer delivery times.

Because every phase requires a 100% completion of all tasks and documentation before transitioning to the next step, projects can take a lot longer to deliver when using this methodology. This disadvantage is the reason why complex assignments tend to avoid using the waterfall model. If an unexpected roadblock occurs, some teams might find themselves back at the starting point once again, creating an even more significant time deficit to manage.

6. It typically works better for small projects.

The waterfall model doesn't work well for significant projects because it struggles to manage size and scope well. It's like looking at the outline for a chapter in a book that an author follows in comparison to what an entire novel requires for composition. Although you could follow the larger structure successfully, the time and labor costs would be massive. You'd need to guarantee the completion of each stage before moving to the next one.
Smaller projects have fewer administrative needs, making it easier for leaders to track the progress made by their teams. It might ignore mid-process users and discourage client feedback with its rigid structures, but you can at least make specification changes when a project isn't oversized.

7. Working models aren't available until the latter stages of a project.

The reason why engineers and construction specialists love to use the waterfall model is that their work isn't reaching completion until the latter stages of a project. It's difficult to test the structural soundness of a building when you only have two walls built for it, after all. That's why software designers prefer to avoid this approach. There can be testing needs that must happen along the way where a working prototype can be useful. This methodology doesn't allow for that outcome to occur until late during the lifecycle.

Q 2. What are the differences between waterfall model and prototype model? [R.T.U. 2015, 2017, 2018]

Ans 2:

Aspect	Waterfall Model	Prototype Model
Development Approach	Sequential and linear. Phases are executed one after another.	Iterative and incremental. The project is divided into small increments.
Requirement Gathering	Comprehensive requirements are gathered and documented at the beginning.	Initial requirements are collected, but the complete set may not be defined initially.
Design and Implementation	Design and coding occur after the requirements phase is completed.	Prototyping is used for early design and implementation, sometimes

		simultaneously with requirements gathering.
Client Involvement	Limited client involvement until the testing phase.	Extensive client involvement from the beginning, as prototypes are developed in collaboration.
Feedback and Changes	Changes to requirements are discouraged after the project starts.	Changes and refinements are expected and encouraged throughout the development process.
Testing and Verification	Testing occurs after the entire system is developed.	Testing and verification are ongoing as each prototype is created.
Delivery Time	Longer delivery time due to sequential phases.	Potentially shorter delivery time as prototypes provide early versions of the software.
Risk Management	Lower flexibility in addressing changing requirements or risks.	More adaptable to changing requirements, which can reduce project risks.
Use Case	Suitable for projects with well-understood, stable requirements.	Suitable for projects with evolving or unclear requirements that benefit from client collaboration.
Documentation	Emphasizes comprehensive documentation.	Documentation is typically less extensive, focusing on prototypes.

Cost of Changes	Changes after the requirement phase can be costly.	Changes are easier to implement and evaluate due to the iterative nature.

Q 3. Explain the waterfall model. Suggest reasons, why it is not a true reflection of the activities which are involved in software development. Boehm came up with an alternative. Briefly explain it. [R.T.U.2018, 2011]

Ans 3: The Waterfall Model is one of the earliest and most well-known software development methodologies. It follows a sequential and linear approach, where the software development process is divided into discrete phases, and each phase must be completed before the next one begins. The typical phases of the Waterfall Model include:

Requirements: The project starts with gathering and documenting all the requirements for the software. This phase aims to create a comprehensive and detailed list of what the software should do.

Design: Once the requirements are established, the design phase begins. Here, the software's architecture, user interface, and data structures are planned.

Implementation: This phase involves the actual coding or implementation of the software based on the design specifications.

Testing: After implementation, the software is thoroughly tested to identify and fix any defects or issues.

Deployment: Once the software passes testing, it is deployed to the end-users or the client.

Maintenance: This is the ongoing phase where the software is maintained, and any necessary updates or changes are made.

Issues with the Waterfall Model:

The Waterfall Model has several limitations, making it less of a true reflection of the complexities involved in software development:

Inflexibility: The Waterfall Model is highly inflexible when it comes to accommodating changing requirements. Once a phase is complete, it discourages making significant changes, which can be problematic in dynamic environments.

Late Client Feedback: It doesn't involve extensive client or user feedback until the testing phase, which can lead to misunderstandings and late-stage revisions.

High Risk: Since it proceeds with minimal client feedback, changes that are identified late in the process can be expensive and risky to address.

Unrealistic Assumptions: It assumes that all requirements can be gathered and defined completely at the project's outset, which is often an unrealistic expectation.

Barry Boehm's Alternative:

Barry Boehm proposed the Spiral Model as an alternative to the Waterfall Model. The Spiral Model is an iterative and risk-driven approach that acknowledges the uncertainty and changing nature of software projects. It consists of several cycles or spirals, each encompassing four major phases: planning, risk analysis, engineering, and evaluation.

The Spiral Model allows for greater flexibility and early identification of risks and issues. It involves clients and stakeholders throughout the process, which results in more frequent opportunities for feedback and adaptation. This makes it a more accurate representation of the activities and challenges involved in software development, especially in projects where requirements are not well-defined from the start.

Q 4. Explain specialized process model. [R.T.U. 2017]

Ans 4: A Specialized Process Model in software engineering refers to a customized or tailored approach to software development that is specifically designed to meet the unique requirements, constraints, and characteristics of a particular project or organization. Unlike generic process models such as the Waterfall Model or Agile, which provide a standardized framework for software development, specialized process models are adapted to address the specific needs and challenges of a particular situation.

Here are some key aspects and characteristics of specialized process models:

Tailoring to Project Needs: Specialized process models are created by selecting and combining elements from different process models or by developing entirely new processes to align with the specific goals and constraints of a project. This tailoring ensures that the software development process is well-suited to the project's requirements.

Industry or Domain Specific: Some specialized models are designed to address the unique demands of specific industries or domains, such as aerospace, healthcare, or finance. These models incorporate domain-specific practices, standards, and regulations.

Complex or Large-Scale Projects: Specialized process models are often applied to complex, large-scale, or mission-critical projects where the standard, off-the-shelf process models may not be sufficient to handle the intricacies of the project.
Risk Management: They may include specialized risk management practices, as risk assessment and mitigation are critical in many complex projects. The model may incorporate strategies to identify, analyze, and mitigate risks effectively.
Compliance and Quality Standards: Some specialized models are designed to ensure compliance with specific quality and regulatory standards, such as ISO 9001, CMMI, or safety-critical standards like DO-178C for aviation software.
Tools and Technologies: Specialized process models may specify the use of particular tools and technologies that are most appropriate for the project's needs, taking into account factors like platform, language, or development environment.
Iterative and Incremental: In some cases, specialized models may incorporate iterative and incremental development approaches, allowing for continuous improvement and refinement of the software.
Highly Collaborative: Specialized models may emphasize close collaboration and communication between cross-functional teams, stakeholders, and clients to ensure that the software meets evolving requirements.
Project-Specific Documentation: They may define specific documentation standards tailored to the project's unique needs, ensuring that project artifacts are relevant and valuable.
Change Control and Adaptation: Specialized process models should include mechanisms for managing changes and adaptations throughout the project's lifecycle, as requirements and circumstances evolve.

Q 5. Discuss the merits & demerits of various model of software engineering models? [R.T.U. 2016, 2017]
Ans 5: Software engineering models are frameworks that guide the development of software applications. Each model has its own set of merits and demerits, and the choice of model depends on the project's specific requirements, constraints, and objectives. Here's an overview of the advantages and disadvantages of various software engineering models:

1. Waterfall Model:
Merits:
Clear and structured approach.
Well-defined phases for easy project management.
Easy to understand and implement, making it suitable for small projects.
Demerits:
Lack of adaptability to changing requirements.
Client feedback is usually received too late.
Potentially long delivery times for complex projects.

2. Agile Model:
Merits:
Highly flexible and adaptive to changing requirements.
Client involvement and continuous feedback.
Rapid development and early delivery of usable software.
Demerits:
Complexity in project management due to frequent iterations.
May require experienced team members to work effectively.
Challenges in documentation and long-term planning.

3. Iterative and Incremental Models (e.g., Spiral Model):
Merits:
Risk management and identification of issues early in the process.
Flexibility and adaptability to changing requirements.
Client engagement in each iteration for feedback.
Demerits:
Can be resource-intensive.
Requires strong project management to handle multiple iterations.
Risk of scope creep if not managed properly.

4. V-Model (Validation and Verification Model):
Merits:
Strong emphasis on testing and validation.

Clear mapping of requirements to test cases.
Structured and well-documented approach.

Demerits:

Limited flexibility in accommodating changes.
Can be time-consuming due to its sequential nature.
Client involvement is not extensive.

5. Big Bang Model:

Merits:

Simple and suitable for small projects.
Quick start without formal phases.

Demerits:

High risk due to lack of formal planning.
Lack of structure and documentation.
May lead to poor project control and quality.

6. Prototype Model:

Merits:

Client involvement and early feedback.
Effective in projects with evolving or unclear requirements.
Enhanced communication between developers and clients.

Demerits:

Can lead to scope creep if not well managed.
Increased complexity due to multiple iterations.
May require additional effort for developing and maintaining prototypes.

7. RAD (Rapid Application Development) Model:

Merits:

Speedy development of applications.
Client feedback and involvement throughout the project.
Suitable for projects with well-understood requirements.

Demerits:

Complexity and resource requirements can be high.
May not be suitable for projects with highly complex or uncertain requirements.
Quality assurance can be challenging.

The choice of software engineering model should be made carefully, considering the specific needs and constraints of the project. Many projects also employ a hybrid approach that combines elements from multiple models to harness their respective merits while mitigating their demerits. Additionally, the experience and expertise of the project team play a significant role in the successful application of a particular model.

Q 6. Explain Spiral model in detail. Also differentiate between prototype model and waterfall model. [R.T.U.2016, 2014]

Ans 6: The Spiral Model is an iterative and risk-driven software development model that combines elements of both waterfall and iterative development approaches. It was introduced by Barry Boehm in 1986 and is designed to address the complexities and uncertainties often associated with large-scale software projects. The Spiral Model consists of multiple cycles or "spirals," each of which encompasses four major phases: planning, risk analysis, engineering, and evaluation.

Phases of the Spiral Model:

Planning: This phase involves setting the project's objectives, constraints, and requirements. The project team identifies alternative approaches and develops a detailed project plan.

Risk Analysis: The most critical aspect of the Spiral Model, this phase involves identifying and analyzing risks. Potential risks are assessed, and strategies for risk mitigation are defined.

Engineering: In this phase, the actual development of the software takes place, following a suitable process model like Waterfall or Agile. The difference in the Spiral Model is that development is guided by risk management and incremental development principles.

Evaluation: After each iteration, the project is evaluated to determine whether it meets its objectives. This phase includes reviewing and assessing the project's progress, quality, and risks. Based on the evaluation, a decision is made to proceed to the next spiral or terminate the project.

Key Differentiating Features of the Spiral Model:

Risk-Driven: Risk analysis is a fundamental component of the Spiral Model, and it influences project planning, execution, and evaluation.
Iterative: The model is inherently iterative, as each spiral represents a cycle of planning, risk analysis, engineering, and evaluation. This iterative nature allows for adjustments and refinements during the project.
Flexibility: The Spiral Model provides flexibility to adapt to changing requirements and evolving project objectives.
Client Involvement: Clients are involved throughout the process, allowing for their feedback and requirements to be incorporated into the software.
Efficient for Large Projects: The Spiral Model is particularly well-suited for large, complex projects where risks and uncertainties are high.

Differences Between Prototype Model and Waterfall Model :

Aspect	Prototype Model	Waterfall Model
Development Approach	Iterative and incremental.	Sequential and linear.
Requirements Gathering	Initial requirements are collected, but the complete set may not be defined initially.	Comprehensive requirements are gathered and documented at the beginning.
Client Involvement	Extensive client involvement from the beginning, as prototypes are developed in collaboration.	Limited client involvement until the testing phase.
Feedback and Changes	Changes and refinements are expected and encouraged throughout the development process.	Changes to requirements are discouraged after the project starts.
Testing and Verification	Testing and verification are ongoing as each prototype is created.	Testing occurs after the entire system is developed.
Delivery Time	Potentially shorter delivery time as prototypes provide early versions of the software.	Longer delivery time due to sequential phases.
Risk Management	Changes are easier to implement and evaluate due to the iterative nature.	Lower flexibility in addressing changing requirements or risks.
Documentation	Documentation is typically less extensive, focusing on prototypes.	Emphasizes comprehensive documentation.

Q 7. Explain the prototype model? Under what circumstances is it beneficial to construct a prototype model? [RTU 2016, 2013]

Ans 7: The Prototype Model is a software development model that emphasizes creating a working, limited-functionality version of the software in order to better understand and refine the requirements, design, and functionality of the final product. It is a type of iterative and incremental model that involves the development of a prototype, which is essentially a "trial version" of the software.

Here's an overview of the Prototype Model and the circumstances in which it can be beneficial:

Key Characteristics of the Prototype Model:

Requirements Gathering: The process begins with the initial gathering of requirements. However, these requirements may not be well-defined or complete, which is common in projects with evolving or unclear requirements.

Prototype Development: A prototype is created based on the initial requirements. This prototype is a working, but usually limited, version of the software that demonstrates key features and functionality.
Client Evaluation: The prototype is shared with clients, stakeholders, and end-users to gather feedback. This step is crucial for understanding whether the initial requirements align with the users' expectations and needs.
Iterative Refinement: Based on the feedback received, the prototype and, subsequently, the requirements and design are iteratively refined. Additional features are often added, and changes are made as the project progresses.
Final Product Development: Once the requirements are well-understood and the prototype has undergone several iterations, the final product is developed, incorporating the refined specifications.
Circumstances Where the Prototype Model is Beneficial:
Unclear or Evolving Requirements: When requirements are not well-defined at the project's outset or are subject to frequent changes, a prototype can help clarify and refine them through feedback.
User Involvement: In projects where user involvement and feedback are crucial, such as in user interface design or customer-centric applications, a prototype model ensures that user expectations are met.
Complex Projects: For complex software systems or projects with intricate functionality, creating a prototype can help in breaking down the complexity and facilitating a more manageable development process.
Risk Mitigation: When a project carries high risks, especially due to uncertainties in requirements or technology, a prototype can help identify and mitigate risks early in the process.
Innovative Projects: In projects that involve the development of innovative or unique solutions, a prototype can provide a platform for experimentation and validation of new concepts.
Large-Scale Projects: For large-scale projects, constructing a prototype can help in managing and understanding the various components and their interdependencies.
Client Confidence: If clients or stakeholders have doubts or concerns about the project's direction, a prototype can reassure them and build confidence in the development process.
Benefits of the Prototype Model:
Enhanced communication between clients and development teams.
Early identification and resolution of issues and misunderstandings.
Better alignment of software with user needs and expectations.
Faster development of a final product once requirements are well-understood.
Challenges of the Prototype Model:
Managing the prototype's scope to prevent scope creep.
Additional time and resources required for prototype development.
The risk of misunderstanding the prototype's limited functionality as the final product.
The Prototype Model is a valuable approach when requirements are uncertain or subject to change and when client or user feedback is vital to the project's success. It allows for flexibility and collaboration throughout the development process, leading to a better understanding of the software's true requirements and functionality.

Q 8. Explain the spiral model with advantages and disadvantages. [R.T.U.2015, 2014]
Ans 8: The Spiral Model is a risk-driven and iterative software development process model. It was introduced by Barry Boehm in 1986 as a response to the limitations of traditional software development models, such as the Waterfall Model. The Spiral Model combines the iterative nature of prototyping with elements of the waterfall model, emphasizing risk management and continuous evaluation throughout the development process.
Key Phases of the Spiral Model:
Planning: In this initial phase, project objectives, constraints, and requirements are determined. The focus is on setting clear project goals and understanding potential risks.
Risk Analysis: This phase involves identifying and analyzing risks associated with the project. Possible risks are evaluated in terms of their impact and probability. Risk management strategies are defined.
Engineering: During this phase, the actual development takes place. It is here that the software is designed, coded, and tested incrementally, addressing the high-priority and high-risk elements first.
Evaluation: After each iteration, the project is evaluated to assess progress, identify potential issues, and ensure that it is on track to meet its objectives. The outcome of this phase influences the decision to proceed to the next iteration.
Advantages of the Spiral Model:
Risk Management: The model explicitly addresses risk, allowing for early identification and mitigation, which can significantly reduce project failures.
Flexibility: The Spiral Model is highly adaptable to changes in requirements, technology, or objectives due to its iterative and incremental nature.

Client Involvement: Clients and stakeholders are involved throughout the process, providing frequent opportunities for feedback and ensuring the software aligns with user expectations.
High-Quality Output: The emphasis on risk analysis and evaluation in each iteration contributes to a higher quality end product.
Progress Visibility: The iterative nature provides clear visibility into the project's progress, making it easier to track and manage.
Disadvantages of the Spiral Model:
Complexity: The model can be complex, particularly for smaller projects or those with well-understood and stable requirements.
Resource-Intensive: The iterative approach can be resource-intensive, requiring continuous effort for risk analysis, planning, and development.
Documentation: Managing documentation and record-keeping can be challenging due to the iterative nature of the model.
Lack of Formality: The flexibility of the model may lead to a lack of formality and structure, which can be a disadvantage in projects where strict adherence to processes is required.
Potentially Prolonged Development: The model may result in a longer development timeline due to the continuous iteration and risk analysis phases.

Q 9. Explain RAD model in detail. Draw suitable diagram to show its activities. [R.T.U.2018]
Ans 9: RAD is a linear sequential software development process model that emphasizes a concise development cycle using an element-based construction approach. If the requirements are well understood and described, and the project scope is a constraint, the RAD process enables a development team to create a fully functional system within a concise time period.
RAD (Rapid Application Development) is a concept that products can be developed faster and of higher quality through:
Gathering requirements using workshops or focus groups
Prototyping and early, reiterative user testing of designs
The re-use of software components
A rigidly paced schedule that refers design improvements to the next product version
Less formality in reviews and other team communication

Fig: RAD Model

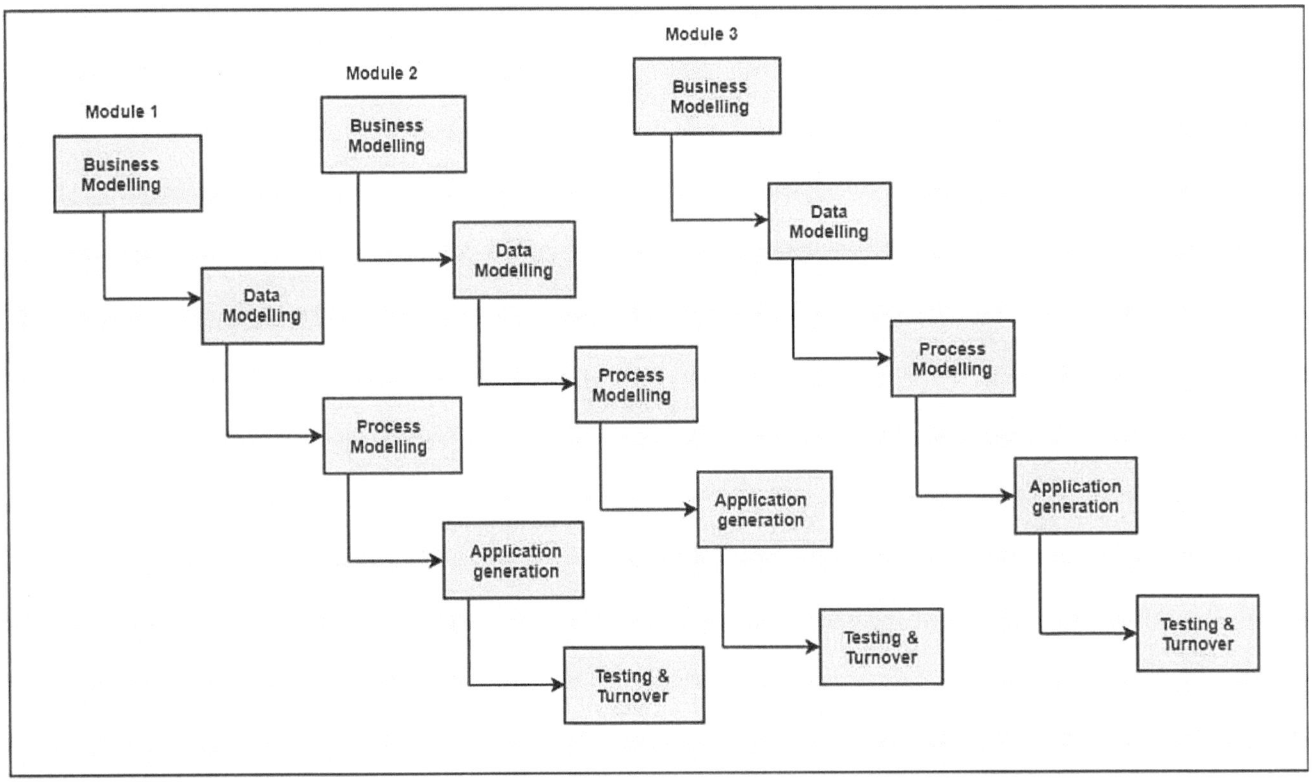

The various phases of RAD are as follows:

1.Business Modelling: The information flow among business functions is defined by answering questions like what data drives the business process, what data is generated, who generates it, where does the information go, who process it and so on.

2. Data Modelling: The data collected from business modeling is refined into a set of data objects (entities) that are needed to support the business. The attributes (character of each entity) are identified, and the relation between these data objects (entities) is defined.

3. Process Modelling: The information object defined in the data modeling phase are transformed to achieve the data flow necessary to implement a business function. Processing descriptions are created for adding, modifying, deleting, or retrieving a data object.

4. Application Generation: Automated tools are used to facilitate construction of the software; even they use the 4th GL techniques.

5. Testing & Turnover: Many of the programming components have already been tested since RAD emphasis reuse. This reduces the overall testing time. But the new part must be tested, and all interfaces must be fully exercised.

When to use RAD Model?

When the system should need to create the project that modularizes in a short span time (2-3 months).

When the requirements are well-known.

When the technical risk is limited.

When there's a necessity to make a system, which modularized in 2-3 months of period.

It should be used only if the budget allows the use of automatic code generating tools.

Q 10. Explain why programs that are developed using evolutionary development are likely to be difficult to maintain. [R.T.U.2018]

Ans 10: Programs developed using Evolutionary Development methodologies, which include practices like rapid prototyping and incremental development, may have certain characteristics that can make them more challenging to maintain over time. Here are some reasons why such programs may be difficult to maintain:

Lack of Comprehensive Documentation: In evolutionary development, the emphasis is often on delivering working software quickly rather than producing extensive documentation. As a result, there may be limited or outdated documentation, making it harder for maintenance teams to understand the code and its underlying design.

Code Complexity: Rapid prototyping and incremental development can lead to code that is evolved quickly and may not always follow the best design practices. This can result in code that is more complex, less modular, and harder to understand and modify.

Quick Fixes and Workarounds: In evolutionary development, it's common to introduce quick fixes and workarounds to meet immediate project goals. Over time, these patches can accumulate and make the codebase more convoluted and difficult to maintain.

Lack of Long-Term Planning: Evolutionary development tends to focus on short-term objectives, often at the expense of long-term planning. This can lead to a lack of consistency and structure in the codebase, making maintenance more challenging.

Feature Creep: As software evolves through iterative development, there's a risk of feature creep, where new features are continually added without a clear architectural plan. This can lead to a bloated and unwieldy codebase that's hard to maintain.

Inadequate Testing: Rapid development may not allow for thorough testing of all code changes. As a result, there may be undiscovered bugs and issues that can make maintenance more challenging.

Dependency on Specific Individuals: In some cases, certain individuals or teams may have in-depth knowledge of the codebase due to their involvement in the rapid development phases. If they leave or are unavailable, it can be difficult for others to maintain the software.

Outdated Technologies: Evolutionary development may involve the use of cutting-edge technologies and frameworks. Over time, these technologies can become outdated or unsupported, leading to compatibility and maintenance issues.

Lack of Version Control: Some evolutionary development practices may not prioritize version control and source code management. Without proper version control, tracking changes and collaborating on maintenance can be challenging.

Frequent Code Changes: Evolutionary development often involves frequent code changes to accommodate evolving requirements. This can create a moving target for maintenance teams, making it harder to stabilize and maintain the software.

Q 11. Write short notes on: [RTU20151]

(i) RAD model

Ans : The Rapid Application Development (RAD) model is a software development methodology that prioritizes speed and flexibility. In the RAD model, the development process is expedited by using pre-built components and prototyping. It emphasizes close collaboration between developers and users, allowing for quick feedback and adjustments. RAD divides the project into small, manageable modules, and these modules are developed in parallel. The model is particularly beneficial for projects with rapidly changing requirements, where fast delivery is essential. However, it may not be suitable for complex, large-scale projects or those with strict regulatory requirements due to its emphasis on speed over comprehensive documentation and formal processes. Overall, the RAD model is a valuable approach for projects that require rapid development and frequent user involvement.

(ii) Prescriptive model

Ans: A Prescriptive Model in software engineering is a structured and standardized approach to software development that provides detailed guidelines, processes, and best practices for every phase of a project. These models offer a step-by-step plan, often with well-defined roles, responsibilities, and deliverables. The Waterfall Model is a classic example of a prescriptive model. While prescriptive models provide clarity and predictability, they can be less flexible in adapting to changing requirements and may not suit projects with evolving needs. These models are well-suited for projects with stable and well-understood requirements, where a structured, sequential approach is desired.

Q 12. Define the following:

(i) Software processes

Ans: In software engineering, software processes refer to the structured and systematic set of activities, workflows, methods, and practices that are used to develop, maintain, and manage software systems throughout their lifecycle. These processes are designed to ensure the efficient and effective creation of high-quality software that meets user needs and adheres to industry standards and best practices. Software processes encompass various phases, including requirements analysis, design, coding, testing, deployment, and maintenance, and are typically guided by specific software development methodologies or models, such as the Waterfall Model, Agile, or DevOps. They aim to improve productivity, manage project risks, and deliver software that is reliable, maintainable, and scalable. Software processes are a fundamental aspect of software engineering, helping teams produce software efficiently and with high quality.

(ii) Software process model

Ans: A software process model in software engineering is a structured framework that guides the development and management of software projects. These models provide a systematic approach to various phases of the software development life cycle, including requirements gathering, design, coding, testing, deployment, and maintenance. Different process models offer distinct strategies for organizing and executing these activities. Some common software process models include:

Waterfall Model: This model follows a linear and sequential approach, where each phase must be completed before the next one begins. It is best suited for projects with well-defined and stable requirements.

Agile Model: Agile models, such as Scrum and Kanban, prioritize flexibility, collaboration, and rapid iterations. They are suitable for projects with changing or evolving requirements.

Iterative and Incremental Models: Models like the Spiral Model involve cycles of planning, risk analysis, development, and evaluation, allowing for risk management and gradual development.

V-Model (Validation and Verification Model): This model associates each development phase with a corresponding testing phase, emphasizing the importance of validation and verification.

Big Bang Model: A simple and informal model where development begins without comprehensive planning. It is suitable for small projects with minimal documentation needs.

Prototyping Model: This model involves creating prototypes to gain user feedback and refine requirements. It is beneficial for projects with unclear or changing requirements.

Rapid Application Development (RAD) Model: RAD focuses on speed and user involvement, emphasizing quick development and feedback.

Incremental Model: Software is developed in smaller increments, each of which adds new functionality to the system.

DevOps: An approach that integrates software development and IT operations to enable continuous delivery and automation of the software development lifecycle.

Lean Software Development: This model emphasizes reducing waste and focusing on value-added activities, leading to more efficient software development.

Q 13. Explain incremental process model. Justify that it is appropriate for business software systems but less appropriate for real time systems. [RTU 2014]

Ans 13: The **Incremental Process Model** is a software development approach in which a system is built in multiple, well-defined increments or iterations. Each increment delivers a portion of the complete system's functionality. The development process is divided into smaller, manageable segments, and each increment is developed and delivered separately. The increments are typically constructed in a way that they can be integrated with the previously delivered ones, eventually leading to the complete system.

Characteristics of the Incremental Process Model:

Phased Development: The development process is divided into phases, with each phase building upon the previous one.

Partial System Functionality: Each increment adds specific, well-defined functionality to the system, allowing for partial system functionality after each increment is completed.

Early Deliveries: Increments can be delivered and deployed as soon as they are developed, providing early value to stakeholders.

Feedback and Iteration: Stakeholder feedback is incorporated into subsequent increments, allowing for adjustments and refinements based on real-world usage.

Risk Management: Risks associated with the entire project are mitigated incrementally rather than all at once.

Appropriateness for Business Software Systems:

Incremental development is well-suited for business software systems for several reasons:

Flexibility: Business requirements can change rapidly. Incremental development allows for flexibility and adaptation as new business needs arise.

Early Deliveries: Incremental development provides an opportunity for early deployment and return on investment, which is valuable in business contexts.

User Involvement: Business software often involves stakeholders from various departments. Incremental development facilitates ongoing feedback and collaboration.

Risk Mitigation: For large-scale business systems, incremental development helps manage project risks and uncertainties effectively.

Modularity: Business software can be structured in a modular fashion, making it suitable for an incremental approach, where each module represents an increment.

Less Appropriateness for Real-Time Systems:

Incremental development may be less appropriate for real-time systems due to the following reasons:

Timing Constraints: Real-time systems often have strict timing requirements and must meet precise deadlines. Incremental development can introduce uncertainties about when critical features will be available.

Complex Integration: In real-time systems, the integration of components must be well-coordinated to ensure that the system meets its time-critical objectives. Incremental development may introduce challenges in achieving this coordination.

Predictability: Real-time systems require a high level of predictability in terms of response times and behavior. Incremental development, with its focus on flexibility, may make it more challenging to predict system behavior.

Testing and Verification: Real-time systems must undergo rigorous testing and verification to ensure they meet timing and correctness requirements. Incremental development can complicate these testing efforts.

High Consequences of Failure: Failure in real-time systems can have severe consequences, making them less tolerant of development issues or delays.

Q 14. Explain the behavior modeling as a part of Structured Analysis of Software Development. [R.T.U. 2016]

Ans 14: Behavior modeling is a fundamental part of structured analysis in software development, which is a technique used to understand and document the behavior of a system. Structured analysis aims to create a clear and detailed representation of how a software system should function, without concerning itself with the specifics of how the system will be implemented. Behavior modeling focuses on defining the logical processes and functionality of a system, and it's typically done using techniques such as data flow diagrams (DFDs) and process specifications. Here's a more detailed explanation of behavior modeling within structured analysis:

Data Flow Diagrams (DFDs): DFDs are a graphical representation that illustrates how data flows within a system. They consist of processes, data stores, data flows, and external entities. Each of these components plays a vital role in representing the behavior of the system:

Processes: Processes in DFDs represent functions or activities within the system. They describe what needs to be done to transform input data into output data. Each process is labeled and typically corresponds to a specific function within the software.

Data Stores: Data stores represent where data is held within the system. These can be databases, files, or other data repositories.

Data Flows: Data flows are arrows that represent the movement of data between processes, data stores, and external entities. They show how data is transformed and transferred as it flows through the system.

External Entities: External entities represent sources or destinations of data that interact with the system. These could be users, other systems, or external services.

Process Specifications: In addition to DFDs, structured analysis often includes process specifications. These are detailed descriptions of the processes shown in the DFDs. Process specifications provide more information about how a process works, including its inputs, outputs, data transformations, and the logic or algorithms involved.

Control Flow: While DFDs primarily focus on data flow, control flow diagrams or flowcharts are sometimes used in conjunction with behavior modeling to represent the flow of control or decision-making within the system. They show the sequence of steps or actions involved in the processes.

The Benefits of Behavior Modeling in Structured Analysis:

Clarity and Understanding: Behavior modeling techniques provide a clear and easily understandable representation of how a system operates, making it easier for stakeholders to grasp the system's functionality.

Communication: DFDs and process specifications serve as a common language between developers, analysts, and users, ensuring that everyone has a shared understanding of the system's behavior.

Documentation: Behavior modeling documents the system's behavior in a systematic and structured manner, facilitating maintenance and future development efforts.

Requirements Elicitation: It helps in eliciting and clarifying system requirements by visualizing how data and control flow within the system, revealing potential issues, and suggesting improvements.

Analysis of Current Systems: Behavior modeling can be used to document and understand the behavior of existing systems, which is crucial when planning system upgrades or replacements.

Risk Identification: It helps in identifying potential risks and issues related to the system's behavior, allowing for proactive risk management.

Q 15. Write short note on behavioral modelling. [R.T.U.2017, 2015]

Ans 15: Behavioral Modeling is a crucial technique in software engineering that focuses on representing and understanding how a software system functions without delving into the specifics of its implementation. This modeling approach uses various visual representations, such as data flow diagrams (DFDs) and control flow diagrams, to illustrate the flow of data and control within the system. By breaking down a complex software system into processes, data stores, data flows, and external entities, behavioral modeling provides a clear and structured overview of the system's behavior. It is a valuable tool for communication between developers, analysts, and stakeholders, as it ensures a shared understanding of how the software operates. Furthermore, behavioral modeling aids in requirements elicitation, risk identification, and the documentation of system behavior, making it an essential step in the software development process.

Q 16. Write short note Finite State Machine (FSM). [RTU 2017, 2016, 2013.12]

Ans 16: A finite state machine (FSM) is a mathematical model used to represent and control the behavior of systems that can exist in a finite number of states at any given time. It is a concept widely used in computer science, engineering, and other fields to design, analyze, and implement systems with discrete and sequential behavior.

Types of FSM

1. Deterministic finite state machine (DFSM)

In a deterministic FSM, each state transition is uniquely determined by the current state and input. This means that given a specific input and current state, only one possible transition to the next state exists.

2. Non-deterministic finite state machine (NDFSM)

Non-deterministic FSMs allow multiple transitions for a given input and current state. This means that the next state is not uniquely determined and the machine can be in multiple states simultaneously.

3. Mealy machine

Mealy machines are FSMs that not only define the states and transitions but also associate outputs with each transition. The outputs in these types of machines rely on both the current state and the input.

Q 17. Explain Finite state Machine (FSSf) Models. [R.T.U.2014]

Ans 17: "Finite State Machine (FSM)" models. A Finite State Machine, also known as a Finite State Automaton, is a mathematical model used to represent and control the behavior of systems, including software and hardware. It is a directed graph in which nodes represent states, and edges represent transitions between states. Finite State Machine models are widely used in software engineering, control systems, and various other fields. Here's an explanation of Finite State Machine models:

Key Components of a Finite State Machine (FSM):

States (Nodes): States represent different conditions or modes in a system. Each state represents a particular situation or configuration of the system.

Transitions (Edges): Transitions define the movement between states. Events or conditions trigger transitions, and they determine the path from one state to another.

Events: Events are the stimuli that initiate state transitions. Events can be external, internal, or time-driven triggers.

Actions (Optional): Actions are associated with transitions and specify what happens when a particular transition occurs. Actions can include changing variables, outputting data, or performing specific functions.

Types of Finite State Machines:

Deterministic Finite State Machine (DFA): In a DFA, for each state and event, there is exactly one transition. This means that the next state is uniquely determined by the current state and the event.

Nondeterministic Finite State Machine (NFA): In an NFA, there can be multiple possible transitions for a given state and event. It is less predictable than a DFA.

Applications of Finite State Machine Models:

Software Design: FSMs are used in software development for tasks such as designing control logic, parsing, and modeling application behavior. They can represent complex decision-making processes, like in compilers or protocol implementations.

Hardware Design: FSMs are employed in digital circuit design to control and manage various hardware components, such as in digital controllers and processors.

Natural Language Processing: FSMs are used for tokenization and parsing in natural language processing and text analysis.

Control Systems: In control systems, FSMs can be used to represent the different states of a system and the transitions between them.

Modeling Real-World Systems: FSMs can model and control various real-world systems, including traffic lights, vending machines, elevator control, and more.

Advantages of Finite State Machine Models:
Simplicity: FSMs are simple and intuitive models, making them easy to understand and analyze.
Clear Representation: They provide a clear and visual representation of system behavior.
Determinism: DFAs are deterministic, meaning that the next state is unambiguously defined by the current state and event.
Limitations of Finite State Machine Models:
Complexity: FSMs can become unwieldy and complex when modeling systems with many states and transitions.
Limited Expressiveness: FSMs are not well-suited for systems with complex decision logic or dynamic behavior.
State Explosion: In some cases, FSMs can suffer from a "state explosion" problem when dealing with large or highly interconnected systems.

Q 18. What is structured analysis? Explain control flow diagram and control process specification by giving a suitable example. Describe software prototyping in detail. [R.T.U.2018]
Ans 18: **Structured Analysis:** Structured Analysis is a systematic approach to software engineering that focuses on understanding and documenting the structure and behavior of a system or software application. It is primarily concerned with visualizing and representing how data flows and how processes (functions) operate within the system. Structured Analysis aims to create a clear and comprehensive model of the software's functionality and data organization before moving on to design and implementation. Two key components of Structured Analysis are Control Flow Diagrams (CFD) and Control Process Specification (CPS).
Control Flow Diagram (CFD): A Control Flow Diagram is a graphical representation used in structured analysis to depict the flow of control or the sequence of operations within a system. It illustrates the logical structure of a system by showing the order in which functions or processes are executed. In a CFD, processes are represented as bubbles or rectangles, and arrows connect them to show the order in which they are executed. The arrows denote the flow of control from one process to another, indicating the logical sequence.
Example: Consider a simple library system. A CFD might depict the following processes in sequence: "User Requests Book," "Check Book Availability," "Issue Book," "Update User Records," and "Print Receipt." Arrows between these processes would show the flow of control from one to the next.
Control Process Specification (CPS): Control Process Specification complements Control Flow Diagrams by providing detailed descriptions of each process or function in a structured manner. CPS documents specify the inputs, outputs, data transformations, and the logic involved in each process. This information is used to define the functionality of each process precisely. CPS is often used in conjunction with CFDs to provide comprehensive documentation.
Example: For the "Issue Book" process in the library system, a Control Process Specification might detail the input data (e.g., book details and user information), the output (e.g., a transaction record), the data transformations (e.g., updating the book's availability status and user records), and the logic (e.g., verifying user eligibility and book availability) involved in this process.
Software Prototyping: Software Prototyping is an iterative and incremental development approach where a basic working model of the software is created to visualize and test the system's functionality. The prototype, often a simplified version of the final system, is used to gather user feedback, validate requirements, and improve the design. There are several types of software prototypes:
Throwaway/Rapid Prototyping: In this approach, a quick and disposable prototype is built solely for the purpose of understanding and refining user requirements. The actual system is developed separately.
Evolutionary Prototyping: In this method, the initial prototype is incrementally improved upon until it eventually evolves into the final system.
Software prototyping is particularly useful when requirements are not well-defined or when user needs are subject to change. It allows for early user involvement, which helps identify and address issues and requirements more effectively. The iterative nature of prototyping aids in reducing the risk of misunderstandings and scope creep, resulting in a system that is more aligned with user expectations. However, prototyping can add complexity to the development process and may not be suitable for all projects, especially those with strict regulatory or performance requirements.

Previous Years Unsolved Questions

Q 1. What is Prototyping Model? What are the shortcomings in it? What are the SDLC models which overcome these shortcomings? [IGNOU, December, 2015]
Q 2. How can spiral life cycle model help to improve the software development process when compared to the waterfall life cycle model? Explain. [IGNOU, December, 2013, 2016]
Q 3. Describe any one model for software estimation. [IGNOU, June, 2017]
Q 4. With reference to the software quality metrics, explain the following:
(i) Defect Metrics
(ii) Maintainability Metrics. [IGNOU, December, 2017]
Q 5. Explain all the phases of the Waterfall Model with the help of a diagram. [IGNOU, December, 2017]
Q 6. With a neat diagram, explain about spiral process model. [Anna University 2022]
Q 7. What is feasibility study? What are the feasibilities to be analyzed in software development? [Anna University 2022]
Q 8. Describe the RAD Model of Software development in detail. Also give the conditions in which Prototype model is used. [MCU 2019]
Q 9. Explain the following: [RGPV June 2020]
i) Linear sequential model
ii) Prototyping model
iii) RAD model
iv) Evolutionary software process model
Q 10. Explain Waterfall Model with advantages and disadvantages. [VTU 2021]

Chapter 5: Agile Software Development

5.1 Introduction Agile Software Development

Agile Software Development is an iterative and incremental approach to software development that emphasizes the importance of delivering a working product quickly and frequently. It involves close collaboration between the development team and the customer to ensure that the product meets their needs and expectations.

The Agile Software Development process typically consists of the following steps:

Requirements Gathering: The customer's requirements for the software are gathered and prioritized.

Planning: The development team creates a plan for delivering the software, including the features that will be delivered in each iteration.

Development: The development team works to build the software, using frequent and rapid iterations.

Testing: The software is thoroughly tested to ensure that it meets the customer's requirements and is of high quality.

Deployment: The software is deployed and put into use.

Maintenance: The software is maintained to ensure that it continues to meet the customer's needs and expectations.

Agile Software Development is widely used by software development teams and is considered to be a flexible and adaptable approach to software development that is well-suited to changing requirements and the fast pace of software development.

Agile is a time-bound, iterative approach to software delivery that builds software incrementally from the start of the project, instead of trying to deliver all at once.

Why Agile? Technology in this current era is progressing faster than ever, enforcing global software companies to work in a fast-paced changing environment. Because these businesses are operating in an ever-changing environment, it is impossible to gather a complete and exhaustive set of software requirements. Without these requirements, it becomes practically hard for any conventional software model to work. The conventional software models such as Waterfall Model that depends on completely specifying the requirements, designing, and testing the system are not geared towards rapid software development. As a consequence, a conventional software development model fails to deliver the required product. This is where agile software development comes to the rescue. It was specially designed to curate the needs of the rapidly changing environment by embracing the idea of incremental development and developing the actual final product.

Principles:

Highest priority is to satisfy the customer through early and continuous delivery of valuable software.

It welcomes changing requirements, even late in development.

Deliver working software frequently, from a couple of weeks to a couple of months, with a preference to the shortest timescale.

Build projects around motivated individuals. Give them the environment and the support they need, and trust them to get the job done.

Working software is the primary measure of progress.

Simplicity the art of maximizing the amount of work not done is essential.

The most efficient and effective method of conveying information to and within a development team is face-to-face conversation.

Development in Agile: Let's see a brief overview of how development occurs in Agile philosophy.

In Agile development, Design and Implementation are considered to be the central activities in the software process.

Design and Implementation phase also incorporates other activities such as requirements elicitation and testing into it.

In an agile approach, iteration occurs across activities. Therefore, the requirements and the design are developed together, rather than separately.

The allocation of requirements and the design planning and development as executed in a series of increments. In contrast with the conventional model, where requirements gathering needs to be completed in order to proceed to the design and development phase, it gives Agile development an extra level of flexibility.

An agile process focuses more on code development rather than documentation.

Example: Let's go through an example to understand clearly how agile actually works. A Software company named **ABC** wants to make a new web browser for the latest release of its operating system. The deadline for the task is 10 months. The company's head assigned two teams named **Team A** and **Team B** for this task. In order to motivate the teams, the company head says that the first team to develop the browser would be given a salary hike and a one-week full-sponsored travel plan. With the dreams of their wild travel fantasies, the two teams set out on the journey of the web browser. Team A decided to play by the book and decided to choose the Waterfall model for the development. Team B after a heavy discussion decided to take a leap of faith and choose Agile as their development model. The Development plan of the Team A is as follows:

Requirement analysis and Gathering – 1.5 Months

Design of System – 2 Months

Coding phase – 4 Months

System Integration and Testing – 2 Months

User Acceptance Testing – 5 Weeks

The Development plan for the Team B is as follows:

Since this was an Agile, the project was broken up into several iterations.

The iterations are all of the same time duration.

At the end of each iteration, a working product with a new feature has to be delivered.

Instead of Spending 1.5 months on requirements gathering, They will decide the core features that are required in the product and decide which of these features can be developed in the first iteration.

Any remaining features that cannot be delivered in the first iteration will be delivered in the next subsequent iteration, based on the priority

At the end of the first iterations, the team will deliver working software with the core basic features.

Both the team have put their best efforts to get the product to a complete stage. But then out of blue due to the rapidly changing environment, the company's head come up with an entirely new set of features and want to be implemented as quickly as possible and wanted to push out a working model in 2 days.

Team A was now in a fix, they were still in their design phase and did not yet start coding and they had no working model to display. And moreover, it was practically impossible for them to implement new features since waterfall model there is not reverting back to the old phase once you proceed to the next stage, which means they would have to start from the square one again. That would incur their heavy cost and a lot of overtime.

Team B was ahead of Team A in a lot of aspects, all thanks to Agile Development. They also had the working product with most of the core requirements since the first increment. And it was a piece of cake for them to add the new requirements. All they had to do is schedule these requirements for the next increment and then implement them.

5.2 Agile Development Models

In earlier days, the Iterative Waterfall Model was very popular for completing a project. But nowadays, developers face various problems while using it to develop software. The main difficulties included handling customer change requests during project development and the high cost and time required to incorporate these changes. To overcome these drawbacks of the Waterfall Model, in the mid-1990s the Agile Software Development model was proposed.

The Agile Model was primarily designed to help a project adapt quickly to change requests. So, the main aim of the Agile model is to facilitate quick project completion. To accomplish this task, agility is required. Agility is achieved by fitting the process to the project and removing activities that may not be essential for a specific project. Also, anything that is a waste of time and effort is avoided.

The Agile Model refers to a group of development processes. These processes share some basic characteristics but do have certain subtle differences among themselves.

Agile SDLC Models/Methods:-

Models: Crystal Agile methodology places a strong emphasis on fostering effective communication and collaboration among team members, as well as taking into account the human elements that are crucial for a successful development process. This methodology is particularly beneficial for projects with a high degree of uncertainty, where requirements tend to change frequently.

Atern: This methodology is tailored for projects with moderate to high uncertainty where requirements are prone to change frequently. Its clear-cut roles and responsibilities focus on delivering working software in short time frames. Governance practices set it apart and make it an effective approach for teams and projects.

Feature-driven development: This approach is implemented by utilizing a series of techniques, like creating feature lists, conducting model evaluations, and implementing a design-by-feature method, to meet its goal. This methodology is particularly effective in ensuring that the end product is delivered on time and that it aligns with the requirements of the customer.

Scrum: This methodology serves as a framework for tackling complex projects and ensuring their successful completion. It is led by a Scrum Master, who oversees the process, and a Product Owner, who establishes the priorities. The Development Team, accountable for delivering the software, is another key player.

Extreme programming (XP): It uses specific practices like pair programming, continuous integration, and test-driven development to achieve these goals. Extreme programming is ideal for projects that have high levels of uncertainty and require frequent changes, as it allows for quick adaptation to new requirements and feedback.

Lean Development: It is rooted in the principles of lean manufacturing and aims to streamline the process by identifying and removing unnecessary steps and activities. This is achieved through practices such as continuous improvement, visual management, and value stream mapping, which helps in identifying areas of improvement and implementing changes accordingly.

Unified Process: Unified Process is a methodology that can be tailored to the specific needs of any given project. It combines elements of both waterfall and Agile methodologies, allowing for an iterative and incremental approach to development. This means that the UP is characterized by a series of iterations, each of which results in a working product increment, allowing for continuous improvement and the delivery of value to the customer.

All Agile methodologies discussed above share the same core values and principles, but they may differ in their implementation and specific practices. Agile development requires a high degree of collaboration and communication among team members, as well as a willingness to adapt to changing requirements and feedback from customers.

In the Agile model, the requirements are decomposed into many small parts that can be incrementally developed. The Agile model adopts Iterative development. Each incremental part is developed over an iteration. Each iteration is intended to be small and easily manageable and can be completed within a couple of weeks only. At a time one iteration is planned, developed, and deployed to the customers. Long-term plans are not made.

Steps in the Agile Model

The agile model is a combination of iterative and incremental process models. The steps involve in agile SDLC models are:

Requirement gathering
Design the Requirements
Construction / Iteration
Testing / Quality Assurance
Deployment
Feedback

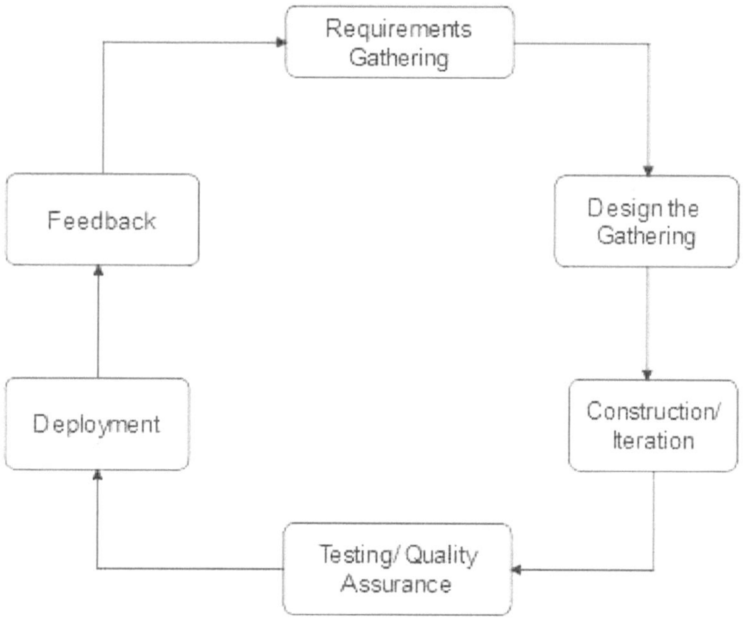

Steps in Agile Model

1. Requirement Gathering:- In this step, the development team must gather the requirements, by interaction with the customer. development team should plan the time and effort needed to build the project. Based on this information you can evaluate technical and economical feasibility.

2. Design the Requirements:- In this step, the development team will use user-flow-diagram or high-level UML diagrams to show the working of the new features and show how they will apply to the existing software. Wireframing and designing user interfaces are done in this phase.

3. Construction / Iteration:- In this step, development team members start working on their project, which aims to deploy a working product.

4. Testing / Quality Assurance:- Testing involves Unit Testing, Integration Testing, and System Testing. A brief introduction of these three tests is as follows:

5. Unit Testing:- Unit testing is the process of checking small pieces of code to ensure that the individual parts of a program work properly on their own. Unit testing is used to test individual blocks (units) of code.

Integration Testing:- Integration testing is used to identify and resolve any issues that may arise when different units of the software are combined.

System Testing:- Goal is to ensure that the software meets the requirements of the users and that it works correctly in all possible scenarios.

5. Deployment:- In this step, the development team will deploy the working project to end users.

6. Feedback:- This is the last step of the Agile Model. In this, the team receives feedback about the product and works on correcting bugs based on feedback provided by the customer.

The time required to complete an iteration is known as a Time Box. Time-box refers to the maximum amount of time needed to deliver an iteration to customers. So, the end date for an iteration does not change. However, the development team can decide to reduce the delivered functionality during a Time-box if necessary to deliver it on time. The Agile model's central principle is delivering an increment to the customer after each Time-box.

Principles of the Agile Model

To establish close contact with the customer during development and to gain a clear understanding of various requirements, each Agile project usually includes a customer representative on the team. At the end of each iteration stakeholders and the customer representative review, the progress made and re-evaluate the requirements.

The agile model relies on working software deployment rather than comprehensive documentation.

Frequent delivery of incremental versions of the software to the customer representative in intervals of a few weeks.

Requirement change requests from the customer are encouraged and efficiently incorporated.

It emphasizes having efficient team members and enhancing communications among them is given more importance.

It is realized that improved communication among the development team members can be achieved through face-to-face communication rather than through the exchange of formal documents.

It is recommended that the development team size should be kept small (5 to 9 people) to help the team members meaningfully engage in face-to-face communication and have a collaborative work environment.

The agile development process usually deploys Pair Programming. In Pair programming, two programmers work together at one workstation. One does coding while the other reviews the code as it is typed in. The two programmers switch their roles every hour or so.

Characteristics of the Agile Process

Agile processes must be adaptable to technical and environmental changes. That means if any technological changes occur, then the agile process must accommodate them.

The development of agile processes must be incremental. That means, in each development, the increment should contain some functionality that can be tested and verified by the customer.

The customer feedback must be used to create the next increment of the process.

The software increment must be delivered in a short span of time.

It must be iterative so that each increment can be evaluated regularly.

When To Use the Agile Model?

When frequent modifications need to be made, this method is implemented.

When a highly qualified and experienced team is available.

When a customer is ready to have a meeting with the team all the time.

when the project needs to be delivered quickly.

Projects with few regulatory requirements or not certain requirements.

projects utilizing a less-than-strict current methodology

Those undertakings where the product proprietor is easily reachable

Flexible project schedules and budgets.

5.3 Advantages and Disadvantages of Agile Methodology

Advantages of Agile Methodology:

In Agile methodology the delivery of software is unremitting.

The customers are satisfied because after every Sprint working feature of the software is delivered to them.

Customers can have a look of the working feature which fulfilled their expectations.

If the customers has any feedback or any change in the feature then it can be accommodated in the current release of the product.

In Agile methodology the daily interactions are required between the business people and the developers.

In this methodology attention is paid to the good design of the product.
Changes in the requirements are accepted even in the later stages of the development.
An Agile/Scrum approach can improve organizational synergy by breaking down organizational barriers and developing a spirit of trust and partnership around organizational goals.

Disadvantages of the Agile Methodology :

In Agile methodology the documentation is less.
Sometimes in Agile methodology the requirement is not very clear hence it's difficult to predict the expected result.
In few of the projects at the starting of the software development life cycle it's difficult to estimate the actual effort required.
Because of the ever-evolving features, there is always a risk of the ever-lasting project.
For complex projects, the resource requirement and effort are difficult to estimate.

5.4 Agile Software Development Life Cycle

Software development life cycle (SDLC) is a phenomenon to design, develop and, test high-quality software. The primary aim of SDLC is to produce high-quality software that fulfills the customer requirement within times and cost estimates.
Agile Software Development Life Cycle (SDLC) is the combination of both iterative and incremental process models. It focuses on process adaptability and customer satisfaction by rapid delivery of working software product. Agile SDLC breaks down the product into small incremental builds. These builds are provided into iterations.

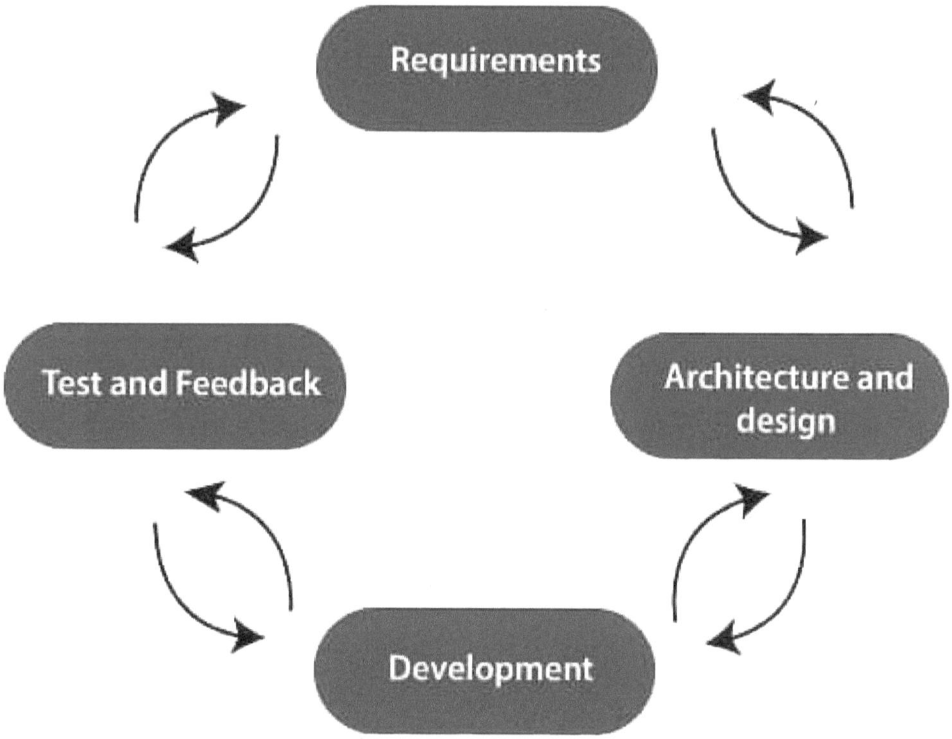

In the agile SDLC development process, the customer is able to see the result and understand whether he/she is satisfied with it or not. This is one of the advantages of the agile SDLC model. One of its disadvantages is the absence of defined requirements so, it is difficult to estimate the resources and development cost.

Each iteration of agile SDLC consists of cross-functional teams working on various phases:

Requirement gathering and analysis
Design the requirements
Construction/ iteration
Deployment
Testing

Feedback

Requirements gathering and analysis: -

In this phase, you must define the requirements. You should explain business opportunities and plan the time and effort needed to build the project. Based on this information, you can evaluate technical and economic feasibility.

Design the requirements: -

When you have identified the project, work with stakeholders to define requirements. You can use the user flow diagram or the high-level UML diagram to show the work of new features and show how it will apply to your existing system.

Construction/ Iteration: -

When the team defines the requirements, the work begins. The designers and developers start working on their project. The aims of designers and developers deploy the working product within the estimated time. The product will go into various stages of improvement, so it includes simple, minimal functionality.

Deployment: -

In this phase, the team issues a product for the user's work environment.

Testing: -

In this phase, the Quality Assurance team examine the product's performance and look for the bug.

Feedback: -

After releasing of the product, the last step is to feedback it. In this step, the team receives feedback about the product and works through the feedback.

The **major factors of agile include according to Agile Manifesto** are following four:

Early customer involvement

Iterative development

Self-organizing teams

Adaptation to change

Agile Testing Methods:

Scrum

Crystal

Dynamic Software Development Method

(DSDM)

Feature Driven Development (FDD)

Lean Software Development

eXtreme Programming (XP)

1. Scrum

SCRUM is an agile development process focused primarily on ways to manage tasks in team-based development conditions.

There are three roles in it, and their responsibilities are:

Scrum Master: The scrum can set up the master team, arrange the meeting and remove obstacles for the process

Product owner: The product owner makes the product backlog, prioritizes the delay and is responsible for the distribution of functionality on each repetition.

Scrum Team: The team manages its work and organizes the work to complete the sprint or cycle.

2. eXtreme Programming (XP)

This type of methodology is used when customers are constantly changing demands or requirements, or when they are not sure about the system's performance.

3. Crystal:

There are three concepts of this method-

Chartering: Multi activities are involved in this phase such as making a development team, performing feasibility analysis, developing plans, etc.

Cyclic delivery: under this, two more cycles consist, these are:

Team updates the release plan.

Integrated product delivers to the users.

Wrap up: According to the user environment, this phase performs deployment, post-deployment.

4. Dynamic Software Development Method (DSDM):

DSDM is a rapid application development strategy for software development and gives an agile project distribution structure. The essential features of DSDM are that users must be actively connected, and teams have been given the right to make decisions. The techniques used in DSDM are:

Time Boxing

MoSCoW Rules
Prototyping

The DSDM project contains seven stages:

Pre-project
Feasibility Study
Business Study
Functional Model Iteration
Design and build Iteration
Implementation
Post-project

5. Feature Driven Development (FDD):

This method focuses on "Designing and Building" features. In contrast to other smart methods, FDD describes the small steps of the work that should be obtained separately per function.

6. Lean Software Development:

Lean software development methodology follows the principle "just in time production." The lean method indicates the increasing speed of software development and reducing costs. Lean development can be summarized in seven phases.

Eliminating Waste
Amplifying learning
Defer commitment (deciding as late as possible)
Early delivery
Empowering the team
Building Integrity
Optimize the whole

Rules to identify the desired SDLC:

There are some rules that the development crew could use to identify the desired SDLC. These include

The size of the crew
Geographical situation
Size of Software
Complication of software
Types of projects
Business strategies
Engineering capability and others where it may be found suitable.

It is also crucial for the crew to study the differences, advantages, and disadvantages of each SDLC before rejecting the decision. An SDLC selection and adoption process are important in that it ensures the organization maximizes its chance for delivering its software successfully.

Exercise

Exercise 1 – MCQ

Q 1. : In Agile methodologies, which role is responsible for removing impediments and ensuring that the team can deliver the project goals?

A. Product Owner B. Scrum Master

C. Development Team D. Project Manager

Q 2. In Agile, what is the purpose of a "stand-up" or "daily scrum" meeting?

A. To plan the entire project B. To inspect and adapt the work

C. To present detailed status reports D. To negotiate contract terms

Exercise 2 – True/ False

Q 1. In Agile, customer collaboration is valued over contract negotiation.

Q2. Agile methodologies prioritize following a rigid project plan over responding to changes.

Exercise 3 – Fill in the blanks

Q 1. Agile methodologies prioritize ___________ and responding to change over following a ___________.

Q 2. Agile practices encourage ___________ teams that work collaboratively and make decisions.

Exercise 4 – Match case

1. Scrum A. Focuses on continuous flow and visualizing work on a Kanban board.
2. Kanban B. Emphasizes short, time-boxed development iterations called sprints.
3. Extreme Programming (XP) C. Promotes pair programming, test-driven development, and continuous integration.
4. Daily Stand-up Meetings D. Writing tests before writing code to ensure code quality and functionality.
5. Test-Driven Development E. Short meetings where team members share progress and discuss obstacles.

Exercise 5 – One word answer

Q 1. What is the main goal of Agile development?

Q 2. What Agile practice involves continuous integration and testing?

Exercise 6 – Small answer

Q 1. What is a key principle of Agile development?

Q 2. What is a Scrum in Agile?

Exercise 7 – Long answer

Q 1. What are the core values and principles of Agile Software Development, and how do they differ from traditional software development approaches?

Q 2. What is the Scrum framework, and how does it fit into Agile Software Development?

Answers

Exercise 1 – MCQ

Ans: 1 B, 2 B

Exercise 2 – True/ False

Ans: 1 True, 2 False

Exercise 3 – Fill in the blanks

Ans: 1 Customer collaboration, 2 Self organizing

Exercise 4 – Match case

Ans: 1 B, 2 A, 3 C, 4 E, 5 D

Exercise 5 – One word answer

Ans: 1 flexibility, 2 Automation

Online Resources

Online Exam Paper:

Link: https://forms.gle/F7Nk6Mcs32sTNnTu5

QR Code:

Chapter 5 Videos Playlist:
Link: https://www.youtube.com/playlist?list=PLzlh_31VWEFrWA5FERgUE8ep4A7EozqHZ **y**
QR Code:

Previous Year Unsolved questions

Q 1. Explain the role of the following for the success of a web application project: [IGNOU, June, 2018]
(i) Webmaster
(ii) Application support team
(iii) Content development team
(iv) Web publisher
Q 2. What are the different techniques for Requirements Gathering? [IGNOU, December, 2016]
Q 3. Explain any two techniques of s/w 10 prototype development. Also mention the pros and cons of prototyping. [IGNOU, December, 2011]
Q 4. Discuss on the pros and cons of Agile software development. [Anna University 2022]
Q 5. List and explain the Principle of Agile Method. [VTU 2021]

Chapter 6: Software Design

6.1 Introduction

Software design is a mechanism to transform user requirements into some suitable form, which helps the programmer in software coding and implementation. It deals with representing the client's requirement, as described in SRS (Software Requirement Specification) document, into a form, i.e., easily implementable using programming language. The software design phase is the first step in SDLC (Software Design Life Cycle), which moves the concentration from the problem domain to the solution domain. In software design, we consider the system to be a set of components or modules with clearly defined behaviors & boundaries.

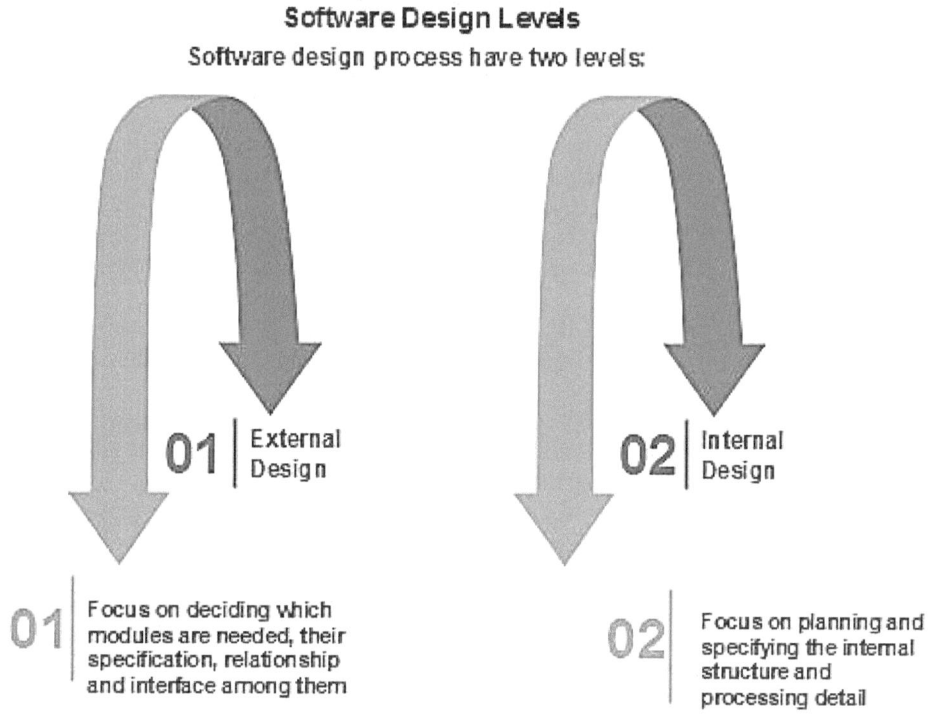

Objectives of Software Design
Following are the purposes of Software design:

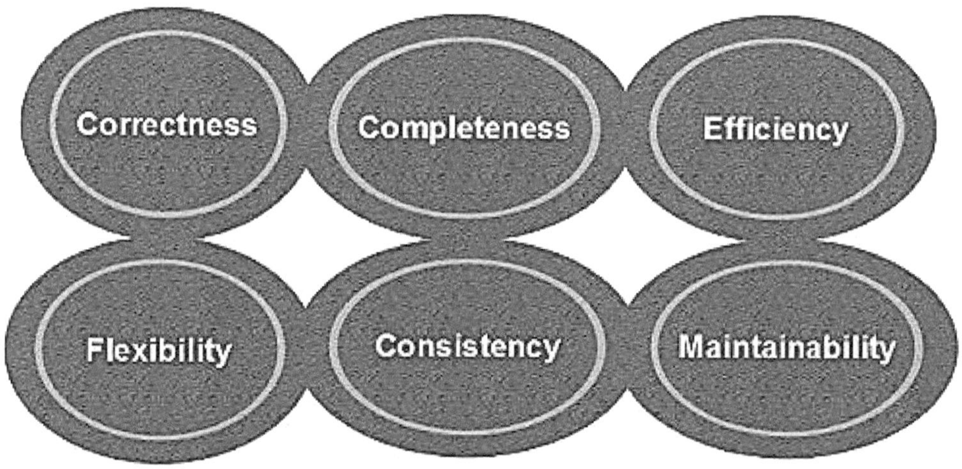

Objectives of Software Design

Correctness: Software design should be correct as per requirement.
Completeness: The design should have all components like data structures, modules, and external interfaces, etc.

Efficiency: Resources should be used efficiently by the program.
Flexibility: Able to modify on changing needs.
Consistency: There should not be any inconsistency in the design.
Maintainability: The design should be so simple so that it can be easily maintainable by other designers.

6.2 Design Process

The design process in software engineering is a crucial phase where the high-level system architecture and detailed system components are defined. It bridges the gap between the requirements specification and the actual implementation of the software. The design process involves several key steps:

Requirements Analysis: Before design begins, it's essential to have a thorough understanding of the software requirements. This includes functional requirements (what the software should do) and non-functional requirements (performance, security, scalability, etc.). The design process is driven by these requirements.

System Architecture Design: This is the top-level design phase where the overall system architecture is defined. It includes decisions about the software's structure, components, and their interactions. Common architectural styles include client-server, microservices, and layered architecture. Key architectural decisions, such as the choice of programming languages, databases, and technology stack, are made at this stage.

Detailed Design: In this step, the high-level architecture is refined into detailed designs for individual system components. Detailed design may include class diagrams, sequence diagrams, database schemas, and data flow diagrams. Design patterns and best practices are applied to ensure the software is modular, maintainable, and extensible.

Data Design: The data design focuses on how data will be stored, accessed, and manipulated within the software. This includes designing database schemas, data models, and data flow diagrams. It's essential to consider data integrity, consistency, and security in this phase.

User Interface (UI) Design: If the software has a user interface, this phase involves designing the user experience. It includes creating wireframes, mockups, and prototypes to visualize how users will interact with the system. UI design also covers usability and accessibility considerations.

Algorithm Design: For software that involves complex computations or data processing, designing efficient algorithms is critical. Algorithm design focuses on optimizing performance and ensuring the software can handle large datasets or complex calculations.

Security Design: Security is a fundamental aspect of software design. It involves identifying potential security threats, vulnerabilities, and implementing security measures to protect the software from malicious attacks. This may include authentication, authorization, encryption, and secure coding practices.

Testing Strategy: The design phase should also consider.

6.2.1 Design and Software Quality

Design and software quality are two interrelated aspects of software engineering that significantly impact the success of a software project. Let's explore how they are connected and their importance:

Design in Software Engineering:

Design in software engineering refers to the process of creating a blueprint or plan for how a software system will be structured, organized, and implemented. It encompasses various levels of design, including system architecture design, detailed component design, database design, user interface design, and algorithm design. Effective design is essential for the following reasons:

Structural Integrity: Good design ensures that the software system is structurally sound, making it easier to understand and maintain. It provides clarity on how different system components interact and collaborate.

Modularity: Modular design divides the software into independent and manageable components. This modularity promotes code reusability, reduces redundancy, and simplifies maintenance.

Scalability: Scalable design allows the software to grow as requirements change. A well-designed system can accommodate new features and increased loads without significant rework.

Maintainability: A well-designed software system is easier to maintain. Changes, updates, and bug fixes can be implemented with minimal impact on other parts of the system.

Usability: User-centric design ensures that the software is user-friendly and provides a positive user experience. This includes considerations for user interface design and usability testing.

Software Quality in Software Engineering:

Software quality refers to the degree to which software meets specified requirements and user expectations. It encompasses various quality attributes, including reliability, performance, security, maintainability, and usability. Achieving high software quality is crucial for the following reasons:

Customer Satisfaction: High-quality software meets or exceeds user expectations. Satisfied users are more likely to use the software, recommend it to others, and remain loyal to the product.
Reliability: Quality software is reliable and operates as expected. It minimizes unexpected crashes, errors, and downtime, ensuring a positive user experience.
Performance: Quality software performs efficiently and responds promptly to user interactions. Performance optimization is crucial, especially for applications with high loads.
Security: Security is a critical quality attribute. Quality software must be secure to protect user data and prevent vulnerabilities and breaches.
Maintainability: Quality software is designed and coded in a way that makes maintenance and updates straightforward. This includes clean code, documentation, and adherence to coding standards.
Usability: High-quality software is user-friendly, ensuring that users can easily navigate and use the system. Usability testing helps identify and address usability issues.
The Relationship Between Design and Software Quality:
The design process plays a pivotal role in determining software quality. Well-designed software is more likely to exhibit the following qualities:
Fewer defects and bugs: A good design can prevent common coding errors and make it easier to identify and address issues during development.
Improved maintainability: Modular and organized design simplifies maintenance and updates, contributing to long-term software quality.
Enhanced usability: Design considerations for user interfaces and user experience directly impact the software's usability and, consequently, its quality.
Performance optimization: Design choices can significantly impact the software's performance, ensuring that it meets performance-related quality criteria.

6.2.2 Evolution of Software Design

The evolution of software design in software engineering has undergone several significant phases over the years, adapting to the changing landscape of technology and development methodologies. Here's an overview of the evolution of software design:
Pre-Software Engineering Era (1940s-1960s):
During the early years of computing, software design was often informal and ad hoc.
Software developers were typically mathematicians and scientists who manually wrote machine-level code.
The focus was on solving specific mathematical or scientific problems with limited software reuse.
Structured Programming Era (late 1960s-1970s):
As software development became more complex, structured programming concepts, such as top-down design, were introduced.
Programmers began to use flowcharts and pseudocode for planning and visualizing program logic.
The goal was to create more organized and maintainable software.
Object-Oriented Programming (OOP) Era (1980s-1990s):
The advent of object-oriented programming led to a fundamental shift in software design.
OOP introduced the concepts of classes, objects, inheritance, and encapsulation.
Design principles like the SOLID principles (Single Responsibility, Open/Closed, Liskov Substitution, Interface Segregation, and Dependency Inversion) emerged.
Design patterns, such as the Gang of Four (GoF) patterns, provided reusable solutions to common design problems.
Component-Based Design Era (late 1990s-early 2000s):
With the rise of component-based development, software design shifted toward creating reusable software components.
Design for reusability and interoperability became essential.
Technologies like COM (Component Object Model) and CORBA (Common Object Request Broker Architecture) were prominent in this era.
UML and Visual Modeling (1990s-Present):
The Unified Modeling Language (UML) was standardized in the mid-1990s, providing a common visual notation for software design.
UML diagrams, such as class diagrams, sequence diagrams, and use case diagrams, became central to design documentation.
Visual modeling tools allowed developers to create and communicate designs more effectively.
Agile and Iterative Design (2000s-Present):

Agile methodologies, like Scrum and Extreme Programming (XP), brought a focus on adaptive and iterative design. Design activities became more integrated into the development process, with shorter design cycles and continuous feedback.

Agile emphasizes working software over comprehensive design documentation.

Microservices and Cloud-Native Design (2010s-Present):

In the era of cloud computing and microservices architecture, software design emphasizes building small, independent services that can be easily deployed and scaled.

Containerization and orchestration technologies, such as Docker and Kubernetes, influence design decisions.

DevOps and Continuous Integration/Continuous Delivery (CI/CD) (2010s-Present):

DevOps practices have blurred the lines between design and development by encouraging collaboration and automation throughout the software lifecycle.

CI/CD pipelines integrate design, coding, testing, and deployment into a seamless process.

User-Centered Design and Human-Centered Design (Ongoing):

Design thinking and user-centered design principles prioritize the user experience in software design.

Usability testing, user feedback, and iterative design are integral to modern software design processes.

Artificial Intelligence and Machine Learning (Ongoing):

The integration of AI and ML into software design introduces new challenges and opportunities.

AI-driven design automation tools are emerging to assist in various design tasks.

6.3 Software Design as a Problem Solving

Software design is a critical aspect of problem-solving in software engineering. It involves the process of transforming requirements and specifications into a well-structured plan for creating software that addresses a specific problem or set of problems. Here's how software design is a form of problem-solving:

Understanding the Problem Domain:

The first step in software design is to thoroughly understand the problem that the software aims to solve. This includes understanding the needs of end-users and stakeholders, as well as the specific challenges and constraints of the problem domain.

Requirement Analysis:

Software designers work closely with stakeholders to gather and analyze requirements. This involves identifying functional and non-functional requirements, constraints, and any existing system or process that the software will interact with.

Decomposition and Abstraction:

The problem is decomposed into smaller, more manageable sub-problems. These sub-problems are abstracted into components or modules that represent different aspects of the solution.

Architectural Design:

The software architect designs the overall structure of the system, which includes defining the major components, their interactions, and the high-level system architecture. This step is crucial for solving the problem efficiently and effectively.

Algorithm and Data Structure Selection:

Depending on the nature of the problem, software designers choose appropriate algorithms and data structures that are best suited to solving the problem efficiently.

User Interface Design:

For software that has a user interface, designers create user-friendly interfaces that allow users to interact with the system easily and intuitively. This is a critical aspect of problem-solving as it directly impacts user satisfaction.

Design Patterns and Best Practices:

Designers apply established design patterns and best practices to solve common problems in software development. These patterns provide reusable solutions to recurring design challenges.

Trade-offs and Constraints:

Designers often face trade-offs between conflicting requirements. For example, optimizing for performance might mean sacrificing simplicity. Making informed decisions about these trade-offs is part of the problem-solving process.

Testing and Validation:

The designed components and modules are tested and validated to ensure they meet the specified requirements and effectively solve the problem. This includes unit testing, integration testing, and validation with real users.

Refinement and Iteration:

Software design is an iterative process. Designers continually refine and improve the design as they discover and address issues during development and testing.

Documentation and Communication:
Clear and concise documentation is created to communicate the design decisions and rationale to developers, testers, and other stakeholders. Effective communication is essential for problem-solving.
Collaboration:
Problem-solving in software design often involves collaboration among team members with different areas of expertise. Effective collaboration ensures that diverse perspectives contribute to the solution.

6.4 Software Design as a Problem Techniques

Software design is a problem-solving process that involves various techniques to create effective and efficient software solutions. Here are some key techniques used in software design as a problem-solving approach:
Decomposition:
Decomposition is the process of breaking down a complex problem into smaller, more manageable sub-problems or modules. Each module can then be designed and implemented independently. This simplifies the overall problem-solving process.
Abstraction:
Abstraction involves simplifying complex systems by focusing on high-level concepts while ignoring irrelevant details. It allows designers to create models of the problem that capture essential aspects without getting bogged down in specifics.
Modularity:
Modularity is the practice of designing software as a collection of independent, interchangeable, and reusable modules. Each module has a specific function, and they interact through well-defined interfaces. Modularity enhances maintainability and scalability.
Architectural Patterns:
Architectural patterns are high-level design templates that provide solutions for organizing and structuring software systems. Examples include the Model-View-Controller (MVC) pattern, layered architecture, and microservices architecture.
Design Patterns:
Design patterns are reusable solutions to common design problems. Examples include the Singleton pattern, Factory pattern, and Observer pattern. These patterns help solve specific issues in a structured and proven way.
Data Flow Diagrams (DFD):
DFDs are graphical representations that illustrate how data flows through a system. They are used to analyze, model, and design information systems. DFDs help in identifying inputs, processes, and outputs in a system.
Entity-Relationship Diagrams (ERD):
ERDs are used to model the data structure and relationships within a system. They help design database schemas and understand how data entities are connected.
Use Case Diagrams:
Use case diagrams are part of Unified Modeling Language (UML) and are used to visualize the interactions between system components and external actors. They help in understanding system functionality from a user's perspective.
Flowcharts:
Flowcharts are diagrams that represent a step-by-step process. They are useful for visually representing algorithms and decision-making processes within the software.
Pseudocode:
Pseudocode is a way to represent the algorithm or logic of a program using a mix of natural language and basic programming concepts. It helps in refining and communicating the logic of the solution before actual coding.
State Diagrams:
State diagrams are used to represent the different states and transitions of an object or system. They are valuable for modeling behavior in software systems.
Collaboration Diagrams:
Collaboration diagrams in UML show the interactions between objects or components in the system, which can be valuable for understanding how different parts of the system work together.
Mockups and Prototyping:
Creating visual mockups and interactive prototypes of user interfaces helps in the design of user-centric software. It allows users and stakeholders to provide feedback and validate the design.
User-Centered Design (UCD):
UCD techniques involve understanding user needs, preferences, and behavior. Techniques like personas, user stories, and usability testing help in designing software that meets user expectations.

Refactoring:
Refactoring is the process of restructuring existing code or design to improve its quality, maintainability, and efficiency. It's a problem-solving technique for addressing issues in the design that emerge during development.

6.5 Software Design Models

In software engineering, various software design models and methodologies are used to guide the process of creating software systems. These models help software engineers and designers plan, structure, and develop software in a systematic and organized manner. Here are some common software design models:

Waterfall Model:
The Waterfall model is a linear and sequential approach to software development. It divides the project into distinct phases such as requirements, design, implementation, testing, and maintenance. Each phase must be completed before the next one begins.

V-Model (Validation and Verification Model):
The V-Model extends the Waterfall model by associating each development phase with a corresponding testing phase. It emphasizes the importance of validation (ensuring the product meets requirements) and verification (ensuring the product is built correctly).

Iterative Model:
The Iterative model divides the project into smaller cycles or iterations. In each iteration, a subset of features is developed, allowing for feedback and refinement. It is flexible and adaptable to changing requirements.

Spiral Model:
The Spiral model combines iterative development with elements of the Waterfall model. It involves a series of cycles, each including planning, risk analysis, engineering, and evaluation phases. This model is particularly useful for large, complex projects.

Agile Model:
Agile methodologies, such as Scrum and Kanban, focus on iterative development with a strong emphasis on customer collaboration, responding to change, and delivering a working product incrementally.

RAD (Rapid Application Development):
RAD is an incremental software development process that puts a premium on rapid prototyping and speedy feedback from end-users. It's often used for small to medium-sized projects.

Object-Oriented Model:
Object-Oriented Design (OOD) involves representing software as a collection of interacting objects. The model promotes reusability, encapsulation, and modeling real-world objects within the software.

Component-Based Development (CBD):
CBD focuses on building software systems by integrating pre-built, reusable components. This approach can save development time and improve maintainability.

Model-Driven Development (MDD):
MDD relies on models as a primary artifact in the software development process. Developers create high-level models that are automatically transformed into code.

Service-Oriented Architecture (SOA):
SOA is an architectural model where software functionality is provided as a set of services that can be accessed and reused by various components and applications. It promotes modularity and interoperability.

Domain-Driven Design (DDD):
DDD is an approach that focuses on understanding and modeling the problem domain within the software. It aims to create a shared understanding of the domain among developers and domain experts.

UML (Unified Modeling Language):
UML is a standardized modeling language used in software design. It includes various diagram types, such as class diagrams, sequence diagrams, and use case diagrams, to represent different aspects of the software.

Use Case-Driven Design:
This design model centers around identifying and designing software features from the perspective of users. Use cases are created to capture the interactions between users and the system.

6.6 General Design Process

The general design process in software engineering is a critical phase in developing a software system. It involves transforming the requirements gathered during the previous phases (such as requirements analysis and specification) into a detailed design that can serve as the blueprint for implementing the software. Here are the key steps in the general design process:

System Architecture Design:
The process typically begins with high-level system architecture design. At this stage, you define the overall structure of the software, including major components, their interactions, and the system's behavior. This can be depicted using architectural diagrams.
Subsystems and Module Design:
Break down the system architecture into smaller subsystems and modules. For each module, design the internal structure, functionality, and interfaces. Use techniques like data flow diagrams, class diagrams, and sequence diagrams to illustrate the module's behavior and relationships.
Data Design:
Design the data structures and databases required for the system. This includes defining the data models, relationships between data entities, and database schemas. Entity-Relationship Diagrams (ERDs) and data flow diagrams are commonly used in this step.
User Interface Design:
If the software has a graphical user interface (GUI), design the layout, controls, and user interaction elements. Prototyping and mockups can help visualize the UI design. Consider usability and user experience (UX) principles.
Algorithm Design:
Specify the algorithms and logic that drive the software's functionality. This includes defining the sequence of steps to perform a task, decision-making processes, and data processing algorithms.
Security Design:
Incorporate security measures into the design to protect the software from potential threats and vulnerabilities. This may involve access control, encryption, authentication, and other security mechanisms.
Error Handling and Exception Design:
Plan for how the software will handle errors and exceptions. Define error messages, recovery strategies, and mechanisms for logging and reporting errors.
Performance Design:
Ensure that the software is designed to meet performance requirements. Address issues related to speed, scalability, and resource utilization. This may include load balancing and caching strategies.
Documentation:
Create design documents that capture the details of the design, including architecture diagrams, data models, interface specifications, and algorithm descriptions. These documents serve as references for developers and future maintenance.
Testing Strategy Design:
Define the testing approach, including unit testing, integration testing, and system testing. Plan how different components and modules will be tested to ensure that they meet the design specifications.
Review and Validation:
Conduct design reviews to ensure that the design aligns with the requirements. Involve peers and stakeholders in the review process to identify and address potential issues early.
Iterative Refinement:
The design process is often iterative. Refine the design based on feedback, changing requirements, and emerging insights. This may involve revisiting and updating design artifacts.
Approach Selection:
Choose the appropriate design paradigms, patterns, and methodologies. For example, you may use object-oriented design principles, design patterns, or other architectural styles based on the nature of the project.
Integration with Development:
The design phase should seamlessly transition into the development phase. Developers use the design specifications to implement the software system.
Tools and Technologies:
Select the tools, programming languages, and technologies that are best suited for implementing the design. Ensure that the chosen tools align with the project's goals and constraints.
Quality Assurance:
Incorporate quality assurance practices into the design process to identify and mitigate quality-related risks and issues.

6.7 Software Design Process

The software design process in software engineering involves the systematic planning and creation of a blueprint for a software system based on the previously gathered requirements. This blueprint serves as a guide for developers during the implementation phase. The software design process typically includes the following stages:

Requirements Analysis:
Begin by analyzing and understanding the functional and non-functional requirements of the software. This step involves discussions with stakeholders to clarify and refine requirements, prioritize features, and identify constraints.
Architectural Design:
Create the high-level architecture of the software. This includes defining the system's structure, components, and their interactions. Common architectural styles include client-server, microservices, and layered architectures.
Detailed Design:
Break down the software into smaller components and modules. For each component, specify the detailed design, including data structures, algorithms, and interfaces. Design patterns may be used to address recurring design problems.
User Interface Design:
If the software has a user interface, design the layout, navigation, and user interactions. Pay attention to user experience (UX) principles and create prototypes or mockups to visualize the design.
Database Design:
Design the data storage and management components of the software. This includes defining the database schema, tables, relationships, and data access methods.
Security Design:
Incorporate security measures to protect the software from threats and vulnerabilities. This may include access controls, encryption, authentication, and input validation.
Error Handling and Exception Design:
Plan how the software will handle errors, exceptions, and edge cases. Define error messages, logging mechanisms, and recovery strategies.
Performance Design:
Address performance-related aspects, such as speed, scalability, and resource optimization. Consider strategies like caching, load balancing, and database indexing.
Testing Strategy Design:
Define the testing approach for the software design. Specify how different components will be tested, including unit testing, integration testing, and system testing.
Documentation:
Create comprehensive design documents that capture the architectural and detailed design, interface specifications, data models, and other relevant details. These documents serve as references for developers.
Quality Assurance:
Integrate quality assurance practices into the design process to identify and mitigate quality-related risks and issues.
Review and Validation:
Conduct design reviews and validations to ensure that the design aligns with the requirements and is feasible to implement. Involve stakeholders and peers in these reviews.
Iteration and Refinement:
Understand that the design process is often iterative. Refine the design based on feedback, changing requirements, or emerging insights. Be prepared to revisit and update design artifacts.
Approach Selection:
Choose the appropriate design paradigms, patterns, and methodologies that best suit the project's goals and constraints. Common approaches include object-oriented design principles and design patterns.
Tools and Technologies:
Select the tools, programming languages, and technologies that align with the project's requirements and the chosen design approach.
Integration with Development:
Ensure a seamless transition from the design phase to the development phase. Developers use the design specifications to build the software system.

6.8 Software design Strategies

Software design strategies in software engineering are approaches or methodologies used to guide the process of creating a software system. These strategies help software designers make critical decisions about the system's architecture, structure, and components. Here are some common software design strategies:
Modular Design:
This strategy involves breaking the software into smaller, independent modules or components. Each module is responsible for a specific function or feature. Modular design promotes reusability, maintainability, and ease of testing.

Layered Architecture:
In a layered architecture, the software is organized into distinct layers, each responsible for a specific aspect of functionality. Common layers include presentation, application logic, and data access. This approach simplifies maintenance and promotes separation of concerns.

Client-Server Architecture:
In client-server architecture, the software is divided into two parts: the client (user interface) and the server (business logic and data storage). This strategy is often used for applications that require distributed computing.

Microservices Architecture:
Microservices involve designing a software system as a collection of small, independent services. Each service handles a specific business capability and communicates with others through APIs. This approach offers flexibility and scalability.

Service-Oriented Architecture (SOA):
SOA focuses on creating reusable, well-defined services that can be used by different parts of the software. It emphasizes interoperability and the use of standard protocols.

Component-Based Design:
Component-based design involves building software using reusable components or objects. Components encapsulate specific functionality and can be reused in different parts of the system.

Model-View-Controller (MVC):
MVC is a design pattern that separates an application into three interconnected components: the Model (data and business logic), the View (user interface), and the Controller (handles user input and updates the model). This separation enhances maintainability.

Object-Oriented Design (OOD):
Object-oriented design is based on the principles of encapsulation, inheritance, and polymorphism. It promotes the modeling of software entities as objects with attributes and methods.

Design Patterns:
Design patterns are recurring solutions to common software design problems. They provide tested and proven approaches to addressing design challenges. Examples include the Singleton pattern, Factory pattern, and Observer pattern.

Database Design Strategies:
For systems with a significant data component, database design strategies focus on structuring data storage, normalization, indexing, and query optimization.

Architectural Patterns:
Architectural patterns, like the Hexagonal Architecture or Clean Architecture, provide high-level guidelines for organizing software systems. They emphasize the separation of concerns and adaptability to changing requirements.

Cross-Platform Design:
In cases where a software system needs to run on multiple platforms (e.g., desktop, web, mobile), the design should consider cross-platform compatibility and consistency.

Scalability and Performance Design:
Software design should address scalability concerns by considering load balancing, caching, and parallel processing to ensure the system can handle increasing loads.

Security Design:
Security design focuses on incorporating security features like encryption, access controls, and input validation to protect the software from potential threats.

User Experience (UX) Design:
UX design emphasizes creating a user-friendly interface and optimizing user interactions for a positive user experience.

Quality Attributes:
Consideration of non-functional requirements, such as reliability, scalability, performance, and maintainability, as part of the design process.

Pattern-Driven Design:
A pattern-driven design approach relies on a catalog of design patterns and uses them to solve specific design challenges in a systematic way.

Agile Design:
In an agile design approach, design is continuously evolving based on feedback and changing requirements, promoting adaptability and responsiveness.

6.9 Algorithms and Its Characteristics

Algorithms are fundamental to computer science and software engineering. They are step-by-step procedures or sets of instructions designed to perform specific tasks or solve particular problems. Here are the key characteristics of algorithms in software engineering:

Input: Algorithms take zero or more inputs, and they produce at least one output. The input represents the data or information on which the algorithm operates. In software engineering, inputs can be provided by users, other software components, or external sources.

Definiteness: Algorithms must have clear, unambiguous, and well-defined instructions. Each step in the algorithm should be precise and understandable, leaving no room for interpretation.

Finiteness: An algorithm must terminate after a finite number of steps. This means that it cannot run indefinitely, and it should eventually reach an endpoint, providing the desired output.

Effectiveness: Algorithms are designed to solve problems or perform tasks effectively. They should lead to the correct and desired result when executed on valid input data. This characteristic is often referred to as "correctness."

Output: As mentioned earlier, algorithms produce at least one output. The output can be a solution to a problem, a specific value, a modified data structure, or any relevant information that the algorithm is intended to generate.

Generality: Algorithms are general solutions to classes of problems, not limited to specific instances. They can be applied to a range of input data, not just one particular set.

Independent: Algorithms should be independent of any specific programming language or hardware. They describe a high-level solution that can be implemented in various programming languages and on different computing platforms.

Uniqueness: For a given problem, there can be multiple algorithms to solve it. The choice of which algorithm to use depends on factors like efficiency, simplicity, and suitability for the problem at hand.

Determinism: Algorithms must be deterministic, meaning that given the same input, they will produce the same output every time. There should be no randomness or uncertainty in the algorithm's behavior.

Efficiency: An efficient algorithm accomplishes the task with minimal time and resource consumption. Efficiency is often measured in terms of time complexity (how long the algorithm takes to run) and space complexity (how much memory it uses).

Optimality: In some cases, an algorithm can be optimal, meaning that it provides the best possible solution or uses the least amount of resources for a specific problem. However, optimality is not always a requirement, as it may come at the cost of complexity.

Analysis: Algorithms can be analyzed to understand their performance characteristics, such as time and space complexity. This analysis helps software engineers choose the most appropriate algorithm for a given problem.

Documentation: It is crucial to document algorithms clearly, including their purpose, input and output specifications, and step-by-step instructions. Proper documentation makes it easier for others to understand, use, and maintain the algorithm.

Reusability: Well-designed algorithms are often reusable in various parts of a software system or in different projects. Reusability can save time and effort in software development.

Exercise

Exercise 1 – MCQ

Q 1. What is the primary goal of software design in software engineering?

A. To identify software requirements
B. To create a detailed blueprint of the software
C. To write code and implement the software
D. To test the software

Q 2. Which software design principle promotes breaking down the system into smaller, manageable modules or components?

A. Modularity
B. Inheritance
C. Abstraction
D. Encapsulation

Exercise 2 – True/ False

Q 1. The primary goal of software design is to write code and implement the software.

Q 2. Abstraction is a design principle that suggests that software components should have a single, well-defined responsibility.

Exercise 3 – Fill in the blanks

Q 1. ____________ is the process of defining the software architecture, components, modules, interfaces, and data for a software system.

Q 2. The primary goal of software design is to transform the requirements defined in the software ____________ into a design that can be implemented in code.

Exercise 4 – Match case

1. Abstraction	A. Ensures that a class has only one instance.
2. Singleton	B. The principle of designing software components that are self-contained and encapsulate their functionality.
3. Factory Method	C. A standardized way to visualize the design of a software system.
4. Cohesion	D. Simplifying complex reality by modeling classes based on their essential characteristics.
5. UML	E. A creational design pattern that provides an interface for creating objects but allows subclasses to alter the type of objects.

Exercise 5 – One word answer

Q 1. What is the process of defining the architecture and structure of a software system?

Answer: Design

Q 2. What design principle suggests that software entities should be open for extension but closed for modification?

Answer: OCP (Open-Closed Principle)

Exercise 6 – Small answer

Q 1. What is software design in the context of software engineering?

Q 2. Why is abstraction an important concept in software design?

Exercise 7 – Long answer

Q 1. Explain the importance of software design in the software development process.

Q 2. What are design patterns in software engineering, and how do they impact software design?

Answers

Exercise 1 – MCQ

Ans: 1 B, 2 A

Exercise 2 – True/ False

Ans: 1 False, 2 False

Exercise 3 – Fill in the blanks

Ans: 1 Software Design, 2 Specification

Exercise 4 – Match case

Ans: 1 D, 2 A, 3 E, 4 B, 5 C

Exercise 5 – One word answer

Ans: 1 Design, 2 OCP (Open-Closed Principle)

Online Resources

Online Exam Paper:

Link: https://forms.gle/Yn3dPdf4HWmi2Dcs6

QR Code:

Chapter 6 Videos Playlist:

Link: https://www.youtube.com/playlist?list=PLzlh_31VWEFom6wCTWdQCnZPkydwJ2q40

QR Code:

Previous Years Solved Questions

Q 1. Explain the following concepts with examples: Modularity, Stepwise Refinement and Information Hiding. [R.T.U.2018]

Ans 1: **1. Modularity:** Modularity is a design principle that involves breaking down a complex software system into smaller, self-contained, and manageable modules or components. Each module serves a specific function and is designed to be independent, meaning that it can be developed, tested, and maintained separately. This approach makes it easier to understand, develop, and maintain software systems. Modularity promotes reusability, as well-structured modules can be used in different parts of the system or even in other projects.

Example: Consider a content management system (CMS) for a website. The CMS can be modularized into separate components, such as user authentication, content creation, database management, and user interface. Each module is responsible for a specific aspect of the CMS's functionality. For instance, the user authentication module handles user logins and permissions, while the content creation module manages content editing and publication. Modularity in the CMS design makes it easier to maintain, upgrade, and extend the system.

2. Stepwise Refinement: Stepwise Refinement, also known as top-down design, is a software design approach that starts with a high-level overview of the system and gradually refines it into finer levels of detail. The process involves breaking down the system into smaller and more manageable subproblems, which are then further refined until they can be implemented as code. It allows developers to focus on one level of detail at a time, simplifying the overall design process.

Example: Imagine you are designing a search engine. Initially, you create a high-level design that outlines the primary components, such as the user interface, search algorithm, and database interaction. You then break down the search algorithm component into subproblems like query processing, relevance ranking, and result retrieval. Each of these subproblems can be further refined until you reach the implementation level. Stepwise refinement ensures that the design is structured, and each level of detail is well-understood before moving on to the next.

3. Information Hiding: Information Hiding, a key principle of software design, focuses on encapsulating and concealing the internal details of a module or component from the rest of the system. It limits access to only the essential information and functionality needed to interact with the module, thereby reducing complexity and promoting a clean separation between modules. This concept helps in minimizing unintended interactions between different parts of the system and enhances the maintainability and scalability of the software.

Example: In an object-oriented programming context, consider a class that represents a car. Information hiding can be applied by making the car's internal details, such as the engine, transmission, and fuel system, private or protected members of the class. The class provides public methods to interact with the car, such as "start," "accelerate," and "stop." These methods expose only the necessary functionality to the external world while concealing the complex internal workings. This design ensures that users of the class do not need to understand or directly manipulate the car's internal components, promoting modularity and maintainability.

Q 2. Describe the role of data and architectural designs in software design. How is flowchart different from box diagram in procedural design? Explain. [R.T.U.2018]

Ans2: **Data Design:** Data design in software engineering involves defining the structure and organization of data within a software system. It focuses on how data is stored, processed, and accessed. The role of data design includes:

Data Structure: Designing data structures such as databases, data tables, records, and fields to represent information in a structured manner.

Data Storage: Determining where and how data will be stored, whether in databases, flat files, or cloud storage.

Data Relationships: Defining relationships between data elements, such as one-to-one, one-to-many, or many-to-many relationships in a database schema.

Data Access: Planning how data will be retrieved and manipulated within the system through queries or API calls.

Data Security: Ensuring data privacy and access control through encryption, authentication, and authorization mechanisms.

Example: In a banking software system, data design includes defining the structure of customer accounts, transaction records, account balances, and their relationships within a relational database.

Architectural Design: Architectural design focuses on defining the overall structure and components of a software system. It determines how the system's components interact and how they are organized to meet functional and non-functional requirements. The role of architectural design includes:

Component Selection: Choosing appropriate components, such as libraries, frameworks, or microservices, to build the system.

System Organization: Deciding how components are organized, including the distribution of responsibilities and communication between them.
Scalability: Designing the system to handle increased loads and growth by distributing components and services as needed.
Performance: Addressing performance considerations, such as response time, throughput, and resource utilization.
Security: Incorporating security measures, like firewalls, authentication, and encryption, to protect the system.
Example: In an e-commerce platform, architectural design may involve selecting a front-end framework, designing a microservices-based back-end, and defining how components like product catalogs, user authentication, and payment processing interact.
Flowchart vs. Box Diagram in Procedural Design:
Flowchart: A flowchart is a visual representation of the flow of control or the sequence of steps in a procedural algorithm or process. It is used to illustrate the logical flow of a program, detailing decisions, loops, and the order of execution. Flowcharts typically include various shapes, such as rectangles (for processes), diamonds (for decisions), and arrows (for control flow). They provide a high-level overview of the entire process and are helpful for understanding the control flow but may not focus on data or data structures.
Box Diagram: A box diagram, also known as a structure chart, is a graphical representation used in procedural design to illustrate the hierarchical structure of a software system or program. It primarily focuses on the organization of program modules or functions and their relationships. In a box diagram, each box represents a module or function, and lines connecting the boxes indicate the calling relationships between them. Unlike flowcharts, box diagrams are primarily concerned with the organization of code and functions and their interactions, making them suitable for representing the software's structural design.

Q 3. Explain any two architectural styles of software design in brief. [RTU 2013, 2012]
Ans 3: **1. Layered Architecture:**
Layered architecture, also known as the "n-tier architecture," is a design style where a software system is organized into distinct layers, each responsible for specific functions. Each layer communicates with the adjacent layers through well-defined interfaces, and this separation of concerns helps in modularizing and managing the system.
Key Characteristics:
Separation of Concerns: The system's functionality is divided into distinct layers, such as presentation, business logic, and data access, each handling specific aspects of the application.
Modularity: Layers can be developed, updated, or replaced independently, facilitating flexibility and maintainability.
Scalability: The system can be easily scaled by adding more instances of specific layers to meet growing demands.
Reusability: Components within each layer can be reused in different parts of the system or even in other projects.
Example: In a web application, the presentation layer handles user interface and user interaction, the business logic layer manages application-specific processes and rules, and the data access layer is responsible for connecting to the database and handling data retrieval and storage.
2. Microservices Architecture:
Microservices architecture is a design style where a complex application is decomposed into a collection of small, independently deployable services that communicate through well-defined APIs. Each service is responsible for a specific, discrete function and operates as a separate, isolated unit.
Key Characteristics:
Service Independence: Each microservice is self-contained and has its database, making it independent of other services.
Decentralization: Teams can develop, deploy, and scale microservices independently, allowing for faster development cycles.
Scalability: Services can be scaled individually based on their specific resource needs.
Fault Isolation: A failure in one microservice does not necessarily impact the entire system, enhancing fault tolerance.
Polyglot Technology: Different services can be built using different technologies and programming languages, as long as they communicate through well-defined APIs.
Example: In an e-commerce platform, different microservices may handle functions like user authentication, product catalog, shopping cart, payment processing, and order fulfillment, each as an independent service.
Both layered architecture and microservices architecture offer solutions to design challenges in different scenarios. Layered architecture provides a structured approach for traditional monolithic applications, while microservices architecture suits complex, large-scale systems where flexibility, independence, and scalability are essential. The choice between these architectural styles depends on the specific requirements and constraints of the project.

Q 4. Explain procedural design in brief. [RTU 2013]

Ans 4: **Procedural design**, also known as procedural programming, is a software design paradigm that focuses on creating software systems by organizing the code into procedures or functions that perform specific tasks. In procedural design, the program's execution is driven by a sequence of procedure calls, each of which may contain a set of instructions for a particular operation or task. This design approach is particularly well-suited for tasks that can be logically broken down into a series of well-defined steps or procedures.

Key Characteristics of Procedural Design:

Modularity: Code is organized into self-contained procedures or functions, each responsible for a specific task. This modularity simplifies code maintenance, promotes code reuse, and makes it easier to understand and test.

Sequential Execution: The program's execution follows a linear sequence of procedure calls. Procedures are called in a specific order, and control flows from one procedure to another as per the sequence.

Data and Logic Separation: Data and logic are often separated. Data is stored in data structures (e.g., arrays or records), and procedures manipulate that data.

Structured Control Flow: Procedural design uses structured control flow constructs like loops and conditional statements to control the program's flow.

Efficiency: Procedural code can be highly efficient because it focuses on performing a specific task with minimal overhead.

Well-Defined Interfaces: Procedures define well-defined interfaces (input and output) to exchange data with other procedures or the main program.

Procedural Abstraction: Procedures encapsulate a specific operation or task, providing a level of abstraction that hides the internal details, making the code easier to work with.

Example: In a procedural design for a simple calculator program, you might have procedures like "add," "subtract," "multiply," and "divide." Each procedure takes specific inputs (operands) and returns a result. The main program would call these procedures based on user input and the desired operation.

Advantages of Procedural Design:

Simplicity: Procedural design is straightforward and easy to understand, making it a suitable choice for small to moderately-sized applications.

Efficiency: The approach tends to be highly efficient because it minimizes overhead.

Code Reusability: Modular procedures can be reused in various parts of the program or even in different programs.

Disadvantages of Procedural Design:

Limited Scalability: Procedural design can become complex and hard to manage as the size of the software system grows.

Code Maintenance: Changes to one part of the program can have unintended consequences on other parts, making maintenance challenging.

Limited Support for Object-Oriented Concepts: Procedural design is less suitable for applications that require complex object-oriented concepts and data structures.

Q 5. Define the meaning of software design, explain the design fundamentals for software design. [R.T. U. 2015]

Ans 5: Software design is the process of defining the architecture, structure, components, interfaces, and data for a software system to satisfy specific requirements. It is a crucial phase in the software development life cycle, occurring after requirements analysis and before coding or implementation. The goal of software design is to create a blueprint that guides developers in building a system that functions efficiently, reliably, and maintainably while meeting the desired functionality and non-functional requirements.

Design Fundamentals for Software Design:

Effective software design requires adherence to certain fundamental principles and practices:

Abstraction: Abstraction involves simplifying complex systems by focusing on high-level concepts and ignoring low-level details. It helps in managing complexity and promoting clarity in design.

Modularity: Modularity is the process of breaking down a complex system into smaller, self-contained modules or components. Each module is responsible for a specific function or aspect of the system, making the design more manageable and facilitating code reuse.

Hierarchy: Hierarchy involves organizing components or modules in a hierarchical structure, with higher-level modules coordinating the activities of lower-level modules. This hierarchical structure simplifies the system's design and understanding.

Decomposition: Decomposition is the process of dividing a problem into smaller, manageable subproblems. Each subproblem can be solved independently, leading to a more efficient and structured design.

Encapsulation: Encapsulation is the practice of bundling data and the methods that operate on that data into a single unit, known as an object in object-oriented design. It promotes data hiding and prevents unauthorized access, ensuring data integrity.
Information Hiding: Information hiding involves concealing the internal details of a module or component, exposing only what is necessary for interaction. This concept minimizes complexity, enhances security, and simplifies maintenance.
Coupling and Cohesion: Coupling measures the degree of interdependence between modules, while cohesion measures how closely related the functions within a module are. Good design strives for low coupling and high cohesion, as it promotes maintainability and flexibility.
Simplicity: Simplicity in design is the practice of keeping the design as simple as possible without sacrificing functionality. A simple design is easier to understand, debug, and maintain.
Scalability: Designing for scalability means ensuring that the system can accommodate growing demands by adding resources or components without a complete redesign.
Flexibility: A flexible design allows for changes and adaptations without major disruptions. It accommodates new features, technologies, or requirements with minimal impact on existing functionality.
Reuse: Reusability promotes the use of existing components or modules in different parts of the system or in other projects. Reusable design elements save time and effort and improve consistency.
Maintainability: Design for maintainability considers the ease of maintaining and updating the software throughout its lifecycle. It includes clear documentation, well-structured code, and modular design.
Performance Optimization: Design considerations should include performance-related factors, such as data structures, algorithms, and resource management, to ensure that the system performs efficiently.

Q 6. Explain the software design process. [R.T.U.2016]
Ans 6: The software design process is a critical phase in software development, where the architecture and structure of the software system are defined. This process involves turning the functional and non-functional requirements, gathered during the requirements analysis phase, into a detailed design that serves as a blueprint for software development. Here's an overview of the software design process:
Requirements Review:
The software design process begins with a review of the requirements gathered during the requirements analysis phase. These requirements form the basis for the design and must be well-understood before proceeding.
System Architecture Design:
At this stage, the high-level architecture of the software system is defined. This includes decisions on the system's components, modules, and their interactions.
Architectural design focuses on structuring the system, identifying major components, and defining how they communicate with each other. Common architectural patterns, such as client-server, microservices, or layered architecture, are selected based on the project's needs.
Detailed Design:
In this phase, each major component or module identified in the architectural design is elaborated in detail.
Detailed design includes creating data models, specifying data structures, defining algorithms, and determining the interfaces between different components.
Design patterns, such as the Singleton pattern for creating a single instance of a class, may be applied to solve common design problems.
Data Design:
Data design focuses on designing the data structures and databases needed to support the software system.
This phase includes defining data entities, relationships, and designing database schemas. It also addresses data storage, retrieval, and data integrity.
User Interface (UI) Design:
If the software has a user interface, the UI design phase focuses on creating wireframes, mockups, and prototypes of the user interface.
UI design includes determining the layout, user interactions, and visual elements of the system's interface to ensure a user-friendly experience.
Component Design:
Component design involves designing individual software components or modules. This includes specifying the internal logic, algorithms, and data structures used within each component.
Component design ensures that each module is self-contained and well-structured.
Security Design:

Security design addresses the identification of potential security threats and the design of security measures to protect the software against vulnerabilities.
Security mechanisms, such as authentication, encryption, and access controls, are defined and integrated into the design.

Quality Assurance and Testing Design:
The design should include plans for quality assurance and testing, specifying test cases, test environments, and criteria for ensuring the software's quality.
Designing for testability helps identify and resolve potential issues early in the development process.

Documentation:
Documentation is created or updated throughout the design process. This includes design documents, architectural diagrams, data dictionaries, and any other relevant documentation needed for implementation, maintenance, and future reference.

Review and Validation:
The design is reviewed and validated to ensure that it meets the requirements and aligns with the architectural decisions.
Reviews may involve stakeholders, including developers, testers, and domain experts.

Refinement and Iteration:
The design may undergo refinements and iterations based on feedback and validation results. This process continues until a robust and complete design is achieved.

Design Verification:
The final design is verified to ensure it meets all design objectives and quality standards.

Q 7. What is software design? [RTU2014]

Ans 7: In software engineering, software design refers to the process of defining the architecture, components, modules, interfaces, and other elements of a software system. It is a critical phase in the software development life cycle that bridges the gap between the requirements analysis and software implementation.
The primary goal of software design is to create a blueprint or detailed plan for the software system that outlines how it will function, how its various components will interact, and how it will meet specific functional and non-functional requirements. This blueprint serves as a guide for developers, providing them with a clear and organized structure for writing the actual code.
Key aspects of software design include:
System Architecture: Deciding on the high-level structure of the system, including how major components or modules will interact. Common architectural patterns, such as layered architecture, microservices, or client-server architecture, may be selected.
Component and Module Design: Designing the individual components, modules, or classes that make up the software system. This involves specifying data structures, algorithms, and the interfaces between components.
Data Design: Defining data structures, databases, and data flow within the system. This includes database schema design, data modeling, and considerations for data storage, retrieval, and processing.
User Interface (UI) Design: If the software has a user interface, this design aspect focuses on creating the layout, interactions, and visual elements of the interface to provide a user-friendly experience.
Security Design: Identifying potential security threats and designing security measures to protect the software against vulnerabilities. Security mechanisms, such as authentication, encryption, and access controls, are defined and integrated into the design.
Quality Assurance and Testing Design: Planning for quality assurance and testing, including specifying test cases, test environments, and criteria for ensuring the software's quality. Designing for testability helps identify and address potential issues early in development.
Documentation: Creating or updating documentation throughout the design process, including design documents, architectural diagrams, data dictionaries, and any other relevant documentation needed for implementation, maintenance, and future reference.

Q 8. What are architectural and procedural software designs? Explain. [RTU 2014]

Ans 8: Architectural Design and Procedural Design are two distinct approaches to organizing and structuring software systems. Let's explain each of them:

Architectural Design:

Definition: Architectural design is a high-level design approach that focuses on defining the overall structure and organization of a software system. It deals with the system's major components, their relationships, and the high-level decisions that guide the system's design.

Key Characteristics:

Component Identification: In architectural design, you identify the major components or modules that make up the system. These components could be functions, classes, or even entire services.

Interaction Patterns: You specify how these components interact with each other. This includes defining communication protocols and data flows between components.

Decisions on Architecture: You choose an architectural style or pattern that best fits the project's needs. Common architectural styles include client-server, microservices, monolithic, and layered architecture.

Scalability and Performance Considerations: Architectural design also includes decisions related to system scalability, performance optimization, and fault tolerance.

Example: In an e-commerce application, the architectural design might involve defining components like the user interface, product catalog, shopping cart, payment processing, and order fulfillment. It would specify how these components communicate and interact to provide the complete e-commerce system.

Procedural Design:

Definition: Procedural design, also known as procedural programming, is an approach where software is structured around procedures or functions that perform specific tasks. In procedural design, the focus is on the sequence of procedures and the flow of control from one procedure to another.

Key Characteristics:

Modular Structure: The software is organized into self-contained procedures or functions, each responsible for a specific operation.

Sequential Flow: Procedures are executed in a predefined order. The program's control follows a linear sequence of procedure calls.

Data and Logic Separation: Data is often stored separately from the procedures, and procedures manipulate that data.

Structured Control Flow: Procedural design uses structured constructs like loops and conditional statements to control the program's flow.

Example: In a procedural design for a calculator application, you might have procedures like "add," "subtract," "multiply," and "divide." The program would call these procedures based on user input and the desired operation.

Key Differences:

Abstraction Level: Architectural design is high-level and focuses on the system's overall structure and components. Procedural design is lower-level and deals with the detailed logic of individual procedures.

Purpose: Architectural design guides how the system's components work together, while procedural design focuses on how specific tasks are carried out within those components.

Flexibility: Architectural design allows for a more flexible and modular approach, making it suitable for larger and more complex systems. Procedural design is often simpler and well-suited for smaller applications or specific tasks within a larger system.

Previous years Unsolved Questions

Q 1. Elaborate the rules for human computer interface design. [IGNOU, December, 2016]
Q 2. List all the elements of a Good Interface 10 design. [IGNOU, December, 2011]
Q 3. State the difference between internal design and external design. [Anna University 2022]
Q 4. What is refactoring? [Anna University 2022]
Q 5. Describe the golden rules for designing user interface design. [Anna University 2022]
Q 6. Discuss the need for component level design. Give examples. [Anna University 2022]
Q 7. Explain in detail about five views of software quality and objectives of SQA. [RGPV June 2020]

Chapter 7: Design Principles

7.1 Design Objectives

Design objectives in software engineering are foundational principles and goals that guide the development of software systems. These objectives define the overarching aims and criteria that a software design must meet to be considered successful. They play a pivotal role in shaping the overall structure, functionality, and quality of the software. Design objectives encompass a range of critical aspects, such as maintainability, scalability, usability, and performance. They ensure that software is not only functional but also reliable, efficient, and adaptable to changing needs. By setting clear design objectives, software engineers and designers can align their efforts with the project's goals, resulting in well-structured, robust, and user-friendly software that meets both the immediate and future requirements of stakeholders.

7.2 Design Principles

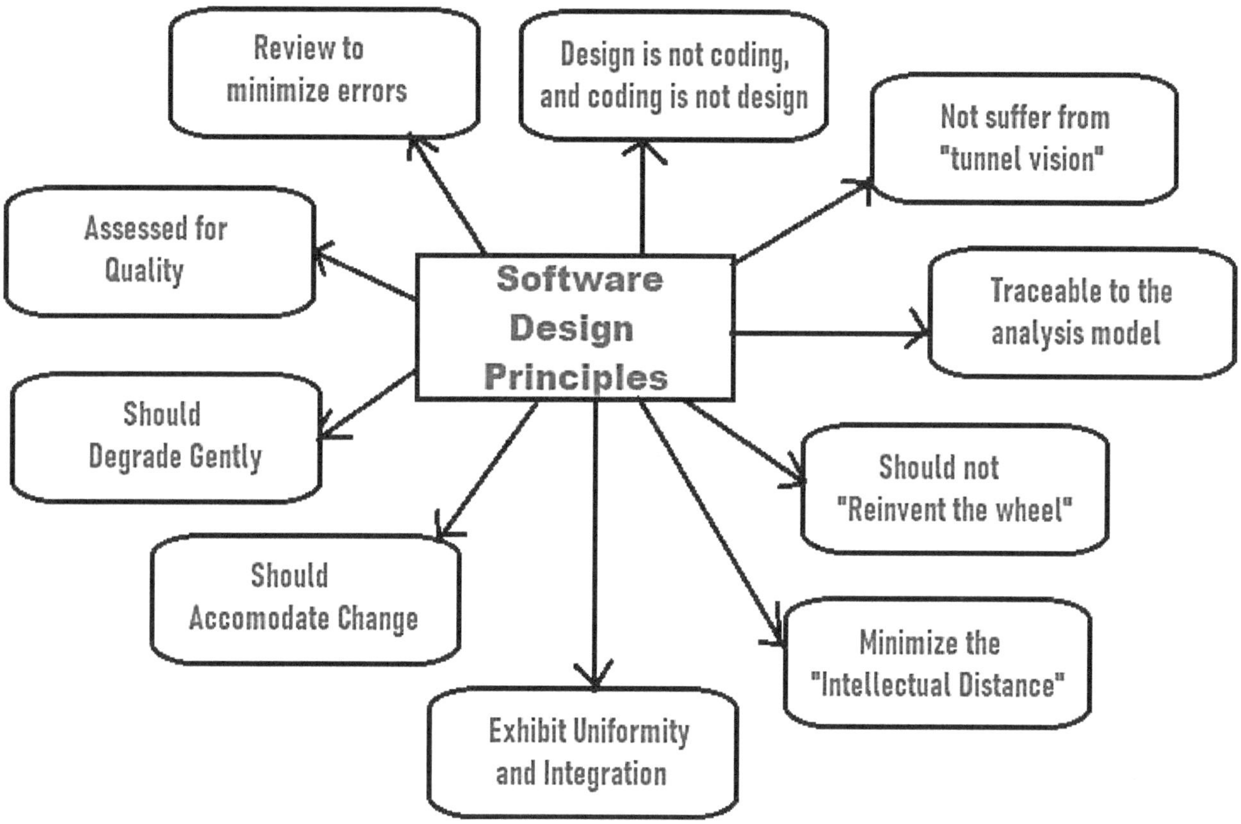

Principles Of Software Design :

Should not suffer from "Tunnel Vision" –

While designing the process, it should not suffer from "tunnel vision" which means that is should not only focus on completing or achieving the aim but on other effects also.

Traceable to analysis model –The design process should be traceable to the analysis model which means it should satisfy all the requirements that software requires to develop a high-quality product.

Should not "Reinvent The Wheel" –The design process should not reinvent the wheel that means it should not waste time or effort in creating things that already exist. Due to this, the overall development will get increased.

Minimize Intellectual distance –The design process should reduce the gap between real-world problems and software solutions for that problem meaning it should simply minimize intellectual distance.

Exhibit uniformity and integration –The design should display uniformity which means it should be uniform throughout the process without any change. Integration means it should mix or combine all parts of software i.e. subsystems into one system.

Accommodate change –The software should be designed in such a way that it accommodates the change implying that the software should adjust to the change that is required to be done as per the user's need.
Degrade gently –The software should be designed in such a way that it degrades gracefully which means it should work properly even if an error occurs during the execution.
Assessed or quality –The design should be assessed or evaluated for the quality meaning that during the evaluation, the quality of the design needs to be checked and focused on.
Review to discover errors –The design should be reviewed which means that the overall evaluation should be done to check if there is any error present or if it can be minimized.
Design is not coding and coding is not design –Design means describing the logic of the program to solve any problem and coding is a type of language that is used for the implementation of a design.

7.3 Constructive Design Principles

Constructive Design Principles in software engineering serve as the foundational guidelines and building blocks for creating high-quality and well-structured software systems. These principles, derived from decades of industry experience and best practices, are essential in the construction phase of the software development life cycle. They provide developers and designers with a structured approach to creating software that is robust, maintainable, and efficient. By following these principles, software engineers ensure that the code is not only functional but also modular, adaptable, and user-friendly. These principles encompass various aspects of software design, including modularity, encapsulation, abstraction, and separation of concerns. They promote best practices that lead to reduced complexity, fewer defects, and increased reusability, ultimately resulting in software that meets the needs of users, adapts to changing requirements, and stands the test of time. Constructive design principles are the cornerstone of well-crafted software, ensuring that it remains a valuable asset throughout its lifecycle.

7.3.1 Modularity Principles

Modularity principles in software engineering are essential guidelines and concepts that focus on breaking down a software system into smaller, self-contained, and interrelated modules. Modularity promotes maintainability, reusability, and understandability in software design and development. Here are key modularity principles:
Single Responsibility Principle (SRP):
Definition: Each module, class, or component should have a single, well-defined responsibility or reason to change.
Benefits: Enhances maintainability, reduces the likelihood of bugs, and makes code more comprehensible.
Open-Closed Principle (OCP):
Definition: Software entities (classes, modules) should be open for extension but closed for modification. You can add new functionality without changing existing code.
Benefits: Encourages the development of flexible and extensible software components.
Dependency Inversion Principle (DIP):
Definition: High-level modules should not depend on low-level modules but should depend on abstractions (e.g., interfaces or abstract classes). This promotes loose coupling.
Benefits: Reduces dependencies, simplifies maintenance, and supports interchangeable components.
Low Coupling:
Definition: Minimize the dependencies between modules or components. A module should rely on the least amount of information about other modules.
Benefits: Reduces the impact of changes in one module on other parts of the system, making the software more adaptable and less error-prone.
High Cohesion:
Definition: Ensure that the elements within a module are related to a single, well-defined purpose. A module should have a clear, cohesive function.
Benefits: Promotes code that is easier to understand, test, and maintain.
Information Hiding:
Definition: Hide the internal details of a module or class from the outside world, exposing only the necessary interfaces.
Benefits: Protects the integrity of the component, allows for easier modifications, and minimizes the impact of changes on other parts of the system.
Abstraction:
Definition: Focus on essential information while hiding the irrelevant details. Abstraction provides a simplified and high-level view of a module's functionality.

Benefits: Simplifies complex systems, enhances comprehensibility, and promotes effective communication between team members.

Separation of Concerns (SoC):

Definition: Divide the software into distinct sections, with each section addressing a specific concern or aspect of the system (e.g., user interface, business logic, data storage).

Benefits: Supports parallel development, facilitates maintenance, and enhances code organization.

Don't Repeat Yourself (DRY):

Definition: Avoid duplicating code or knowledge. Reuse code and information to reduce redundancy and maintenance effort.

Benefits: Reduces the likelihood of inconsistencies, simplifies maintenance, and makes the code more maintainable.

7.3.2 Implementability Principles

In software engineering, implementability principles refer to the guidelines and best practices that focus on making software designs and systems more practical to implement. These principles help ensure that the software can be efficiently and effectively developed, maintained, and extended by software developers. Here are some key implementability principles:

Modularity and Decomposition:

Principle: Divide the software into smaller, self-contained modules or components.

Benefits: Enhances code reusability, simplifies development, and allows teams to work on different modules simultaneously.

Consistency and Standardization:

Principle: Maintain a consistent coding style and adhere to coding standards.

Benefits: Makes the codebase more understandable, reduces errors, and aids in collaborative development.

Code Simplicity:

Principle: Write code that is simple and straightforward, avoiding unnecessary complexity.

Benefits: Reduces the likelihood of errors, eases debugging, and makes the software more maintainable.

Clear Documentation:

Principle: Provide comprehensive and well-maintained documentation for the software, including comments, user manuals, and API documentation.

Benefits: Assists developers in understanding the codebase and helps users make effective use of the software.

Automated Testing:

Principle: Implement automated testing (unit tests, integration tests, etc.) as part of the development process.

Benefits: Ensures software reliability, facilitates regression testing, and supports ongoing maintenance.

Version Control and Collaboration:

Principle: Use version control systems (e.g., Git) to manage code changes and promote collaboration among team members.

Benefits: Helps track code changes, facilitates collaboration, and simplifies the process of merging code from multiple developers.

Error Handling:

Principle: Implement robust error handling and reporting mechanisms to handle unexpected situations gracefully.

Benefits: Enhances the software's robustness, provides users with informative error messages, and eases debugging.

Scalability and Performance Optimization:

Principle: Design software to be scalable and optimize performance as needed.

Benefits: Allows the software to grow with increased demand and ensures it performs efficiently.

Security Best Practices:

Principle: Incorporate security best practices from the early stages of development to protect against vulnerabilities and threats.

Benefits: Safeguards sensitive data, mitigates security risks, and enhances user trust.

Code Review and Quality Assurance:

Principle: Perform regular code reviews and quality assurance activities to identify and rectify issues.

Benefits: Ensures code quality, identifies defects early, and maintains software reliability.

Extensibility and Future-Proofing:

Principle: Design software with extensibility in mind, making it easier to add new features or accommodate changing requirements.

Benefits: Reduces the cost and effort required for future enhancements and updates.

Deployment and Configuration Management:

Principle: Automate the deployment and configuration management processes to ensure consistency and reliability in different environments.
Benefits: Streamlines the deployment process, minimizes configuration errors, and supports scalability.
Logging and Monitoring:
Principle: Implement logging and monitoring to track software behavior, performance, and security.
Benefits: Helps diagnose issues, identify trends, and maintain software health.

7.3.3 Conflicts Between Software Design Principles

In software engineering, there can be conflicts or tensions between different software design principles due to the complex and multifaceted nature of software development. These conflicts often arise when trying to balance multiple design objectives, each of which may pull in different directions. Here are some common conflicts between software design principles:
Simplicity vs. Flexibility:
Simplicity: A simple design is easy to understand and maintain.
Flexibility: A highly flexible design can accommodate changing requirements and support various use cases.
Conflict: While simplicity is desirable for maintainability, excessive flexibility can introduce complexity and make the software harder to comprehend.
Modularity vs. Performance:
Modularity: A modular design enhances reusability and ease of maintenance.
Performance: High-performance systems often require tight integration, which can lead to less modularity.
Conflict: Striking a balance between modularity and performance can be challenging. Highly modular systems may have performance overhead due to the need for inter-module communication.
Abstraction vs. Transparency:
Abstraction: Abstraction hides complex details, providing a high-level view of the system.
Transparency: Transparency provides visibility into the internal workings of the system.
Conflict: Abstraction simplifies the understanding of the system, while transparency may be necessary for debugging and troubleshooting, but it can also introduce complexity.
Security vs. Usability:
Security: Emphasizes protecting the system from vulnerabilities and attacks.
Usability: Focuses on providing a user-friendly experience.
Conflict: Stricter security measures can sometimes lead to a less user-friendly interface or workflow. Striking a balance is essential to ensure both security and usability.
Extensibility vs. Simplicity:
Extensibility: Designing for extensibility allows for easy addition of new features.
Simplicity: Keeping the system simple can make it more understandable and maintainable.
Conflict: Highly extensible systems can become complex and harder to maintain. Balancing extensibility with simplicity is a challenge.
Granularity vs. Performance:
Granularity: Fine-grained components can lead to more modular and maintainable code.
Performance: Coarser-grained components can reduce the overhead of component interaction.
Conflict: Fine-grained components can lead to more method calls, which may impact performance. Coarser-grained components may sacrifice modularity.
Consistency vs. Diversity:
Consistency: A consistent design promotes predictability and ease of use.
Diversity: Diversity in design elements can enhance creativity and meet specific user needs.
Conflict: Overemphasizing consistency can lead to a lack of innovation and diversity in user interfaces, while excessive diversity can make the software inconsistent and confusing.

7.4 Effective Modular Design

7.4.1 Functional Independence

Functional independence in software engineering means that when a module focuses on a single task, it should be able to accomplish it with very little interaction with other modules.
In software engineering, if a module is functionally independent of other module, then it means it has high cohesion and low coupling.
Functional independence is essential for good software design.
Example of functional independence

We will take an example of simple college level project to explain concept of functional independence.
Suppose you and your friends are asked to work on a calculator project as a team. Here we need to develop each calculator functionality in form of modules taking two user inputs.
So, our modules are addition Module, subtraction Module, division Module, multiplication Module. Each one of you pick up one module for development purpose.
Before you enter into development phase, you and your team need to make sure to design the project in such a way that each of the module that you develop individually should be able to perform its assigned task without requiring much or no interaction with your friend's module. What I intend to say is, if you are working on addition Module then your module should be able to independently perform addition operation on receiving user input. It should not require to make any interaction with other modules like subtraction Module, multiplication Module or etc.
This is actually the concept of having module as functional independence of other modules.

7.4.2 Cohesion and Coupling

Module Coupling

In software engineering, the coupling is the degree of interdependence between software modules. Two modules that are tightly coupled are strongly dependent on each other. However, two modules that are loosely coupled are not dependent on each other. **Uncoupled modules** have no interdependence at all within them.

The various types of coupling techniques are shown in fig:

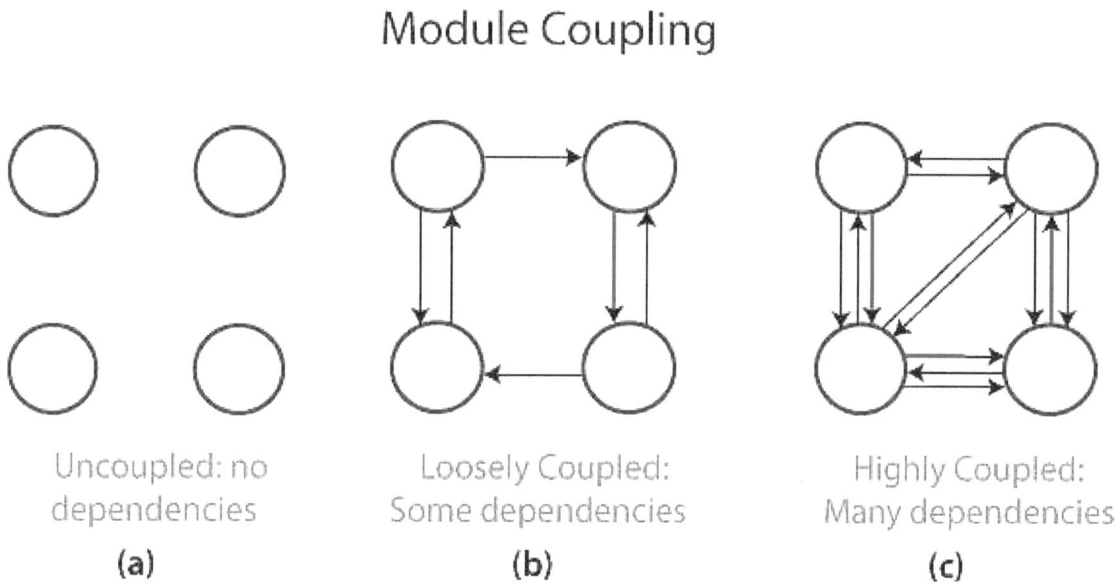

A good design is the one that has low coupling. Coupling is measured by the number of relations between the modules. That is, the coupling increases as the number of calls between modules increase or the amount of shared data is large. Thus, it can be said that a design with high coupling will have more errors.

Types of Module Coupling

Types of Modules Coupling

There are various types of module Coupling are as follows:

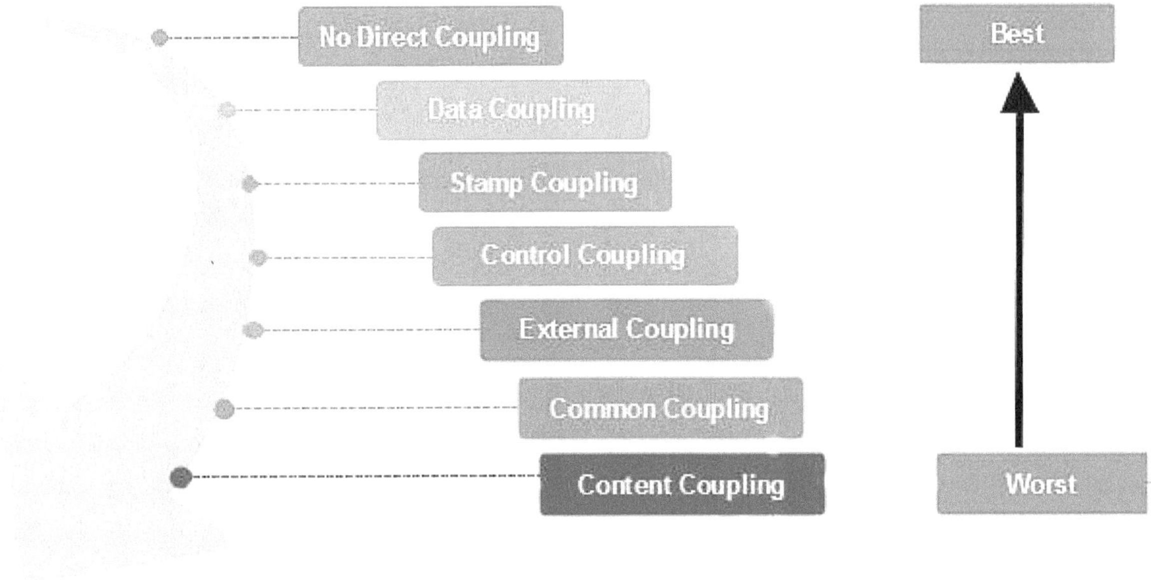

1. No Direct Coupling: There is no direct coupling between M1 and M2.

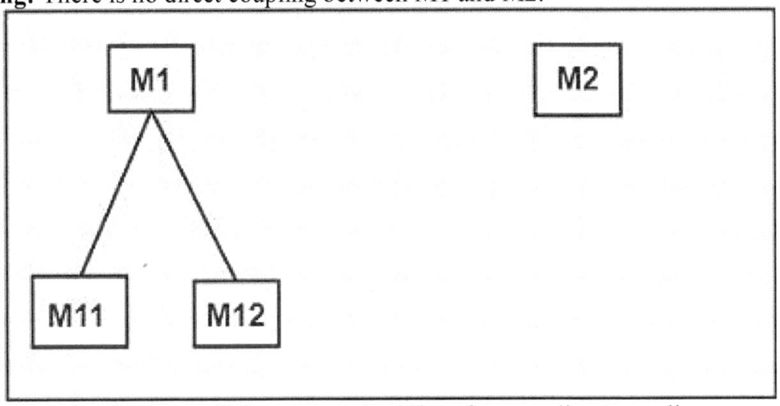

In this case, modules are subordinates to different modules. Therefore, no direct coupling.

2. Data Coupling: When data of one module is passed to another module, this is called data coupling.

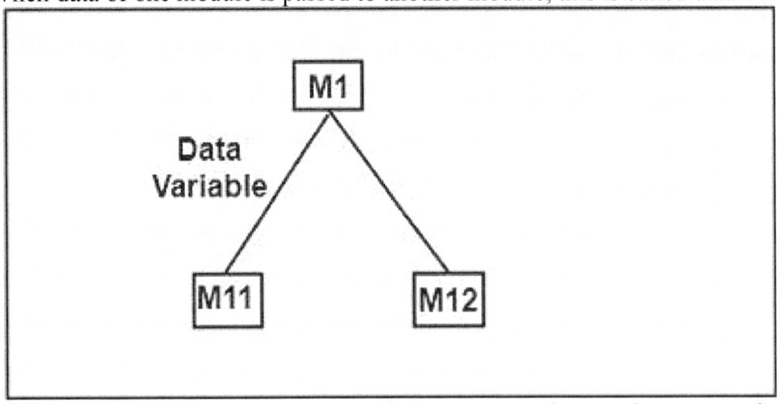

3. Stamp Coupling: Two modules are stamp coupled if they communicate using composite data items such as structure, objects, etc. When the module passes non-global data structure or entire structure to another module, they are said to be stamp coupled. For example, passing structure variable in C or object in C++ language to a module.

4. Control Coupling: Control Coupling exists among two modules if data from one module is used to direct the structure of instruction execution in another.

5. External Coupling: External Coupling arises when two modules share an externally imposed data format, communication protocols, or device interface. This is related to communication to external tools and devices.

6. Common Coupling: Two modules are common coupled if they share information through some global data items.

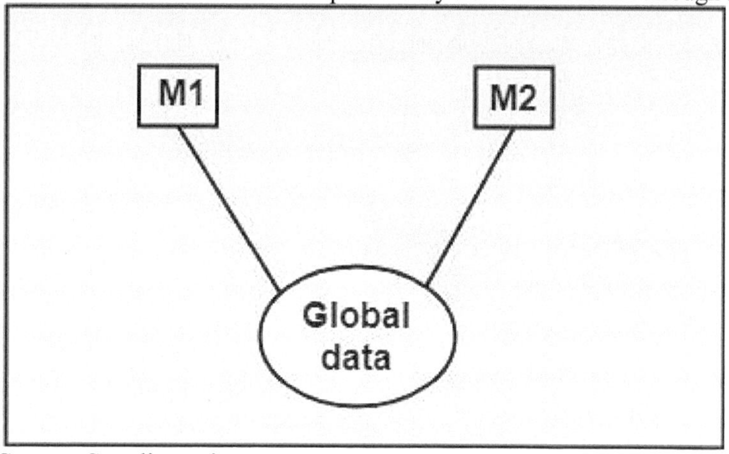

7. Content Coupling: Content Coupling exists among two modules if they share code, e.g., a branch from one module into another module.

Module Cohesion

In computer programming, cohesion defines to the degree to which the elements of a module belong together. Thus, cohesion measures the strength of relationships between pieces of functionality within a given module. For example, in highly cohesive systems, functionality is strongly related.

Cohesion is an ordinal type of measurement and is generally described as "high cohesion" or "low cohesion."

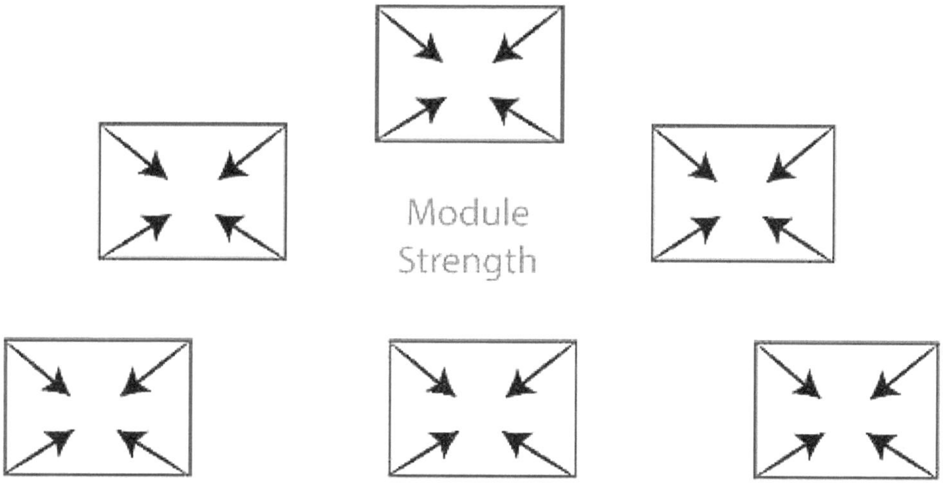

Cohesion= Strength of relations within Modules

Types of Modules Cohesion

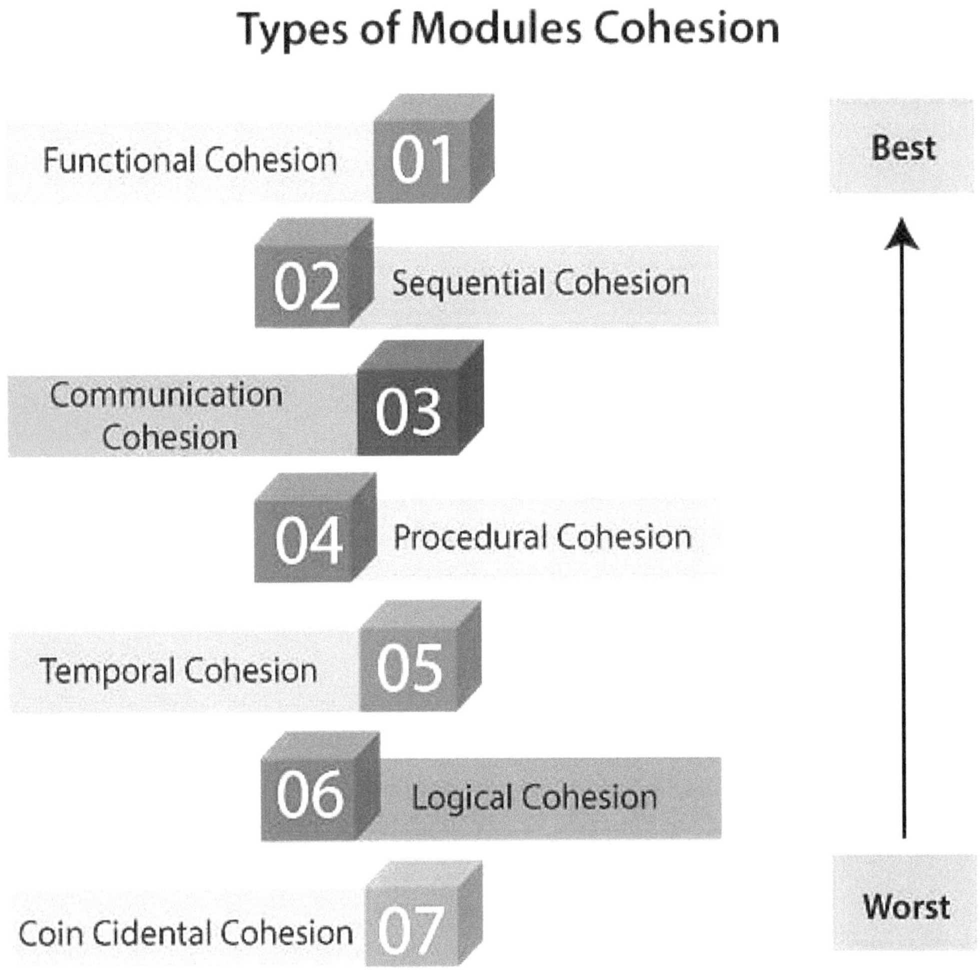

Functional Cohesion: Functional Cohesion is said to exist if the different elements of a module, cooperate to achieve a single function.
Sequential Cohesion: A module is said to possess sequential cohesion if the element of a module form the components of the sequence, where the output from one component of the sequence is input to the next.
Communicational Cohesion: A module is said to have communicational cohesion, if all tasks of the module refer to or update the same data structure, e.g., the set of functions defined on an array or a stack.
Procedural Cohesion: A module is said to be procedural cohesion if the set of purpose of the module are all parts of a procedure in which particular sequence of steps has to be carried out for achieving a goal, e.g., the algorithm for decoding a message.
Temporal Cohesion: When a module includes functions that are associated by the fact that all the methods must be executed in the same time, the module is said to exhibit temporal cohesion.
Logical Cohesion: A module is said to be logically cohesive if all the elements of the module perform a similar operation. For example Error handling, data input and data output, etc.
Coincidental Cohesion: A module is said to have coincidental cohesion if it performs a set of tasks that are associated with each other very loosely, if at all.

Differentiate between Coupling and Cohesion

Coupling	Cohesion
Coupling is also called Inter-Module Binding.	Cohesion is also called Intra-Module Binding.
Coupling shows the relationships between modules.	Cohesion shows the relationship within the module.

Coupling shows the relative **independence** between the modules.	Cohesion shows the module's relative **functional** strength.
While creating, you should aim for low coupling, i.e., dependency among modules should be less.	While creating you should aim for high cohesion, i.e., a cohesive component/ module focuses on a single function (i.e., single-mindedness) with little interaction with other modules of the system.
In coupling, modules are linked to the other modules.	In cohesion, the module focuses on a single thing.

7.5 Design Heuristics for Effective Modularity

Design heuristics for effective modularity in software engineering are guiding principles and rules of thumb that help software designers and architects create modular systems. Effective modularity enhances maintainability, reusability, and overall software quality. Here are some design heuristics to achieve effective modularity:

Single Responsibility Principle (SRP):

Heuristic: Each module or component should have a single, well-defined responsibility or reason to change.

Benefits: Promotes clear and focused modules that are easier to understand, maintain, and reuse.

Low Coupling:

Heuristic: Minimize the dependencies between modules. A module should rely on the least amount of information about other modules.

Benefits: Reduces the impact of changes in one module on other parts of the system, making the software more adaptable and less error-prone.

High Cohesion:

Heuristic: Ensure that the elements within a module are related to a single, well-defined purpose. A module should have a clear, cohesive function.

Benefits: Promotes code that is easier to understand, test, and maintain.

Abstraction and Encapsulation:

Heuristic: Hide complex details and expose only relevant and necessary information through well-defined interfaces.

Benefits: Enhances security, simplifies module interactions, and supports future changes.

Orthogonality:

Heuristic: Ensure that modules have minimal or no interaction with each other beyond their specified interfaces.

Benefits: Minimizes unintended side effects and facilitates independent development and testing.

Information Hiding:

Heuristic: Conceal the internal details of a module or class from the outside world, exposing only the necessary interfaces.

Benefits: Protects the integrity of the component, allows for easier modifications, and minimizes the impact of changes on other parts of the system.

Namespace Control:

Heuristic: Maintain strict control over naming and namespaces to prevent naming conflicts and to provide clear, organized access to modules and components.

Benefits: Enhances code organization and prevents unintended interference between modules.

Use of Dependency Injection:

Heuristic: Instead of creating dependencies within a module, inject dependencies from external sources, making it easier to change behavior or components.

Benefits: Promotes modularity, testability, and flexibility in software systems.

Design by Contract (DbC):

Heuristic: Specify and verify the expected behavior of modules through preconditions, postconditions, and invariants.

Benefits: Ensures that modules meet their contracts and behave predictably.

Clear Interfaces and API Design:

Heuristic: Design clear and intuitive interfaces for modules, classes, and components, ensuring they are easy to use and understand.

Benefits: Facilitates effective communication between developers, improves code maintainability, and enhances reusability.

Dependency Inversion Principle (DIP):
Heuristic: High-level modules should not depend on low-level modules but should depend on abstractions (e.g., interfaces or abstract classes).
Benefits: Reduces dependencies, simplifies maintenance, and supports interchangeable components.

7.6 Design Model

Definition:
Design modeling in software engineering represents the features of the software that helps engineer to develop it effectively, the architecture, the user interface, and the component level detail. Design modeling provides a variety of different views of the system like architecture plan for home or building. Different methods like data-driven, pattern-driven, or object-oriented methods are used for constructing the design model.
It is mainly classified into four categories – Data design, architectural design, interface design, and component-level design.
Data design: It represents the data objects and their interrelationship in an entity-relationship diagram. Entity-relationship consists of information required for each entity or data objects as well as it shows the relationship between these objects. It shows the structure of the data in terms of the tables. It shows three type of relationship – One to one, one to many, and many to many. In one-to-one relation, one entity is connected to another entity. In one many relations, one Entity is connected to more than one entity. un many to many relations one entity is connected to more than one entity as well as other entity also connected with first entity using more than one entity.
Architectural design: It defines the relationship between major structural elements of the software. It is about decomposing the system into interacting components. It is expressed as a block diagram defining an overview of the system structure – features of the components and how these components communicate with each other to share data. It defines the structure and properties of the component that are involved in the system and also the inter-relationship among these components.
User Interfaces design: It represents how the Software communicates with the user i.e., the behavior of the system. It refers to the product where user interact with controls or displays of the product. For example, Military, vehicles, aircraft, audio equipment, computer peripherals are the areas where user interface design is implemented. UI design becomes efficient only after performing usability testing. This is done to test what works and what does not work as expected. Only after making the repair, the product is said to have an optimized interface.
Component level design: It transforms the structural elements of the software architecture into a procedural description of software components. It is a perfect way to share a large amount of data. Components need not be concerned with how data is managed at a centralized level i.e. components need not worry about issues like backup and security of the data.

7.7 Design Implementation

Design implementation in software engineering refers to the process of turning a software design into actual code or a functional system. It's the phase where developers and programmers take the high-level design and transform it into a concrete and executable software solution. Here's an overview of design implementation in software engineering:
Code Writing: The primary activity in design implementation is writing code. Developers use programming languages and frameworks to translate the design specifications into executable software. They follow coding standards and best practices to ensure code quality and maintainability.
Programming Paradigms: The choice of programming paradigms, such as procedural, object-oriented, or functional programming, plays a crucial role in implementing the software design. The selected paradigm aligns with the design's architectural choices.
Development Environment: Developers work within an integrated development environment (IDE) or code editor that supports syntax highlighting, code completion, debugging, and version control. These tools enhance productivity and code quality.
Development Methodology: The development methodology, whether it's Agile, Waterfall, or another approach, impacts the implementation process. Agile methodologies involve iterative and incremental coding, while Waterfall follows a more sequential approach.
Version Control: Developers use version control systems like Git to manage code changes, track revisions, and collaborate with team members. Version control helps in maintaining a history of the codebase.
Testing: Developers perform unit testing to ensure that individual modules or components work as intended. Automated testing frameworks are often used to catch and fix bugs early in the development process.

Integration and Build: As individual modules are developed and tested, they are integrated into the larger system. Continuous integration (CI) and build tools are employed to automate this process and ensure that the software is always in a functional state.

Code Reviews: Code reviews involve peers or team members scrutinizing the code for quality, adherence to coding standards, and potential issues. Code reviews help improve code quality and knowledge sharing.

Documentation: Developers create and maintain documentation for the code, including inline comments, API documentation, and user manuals. This documentation is essential for understanding and maintaining the code.

Performance Optimization: Developers often need to optimize code for performance. This may involve profiling, identifying bottlenecks, and implementing efficiency improvements.

Security: Implementing security measures, such as input validation, authentication, and encryption, is essential to protect the software from vulnerabilities and attacks.

Error Handling: Robust error handling and logging mechanisms are implemented to provide meaningful error messages and facilitate debugging.

Scalability and Extensibility: Developers design the code with scalability and extensibility in mind to accommodate future requirements and growth.

Deployment and Configuration: Preparing the software for deployment includes setting up environments, configuring servers, and ensuring that the software functions correctly in different deployment scenarios.

Quality Assurance: Quality assurance teams conduct testing beyond unit testing, including integration testing, system testing, and user acceptance testing, to ensure that the software meets the specified requirements.

Exercise

Exercise 1 – MCQ

Q 1 Which design principle focuses on separating the software into smaller, reusable components to promote modularity and reusability?

a. Encapsulation b. Inheritance
c. Abstraction d. Composition

Q 2 What design principle emphasizes that software entities should be open for extension but closed for modification?

a. Single Responsibility Principle (SRP) b. Open-Closed Principle (OCP)
c. Liskov Substitution Principle (LSP) d. Interface Segregation Principle (ISP)

Exercise 2 – True/ False

Q 1 The Single Responsibility Principle (SRP) suggests that a class should have only one reason to change.

Q 2 True or False: The Liskov Substitution Principle (LSP) states that derived classes must always add new methods, not override existing ones.

Exercise 3 – Fill in the blanks

Q 1 The ___________ principle suggests that a class should have only one reason to change.

Q 2 The ___________ principle advocates that software entities should be open for extension but closed for modification.

Exercise 4 – Match case

1. Single Responsibility Principal	A. This principle states that a class should have only one reason to change, promoting high cohesion and modularity.
2. Open-Closed Principle	B. This principle encourages software entities to be open for extension but closed for modification, allowing for easy addition of new features.
3. Liskov Substitution Principle	C. Derived classes must be substitutable for their base classes without altering program correctness.
4. Interface Segregation Principle	D. This principle suggests that clients should not be forced to depend on interfaces they do not use.
5. Dependency Inversion Principle	E. High-level modules should not depend on low-level modules; both should depend on abstractions.

Exercise 5 – One word answer

Q 1 What principle suggests that a class should have only one reason to change?

Q 2 Which principle encourages software entities to be open for extension but closed for modification?

Exercise 6 – Small answer

Q 1 What is the Single Responsibility Principle (SRP)?

Q 2 What is the Liskov Substitution Principle (LSP) about?

Exercise 7 – Long answer

Q 1 What is the Single Responsibility Principle (SRP) in software engineering, and why is it important?

Q 2 Could you explain the Dependency Inversion Principle (DIP) and its role in reducing coupling in software systems?

Answers

Exercise 1 – MCQ

Ans: 1 d, 2 b

Exercise 2 – True/ False

Ans: 1 True, 2 False

Exercise 3 – Fill in the blanks

Ans: 1 Single Responsibility Principle (SRP), 2 Open-Closed Principle (OCP)

Exercise 4 – Match case

Ans: 1 a, 2 b, 3 c, 4 d

Exercise 5 – One word answer

Ans: 1 SRP (Single Responsibility Principle), 2 OCP (Open-Closed Principle)

Online Resources

Online Exam Paper:
Link: https://forms.gle/UXUTugkdBdtcrdQj8
QR Code:

Chapter 7 Videos Playlist:
Link: https://www.youtube.com/playlist?list=PLzlh_31VWEFoXz4gGbaKXut7wXzat2rEU
QR Code:

Previous Years Solved Questions

Q 1. How are coupling and software portability related? Give an example. [R.T.U. 2018]

Ans 1: Coupling and software portability are related in the context of software design and architecture. The degree of coupling in a software system can impact its portability, which refers to the ability of software to run on different platforms or environments without modification. Let's explore this relationship with an example:

Example: Database Coupling and Software Portability

Consider a software application that interacts with a database. The way the software is coupled with the database can affect its portability.

Low Coupling and High Portability:

If the software is designed with low coupling to the specific database system, it is more likely to be portable. Low coupling means that the software does not have direct dependencies on the database's internal structure or proprietary features.

For example, the software uses standard SQL for database interactions and relies on a database abstraction layer or an Object-Relational Mapping (ORM) framework that can work with multiple database systems. In this case, the software can be easily ported to different databases without significant code changes.

High Coupling and Low Portability:

If the software is tightly coupled to a specific database system, it may be less portable. High coupling implies that the software relies on database-specific features, functions, or syntax.

For instance, the software uses stored procedures, triggers, or SQL queries that are optimized for a particular database, and the code assumes the presence of these database-specific features. If you attempt to port this software to a different database, you may encounter issues as the code won't work without significant modifications.

The degree of coupling extends beyond just the database example. Coupling can also be related to the operating system, hardware dependencies, external libraries, or even proprietary APIs. In general, the more a software system is tightly coupled to specific technologies, the less portable it becomes.

Q 2. What is a "Design Walk through Is it different from a "Design Inspection "? [R.T.U.2018]

Ans 2: **Design Walkthrough** and **Design Inspection** are both software engineering practices used to review and evaluate the design of a software system to ensure quality and adherence to requirements. While they share similar goals, they are different in terms of their approach and formality.

Design Walkthrough:

A **design walkthrough** is an informal and collaborative review process where the design is presented to a group of stakeholders, including developers, architects, and sometimes users or clients. The goal of a design walkthrough is to have a structured discussion about the design, identify potential issues, and gather feedback. It is a less formal and more open process than an inspection.

Key characteristics of a design walkthrough:

Informal: Design walkthroughs are typically informal, and the focus is on discussion and feedback rather than rigid processes and checklists.

Presentation: The designer or a representative presents the design, explains the decisions made, and answers questions.

Feedback and Discussion: Participants provide feedback, ask questions, and engage in discussions about the design. It is a collaborative process.

Less Formal Documentation: The documentation used in a walkthrough may be less formal and may serve as a basis for discussion rather than a strict checklist.

Design Inspection:

A design inspection is a formal and structured review process with specific guidelines, checklists, and criteria for evaluating the design. The inspection process is often more focused on identifying defects and deviations from design standards.

Key characteristics of a design inspection:

Formal: Design inspections are more formal and structured. There are specific roles, responsibilities, and predefined checklists.

Checklists: Inspections typically use checklists or criteria to evaluate the design. These checklists can be based on design principles, standards, or best practices.

Defect Identification: The primary goal of an inspection is to identify defects or issues in the design. These defects may include violations of design standards, architectural problems, or design flaws.

Documentation Focus: Inspections place a strong emphasis on the quality of design documentation, which should be detailed, consistent, and conform to the established standards.

Q 3. What are the importance of design documentation in software engineering? [R.T.U.2018]

Ans 3: Design documentation plays a crucial role in software engineering, providing a structured and organized way to capture and communicate the design decisions, details, and rationale throughout the software development process. The importance of design documentation can be summarized as follows:

Communication: Design documents serve as a means of communication among team members, stakeholders, and future developers. They convey the design choices, architecture, and decisions in a clear and concise manner, ensuring everyone is on the same page.

Documentation of Design Rationale: Design documentation captures the reasoning behind specific design decisions. This is essential for understanding why certain choices were made and helps in future design modifications or maintenance.

Knowledge Transfer: Design documentation is valuable for knowledge transfer within a development team. New team members can quickly familiarize themselves with the system's design and architecture, reducing the learning curve.

Guidance for Implementation: Design documents serve as a roadmap for developers during the implementation phase. They provide clear guidance on how the software components and modules should be built, which contributes to consistent coding practices.

Quality Assurance: Design documentation can be used as a reference for quality assurance and code reviews. It helps in ensuring that the implementation aligns with the design and that coding standards are followed.

Maintenance and Updates: As software evolves, design documents support future maintenance and updates. They provide insights into the original design intent, making it easier to assess the impact of changes on the system.

Risk Mitigation: Having well-documented designs allows for early identification of potential design flaws or issues. This proactive approach can help mitigate risks and reduce the likelihood of costly design changes in later stages of development.

Cost and Time Savings: Design documentation reduces the chances of misunderstanding or misinterpretation of the design, thereby reducing development errors and the time and cost associated with rework.

Scalability and Extensibility: Design documents help in planning for scalability and extensibility. They provide a foundation for future system expansion and allow developers to make informed decisions regarding enhancements.

Regulatory Compliance: In industries with regulatory requirements, such as healthcare or finance, detailed design documentation may be necessary for compliance and auditing purposes.

Knowledge Preservation: Design documents serve as a historical record of the software's evolution. They help in preserving institutional knowledge, which can be invaluable when addressing legacy systems or revisiting past projects.

Collaboration and Decision-Making: Design documentation facilitates collaboration among multidisciplinary teams, including designers, developers, testers, and stakeholders. It supports informed decision-making and ensures that design changes are well-considered and documented.

Q 4. Explain Cohesion and Coupling. [R.T.U.2017]

Ans 4: In software engineering, the coupling is the degree of interdependence between software modules. Two modules that are tightly coupled are strongly dependent on each other. However, two modules that are loosely coupled are not dependent on each other. Uncoupled modules have no interdependence at all within them.

The various types of coupling techniques are shown in fig:

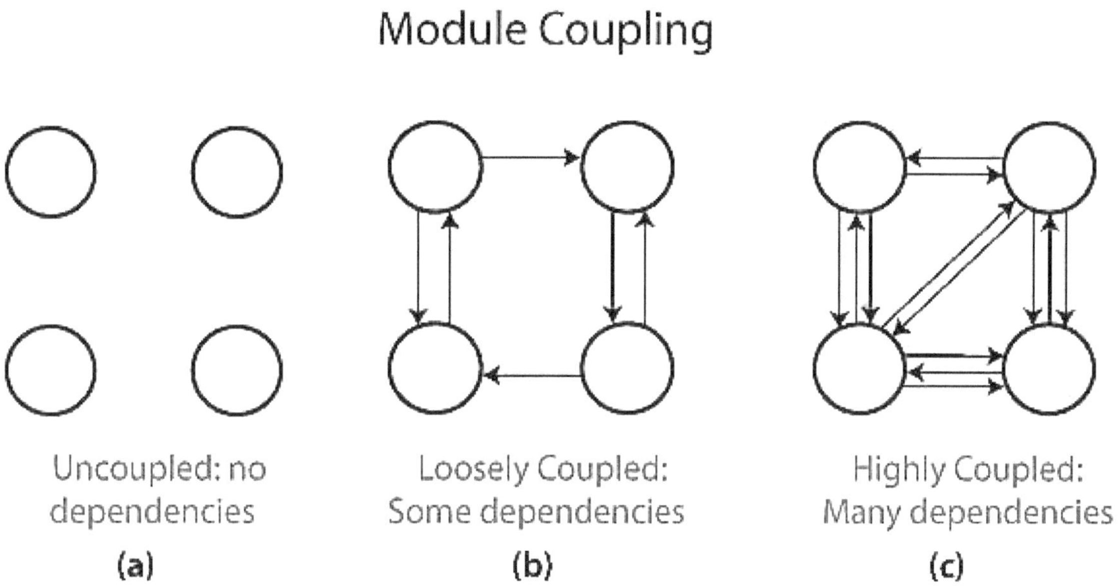

A good design is the one that has low coupling. Coupling is measured by the number of relations between the modules. That is, the coupling increases as the number of calls between modules increase or the amount of shared data is large. Thus, it can be said that a design with high coupling will have more errors.

Types of Module Coupling

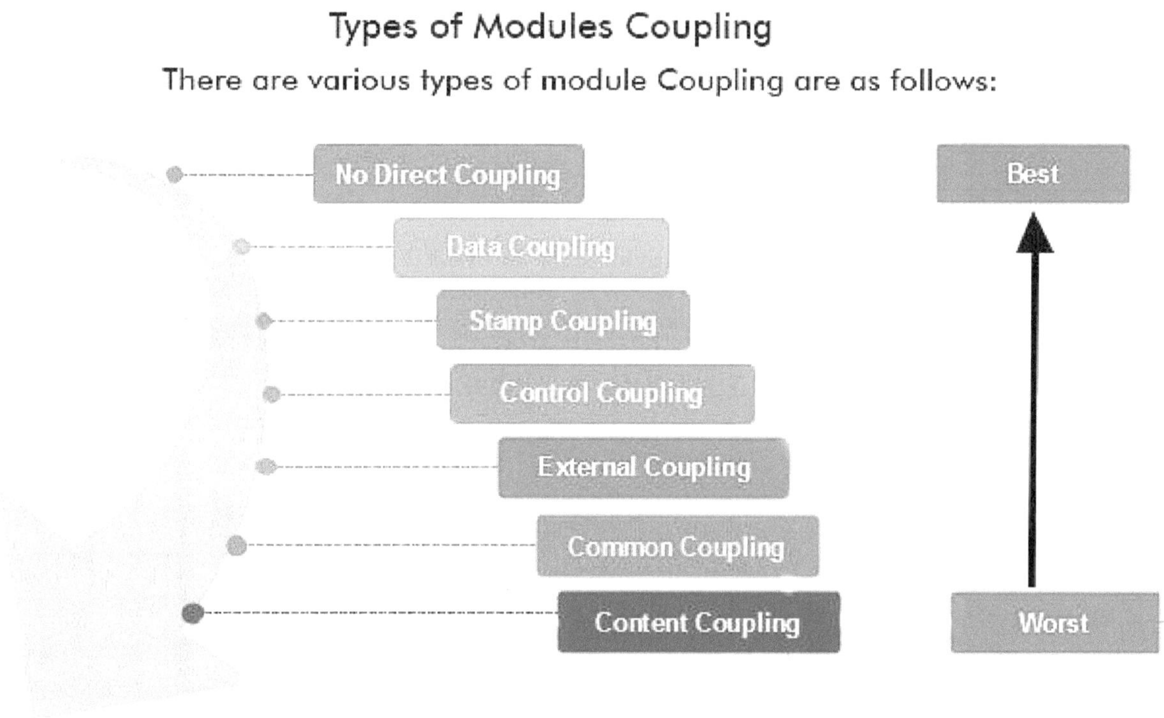

1. No Direct Coupling: There is no direct coupling between M1 and M2.

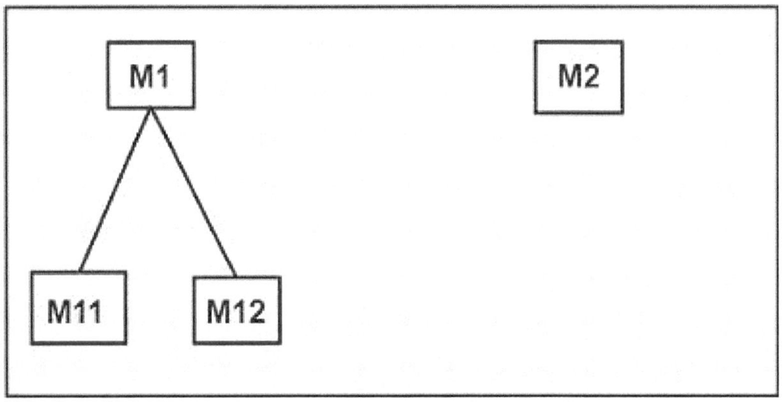

In this case, modules are subordinates to different modules. Therefore, no direct coupling.

2. Data Coupling: When data of one module is passed to another module, this is called data coupling.

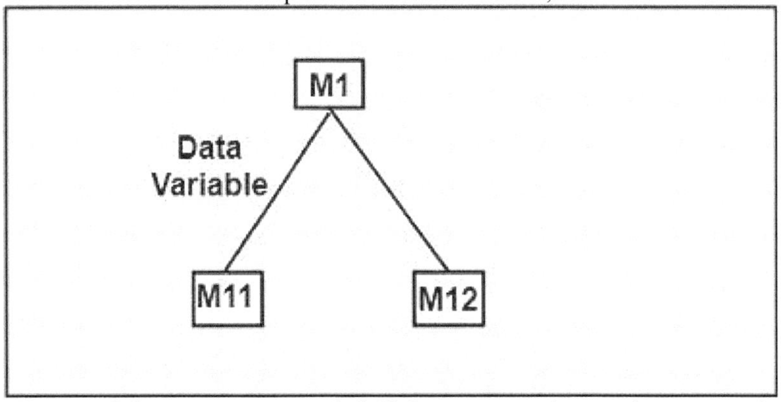

3. Stamp Coupling: Two modules are stamp coupled if they communicate using composite data items such as structure, objects, etc. When the module passes non-global data structure or entire structure to another module, they are said to be stamp coupled. For example, passing structure variable in C or object in C++ language to a module.

4. Control Coupling: Control Coupling exists among two modules if data from one module is used to direct the structure of instruction execution in another.

5. External Coupling: External Coupling arises when two modules share an externally imposed data format, communication protocols, or device interface. This is related to communication to external tools and devices.

6. Common Coupling: Two modules are common coupled if they share information through some global data items.

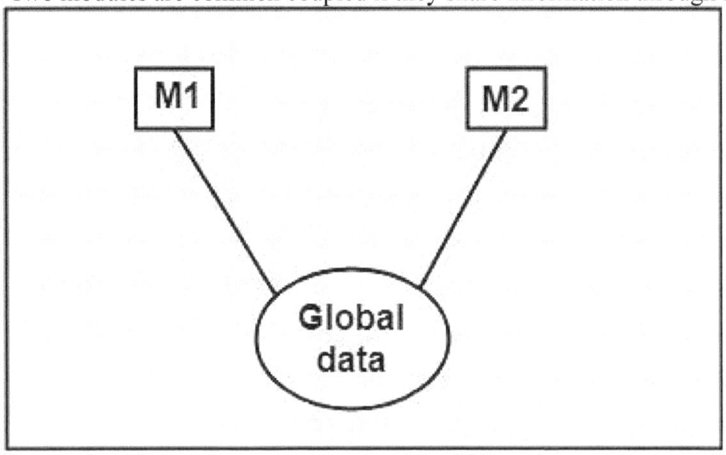

7. Content Coupling: Content Coupling exists among two modules if they share code, e.g., a branch from one module into another module.

Module Cohesion

In computer programming, cohesion defines to the degree to which the elements of a module belong together. Thus, cohesion measures the strength of relationships between pieces of functionality within a given module. For example, in highly cohesive systems, functionality is strongly related.

Cohesion is an **ordinal** type of measurement and is generally described as "high cohesion" or "low cohesion."

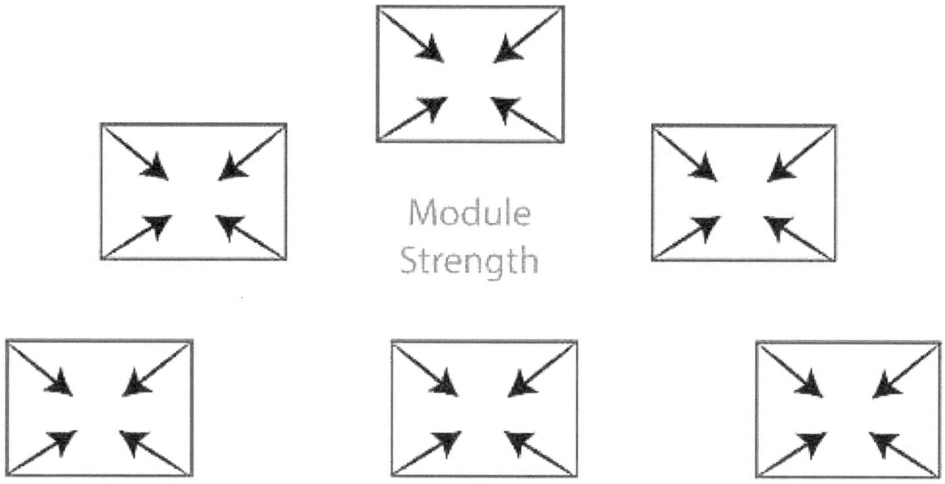

Cohesion= Strength of relations within Modules

Types of Modules Cohesion

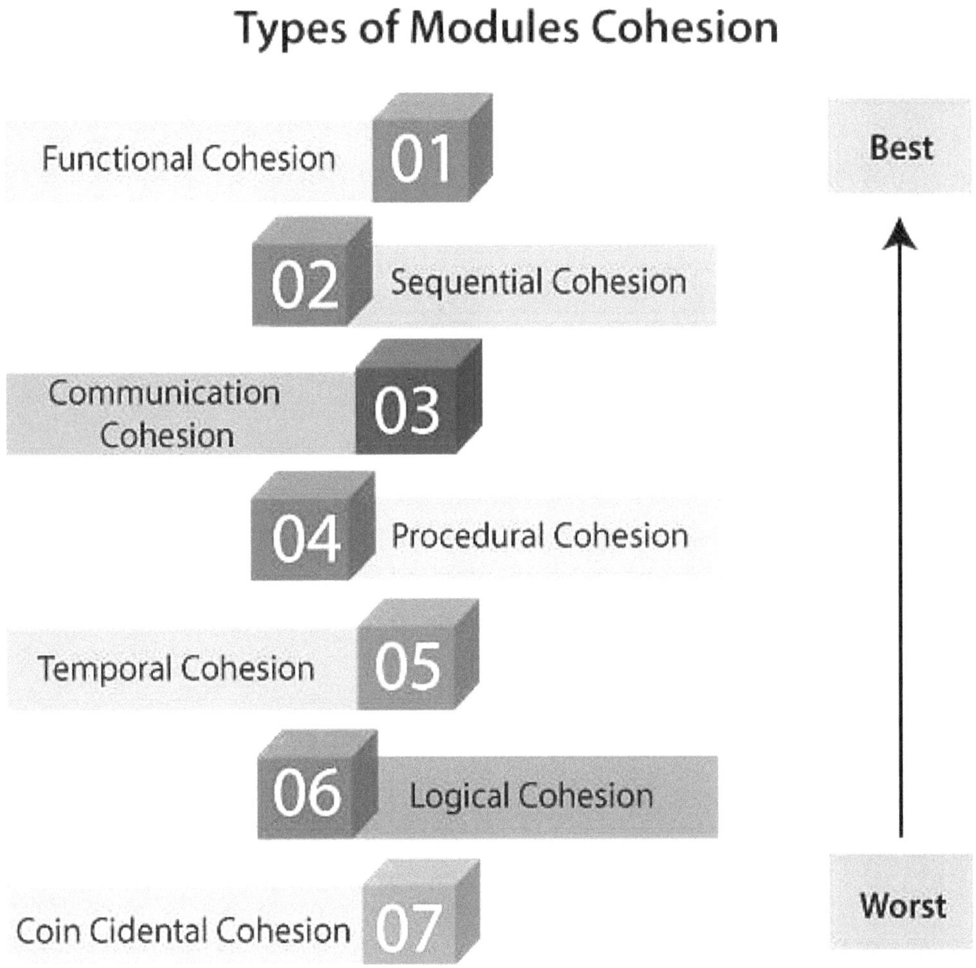

Functional Cohesion: Functional Cohesion is said to exist if the different elements of a module, cooperate to achieve a single function.
Sequential Cohesion: A module is said to possess sequential cohesion if the element of a module form the components of the sequence, where the output from one component of the sequence is input to the next.
Communicational Cohesion: A module is said to have communicational cohesion, if all tasks of the module refer to or update the same data structure, e.g., the set of functions defined on an array or a stack.
Procedural Cohesion: A module is said to be procedural cohesion if the set of purpose of the module are all parts of a procedure in which particular sequence of steps has to be carried out for achieving a goal, e.g., the algorithm for decoding a message.
Temporal Cohesion: When a module includes functions that are associated by the fact that all the methods must be executed in the same time, the module is said to exhibit temporal cohesion.
Logical Cohesion: A module is said to be logically cohesive if all the elements of the module perform a similar operation. For example Error handling, data input and data output, etc.
Coincidental Cohesion: A module is said to have coincidental cohesion if it performs a set of tasks that are associated with each other very loosely, if at all.

Q 5. Explain different types of cohesion that a module must exhibit. How is it different front coupling? [R.T.U.2018]
Ans 5: In software design and modular programming, **cohesion** and **coupling** are two key concepts that influence the structure and organization of software systems. Cohesion refers to the degree to which the elements (e.g., functions, classes, or modules) within a module are related to each other, while coupling refers to the degree of interdependence between modules or components.

Cohesion is about how closely the elements within a module work together, while coupling is about how modules interact with each other. There are different types of cohesion, each describing a different relationship between the elements within a module. The different types of cohesion, ranked from the highest (most desirable) to the lowest (least desirable), are as follows:

Functional Cohesion: In a module exhibiting functional cohesion, all elements (e.g., functions or methods) are related and work together to perform a single, well-defined function or task. This is the highest level of cohesion and is considered the most desirable.

Sequential Cohesion: In a module with sequential cohesion, elements are related and execute in a specific sequence, with the output of one element feeding into the next. While not as desirable as functional cohesion, it is still reasonably cohesive.

Communicational Cohesion: This type of cohesion occurs when elements in a module operate on the same data but perform different functions. While they share data, their functions are not directly related. It's less desirable than sequential cohesion.

Procedural Cohesion: In a module exhibiting procedural cohesion, elements perform a set of related tasks, but these tasks do not form a single, well-defined function. Elements are grouped together for convenience, and their functions may not be directly related.

Temporal Cohesion: In a module with temporal cohesion, elements are related because they are executed at the same time, such as within the same program loop. However, their functions may not be directly connected.

Logical Cohesion: In a module with logical cohesion, elements are grouped together based on some logical criteria, such as they all need to be executed in the same part of the program. However, their functions may not be directly related.

Coincidental Cohesion: Coincidental cohesion is the lowest level of cohesion and occurs when elements in a module are unrelated and grouped together purely by coincidence. This is highly undesirable.

Differentiate between Coupling and Cohesion

Coupling	**Cohesion**
Coupling is also called Inter-Module Binding.	Cohesion is also called Intra-Module Binding.
Coupling shows the relationships between modules.	Cohesion shows the relationship within the module.
Coupling shows the relative **independence** between the modules.	Cohesion shows the module's relative **functional** strength.
While creating, you should aim for low coupling, i.e., dependency among modules should be less.	While creating you should aim for high cohesion, i.e., a cohesive component/ module focuses on a single function (i.e., single-mindedness) with little interaction with other modules of the system.
In coupling, modules are linked to the other modules.	In cohesion, the module focuses on a single thing.

Q 6. Explain cohesion and coupling in modular design. [RTU 2013]

Ans 6: Cohesion and coupling are two fundamental principles in modular design in software engineering. They play a significant role in shaping the structure and organization of software systems.

Cohesion:

Cohesion refers to the degree to which the elements within a module (such as functions, classes, or components) are related to each other and work together to perform a well-defined and focused set of tasks. The goal of cohesion is to ensure that the elements within a module are tightly connected, sharing a common purpose and responsibility. Cohesion can be categorized into different types, ranging from high to low:

Functional Cohesion: In a module with functional cohesion, all elements work together to perform a single, well-defined function or task. This is the highest level of cohesion and is considered the most desirable.

Sequential Cohesion: Elements in a module with sequential cohesion are related because they execute in a specific sequence, with the output of one element feeding into the next.
Communicational Cohesion: In communicational cohesion, elements share common data, but they perform different, unrelated functions on that data.
Procedural Cohesion: Procedural cohesion occurs when elements within a module perform a set of related tasks, but these tasks do not form a single, well-defined function.
Temporal Cohesion: Elements exhibit temporal cohesion when they are grouped together because they need to be executed at the same time, such as within the same program loop.
Logical Cohesion: Logical cohesion is based on some logical criteria, like all elements need to be executed in the same part of the program. However, their functions may not be directly related.
Coincidental Cohesion: Coincidental cohesion is the lowest level of cohesion and occurs when elements in a module are unrelated and are grouped together purely by coincidence. This is highly undesirable.
Coupling:
Coupling, on the other hand, refers to the degree of interdependence and interaction between modules or components in a software system. It measures how tightly or loosely connected different parts of the system are. Low coupling is desirable because it indicates a higher level of independence and modularity.
Low Coupling: Modules are loosely connected, and changes in one module have minimal impact on others. This promotes maintainability and ease of change.
High Coupling: Modules are tightly connected, and changes in one module may necessitate changes in multiple other modules. High coupling can lead to a fragile and difficult-to-maintain system.

Q 7. Distinguish between cohesion and coupling. Explain both cohesion and coupling spectrums. [RTU 2016, 2011]
Ans 7:

Coupling	**Cohesion**
Coupling is also called Inter-Module Binding.	Cohesion is also called Intra-Module Binding.
Coupling shows the relationships between modules.	Cohesion shows the relationship within the module.
Coupling shows the relative **independence** between the modules.	Cohesion shows the module's relative **functional** strength.
While creating, you should aim for low coupling, i.e., dependency among modules should be less.	While creating you should aim for high cohesion, i.e., a cohesive component/ module focuses on a single function (i.e., single-mindedness) with little interaction with other modules of the system.
In coupling, modules are linked to the other modules.	In cohesion, the module focuses on a single thing.

In software engineering, both cohesion and coupling are important principles that influence the design and structure of software systems. They are often described using spectrums that illustrate the varying degrees of cohesion and coupling within a system:
Cohesion Spectrum:
The cohesion spectrum represents the various levels of cohesion, ranging from high cohesion to low cohesion:
High Cohesion: At one end of the spectrum is high cohesion, where the elements within a module (e.g., functions, classes, or components) are closely related, share a common purpose, and work together to perform a single, well-defined function or task. High cohesion is the most desirable and indicates that a module has a clear and focused responsibility.
Moderate Cohesion: In the middle of the spectrum, you may find modules with moderate cohesion. Elements in such modules are related and perform a set of tasks, but these tasks may not form a single, well-defined function. The module's responsibilities are broader compared to highly cohesive modules.

Low Cohesion: Towards the other end of the spectrum is low cohesion, where elements within a module are loosely related or even unrelated. In low-cohesion modules, the elements may have a wide range of responsibilities that are not logically connected. Low cohesion is generally undesirable because it can lead to a lack of clarity and maintainability.

No Cohesion: At the extreme end of the spectrum, you have modules with no cohesion. In this case, the elements within a module have no logical or functional connection. They are grouped together arbitrarily or coincidentally.

Coupling Spectrum:

The coupling spectrum represents the levels of interdependence or interaction between modules in a software system:

Low Coupling: Low coupling indicates that modules have minimal interdependence and are loosely connected. Changes in one module have little to no impact on other modules. Low coupling promotes modularity and ease of maintenance.

Moderate Coupling: In the middle of the spectrum, you find modules with moderate coupling. These modules have some interdependence but are not excessively entangled. Changes in one module may require changes in a few related modules.

High Coupling: High coupling signifies that modules are tightly connected and have a significant interdependence. Changes in one module may necessitate changes in many other modules. High coupling can lead to a fragile and difficult-to-maintain system.

Balancing Cohesion and Coupling:

The goal in software design is to achieve high cohesion within modules (each module should have a clear and focused responsibility) and low coupling between modules (minimizing interdependencies). High cohesion promotes clarity, while low coupling promotes maintainability and flexibility.

Q 8. Explain effective modular design in context of the following: Cohesion and Coupling? [RTU 2010, 2009; Raj. Univ. 2007, 2006, 2005]

Ans 9: Effective modular design in software engineering involves achieving the right balance between **cohesion** and **coupling**. Cohesion and coupling are critical concepts in modular design that determine the organization and relationships between modules (components, classes, functions, or other building blocks of a software system). Let's explore how effective modular design relates to cohesion and coupling:

Cohesion in Effective Modular Design:

High Cohesion: Effective modular design promotes high cohesion within modules. Modules should be organized so that their elements (functions, classes, or components) are closely related and work together to achieve a well-defined and focused function or task. This ensures that each module has a clear and specific purpose.

Advantages of High Cohesion:

Improved maintainability: High-cohesion modules are easier to understand, modify, and maintain because their functionality is well-defined and self-contained.

Reusability: Modules with high cohesion can often be reused in different parts of the system or in other projects because their purpose is clear.

Testability: High-cohesion modules are easier to test since their functionality is well-isolated.

Examples of High Cohesion:

A "Payment Processor" module that handles all payment-related tasks.

A "User Authentication" module responsible for user login, registration, and authentication.

Challenges to Avoid:

Modules with too many unrelated functions.

Modules with "kitchen sink" functionality, where everything is thrown together without a clear focus.

Coupling in Effective Modular Design:

Low Coupling: Effective modular design aims for low coupling between modules. Low coupling means that modules have minimal interdependence and interact with each other as independently as possible. Changes in one module should have minimal impact on other modules.

Advantages of Low Coupling:

Ease of maintenance: Low-coupling modules can be modified or replaced without affecting the entire system.

Scalability: Low coupling supports system growth as new modules can be added with minimal disruption.

Flexibility: Low-coupling modules are adaptable to changes and allow for reconfiguration without extensive adjustments.

Examples of Low Coupling:

Modules that communicate through well-defined interfaces or APIs without exposing their internal details.

Use of abstract classes or interfaces to decouple modules from concrete implementations.

Challenges to Avoid:

Modules that tightly depend on specific implementation details of other modules.
Modules that have many direct dependencies on other modules.

Q 9. What is design documentation in software engineering? Explain along with its importance in detail. [R.T.U.2017, 2004]

Ans 9: Design documentation in software engineering refers to the set of documents, diagrams, and artifacts created during the design phase of a software development project. These documents capture the architectural and detailed design of the software system, providing a blueprint for how the software will be constructed, organized, and function. Design documentation is an essential part of the software development process and plays a critical role in ensuring the success of a project.

The importance of design documentation in software engineering can be explained in detail as follows:

Communication: Design documentation serves as a means of communication among various stakeholders, including developers, architects, project managers, quality assurance teams, and clients or end-users. It conveys the design decisions, structures, and rationale, ensuring that all team members are on the same page regarding the system's design.

Design Rationale: Design documents capture the reasoning and justifications behind specific design decisions. This is critical for understanding why certain choices were made and the expected outcomes. It provides context for the design and helps in making informed decisions during development.

Knowledge Transfer: Design documentation facilitates knowledge transfer within the development team. New team members or those working on specific aspects of the project can quickly understand the system's design and architecture, reducing the learning curve and enabling them to be productive more quickly.

Guidance for Implementation: Design documents serve as a roadmap for developers during the implementation phase. They provide clear guidance on how the software components, modules, and classes should be constructed. This clarity results in code that is more consistent and aligns with the design.

Quality Assurance and Testing: Design documentation is a valuable reference for quality assurance and testing. It ensures that testing efforts are based on an understanding of the design and that the implementation aligns with the design specifications. It supports the development of test cases and validation processes.

Maintenance and Updates: As software evolves, design documentation helps in future maintenance and updates. It provides insights into the original design intent, making it easier to assess the impact of changes on the system and ensure that they are consistent with the design.

Risk Mitigation: Well-documented designs allow for early identification of potential design flaws or issues. This proactive approach helps in mitigating risks and reducing the likelihood of costly design changes in later stages of development.

Cost and Time Savings: Design documentation reduces the chances of misunderstanding or misinterpretation of the design. By providing a clear and organized structure for the development process, it reduces development errors and, in turn, the time and cost associated with rework.

Scalability and Extensibility: Design documents support planning for scalability and extensibility. They provide a foundation for future system expansion, allowing developers to make informed decisions regarding enhancements and modifications.

Regulatory Compliance: In industries with regulatory requirements (e.g., healthcare or finance), detailed design documentation may be necessary for compliance and auditing purposes.

Historical Record: Design documentation serves as a historical record of the software's evolution. It helps in preserving institutional knowledge, which can be invaluable when addressing legacy systems or revisiting past projects.

Q 10. Describe the top down and bottom-up approach in effective modular design with example. [R.T.U.2017]

Ans 10: Top-down and bottom-up are two different approaches to designing and building modular software systems. These approaches have their own advantages and are often used in combination. Let's explain each approach and provide an example for each:

Top-Down Approach:

In the top-down approach, the design process starts at a high-level view of the system and progressively drills down into lower-level details. The top-down approach typically begins with the system's overall architecture, identifying major modules or components. Each of these major modules is then further divided into sub-modules or sub-components until the design becomes detailed enough for implementation.

Example: Consider the development of a web-based e-commerce platform. In the top-down approach:

High-Level Design: Begin by designing the system's architecture, defining major modules like "User Authentication," "Product Catalog," "Shopping Cart," and "Order Processing."

Sub-Module Design: For the "User Authentication" module, further break it down into sub-modules like "User Registration," "User Login," and "User Profile Management."
Low-Level Design: Continue drilling down into specific components or classes for each sub-module. For "User Registration," you would design components for data validation, database interactions, and user notification.
The top-down approach starts with a big picture and gradually refines the design until it's suitable for implementation.
Bottom-Up Approach:
The bottom-up approach, in contrast, begins with designing and implementing lower-level components or modules first. These lower-level components are then combined to form higher-level modules and eventually the entire system.
Example: In the same e-commerce platform development project:
Low-Level Components: Start by designing and implementing specific low-level components, such as a "User Validation" component, a "Product Retrieval" component, and a "Cart Management" component.
Module Construction: Combine these low-level components to create higher-level modules like "User Management" and "Shopping."
System Assembly: Assemble the modules to build the complete e-commerce platform.
The bottom-up approach focuses on creating functional building blocks and incrementally building up to the top-level architecture.

Q 11. Explain the design documentation with example. [R.T.U. 2015, 2010]
Ans 11. Design documentation in software engineering is a comprehensive set of documents, diagrams, and artifacts created during the design phase of a software development project. These documents capture the architectural and detailed design of the software system, providing a roadmap for how the software will be constructed, organized, and function. Design documentation is essential for understanding, communicating, and guiding the development of a software system. Let's explore design documentation with an example:
Example: Design Documentation for an E-commerce Website
Consider the development of an e-commerce website, where customers can browse and purchase products online. Here is an example of design documentation elements that would be created for this project:
High-Level Architecture Diagram:
A visual representation of the system's high-level architecture, showing the major components and their interactions.
Example: A diagram that illustrates the web server, application server, database server, and their connections.
Use Case Diagrams:
Diagrams depicting various use cases, actors (e.g., customers, administrators), and their interactions with the system.
Example: A use case diagram that outlines the "Customer Registration" use case, "Product Search and Purchase," and "Order Management."
Class Diagrams:
Detailed diagrams that represent the classes, their attributes, methods, and relationships within the system.
Example: Class diagrams for "User," "Product," "Shopping Cart," and "Order" classes, including their attributes and methods.
Sequence Diagrams:
Diagrams that show the interactions and communication between objects or components for specific scenarios.
Example: A sequence diagram that illustrates the steps involved in a customer's product selection and purchase process.
Database Schema Design:
Detailed documentation of the database structure, including tables, columns, relationships, and data types.
Example: A SQL script that outlines the database schema for storing product information, user accounts, and order data.
Component Diagrams:
Diagrams showing how software components, such as libraries, APIs, or microservices, are organized and connected within the system.
Example: A component diagram depicting the integration of payment gateways, email services, and third-party analytics tools.
Interface Design:
Mockups or wireframes illustrating the graphical user interface (GUI) design, including page layouts, navigation, and user interactions.
Example: Mockups of the website's homepage, product listing page, and shopping cart interface.
Data Flow Diagrams (DFD):
Diagrams that depict how data flows through the system, including data sources, processes, and data destinations.

Example: A DFD illustrating the flow of customer order data from the website to the order processing system.

API Documentation:

Detailed documentation for any APIs or services exposed by the system for integration with external systems or mobile apps.

Example: Swagger documentation for the RESTful API used to fetch product details.

Design Guidelines and Standards:

Documentation outlining coding standards, naming conventions, architectural principles, and design patterns to be followed by the development team.

Example: A document specifying that the project will adhere to the Model-View-Controller (MVC) architectural pattern.

Q12. Explain modularity in context of software design. [RTU 2013]

Ans 12: Modularity in software design is a fundamental principle that promotes the organization of a software system into separate, self-contained, and independent modules or components. These modules are designed to perform specific, well-defined functions within the system while minimizing their interactions with other modules. Modularity is a key design concept that contributes to the development of maintainable, scalable, and flexible software systems. Here's a more detailed explanation of modularity in the context of software design:

Encapsulation of Functionality: Modularity involves encapsulating related functionality and data within discrete modules. Each module should have a clear, specific purpose or responsibility. For example, a module might handle user authentication, product catalog management, or payment processing.

Clear Interfaces: Modules typically communicate with each other through well-defined interfaces or APIs. This separation of concerns ensures that modules can interact without exposing their internal details. Clear interfaces make it easier to understand how modules interact and facilitate changes or updates to a module without affecting other parts of the system.

Information Hiding: Modularity often includes the concept of information hiding, where the internal details and implementation of a module are hidden from external modules. This helps in managing complexity and ensures that other modules only need to know how to use the module, not how it works internally.

Reusability: Modular design encourages the creation of reusable components. Modules can be designed to be self-contained and independent, making it easier to use them in different parts of the system or in other projects.

Maintainability: With well-defined modules, it becomes easier to maintain and update a software system. Changes and bug fixes can be localized to specific modules, reducing the risk of unintended side effects in other parts of the system.

Scalability: Modularity supports scalability because it allows for the addition of new modules to extend the system's functionality. New modules can be developed independently and integrated with existing ones.

Flexibility: A modular design provides flexibility in terms of replacing or upgrading individual modules. For example, you can replace a database module with a different one without affecting the rest of the system, as long as the interface remains the same.

Collaborative Development: Modular design encourages collaboration among development teams. Different teams can work on different modules concurrently, and as long as they adhere to the defined interfaces, their modules can be integrated seamlessly.

Testing and Quality Assurance: Modules can be tested independently, which simplifies the testing process. Testing can focus on each module's functionality and interactions, allowing for easier debugging and validation.

Q 13. Describe effective Modular design in detail [R.T.U. 2015, 2009, 2016, Raj. Univ. 2007, 2000]

Ans 13. module (e.g., functions, classes, or components) are closely related and work together to achieve a well-defined function or task. High cohesion ensures that a module has a clear, specific purpose, and its functionality is focused.

Low Coupling: Modules should have low coupling, which means that their interactions and dependencies with other modules are minimized. Low coupling ensures that changes in one module have minimal impact on other modules. This promotes isolation and modularity.

Clear Interfaces: Modules communicate with each other through well-defined and clear interfaces. These interfaces specify how data and functionality are exchanged between modules, abstracting the implementation details. Clear interfaces enable modules to interact seamlessly and facilitate integration.

Encapsulation: Modules encapsulate their internal details, hiding the implementation from other modules. This concept is often referred to as information hiding. Encapsulation ensures that the internal workings of a module are protected, and other modules only need to know how to use the module, not how it's implemented.

Reusability: Modular design encourages the creation of reusable components. Modules can be designed to be self-contained and independent, making it easier to reuse them in different parts of the system or in other projects. Reusability reduces redundancy and development effort.

Separation of Concerns: Modular design promotes the separation of concerns, where each module is responsible for a specific aspect of the system. This separation enhances the system's maintainability, as changes to one concern are isolated from others.

Scalability: A modular system is more scalable because new modules can be added to extend its functionality. These new modules can be developed independently and integrated into the system, allowing it to grow and adapt to changing requirements.

Testing and Quality Assurance: Modules can be tested independently, simplifying the testing process. Quality assurance efforts can focus on individual modules, ensuring that they function correctly and meet their defined interfaces.

Flexibility: Effective modular design provides flexibility for making changes and updates. A well-designed module can be replaced or upgraded without affecting other parts of the system, as long as the interface remains the same.

Documentation: Comprehensive documentation is crucial for effective modular design. Documenting each module's purpose, interface, and implementation details helps developers, maintainers, and users understand and work with the modules effectively.

Collaboration: Modular design facilitates collaborative development. Different teams or developers can work on different modules concurrently, provided they adhere to the defined interfaces. This parallel development accelerates project progress.

Maintainability: A modular design significantly enhances the maintainability of a software system. Changes and bug fixes can be localized to specific modules, reducing the risk of unintended side effects in other parts of the system.

Previous Years Unsolved Questions

Q 1. Differentiate between Cohesion and Coupling. Also explain three different types of coupling and cohesion with a suitable example for each. [IGNOU.June,2018] [Anna university 2022]
Q 2. Define "Software Quality" and "Software Reliability". Is it possible to achieve both? Justify your answer. [IGNOU, December, 2015]
Q 3. Define Cohesion and Coupling. Explain various types in each of them. [IGNOU, June, 2016, 2015, December 2012]
Q 4. Write down the several aspects of creating a good design. Explain each step. [IGNOU, December, 2012]
Q 5. List some examples for software defects? [Anna University 2017]
Q 6. Define Coupling? [Kota University 2021]
Q 7. Explain about the cardinality and modularity with the suitable examples. [Kota University 2021]
Q 8. Explain the term cohesion and coupling with appropriate examples: [RGPV June 2020]

Chapter 8: Design Concept

8.1 Introduction

Design concepts in software engineering encompass the fundamental principles and ideas that guide the process of creating software systems. These concepts play a crucial role in shaping the structure, functionality, and quality of software applications. Here's an introduction to some of the key design concepts in software engineering:

Abstraction: Abstraction involves simplifying complex systems by focusing on essential features while ignoring non-essential details. It allows developers to create models and representations of the software that emphasize what the software does, rather than how it does it. Abstraction is a critical concept that helps manage the complexity of software.

Modularity: Modularity is the practice of breaking down a software system into smaller, self-contained modules or components. Each module has a well-defined purpose and can be developed, tested, and maintained independently. Modularity enhances code reusability and maintainability.

Encapsulation: Encapsulation is the concept of bundling data (attributes) and the methods (functions) that operate on that data into a single unit known as a class. It enforces data hiding and abstraction, preventing direct access to an object's internal data. Encapsulation promotes information hiding and reduces dependencies between components.

Decomposition: Decomposition involves dividing a large, complex problem into smaller, more manageable subproblems. Each subproblem can be tackled separately, making it easier to understand and solve. Decomposition is an essential step in the software design process.

Hierarchy: Hierarchy is a way to organize software components into a structured and meaningful order. In object-oriented design, classes often form a hierarchy, with inheritance relationships. Hierarchy is important for understanding relationships between components and creating a clear, organized design.

Design Patterns: Design patterns are proven solutions to recurring design problems in software development. These patterns offer well-established templates for solving common architectural and design challenges. Using design patterns can improve software quality, maintainability, and scalability.

Reuse: The concept of reuse involves creating software components and modules that can be utilized in multiple projects. Reusable code saves time and effort in software development and maintenance. It is closely related to the principles of modularity and encapsulation.

Cohesion and Coupling: Cohesion refers to the degree to which the elements within a module or component are related to one another. High cohesion implies that the elements within a module work together toward a common goal. Coupling refers to the interdependencies between modules or components. Low coupling suggests that modules are loosely connected, making the software more flexible and maintainable.

Scalability: Designing for scalability means ensuring that the software can handle increased workloads, data volumes, and user numbers without a major redesign. Scalability is an important consideration for software systems that are expected to grow over time.

SOLID Principles: The SOLID principles are a set of five design principles that promote the development of maintainable and scalable software. They include Single Responsibility, Open/Closed, Liskov Substitution, Interface Segregation, and Dependency Inversion principles.

8.2 Design Concepts

8.2.1 Abstraction

Abstraction is a fundamental design concept in software engineering that plays a crucial role in managing the complexity of software systems. It involves simplifying complex systems by focusing on essential features while ignoring non-essential details. Abstraction provides a high-level view of a system and allows developers to create models and representations that emphasize "what" the software does rather than "how" it does it. Here's a deeper look into the abstraction design concept in software engineering:

Key Aspects of Abstraction:

Focus on Relevant Information: Abstraction helps in concentrating on the most relevant aspects of a software system while excluding unnecessary or intricate details. This is achieved by identifying and highlighting the essential components, functions, and interactions.

Hide Implementation Details: Abstraction enables the hiding of the internal workings of a system. It encapsulates the complexity within well-defined interfaces or boundaries. For example, in object-oriented programming, classes encapsulate both data (attributes) and methods (functions), exposing only what is necessary.

Modeling: Abstraction is often used for creating models of software systems. These models can be diagrams, charts, or representations that provide a simplified view of the system's structure, behavior, or data flow. Common modeling techniques include Unified Modeling Language (UML) diagrams.

Levels of Abstraction: Software systems can be abstracted at multiple levels. High-level abstraction provides an overview of system functionality, while lower-level abstractions dive into specific details of components and interactions. The choice of abstraction level depends on the context and purpose.

Generalization: Abstraction allows the creation of general concepts or entities that represent a class of specific instances. For instance, an abstract class in object-oriented programming represents a common structure shared by multiple derived classes.

Simplification: By removing unessential details and complexities, abstraction simplifies the understanding and maintenance of software systems. It aids in reducing cognitive load and improves communication among team members and stakeholders.

Benefits of Abstraction:

Complexity Management: Abstraction helps in breaking down a complex system into manageable, understandable parts. It reduces the cognitive load on developers and makes it easier to design, implement, and maintain software.

Modularity: Abstraction supports the creation of modular software, where each module represents an abstracted entity with a specific purpose. These modules can be developed, tested, and maintained independently.

Reusability: Abstraction allows for the creation of reusable components and patterns. Generalized abstractions can be applied to different parts of the software or in entirely different projects, promoting code reusability.

Scalability: Abstraction supports the scalability of software systems. When the core functionalities are well abstracted, it becomes easier to extend and adapt the system to meet evolving requirements.

8.2.2 Refinement

Refinement is an important design concept in software engineering that involves the process of elaborating and detailing a high-level design into a more concrete and implementable form. It allows designers to gradually transform abstract system specifications into a well-structured and executable design. The refinement process typically occurs in stages, with each stage adding more detail and precision to the design. Here's a closer look at the refinement design concept:

Key Aspects of Refinement:

Stepwise Elaboration: Refinement is an iterative process where a high-level design is refined step by step. Each step results in a more detailed design representation. Designers start with a broad overview and gradually add more specifics.

Top-Down Approach: Refinement often follows a top-down approach, where the initial design starts with an abstract system view. Successive refinements break down the system into smaller components, modules, and sub-modules, each with increasing detail.

Decomposition: Decomposition is a fundamental aspect of refinement. Designers break down complex components into smaller, manageable parts. This simplifies the design and allows different parts of the system to be developed in parallel.

Abstraction Levels: Refinement occurs at multiple abstraction levels. It begins with a high-level architectural design and proceeds to lower-level details, such as component interactions, data structures, and algorithms.

Data and Control Flow: During refinement, data flows and control flows are specified in more detail. This includes defining data structures, interfaces, and dependencies between components.

Prototyping: In some cases, prototyping is used as a refinement technique. Prototypes provide a tangible representation of the system's functionality, allowing designers to gather feedback and validate design decisions.

Benefits of Refinement:

Detail Clarification: Refinement helps clarify the details of a software design, making it more explicit and precise. This ensures that all aspects of the system are thoroughly considered.

Error Detection: As the design becomes more detailed, it becomes easier to identify errors, ambiguities, or inconsistencies in the design. This early error detection can save time and resources during implementation and testing.

Parallel Development: By decomposing the system into smaller parts, refinement supports parallel development. Different teams or individuals can work on various components simultaneously, speeding up the development process.

Traceability: Each refinement step should be traceable back to the higher-level design, ensuring that the detailed design aligns with the overall system requirements and architecture.

Risk Mitigation: Refinement allows designers to address and mitigate potential risks early in the design process. Risks associated with complex or critical components can be identified and managed more effectively.

Change Management: If requirements change or new information becomes available, the refinement process makes it easier to adapt the design. Modifications can be applied at the appropriate level without affecting the entire system.

Examples of Refinement:

In the context of object-oriented design, refining a class diagram involves specifying the attributes, methods, and relationships for each class in greater detail.

In database design, refining an entity-relationship diagram (ERD) involves defining data types, constraints, primary keys, foreign keys, and indexes for each entity.

In architectural design, refining a system architecture involves specifying the components, their interfaces, and communication protocols.

8.2.3 Modularity

Modularity is a fundamental design concept in software engineering that promotes the organization of a software system into separate, self-contained modules or components. These modules are designed to perform specific functions or encapsulate related data, and they interact with each other through well-defined interfaces. Modularity is crucial for managing complexity, enhancing maintainability, and facilitating collaboration in software development. Here's a more detailed look at the concept of modularity:

Key Aspects of Modularity:

Encapsulation: Each module should encapsulate a set of related functionalities and data. This means that the internal details of a module are hidden from other modules, and interactions occur through clearly defined interfaces.

High Cohesion: Modules should exhibit high cohesion, meaning that the elements within a module are closely related and work together to achieve a common purpose. This promotes a focused and organized design.

Loose Coupling: Modules should be loosely coupled, which means that they should have minimal dependencies on other modules. Loose coupling reduces the impact of changes in one module on other parts of the system.

Abstraction: Modules provide an abstraction that simplifies the understanding of the system. They offer a high-level view of the system's components and their interactions.

Reusability: Well-designed modules can be reused in different parts of the software system or even in other projects, which can significantly reduce development time and effort.

Scalability: Modularity supports system scalability. New features or components can be added by creating new modules or extending existing ones without affecting the entire system.

Isolation of Faults: If an issue arises in one module, it is easier to isolate and debug the problem without affecting the functionality of other modules.

Benefits of Modularity:

Ease of Maintenance: When modules are self-contained and have clear interfaces, maintenance and updates become more manageable. Developers can work on one module without affecting others.

Collaboration: Modularity promotes parallel development. Different teams or individuals can work on separate modules, reducing bottlenecks in the development process.

Reuse: Modules that are designed with reusability in mind can save development time and costs. Reusable components can be leveraged in multiple projects.

Simplicity: Modular systems are often easier to understand and reason about, as they break down complex systems into smaller, more comprehensible parts.

Testing: Modules can be individually tested, making it easier to verify that each component functions correctly.

Evolvability: As requirements change, adding or modifying modules is more straightforward than overhauling an entire monolithic system.

Examples of Modularity:

In object-oriented programming, classes and objects serve as modules. Each class encapsulates data and behavior into a self-contained unit.

In web development, components in modern frameworks like React or Angular are examples of modular units. Each component manages its state and functionality, and they can be combined to build complex web applications.

In software architecture, microservices are a modular architectural style where each microservice handles a specific aspect of a system's functionality, and they communicate through well-defined APIs.

8.2.4 Software Architecture

In software engineering, **architecture** refers to the high-level structural design of a software system or application. It encompasses the organization and arrangement of system components, the relationships between them, and the principles guiding their design. Software architecture serves as a blueprint for the software's construction and provides a conceptual framework for understanding its overall structure and behavior.

Key aspects of software architecture include:
Components: Identifying the major components or modules that make up the software system. These components are responsible for specific functions and often correspond to different parts of the system.
Interactions: Determining how the components interact with each other. This includes defining the communication patterns, data flow, and dependencies between components.
Abstraction: Using abstractions to simplify the system's complexity. Abstractions can help manage the details of individual components while focusing on their interactions and interfaces.
Design Patterns: Applying established design patterns and architectural styles to solve common problems. These patterns provide proven solutions to recurring design challenges.
Scalability: Ensuring that the architecture can accommodate growth and evolving requirements. A well-designed architecture allows for the addition of new features and components without extensive rework.
Performance: Addressing performance considerations by optimizing resource usage, data storage, and processing efficiency within the architecture.
Security: Incorporating security measures to protect the software system from potential threats and vulnerabilities.
Maintainability: Designing the architecture with maintainability in mind, making it easy to modify, update, and extend the system as needed.
Software architecture is often represented through various architectural views or diagrams, such as:
High-Level Overview: Provides an overall view of the system's major components and their relationships.
Component Diagrams: Focus on the structure and organization of system components.
Deployment Diagrams: Describe the physical deployment of software components across hardware resources.
Sequence Diagrams: Illustrate the interactions and communication sequences between components or objects over time.
Class Diagrams: Depict the static structure of the system by showing classes, their attributes, and relationships.
Architectural patterns and styles play a significant role in software architecture. Examples include:
Client-Server: Separating the presentation and user interface (client) from the data and application logic (server).
Layered Architecture: Dividing the system into layers, such as presentation, business logic, and data access layers.
Microservices: Decomposing the application into small, independent services that communicate through APIs.
Event-Driven Architecture: Building systems that react to events or messages, often used in real-time or reactive systems.
Software architecture is a critical phase in the software development process, as it lays the foundation for the entire project. A well-designed architecture can lead to a more maintainable, scalable, and robust software system. It guides the development team's efforts and facilitates communication between team members and stakeholders.

8.2.5 Control Hierarchy

In software engineering, the control hierarchy is a design concept that focuses on organizing and structuring the control flow or the sequence of operations in a software system. This concept plays a critical role in designing the control structure of a program or system, making it easier to understand, manage, and maintain. Here's a closer look at control hierarchy:
Key Aspects of Control Hierarchy:
Hierarchical Structure: The control hierarchy typically follows a hierarchical or tree-like structure, where higher-level elements control the flow and execution of lower-level elements. This hierarchy can have several levels, with the main control unit at the top and more detailed sub-controls below.
Top-Down Design: Control hierarchy often follows a top-down design approach, where you start with the highest-level control or main function and progressively decompose it into smaller, more manageable sub-functions. This decomposition continues until you reach the lowest level, which consists of elementary operations.
Dividing Complex Problems: Control hierarchy is useful for breaking down complex problems into smaller, more manageable tasks or functions. This simplifies the design process by isolating specific concerns at different levels of the hierarchy.
Abstraction: Higher-level controls provide an abstraction of the system's functionality, while lower-level controls handle the implementation details. This separation of concerns enhances the system's comprehensibility and maintainability.
Benefits of Control Hierarchy:
Modularity: Control hierarchy promotes modularity by dividing a system into smaller, independent units. Each unit or module is responsible for a specific aspect of the system's behavior.
Readability: A well-defined control hierarchy enhances the readability of the software. It's easier for developers to understand the system's flow when it's structured hierarchically.

Scalability: As the system evolves or grows, the hierarchical structure allows for the addition or modification of control elements at various levels without disrupting the entire system.
Debugging and Testing: Control hierarchy facilitates debugging and testing because issues can be isolated to specific parts of the hierarchy. This simplifies the identification and resolution of problems.
Maintenance: When changes or updates are needed, it's easier to identify the relevant control elements and make modifications without affecting the entire system.
Examples of Control Hierarchy:
In a software application, the main function at the highest level of control coordinates the overall program flow. It calls various sub-functions to handle specific tasks.
In a web application, the control hierarchy can be represented by the routing system, where the main router directs incoming requests to the appropriate controllers and actions.
In a microservices architecture, each microservice can have its own control hierarchy, managing its internal operations independently.
The control hierarchy is an essential design concept that contributes to the overall structure, readability, and maintainability of a software system. When software engineers establish a clear and well-organized control hierarchy, they create systems that are easier to develop, understand, and adapt to changing requirements.

8.2.6 Structural Partitioning

Structural partitioning is a design concept in software engineering that involves breaking down a complex software system into manageable parts or modules. These modules are organized based on their functions, responsibilities, or related features, and this partitioning helps in simplifying the overall system design, making it easier to understand, develop, and maintain. Here are some key aspects of structural partitioning:
Modularity: The core principle of structural partitioning is modularity. Modularity means that the software system is divided into modules, where each module is a self-contained unit with a well-defined purpose and a clear interface for interaction with other modules.
Abstraction: Structural partitioning relies on abstraction, where each module abstracts away the internal complexities of its implementation, exposing only the necessary details through a well-defined interface or API. This simplifies how other modules interact with it.
Encapsulation: Encapsulation is another important concept that ensures that the internal details and data of a module are hidden from other modules. It enforces data hiding and encapsulates the module's functionality.
Information Hiding: Modules should provide information hiding, allowing them to reveal only what is necessary for other modules to interact with them. This concept promotes a clear separation of concerns.
Functional Cohesion: Modules should exhibit functional cohesion, meaning that the functions or methods within a module are related and serve a common purpose. This promotes clarity and maintainability.
Low Coupling: Structural partitioning aims to achieve low coupling between modules. Low coupling means that modules have minimal dependencies on each other, making it easier to change or replace one module without affecting others.
High Cohesion: Modules should have high cohesion, which means that each module should focus on performing a specific set of related tasks without unnecessary or unrelated functions.
Ease of Maintenance: The modularity achieved through structural partitioning makes it easier to maintain and enhance the software system. Changes and updates can be isolated to specific modules, reducing the risk of unintended consequences.
Parallel Development: Structural partitioning enables parallel development, allowing different teams or individuals to work on different modules simultaneously, speeding up the development process.
Reuse: Modular design encourages the reuse of modules in other parts of the software or in other projects, promoting efficiency and consistency.
Structural partitioning can be applied at various levels of the software design process. It can be used to partition a large system into subsystems, which are further partitioned into modules. Each module may consist of classes or functions that implement specific features or functions.

8.3 Major Outlines of Design Specifications

Design specifications in software engineering outline the technical details and requirements for building a software system or component. These specifications are crucial for guiding the development process and ensuring that the final product meets the desired functionality and quality standards. Here are the major outlines of design specifications:
Introduction:

Brief overview: Start with an introduction that provides a high-level description of the software system or component being designed. This should include its purpose and context within the larger project.

System Architecture:

High-level architecture: Describe the overall structure of the software system, including its major components and their interactions.

Data flow: Explain how data will be processed, stored, and transferred within the system.

Communication protocols: Specify the communication mechanisms and protocols used for interaction with other systems or components.

Functional Requirements:

Use cases or scenarios: Detail the specific functionalities and features the software must support. Use cases or scenarios illustrate how the software will be used in practice.

Functional dependencies: Describe any dependencies between different functions or features.

Non-Functional Requirements:

Performance: Specify performance criteria, such as response times, throughput, and resource utilization.

Reliability: Define reliability and availability requirements, including error handling and fault tolerance.

Security: Outline security measures and access controls to protect the software and its data.

Scalability: Describe how the system can scale to handle increased loads or users.

Usability: Detail user interface requirements and usability guidelines.

Compatibility: Specify compatibility with hardware, software, and operating systems.

Compliance: Identify any regulatory or industry-specific compliance requirements.

Data Design:

Data models: Describe the structure of data used by the software, including entities, attributes, and relationships.

Data storage: Specify how data will be stored, retrieved, and managed, including databases and file systems.

Data validation: Outline data validation rules and constraints.

Software Components:

Modules and classes: List and describe the software modules or classes that make up the system.

Interfaces: Define the interfaces (APIs) between different components, including input and output formats.

Third-party components: Identify any third-party libraries or components used in the system.

Design Patterns and Techniques:

Describe any design patterns, architectural styles, or development methodologies that should be followed.

Testing and Quality Assurance:

Testing requirements: Specify the testing strategies, including unit testing, integration testing, and acceptance testing.

Quality assurance measures: Detail quality control processes, coding standards, and code review guidelines.

Performance and Optimization:

Performance considerations: Highlight performance bottlenecks and optimization strategies.

Resource utilization: Specify memory and processing resource requirements.

Error Handling and Recovery:

Error codes and messages: Define error codes and messages for different scenarios.

Recovery procedures: Explain how the software should handle errors and exceptions.

Documentation:

Documentation requirements: Specify the types of documentation needed, such as user manuals, developer guides, and API documentation.

Dependencies:

List any external dependencies, such as libraries, frameworks, or APIs.

Constraints:

Identify constraints, such as budgetary constraints, time constraints, or hardware limitations.

Exercise

Exercise 1 – MCQ

Q 1. Which design concept focuses on breaking a software system into smaller, manageable components?

A. Abstraction B. Encapsulation

C. Modularity D. Inheritance

Q 2. Which design concept represents the ability of an object to take on multiple forms and behaviors?

A. Polymorphism B. Inheritance

C. Encapsulation D. Abstraction

Exercise 2 – True/ False

Q 1. The primary goal of software design is to write detailed code.

Q 2. Modularity in software design involves breaking a software system into smaller, manageable components.

Exercise 3 – Fill in the blanks

Q 1. ___ is the process of representing essential features without including the background details.

Q 2. ________is the principle that every piece of knowledge or logic should exist in a single, unambiguous location within the system.

Exercise 4 – Match case

1. Abstraction A. Dividing a system into self-contained components or modules for easier development and maintenance.
2. Modularity B. Simplifying complex systems by focusing on essential features and suppressing irrelevant details.
3. Inheritance C. Allowing one class to inherit properties and behaviors from another class.
4. Encapsulation D. Bundling data and methods into objects, hiding internal details, and exposing relevant functionality.

Exercise 5 – One word answer

Q 1. What is the term for bundling data and methods that operate on that data into a single unit?

Q 2. What is the concept of dividing a system into smaller, manageable components or modules?

Exercise 6 – Small answer

Q 1. What is the primary purpose of abstraction in software design?

Q 2. What is the term for bundling data and methods that operate on that data into a single unit?

Exercise 7 – Long answer

Q 1. What are the key principles of object-oriented design, and how do they contribute to effective software design?

Q 2. Discuss the significance of modularity in software engineering. How does modularity contribute to efficient software design and development?

Answers

Exercise 1 – MCQ

Ans: 1 C, 2 A

Exercise 2 – True/ False

Ans: 1 False, 2 True

Exercise 3 – Fill in the blanks

Ans: Abstraction, 2 DRY (Don't Repeat Yourself)

Exercise 4 – Match case

Ans: 1 B, 2 A, 3 C, 4 D

Exercise 5 – One word answer

Ans: 1 Encapsulation, 2 Modularity

Online Resources

Online Exam Paper:

Link: https://forms.gle/ALL2MAsCpKxPeaoDA

QR Code:

Chapter 8 Videos Playlist:
Link: https://www.youtube.com/playlist?list=PLzlh_31VWEFriJeCZcFzN9UH8yi15QlPt
QR Code:

Previous Years Unsolved Questions

Q 1. What are the Software Design Concepts? Describe software design principles. [MCU 2019]
Q 2. Top Down and Bottom-Up approaches of Software Design. [MCU 2019]
Q 3. Explain the role of system analyst to design a software. [RGPV June 2020]

Chapter 9: Software Project Management (SPM)

9.1 Introduction Software Project Management (SPM)

Software Project Management (SPM) is a proper way of planning and leading software projects. It is a part of project management in which software projects are planned, implemented, monitored, and controlled.

What is Need for Software Project Management?

Software is a non-physical product. Software development is a new stream in business and there is very little experience in building software products. Most of the software products are made to fit clients' requirements. The most important is that basic technology changes and advances so frequently and rapidly that the experience of one product may not be applied to the other one. Such types of business and environmental constraints increase risk in software development hence it is essential to manage software projects efficiently. It is necessary for an organization to deliver quality products, keep the cost within the client's budget constraint, and deliver the project as per schedule. Hence in order, software project management is necessary to incorporate user requirements along with budget and time constraints.

Different Types of Management in SPM

Conflict Management: Conflict management is the process to restrict the negative features of conflict while increasing the positive features of conflict. The goal of conflict management is to improve learning and group results including efficacy or performance in an organizational setting. Properly managed conflict can enhance group results.

Risk Management: Risk management is the analysis and identification of risks that is followed by synchronized and economical implementation of resources to minimize, operate and control the possibility or effect of unfortunate events or to maximize the realization of opportunities.

Requirement Management: It is the process of analyzing, prioritizing, tracking, and documenting requirements and then supervising change and communicating to pertinent stakeholders. It is a continuous process during a project.

Change Management: Change management is a systematic approach to dealing with the transition or transformation of an organization's goals, processes, or technologies. The purpose of change management is to execute strategies for effecting change, controlling change, and helping people to adapt to change.

Software Configuration Management: Software configuration management is the process of controlling and tracking changes in the software, part of the larger cross-disciplinary field of configuration management. Software configuration management includes revision control and the inauguration of baselines.

Release Management: Release Management is the task of planning, controlling, and scheduling the build-in deploying releases. Release management ensures that the organization delivers new and enhanced services required by the customer while protecting the integrity of existing services.

Aspects of Software Project Management

The list of focus areas it can tackle and the broad upsides of Software Project Management is:

Planning: The software project manager lays out the complete project's blueprint. The project plan will outline the scope, resources, timelines, techniques, strategy, communication, testing, and maintenance steps. SPM can aid greatly here.

Leading: A software project manager brings together and leads a team of engineers, strategists, programmers, designers, and data scientists. Leading a team necessitates exceptional communication, interpersonal, and leadership abilities. One can only hope to do this effectively if one sticks with the core SPM principles.

Execution: SPM comes to the rescue here also as the person in charge of software projects (if well versed with SPM/Agile methodologies) will ensure that each stage of the project is completed successfully. measuring progress, monitoring to check how teams' function, and generating status reports are all part of this process.

Time management: Abiding by a timeline is crucial to completing deliverables successfully. This is especially difficult when managing software projects because changes to the original project charter are unavoidable over time.

Budget: Software project managers, like conventional project managers, are responsible for generating a project budget and adhering to it as closely as feasible, regulating spending, and reassigning funds as needed. SPM teaches us how to effectively manage the monetary aspect of projects to avoid running into a financial crunch later on in the project.

Maintenance: Software project management emphasizes continuous product testing to find and repair defects early, tailor the end product to the needs of the client, and keep the project on track. The software project manager makes ensuring that the product is thoroughly tested, analyzed, and adjusted as needed. Another point in favor of SPM.

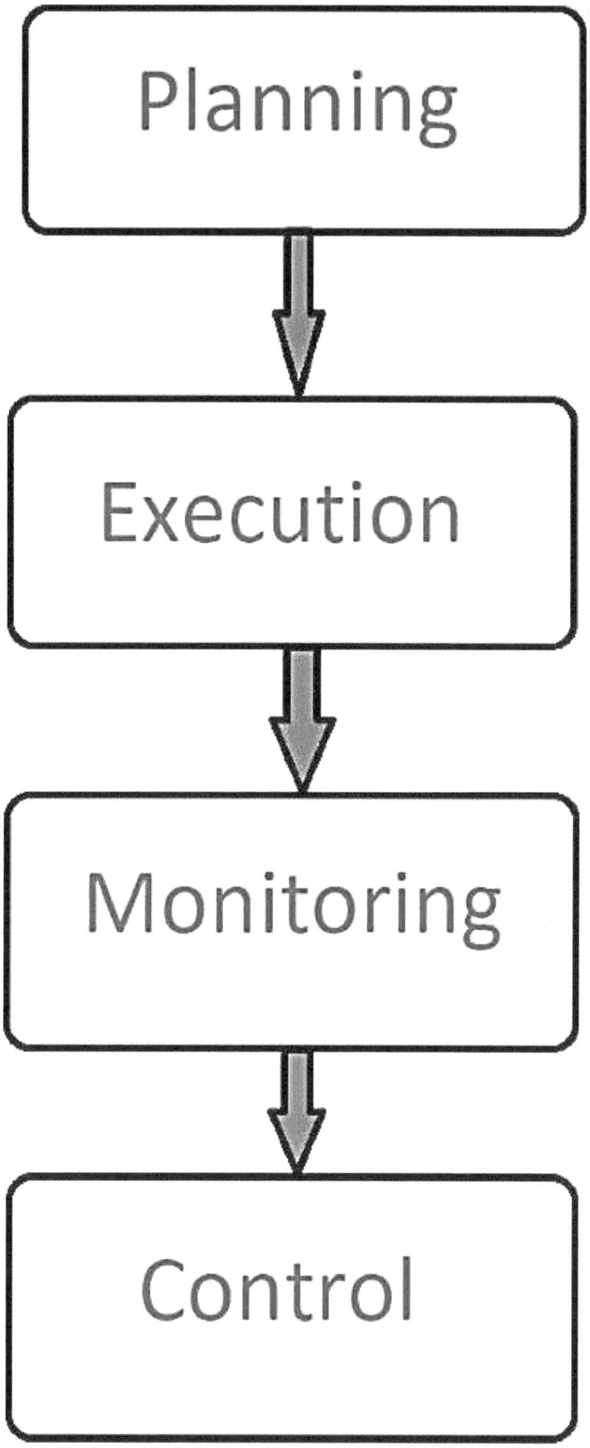

Aspects of Project Management

Downsides of Software Project Management

Numerous issues can develop if a Software project manager lacks the necessary expertise or knowledge. Software Project management has several drawbacks, including resource loss, scheduling difficulty, data protection concerns, and interpersonal conflicts between Developers/Engineers/Stakeholders. Furthermore, outsourcing work or recruiting additional personnel to complete the project may result in hefty costs for one's company.

Costs are high: Consider spending money on various kinds of project management tools, software, & services if ones engage in Software Project Management strategies. These initiatives can be expensive and time-consuming to put in place. Because your team will be using them as well, they may require training. One may need to recruit subject matter experts or specialists to assist with a project, depending on the circumstances. Stakeholders will frequently press for the inclusion of features that were not originally envisioned. All of these factors can quickly drive up a project's cost.
Complexity will be increased: Software Project management is a multi-stage, complex process. Unfortunately, some specialists might have a propensity to overcomplicate everything, which can lead to confusion among teams and lead to delays in project completion. Their expressions are very strong and specific in their ideas, resulting in a difficult work atmosphere. Projects having a larger scope are typically more arduous to complete, especially if there isn't a dedicated team committed completely to the project. Members of cross-functional teams may lag far behind their daily tasks, adding to the overall complexity of the project being worked on.
Overhead in Communication: Recruits enter your organization when we hire software project management personnel. This provides a steady flow of communication that may or may not match a company's culture. As a result, it is advised that you maintain your crew as small as feasible. The communication overhead tends to skyrocket when a team becomes large enough. When a large team is needed for a project, it's critical to identify software project managers who can conduct effective communication with a variety of people.
Lack of originality: Software Project managers can sometimes provide little or no space for creativity. Team leaders either place an excessive amount of emphasis on management processes or impose hard deadlines on their employees, requiring them to develop and operate code within stringent guidelines. This can stifle innovative thought and innovation that could be beneficial to the project. When it comes to Software project management, knowing when to encourage creativity and when to stick to the project plan is crucial. Without Software project management personnel, an organization can perhaps build and ship code more quickly. However, employing a trained specialist to handle these areas, on the other hand, can open up new doors and help the organization achieve its objectives more quickly and more thoroughly.

9.2 Project Management Process

Project Management is a discipline about planning, monitoring, and controlling software projects, identifying the scope, estimating the work involved, and creating a project schedule. Along with it is also responsible to keep the team up to date on the project's progress and handle problems and discuss solutions.
The Project Management Process consists of the following 4 stages:
Feasibility study
Project Planning
Project Execution
Project Termination

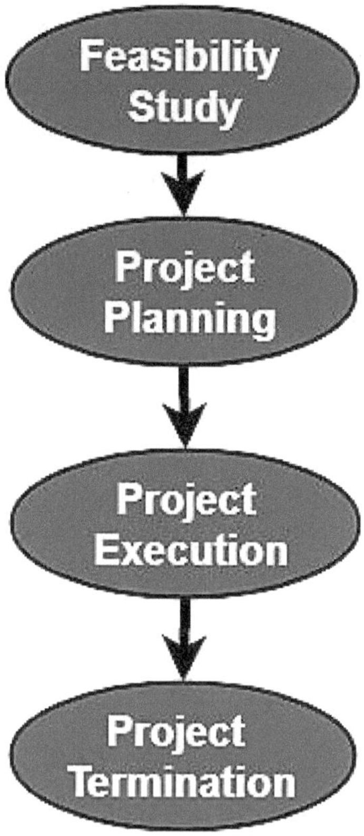

Feasibility Study: A feasibility study explores system requirements to determine project feasibility. There are several fields of feasibility study including economic feasibility, operational feasibility, and technical feasibility. The goal is to determine whether the system can be implemented or not. The process of feasibility study takes as input the required details as specified by the user and other domain-specific details. The output of this process simply tells whether the project should be undertaken or not and if yes, what would the constraints be. Additionally, all the risks and their potential effects on the projects are also evaluated before a decision to start the project is taken.

Project Planning: A detailed plan stating a stepwise strategy to achieve the listed objectives is an integral part of any project. Planning consists of the following activities:

Set objectives or goals
Develop strategies
Develop project policies
Determine courses of action
Making planning decisions
Set procedures and rules for the project
Develop a software project plan
Prepare budget
Conduct risk management
Document software project plans

This step also involves the construction of a work breakdown structure(WBS). It also includes size, effort, schedule, and cost estimation using various techniques.

Principles of effective project planning:

Project should be effective so that the project begins with well-defined tasks. Effective project planning helps to minimize the additional costs incurred on the project while it is in progress.

Planning is necessary: Planning should be done before a project begins.

Risk analysis: Before starting the project, senior management and the project management team should consider the risks that may affect the project.

Tracking of project plan: Once the project plan is prepared, it should be tracked and modified accordingly.

Most quality standards and produce quality deliverables: The project plan should identify processes by which the project management team can ensure quality in software.

Description of flexibility to accommodate changes: The result of project planning is recorded in the form of a project plan, which should allow new changes to be accommodated when the project is in progress

Project Execution: A project is executed by choosing an appropriate software development lifecycle model(SDLC). It includes a number of steps including requirements analysis, design, coding, testing and implementation, testing, delivery, and maintenance. There are a number of factors that need to be considered while doing so including the size of the system, the nature of the project, time and budget constraints, domain requirements, etc. An inappropriate SDLC can lead to the failure of the project.

Project Termination: There can be several reasons for the termination of a project. Though expecting a project to terminate after successful completion is conventional, at times, a project may also terminate without completion. Projects have to be closed down when the requirements are not fulfilled according to given time and cost constraints. Some of the reasons for failure include:

Fast-changing technology

Project running out of time

Organizational politics

Too much change in customer requirements

Project exceeding budget or funds

Once the project is terminated, a post-performance analysis is done. Also, a final report is published describing the experiences, lessons learned, and recommendations for handling future projects.

Project management is a systematic approach to planning, organizing, and controlling the resources required to achieve specific project goals and objectives. The project management process involves a set of activities that are performed to plan, execute, and close a project. The project management process can be divided into several phases, each of which has a specific purpose and set of tasks.

The main phases of the project management process are:

Initiation: This phase involves defining the project, identifying the stakeholders, and establishing the project's goals and objectives.

Planning: In this phase, the project manager defines the scope of the project, develops a detailed project plan, and identifies the resources required to complete the project.

Execution: This phase involves the actual implementation of the project, including the allocation of resources, the execution of tasks, and the monitoring and control of project progress.

Monitoring and Control: This phase involves tracking the project's progress, comparing actual results to the project plan, and making changes to the project as necessary.

Closing: This phase involves completing the project, documenting the results, and closing out any open issues.

Effective project management requires a clear understanding of the project management process and the skills necessary to apply it effectively. The project manager must have the ability to plan and execute projects, manage resources, communicate effectively, and handle risks and issues.

Advantages of the project management process:

Provides a structured approach to managing projects.

Helps to define project objectives and requirements.

Facilitates effective communication and collaboration among team members.

Helps to manage project risks and issues.

Ensures that the project is delivered on time and within budget.

Disadvantages of the project management process:

Can be time-consuming and bureaucratic

May be inflexible and less adaptable to changes

Requires a skilled project manager to implement effectively

May not be suitable for small or simple projects.

Responsibilities of software project manager:

-Proper project management is essential for the successful completion of a software project and the person who is responsible for it is called project manager.

-To do his job effectively, the project manager must have certain set of skills. This section discusses both the job responsibilities of project manager and the skills required by him.

Job Responsibilities :

-Involves with the senior managers in the process of appointing team members.

-Builds the project team and assigns tasks to various team members.

-Responsible for effective project planning and scheduling, project monitoring and control activities in order to achieve the project objectives.

-Acts as a communicator between the senior management and the other persons involved in the project like the development team and internal and external stakeholders.
-Effectively resolves issues that arise between the team members by changing their roles and responsibilities.
-Modifies the project plan(if required)to deal with the situation.

9.3 Project size estimation techniques

Project size estimation is a crucial aspect of software engineering, as it helps in planning and allocating resources for the project. Here are some of the popular project size estimation techniques used in software engineering:

Expert Judgment: In this technique, a group of experts in the relevant field estimates the project size based on their experience and expertise. This technique is often used when there is limited information available about the project.

Analogous Estimation: This technique involves estimating the project size based on the similarities between the current project and previously completed projects. This technique is useful when historical data is available for similar projects.

Bottom-up Estimation: In this technique, the project is divided into smaller modules or tasks, and each task is estimated separately. The estimates are then aggregated to arrive at the overall project estimate.

Three-point Estimation: This technique involves estimating the project size using three values: optimistic, pessimistic, and most likely. These values are then used to calculate the expected project size using a formula such as the PERT formula.

Function Points: This technique involves estimating the project size based on the functionality provided by the software. Function points consider factors such as inputs, outputs, inquiries, and files to arrive at the project size estimate.

Use Case Points: This technique involves estimating the project size based on the number of use cases that the software must support. Use case points consider factors such as the complexity of each use case, the number of actors involved, and the number of use cases.

Each of these techniques has its strengths and weaknesses, and the choice of technique depends on various factors such as the project's complexity, available data, and the expertise of the team.

Estimation of the size of the software is an essential part of Software Project Management. It helps the project manager to further predict the effort and time which will be needed to build the project. Various measures are used in project size estimation. Some of these are:

Lines of Code
Number of entities in ER diagram
Total number of processes in detailed data flow diagram
Function points

1. Lines of Code (LOC): As the name suggests, LOC counts the total number of lines of source code in a project. The units of LOC are:

KLOC- Thousand lines of code
NLOC- Non-comment lines of code
KDSI- Thousands of delivered source instruction

The size is estimated by comparing it with the existing systems of the same kind. The experts use it to predict the required size of various components of software and then add them to get the total size.

It's tough to estimate LOC by analyzing the problem definition. Only after the whole code has been developed can accurate LOC be estimated. This statistic is of little utility to project managers because project planning must be completed before development activity can begin.

Two separate source files having a similar number of lines may not require the same effort. A file with complicated logic would take longer to create than one with simple logic. Proper estimation may not be attainable based on LOC.

The length of time it takes to solve an issue is measured in LOC. This statistic will differ greatly from one programmer to the next. A seasoned programmer can write the same logic in fewer lines than a newbie coder.

Advantages:

Universally accepted and is used in many models like COCOMO.
Estimation is closer to the developer's perspective.
Both people throughout the world utilize and accept it.
At project completion, LOC is easily quantified.
It has a specific connection to the result.
Simple to use.

Disadvantages:

Different programming languages contain a different number of lines.

No proper industry standard exists for this technique.
It is difficult to estimate the size using this technique in the early stages of the project.
When platforms and languages are different, LOC cannot be used to normalize.

2. Number of entities in ER diagram: ER model provides a static view of the project. It describes the entities and their relationships. The number of entities in ER model can be used to measure the estimation of the size of the project. The number of entities depends on the size of the project. This is because more entities needed more classes/structures thus leading to more coding.

Advantages:

Size estimation can be done during the initial stages of planning.
The number of entities is independent of the programming technologies used.

Disadvantages:

No fixed standards exist. Some entities contribute more to project size than others.
Just like FPA, it is less used in the cost estimation model. Hence, it must be converted to LOC.

3. Total number of processes in detailed data flow diagram: Data Flow Diagram(DFD) represents the functional view of software. The model depicts the main processes/functions involved in software and the flow of data between them. Utilization of the number of functions in DFD to predict software size. Already existing processes of similar type are studied and used to estimate the size of the process. Sum of the estimated size of each process gives the final estimated size.

Advantages:

It is independent of the programming language.
Each major process can be decomposed into smaller processes. This will increase the accuracy of the estimation

Disadvantages:

Studying similar kinds of processes to estimate size takes additional time and effort.
All software projects are not required for the construction of DFD.

4. Function Point Analysis: In this method, the number and type of functions supported by the software are utilized to find FPC(function point count). The steps in function point analysis are:

Count the number of functions of each proposed type.
Compute the Unadjusted Function Points(UFP).
Find the Total Degree of Influence(TDI).
Compute Value Adjustment Factor(VAF).
Find the Function Point Count(FPC).

The explanation of the above points is given below:

Count the number of functions of each proposed type: Find the number of functions belonging to the following types:

External Inputs: Functions related to data entering the system.
External outputs: Functions related to data exiting the system.
External Inquiries: They lead to data retrieval from the system but don't change the system.
Internal Files: Logical files maintained within the system. Log files are not included here.
External interface Files: These are logical files for other applications which are used by our system.

Compute the Unadjusted Function Points(UFP): Categorise each of the five function types like simple, average, or complex based on their complexity. Multiply the count of each function type with its weighting factor and find the weighted sum. The weighting factors for each type based on their complexity are as follows:

Function type	Simple	Average	Complex
External Inputs	3	4	6
External Output	4	5	7
External Inquiries	3	4	6
Internal Logical Files	7	10	15

External Interface Files	5	7	10

Find Total Degree of Influence: Use the '14 general characteristics' of a system to find the degree of influence of each of them. The sum of all 14 degrees of influence will give the TDI. The range of TDI is 0 to 70. The 14 general characteristics are: Data Communications, Distributed Data Processing, Performance, Heavily Used Configuration, Transaction Rate, On-Line Data Entry, End-user Efficiency, Online Update, Complex Processing Reusability, Installation Ease, Operational Ease, Multiple Sites and Facilitate Change.
Each of the above characteristics is evaluated on a scale of 0-5.
Compute Value Adjustment Factor(VAF): Use the following formula to calculate VAF
VAF = (TDI * 0.01) + 0.65
Find the Function Point Count: Use the following formula to calculate FPC
FPC = UFP * VAF
Advantages:
It can be easily used in the early stages of project planning.
It is independent of the programming language.
It can be used to compare different projects even if they use different technologies (database, language, etc).
Disadvantages:
It is not good for real-time systems and embedded systems.
Many cost estimation models like COCOMO use LOC and hence FPC must be converted to LOC.

9.4 System configuration Management

System Configuration Management (SCM) is an arrangement of exercises which controls change by recognizing the items for change, setting up connections between those things, making/characterizing instruments for overseeing diverse variants, controlling the changes being executed in the current framework, inspecting and revealing/reporting on the changes made. It is essential to control the changes in light of the fact that if the changes are not checked legitimately then they may wind up undermining a well-run programming. In this way, SCM is a fundamental piece of all project management activities. Processes involved in SCM – Configuration management provides a disciplined environment for smooth control of work products. It involves the following activities:
Identification and Establishment – Identifying the configuration items from products that compose baselines at given points in time (a baseline is a set of mutually consistent Configuration Items, which has been formally reviewed and agreed upon, and serves as the basis of further development). Establishing relationship among items, creating a mechanism to manage multiple level of control and procedure for change management system.
Version control – Creating versions/specifications of the existing product to build new products from the help of SCM system. A description of version is given below:

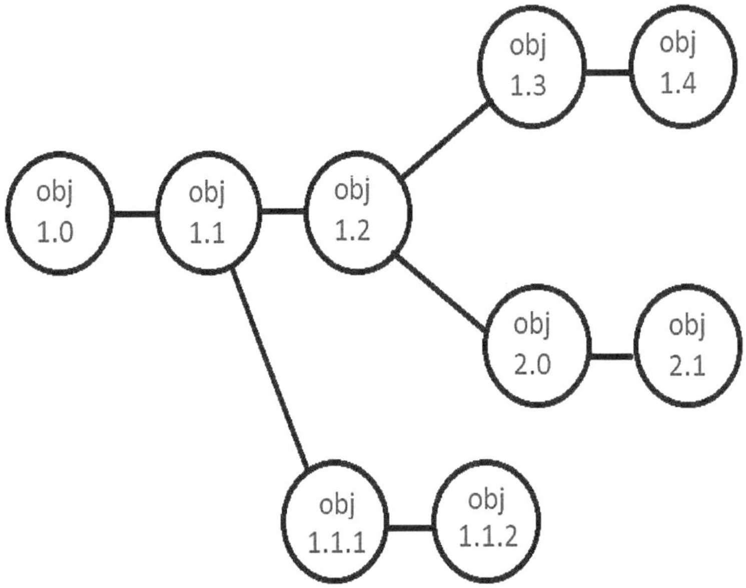

Suppose after some changes, the version of configuration object changes from 1.0 to 1.1. Minor corrections and changes result in versions 1.1.1 and 1.1.2, which is followed by a major update that is object 1.2. The development of object 1.0 continues through 1.3 and 1.4, but finally, a noteworthy change to the object results in a new evolutionary path, version 2.0. Both versions are currently supported.

Change control – Controlling changes to Configuration items (CI). The change control process is explained in Figure below:

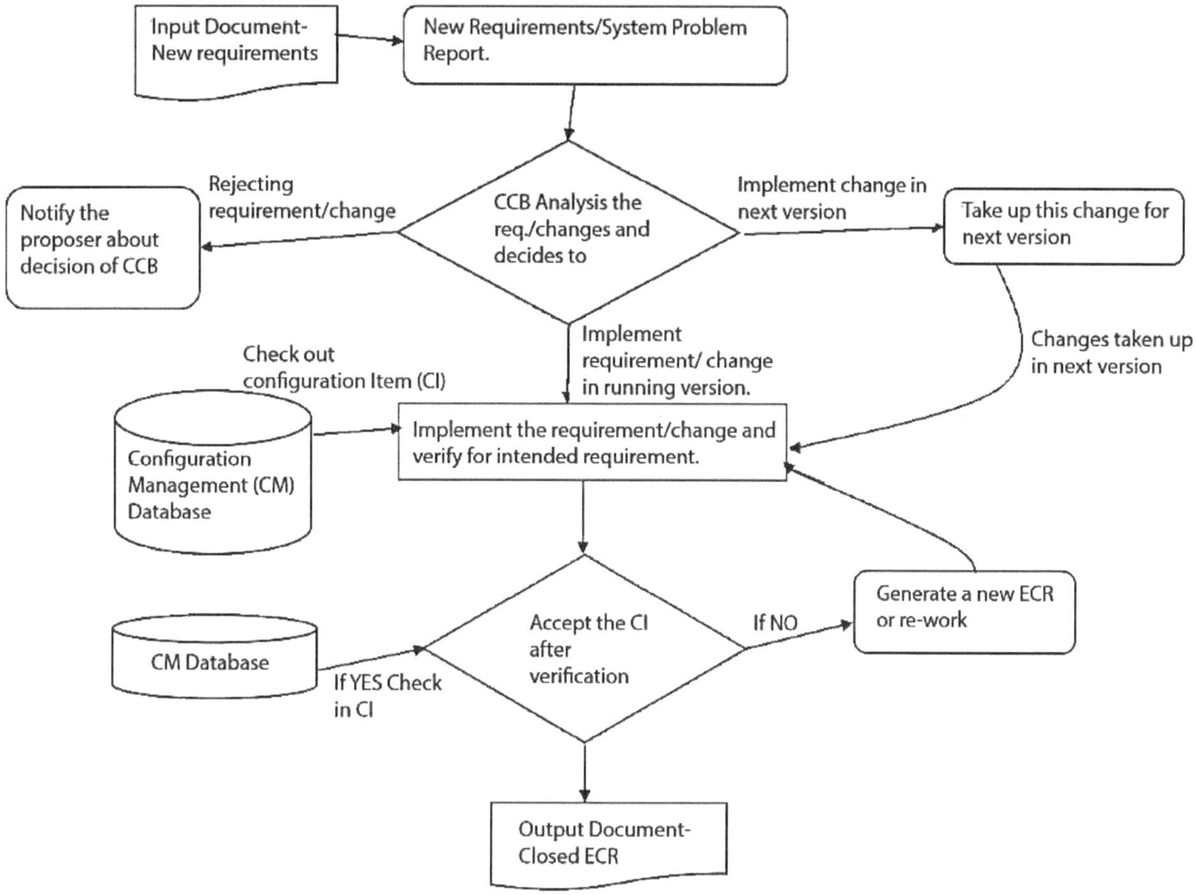

A change request (CR) is submitted and evaluated to assess technical merit, potential side effects, overall impact on other configuration objects and system functions, and the projected cost of the change. The results of the evaluation are presented as a change report, which is used by a change control board (CCB) —a person or group who makes a final decision on the status and priority of the change. An engineering change Request (ECR) is generated for each approved change. Also CCB notifies the developer in case the change is rejected with proper reason. The ECR describes the change to be made, the constraints that must be respected, and the criteria for review and audit. The object to be changed is "checked out" of the project database, the change is made, and then the object is tested again. The object is then "checked in" to the database and appropriate version control mechanisms are used to create the next version of the software.

Configuration auditing – A software configuration audit complements the formal technical review of the process and product. It focuses on the technical correctness of the configuration object that has been modified. The audit confirms the completeness, correctness and consistency of items in the SCM system and track action items from the audit to closure.

Reporting – Providing accurate status and current configuration data to developers, tester, end users, customers and stakeholders through admin guides, user guides, FAQs, Release notes, Memos, Installation Guide, Configuration guide etc

System Configuration Management (SCM) is a software engineering practice that focuses on managing the configuration of software systems and ensuring that software components are properly controlled, tracked, and stored. It is a critical aspect of software development, as it helps to ensure that changes made to a software system are properly coordinated and that the system is always in a known and stable state.

SCM involves a set of processes and tools that help to manage the different components of a software system, including source code, documentation, and other assets. It enables teams to track changes made to the software system, identify when and why changes were made, and manage the integration of these changes into the final product.

The key objectives of SCM are to:
Control the evolution of software systems: SCM helps to ensure that changes to a software system are properly planned, tested, and integrated into the final product.
Enable collaboration and coordination: SCM helps teams to collaborate and coordinate their work, ensuring that changes are properly integrated and that everyone is working from the same version of the software system.
Provide version control: SCM provides version control for software systems, enabling teams to manage and track different versions of the system and to revert to earlier versions if necessary.
Facilitate replication and distribution: SCM helps to ensure that software systems can be easily replicated and distributed to other environments, such as test, production, and customer sites.
SCM is a critical component of software development, and effective SCM practices can help to improve the quality and reliability of software systems, as well as increase efficiency and reduce the risk of errors.

9.5 Capability maturity model (CMM)

Capability Maturity Model (CMM) was developed by the Software Engineering Institute (SEI) at Carnegie Mellon University in 1987. It is not a software process model. It is a framework that is used to analyze the approach and techniques followed by any organization to develop software products. It also provides guidelines to further enhance the maturity of the process used to develop those software products.
It is based on profound feedback and development practices adopted by the most successful organizations worldwide. This model describes a strategy for software process improvement that should be followed by moving through 5 different levels. Each level of maturity shows a process capability level. All the levels except level 1 are further described by Key Process Areas (KPA).
Principles of Capability Maturity Model (CMM)
People's capability is a competitive issue. Competition arises when different organizations are performing the same task (such as software development). In such a case, the people of an organization are sources of strategy and skills, which in turn results in better performance of the organization.
The people's capability should be defined in relation to the business objectives of the organization.
An organization should invest in improving the capabilities and skills of the people as they are important for its success.
The management should be responsible for enhancing the capability of the people in the organization.
The improvement in the capability of people should be done as a process. This process should incorporate appropriate practices and procedures.
The organization should be responsible for providing improvement opportunities so that people in the organization can take advantage of them.
Since new technologies and organizational practices emerge rapidly, organizations should continually improve their practices and develop the abilities of people.
Shortcomings of the Capability Maturity Model (CMM)
It encourages the achievement of a higher maturity level in some cases by displacing the true mission, which is improving the process and overall software quality.
It only helps if it is put into place early in the software development process.
It has no formal theoretical basis and in fact, is based on the experience of very knowledgeable people.
It does not have good empirical support and this same empirical support could also be constructed to support other models.
Difficulty in measuring process improvement: The SEI/CMM model may not provide an accurate measure of process improvement, as it relies on self-assessment by the organization and may not capture all aspects of the development process.
Focus on documentation rather than outcomes: The SEI/CMM model may focus too much on documentation and adherence to procedures, rather than on actual outcomes such as software quality and customer satisfaction.
May not be suitable for all types of organizations: The SEI/CMM model may not be suitable for all kinds of organizations, particularly those with smaller development teams or those with less structured development processes.
May not keep up with rapidly evolving technologies: The SEI/CMM model may not be able to keep up with rapidly evolving technologies and development methodologies, which could limit its usefulness in certain contexts.
Lack of agility: The SEI/CMM model may not be agile enough to respond quickly to changing business needs or customer requirements, which could limit its usefulness in dynamic and rapidly changing environments.
Key Process Areas (KPA)
Each of these KPA (Key Process Areas) defines the basic requirements that should be met by a software process in order to satisfy the KPA and achieve that level of maturity.

Conceptually, key process areas form the basis for management control of the software project and establish a context in which technical methods are applied, work products like models, documents, data, reports, etc. are produced, milestones are established, quality is ensured and change is properly managed.

Levels of Capability Maturity Model (CMM)

There are basically 5 levels of Capability Maturity Models. We will discuss each one of them in detail.

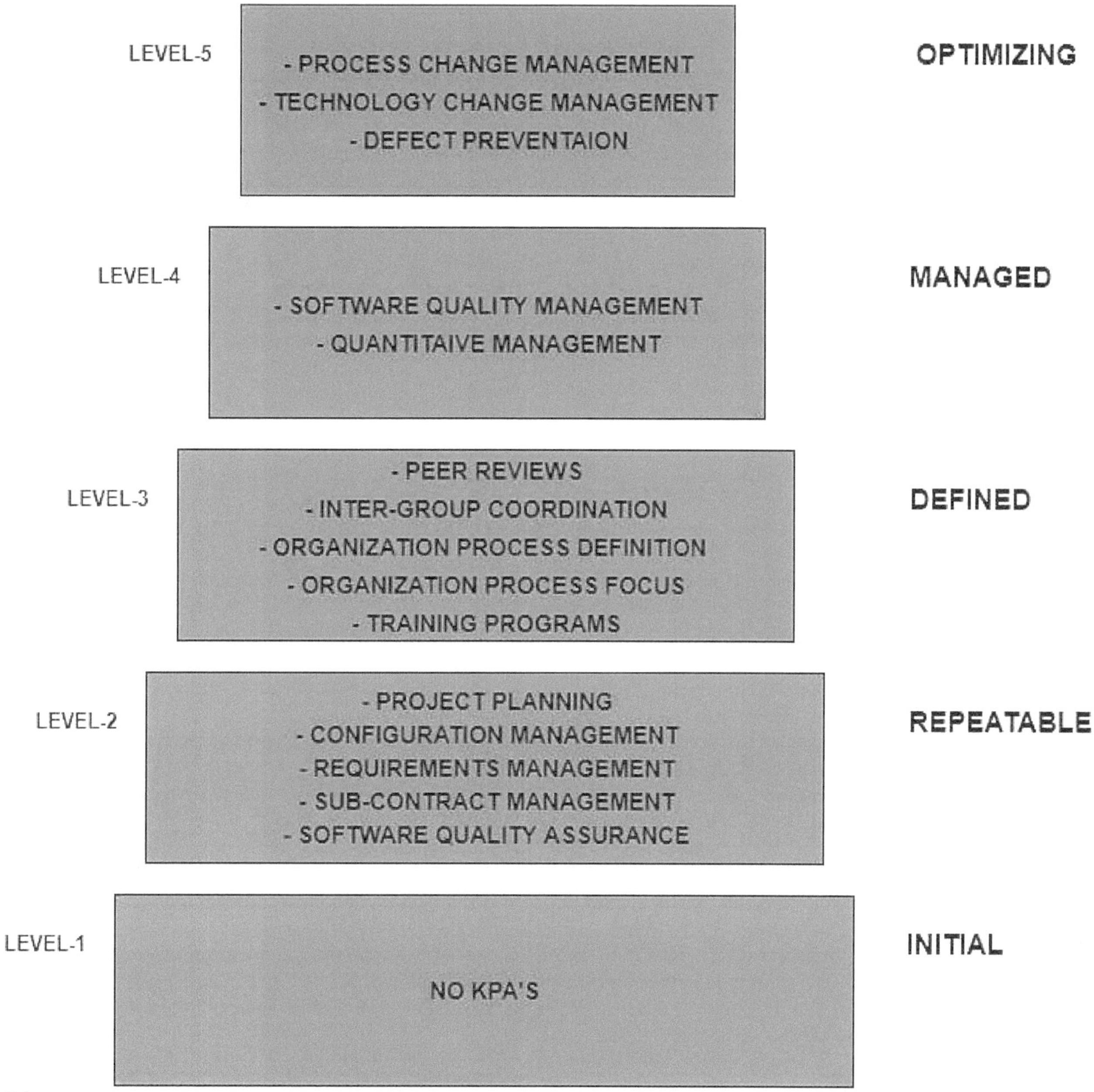

CMM

Level-1: Initial

No KPIs defined.

Processes followed are Adhoc and immature and are not well defined.

Unstable environment for software development.

No basis for predicting product quality, time for completion, etc.

Limited project management capabilities, such as no systematic tracking of schedules, budgets, or progress.

We have limited communication and coordination among team members and stakeholders.

No formal training or orientation for new team members.

Little or no use of software development tools or automation.
Highly dependent on individual skills and knowledge rather than standardized processes.
High risk of project failure or delays due to a lack of process control and stability.

Level-2: Repeatable

Focuses on establishing basic project management policies.
Experience with earlier projects is used for managing new similar-natured projects.

Project Planning- It includes defining resources required, goals, constraints, etc. for the project. It presents a detailed plan to be followed systematically for the successful completion of good-quality software.

Configuration Management- The focus is on maintaining the performance of the software product, including all its components, for the entire lifecycle.

Requirements Management- It includes the management of customer reviews and feedback which result in some changes in the requirement set. It also consists of accommodation of those modified requirements.

Subcontract Management- It focuses on the effective management of qualified software contractors i.e. it manages the parts of the software developed by third parties.

Software Quality Assurance- It guarantees a good quality software product by following certain rules and quality standard guidelines while developing.

Level-3: Defined

At this level, documentation of the standard guidelines and procedures takes place.
It is a well-defined integrated set of project-specific software engineering and management processes.

Peer Reviews: In this method, defects are removed by using a number of review methods like walkthroughs, inspections, buddy checks, etc.

Intergroup Coordination: It consists of planned interactions between different development teams to ensure efficient and proper fulfillment of customer needs.

Organization Process Definition: Its key focus is on the development and maintenance of standard development processes.

Organization Process Focus: It includes activities and practices that should be followed to improve the process capabilities of an organization.

Training Programs: It focuses on the enhancement of knowledge and skills of the team members including the developers and ensuring an increase in work efficiency.

Level-4: Managed

At this stage, quantitative quality goals are set for the organization for software products as well as software processes. The measurements made help the organization to predict the product and process quality within some limits defined quantitatively.

Software Quality Management: It includes the establishment of plans and strategies to develop quantitative analysis and understanding of the product's quality.

Quantitative Management: It focuses on controlling the project performance in a quantitative manner.

Level-5: Optimizing

This is the highest level of process maturity in CMM and focuses on continuous process improvement in the organization using quantitative feedback.

The use of new tools, techniques, and evaluation of software processes is done to prevent the recurrence of known defects.

Process Change Management: Its focus is on the continuous improvement of the organization's software processes to improve productivity, quality, and cycle time for the software product.

Technology Change Management: It consists of the identification and use of new technologies to improve product quality and decrease product development time.

Defect Prevention It focuses on the identification of causes of defects and prevents them from recurring in future projects by improving project-defined processes.

CMM (Capability Maturity Model) vs CMMI (Capability Maturity Model Integration)

Aspects	Capability Maturity Model (CMM)	Capability Maturity Model Integration (CMMI)
Scope	Primarily focused on software engineering processes.	Expands to various disciplines like systems engineering, hardware development, etc.

Maturity Levels	Had a five-level maturity model (Level 1 to Level 5).	Initially had a staged representation; introduced continuous representation later.
Flexibility	More rigid structure with predefined practices.	Offers flexibility to tailor process areas to organizational needs.
Adoption and Popularity	Gained popularity in software development industry.	Gained wider adoption across industries due to broader applicability.

Levels of CMMI

There are basically 5 performance levels of the CMMI Model.

Level 1: Initial: Processes are often ad hoc and unpredictable. There is little or no formal process in place.

Level 2: Managed: Basic project management processes are established. Projects are planned, monitored, and controlled.

Level 3: Defined: Organizational processes are well-defined and documented. Standardized processes are used across the organization.

Level 4: Quantitatively Managed: Processes are measured and controlled using statistical and quantitative techniques. Process performance is quantitatively understood and managed.

Level 5: Optimizing: Continuous process improvement is a key focus. Processes are continuously improved based on quantitative feedback.

9.6 Size Estimation and Cost Estimation

Size Estimation

Size estimation in software engineering is the process of determining the size or extent of a software project or its individual components. Estimating size is a crucial step in project planning and management, as it helps in assessing the effort, time, and resources required for the development and maintenance of software. There are several methods and metrics used for size estimation in software engineering, including:

Lines of Code (LOC): This is a common metric that counts the number of lines of code in a software program. It provides a basic measure of the software's size, although it may not reflect the complexity or functionality accurately.

Function Points (FP): Function point analysis is a more comprehensive size metric that considers the functionality of the software. It assesses the number of inputs, outputs, user interactions, and data storage requirements. Function points provide a more accurate estimate of the software's size.

Use Case Points (UCP): UCP is a size estimation method based on the number of use cases and actors in a software system. It takes into account the user interactions and system functionality to determine size.

Story Points: Story points are commonly used in agile development and are a subjective measure of the complexity and effort required to complete a user story or task.

Object Points: This method assesses the complexity of software components, such as objects or classes, to estimate size.

Cyclomatic Complexity: Cyclomatic complexity measures the complexity of a software program's control flow. It can be used to estimate the size of code based on the number of decision points and paths through the code.

Data Points: Data points estimate the size of a software system based on data volume and the complexity of data processing.

Feature Points: Feature points consider the features and functionality of a software product to estimate its size.

Size estimation is essential for various purposes, including project planning, cost estimation, resource allocation, scheduling, and risk assessment. Accurate size estimation helps in delivering software projects on time and within budget while managing expectations and ensuring that the software meets user requirements. Different projects and organizations may use various size estimation methods based on their specific needs and practices.

Cost Estimation

For any new software project, it is necessary to know how much it will cost to develop and how much development time will it take. These estimates are needed before development is initiated, but how is this done? Several estimation procedures have been developed and are having the following attributes in common.

Project scope must be established in advanced.

Software metrics are used as a support from which evaluation is made.

The project is broken into small PCs which are estimated individually. To achieve true cost & schedule estimate, several option arise.

Delay estimation

Used symbol decomposition techniques to generate project cost and schedule estimates.

Acquire one or more automated estimation tools.

Uses of Cost Estimation

During the planning stage, one needs to choose how many engineers are required for the project and to develop a schedule.

In monitoring the project's progress, one needs to access whether the project is progressing according to the procedure and takes corrective action, if necessary.

9.6.1 Methods of Size Estimation (LOC, FP, etc.)

Accurate estimation of the problem size is fundamental to satisfactory estimation of effort, time duration and cost of a software project. In order to be able to accurately estimate the project size, some important metrics should be defined in terms of which the project size can be expressed. The size of a problem is obviously not the number of bytes that the source code occupies. It is neither the byte size of the executable code. The project size is a measure of the problem complexity in terms of the effort and time required to develop the product.

Currently two metrics are popularly being used widely to estimate size:

1- lines of code (LOC)

2- function point (FP)

The usage of each of these metrics in project size estimation has its own advantages and disadvantages.

1. LINES OF CODE (LOC)

LOC is the simplest among all metrics available to estimate project size. This metric is very popular because it is the simplest to use. Using this metric, the project size is estimated by counting the number of source instructions in the developed program. Obviously, while counting the number of source instructions, lines used for commenting the the code and the header lines should be ignored. Determining the LOC count at the end of a project is a very simple job. However, accurate estimation of the LOC count at the beginning of a project is very difficult. In order to estimate the LOC count at the beginning of a project, project managers usually divide the problem into modules, and each module into submodules and so on, until the sizes of the different leaf-level modules can be approximately predicted. To be able to do this, past experience in developing similar products is helpful. By using the estimation of the lowest level modules, project managers arrive at the total size estimation.

2. FUNCTION POINT (FP)

Function point metric was proposed by Albrecht [1983]. This metric overcomes many of the shortcomings of the LOC metric. Since its inception in late 1970s, function point metric has been slowly gaining popularity. One of the important advantages of using the function point metric is that it can be used to easily estimate the size of a software product directly from the problem specification. This is in contrast to the LOC metric, where the size can be accurately determined only after the product has fully been developed. The conceptual idea behind the function point metric is that the size of a software product is directly dependent on the number of different functions or features it supports. A software product supporting many features would certainly be of larger size than a product with less number of features. Each function when invoked reads some input data and transforms it to the corresponding output data. For example, the issue book feature (as show in figure) of a Library Automation Software takes the name of the book as input and displays its location and the number of copies available. Thus, a computation of the number of input and the output data values to a system gives some indication of the number of functions supported by the system. Albrecht postulated that in addition to the number of basic functions that a software performs, the size is also dependent on the number of files and the number of interfaces

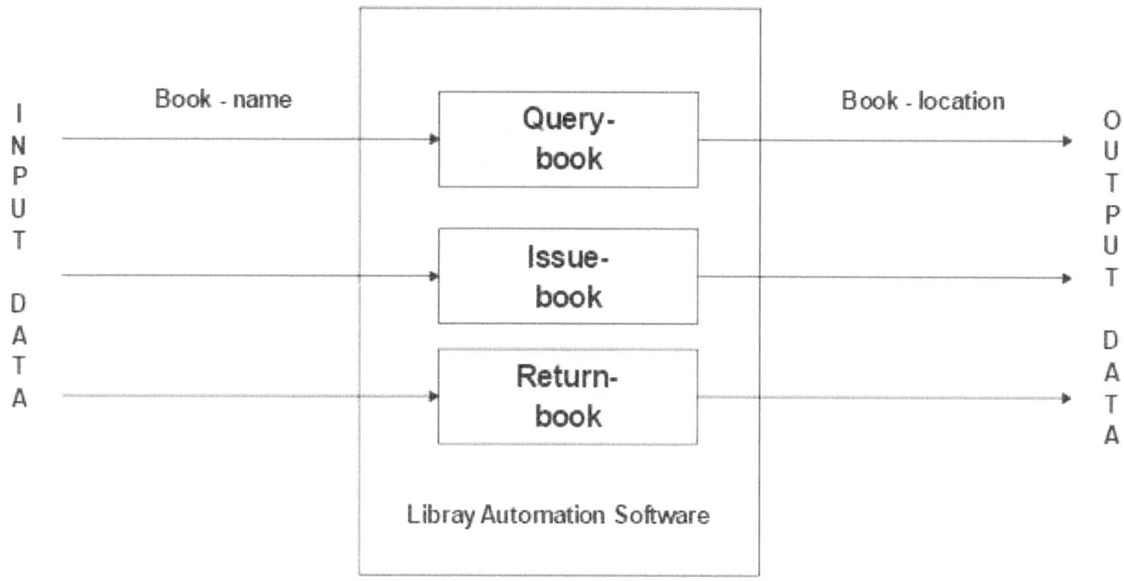

System function as a map of input data to output data

Besides using the number of input and output data values, function point metric computes the size of a software product (in units of functions points or FPs) using three other characteristics of the product as shown in the following expression. The size of a product in function points (FP) can be expressed as the weighted sum of these five problem characteristics. The weights associated with the five characteristics were proposed empirically and validated by the observations over many projects. Function point is computed in two steps. The first step is to compute the unadjusted function point (UFP).

UFP = (Number of inputs)*4 + (Number of outputs)*5 + (Number of inquiries)*4 +
(Number of files)*10 + (Number of interfaces)*10

Number of inputs: Each data item input by the user is counted. Data inputs should be distinguished from user inquiries. Inquiries are user commands such as print-account-balance. Inquiries are counted separately. It must be noted that individual data items input by the user are not considered in the calculation of the number of inputs, but a group of related inputs are considered as a single input. For example, while entering the data concerning an employee to an employee pay roll software; the data items name, age, sex, address, phone number, etc. are together considered as a single input. All these data items can be considered to be related, since they pertain to a single employee.

Number of outputs: The outputs considered refer to reports printed, screen outputs, error messages produced, etc. While outputting the number of outputs the individual data items within a report are not considered, but a set of related data items is counted as one input.

Number of inquiries: Number of inquiries is the number of distinct interactive queries which can be made by the users. These inquiries are the user commands which require specific action by the system.

Number of files: Each logical file is counted. A logical file means groups of logically related data. Thus, logical files can be data structures or physical files.

Number of interfaces: Here the interfaces considered are the interfaces used to exchange information with other systems. Examples of such interfaces are data files on tapes, disks, communication links with other systems etc.

Once the unadjusted function point (UFP) is computed, the technical complexity factor (TCF) is computed next. TCF refines the UFP measure by considering fourteen other factors such as high transaction rates, throughput, and response time requirements, etc. Each of these 14 factors is assigned from 0 (not present or no influence) to 6 (strong influence). The resulting numbers are summed, yielding the total degree of influence (DI).

Now, TCF is computed as (0.65+0.01*DI). As DI can vary from 0 to 70, TCF can vary from 0.65 to 1.35.

Finally, FP=UFP*TCF

Shortcomings of function point (FP) metric

LOC as a measure of problem size has several shortcomings:

• LOC gives a numerical value of problem size that can vary widely with individual coding style – different programmers lay out their code in different ways. For example, one programmer might write several source instructions on a single line whereas another might split a single instruction across several lines. Of course, this problem can be easily overcome by counting the language tokens in the program rather than the lines of code. However, a more intricate problem arises because the length of a program depends on the choice of instructions used in writing the program. Therefore, even for the same problem, different programmers might come up with programs having different LOC counts. This situation does not improve even if language tokens are counted instead of lines of code.

• A good problem size measure should consider the overall complexity of the problem and the effort needed to solve it. That is, it should consider the local effort needed to specify, design, code, test, etc. and not just the coding effort. LOC, however, focuses on the coding activity alone; it merely computes the number of source lines in the final program. We have already seen that coding is only a small part of the overall software development activities. It is also wrong to argue that the overall product development effort is proportional to the effort required in writing the program code. This is because even though the design might be very complex, the code might be straightforward and vice versa. In such cases, code size is a grossly improper indicator of the problem size.

• LOC measure correlates poorly with the quality and efficiency of the code. Larger code size does not necessarily imply better quality or higher efficiency. Some programmers produce lengthy and complicated code as they do not make effective use of the available instruction set. In fact, it is very likely that a poor and sloppily written piece of code might have larger number of source instructions than a piece that is neat and efficient

• LOC metric measures the lexical complexity of a program and does not address the more important but subtle issues of logical or structural complexities. Between two programs with equal LOC count, a program having complex logic would require much more effort to develop than a program with very simple logic. To realize why this is so, consider the effort required to develop a program having multiple nested loop and decision constructs with another program having only sequential control flow.

• It is very difficult to accurately estimate LOC in the final product from the problem specification. The LOC count can be accurately computed only after the code has been fully developed. Therefore, the LOC metric is little use to the project managers during project planning, since project planning is carried out even before any development activity has started. This possibly is the biggest shortcoming of the LOC metric from the project manager's perspective

9.6.2 Cost Estimation Models

Cost Estimation Models

A model may be static or dynamic. In a static model, a single variable is taken as a key element for calculating cost and time. In a dynamic model, all variable are interdependent, and there is no basic variable.

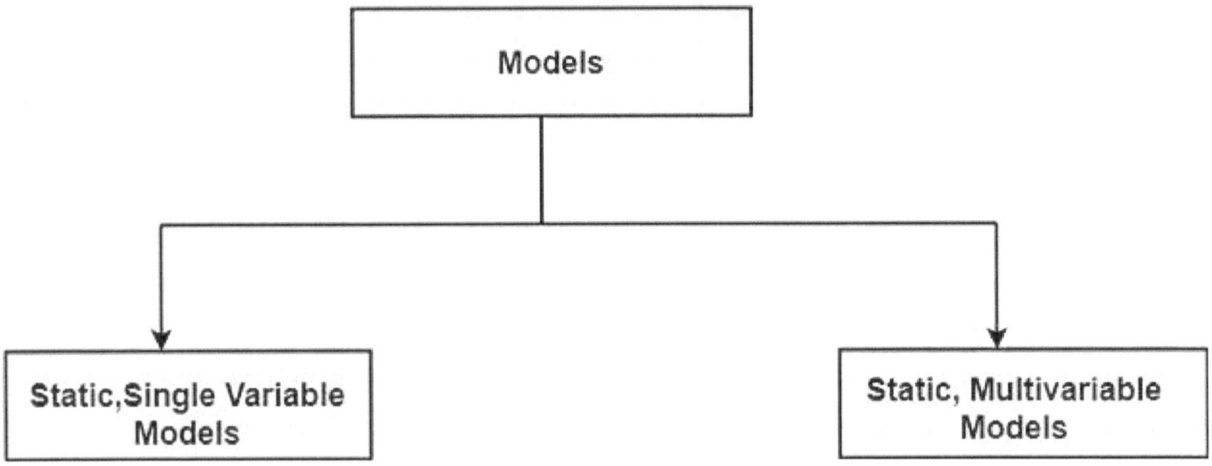

Static, Single Variable Models: When a model makes use of single variables to calculate desired values such as cost, time, efforts, etc. is said to be a single variable model. The most common equation is:

$$C=aL^b$$

Where C = Costs
L= size
a and b are constants

The Software Engineering Laboratory established a model called SEL model, for estimating its software production. This model is an example of the static, single variable model.

$E=1.4L^{0.93}$

$DOC=30.4L^{0.90}$

$D=4.6L^{0.26}$

Where E= Efforts (Person Per Month)

DOC=Documentation (Number of Pages)

D = Duration (D, in months)

L = Number of Lines per code

Static, Multivariable Models: These models are based on method (1), they depend on several variables describing various aspects of the software development environment. In some model, several variables are needed to describe the software development process, and selected equation combined these variables to give the estimate of time & cost. These models are called multivariable models.

WALSTON and FELIX develop the models at IBM provide the following equation gives a relationship between lines of source code and effort:

$E=5.2L^{0.91}$

In the same manner duration of development is given by

$D=4.1L^{0.36}$

The productivity index uses 29 variables which are found to be highly correlated productivity as follows:

$$I = \sum_{i=1}^{29} W_i X_i$$

Where W_i is the weight factor for the i^{th}variable and X_i={-1,0,+1} the estimator gives $X_i$one of the values -1, 0 or +1 depending on the variable decreases, has no effect or increases the productivity.

Example: Compare the Walston-Felix Model with the SEL model on a software development expected to involve 8 person-years of effort.

Calculate the number of lines of source code that can be produced.

Calculate the duration of the development.

Calculate the productivity in LOC/PY

Calculate the average manning

Solution:

The amount of manpower involved = 8PY=96persons-months

(a)Number of lines of source code can be obtained by reversing equation to give:

L = (E/a) 1/b

Then

L (SEL) = (96/1.4)1/0.93=94264 LOC

L (SEL) = (96/5.2)1/0.91=24632 LOC

(b)Duration in months can be calculated by means of equation

D (SEL) = 4.6 (L) 0.26

= 4.6 (94.264)0.26 = 15 months

D (W-F) = 4.1 $L^{0.36}$

= 4.1 (24.632)0.36 = 13 months

(c) Productivity is the lines of code produced per persons/month (year)

P(SEL) = 94264/8 = 11783 LOC/Person – Years

P(SEL) = 24632/8 = 3079 LOC/Person -Years

(d)Average manning is the average number of persons required per month in the project

M(SEL) = 96P-M/15M = 6.4Persons

M(W-F) = 96P-M/13M = 7.4Persons

9.6.3 COCOMO Model (Introduction)

COCOMO: The COCOMO (Constructive Cost Estimation Model) is proposed by DR. Berry Boehm in 1981 and that's why it is also known as COCOMO'81. It is a method for evaluating the cost of a software package. According to him software cost estimation should be done through three stages:

Basic COCOMO Model

Intermediate COCOMO Model

Complete/Detailed COCOMO Model

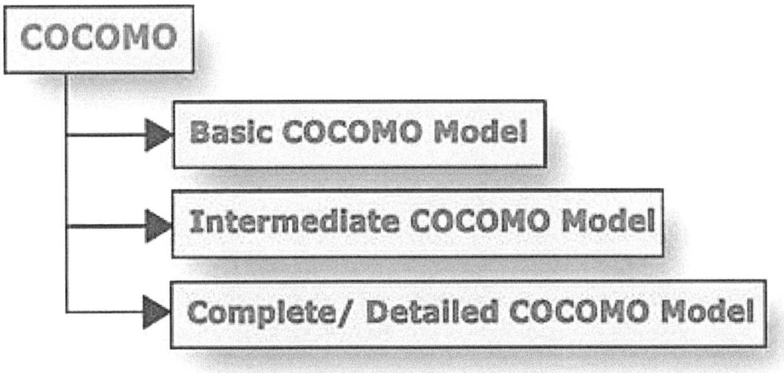

COCOMO'81 models depend upon the two main equations:
Development Effort : MM = a * KDSI b
Which is based on MM - man-month / person month / staff-month is one month of effort by one person.
Note: In COCOMO'81, there are 152 hours per Person month. According to organization this values may differ from the standard by 10% to 20%.
Efforts and Development Time (TDEV) : TDEV = 2.5 * MM c
Note: The coefficients a, b and c depend on the mode of the development.

DEVELOPMENT MODES:
There are three modes of development:
Organic Mode:
Relatively Small, Simple Software projects.
Small teams with good application experience work to a set of less than rigid requirements.
Similar to previously developed projects.
Relatively small and require little innovation.
Semidetached Mode:
Intermediate (in size and complexity) software projects in which teams with mixed experience levels must meet a mix of rigid and less than rigid requirements.
Embedded Mode:
Software projects that must be developed within set of tight hardware, software and operational Constraints.
Development Mode with Project Characteristics:

Development Mode	**Project Characteristics**			
	Size	**Innovation**	**Deadline**	**Dev. Environment**
ORGANIC	Small	Little	Not Tight	Stable
SEMI-DITACHED	Medium	Medium	Medium	Medium
EMBEDDED	Large	Greater	Tight	Complex Hardware

The values of a1, a2, b1, b2 for different categories of products (i.e. organic, semidetached, and embedded) as given by Boehm [1981] are summarized below. He derived the above expressions by examining historical data collected from a large number of actual projects.
BASIC COCOMO MODEL: Basic COCMO Model is good for quick, early, rough order of magnitude estimate of software cost. It does not account for differences in hardware constraints, personal Quality and experience, use of modern tools and techniques, and other project attribute known to have a significant influence on software cost, which limits its accuracy. It gives an approximate estimate of the project parameters. The basic COCOMO estimation model is given by the following expressions:
Effort = $a_1 \times (KLOC)^{a_2}$PM
Tdev = $b_1 \times (Effort)^{b_2}$ Months
Where,
KLOC is the estimated size of the software product expressed in Kilo Lines of Code,

a_1, a_2, b_1, b_2 are constants for each category of software products,
Tdev is the estimated time to develop the software, expressed in months,
Effort is the total effort required to develop the software product, expressed in person months (PMs).

Estimation of development effort:

For the three classes of software products, the formulas for estimating the effort based on the code size are shown below:

Organic: Effort = $2.4(KLOC)^{1.05}$ PM
Semi-Detached: Effort = $3.0(KLOC)^{1.12}$ PM
Embedded: Effort = $3.6(KLOC)^{1.20}$ PM

PM: Person Months

Estimation of development time:

For the three classes of software products, the formulas for estimating the development time based on the effort are given below:

Organic: Tdev = $2.5(Effort)^{0.38}$ Months
Semi-detached: Tdev = $2.5(Effort)^{0.35}$ Months
Embedded: Tdev = $2.5(Effort)^{0.32}$ Months

The effort estimation is expressed in units of person-months (PM). It is the area under the person-month plot as shown in figure below. It should be carefully noted that an effort of 100 PM does not imply that 100 persons should work for 1 month nor does it imply that 1 person should be employed for 100 months, but it denotes the area under the person-month curve.

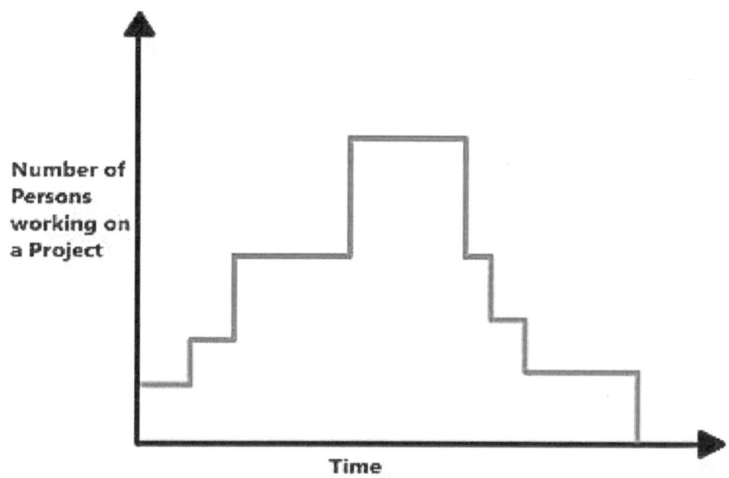

Fig. Person Month Curve

From the following figure which shows a plot of estimated effort versus product size. We can observe that the effort is somewhat superlinear in the size of the software product. Thus, the effort required to develop a product increases very rapidly with project size.

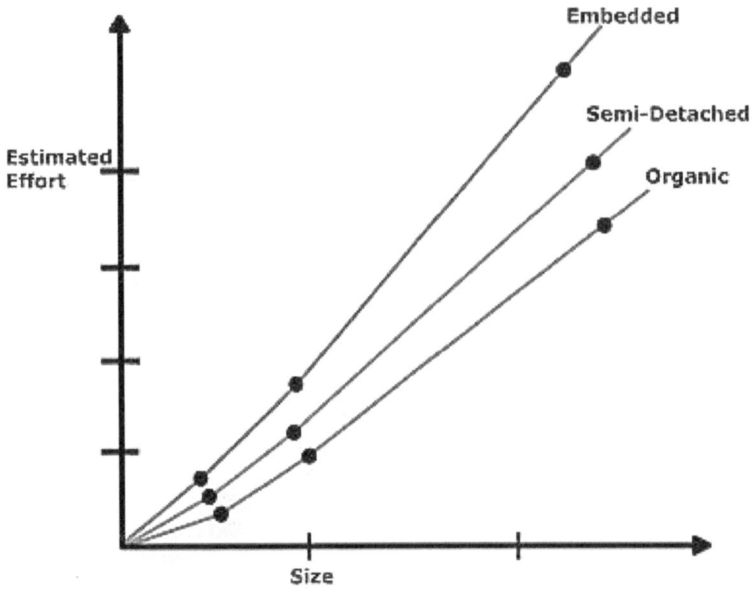

Fig. Effort Verses Product size

Now the following figure plots the development time versus the product size in KLOC can be observed that the development time is a sublinear function of the size of the product, i.e. when the size of the product increases by two times, the time to develop the product does not double but rises moderately.

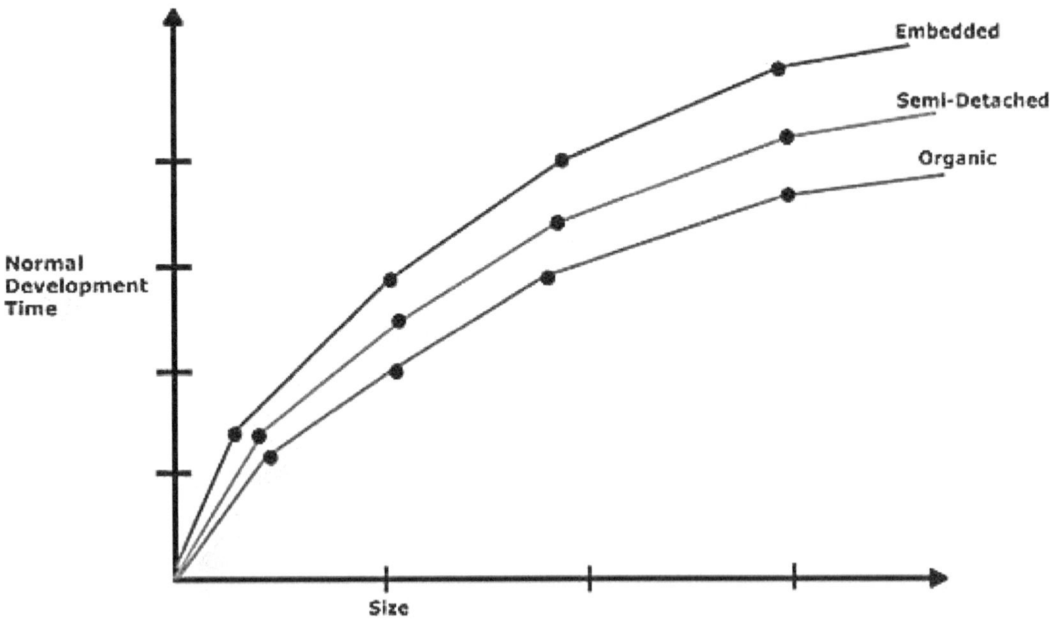

Fig. Development time Verses size

Note: It is to be noted that the effort and the duration estimations obtained using the COCOMO model are called as nominal effort estimate and nominal duration estimate.

Let's see an Example:

Problem: Assume that the size of an organic type software product has been estimated to be 32,000 lines of source code. Assume that the average salary of software engineers be Rs. 15,000/- per month. Determine the effort required to develop the software product and the nominal development time.

Solution: As per the basic COCOMO estimation formula for organic software:

Effort = $2.4 * (32)^{1.05}$ = 91 PM

Nominal development time = $2.5 * (91)^{0.38}$ = 14 months

Cost required to develop the product = 14 * 15,000

= Rs. 210,000/-

INTERMEDIATE COCOMO MODEL: The intermediate COCOMO model takes the basic COCOMO model as its starting point which means that it is slightly different coefficients for the effort equation than the Basic model. After that it multiplies the basic estimate by an Effort Adjustment Factor which is calculated as the product of 15 multipliers (cost drivers) which take into account factors such as required product reliability, database size, execution and storage constraints, personnel aptitude, and the use of software tools. It produces better results than the Basic model because the user supplies settings for cost drivers that determine the effort and duration of the software projects. The Intermediate model also allows the system to be divided and estimated in components. DSI values and cost drivers can be chosen for individual components instead of for the system as a whole.

Effort Adjustment factor

The effort adjustment factor use 15 cost drivers that are grouped into four categories:

Product

Computer

Personnel

Project

Note: Each cost driver has been rated on a six-point ordinal scale ranging from low to high importance. Product of all effort multipliers leads to EAF.

Estimation of development effort:

For the three classes of software products, the formulas for estimating the effort based on the code size are shown below:

Organic: Effort = $3.2(KLOC)^{1.05}$ PM

Semi-Detached: Effort = $3.0(KLOC)^{1.12}$ PM

Embedded: Effort = $2.8(KLOC)^{1.20}$ PM

PM: Person Months

Estimation of development time:

For the three classes of software products, the formulas for estimating the development time based on the effort are given below:

Organic: Tdev = $2.5(Effort)^{0.38}$ Months

Semi-detached: Tdev = $2.5(Effort)^{0.35}$ Months

Embedded: Tdev = $2.5(Effort)^{0.32}$ Months

DETAILED/ADVANCED COCOMO MODEL: A major shortcoming of both the basic and intermediate COCOMO models is that they consider a software product as a single homogeneous entity. However, most large systems are made up several smaller sub-systems. These sub-systems may have widely different characteristics.

The Detailed COCOMO Model differs from the Intermediate COCOMO model in that it uses effort multipliers for each phase of the project. These phase dependent effort multipliers yield better estimates because the cost driver ratings may be different during each phase.

In Advanced COCOMO Model the cost of each subsystem is estimated separately. This approach reduces the margin of error in the final estimate.

Example: A distributed Management Information System (MIS) product for an organization having offices at several places across the country can have the following sub-components:

Database part

Graphical User Interface (GUI) part

Communication part

Of these, the communication part can be considered as Embedded software. The database part could be Semi-detached software, and the GUI part Organic software. The costs for these three components can be estimated separately, and summed up to give the overall cost of the system.

Advantages of COCOMO'81 Model:

COCOMO is transparent, one can see how it works unlike other models such as SLIM

Drivers are particularly helpful to the estimator to understand the impact of different factors that affect project costs.

Limitations of COCOMO'81 Model:

It is hard to accurately estimate KDSI early on in the project, when most effort estimates are required.

KDSI, actually, is not a size measure it is a length measure.

Extremely vulnerable to mis-classification of the development mode.

Success depends largely on tuning the model to the needs of the organization, using historical data which is not always available.

9.6.4 Estimating Risks and Contingencies

Estimating risks and contingencies in software engineering is a crucial aspect of project management. It involves identifying potential risks that could impact the software development project and developing contingency plans to mitigate these risks. Here's a detailed explanation of the process:

Risk Identification:

The first step in estimating risks is to identify potential risks. These risks can be categorized into various types, such as technical risks, project management risks, business risks, and external risks.

Technical risks can include issues related to software complexity, technology adoption, or integration challenges.

Project management risks can involve factors like scope changes, resource constraints, or schedule delays.

Business risks may relate to changes in market conditions, competition, or changes in project stakeholders' requirements.

External risks can include factors beyond the project team's control, such as regulatory changes or natural disasters.

Risk Assessment:

Once risks are identified, they need to be assessed in terms of their impact and probability. This assessment helps in prioritizing risks based on their potential consequences.

Risks with a high impact and high probability should be given the highest priority.

Risk Quantification:

Some risks can be quantified in terms of potential financial impact or schedule delays. This quantification helps in understanding the potential cost associated with specific risks.

Tools and techniques like Monte Carlo simulations or decision trees can be used for quantitative risk analysis.

Contingency Planning:

Contingency planning involves developing strategies to deal with identified risks.

For each high-priority risk, a contingency plan is created. The plan outlines specific actions that can be taken to mitigate the risk if it occurs.

Risk Mitigation:

Risk mitigation is the process of reducing the probability or impact of identified risks.

Various mitigation strategies can be employed, such as thorough testing, early issue identification, adopting best practices, or using alternative technologies.

Monitoring and Control:

Continuous monitoring of risks and the effectiveness of contingency plans is essential. This ensures that the project team is aware of potential issues as they arise.

Regular risk reviews and status updates should be conducted to ensure that the project stays on track.

Risk Response Strategies:

There are several risk response strategies that can be employed:

Avoidance: The risk is eliminated by changing the project plan.

Transfer: The risk is transferred to a third party, such as through insurance or outsourcing.

Mitigation: Steps are taken to reduce the risk's impact or probability.

Acceptance: Some risks may be accepted if their impact is low or if the cost of mitigation is too high.

Documentation:

All identified risks, their assessments, and contingency plans should be documented and regularly updated as the project progresses.

Communication:

Effective communication with stakeholders is crucial. They should be informed about potential risks and the actions being taken to mitigate them.

Lessons Learned:

After the project is completed, it's essential to conduct a lessons-learned session to evaluate how well risks were managed. This information can be invaluable for future projects.

9.7 Software Project Planning

Software Project Planning

A Software Project is the complete methodology of programming advancement from requirement gathering to testing and support, completed by the execution procedures, in a specified period to achieve intended software product.

Need of Software Project Management

Software development is a sort of all new streams in world business, and there's next to no involvement in structure programming items. Most programming items are customized to accommodate customer's necessities. The most significant is that the underlying technology changes and advances so generally and rapidly that experience of one element may not be connected to the other one. All such business and ecological imperatives bring risk in software development; hence, it is fundamental to manage software projects efficiently.

Software Project Manager

Software manager is responsible for planning and scheduling project development. They manage the work to ensure that it is completed to the required standard. They monitor the progress to check that the event is on time and within budget. The project planning must incorporate the major issues like size & cost estimation scheduling, project monitoring, personnel selection evaluation & risk management. To plan a successful software project, we must understand:

Scope of work to be completed

Risk analysis

The resources mandatory

The project to be accomplished

Record of being followed

Software Project planning starts before technical work start. The various steps of planning activities are:

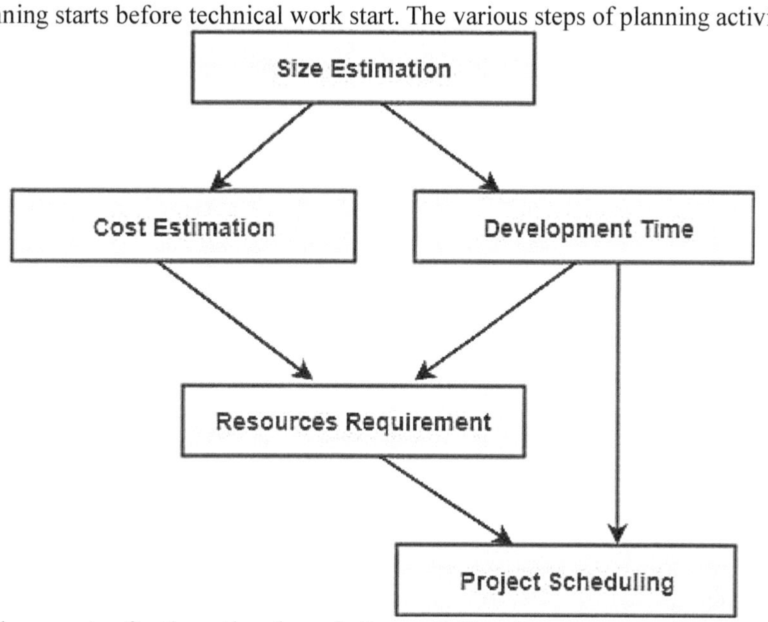

The size is the crucial parameter for the estimation of other activities. Resources requirement are required based on cost and development time. Project schedule may prove to be very useful for controlling and monitoring the progress of the project. This is dependent on resources & development time.

9.7.1 Project Initiation

Project initiation is set by the Project Management Institute as the first of five project management phases: initiation, planning, execution, performance, and closure. The main objectives of the project initiation phase are:

Ensure the buy-in of the decision-makers at your company

Secure the resources you need to finish the project

Set the expectations for everyone involved in the project

The trick here is to flesh out your project enough to communicate it without going into the actual planning phase. Think of the initiation phase of a project as developing a big-picture view. It's not the moment when you start pumping out Gantt charts or assigning Fred a long, long list of tasks. That happens later, during project planning and execution. The reason why you want to stick with big picture in the initiation phase of project management is that your project may not even secure the green lights—or the green bills—it needs to be implemented. Use this phase to get a feel for whether people are on board with the project or not interested at all.

Here are the five steps to kick off your project management initiation phase:

Define your business case

Draft a project charter

Run a feasibility study

Pick your team

Choose the workplace and the tools

1. Define your business case

Let's generalize for a minute: companies love things that increase profits, reduce costs, or reduce risk. And there are many ways to achieve this: new products or services may increase profits, automating workflows may reduce costs, and switching to more reliable suppliers may reduce risk.

Constructing a business case is about tuning in your project to what your company needs. How will this project increase profits, reduce costs, or reduce risk? The benefits of your project may not be obvious, so use your creativity and your research skills to build a compelling case.

Now create a project initiation document, and follow this outline:

Executive briefing. Write a couple of paragraphs that summarize your project.

Projected costs. Set down the number of people you will need, along with a ballpark budget.

Expected benefits. Show how this project will positively impact the business, but don't forget to mention the risks involved.

Conclusion and overview of next steps. Write down what you'll do once someone gives you the green light to go to the next stage.

Here are some tips for and questions to ask during project initiation to help build your business case:

Why is this project necessary?

Why should we spend money or time building it?

What results do you want to achieve?

For smaller projects, you can get away with giving an overview of what you're planning. But if you're suggesting something bigger and riskier, look for data to base your claims on. Find studies online or similar initiatives in other companies, and do some risk assessment to get a clearer picture.

A business case is a general overview, but it can't be vague. Be as specific as you can.

Once you have your business case complete, take it to the person who has the power to give you the approval and resources to complete it. It's usually someone directly above you in the hierarchy or someone at the executive level. Be persuasive. Show the value of your project, but don't forget that you're not implementing it only for your own good. If you show you understand and care about the business, you're already one step closer to getting that nod.

2. Draft a project charter

Ok, your business case raised some eyebrows and got people talking. You had some face time with coworkers, and they want to know more. What's the next step? Drafting a project charter. This is where you:

Define the goals of the project

List the deliverables

Set the scope

Decide on a rough timeline

Add a more detailed budget

Table of contents
Goal
Description
Major Requirements & deliverables

Budget
Success factors
Risks
Milestones & schedule
Assumptions & constraints
Project manager & team members
Approval

A project charter template from Notion

Here, you're mapping the road ahead with a little bit more resolution than before. Be careful though: it's really easy to go into full-blown project planning. Don't slip into that yet if you don't have complete approval (approval is half the battle when it comes to project management initiation). To help, grab a project charter template from your documentation tool—apps like Notion usually have them built in.

The objective of the project charter is to show not only that the project can be completed, but that you know the steps to take to reach the end.

3. Run a feasibility study

You know why you're doing this project, and you have an outline of what you need to do to complete it. Don't get too excited: it's time to analyze the potential risks ahead.

Your project has merit, but there may be obstacles strong enough to break it. Similarly, while the idea may look great on paper, the return on investment or the projected benefits may be so negligible that it's not worth it to even begin.

Turn on your "better safe than sorry" approach:

Is now the right time to implement the project?

Is the cost too high?

Does it demand too many people (and could it delay other projects or work)?

How soon will you see some return on investment?

Do you have all the people you need? Do they have the skillsets required to complete the project successfully?

Put your budget, the projected return on investment, and the timeline side by side. Is the project's result worth your company's money and your effort? Are the changes going to be noticeable?

The bigger the project is, the more detailed the feasibility study needs to be. Again, base everything on data. For example, find other companies that may have implemented what you're about to, and see if you can find case studies on their results.

4. Pick your team

People can make or break projects, which is why it's important to assemble a group with the right skills and set a hierarchy that makes sense for what you're trying to accomplish. It's time to build the dream team.

List the skills needed to complete the project. Will you need design skills? Writing? Product design? Sales? Think about who in your company has these skills, and list their names. At the same time, think about hierarchy: Who will lead the team? Will it be you? A project manager? Think about who reports to whom and how those processes will be carried out. Having these details set up from the beginning can save you a lot of trouble and tension during execution.

If you're having a hard time coming up with the list, start talking with some of the people you're sure about. Ask them if they know anyone within the company that has the skills you're looking for. Depending on which people you deal with more frequently, you may not be aware of everyone's skillsets, so use the knowledge of your coworkers to find everyone you need. It may also be the case that you need new hires, so remember to update your budget if that's the case.

5. Choose the workplace and the tools

While smaller projects won't motivate people to camp out in that nice conference room upstairs, bigger ones may require finding a new space. Where will your team work? If you're working at an office, will you move your desks and chairs to a new room? Or will you keep to your desks and meet in a meeting room as necessary? How often will that happen?

Maybe you're working with a remote team. In that case, it's important to find the collection of apps you'll use to get everything done. For communication, you'll definitely need a video conferencing app and team chat app, if you don't already have them. You'll also want screen recording software or screen sharing software since folks can't stand over your shoulder.

But regardless of working at the office or doing the same from home, you'll need to track tasks, documents, and deliverables. Consider adding an all-in-one workspace app or a project management app to the mix to create a single source of truth for the whole team.

And finally, be sure to automate where you can, so you can keep your eye on the prize.

9.7.2 Planning Scope Management

Managing the scope of a project is like driving a car. If you don't keep your eyes in front of you, the car veers off the road. Similarly, if you don't control your project scope, the project gets off track. A scope management plan outlines the processes involved in executing your project and serves as a guideline to keep the project within specific limits.

As a project manager, it's your responsibility to guide your team through the project life cycle. In this article, we'll explain what a scope management plan is and how it can assist you in the planning phase. Once you understand the scope management process, your plan will set you and your team up for success.

What is the purpose of a scope management plan?

The purpose of a scope management plan is to create project structure by documenting the resources required to achieve the project objectives. Your scope management plan will also reduce the chance of scope creep.

A scope management process helps you avoid common problems, including:

Constantly changing requirements

Overspending

Wasted time

Failure to meet deadlines

What is project scope?

Your project scope sets the boundaries for your project and defines the project goals, deadlines, and deliverables. When you clarify your project scope, you're structuring your project around what your team will and won't do and providing goals and objectives for them to work toward.

The entire team should be involved in defining the project scope. This means communicating with key stakeholders and writing up a project scope statement that outlines requirements of the project. For example, if you're defining a scope for a new advertising campaign, you'll want to ensure the design team, the content team, and the digital marketing team all agree on the details in the scope statement.

What is scope creep?

Scope creep occurs when your project exceeds your initial scope statement. For example, scope creep may occur if a stakeholder adds an additional project deliverable after the project has begun.

Unexpected project changes can lead to increased project risks like missed timelines, increased budgets, overwork, or a low-quality end product. There are various reasons why scope creep can occur. Some reasons include:

Unclear project scope

Unrealistic project objectives

Too many stakeholders

Poor scope management

Poor communication with stakeholders

To avoid scope creep, you need to plan against it, which is where a strong scope management plan comes into play.

6 steps to create a project scope management plan

The Project Management Institute's (PMI) Project Management Body of Knowledge (PMBOK® Guide) offers a standard, six step project scope management process. These six steps help you create a solid scope management plan to keep your project on track.

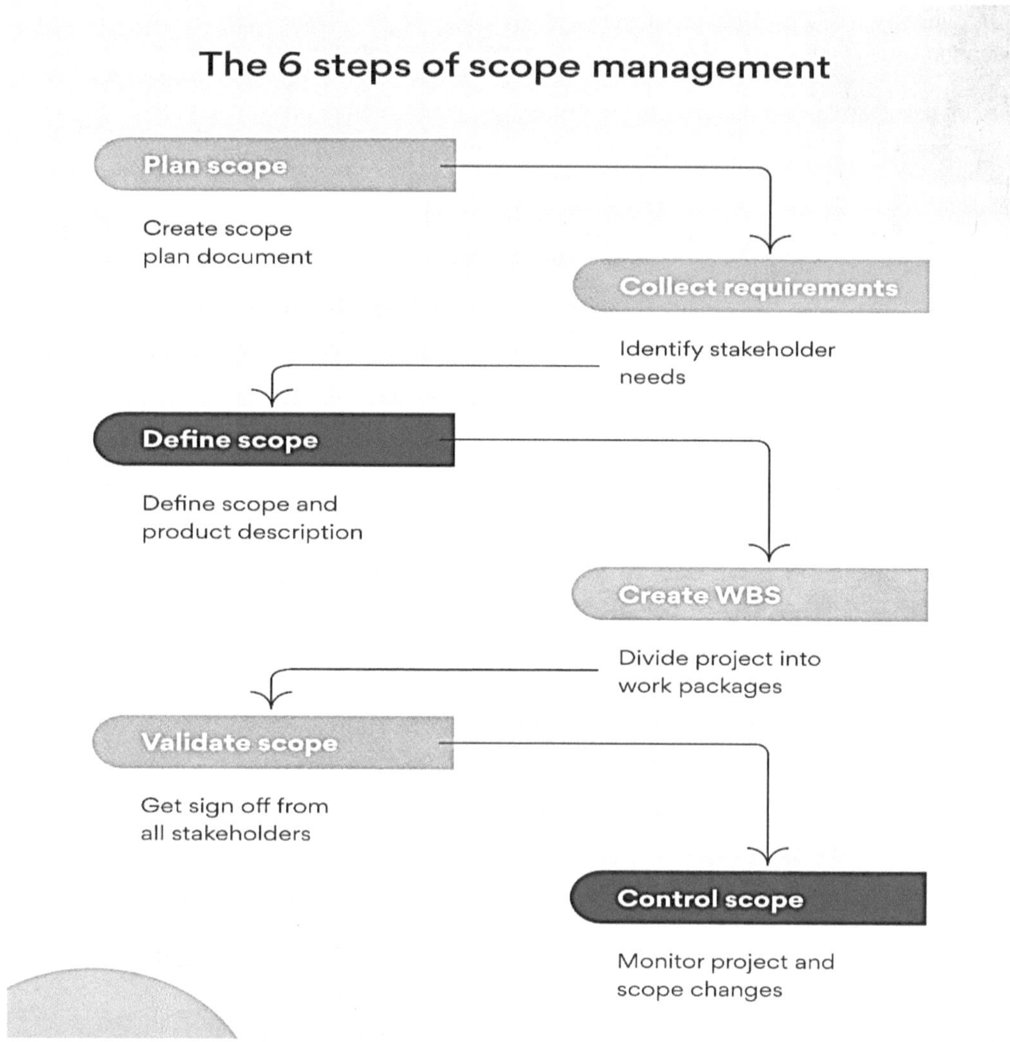

1. Create your scope plan

The first step in the planning process involves creating your scope plan document. This document should include your scope statement, a breakdown of project requirements, and any expected deliverables for the project.

Your scope plan document may also include a change control process, which is a process for change requests that can prevent scope creep. This is a document you can refer to in later stages of project planning. You may need this document for complex projects, projects where you think stakeholders will want many deliverables, or when there's a lot of flux in what your deliverables might be.

Tips for creating a scope plan:

Incorporate expert judgement: To create your scope planning document, you need to consider all parts of the organizational process. Check in with cross-functional and executive stakeholders to ensure you have all of the information you need.

Hold scope kickoff meetings: Before you lock your scope document, make sure you have buy-in from all stakeholders. Share your scope plan document asynchronously, or host a kickoff meeting so that other managers and team members involved in the project can contribute to the initial scope statement.

2. Collect project requirements

In this step of the process, you'll identify stakeholders' needs so you can meet project objectives. Your goal should be to gather an in-depth list of requirements from stakeholders so that you can prevent scope changes down the line.

Tips for collecting project requirements:

Create a project charter: Create a project charter, or an elevator pitch, so stakeholders can clearly understand the project and ensure their expectations match the project's objectives.

Hold focus groups or workshops: Hold focus groups or workshops to give stakeholders a better understanding of your project. Communicating your project objectives to stakeholders is essential if you want them to buy into your project scope.

Develop prototypes: Develop a prototype of your project deliverable before presenting your project to stakeholders. This way, stakeholders can visualize the end product and voice their concerns or list additional requirements early on.

3. Define scope

Once you've collected requirements from stakeholders, turn that information into a well-defined scope and a detailed product description. This document clarifies the expectations and deliverables for the project so that all team members know what they must accomplish.

Tips for defining scope:

Try product analysis: Before you can define your scope and write a detailed product description, you need to do an in-depth product analysis. Analyze the product you plan to create from the eyes of the customer or client in order to determine whether it will meet their expectations.

Generate alternatives: You'll also want to generate alternatives in case your project encounters risks. For example, how will you meet stakeholder needs if you're planning a new product launch and your launch date gets delayed?

Facilitate workshops: Host brainstorming workshops to clarify the scope of the project and to encourage collaboration among team members.

4. Create a work breakdown structure

A work breakdown structure (WBS) is a way to divide your project into levels of tasks. When you create a WBS, your team can clearly visualize each component of the project and assess what needs to get done.

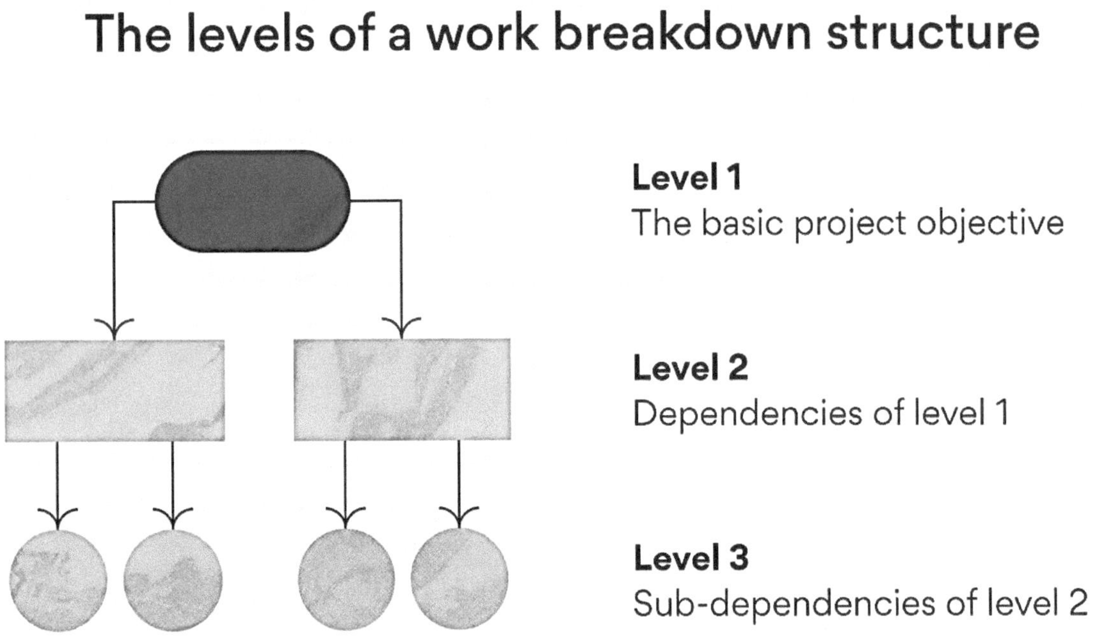

A work breakdown structure creates a hierarchical structure of tasks. From there, you can schedule, monitor, and control your project.

Tips for creating a WBS:

Decompose your project objective: A WBS decomposes, or breaks down, your project objective into dependencies and sub-dependencies. These smaller groups of tasks are often referred to as work packages. Once you break your tasks down, you have clear insight into everything your project needs, including the hours, equipment, tools, and expenses.

Automate workflows: Automating team member workflows can streamline coordination on projects and enhance project visibility. Using software to automate these workflows will also reduce manual information-gathering and duplicative work.

5. Validate scope

Validating your scope simply means getting sign-off from all stakeholders involved in the project. Make sure stakeholders clearly understand your project deliverables to avoid future scope creep. If possible, get feedback or advice on any changes and improvements.

Tips to validate scope:

Inspect your plan: Because validation is the final sign-off for your scope management plan, you'll want to review and inspect it thoroughly. Team members can help you inspect the plan before sending it off to stakeholders, but stakeholders should also participate in a final inspection so that the plan gets as many eyes on it as possible.

6. Control scope

The last step in your scope management plan is scope control. As your project continues into the execution phase, monitor the status of the project and manage changes to the scope. The best way to streamline scope control is to use project management software. These tools can share feedback, files, and status updates on your project so you're aware of any scope changes in real time.

Tips to control scope:

Analyze variance: In this part of the scope management plan, assess how much variance in scope occurs. Analyzing the actual performance of your scope versus the planned performance will give you insight for future projects.

Refer to change control document: You created a change control process earlier in the planning phase. Remember to refer to this document so you can track the flow of information when it comes to project changes.

9.7.3 Work Breakdown Structure (WBS)

A work breakdown structure (WBS) is a project management tool that decomposes the total work required to deliver a product, service, or project into smaller, more manageable components. A WBS provides a hierarchical view of your project's scope, translating overall strategies and objectives into specific goals, workflows, project phases, and action plans.

What is the purpose of a work breakdown structure?

In project management, you'll use work breakdown structures for several reasons:

To identify the project tasks that make up the critical path of your project

To schedule activities that comprise the performance measurement baseline (PMB)

To define the deliverables for your project

To plan your resources, timelines, and priorities

To get a clearer picture of the risks the project may face as it progresses

Project planning, scheduling, and budgeting

The **top level** of your WBS represents the project's final deliverable, or end product. It represents the project scope statement. The **lower levels** break down the scope into more detailed deliverables and individual tasks. All these **sub-elements** can have time and cost estimates associated with them. When combined, they form a total estimate of what's required for the project team to complete the project within its defined scope. This makes it possible for you to plan, schedule, and form budgets based on the details of the project, rather than relying on high-level guesstimates.

Risk management, resource management, task management, and team management

The work breakdown structure lets you dissect the project to understand how it all fits together and create a Gannt chart that provides clear focus and critical path requirements.

When you create a WBS, you're required to think through each activity in detail to define all the work necessary to complete it. In doing so, you'll identify risks that may impact your project. These can go on the risk register, and you can then form an appropriate project risk plan.

You will also identify the resources needed to complete each task, which will help you plan how many people you need on your team and when you need them. This will help you manage your team during the project life cycle because you can assign each task to a team member with the required expertise.

Benefits of using a work breakdown structure

Better communication with your team members regarding tasks

Clearer definition of the deliverables that need to be produced during each project stage

More accurate time estimates for each task because you can see precisely what needs to be done for each step of the project

Easier identification of critical path items, so you can take steps to reduce risks to these tasks (e.g., add resources or assign another team member to help complete it)

More easily identify which tasks should be done by whom because you can see where the expertise is needed most.

Types of WBS

There are different types of work breakdown structures that you can use to define deliverables and schedule tasks:

1. Process-oriented WBS

A process-oriented WBS decomposes work into the processes needed to accomplish it, such as requirements, design, development, and testing. The advantage of this type of breakdown structure is that it clarifies tasks and assigns task owners. It also makes it easy to assign resources and estimate time because they can be assigned at each level of the structure. Process-oriented WBS provides clear milestones and thus is often preferred by clients.

2. Phase-based work breakdown structure

Similar to a process-oriented WBS, a phase-based WBS is a project management approach that breaks projects down into phases, each of which has its own purpose and features. The phases are usually broken down into smaller tasks, which are typically broken down even further into simpler tasks.

3. Deliverable-oriented WBS

A deliverable-oriented WBS is a hierarchical tree structure of the project and its components. It decomposes work into tangible products or services, such as database schema, and user manuals. It shows the connection between the high-level deliverables and the work to be done. The deliverable-based WBS organizes the work horizontally as related activities, providing a view of the entire project from start to finish.

The advantage of this type of breakdown structure is that it gives an overview of the deliverables required for a project. This type of WBS is most appreciated by project teams and management.

4. Resource breakdown structure

The resource breakdown structure (RBS) is used to identify all of the resources required to complete each work package in the WBS and for the project. It can be developed by starting with the work packages in the WBS, then collecting all of the resources needed to complete each work package, and finally organizing them into a hierarchical structure based on their similarity or specialty.

The goal of the RBS is to ensure that all necessary resources are available to carry out the project and that there are no conflicts in their usage, which could delay the project.

5. Risk breakdown structure

A risk breakdown structure (Risk BS) is used to organize risks into categories and subcategories in a way that helps you manage them effectively. Risk categories may be defined by type, risk source, or other means deemed appropriate for your project.

A risk category would be something like cost, schedule, quality, or scope. Risk subcategories would be more specific risk types within each category. For example, under cost risks, you might have subcategories like labor rates, material costs, or budget overruns.

6. Cost breakdown structure

A cost breakdown structure (CBS) shows the estimated cost of each element of the project. For example, the cost of a website is made up of hosting, programming, design, and content creation. The CBS makes it easier to estimate a project budget and control costs.

7. Organizational breakdown structure

An organizational breakdown structure (OBS) shows how roles are assigned within an organization. For example, a medium-sized online business might have a chief technology officer, chief operating officer, chief executive officer, and other roles, each with different responsibilities.

What are the elements of work breakdown structure?

A work breakdown structure is comprised of several key components:

WBS dictionary: The WBS dictionary documents each component with its definition, estimated effort, and performance measurements. It allows you to define each step of the WBS and how it will be executed.

WBS levels: The WBS levels provide context for each portion of the project and determine the hierarchy of tasks and deliverables.

Project deliverables: Project deliverables are the desired outcomes of project tasks. They are grouped into work packages.

Work packages: A work package is the lowest level in the WBS. It represents the work needed to accomplish a specific deliverable. Work packages describe activities that can be planned, scheduled, and controlled by one person. Once completed, it should be possible to hand over the work package to another person.

Planning packages: are used as an independent planning horizon for one or more work packages that will be completed in the future. They help to summarize the project plan at different levels.

Control accounts: Control accounts help control costs and schedules on projects with very large budgets or when a large part of the budget or duration applies to only one or two major deliverables. Control accounts function like work packages with some additional requirements. Control accounts are usually created for major parts of the project, such as phases and key deliverables.

Tasks: Tasks are work packages broken down into smaller activities so they can be scheduled, monitored, and controlled by one person.

How to create a work breakdown structure

A WBS helps everyone on the project team understand what needs to be completed, who's responsible for each task, how tasks relate to one another, when things should be done, and how much they will cost. Follow these steps to create a WBS.

1. Define the project scope.

Start by identifying the overall project goal, the deliverables, boundaries, and deadlines. What are the major outcomes that your team needs to achieve in order to complete the project? What does the project include and exclude?

2. Gather critical documents.

Gather critical documents, including:

Project management plan, outlining the project's execution, monitoring, scheduling, and resources.

Risk register, detailing potential risks and mitigation strategies.

Project scope statement, outlining the project's objectives, deliverables, and boundaries.

3. Create a hierarchy.

Organize the project into a hierarchical structure, with the major deliverables as the highest level.

4. Decompose project components.

Break down each deliverable into smaller, manageable tasks or work packages that can be assigned and tracked.

5. Identify key team members.

Determine the individual or team who'll be responsible for each task. This step will ensure accountability and help project team members communicate effectively.

6. Create the WBS dictionary.

After decomposition, create the WBS dictionary that documents the project's key information, including the time and resources needed for each task and the relationships between each tasks. The WBS dictionary can be represented as an outline or a diagram. Use boxes for each work package and lines to indicate the relationships between them.

7. Create a Gantt chart schedule.

After reviewing and validating the WBS thus far, create a Gannt chart schedule. The schedule is one of the most important components of a project management plan and will be used to monitor progress throughout the life of the project.

9.7.4 Creating a Project Schedule

Identify tasks you need to accomplish

Before creating a project schedule, you need to identify all the tasks you should accomplish to complete the project. It may seem like a challenging task, but there are a few ways to make it simpler. First, take a close look at the project goals and objectives. It will give you a good idea of what you need to do to achieve the desired outcome.

Next, break the project down into smaller manageable parts. Once you have a list of all the tasks you need to finish, you can start creating your project schedule. Common examples in software engineering in this phase could be developing use cases, creating class diagrams, writing code, etc.

Estimate the duration of each task

Next, you will need to estimate the time required to complete each task. You can do this using a bottom-up estimation technique, which involves breaking each task into smaller subtasks and assessing the time required for each subtask. Once you have estimated the time needed for each task, you can create a project timeline by assigning start and end dates to each task.

Allocate resources

One of the most critical steps in creating a project schedule is allocating resources. It includes identifying the human, financial, and material resources necessary to complete the project.

Once you have identified these resources, it is essential to determine how to use them. For example, if a project requires many materials, it may be necessary to purchase them in advance. Similarly, hiring additional staff or bringing in outside contractors may be needed if a project requires a great deal of labor.

By carefully allocating resources, it is possible to create a project schedule that meets the project's needs while staying within budget.

9.7.5 Risk Identification and Management

Risk identification is not a rigid process that you follow step-by-step. Instead, good risk identification comes from communication and collaboration with all project stakeholders.

Moreover, you need to educate others on how to use your risk management process.

Let me explain how it works in the real world with real people.

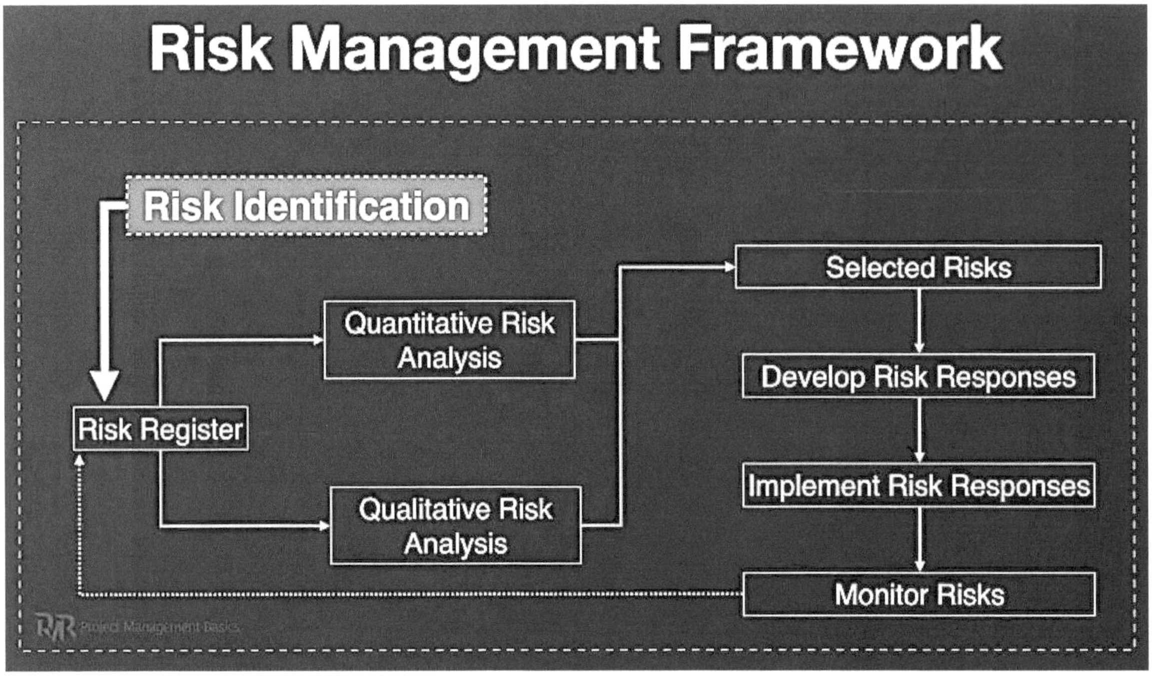

What is Risk Identification?

Risk identification is an effort to discover threats and opportunities that may impact a project, its feasibility, or its management plan by applying risk identification techniques.

As a result, you need to capture all identified risks into a Risk Register.

Note that risk identification is the first step in the process. You will continue analyzing risks in the next steps of your risk management process.

The project organiser must identify the project's risk as early as feasible to minimize the risk's impact via appropriate risk management planning.

A project can be favourable to a wide range of risks. To detect a significant risk that could have an impact on a project. It is essential to categorize the risks into various risk classes.

Several types of risks can impact a software product; a few of them are defined below:

Technology Risks: Risks arising from the software or hardware technologies utilised to construct the system.

People Risks: Risks associated with an individual of the development team.

Organizational Risks: Risks arise due to the organization in which the software is being produced.

Tools Risks: Risks arising from the software tools and other support software used to build the system.

Requirement Risks: Risks associated with changes in client requirements and the process of managing those changes.

Estimation Risks: Risks arising from management estimates of the resources necessary to create the system.

When Do You Perform Risk Identification?

In practice, you should use an integrated risk management approach. This means that you should talk through possible risks for each and every activity during the project.

For example, when you collect requirements and write specifications, you and your team should always be on the lookout for risks:

Track all the assumptions you make.

Check if the requirements are ambiguous, i.e., do people understand the exact same requirements differently?

Don't hide uncertainties. Instead, transform them into risks.

But that's not enough. You also need in-depth risk identification sessions at specific critical points in project planning where you take a broader look at the project as a whole.

For example, here are some important moments at which to consider the need for dedicated risk identification sessions:

When clients identified the project goal.

After you've identified key stakeholders.

When you've reviewed risk categories for the first time.

After you've collected most of the requirements.

After you've created a draft of the work breakdown structure (WBS).

After you've identified the required resources.

After you've drafted the project schedule.
After you've drafted the project budget.

How to Identify a Risk?

Risk identification technique is an approach to discovering threats you were unaware of by collaborating with project stakeholders.
We use just a handful of risk identification techniques in practice. The most popular risk identification techniques are:
Talking about risks (not a real technique, but I'll explain it below).
Checklists (risk categories).
Document analysis.
Root cause analysis.
Assumptions analysis.
Brainstorming.
Interviews.
Now, you need to understand when to use them and how to apply them to your project management documentation.
You'll capture all identified risks into the Risk Register.

How to Use Risk Identification Techniques

Some techniques, like brainstorming, are universal. You can apply them to anything on a project.
Other techniques, like requirements analysis, are specific to a piece of project documentation, and you do it once.
You don't always use all the techniques on everything. However, you might apply several techniques to one input. For example:
You can review the project schedule with the team **(#1)** and brainstorm **(#2)** possible threats. After that, you'll check common risk sources in the risk categories **(#3)**. Then, you'll take the schedule to a senior project manager and interview **(#4)** her to get her insights.
Notice how we used four different techniques on the same piece of project documentation. Of course, not all artifacts require so much attention. However, for example, I recommend putting more effort into the project budget and schedule.
Overall, it all boils down to efficiently using your time and resources. Keep in mind that risk management is not free of charge. You use time and resources from your project.
Now, let me give you some real-life examples.

Risk Identification Examples

In real life, it's tough to make risk identification techniques timely and efficient. The key is to keep things simple. Team members and stakeholders should be able to use them without special training or experience.
That's why I've selected these seven techniques you can use on any project, no matter how experienced you are.

1: Continuously Discuss Possible Risks

In the real world, we continuously identify risks. It's the most effective approach.
But it's not a casual conversation. It has specific rules and agreements. That's why you need to educate all team members and stakeholders in your risk management process.
In essence, you need to ensure that everyone has the same understanding of the following:
Importance of risk management.
Responsibility of each person in risk management.
What is a risk, and what is a fact?
How do we capture risks in the risk register?
How do we handle risks in general?
It will ensure that you use the same terminology and mean the same thing when talking about project risks.
Therefore, when you have a shared vision of risk management, you can incorporate risk identification into every project activity. For example, you can ask something along the lines of:
Do you see any risks here?
How risky is this approach?
Please provide a list of risks along with estimates.
Let's think about possible risks.
What may go wrong with this plan?
So, all other techniques below will have sporadic or one-time appearances. However, talking about risks happens daily.

2: Analyze Risk Categories to Discover Typical Risks

Most organizations carry out projects of a similar nature. Processes and policies are the same. Some stakeholders never change. So, a new project inherits all the same sources of risks from your environment.

Risk categories are just a list of these common sources of risks in your organization.

In practice, that means all organizations in the same niche share the same sources of risks. So, this technique is really worth your time because you can reuse it throughout your whole career.

The list of risk categories comes from lessons learned in risk management. Ideally, project managers should share these lessons with others. However, that is rarely the case.

That's why you won't find such a list in your organization. What's even worse, for the same reasons, you probably don't even have your own list of risk categories right now. But I've got you covered. You can use my list of categories.

So, risk categories technique:

helps you to identify risks that you may not be aware of;

prevents you from forgetting about some risk sources; and

structures your risk identification efforts.

The process is simple – you need to get through the list to identify risks that may apply to your current project. You can approach this in different ways.

You may review the list alone and shortlist the categories, then discuss the shortlist with your team. Or, you can brainstorm through the whole list with your team. Usually, the best time to do this is when you already know the project's scope of work.

I also recommend keeping the list close at hand as a cheat sheet or template for other risk identification sessions. It will be a good starting point for identifying new possible sources of risks.

3: Perform Requirements Review

A requirements review is just one part of assessing the project documentation, but I want to focus on it separately because it's critical.

Requirements contain significant risks for a project. Therefore, you need to analyze them to find any ambiguous or unclear aspects. This review will help you assess how much work is required to fulfill each requirement.

Poor requirements are the number one cause of project failure. However, it's not just their quality and level of detail: It's also important to have enough time to analyze the project specifications.

You need to have a chance to review and discuss each requirement with the team, with the big picture in mind. You need to ensure that the requirements don't conflict with one another. Not giving yourself the time to do all of this is a risk in itself!

In the real world, you clarify requirements throughout the whole project's lifetime. Therefore, you need to re-evaluate the risks progressively here. So, here's what you need to do in practice:

Select some requirements.

Select a group for analysis (the whole team or just group leaders).

Let them read through the specifications, designs, and emails.

Plan a meeting to analyze the requirements.

Let one person explain the requirements to the others.

Clarify requirements to the point where everyone has the same understanding.

If you have never done this before, try it at least once, even if just out of curiosity. You'll notice that different people read the same words and sentences differently.

Likewise, I'm a big fan of visualizing workflows, information flows, and user experience.

If your product, service, or result has a user interface or any tangible form, take time to draw it out. You will identify a lot of new use cases, weak spots in requirements, and inconsistencies. As the old saying goes, a picture is worth a thousand words.

4: Review the Project Management Plan with the Team

This is the more general part of reviewing project documentation that can be applied to any assessment of risks.

So, what documents should you review to find risks? The answer is every one! For example, once you have a first draft of the project management plan, review it with your team.

First of all, engaging the project team in the planning activities is vital. So you need to ensure their buy-in from the start. A disengaged and unmotivated team that doesn't believe in the project plan is a huge risk by itself.

On the other hand, your team is the primary source of information and risks. When you walk the whole team through the project plan, I can promise that each person will find at least one risk related to them. It's better to find out such risks early and adjust the plan accordingly.

There are many aspects that you need to talk about with the team. At the very least, you need to discuss the following:

Units of measurement. Did they provide estimates in effective or ideal hours, working days, etc.?

What did they include in those estimates? Is there a buffer?

Do they know how to report the money they spend?

Do they know how to log their progress and when?

Do they know your project management approach in general? What about risk management?
Do they understand the definition of a completed task?
The list goes on and on. Never assume that team members see and understand your plan the same way as you do. Moreover, don't assume that all team members have a common understanding of all project activities.

Risk Management Plan Template

(For Software Projects)

Most software project managers don't know what goes into a Risk Management Plan. So, they simply don't write it out. **Unfortunately, this often leads to problems.**

Get my template and use it as a starting point. In addition, you get access to all related risk management resources I have.

This template will eliminate the guesswork for you. With minor adjustments, you'll be proud to present your risk management plan to the team and stakeholders.

Once I have a draft of a schedule, I show it to the team. They review dependencies, the flow of tasks, and any buffers that we have. They also think through their personal plans, vacations, and other errands.

For example, a team member sees the project schedule. He has several critical tasks next week. Then, suddenly, he remembers that he's planning an important trip he has not told you about yet. You can then adjust the schedule to allow for his absence.

Moreover, different parts of your project always depend on others, and you want to make sure that nothing blocks your progress. So, team members may discover hard dependencies that I've missed. Therefore, it helps me to correct the plan early on and include these possible delays.

I use the same process to verify our Work Breakdown Structure (WBS). Draft after draft, I collect feedback from the team and correct the WBS. This often reveals insufficient details in requirements. Therefore, we need to take a step back. Occasionally, we discover a new piece of work when we look at the product as a whole.

I also recommend creating and reviewing project workflows. At the very least, you need them for the following:
starting, reporting on, and finishing a task;
identifying and controlling risks;
reporting on project status;
identifying and fixing defects;
integrating a change request; and
elaborating requirements from concept to an approved specification.

5: Use Brainstorming and Interviews Techniques for Deeper Analysis

In general, I don't like to identify risks with wild brainstorming. However, there are critical points in project planning when I use brainstorming for risk identification on a higher level. These are:
when analyzing essential requirements;
while reviewing the WBS;
when reviewing the schedule and HR plan;
while creating a quality management plan; and
before finalizing the whole project management plan.

6: Apply Root Cause Analysis for Systematic Risks

In practice, I use root cause analysis for risk identification in three scenarios:

To analyze severe problems of past projects. It might be my previous project. It might be a similar one in the organization carried out by another project manager. It can also be relevant notes from lessons learned or a list of risk categories.

When I'm trying to solve a systematic problem. This usually relates to inefficient communications, poor-quality, inaccurate estimates; or ambiguity in requirements.

To group all identified risks by the root cause. It helps to see the primary sources of problems and identify even more risks.

So, in a real-world project, you don't carry out root cause analysis during planning. Usually, it's a post-mortem or analysis after a significant problem.

7: Analyze Assumptions to Identify the Most Impactful Risks

By nature, assumptions involve risks. If an assumption is wrong, a project is in trouble.

So, first of all, you need to keep track of all major assumptions. I keep a separate list of project-level assumptions. In addition, I log all assumptions related to specific requirements right in the specification document. After that, you need to review and validate the assumptions regularly.

We make assumptions all the time. But most are made right at the start of a project. So, they may impact the project later down the road. Assumptions that you make due to problems in the organization are the most risky. These include the following:
An assumption that you'll get the required resources in time. Why?! Do recruiters always hire people quickly?
An assumption that your SME will be available for your project. But what if he's assigned full time to another critical project?
An assumption that a third party will provide their deliverables on time. Usually, they don't, and the whole project stalls.
You need to work hard to validate an assumption and either make it a fact or transform it into a known risk.

Risk Management

A risk is a probable problem- it might happen or it might not. There are main two characteristics of risk
Uncertainty- the risk may or may not happen that means there are no 100% risks.
loss – If the risk occurs in reality , undesirable result or losses will occur.
Risk management is a sequence of steps that help a software team to understand , analyze and manage uncertainty.
Risk management consists of
Risk Identification
Risk analysis
Risk Planning
Risk Monitoring

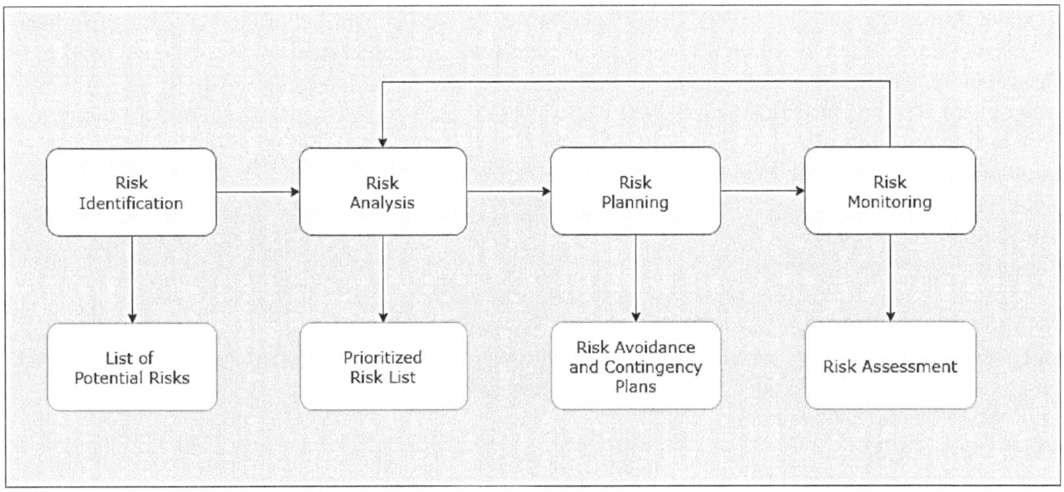

A computer code project may be laid low with an outsized sort of risk. so as to be ready to consistently establish the necessary risks which could have an effect on a computer code project, it's necessary to reason risks into completely different categories. The project manager will then examine the risks from every category square measure relevant to the project.
There are mainly 3 classes of risks that may have an effect on a computer code project:
Project Risks:
Project risks concern various sorts of monetary funds, schedules, personnel, resource, and customer-related issues. a vital project risk is schedule slippage. Since computer code is intangible, it's terribly tough to observe and manage a computer code project. it's terribly tough to manage one thing that can not be seen. For any producing project, like producing cars, the project manager will see the merchandise taking form.
For example, see that the engine is fitted, at the moment the area of the door unit fitted, the automotive is obtaining painted, etc. so he will simply assess the progress of the work and manage it. The physical property of the merchandise being developed is a vital reason why several computer codes come to suffer from the danger of schedule slippage.
Technical Risks:
Technical risks concern potential style, implementation, interfacing, testing, and maintenance issues. Technical risks conjointly embody ambiguous specifications, incomplete specification, dynamic specification, technical uncertainty, and technical degeneration. Most technical risks occur thanks to the event team's lean information concerning the project.
Business Risks:

This type of risk embodies the risks of building a superb product that nobody needs, losing monetary funds or personal commitments, etc.

Other risk categories

1. Known risks: Those risks that can be uncovered after careful assessment of the project program, the business and technical environment in which the plan is being developed, and more reliable data sources (e.g., unrealistic delivery date)

2. Predictable risks: Those risks that are hypothesized from previous project experience (e.g., past turnover)

3. Unpredictable risks: Those risks that can and do occur, but are extremely tough to identify in advance.

Principle of Risk Management

Global Perspective: In this, we review the bigger system description, design, and implementation. We look at the chance and the impact the risk is going to have.

Take a forward-looking view: Consider the threat which may appear in the future and create future plans for directing the next events.

Open Communication: This is to allow the free flow of communications between the client and the team members so that they have certainty about the risks.

Integrated management: In this method risk management is made an integral part of project management.

Continuous process: In this phase, the risks are tracked continuously throughout the risk management paradigm.

9.7.6 RMMM (Risk Mitigation, Monitoring, and Management)

9.7.6.1 Risk Mitigation for Risk m

In this section several different software development risks will be identified, a plan will be created to avoid these risks. We will think of the risks possible and of the way to keep the software development process from encountering these risks. It is important to have mitigation plan to avoid risks once and for all. Goal is to attack the risk even before it comes into existence. The plan will help in identifying the possible risks and to monitor them.

Product Size

In this risk concern is of under or overestimation (mainly underestimation) of the number of Function Points. If we estimate too few LOC (line of code) necessary for the project we may get wrong cost figures which can prove fatal to the software development plan. To avoid this from happening we will use conservative figures to reduce the probability of the risk. This means we will overestimate the LOC a little. If we end up finishing the project earlier than that will not create any troubles. If the software cost estimations are passed with higher than actual cost required to deliver the product, the software development team can get credited for finishing the product sooner. Also for any reason the delivery dates get pushed back development team can still deliver the product on the time. In normal circumstances companies are not picky about the product size, so increasing the number will not cause any troubles in getting approval for the project.

Business Impact

In this risk category we are concerned about the quality of the final product. As mitigation step we will spend more time with the users to understand their needs. This way we can gather all the information necessary for the project to be successful. We will try to understand business environment and can try to provide the user with help in defining software requirements. More the time team spends with the customer better the understating the team will have regarding the software inspection.

Customer (User) Risks

If the users of the product fail to participate during the different phases of the software development we fail to recognize problems with the software. To avoid this in the mitigation phase we will try to meet the customer frequently and present software in phases so that customer and we can have better understanding the software being developed. More the time team spends with the customer better the understating the team will have regarding the software. This will help in coming up with just right product at right price for the customer. If customer fails to mention some special operations that have to performed with totally separate checklist and have to be stored separately, software development team does not know anything about it thus leaving big problem in the software.

Process Risks

We want quality of the product to be as high as possible. To achieve this we will set up guidelines to be followed for each of the team members during all the phases of the software development cycle. The standard will be set and defined for all of the software development. This will help the team in delivering the high quality product thus increasing our reputation in the market. This will help bring in more clients in the future. It will also save customer from getting low quality product. For example, palm size PC checklists are easy to get used too. If inspector can not get used to the forms in the PC they may go back to using pen and paper which is not good for the reputation of the team.

Technology Risks
To avoid risk of using technology that may become obsolete in few years after the product have been developed. We will do excessive research on what technology to use for software development and will use the latest technology (programming languages etc.) to avoid this risk. Software development team has to make sure that the equipment requested (i.e. Palm-size PC) are current and will not be obsolete in near future.
Development Risks
If the necessary tools are not provided to all of the team members, their work will lack quantity and quality. As mitigation phase we will make sure that the budget includes cost for latest technology and tools needed to achieve the desired product. For example if the government refused to deliver the Palm-size PC to the DEQ the PC integration part will be useless until the units are actually bought.
Employee Risks (Team members)
This risk concerns the knowledge and of the employees and their willingness to help make the project succeed. As mitigation step of this risk, we will make sure that someone in all of the project development phases knows exactly what to do and the tools to use to achieve the goals. If the employees that have little knowledge in the main software implementation language fails to learn it, it may cause big problems when coding part begins.
9.7.6.2 Risk Monitoring for Risk m
In this section we will identify the conditions to monitor to determine whether risk m is becoming more or less likely.
Product Size
To monitor the risk here, we will keep track of the number of functions necessary for the program throughout the entire development cycle. This will tell us if the project may come across risk in future. We will keep tack of the Visual Basic code produced during the coding. We will also keep stack of the code required for the integration of the Palm size PC. We will also be concerned about the size of the database. The number of table and number of tuples in each table. All of the above will help us in monitoring the size of the product.
Business Impact
As monitoring step in this risk, we will setup user meetings to show them the work that has been completed and to get user input on the work. We will have meetings every other week to present the work that has been done from the time of the last meeting. This will help team in staying in touch with the customers and will also be very efficient way to derive customer's input on the progress made. It will also be a way to get customer insight on the project, which will help us determine the changes that we may have to make to the software upon customer's request.
Customer (User) Risks
To monitor this risk, we will monitor the successes of the meeting by keeping track of people that have attended the meeting. If the outcome of the meeting is low, we can contact responsible person to help us overcome this problem. We will also have the login charts to show the customer who is attending the meetings and who needs to be reminded to start attending meetings.
Process Risks
To monitor the risk here we will review each other's work to find the problems and to help each other in achieving better product quality. We will also have the general guidelines set for all of the work to be carried on for the software development. Software development team will constantly check each other's work; will compare it with the set guidelines, and will inform a team member who is failing to participate in following the guidelines.
Technology Risks
For monitoring phase during the development of the software we will keep eye on new technology. This will help us to keep up with new technology. For example, plan will be drawn to use multiple set of the Palm-size PC so team can see if the different brand PC with same operation system is capable of carrying the task needed to perform checklist operations.
Development Risks
For monitoring phase during the development of the software we will keep eye on tools being used and their effectiveness. This will help us to keep up with new technology. We will keep track of the new equipment being brought into use at DEQ. We will also look r the availability of the inexpensive equipment that may provide help in completion of this project.
Employee Risks (Teammates)
Monitoring and managing of this risk will include looking out for each other, that is if some team-member is having difficulties in performing some tasks or using particular tool or technique other members of that team will help him out. This is where team members may have to spend little time with each other learning or teaching what others know.
9.7.6.3 Risk Management for Risk m
In this section we will identify several different software development risks and will try to create a plan to manage these risks if they do occur.

Product Size

After careful monitoring of the process, if we still end up with underestimation of the FP we will put more man-hours into the project. This is the only way that we think we can manage the risk.

Business Impact

If a mistake has been made, user input on the completed work will provide us with information to fix or improve the software. We have done very many meeting with the clients and plan to do meeting every two weeks; this should clear any misunderstandings between the software development team and customers. This is the best way to go at since the work that is done on the project is revealed during the meetings and customer gets chance to make adjustments necessary.

Customer (User) Risks

If the turn out in the meetings is not encouraging, we will pass out questionnaire to easily gather customers' view. We will ask them question rather than waiting for them to ask us questions. We will also talk to the manager at the DEQ to help us come up with plan that will increase the attendance during the meeting. If the outcomes of the meetings is satisfactory there should not be any major difficulties regarding customer risks.

Process Risks

If the problem exists with the quality of the work, the quality assurance plan will be revised in the risk management phase. Other team member will attempt to take over or swap the work of the member whose work does not meet the quality standards.

Technology Risks

For monitoring phase during the development of the software we will keep eye on new technology. If we spot new techniques that can be implement without major changes in our project, we will include such techniques in the development of the project. We will also keep a look out for major shifts in the technology and how it affects the software that we are working on. If there is a need change in the technology will be discussed among team members and will be presented to the client. If client agrees necessary changes will be made with the existing technology.

Development Risks

In the management phase if the funding for the technology and tools are not enough, we will have to reschedule the phases of software development cycle to allow more time to coding phase. We will provide information on the several different Palm-size PC's and will let the customer to choose the one that is most appropriate for the customer to buy. We will also make sure that the equipment is allowed to be purchased under government controls and contracts.

Employee Risks (Team members)

Monitoring and managing of this risk will include looking out for each other, that is if some team-member is having difficulties in performing some tasks or using particular tool or technique other members of that team will help him out.

Drawbacks of RMMM:

It incurs additional project costs.

It takes additional time.

For larger projects, implementing an RMMM may itself turn out to be another tedious project.

RMMM does not guarantee a risk-free project, infact, risks may also come up after the project is delivered.

9.8 Component- Based Software Engineering

Component-Based Software Engineering (CBSE) is an approach to software development where software systems are built by assembling pre-existing software components. These components can be individual modules, libraries, or even full-fledged software systems that are designed to work together. The CBSE process involves the selection, adaptation, and integration of these components to create a new software system. Here's an example to illustrate the CBSE process:

Example: Building an E-commerce Website using CBSE

Imagine a software development team tasked with building an e-commerce website. Instead of developing every aspect of the website from scratch, they decide to use the CBSE approach.

1. Component Identification:

Component 1: The team identifies a pre-existing e-commerce shopping cart component, which provides features like adding products to a cart, managing the cart contents, and handling transactions.

Component 2: They also identify a user authentication component, allowing users to register, log in, and manage their profiles.

Component 3: A payment gateway component is chosen to handle payment processing.

2. Component Selection:

The team evaluates various available components and selects those that best meet the project's requirements and are compatible with each other.
They choose a shopping cart component developed by a third-party vendor, an open-source user authentication component, and a payment gateway service with an API.

3. Component Adaptation:

While the selected components provide most of the required functionality, they may need to be adapted or customized to fit the specific needs of the e-commerce website.
For the user authentication component, the team may customize the login and registration pages to match the website's design and branding.

4. Integration:

The team integrates the selected components into the e-commerce website project. This includes connecting the user authentication system to the shopping cart and payment gateway.
They ensure that data flows seamlessly between components, and APIs are used effectively.

5. Testing:

Rigorous testing is performed to ensure that the integrated components work together without issues. This involves functional testing, integration testing, and testing various use cases, such as adding products to the cart, making payments, and user account management.

6. Deployment:

After successful testing, the e-commerce website, built by integrating components, is deployed to a production server and made available to users.

7. Maintenance and Updates:

The team regularly monitors and maintains the e-commerce website, keeping the integrated components up-to-date.
If a security update is released for the user authentication component, they apply the update to maintain security.
In this example, CBSE allows the development team to leverage existing, well-tested components for the e-commerce website, which can significantly reduce development time, costs, and risks. It also ensures that the website benefits from the reliability and scalability of components that have been used in other projects.

Exercise

Exercise 1 – MCQ

Q 1. Which of the following is NOT a key knowledge area in software project management according to the Project Management Institute (PMI)?

A. Scope management B. Time management
C. Quality management D. Budget management

Q 2. Which software project management activity involves defining and documenting the features and functions of the software product?

A. Risk management B. Schedule management
C. Scope management D. Cost management

Exercise 2 – True/ False

Q 1. True or False: The critical path in a project's schedule is the sequence of tasks that determines the project's overall duration.

Q 2. A project charter is used to track the project's budget.

Exercise 3 – Fill in the blanks

Q 1. A project manager creates a __________ to illustrate the sequence and dependencies of project activities.

Q 2. __________ is a software project management process that defines how to deal with issues and changes as they occur during the project.

Exercise 4 – Match case

1. Project Scope A. A sequence of tasks that, if delayed, would delay the project's completion.
2. Critical Path B. Document outlining the project's objectives, deliverables, and constraints.
3. Stakeholder C. Individuals or groups who have an interest in the project's outcome.
4. Risk Assessment D. A collaborative approach to software development emphasizing individuals and interactions.
5. Agile Manifesto E. The process of identifying and evaluating potential project risks.

Exercise 5 – One word answer

Q 1. What type of project management chart shows the relationship between a project's tasks?

PERT (Program Evaluation and Review Technique)

Q 2. What do you call the individual responsible for overseeing the entire project from initiation to completion?

Project Manager

Exercise 6 – Small answer

Q 1. What does the term "Work Breakdown Structure" (WBS) refer to in project management?

Q 2. What is the critical path in project scheduling?

Exercise 7 – Long answer

Q 1. What are the key activities involved in the project initiation phase of Software Project Management, and why is it essential for project success?

Q 2. Risk management is a critical aspect of Software Project Management. Discuss the risk management process in software projects, including risk identification, analysis, mitigation, and monitoring. Provide real-world examples of software project risks and how they were effectively managed

Answers

Exercise 1 – MCQ

Ans: 1 C, 2 C

Exercise 2 – True/ False

Ans: 1 True, 2 False

Exercise 3 – Fill in the blanks

Ans: 1 Gantt chart, 2 change control

Exercise 4 – Match case

Ans: 1 B, 2 A, 3 C, 4 E, 5 D

Exercise 5 – One word answer

Ans: 1 PERT (Program Evaluation and review technique), 2 Project manager

Online Resources

Online Exam Paper:
Link: https://forms.gle/jBks862q2VDN1GU98
QR Code:

Chapter 9 Videos Playlist:
Link: https://www.youtube.com/playlist?list=PLzlh_31VWEFow9HYgM3oguN1hUEq3UkC4
QR Code:

Previous Years Solved Questions

Q 1. Write the objective of software project planning. [R.T.U.2018]

Ans 1: The objective of software project planning is to establish a well-structured and organized approach for successfully delivering a software project. Effective project planning aims to achieve the following key goals:

Define Project Scope: Clearly outline the project's objectives, requirements, and deliverables. This includes understanding what the software should do, who the stakeholders are, and what success looks like.

Set Realistic Goals: Establish achievable project goals, such as timelines, budgets, and quality standards. Objectives should be based on a thorough understanding of the project's complexity and constraints.

Allocate Resources: Determine the necessary resources for the project, including personnel, hardware, software, and budget. Resource allocation should align with the project's scope and objectives.

Identify Risks: Identify potential risks and challenges that could impact the project's success. This includes technical, operational, and external risks. The goal is to develop strategies to mitigate or manage these risks.

Create a Project Plan: Develop a detailed project plan that outlines tasks, milestones, dependencies, and timelines. The plan should provide a roadmap for project execution, helping the team stay on track.

Allocate Responsibilities: Clearly define roles and responsibilities for team members, stakeholders, and other contributors. This ensures that everyone knows their part in the project.

Monitor and Control: Establish monitoring and control mechanisms to track project progress, identify deviations from the plan, and take corrective actions when necessary. This involves regular reporting and status updates.

Quality Assurance: Define quality standards and processes to ensure that the software meets user requirements and industry best practices. Quality assurance activities should be integrated into the project plan.

Communication: Develop a communication plan that outlines how project-related information will be shared among team members, stakeholders, and management. Effective communication is critical for project success.

Change Management: Establish processes for handling changes in project scope, requirements, or objectives. Changes should be evaluated, documented, and approved before implementation.

Budget Management: Monitor and manage the project budget to ensure that it remains on track. This involves tracking expenses, cost estimation, and controlling project costs.

Documentation: Ensure that all project-related information, including plans, reports, and documentation, is well-maintained and readily accessible to project stakeholders.

Client/Stakeholder Satisfaction: Ensure that the software project planning aligns with the needs and expectations of clients and stakeholders. Customer satisfaction is a primary objective.

Risk Management: Identify, assess, and manage risks to minimize their impact on the project's success. This includes proactive risk mitigation and contingency planning.

Adaptability: Design the project plan with a degree of adaptability to accommodate changing requirements or unforeseen challenges without disrupting the project's overall trajectory.

Timely Delivery: The ultimate objective is to deliver the software project on time, within budget, and meeting quality standards.

Stakeholder Communication: Keep stakeholders informed about project progress, challenges, and changes, ensuring that they have realistic expectations and can provide feedback.

Team Motivation and Collaboration: Create an environment that motivates and encourages the project team to collaborate effectively, fostering creativity and productivity.

Q 2. List any three common types risks that typical software might suffer from. Explain how you can identify the risks that your project is susceptible to, suppose you are the project manager of a large software development project. Point out the main steps you would follow to manage the risks in your project. [R.T.U.2018]

Ans 2: Three common types of risks that typical software development projects might suffer from include:

Technical Risks: These involve issues related to technology, such as programming languages, frameworks, and tools. Technical risks may include challenges in integrating third-party components, optimizing performance, or handling complex algorithms.

Schedule Risks: These risks are associated with project timelines and deadlines. Delays in development, resource constraints, or unexpected issues can lead to schedule risks that impact project delivery.

Scope Risks: Scope risks pertain to changes in project requirements, features, or objectives. These changes can result in scope creep, where the project grows beyond its initial boundaries, affecting timelines and budgets.

To identify risks in a software development project as a project manager, follow these steps:

Risk Identification:

Gather the project team, stakeholders, and subject matter experts.

Brainstorm potential risks that could affect the project's success.

Categorize risks as technical, schedule, scope, resource, external, or other relevant categories.

Document identified risks with descriptions, potential impacts, and likelihood ratings.

Risk Assessment:

Evaluate the identified risks based on their potential impact on project objectives (e.g., schedule, budget, quality).

Assess the likelihood of each risk occurring.

Prioritize risks based on their significance and potential consequences.

Develop a risk matrix to help quantify and visualize the risks.

Risk Mitigation Planning:

Develop risk mitigation plans for the most significant and likely risks. Mitigation plans should include specific actions to reduce the likelihood or impact of each risk.

Assign responsible parties for each risk mitigation plan.

Establish contingency plans for risks that cannot be entirely mitigated.

Risk Monitoring:

Continuously monitor the project to identify early warning signs of potential risks.

Regularly review and update the risk assessment and mitigation plans.

Maintain open communication with the project team and stakeholders to stay informed about emerging risks or changes in risk factors.

Risk Response and Contingency:

Implement risk mitigation plans as needed when risks materialize.

Activate contingency plans for unanticipated risks or situations that are difficult to mitigate.

Communicate with stakeholders about risk status and the steps being taken to address them.

Risk Documentation:

Maintain a comprehensive risk register that includes the details of all identified risks, their assessment, mitigation plans, and status.

Regularly update the risk register to reflect changes in risk assessments or new risks that emerge.

Lessons Learned:

After project completion, conduct a lessons-learned session to evaluate how risks were managed and what could be improved in future projects.

Document the lessons learned for reference in future projects.

Q 3. Explain risk analysis process in detail. [R.T.U.2018]

Ans 3: Risk analysis is an essential process in software engineering that involves identifying, assessing, and mitigating potential risks that could impact a software project's success. The goal is to proactively manage uncertainties and challenges that may arise during the project. Here's a detailed explanation of the risk analysis process:

Risk Identification:

Gather Stakeholders: Start by involving stakeholders, project team members, and subject matter experts. Different perspectives can help identify a wide range of potential risks.

Brainstorming: Conduct brainstorming sessions or workshops to generate a list of possible risks. Encourage open discussions and consider various categories of risks, including technical, schedule, scope, resource, and external risks.

Documentation: Document each identified risk, providing a clear description and context. Include details about the risk's source, its potential impacts, and the likelihood of occurrence.

Risk Categorization:

Categorize Risks: Organize the identified risks into categories (e.g., technical, schedule, scope, quality, cost, legal, or other relevant categories). Categorization helps in managing and addressing risks more effectively.

Risk Assessment:

Impact Assessment: Evaluate the potential impact of each identified risk on project objectives. Consider how a risk could affect the project in terms of scope, schedule, budget, quality, and other critical factors.

Likelihood Assessment: Assess the likelihood or probability of each risk occurring. Use historical data, expert judgment, and available information to estimate the chances of a risk materializing.

Risk Prioritization: Prioritize risks based on their significance. Some risks may have high impacts and high likelihood, making them top priority. Create a risk matrix to visualize the prioritized risks.

Risk Mitigation Planning:

Risk Mitigation Strategies: Develop risk mitigation plans for the most significant and likely risks. Mitigation strategies should outline specific actions to reduce the likelihood or impact of each risk.

Contingency Planning: For risks that cannot be entirely mitigated, establish contingency plans that describe how the project will respond if the risk materializes. Contingency plans may include alternative approaches or fallback options.

Risk Monitoring and Control:

Regular Monitoring: Continuously monitor the project to identify early warning signs of potential risks. Regularly review and update the risk assessment and mitigation plans to reflect the current project status.

Communication: Maintain open and transparent communication with the project team and stakeholders. Ensure that everyone is aware of the identified risks, their status, and the actions being taken to address them.

Risk Response and Contingency:

Risk Response Execution: Implement risk mitigation plans as needed when risks materialize. Take action to reduce the impact or likelihood of the risk.

Contingency Activation: If unanticipated risks or challenges arise, or if risks cannot be effectively mitigated, activate contingency plans. These plans provide a predefined response to handle the risk's impact.

Documentation and Reporting:

Risk Register: Maintain a comprehensive risk register that includes all identified risks, their assessments, mitigation plans, current status, and any changes that occur over the project's lifecycle.

Regular Reporting: Regularly report the status of identified risks and risk management activities to project stakeholders.

Lessons Learned:

After project completion, conduct a lessons-learned session to evaluate how risks were managed and what could be improved in future projects.

Document the lessons learned for reference in future projects to continually improve the risk analysis process.

Q 4. Explain project estimation technique. [R.T.U.2018]

Ans 4: Project estimation techniques in software engineering are methods used to predict the various aspects of a software development project, such as its size, duration, effort, cost, and resource requirements. Accurate estimation is essential for effective project planning, resource allocation, and risk management. Several techniques are commonly used for project estimation:

Expert Judgment: Expert judgment involves seeking input from experienced individuals who have worked on similar projects. These experts provide insights into project estimation based on their knowledge and past experiences. While subjective, expert judgment can be a valuable resource for making informed estimates.

Analogous Estimation: Analogous estimation, also known as top-down estimation, relies on comparing the current project with previous, similar projects. It uses historical data and project characteristics to estimate factors like effort, duration, and cost. This technique assumes that past projects can provide reliable benchmarks for future ones.

Parametric Estimation: Parametric estimation, also known as bottom-up estimation, is a mathematical model-based approach. It involves identifying project parameters and creating a formula or algorithm to calculate the estimate. Common parameters include lines of code, function points, or complexity metrics.

Function Point Analysis: Function Point Analysis (FPA) is a widely used method for estimating the size and complexity of software projects. It quantifies the functionality provided by a software application based on user inputs, outputs, inquiries, files, and interfaces. FPA is particularly useful for estimating effort and resource requirements.

COCOMO (Constructive Cost Model): COCOMO is a well-known cost estimation model that was developed by Barry Boehm. It uses a set of mathematical equations to estimate effort, duration, and cost based on various factors, including project size, complexity, and development environment.

PERT (Program Evaluation and Review Technique): PERT is a project management technique used for estimating the duration and scheduling of tasks. It uses three time estimates for each task: optimistic, pessimistic, and most likely. These estimates are combined to calculate expected durations and create a probabilistic project schedule.

Expert Estimation Panels: In this approach, a panel of experts collaborates to estimate different aspects of the project. They provide individual estimates and then discuss and reconcile their estimates to arrive at a consensus. This method combines expert judgment with a structured approach.

Delphi Method: The Delphi Method is a structured approach to estimation that involves multiple rounds of feedback and consensus-building among a group of experts. It helps reduce bias and reach a more accurate estimate through iterative discussions.

Monte Carlo Simulation: Monte Carlo simulation uses random sampling and probability distributions to model project uncertainty. It can generate multiple estimates based on different scenarios, offering a probabilistic view of project outcomes.

Use Case Points: This technique estimates the size and complexity of a software project based on the number and complexity of use cases or user scenarios. Use Case Points help in estimating the effort and resources needed for requirements analysis, design, and development.

Q 5. What are the objectives of the software project management. [R.T.U.2018]

Ans 5: The objectives of software project management in software engineering are to ensure the successful planning, execution, and completion of a software development project while meeting its quality, cost, and schedule targets. Effective software project management aims to achieve the following objectives:

Project Planning: Create a well-defined project plan that outlines the project's scope, objectives, requirements, and deliverables. The plan should specify the project's timeline, resource allocation, budget, and quality standards.

Resource Management: Efficiently allocate and manage project resources, including personnel, hardware, software, and budget. Ensure that resources are used effectively to meet project goals.

Risk Management: Identify, assess, and mitigate potential risks that could impact the project's success. Develop strategies to minimize the impact of uncertainties and challenges.

Quality Assurance: Establish and maintain quality standards and processes to ensure that the software product meets user requirements and industry best practices. Implement testing, reviews, and quality control measures.

Scope Management: Define, document, and control the project's scope to prevent scope creep (uncontrolled expansion of project scope). Ensure that the project stays within its boundaries.

Cost Management: Monitor and manage the project budget to keep it within approved limits. This involves tracking expenses, cost estimation, and controlling project costs.

Schedule Management: Develop and manage the project schedule to ensure that tasks are completed on time. Track progress, identify delays, and take corrective actions to meet project timelines.

Communication: Establish a communication plan that outlines how project-related information will be shared among team members, stakeholders, and management. Effective communication is essential for project success.

Change Management: Establish processes for handling changes in project scope, requirements, or objectives. Changes should be evaluated, documented, and approved before implementation.

Client/Stakeholder Satisfaction: Ensure that the software project management aligns with the needs and expectations of clients and stakeholders. Customer satisfaction is a primary objective.

Team Motivation and Collaboration: Create an environment that motivates and encourages the project team to collaborate effectively, fostering creativity and productivity.

Risk Management: Identify, assess, and manage risks to minimize their impact on the project's success. This includes proactive risk mitigation and contingency planning.

Adaptability: Design the project plan with a degree of adaptability to accommodate changing requirements or unforeseen challenges without disrupting the project's overall trajectory.

Timely Delivery: The ultimate objective is to deliver the software project on time, within budget, and meeting quality standards.

Stakeholder Communication: Keep stakeholders informed about project progress, challenges, and changes, ensuring that they have realistic expectations and can provide feedback.

Lessons Learned: After project completion, conduct a lessons-learned session to evaluate what went well and what could be improved in future projects. Document the lessons learned for reference.

By addressing these objectives, software project management ensures that projects are well-organized, resources are utilized efficiently, risks are managed effectively, and the software product meets user expectations while being delivered on time and within budget.

Q 6. Consider a software project of full screen editor. the major components identified are : [R.T.U.2018]

(i) Screen Edit
(ii) Command Language Interpreter
(iii) File Input and Output
(iv) Cursor Movement and
(v) Screen Movement

The sizes for these components are estimated to be 6K, 7K, 2K, 4K and 3K LOC Assume cost driver values as 1.0. Use intermediate COCOMO model to determine:

(i) Final effort
(ii) Efforts estimates for different phases
(iii) Total time
(iv) Time estimates for different phases

Ans 7: To determine the final effort, effort estimates for different phases, total time, and time estimates for different phases using the intermediate COCOMO model, you can follow these steps:
Given data:
Sizes (in KLOC): (i) Screen Edit: 6K LOC (ii) Command Language Interpreter: 7K LOC (iii) File Input and Output: 2K LOC (iv) Cursor Movement: 4K LOC (v) Screen Movement: 3K LOC
Cost driver values: All cost driver values are assumed to be 1.0.
The intermediate COCOMO model formula is as follows: Effort (E) = a * (KLOC)^b Development Time (D) = c * (E)^d
Let's calculate the values step by step:
(i) Final Effort: Calculate the total KLOC (Kilo Lines of Code) by summing the sizes of all components: Total KLOC = 6K + 7K + 2K + 4K + 3K = 22K LOC
Now, calculate the final effort (E) using the COCOMO formula: E = a * (KLOC)^b E = 2.8 * (22)^1.20 E ≈ 2.8 * 50.27 E ≈ 140.70 Person-Months
(ii) Effort Estimates for Different Phases: The COCOMO model typically divides effort estimates into different phases, such as Planning, Design, Coding, Testing, and Maintenance. You can determine the effort for each phase as a percentage of the total effort. These percentages can vary based on the project and organization, but a common breakdown is as follows:
Planning: 10% of total effort
Design: 20% of total effort
Coding: 30% of total effort
Testing: 30% of total effort
Maintenance: 10% of total effort
Effort for each phase:
Planning Effort = 0.10 * 140.70 ≈ 14.07 Person-Months
Design Effort = 0.20 * 140.70 ≈ 28.14 Person-Months
Coding Effort = 0.30 * 140.70 ≈ 42.21 Person-Months
Testing Effort = 0.30 * 140.70 ≈ 42.21 Person-Months
Maintenance Effort = 0.10 * 140.70 ≈ 14.07 Person-Months
(iii) Total Time: Calculate the total time (D) using the COCOMO formula: D = c * (E)^d D = 2.5 * (140.70)^0.35 D ≈ 2.5 * 3.3509 D ≈ 8.38 Months
(iv) Time Estimates for Different Phases: You can determine the time for each phase by applying the same phase percentages to the total time.
Planning Time = 0.10 * 8.38 ≈ 0.84 Months
Design Time = 0.20 * 8.38 ≈ 1.68 Months
Coding Time = 0.30 * 8.38 ≈ 2.51 Months
Testing Time = 0.30 * 8.38 ≈ 2.51 Months
Maintenance Time = 0.10 * 8.38 ≈ 0.84 Months

Q 7. Write a detailed note on COCOMO Model. Explain its types. [R.T.U.2018]

Ans 7: COCOMO, which stands for "COnstructive COst MOdel," is a widely used model in software engineering for estimating the effort, cost, and schedule of a software development project. It was initially developed by Dr. Barry Boehm in the 1980s and has since evolved into various versions to accommodate different project types and complexities. COCOMO models provide a systematic and structured approach to software project estimation. There are three main types of COCOMO models:

Basic COCOMO:

Basic COCOMO is the original version and is suitable for estimating small to medium-sized software projects.
It estimates effort, cost, and duration as a function of the project's size in lines of code (LOC).
The formula for Basic COCOMO is: **E = a * (KLOC)^b**, where **E** is the effort in person-months, **KLOC** is the project size in Kilo Lines of Code, and **a** and **b** are constants.
Basic COCOMO uses a single cost driver, which is a multiplicative factor to account for project-specific attributes. All cost drivers are assumed to have a value of 1.0.

Intermediate COCOMO:

Intermediate COCOMO is an extension of the Basic COCOMO model and is used for medium-sized projects.
It includes more cost drivers to consider project-specific factors, such as personnel capability, software reliability, complexity, and development flexibility.
The formula for Intermediate COCOMO is more complex and accounts for multiple cost drivers.

Intermediate COCOMO provides more accurate estimates than Basic COCOMO because it considers additional project attributes.

Detailed COCOMO:

Detailed COCOMO, also known as COCOMO II, is the most comprehensive version and is suitable for projects of any size, including large and complex projects.

It provides a detailed analysis of various cost factors, effort distribution, and project phases.

Detailed COCOMO considers a wide range of cost drivers, including product, hardware, personnel, project, and platform factors.

The formula for Detailed COCOMO is highly detailed, accounting for numerous cost drivers and their interactions.

Detailed COCOMO is the most accurate version of the model but also the most complex.

Key components of COCOMO models include:

Effort Estimation: Estimating the person-months (effort) required to complete a software project.

Schedule Estimation: Estimating the project schedule in terms of months or years.

Cost Estimation: Estimating the project cost, which includes labor costs, hardware and software costs, and other expenses.

Phase-wise Estimates: COCOMO models typically provide effort and time estimates for different project phases, including planning, design, coding, testing, and maintenance.

Risk Management: COCOMO models encourage identifying and managing project risks, such as uncertainty in requirements, technology challenges, and external dependencies.

Q 8. Write detailed note on software project scheduling. [R.T.U.2018]

Ans 8: Software project scheduling is a critical aspect of software project management. It involves planning and organizing tasks, resources, and timelines to ensure that a software development project is completed on time and within budget while meeting its quality and scope objectives. Effective project scheduling is essential for successful project execution. Here's a detailed note on software project scheduling:

Key Components of Software Project Scheduling:

Project Work Breakdown Structure (WBS): Before creating a schedule, the project is broken down into smaller, manageable components, known as work breakdown structure (WBS). This hierarchical decomposition helps in organizing and categorizing tasks.

Task Identification and Sequencing: Each component in the WBS is analyzed to identify specific tasks and activities required for the project. Tasks are sequenced based on dependencies, priorities, and logical order.

Task Estimation: Estimating the time and effort required for each task is a critical step. This can be done using techniques such as expert judgment, historical data, or parametric estimation models like COCOMO.

Resource Allocation: Identify and allocate resources (such as human resources, equipment, software, and facilities) to each task. Resource allocation should be realistic, considering availability and capacity.

Task Dependencies: Define task dependencies, including:

Finish-to-Start (FS): The successor task cannot start until the predecessor task is complete.

Start-to-Start (SS): The successor task can start as soon as the predecessor task starts.

Finish-to-Finish (FF): The successor task can finish when the predecessor task finishes.

Start-to-Finish (SF): The successor task can finish when the predecessor task starts.

Critical Path Analysis: Identify the critical path, which is the longest sequence of tasks that determines the minimum duration of the project. Delaying any task on the critical path will result in a project delay.

Contingency Planning: Develop contingency plans for high-risk tasks or situations where delays are possible. These plans outline how to mitigate risks and respond to unforeseen challenges.

Schedule Development: Use scheduling tools and techniques (e.g., Gantt charts, network diagrams, project management software) to create a detailed project schedule. This schedule includes task start and end dates, resource allocation, and task dependencies.

Important Considerations in Software Project Scheduling:

Resource Constraints: Ensure that resource allocation matches resource availability. Overloading or underutilizing resources can lead to inefficiencies and project delays.

Scope Changes: Be prepared to adapt the schedule when changes in project scope occur. Proper change management processes should be in place to assess the impact of scope changes on the schedule.

Risk Management: Anticipate and manage risks that could impact the schedule. Include risk response plans in the scheduling process to address potential delays.

Communication: Effective communication is crucial. Keep team members, stakeholders, and management informed about schedule progress, delays, and changes. Regular status meetings can help.

Project Monitoring: Continuously monitor the project's progress against the schedule. Identify variances and take corrective actions to keep the project on track.
Milestone Tracking: Use project milestones to mark key achievements and track overall progress. Milestones help assess whether the project is meeting its objectives.
Buffer and Slack: Include buffers and slack in the schedule to account for unforeseen delays or uncertainties. This provides flexibility in case things don't go as planned.
Baseline Schedule: Establish a baseline schedule as a reference point. It serves as the standard against which you can compare actual progress.

Previous Year Unsolved Questions

Q 1. With the help of an example, explain the component-based software engineering process. [IGNOU June, 2018]
Q 2. Describe the COCOMO Model in detail with an example for Software Cost Estimation. [IGNOU, December 2013, 2015, June 2016, 2018] [Anna University 2022] [Kota University 2021] [VTU 2021]
Q 3. Explain any two project scheduling techniques with examples. [IGNOU, December, 2015] [Anna University 2022]
Q 4. Explain any one of the Risk Management Techniques. [IGNOU, December, 2015, 2017] [VTU 2021]
Q 5. What is a risk? Explain different types of software risks. [IGNOU, December, 2013, 2016]
Q 6. Briefly explain any two techniques of scheduling in software engineering. [IGNOU, December, 2016]
Q 7. What is Software Project Management model? [IGNOU, June, 2016]
Q 8. With a neat diagram, explain Software Project estimation in detail and what are the techniques also? [IGNOU, June 2016, December 2012]
Q 9. Explain the various levels in SEI-CMM. [IGNOU, June, 2016]
Q 10. Write a brief note about change control. [IGNOU, December, 2017]
Q 11. What are the different levels of Capability Maturity Model? Describe them. [IGNOU, December, 2017]
Q 12. What are the different methods used for estimating Cost and Effort required for completing a project successfully? Explain any one method in detail. [IGNOU, June, 2015]
Q 13. Bring the importance between COCOMO I and II. [Anna University 2022]
Q 14. What are the risks in software development? Explain how risk is identifies? [Anna University 2022]
Q 15. What is Software Cost Estimation Model? What are the various software Project Matrices for this? Describe. [MCU 2019]
Q 16. What is Software Capability Maturity Model? What are its different levels ? [MCU 2019]
Q 17. Process-Based Estimation Vs Tool-Based Estimation. Explain. [RGPV June 2020]
Q 18. Explain the various activities covered by software project management. [RGPV June 2020]

Chapter 10: Software Testing, Debugging and Maintenance

10.1 Testing Objectives

In software engineering, testing objectives are specific goals and purposes for conducting testing activities throughout the software development process. These objectives are critical for ensuring the quality and reliability of the software product. The primary testing objectives include:

Defect Detection: Identify and locate defects or issues in the software, such as bugs, errors, or inconsistencies. The goal is to find and document as many defects as possible to improve the software's quality.

Quality Assurance: Ensure that the software meets specified quality standards and requirements. This includes verifying that the software performs its intended functions correctly and reliably.

Verification and Validation: Confirm that the software meets the defined specifications (verification) and satisfies the end-users' needs and expectations (validation). Verification ensures that the software is built right, while validation ensures it is the right software for the users.

Risk Mitigation: Mitigate potential risks associated with software development. Testing helps identify and address issues early in the development process, reducing the likelihood of major problems later.

Error Prevention: Detecting and fixing errors during the testing phase helps prevent these errors from propagating to later stages of development and, ultimately, into the released software.

User Satisfaction: Ensure that the software is user-friendly, meets user needs, and provides a positive user experience. User satisfaction is a crucial objective of testing, especially for software products with a significant user base.

Conformance to Standards: Ensure that the software complies with industry standards, regulations, and best practices, such as security standards, accessibility guidelines, or coding conventions.

Performance Evaluation: Assess the software's performance characteristics, including speed, responsiveness, scalability, and resource usage. Performance testing helps ensure that the software performs optimally under expected and peak conditions.

10.2 Types of Software Testing

What is Software Testing?

Software Testing is a method to assess the functionality of the software program. The process checks whether the actual software matches the expected requirements and ensures the software is bug-free. The purpose of software testing is to identify the errors, faults, or missing requirements in contrast to actual requirements. It mainly aims at measuring the specification, functionality, and performance of a software program or application.

Software testing can be divided into two steps:

Verification: It refers to the set of tasks that ensure that the software correctly implements a specific function. It means "Are we building the product right?".

Validation: It refers to a different set of tasks that ensure that the software that has been built is traceable to customer requirements. It means "Are we building the right product?".

Different Types Of Software Testing

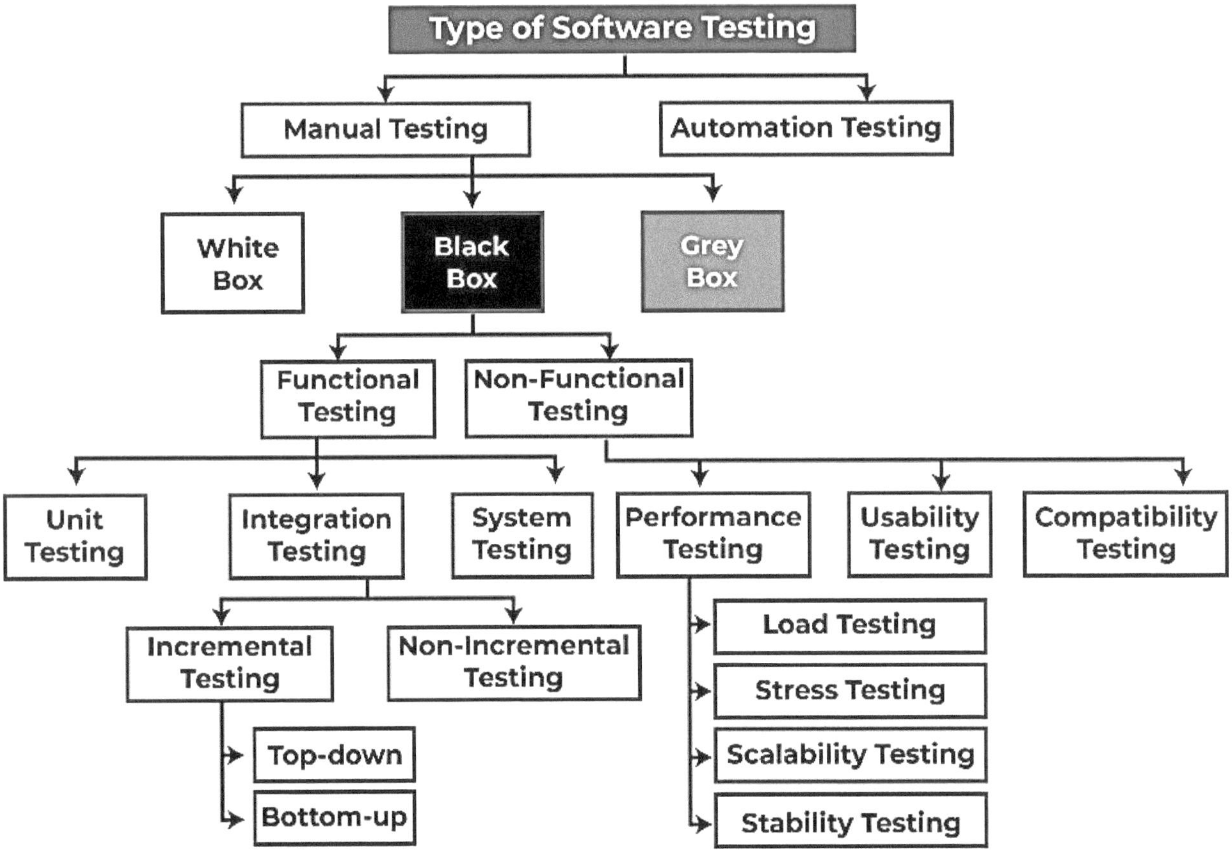

Software Testing can be broadly classified into 3 types:

Functional Testing: Functional testing is a type of software testing that validates the software systems against the functional requirements. It is performed to check whether the application is working as per the software's functional requirements or not. Various types of functional testing are Unit testing, Integration testing, System testing, Smoke testing, and so on.

Non-functional Testing: Non-functional testing is a type of software testing that checks the application for non-functional requirements like performance, scalability, portability, stress, etc. Various types of non-functional testing are Performance testing, Stress testing, Usability Testing, and so on.

Maintenance Testing: Maintenance testing is the process of changing, modifying, and updating the software to keep up with the customer's needs. It involves regression testing that verifies that recent changes to the code have not adversely affected other previously working parts of the software.

There are 2 types of Testing: -

Manual Testing

Automation Testing

Manual Testing: Manual testing includes testing software manually, i.e., without using any automation tool or script. In this type, the tester takes over the role of an end-user and tests the software to identify any unexpected behavior or bug. There are different stages for manual testing such as unit testing, integration testing, system testing, and user acceptance testing. Testers use test plans, test cases, or test scenarios to test software to ensure the completeness of testing. Manual testing also includes exploratory testing, as testers explore the software to identify errors in it.

Steps in Manual Testing

The below diagram lists the steps in the manual testing process:

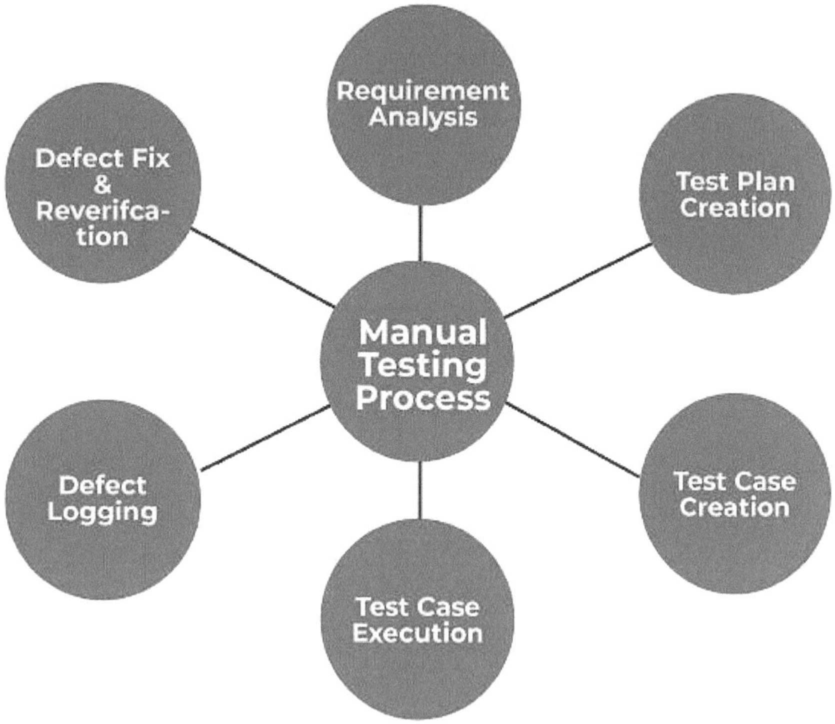

Requirement Analysis: Study the software project documentation, guides, and Application Under Test (AUT). Analyze the requirements from SRS.

Test Plan Creation: Create a test plan covering all the requirements.

Test Case Creation: Design the test cases that cover all the requirements described in the documentation.

Test Case Execution: Review and baseline the test cases with the team lead and client. Execute the test cases on the application under test.

Defect Logging: Detect the bugs, log and report them to the developers.

Defect Fix and Re-verification: When bugs are fixed, again execute the failing test cases to verify they pass.

Types of Manual Testing

There are different methods to implement manual testing but it is broadly classified into three types of manual testing:

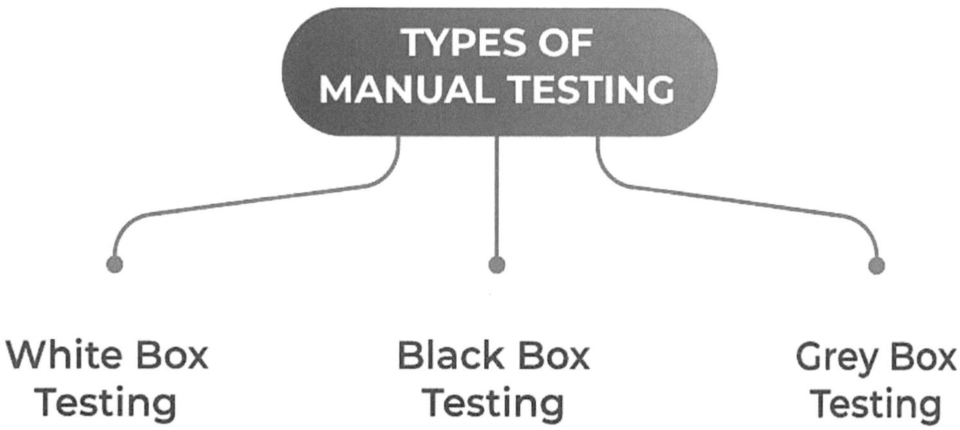

Black Box Testing: In this technique, the tester or the QA analyst will only check the functionality of the particular module or particular method or sometimes the entire application by providing the different test cases manually. Here, the tester will give the input for the application and test it manually. If it returns the expected output then the tester will proceed with another set of inputs and report all the results to the team. If the input given by the user manually is failed during the testing then he/she will report this issue to the development team.

White Box Testing: In this technique, the person will check the internal structure of the system like designs, coding, etc., manually. Here, the development team will review the entire coding part line by line to ensure the correctness of the code. If he/she finds anything dissimilarities or errors in the code, they will correct or fix the errors in the coding or designs. Here, the process is entirely carried out manually and the process is efficient since the checking code or design is manually checked by humans.

Gray Box Testing: This technique is the combination of both white-box testing and black-box testing. Here, the internal structure of the application is partially known by the tester. The tester will check both the internal structure and the functionality of the application manually. The tester will check the coding part as well as test the application by providing different test cases manually. If the input fails at some stage the tester will then make the changes in the coding part.

S. No.	Black Box Testing	Gray Box Testing	White Box Testing
1.	This testing has Low granularity.	This testing has a medium level of granularity.	This testing has high-level granularity.
2.	It is done by end-users and also by the tester and developers.	It is done by end-users (called user acceptance testing) and also by testers and developers.	It is generally done by testers and developers.
3.	Here, Internals are not required to be known.	Here, Internals relevant to the testing are known.	Here, the Internal code of the application and database is known.
4.	It is likely to be less exhaustive than the other two.	It is kind of in-between.	Most exhaustive among all three.
5.	It is based on requirements, and test cases on the functional specifications, as the internals are not known.	It provides better variety/depth in test cases on account of high-level knowledge of the internals.	It can exercise code with a relevant variety of data.
6.	If algorithm testing is not suited best for that.	If used algorithm testing is also not suited best for that.	If algorithm testing is, it is suited best for that.
7.	It is suited for functional or business testing.	It is suited for functional or business domain testing deeply.	It is used for all.
8.	This testing involves validating the outputs for given inputs, the application being tested as a black-box technique.	Herein, we have a better variety of inputs and the ability to extract test results from the database for comparison with expected results.	It involves structural testing and enables logic coverage, decisions, etc. within the code.

9.	This is also called Opaque-box testing, Closed-box testing, input-output testing, Data-driven testing, Behavioral, Functional testing	This is also called translucent box testing	This is also called Glass-box testing, Clear-box testing, Design-based testing, Logic-based testing, Structural testing, and Code-based testing.
10.	**Black-box test design techniques-** • Decision table testing • All-pairs testing • Equivalence partitioning • Error guessing	**Gray box test design techniques-** • Matrix testing • Regression testing • Pattern testing • Orthogonal Array Testing	**White-box test design techniques-** • Control flow testing • Data flow testing • Branch testing

Tools Used for Manual Testing

TestLink: It is a web-based test management system that facilitates software quality assurance and it is one of the most user-friendly programs. It is available through a browser connected to the internet.

Bugzilla: It is a web-based bug-tracking tool that is developed by Mozilla. It has a simple bug search that searches the complete text of the bug.

Jira: It is a manual testing tool that helps teams assign, track, report, and manage work and bring teams together. This tool is compatible with agile software projects also.

LoadRunner: It is one of the most widely used performance testing tools. The primary purpose of this tool is to categorize the most prevalent causes of performance problems.

Apache JMeter: It is an open-source load testing tool for analyzing and measuring the performance of a variety of services. It has an easy-to-use user interface.

Manual Testing vs Automation Testing

Below are the differences between manual testing and automation testing:

Parameters	**Manual Testing**	**Automation Testing**
Definition	It is the process of manually testing the software.	It involves the usage of automation tools for executing the test cases.
Test case execution	Test cases are executed manually by the QA Testers.	Test cases are executed automatically using automation tools and scripts.
Efficiency	Manual testing is less-efficient and time-consuming.	Automation testing is more efficient and less time-consuming.
Test coverage	It is difficult to ensure 100% test coverage.	More test coverage can be ensured in automation testing.
Programming knowledge	There is no need to have programming knowledge, only product knowledge is required.	It is important to have programming knowledge to write test scripts.

Automation Testing:

Automated Testing is a technique where the Tester writes scripts on their own and uses suitable Software or Automation Tool to test the software. It is an Automation Process of a Manual Process. It allows for executing repetitive tasks without the intervention of a Manual Tester.

It is used to automate the testing tasks that are difficult to perform manually.
Automation tests can be run at any time of the day as they use scripted sequences to examine the software.
Automation tests can also enter test data can compare the expected result with the actual result and generate detailed test reports.
The goal of automation tests is to reduce the number of test cases to be executed manually but not to eliminate manual testing.
It is possible to record the test suit and replay it when required.

Types of Automation Testing

Unit testing: Unit testing is a phase in software testing to test the smallest piece of code known as a unit that can be logically isolated from the code. It is carried out during the development of the application.

Integration testing: component: Integration testing is a phase in software testing in which individual software components are combined together and tested as a group. It is carried out to check the compatibility of the component with the specified functional requirements.

Smoke testing: Smoke testing is a type of software testing that determines whether the built software is stable or not. It is the preliminary check of the software before its release in the market.

Performance testing: Performance testing is a type of software testing that is carried out to determine how the system performs in terms of stability and responsiveness under a particular load.

Regression testing: Regression testing is a type of software testing that confirms that previously developed software still works fine after the change and that the change has not adversely affected existing features.

Security testing: Security testing is a type of software testing that uncovers the risks, and vulnerabilities in the security mechanism of the software application. It helps an organization to identify the loopholes in the security mechanism and take corrective measures to rectify the gaps in security.

Acceptance testing: Acceptance testing is the last phase of software testing that is performed after the system testing. It helps to determine to what degree the application meets end users' approval.

API testing: API testing is a type of software testing that validates the Application Programming Interface(API) and checks the functionality, security, and reliability of the programming interface.

UI Testing: UI testing is a type of software testing that helps testers ensure that all the fields, buttons, and other items on the screen function as desired.

Automation Testing Process

Test Tool Selection: There will be some criteria for the Selection of the tool. The majority of the criteria include: Do we have skilled resources to allocate for automation tasks, Budget constraints, and Do the tool satisfies our needs?

Define Scope of Automation: This includes a few basic points such as the Framework should support Automation Scripts, Less Maintenance must be there, High Return on Investment, Not many complex Test Cases

Planning, Design, and Development: For this, we need to Install particular frameworks or libraries, and start designing and developing the test cases such as NUnit, JUnit, QUnit, or required Software Automation Tools

Test Execution: Final Execution of test cases will take place in this phase and it depends on Language to Language for .NET, we'll be using NUnit, for Java, we'll be using JUnit, for JavaScript, we'll be using QUnit or Jasmine, etc.

Maintenance: Creation of Reports generated after Tests and that should be documented so as to refer to that in the future for the next iterations.

Automation Tools

Selenium: Selenium is an automated testing tool that is used for Regression testing and provides a playback and recording facility. It can be used with frameworks like JUnit and Test NG. It provides a single interface and lets users write test cases in languages like Ruby, Java, Python, etc.

QTP: Quick Test Professional (QTP) is an automated functional testing tool to test both web and desktop applications. It is based on the VB scripting language and it provides functional and regression test automation for software applications.

Sikuli: It is a GUI-based test automation tool that is used for interacting with elements of web pages. It is used to search and automate graphical user interfaces using screenshots.

Appium: Apium is an open-source test automation framework that allows QAs to conduct automated app testing on different platforms like iOS, Android, and Windows SDK.

Jmeter: Apache JMeter is an open-source Java application that is used to load test the functional behavior of the application and measure the performance.

Different Levels of Software Testing

Software level testing can be majorly classified into 4 levels:

Unit Testing: Unit testing is a level of the software testing process where individual units/components of a software/system are tested. The purpose is to validate that each unit of the software performs as designed.

Integration Testing: Integration testing is a level of the software testing process where individual units are combined and tested as a group. The purpose of this level of testing is to expose faults in the interaction between integrated units.

System Testing: System testing is a level of the software testing process where a complete, integrated system/software is tested. The purpose of this test is to evaluate the system's compliance with the specified requirements.

Acceptance Testing: Acceptance testing is a level of the software testing process where a system is tested for acceptability. The purpose of this test is to evaluate the system's compliance with the business requirements and assess whether it is acceptable for delivery.

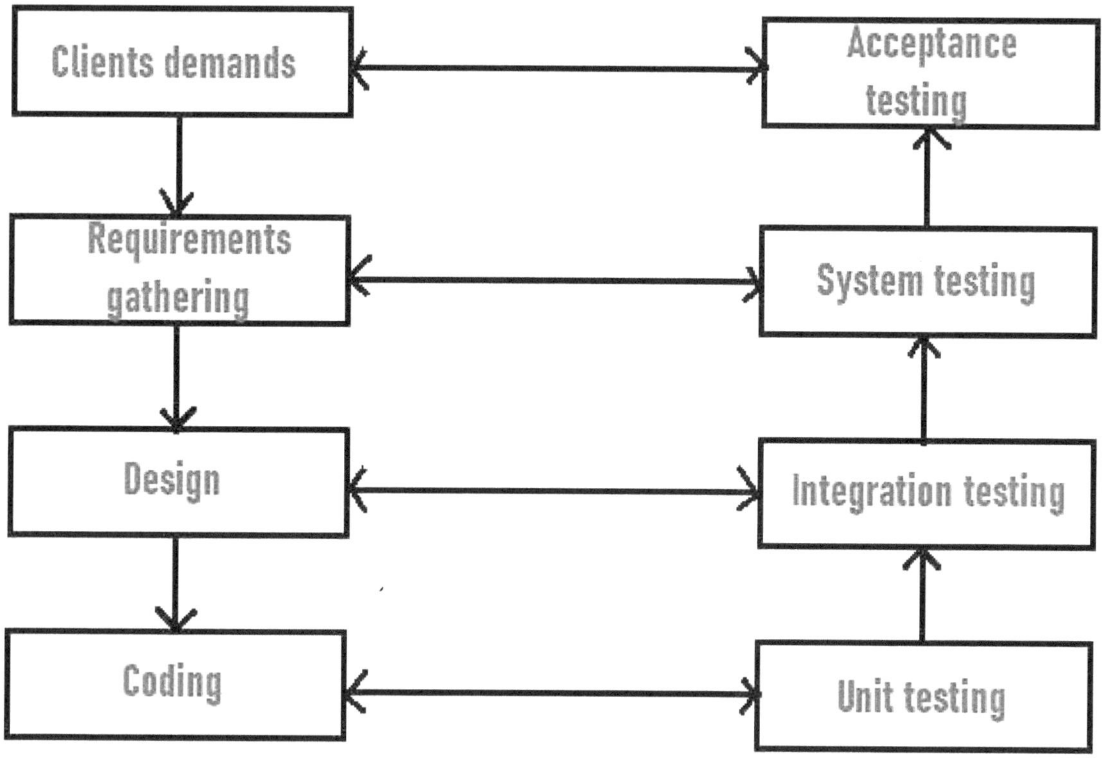

LEVELS OF TESTING

10.3 Seven Principles of software testing

7 Principles of Software Testing

Testing shows presence of defects

Exhaustive testing is not possible

Early testing

Defect clustering

Pesticide paradox

Testing is context dependent

Absence of errors fallacy

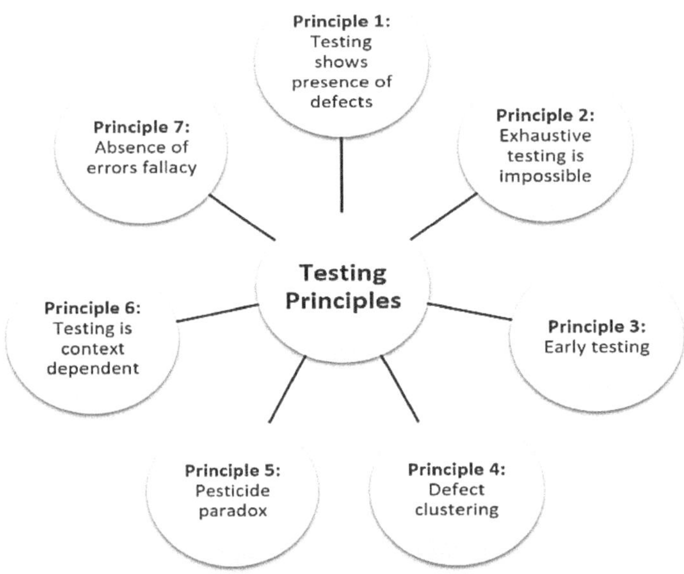

Testing shows the presence of defects: The goal of software testing is to make the software fail. Software testing reduces the presence of defects. Software testing talks about the presence of defects and doesn't talk about the absence of defects. Software testing can ensure that defects are present but it can not prove that software is defect-free. Even multiple testing can never ensure that software is 100% bug-free. Testing can reduce the number of defects but not remove all defects.

Exhaustive testing is not possible: It is the process of testing the functionality of the software in all possible inputs (valid or invalid) and pre-conditions is known as exhaustive testing. Exhaustive testing is impossible means the software can never test at every test case. It can test only some test cases and assume that the software is correct and it will produce the correct output in every test case. If the software will test every test case then it will take more cost, effort, etc., which is impractical.

Early Testing: To find the defect in the software, early test activity shall be started. The defect detected in the early phases of SDLC will be very less expensive. For better performance of software, software testing will start at the initial phase i.e. testing will perform at the requirement analysis phase.

Defect clustering: In a project, a small number of modules can contain most of the defects. Pareto Principle to software testing state that 80% of software defect comes from 20% of modules.

Pesticide paradox: Repeating the same test cases, again and again, will not find new bugs. So it is necessary to review the test cases and add or update test cases to find new bugs.

Testing is context-dependent: The testing approach depends on the context of the software developed. Different types of software need to perform different types of testing. For example, The testing of the e-commerce site is different from the testing of the Android application.

Absence of errors fallacy: If a built software is 99% bug-free but it does not follow the user requirement then it is unusable. It is not only necessary that software is 99% bug-free but it is also mandatory to fulfill all the customer requirements.

10.4 Testing Guidelines

Define clear and measurable testing goals: Establish what needs to be tested and what constitutes a pass or fail for each test.

Write comprehensive test cases: Develop a set of test cases that cover all possible scenarios, including edge cases and negative test cases.

Create test data: Create test data that represents the expected and unexpected data that the software will encounter during normal operation.

Automate testing: Automate as much of the testing as possible to increase efficiency and reduce human error.

Use multiple testing techniques: Use a combination of different testing techniques such as unit testing, integration testing, system testing, and acceptance testing to provide a comprehensive test coverage.

Use test-driven development: This is a method where the tests are written before the code, this approach helps in verifying that the code meets the requirement and also helps in refactoring the code.
Document the testing process: Keep detailed records of the testing process, including test cases, test data, and test results. This can be helpful for debugging and maintaining the software.
Continuously test and monitor: Continuously test and monitor the software during development and after release to ensure that it continues to function as expected.
Involve the end-users: Get the end-users involved in testing to ensure that the software meets their needs and is easy to use.
Use a testing framework: Use a testing framework to help organize and automate the testing process.

10.5 White Box and Black Box Testing

White box testing techniques analyze the internal structures the used data structures, internal design, code structure, and the working of the software rather than just the functionality as in black box testing. It is also called glass box testing or clear box testing or structural testing. White Box Testing is also known as transparent testing or open box testing.
White box testing is also known as structural testing or code-based testing, and it is used to test the software's internal logic, flow, and structure. The tester creates test cases to examine the code paths and logic flows to ensure they meet the specified requirements.
White Box Testing is coverage of the specification in the code:
1. Code coverage
2. Segment coverage: Ensure that each code statement is executed once.
3. Branch Coverage or Node Testing: Coverage of each code branch in from all possible was.
4. Compound Condition Coverage: For multiple conditions test each condition with multiple paths and combination of the different path to reach that condition.
5. Basis Path Testing: Each independent path in the code is taken for testing.
6. Data Flow Testing (DFT): In this approach you track the specific variables through each possible calculation, thus defining the set of intermediate paths through the code.DFT tends to reflect dependencies but it is mainly through sequences of data manipulation. In short, each data variable is tracked and its use is verified. This approach tends to uncover bugs like variables used but not initialize, or declared but not used, and so on.
7. Path Testing: Path testing is where all possible paths through the code are defined and covered. It's a time-consuming task.
8. Loop Testing: These strategies relate to testing single loops, concatenated loops, and nested loops. Independent and dependent code loops and values are tested by this approach.
Types and Techniques of White Box Testing
There are several types and different methods for each white box testing type.

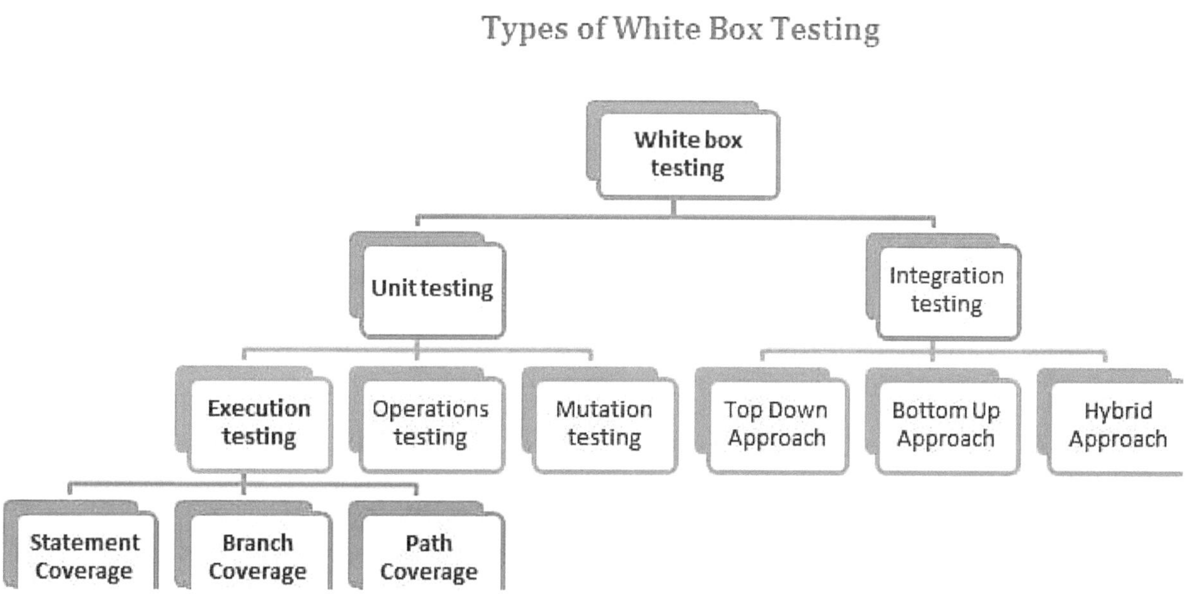

3 Main White Box Testing Techniques:
Statement Coverage
Branch Coverage
Path Coverage
Note that the statement, branch or path coverage does not identify any bug or defect that needs to be fixed. It only identifies those lines of code which are either never executed or remains untouched. Based on this further testing can be focused on.
Let's understand these techniques one by one with a simple example.
1) Statement coverage:
In a programming language, a statement is nothing but the line of code or instruction for the computer to understand and act accordingly. A statement becomes an executable statement when it gets compiled and converted into the object code and performs the action when the program is in a running mode.
Hence *"Statement Coverage"*, as the name itself suggests, it is the method of validating whether each and every line of the code is executed at least once.
2) Branch Coverage:
"Branch" in a programming language is like the "IF statements". An IF statement has two branches: True and False. So in Branch coverage (also called Decision coverage), we validate whether each branch is executed at least once.
In case of an "IF statement", there will be two test conditions:
One to validate the true branch and,
Other to validate the false branch.
Hence, in theory, Branch Coverage is a testing method which is when executed ensures that each and every branch from each decision point is executed.
3) Path Coverage
Path coverage tests all the paths of the program. This is a comprehensive technique which ensures that all the paths of the program are traversed at least once. Path Coverage is even more powerful than Branch coverage. This technique is useful for testing the complex programs.
White Box Testing Example
Consider the below simple pseudocode:
INPUT A & B
C = A + B
IF C>100
PRINT "ITS DONE"
For Statement Coverage – we would only need one test case to check all the lines of the code.
That means:
If I consider TestCase_01 to be (A=40 and B=70), then all the lines of code will be executed.
Now the question arises:
Is that sufficient?
What if I consider my Test case as A=33 and B=45?
Because Statement coverage will only cover the true side, for the pseudo code, only one test case would NOT be sufficient to test it. As a tester, we have to consider the negative cases as well.
Hence for maximum coverage, we need to consider "Branch Coverage", which will evaluate the "FALSE" conditions.
In the real world, you may add appropriate statements when the condition fails.
So now the pseudocode becomes:
INPUT A & B

C = A + B
IF C>100
PRINT "ITS DONE"
ELSE

PRINT "ITS PENDING"
Since Statement coverage is not sufficient to test the entire pseudo code, we would require Branch coverage to ensure maximum coverage.
So for Branch coverage, we would require two test cases to complete the testing of this pseudo code.
TestCase_01: A=33, B=45

TestCase_02: A=25, B=30
With this, we can see that each and every line of the code is executed at least once.

Here are the Conclusions that are derived so far:

Branch Coverage ensures more coverage than Statement coverage.
Branch coverage is more powerful than Statement coverage.
100% Branch coverage itself means 100% statement coverage.
But 100 % statement coverage does not guarantee 100% branch coverage.
Now let's move on to Path Coverage:
As said earlier, Path coverage is used to test the complex code snippets, which basically involve loop statements or combination of loops and decision statements.

Consider this pseudocode:

```
INPUT A & B
C = A + B
IF C>100
PRINT "ITS DONE"

END IF
IF A>50
PRINT "ITS PENDING"
END IF
```

Now to ensure maximum coverage, we would require 4 test cases.
How? Simply – there are 2 decision statements, so for each decision statement, we would need two branches to test. One for true and the other for the false condition. So for 2 decision statements, we would require 2 test cases to test the true side and 2 test cases to test the false side, which makes a total of 4 test cases.

To simplify these let's consider below flowchart of the pseudo code we have:

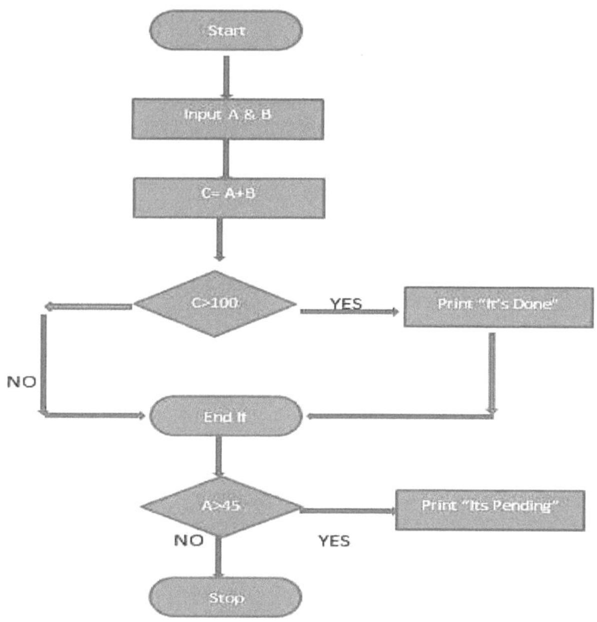

Path Coverage

In order to have the full coverage, we would need following test cases:
TestCase_01: A=50, B=60
TestCase_02: A=55, B=40
TestCase_03: A=40, B=65
TestCase_04: A=30, B=30
So the path covered will be:

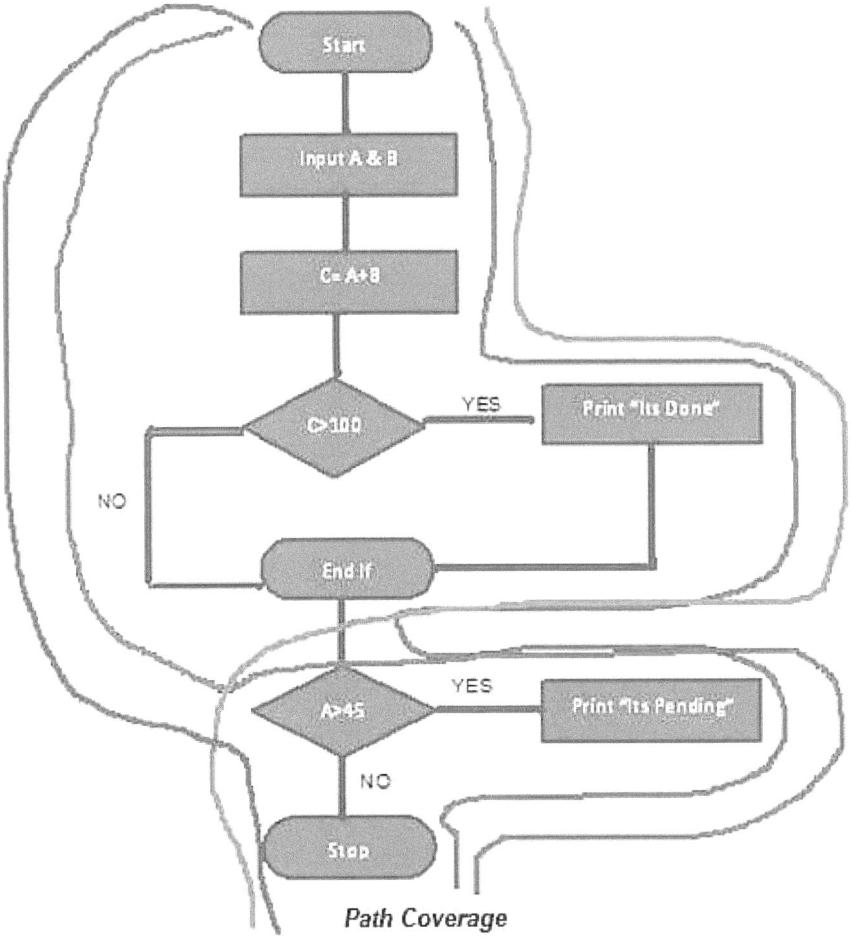

Path Coverage

Red Line – TestCase_01 = (A=50, B=60)
Blue Line = TestCase_02 = (A=55, B=40)
Orange Line = TestCase_03 = (A=40, B=65)
Green Line = TestCase_04 = (A=30, B=30)

Black box Testing

Black Box Testing is a software testing method in which testers evaluate the functionality of the software under test without looking at the internal code structure. This can be applied to every level of software testing such as Unit, Integration, System, and Acceptance Testing.

Black Box Testing Techniques:

Equivalence Partitioning
Boundary Value Analysis
Decision Table
State Transition

Equivalence Partitioning:

Equivalence Partitioning is also known as Equivalence Class Partitioning. In equivalence partitioning, inputs to the software or system are divided into groups that are expected to exhibit similar behavior, so they are likely to be proposed in the same way. Hence selecting one input from each group to design the test cases. Click here to see a detailed post on equivalence partitioning.

Boundary Value Analysis:

Boundary value analysis (BVA) is based on testing the boundary values of valid and invalid partitions. The Behavior at the edge of each equivalence partition is more likely to be incorrect than the behavior within the partition, so boundaries are an area where testing is likely to yield defects. Click here to see a detailed post on boundary value analysis.

Decision Table:

The decision Table is aka Cause-Effect Table. This test technique is appropriate for functionalities which has logical relationships between inputs (if-else logic). In the Decision table technique, we deal with combinations of inputs. To identify the test cases with the decision table, we consider conditions and actions. We take conditions as inputs and actions as outputs. Click here to see a detailed post on the decision table.

State Transition:

Using state transition testing, we pick test cases from an application where we need to test different system transitions. We can apply this when an application gives a different output for the same input, depending on what has happened in the earlier state. Click here to see a detailed post on the state transition technique.

Types of Black Box Testing:

Functionality Testing

Non-functionality Testing

Functional Testing vs Non-Functional Testing:

Functional Testing	**Non-functional Testing**
What the system actually does is functional testing	How well the system performs is non-functionality testing
To ensure that your product meets customer and business requirements and doesn't have any major bugs	To ensure that the product stands up to customer expectations
To verify the accuracy of the software against expected output	To verify the behavior of the software at various load conditions
It is performed before non-functional testing	It is performed after functional testing
Example of functional test case is to verify the login functionality	Example of non-functional test case is to check whether the homepage is loading in less than 2 seconds
Testing types are • Unit testing • Smoke testing • User Acceptance • Integration Testing • Regression testing • Localization • Globalization • Interoperability	Testing types are • Performance Testing • Volume Testing • Scalability • Usability Testing • Load Testing • Stress Testing • Compliance Testing • Portability Testing • Disaster Recover Testing
It can be performed either manual or automated way	It can be performed efficiently if automated

10.6 Levels of Testing

10.6.1 Unit Testing

Unit Testing is a software testing technique by means of which individual units of software i.e. group of computer program modules, usage procedures, and operating procedures are tested to determine whether they are suitable for use or not. It is a testing method using which every independent module is tested to determine if there is an issue by the developer himself. It is correlated with the functional correctness of the independent modules.

Unit Testing is defined as a type of software testing where individual components of a software are tested. Unit Testing of the software product is carried out during the development of an application. An individual component may be either an individual function or a procedure.

Unit Testing is typically performed by the developer. In SDLC or V Model, Unit testing is the first level of testing done before integration testing.

Unit testing is such a type of testing technique that is usually performed by developers. Although due to the reluctance of developers to test, quality assurance engineers also do unit testing.

Objective of Unit Testing:

The objective of Unit Testing is:

To isolate a section of code.

To verify the correctness of the code.

To test every function and procedure.
To fix bugs early in the development cycle and to save costs.
To help the developers to understand the code base and enable them to make changes quickly.
To help with code reuse.

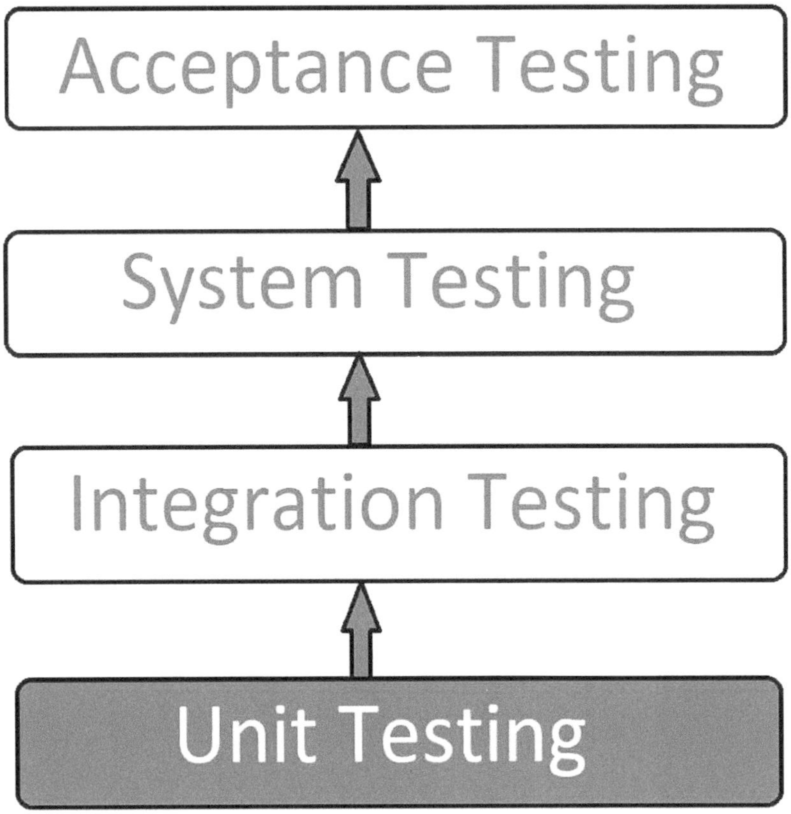

Types of Unit Testing:
There are 2 types of Unit Testing: Manual, and Automated.

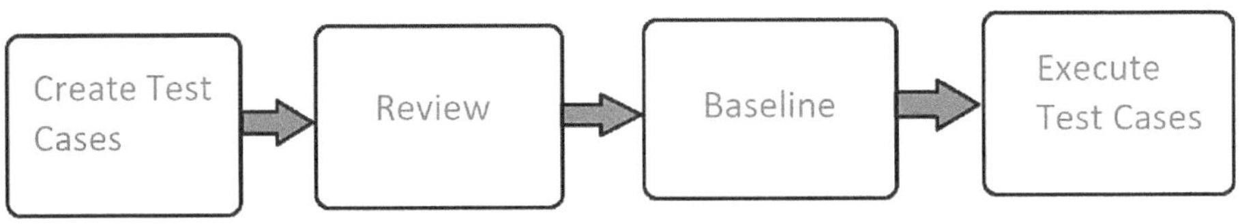

Workflow of Unit Testing:

Unit Testing Techniques:
There are 3 types of Unit Testing Techniques. They are
Black Box Testing: This testing technique is used in covering the unit tests for input, user interface, and output parts.
White Box Testing: This technique is used in testing the functional behavior of the system by giving the input and checking the functionality output including the internal design structure and code of the modules.
Gray Box Testing: This technique is used in executing the relevant test cases, test methods, test functions, and analyzing the code performance for the modules.

Unit Testing Tools:
Here are some commonly used Unit Testing tools:
Jtest
Junit
NUnit
EMMA
PHPUnit

10.6.2 System Testing

System Testing is a type of software testing that is performed on a complete integrated system to evaluate the compliance of the system with the corresponding requirements. In system testing, integration testing passed components are taken as input. The goal of integration testing is to detect any irregularity between the units that are integrated together. System testing detects defects within both the integrated units and the whole system.
System Testing is carried out on the whole system in the context of either system requirement specifications or functional requirement specifications or in the context of both.
System Testing is basically performed by a testing team that is independent of the development team that helps to test the quality of the system impartial. It has both functional and non-functional testing.
System Testing is a black-box testing. System Testing is performed after the integration testing and before the acceptance testing.

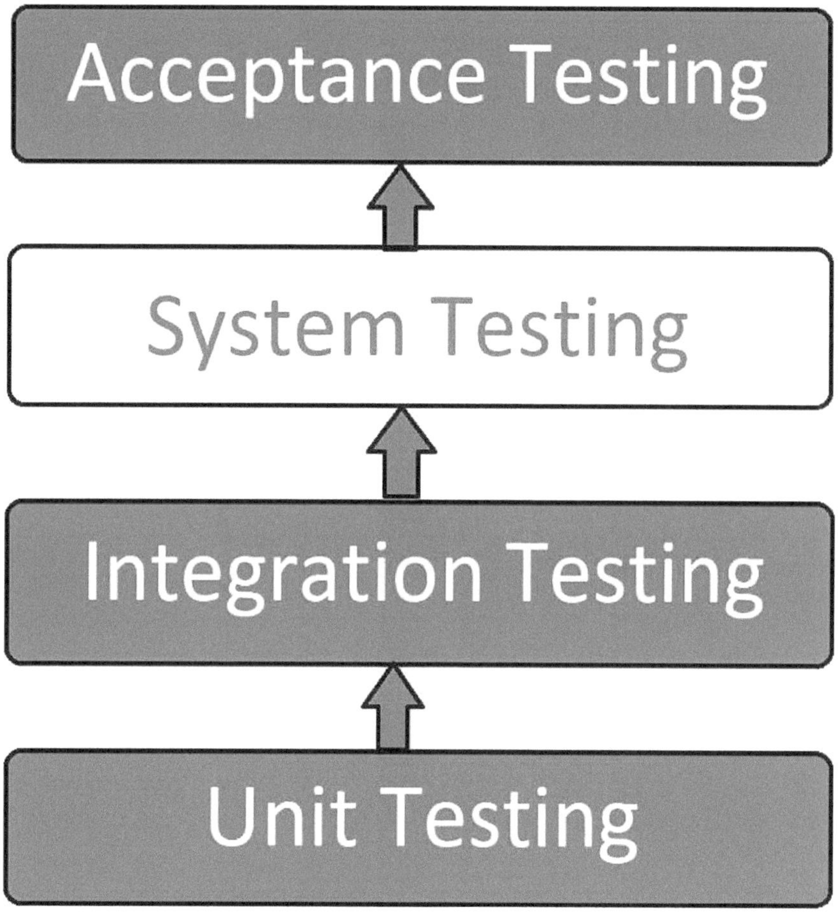

System Testing Process: System Testing is performed in the following steps:
Test Environment Setup: Create testing environment for the better quality testing.
Create Test Case: Generate test case for the testing process.
Create Test Data: Generate the data that is to be tested.
Execute Test Case: After the generation of the test case and the test data, test cases are executed.
Defect Reporting: Defects in the system are detected.
Regression Testing: It is carried out to test the side effects of the testing process.
Log Defects: Defects are fixed in this step.
Retest: If the test is not successful then again test is performed.

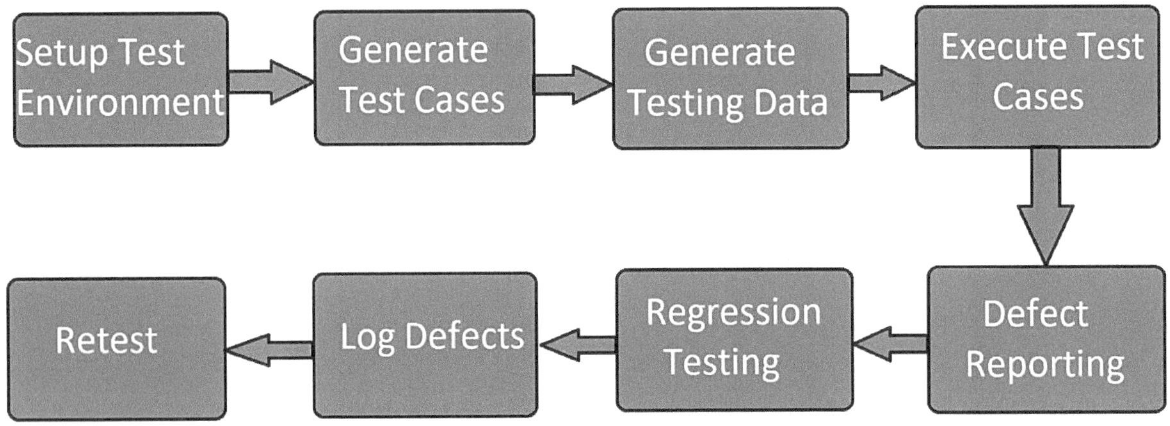

Types of System Testing:

Performance Testing: Performance Testing is a type of software testing that is carried out to test the speed, scalability, stability and reliability of the software product or application.

Load Testing: Load Testing is a type of software Testing which is carried out to determine the behavior of a system or software product under extreme load.

Stress Testing: Stress Testing is a type of software testing performed to check the robustness of the system under the varying loads.

Scalability Testing: Scalability Testing is a type of software testing which is carried out to check the performance of a software application or system in terms of its capability to scale up or scale down the number of user request load.

Tools used for System Testing :

JMeter
Gallen Framework
Selenium

Here are a few common tools used for System Testing:

HP Quality Center/ALM
IBM Rational Quality Manager
Microsoft Test Manager
Selenium
Appium
LoadRunner
Gatling
JMeter
Apache JServ
SoapUI

Note: The choice of tool depends on various factors like the technology used, the size of the project, the budget, and the testing requirements.

10.6.3 Integration Testing

Integration testing is the second level of the software testing process comes after unit testing. In this testing, units or individual components of the software are tested in a group. The focus of the integration testing level is to expose defects at the time of interaction between integrated components or units.

Unit testing uses modules for testing purpose, and these modules are combined and tested in integration testing. The Software is developed with a number of software modules that are coded by different coders or programmers. The goal of integration testing is to check the correctness of communication among all the modules.

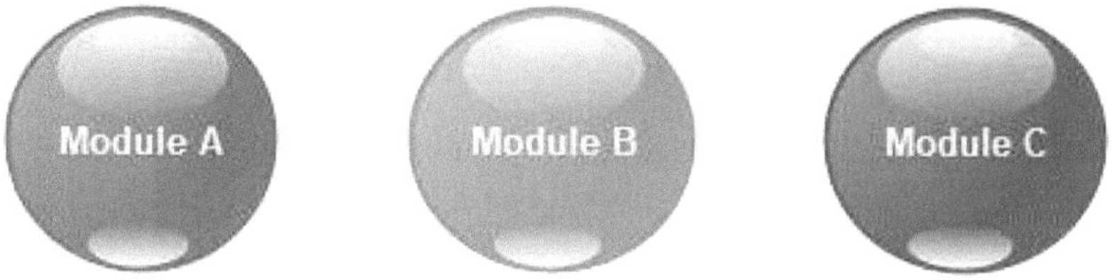

Tested in Unit Testing

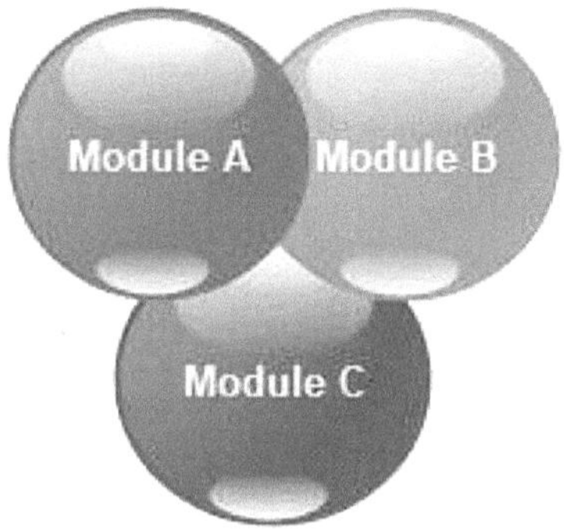

Under Integration Testing

Once all the components or modules are working independently, then we need to check the data flow between the dependent modules is known as integration testing.
Let us see one sample example of a banking application, as we can see in the below image of amount transfer.

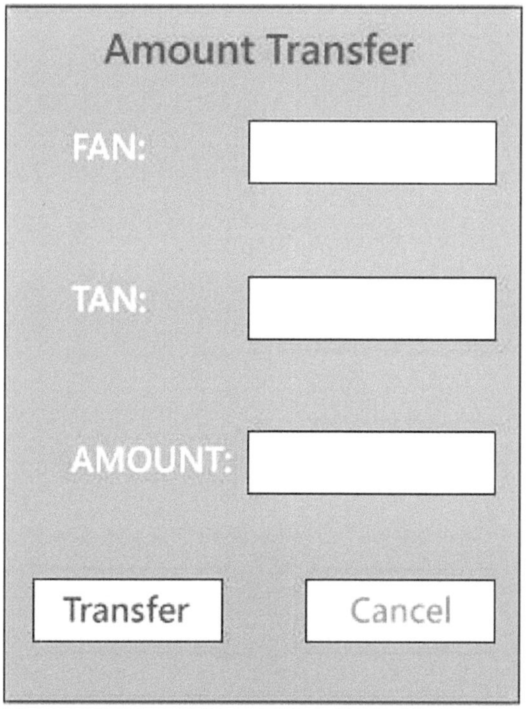

First, we will login as a user P to amount transfer and send Rs200 amount, the confirmation message should be displayed on the screen as amount transfer successfully. Now logout as P and login as user Q and go to amount balance page and check for a balance in that account = Present balance + Received Balance. Therefore, the integration test is successful.

Also, we check if the amount of balance has reduced by Rs200 in P user account.

Click on the transaction, in P and Q, the message should be displayed regarding the data and time of the amount transfer.

Guidelines for Integration Testing

We go for the integration testing only after the functional testing is completed on each module of the application.

We always do integration testing by picking module by module so that a proper sequence is followed, and also we don't miss out on any integration scenarios.

First, determine the test case strategy through which executable test cases can be prepared according to test data.

Examine the structure and architecture of the application and identify the crucial modules to test them first and also identify all possible scenarios.

Design test cases to verify each interface in detail.

Choose input data for test case execution. Input data plays a significant role in testing.

If we find any bugs then communicate the bug reports to developers and fix defects and retest.

Perform positive and negative integration testing.

Here positive testing implies that if the total balance is Rs15, 000 and we are transferring Rs1500 and checking if the amount transfer works fine. If it does, then the test would be a pass.

And negative testing means, if the total balance is Rs15, 000 and we are transferring Rs20, 000 and check if amount transfer occurs or not, if it does not occur, the test is a pass. If it happens, then there is a bug in the code, and we will send it to the development team for fixing that bug.

Note: Any application in this world will do functional testing compulsory, whereas integration testing will be done only if the modules are dependent on each other. Each integration scenarios should compulsorily have source→ data→destination. Any scenarios can be called as integration scenario only if the data gets saved in the destination.

For example: In the Gmail application, the Source could be Compose, Data could be Email and the Destination could be the Inbox.

Example of integration testing

Let us assume that we have a Gmail application where we perform the integration testing.

First, we will do functional testing on the login page, which includes the various components such as username, password, submit, and cancel button. Then only we can perform integration testing.

The different integration scenarios are as follows:

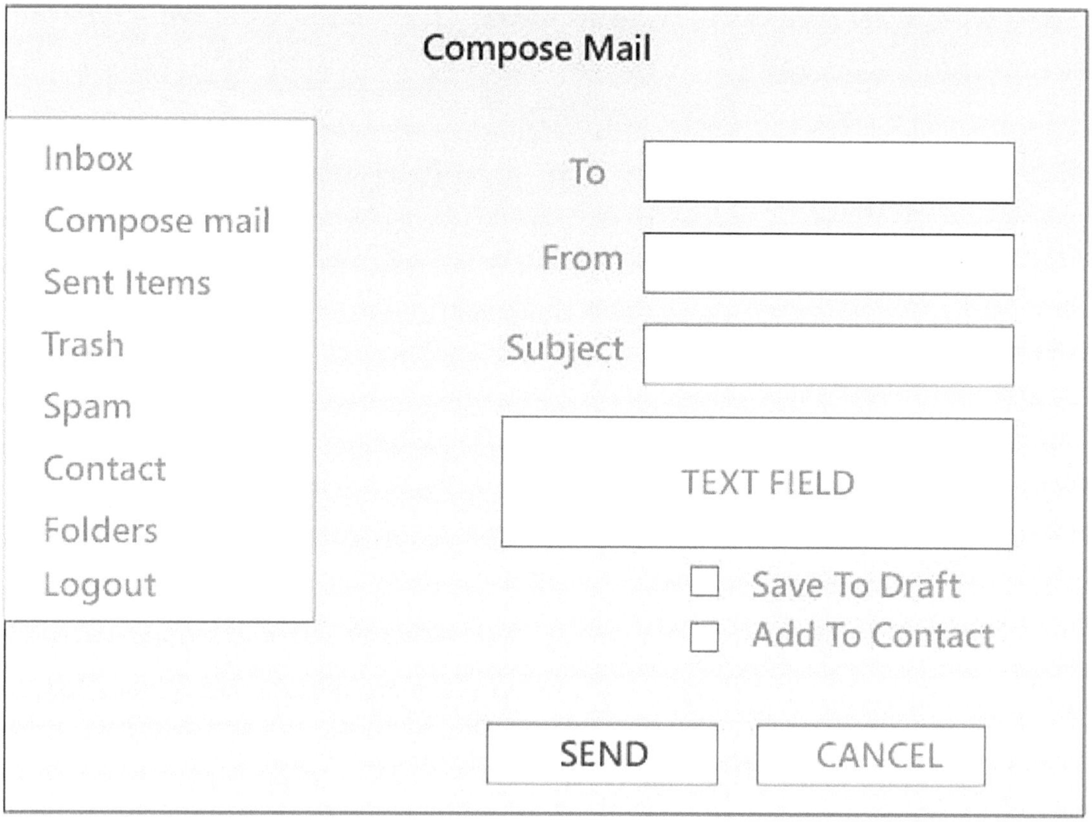

Scenarios1:
First, we login as P users and click on the Compose mail and performing the functional testing for the specific components.
Now we click on the Send and also check for Save Drafts.
After that, we send a mail to Q and verify in the Send Items folder of P to check if the send mail is there.
Now, we will log out as P and login as Q and move to the Inbox and verify that if the mail has reached.
Secanrios2: We also perform the integration testing on Spam folders. If the particular contact has been marked as spam, then any mail sent by that user should go to the spam folder and not in the inbox.
Note: We will perform functional testing for all features, such as to send items, inbox, and so on.
As we can see in the below image, we will perform the functional testing for all the text fields and every feature. Then we will perform integration testing for the related functions. We first test the add user, list of users, delete user, edit user, and then search user.

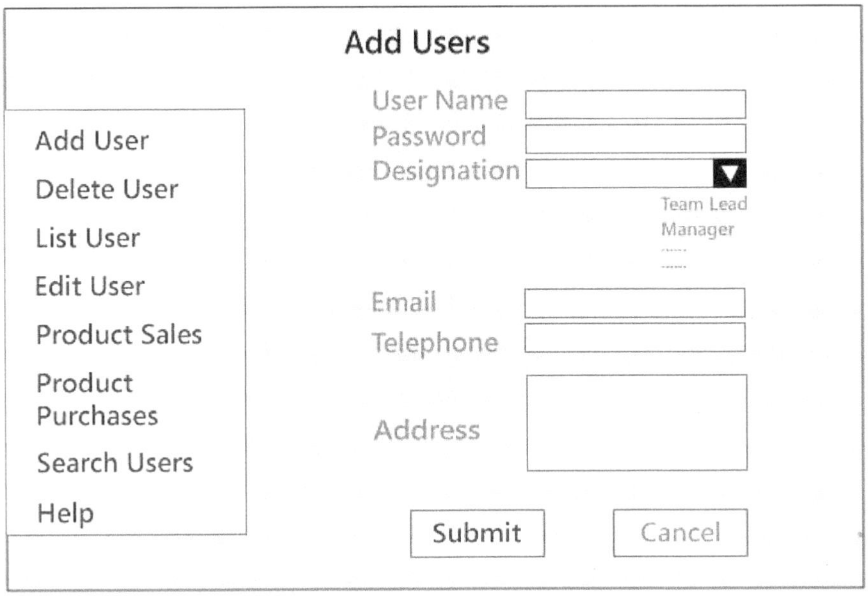

Note:
There are some features, we might be performing only the functional testing, and there are some features where we are performing both functional and integration testing based on the feature's requirements.
Prioritizing is essential, and we should perform it at all the phases, which means we will open the application and select which feature needs to be tested first. Then go to that feature and choose which component must be tested first. Go to those components and determine what values to be entered first.
And don't apply the same rule everywhere because testing logic varies from feature to feature.
While performing testing, we should test one feature entirely and then only proceed to another function.
Among the two features, we must be performing only positive integrating testing or both positive and negative integration testing, and this also depends on the features need.

Reason Behind Integration Testing

Although all modules of software application already tested in unit testing, errors still exist due to the following reasons:
Each module is designed by individual software developer whose programming logic may differ from developers of other modules so; integration testing becomes essential to determine the working of software modules.
To check the interaction of software modules with the database whether it is an erroneous or not.
Requirements can be changed or enhanced at the time of module development. These new requirements may not be tested at the level of unit testing hence integration testing becomes mandatory.
Incompatibility between modules of software could create errors.
To test hardware's compatibility with software.
If exception handling is inadequate between modules, it can create bugs.

Integration Testing Techniques

Any testing technique (Blackbox, Whitebox, and Greybox) can be used for Integration Testing; some are listed below:
Black Box Testing
State Transition technique
Decision Table Technique
Boundary Value Analysis
All-pairs Testing
Cause and Effect Graph
Equivalence Partitioning
Error Guessing
White Box Testing
Data flow testing
Control Flow Testing
Branch Coverage Testing

Decision Coverage Testing

Types of Integration Testing

Integration testing can be classified into two parts:

Incremental integration testing

Non-incremental integration testing

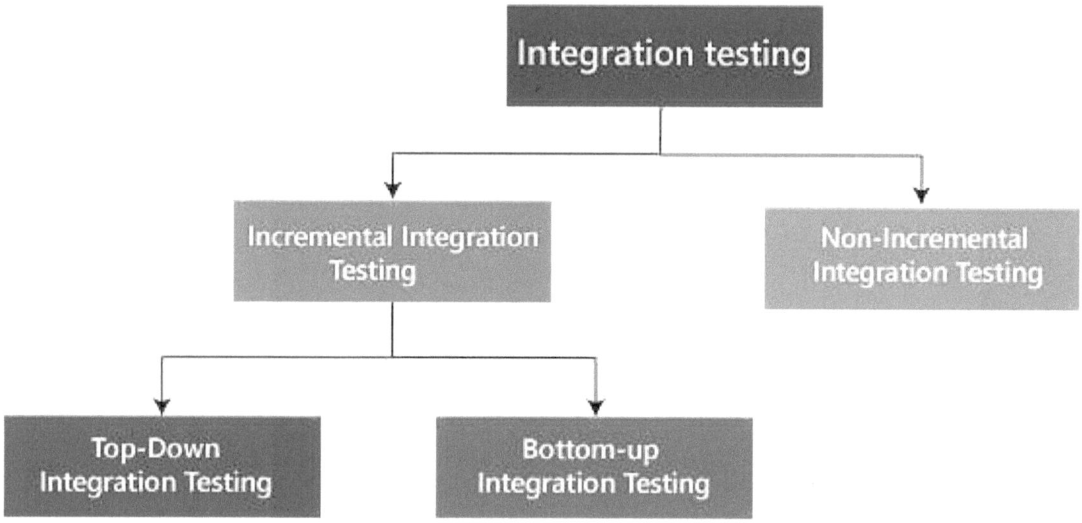

Incremental Approach

In the Incremental Approach, modules are added in ascending order one by one or according to need. The selected modules must be logically related. Generally, two or more than two modules are added and tested to determine the correctness of functions. The process continues until the successful testing of all the modules.

OR

In this type of testing, there is a strong relationship between the dependent modules. Suppose we take two or more modules and verify that the data flow between them is working fine. If it is, then add more modules and test again.

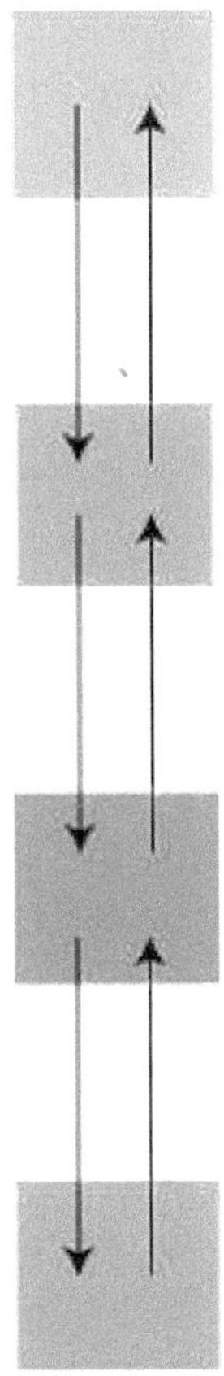

For example: Suppose we have a Flipkart application, we will perform incremental integration testing, and the flow of the application would like this:

Flipkart→ Login→ Home → Search→ Add cart→Payment → Logout

Incremental integration testing is carried out by further methods:

Top-Down approach

Bottom-Up approach

Top-Down Approach

The top-down testing strategy deals with the process in which higher level modules are tested with lower level modules until the successful completion of testing of all the modules. Major design flaws can be detected and fixed early because critical modules tested first. In this type of method, we will add the modules incrementally or one by one and check the data flow in the same order.

Top-Down Approach

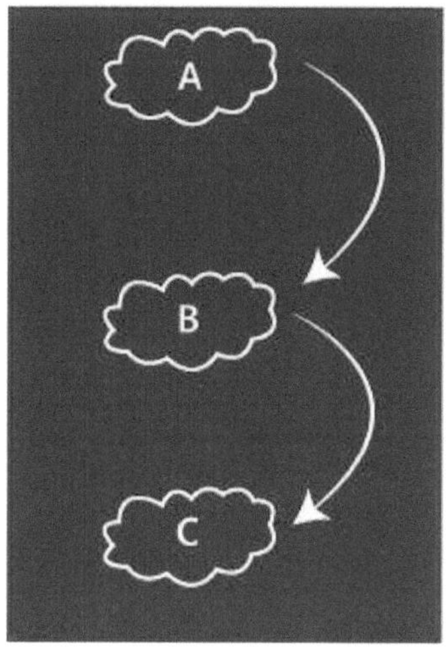

In the top-down approach, we will be ensuring that the module we are adding is the child of the previous one like Child C is a child of Child B and so on as we can see in the below image:

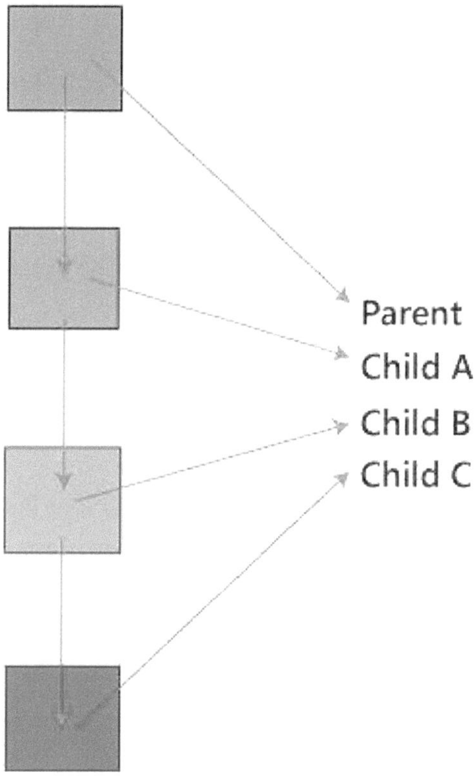

Advantages:
Identification of defect is difficult.
An early prototype is possible.
Disadvantages:
Due to the high number of stubs, it gets quite complicated.
Lower level modules are tested inadequately.
Critical Modules are tested first so that fewer chances of defects.
Bottom-Up Method

The bottom to up testing strategy deals with the process in which lower level modules are tested with higher level modules until the successful completion of testing of all the modules. Top level critical modules are tested at last, so it may cause a defect. Or we can say that we will be adding the modules from **bottom to the top** and check the data flow in the same order.

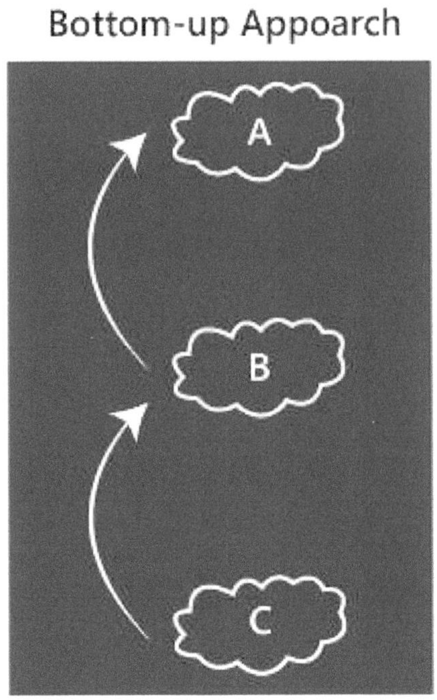

In the bottom-up method, we will ensure that the modules we are adding are the parent of the previous one as we can see in the below image:

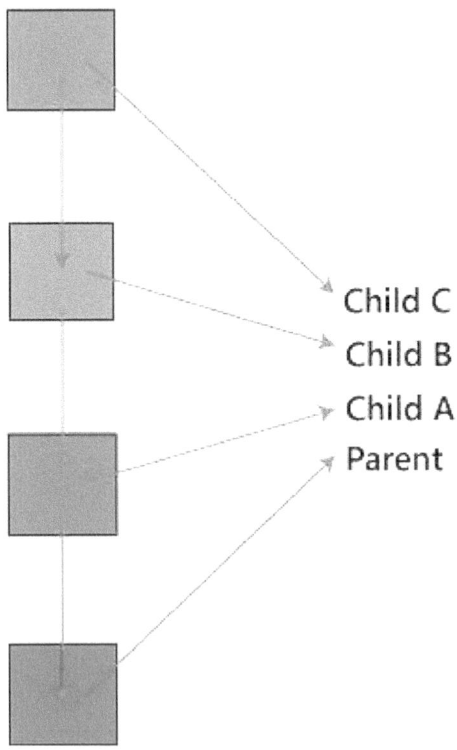

Advantages

Identification of defect is easy.

Do not need to wait for the development of all the modules as it saves time.

Disadvantages

Critical modules are tested last due to which the defects can occur.

There is no possibility of an early prototype.

In this, we have one addition approach which is known as hybrid testing.

Hybrid Testing Method

In this approach, both Top-Down and Bottom-Up approaches are combined for testing. In this process, top-level modules are tested with lower level modules and lower level modules tested with high-level modules simultaneously. There is less possibility of occurrence of defect because each module interface is tested.

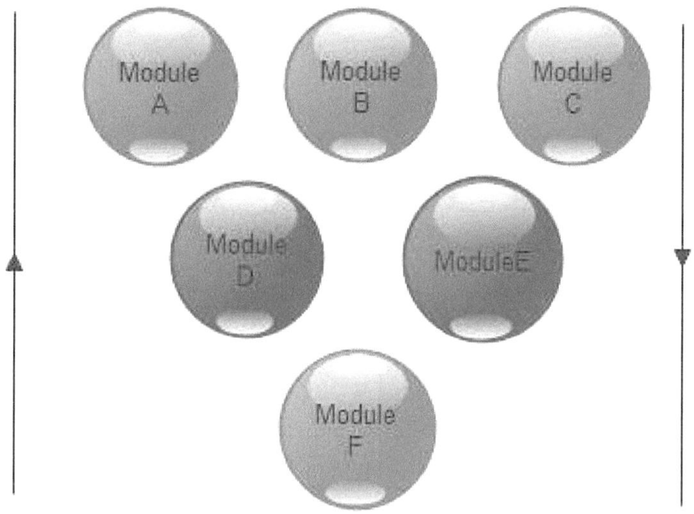

Hybrid Method

Advantages

The hybrid method provides features of both Bottom Up and Top Down methods.

It is most time reducing method.

It provides complete testing of all modules.

Disadvantages

This method needs a higher level of concentration as the process carried out in both directions simultaneously.

Complicated method.

Non- incremental integration testing

We will go for this method, when the data flow is very complex and when it is difficult to find who is a parent and who is a child. And in such case, we will create the data in any module bang on all other existing modules and check if the data is present. Hence, it is also known as the Big bang method.

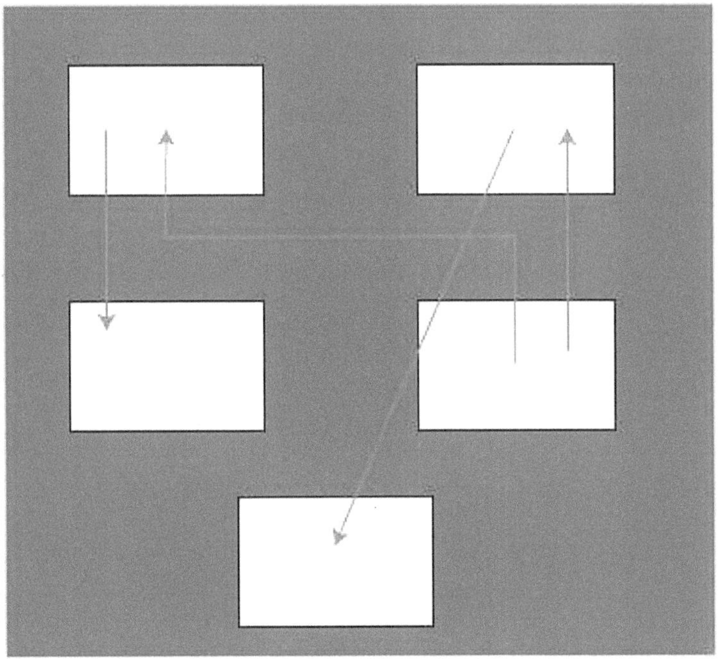

Big Bang Method

In this approach, testing is done via integration of all modules at once. It is convenient for small software systems, if used for large software systems identification of defects is difficult.

Since this testing can be done after completion of all modules due to that testing team has less time for execution of this process so that internally linked interfaces and high-risk critical modules can be missed easily.

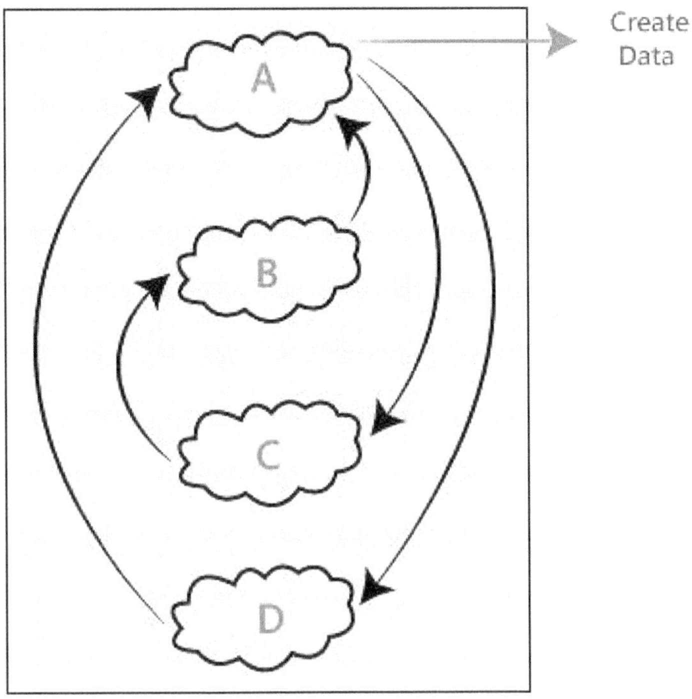

Advantages:

It is convenient for small size software systems.

Disadvantages:

Identification of defects is difficult because finding the error where it came from is a problem, and we don't know the source of the bug.
Small modules missed easily.
Time provided for testing is very less.
We may miss to test some of the interfaces.
Let us see examples for our better understanding of the non-incremental integrating testing or big bang method:

Example1

In the below example, the development team develops the application and sends it to the CEO of the testing team. Then the CEO will log in to the application and generate the username and password and send a mail to the manager. After that, the CEO will tell them to start testing the application.
Then the manager manages the username and the password and produces a username and password and sends it to the **test** leads. And the test leads will send it to the test engineers for further testing purposes. This order from the CEO to the test engineer is top-down incremental integrating testing.
In the same way, when the test engineers are done with testing, they send a report to the test leads, who then submit a report to the manager, and the manager will send a report to the CEO. This process is known as Bottom-up incremental integration testing as we can see in the below image:
Note: The combination incremental integration testing (I.I.T) and non-incremental integration testing is known as sandwich testing.

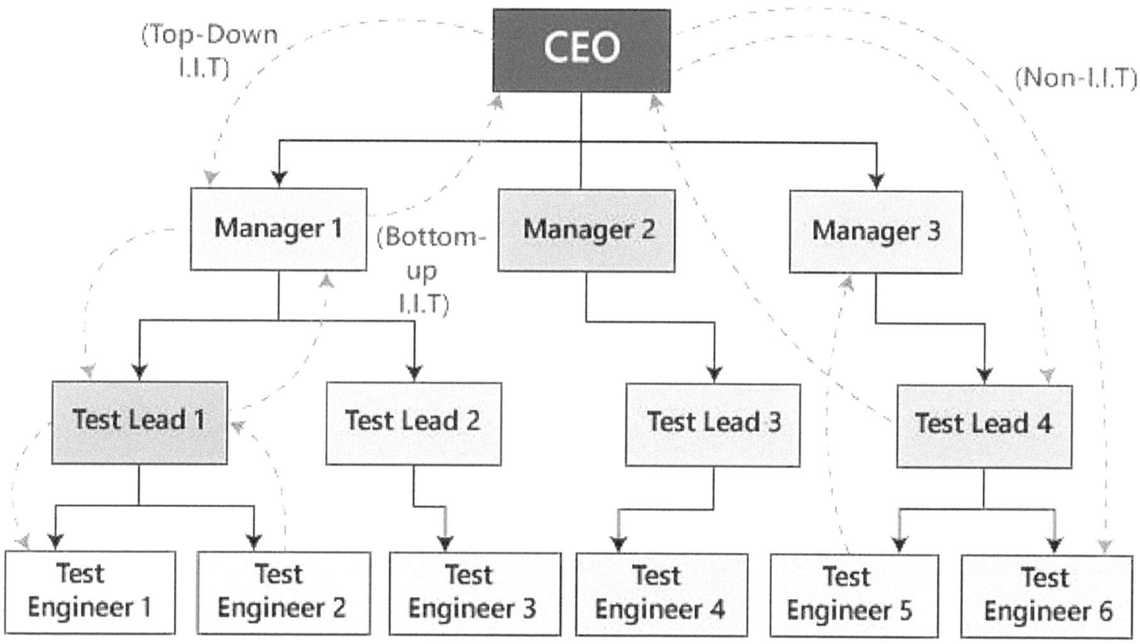

Example2

The below example demonstrates a home page of Gmail's Inbox, where we click on the Inbox link, and we are moved to the inbox page. Here we have to do non- incremental integration testing because there is no parent and child concept.

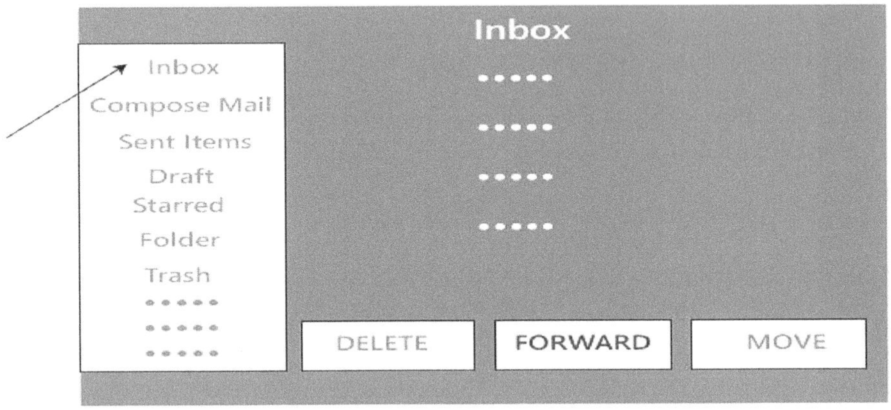

Note: -

Stub and driver

The **stub** is a dummy module that receives the data and creates lots of probable data, but it performs like a real module. When a data is sent from module P to Stub Q, it receives the data without confirming and validating it, and produce the estimated outcome for the given data.

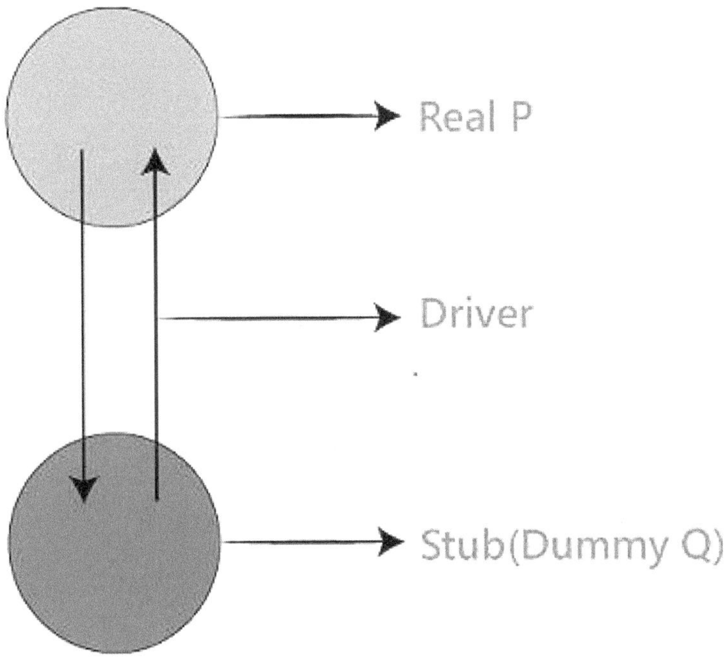

The function of a driver is used to verify the data from P and sends it to stub and also checks the expected data from the stub and sends it to P.

The **driver** is one that sets up the test environments and also takes care of the communication, evaluates results, and sends the reports. We never use the stub and driver in the testing process.

In White box testing, bottom-up integration testing is ideal because writing drivers is accessible. And **in black box testing**, no preference is given to any testing as it depends on the application.

10.6.4 Acceptance Testing

Acceptance Testing can be defined as the level of software testing where your system will be tested for acceptability, or you can say suitability.

These types of tests in products are done for evaluating the compliance of the system with business needs and check if it's suitable for delivery or not.

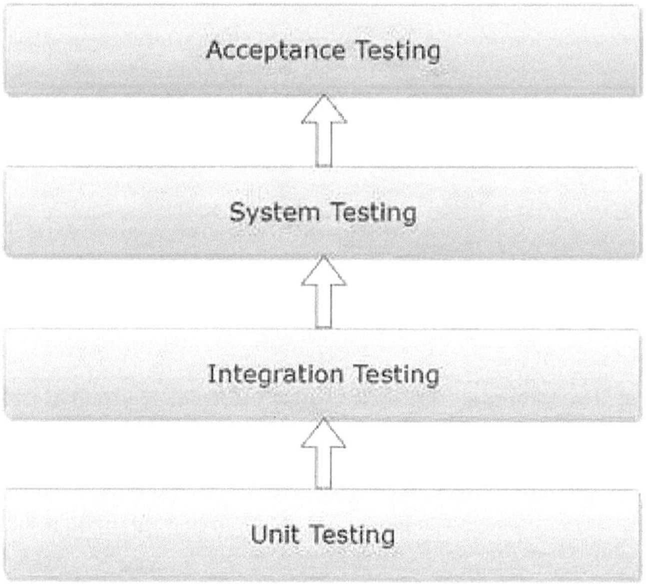

Levels of Testing

Typically, a Black box testing technique needs to be implemented for Acceptance Test. Though it doesn't usually pursue a strict practice still, you can follow this testing technique to better accept your product by users.

Tasks to Be Done Through Acceptance Testing

Plan for acceptance test:
Prepare
Review
Rework
Baseline
The cycle must be followed to achieve acceptance testing plan:
Cases for acceptance test:
Prepare
Review
Rework
Baseline
Acceptance Test to be carried on:
Perform

When to Perform Acceptance Test?

This test can be performed after the system test and before making available your system for use.

Attributes for Acceptance Testing and Reporting

Here are the report attributes that can be followed to create an acceptance testing report:
Set a report identifier
Grab and put all the summary of results
Variations found
Recommendations are given
To-Do List summary
Approval Decision

10.6.5 Alpha Testing

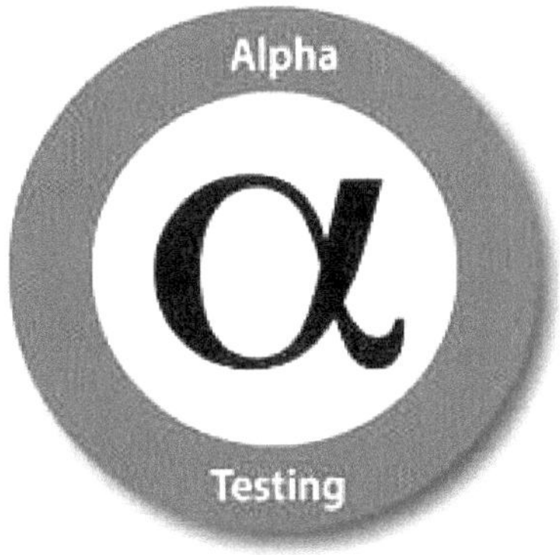

Alpha testing is conducted in the organization and tested by a representative group of end-users at the developer's side and sometimes by an independent team of testers.
Alpha testing is simulated or real operational testing at an in-house site. It comes after the unit testing, integration testing, etc. Alpha testing used after all the testing are executed.
It can be a white box, or Black-box testing depends on the requirements - particular lab environment and simulation of the actual environment required for this testing.

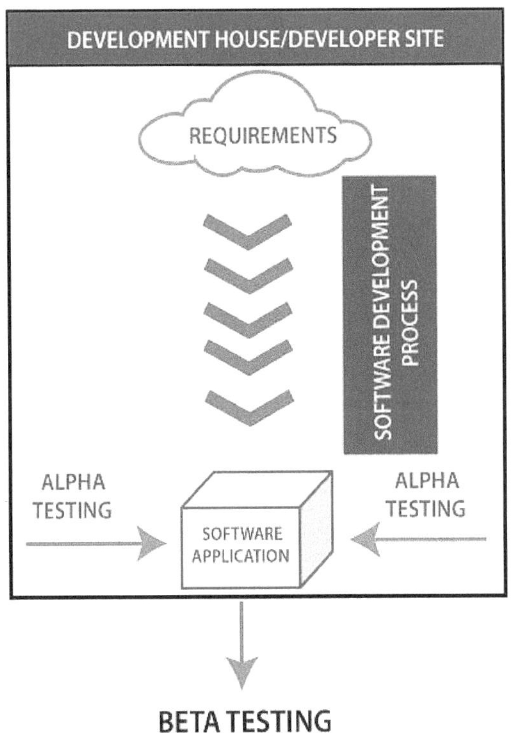

What is the alpha testing process?
Alpha testing follows the following process:
Requirement Review: Review the design of the specification and functional requirement
Test Development: Test development is base on the outcome of the requirement review. Develop the test cases and test plan.
Test case design: Execute the test plan and test cases.
Logging Defects: Logging the identified and detected bug found in the application.
Bug Fixation: When all the bugs are identified and logged, then there is a need to fix the bug.
Retesting: When all the issues are solved, and fixed retesting is done.

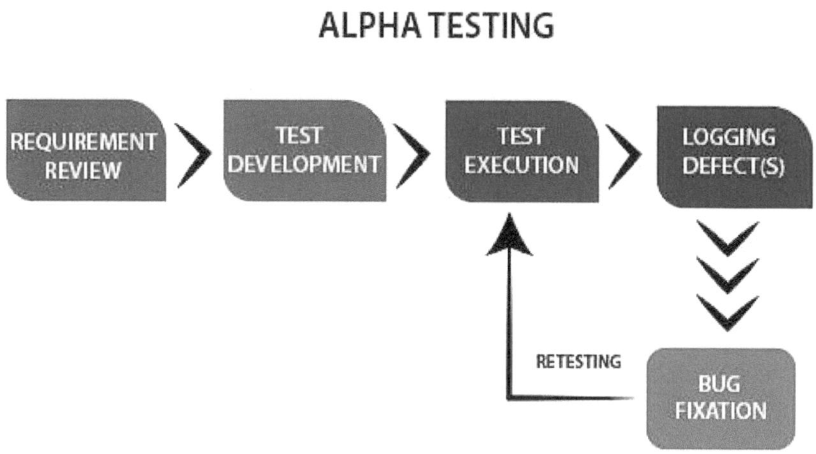

What are the phases of alpha testing?

Alpha testing ensures that the software performs flawlessly and does not impact the reputation of the organization; the company implements final testing in the form of alpha testing. This testing executed into two phases.

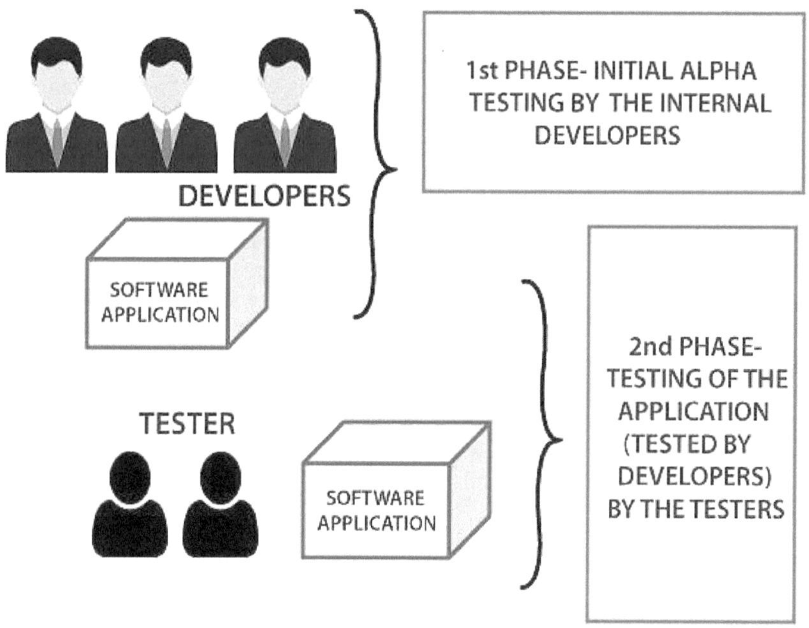

There are two phases of alpha testing.

First Phase: In-house developers of software engineers do the first phase of testing. In this phase, the tester used hardware debugger or hardware aided debugger to catches the bugs quickly. During the alpha testing, a tester finds a lot of bugs, crashes, missing features, and docs.

Second Phase: The second phase involves the quality assurance staff performs the alpha testing by involving black box and white box techniques.

When to perform alpha testing?

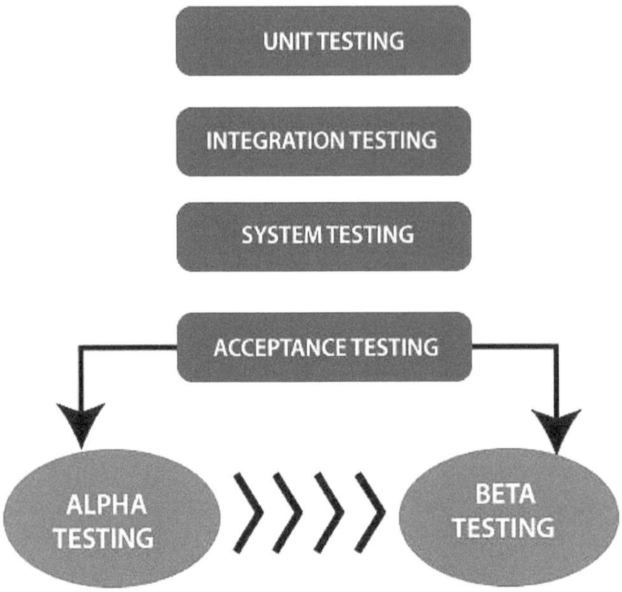

Alpha testing is user acceptance testing. Alpha testing performed once the product has gone through stages of testing and prepared for release. It is executing before beta testing, which is also a part of acceptance testing and can define as field testing. During this testing, we can make changes in the software to improve its quality and functionality. Alpha testing done from the developer's site where independent developers can monitor and record user experience and make necessary changes to enhance the performance.

What are the reasons to perform Alpha Testing?

Alpha testing is the final stage of the testing. Alpha testing is an essential and popular testing technique that helps the team to deliver quality and useful software. This testing performed before the release of the product. Alpha testing can define as the first round of independent testing that ensures that the software run as per the requirement plan.

Reasons for alpha testing are:

Refines the software product by finding and rectifying bugs that weren't discovered through previous tests.

Alpha testing allows the team to test the software in a real-world environment.

One of the reasons to do alpha testing is to ensure the success of the software product.

Alpha testing validates the quality, functionality of the software, and effectiveness of the software before it released in the real world.

10.6.6 Beta Testing

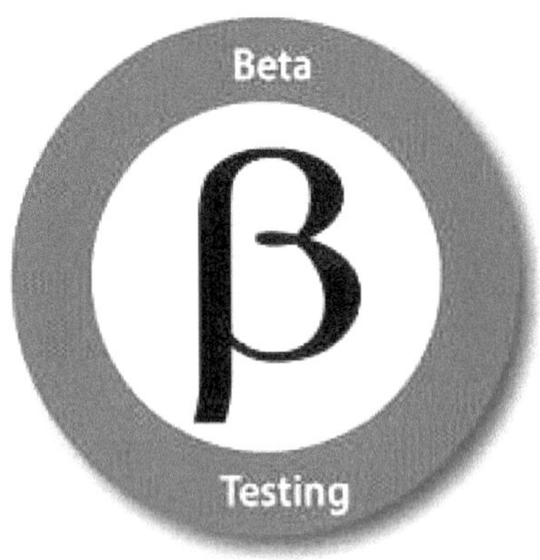

Beta testing is a type of User Acceptance Testing among the most crucial testing, which performed before the release of the software.

Beta Testing is a type of Field Test. This testing performs at the end of the software testing life cycle. This type of testing can be considered as external user acceptance testing. It is a type of salient testing. Real users perform this testing.

This testing executed after the alpha testing. In this the new version, beta testing is released to a limited audience to check the accessibility, usability, and functionality, and more.

Beta testing is the last phase of the testing, which is carried out at the client's or customer's site.

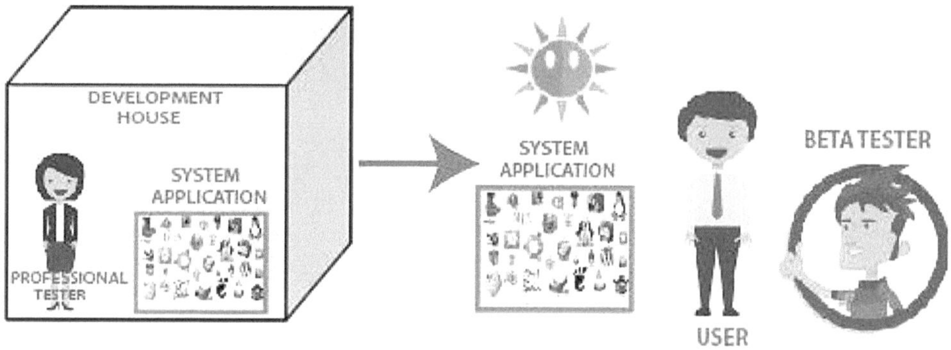

BETA TESTING OF THE PRODUCT IN REAL WORLD ENVIRONMENT

Features of beta testing are:

Beta testing used in a real environment at the user's site. Beta testing helps in providing the actual position of the quality.

Testing performed by the client, stakeholder, and end-user.

Beta testing always is done after the alpha testing, and before releasing it into the market.

Beta testing is black-box testing.

Beta testing performs in the absence of tester and the presence of real users

Beta testing is performed after alpha testing and before the release of the final product.

Beta testing generally is done for testing software products like utilities, operating systems, and applications, etc.

What is a beta version of the software?

The beta version of the software is delivered to a restricted number of users to accept their feedback and suggestions on quality improvement. Hence, there are two types of beta version:

1) Closed beta version: Closed beta version, also known as a private beta, it is released to a group of selected and invited people. Those people will test the software and evaluate their features and specifications. This beta version represents the software which is capable of delivering value, but it is not ready to be used by everyone. Because it shows the issues like lack of documentation or missing vital features.

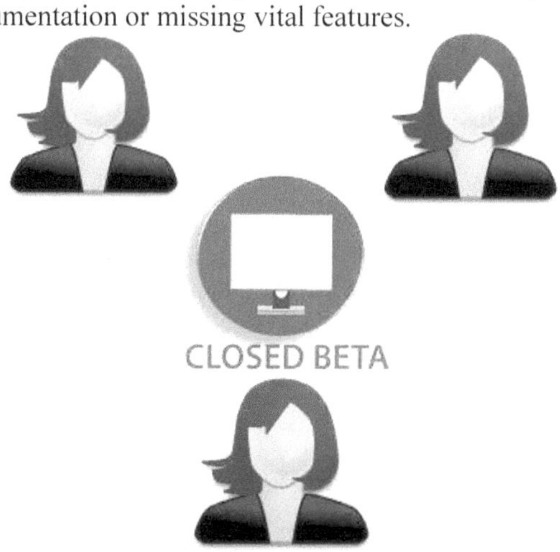

2) Open beta version: Open beta is also known as a public beta. The open beta opened to the public. Any user as a tester can assess the beta version to provide the relevant feedback and reviews. Open beta version improves the quality of the final release. This version helps to find the various undetected errors and issues.

The beta testing process orients this beta version.

What is the lifecycle of Beta Testing?

A group of end-users performs beta testing. This process can't execute without any strategy or test plan. Before the testers, the end-user executes this type of testing.

The process of beta testing follows the following steps:

Planning: Like another testing process, beta testing also supports proper planning. In this stage, the team prepares a testing strategy and defines the goal of testing. In this case, the team establishes the need of users for testing, duration, and necessary details related to the process.

Participant Recruitment: This is the second stage of the beta process in which the team recruits a group of selected end-users for testing. This group can change as per the requirement of the organization and the product.

Product Launch: When a team of users (testers) recruited. The beta version of the product is launched or installed at the client or user side, and users will test the product for quality assurance.

Collect and Evaluate Feedback: When the testing finished, developers will collect the feedback provided by the testers and evaluate it. In the end, based on the feedback, issues, and bugs are fixed and resolved by the responsible individual team.

Closure: When all the problems fixed and the organization meets the exit criteria, beta testing achieved, and the rewards offered to the testing team.

What are the types of beta testing?

Beta testing has six types. Each type has different aspects of the software. All these help developers to improve the quality of the software and allow them to deliver a product that offers excellent user experience. Here are the different types of beta testing:

Open Beta Testing: Open beta testing involves testing the software product by a large number of people before the final release. The organization decides to make a software product open to the public before releasing the product. Open Beta includes the extensive participation of the public to use and evaluate software product accordingly. Users report the bug to the organization, along with a suggestion to improve the quality of the software.

Closed Beta Testing: Opposite to the open beta testing. Closed beta testing performed by the selective and limited number of persons. The organization recruits these. In this testing software product is not open to the public.

Traditional Beta Testing: In this testing, a software product delivered to the target market, and the feedback from the users collected. This type of testing assistance the beta testing, the quality of the software is improved, and developers can make the changes.

Public Beta Testing: This type of testing is similar to open testing. Public beta testing also allows the product is delivering to the end-users worldwide, with the aid of various online channels available in the world. From this, the feedback and evaluated data also collected and based on the requirement changes, and the development team implements modifications.

Technical Beta Testing: Technical beta testing is also an essential type of beta testing. This testing involves delivering the software product to the internal groups of the organization. However, the data and feedback provided by the employees of the organization.

Focused Beta Testing: This type of testing focused on monitoring and evaluating a specific feature or component of the software. In focused beta testing, the software released to the market and user's experience assessed and collected to make the required changes.

Post-Release Beta Testing: In this testing, the product delivered to the market for the use of the end-users. Their feedback, reactions, and experience are collect for the future release of the software.

What is a Beta Test plan?

A beta test plan can be written in many ways,

Objective: We should have to mention the aim of the project why there is a need for beta testing even after performing the internal testing.

Scope: In this plan, we should mention the areas to be tested or not.

Test Approach: We should have to mention clearly that the testing is in the deep, what to focus on - functionality, UI, response, etc.

Schedule: We have to specify, clearly the start and ending date with time, number of cycles, and duration per cycle.

Tools: Bug logging tools and the usage of the machines should identify.

Budget: Incentive of the bugs based on the severity.

Feedback: Collecting feedback and evaluating methods.

Identify and review the entry and exit criteria.

What are the entry criteria for Beta Testing?

Sign off the document from alpha testing.

Beta version of the software should ready.

The environment should be ready to release the software application to the public.

To capture the real-time faults environment should be ready.

What are the exit criteria for Beta Testing?

All the major and minor issues resolved.

The feedback report should prepare.

The delivery of beta test summary report.

10.6.7 Regression Testing

Regression Testing is defined as a type of software testing to confirm that a recent program or code change has not adversely affected existing features. Regression Testing is nothing but a full or partial selection of already executed test cases that are re-executed to ensure existing functionalities work fine.

Why Regression Testing?

There is a need for regression testing whenever the code is changed, and you need to determine whether the modified code will affect other parts of the software application. Moreover, regression testing is needed when a new feature is added to the software application. Regression tests may also be performed when a functional or performance defect/issue is fixed.

How to do Regression Testing in Software Testing

In order to do Regression Testing process, we need to first debug the code to identify the bugs. Once the bugs are identified, required changes are made to fix it, then the regression testing is done by selecting relevant test cases from the test suite that covers both modified and affected parts of the code.

Software maintenance is an activity which includes enhancements, error corrections, optimization and deletion of existing features. These modifications may cause the system to work incorrectly. Therefore, Regression Testing becomes necessary. Regression testing, and specifically various regression testing techniques, can be carried out for effective software quality assurance:

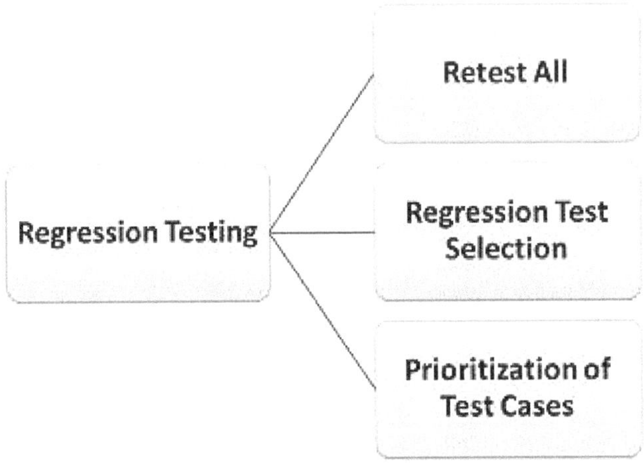

Retest All

This is one of the methods for Regression Testing, specifically employing a regression testing suite, in which all the tests in the existing test bucket or suite should be re-executed. This is very expensive as it requires huge time and resources.

Regression Test Selection

Regression Test Selection is a technique in which some selected test cases from test suite are executed to test whether the modified code affects the software application or not. Test cases are categorized into two parts, reusable test cases which can be used in further regression cycles and obsolete test cases which can not be used in succeeding cycles.

Prioritization of Test Cases

Prioritize the test cases depending on business impact, critical & frequently used functionalities. Selection of test cases based on priority will greatly reduce the regression test suite.

Selecting test cases for regression testing

It was found from industry data that a good number of the defects reported by customers were due to last minute bug fixes creating side effects and hence selecting the Test Case for regression testing is an art and not that easy. Effective Regression Tests can be done by selecting the following test cases –

Test cases which have frequent defects
Functionalities which are more visible to the users
Test cases which verify core features of the product
Test cases of Functionalities which has undergone more and recent changes
All Integration Test Cases
All Complex Test Cases
Boundary value test cases
A sample of Successful test cases
A sample of Failure test cases

Regression Testing Tools

If your software undergoes frequent changes, regression testing costs will escalate. In such cases, Manual execution of test cases increases test execution time as well as costs. Automation of regression test cases is the smart choice in such cases. The extent of automation depends on the number of test cases that remain re-usable for successive regression cycles.

Following are the most important tools used for both functional and regression testing in software engineering:

1) testRigor
2) Avo Assure
3) Subject7
4) Selenium: This is an open source tool used for automating web applications. Selenium can be used for browser-based regression testing.

Types of Regression Testing

Here are the different kinds of regression testing:

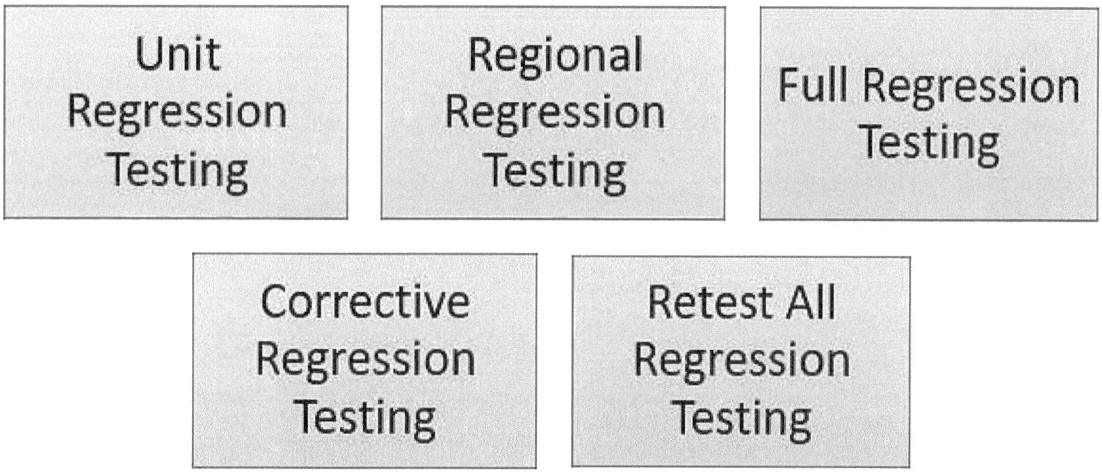

10.6.8 Mutation Testing

The mutation is a small modification in a program; these minor modifications are planned to typical low-level errors which are happened at the time of coding process.

Generally, we deliberate the mutation operators in the form of rules which match the data and also generate some efficient environment to produce the mutant.

Types of mutation testing

Mutation testing can be classified into three parts, which are as follows:

Decision mutations

value mutations

Statement mutations

Let us understand them one by one:

Decision mutations

In this type of mutation testing, we will check the design errors. And here, we will do the modification in arithmetic and logical operator to detect the errors in the program.

Like if we do the following changes in arithmetic operators:

plus(+)→ minus(-)

asterisk(*)→ double asterisk(**)

plus(+)→incremental operator(i++)

Like if we do the following changes in logical operators
Exchange P > → P<, OR P>=
Now, let see one example for our better understanding:

Original Code	Modified Code
if(p >q)	if(p < q)
r= 5;	r = 5;
else	else
r= 15;	r = 15;

Value mutations
In this, the values will modify to identify the errors in the program, and generally, we will change the following:
Small value à higher value
Higher value àSmall value.
For Example:

Original Code	Modified Code
int add =9000008;	int mod = 9008;
int p = 65432;	int p = 65432;
int q =12345;	int q =12345;
int r = (p+ q);	int r= (p + q);

Statement Mutations
Statement mutations means that we can do the modifications into the statements by removing or replacing the line as we see in the below example:

Original Code	Modified Code
if(p * q)	if(p* q)
r = 15;	s = 15;
else	else
r = 25;	s = 25;

In the above case, we have replaced the statement r=15 by s=15, and r=25 by s=25.
How to perform mutation testing
To perform mutation testing, we will follow the below process:

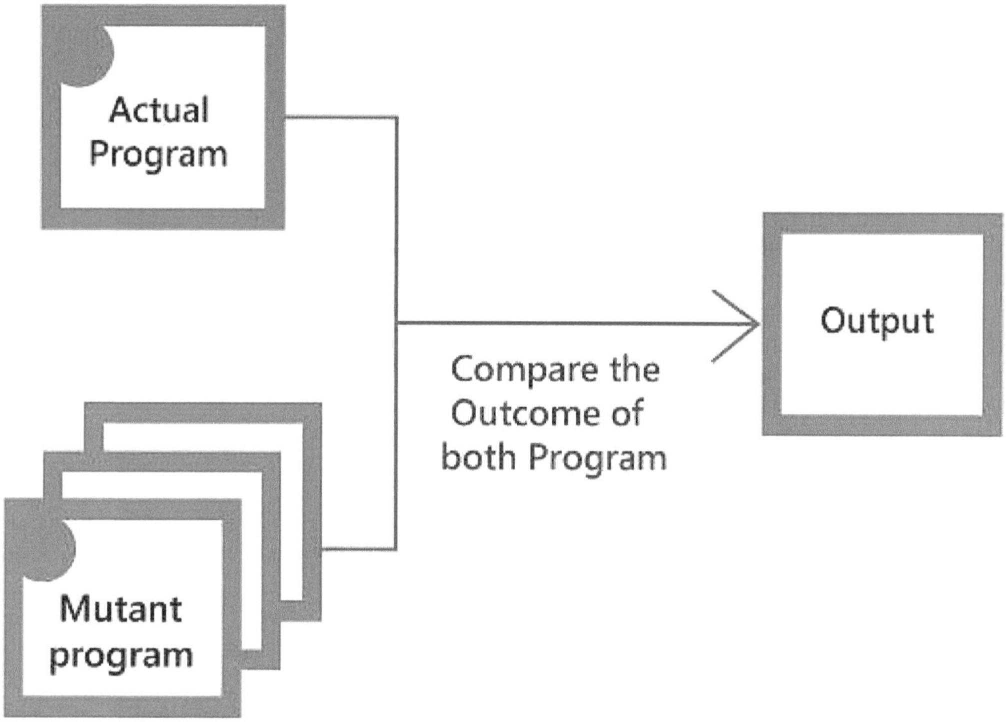

In this, firstly, we will add the errors into the source code of the program by producing various versions, which are known mutants. Here every mutant having the one error, which leads the mutant kinds unsuccessful and also validates the efficiency of the test cases.
After that, we will take the help of the test cases in the mutant program and the actual application will find the errors in the code.
Once we identify the faults, we will match the output of the actual code and mutant code.
After comparing the output of both actual and mutant programs, if the results are not matched, then the mutant is executed by the test cases. Therefore the test case has to be sufficient for identifying the modification between the actual program and the mutant program.
And if the actual program and the mutant program produced the exact result, then the mutant is saved. And those cases are more active test cases because it helps us to execute all the mutants.

10.7 Debugging

Debugging is the process of identifying and resolving errors, or bugs, in a software system. It is an important aspect of software engineering because bugs can cause a software system to malfunction, and can lead to poor performance or incorrect results. Debugging can be a time-consuming and complex task, but it is essential for ensuring that a software system is functioning correctly.
There are several common methods and techniques used in debugging, including:
Code Inspection: This involves manually reviewing the source code of a software system to identify potential bugs or errors.
Debugging Tools: There are various tools available for debugging such as debuggers, trace tools, and profilers that can be used to identify and resolve bugs.
Unit Testing: This involves testing individual units or components of a software system to identify bugs or errors.
Integration Testing: This involves testing the interactions between different components of a software system to identify bugs or errors.
System Testing: This involves testing the entire software system to identify bugs or errors.
Monitoring: This involves monitoring a software system for unusual behavior or performance issues that can indicate the presence of bugs or errors.
Logging: This involves recording events and messages related to the software system, which can be used to identify bugs or errors.
Debugging Process: Steps involved in debugging are:

Problem identification and report preparation.
Assigning the report to the software engineer defect to verify that it is genuine.
Defect Analysis using modeling, documentation, finding and testing candidate flaws, etc.
Defect Resolution by making required changes to the system.
Validation of corrections.

The debugging process will always have one of two outcomes :

The cause will be found and corrected.
The cause will not be found.

Later, the person performing debugging may suspect a cause, design a test case to help validate that suspicion and work toward error correction in an iterative fashion.

During debugging, we encounter errors that range from mildly annoying to catastrophic. As the consequences of an error increase, the amount of pressure to find the cause also increases. Often, pressure sometimes forces a software developer to fix one error and at the same time introduce two more.

Debugging Approaches/Strategies:

Brute Force: Study the system for a larger duration in order to understand the system. It helps the debugger to construct different representations of systems to be debugged depending on the need. A study of the system is also done actively to find recent changes made to the software.

Backtracking: Backward analysis of the problem which involves tracing the program backward from the location of the failure message in order to identify the region of faulty code. A detailed study of the region is conducted to find the cause of defects.

Forward analysis of the program involves tracing the program forwards using breakpoints or print statements at different points in the program and studying the results. The region where the wrong outputs are obtained is the region that needs to be focused on to find the defect.

Using past experience with the software debug the software with similar problems in nature. The success of this approach depends on the expertise of the debugger.

Cause elimination: it introduces the concept of binary partitioning. Data related to the error occurrence are organized to isolate potential causes.

Static analysis: Analyzing the code without executing it to identify potential bugs or errors. This approach involves analyzing code syntax, data flow, and control flow.

Dynamic analysis: Executing the code and analyzing its behavior at runtime to identify errors or bugs. This approach involves techniques like runtime debugging and profiling.

Collaborative debugging: Involves multiple developers working together to debug a system. This approach is helpful in situations where multiple modules or components are involved, and the root cause of the error is not clear.

Logging and Tracing: Using logging and tracing tools to identify the sequence of events leading up to the error. This approach involves collecting and analyzing logs and traces generated by the system during its execution.

Automated Debugging: The use of automated tools and techniques to assist in the debugging process. These tools can include static and dynamic analysis tools, as well as tools that use machine learning and artificial intelligence to identify errors and suggest fixes.

Debugging Tools:

Debugging tool is a computer program that is used to test and debug other programs. A lot of public domain software like gdb and dbx are available for debugging. They offer console-based command-line interfaces. Examples of automated debugging tools include code-based tracers, profilers, interpreters, etc. Some of the widely used debuggers are:

Radare2
WinDbg
Valgrind

Difference Between Debugging and Testing:

Testing	**Debugging**
Testing is the process to find bugs and errors.	Debugging is the process of correcting the bugs found during testing.
It is the process to identify the failure of implemented code.	It is the process to give absolution to code failure.

Testing is the display of errors.	Debugging is a deductive process.
Testing is done by the tester.	Debugging is done by either programmer or the developer.
There is no need of design knowledge in the testing process.	Debugging can't be done without proper design knowledge.
Testing can be done by insiders as well as outsiders.	Debugging is done only by insiders. An outsider can't do debugging.
Testing can be manual or automated.	Debugging is always manual. Debugging can't be automated.
It is based on different testing levels i.e. unit testing, integration testing, system testing, etc.	Debugging is based on different types of bugs.
Testing is a stage of the software development life cycle (SDLC).	Debugging is not an aspect of the software development life cycle, it occurs as a consequence of testing.
Testing is composed of the validation and verification of software.	While debugging process seeks to match symptoms with cause, by that it leads to error correction.
Testing is initiated after the code is written.	Debugging commences with the execution of a test case.
Testing process based on various levels of testing-system testing, integration testing, unit testing, etc.	Debugging process based on various types of bugs is present in a system.

Exercise

Exercise 1 – MCQ

Q 1. Which of the following is a fundamental goal of software testing?

a. Debugging the code
b. Checking for coding style conformity
c. Verifying that the software meets requirements
d. Writing documentation

Q2. What is the primary purpose of debugging in software development?

a. To add new features to the software
b. To optimize the code for performance
c. To identify and fix defects or errors in the code
d. To write user documentation

Exercise 2 – True/ False

Q 1. Unit testing involves testing individual components or functions in isolation from the rest of the system.

Q 2. Usability testing focuses on evaluating the system's security and performance.

Exercise 3 – Fill in the blanks

Q 1. ____________ testing focuses on evaluating the software's functionality, usability, and conformance to specifications.

Q 2. In ____________ maintenance, the primary goal is to enhance the software's functionality by adding new features or capabilities.

Exercise 4 – Match case

A. Acceptance Testing	Process of identifying and fixing defects or errors in the code.
B. Debugging	Focuses on evaluating the software's functionality, usability, and conformance to specifications.
C. Perfective Maintenance	Involves testing individual components or functions in isolation from the rest of the system.
D. Unit Testing	In this type of maintenance, the primary goal is to enhance the software's functionality by adding new features or capabilities.
E. Regression Testing	Testing that verifies that new changes have not adversely affected existing functionality.

Exercise 5 – One word answer

Q 1. What is the process of finding and fixing errors or defects in software code?

Q 2. What is a planned and systematic approach for evaluating software quality by checking if it meets specified requirements?

Exercise 6 – Small answer

Q 1. What is the purpose of debugging in software development?

Q 2. What is regression testing?

Exercise 7 – Long answer

Q 1. Describe the major phases involved in the software testing process.

Q 2. Explain the differences between white-box and black-box testing approaches.

Answers

Exercise 1 – MCQ

Ans: 1 C, 2 C

Exercise 2 – True/ False

Ans: 1 True, 2 False

Exercise 3 – Fill in the blanks

Ans: 1 Acceptance, 2 Perfective

Exercise 4 – Match case

Ans: 1 B, 2 A, 3 D, 4 C, 5 E

Exercise 5 – One word answer

Ans: 1 Debugging, 2 Testing

ONLINE RESOURCES

Online Exam Paper:
Link: https://forms.gle/2tG88jfvKEnoX9Lb7
QR Code:

Chapter 10 Videos Playlist:
Link: https://www.youtube.com/playlist?list=PLzlh_31VWEFr0zXl2bGwqt2jwSMFGMzDD
QR Code:

Previous Years Unsolved Questions

Q 1. With the help of an example program segment, explain Mutation Testing. [IGNOU, June 2018, December 2011]

Q 2. Write short notes on the following: [IGNOU June, 2018

(a) Prototyping Model

(b) Boundary Value Analysis

(c) Regression Testing

Q 3. Explain the following testing techniques: [IGNOU, December, 2015]

(i) Unit Testing (ii) Stress Testing

Q 4. Explain black-box testing with an example. [IGNOU, December, 2016] [VTU 2021]

Q 5. Define debugging. Explain the characteristics of bugs in detail. [IGNOU, December, 2016]

Q 6. Define "Baseline". What is its significance? How can it be changed? [IGNOU, December, 2017]

Q 7. Define "Black Box Testing" and "White Box. Testing". Explain the differences between them. [IGNOU, December, 2017, 2012] [VTU 2021]

Q 8. What are the steps involved in the process 10 of debugging? Explain. [IGNOU, December, 2011]

Q 9. Define regression testing. [Anna University 2022]

Q10. Explain the various levels of software testing with suitable example. [Anna University 2022]

Q 11. With suitable example, explain boundary value analysis. [Anna University 2022, 2017] [VTU 2021]

Q 12. How static test is different from structural testing? [Anna University 2017]

Q 13. Who are all involved in acceptance testing? Comment. [Anna University 2017]

Q 14. Differentiate between the alpha and beta testing. [Anna University 2017]

Q 15. List out the various components of test plan. [Anna University 2022]

Q 16. Explain the various software testing principles. [Anna University 2017]

Q 17. With a sample flow chart, detail different ways to find the number of test cases necessary to do the testing of a code using white box testing approach. [Anna University 2017]

Q 18. With a sample flow chart, detail different ways to find the number of test cases necessary to do the testing of a code using white box testing approach. [Anna University 2017]

Q 19. With a neat diagram, explain the unit testing, its planning and designing concepts. [Anna University 2017]

Q 20. What do you understand by Functional Testing? Describe with an example. [MCU 2019]

Q 21. What is software testing? Explain clearly the system testing. [Kota University 2021]

Q 22. Explain the following: [RGPV June 2020]

i) Unit Testing

ii) Integration testing

iii) Validation testing

iv) System testing

Chapter 11: Software Verification and Validation

11.1 Introduction

Verification and Validation is the process of investigating whether a software system satisfies specifications and standards and fulfills the required purpose. Barry Boehm described verification and validation as the following:

Verification: Are we building the product right?

Validation: Are we building the right product?

Verification

Verification is the process of checking that software achieves its goal without any bugs. It is the process to ensure whether the product that is developed is right or not. It verifies whether the developed product fulfills the requirements that we have. Verification is simply known as Static Testing.

Static Testing

Verification Testing is known as Static Testing and it can be simply termed as checking whether we are developing the right product or not and also whether our software is fulfilling the customer's requirement or not. Here are some of the activities that are involved in verification.

Inspections
Reviews
Walkthroughs
Desk-checking

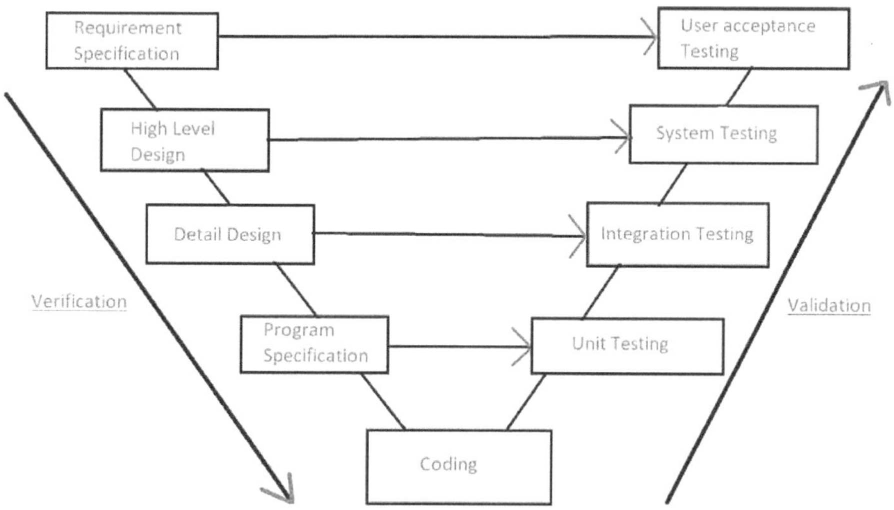

Verification and Validation

Validation

Validation is the process of checking whether the software product is up to the mark or in other words product has high-level requirements. It is the process of checking the validation of the product i.e. it checks what we are developing is the right product. It is a validation of actual and expected products. Validation is simply known as **Dynamic Testing.**

Dynamic Testing

Validation Testing is known as Dynamic Testing in which we examine whether we have developed the product right or not and also about the business needs of the client. Here are some of the activities that are involved in Validation.

Black Box Testing
White Box Testing
Unit Testing
Integration Testing

Note: Verification is followed by Validation.

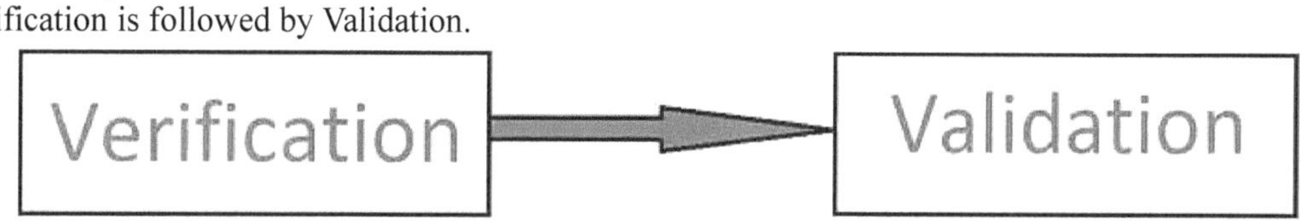

11.2 Role of Verification and Verification in SDLC

The various roles of Verification and Validation(V&V) in SDLC in the software testing process are given below:

Traceability Analysis

Traceability can be defined as a property that describes the degree to which it can be traced to its point of origin. It also describes the ability to establish a predecessor-successor relationship between one work product and another. It helps us in tracing every software requirement back to its original system requirements established in the concept activity. The thing is to ensure that every requirement correctly satisfies the system requirements and that no extra things of software requirements are included. In this technique, we also determine whether any derived requirements are consistent with the original objectives, physical laws, and technologies described in the system document.

Interface Analysis

It is the detailed analysis of the interface requirements specifications in the software development lifecycle. It also helps us in identifying the interfaces between the applications to determine the requirements for ensuring that the components interact with each other effectively. The evaluation criteria are the same as those for requirements specification as it helps us in determining the requirements for interoperability. The main target of this analysis is the interfaces between the software, hardware, and user.

Criticality Analysis

The criticality is given to each and every software requirement and when the requirements are combined into functions, the combined criticality of requirements forms the criticality for the aggregate function. Criticality analysis is updated regularly after there have been any new requirement changes. This is because such changes can cause an increase or decrease in a function's criticality which depends on how the revised requirement impacts system criticality.

The Criticality analysis has the following steps:

Step 1: The first step is to construct a control flow diagram (CFD) of the system with its elements where every block will represent only one software function.

Step 2: Then next, it will trace every critical function or its quality requirement with the help of a control flow diagram.

Step 3: Classify all traced software functions as critical to the proper execution of critical software functions & quality requirements.

Step 4: Focus additional analysis on these traced critical software functions.

Step 5: Lastly, it will repeat the criticality analysis for every life cycle process to check whether the implementation details shifted the emphasis of the criticality.

Hazard and Risk Analysis

Hazard and Risk analysis is done during the requirements definition activity. In this analysis, the hazards or risks are identified by refining the requirements of the system into detailed software requirements.

11.3 Requirements Validation Techniques

Requirements Validation Techniques are used to ensure that the software requirements are complete, consistent, and correct. In this article, we will discuss the Requirements Validation Technique in detail. We will also see the advantages and disadvantages of Software Validation Techniques.

Common Techniques used in Software Engineering

Inspection: This technique involves reviewing the requirements document with a group of experts, looking for errors, inconsistencies, and missing information.

Walkthrough: Walkthrough technique involves a group of experts reviewing the requirements document and walking through it line by line, discussing any issues or concerns that arise.

Formal Verification: This technique involves mathematically proving that the requirements are complete and consistent and that the system will meet the requirements.

Model-Based Verification: Model-Based Verification involves creating a model of the system and simulating it to see if it meets the requirements.

Prototyping: This technique involves creating a working prototype of the system and testing it to see if it meets the requirements.

Black-box Testing: Black Box testing technique involves testing the system without any knowledge of its internal structure or implementation, to see if it meets the requirements.

Acceptance Testing: Accepting Testing technique involves testing the system with real users to see if it meets their needs and requirements.

User Feedback: This technique involves gathering feedback from the users and incorporating their suggestions and feedback into the requirements.

What is Traceability?

This technique involves tracing the requirements throughout the entire software development life cycle to ensure that they are being met and that any changes are tracked and managed.

What is Agile Methodologies?
Agile Methodologies such as Scrum and Kanban, provide an iterative approach to validate requirements by delivering small chunks of functionality and getting feedback from the customer.
It is important to note that no single technique is sufficient on its own and a combination of different techniques is usually used to validate software requirements effectively.
What is Requirements Validation?
Requirements validation is the process of checking that requirements defined for development, define the system that the customer really wants. To check issues related to requirements, we perform requirements validation. We usually use requirements validation to check errors at the initial phase of development as the error may increase excessive rework when detected later in the development process. In the requirements validation process, we perform a different type of test to check the requirements mentioned in the Software Requirements Specification (SRS), these checks include:
Completeness checks
Consistency checks
Validity checks
Realism checks
Ambiguity checks
Verifiability
The output of requirements validation is the list of problems and agreed-on actions of detected problems. The lists of problems indicate the problem detected during the process of requirement validation. The list of agreed actions states the corrective action that should be taken to fix the detected problem. There are several techniques that are used either individually or in conjunction with other techniques to check to check entire or part of the system:
Test case generation: The requirement mentioned in the SRS document should be testable, the conducted tests reveal the error present in the requirement. It is generally believed that if the test is difficult or impossible to design, this usually means that the requirement will be difficult to implement and it should be reconsidered.
Prototyping: In this validation technique the prototype of the system is presented before the end-user or customer, they experiment with the presented model and check if it meets their need. This type of model is generally used to collect feedback about the requirement of the user.
Requirements Reviews: In this approach, the SRS is carefully reviewed by a group of people including people from both the contractor organizations and the client side, the reviewer systematically analyses the document to check errors and ambiguity.
Automated Consistency Analysis: This approach is used for the automatic detection of an error, such as non-determinism, missing cases, a type error, and circular definitions, in requirements specifications. First, the requirement is structured in formal notation then the CASE tool is used to check the in-consistency of the system, The report of all inconsistencies is identified and corrective actions are taken.
Walk-through: A walkthrough does not have a formally defined procedure and does not require a differentiated role assignment.
Checking early whether the idea is feasible or not.
Obtaining the opinions and suggestions of other people.
Checking the approval of others and reaching an agreement.

11.4 Difference between Verification Validation

Verification	Validation
Are we building the product right?	Are we building the right product?
It includes checking documents, design, codes and programs.	It includes testing and validating the actual product.
Verification is the static testing.	Validation is the dynamic testing.
It does not include the execution of the code.	It includes the execution of the code.
It checks whether the software conforms to specifications or not.	It checks whether the software meets the requirements and expectations of a customer or not.

It can find the bugs in the early stage of the development.	It can only find the bugs that could not be found by the verification process.
The goal of verification is application and software architecture and specification.	The goal of validation is an actual product.
Quality assurance team does verification.	Validation is executed on software code with the help of testing team.
It comes before validation.	It comes after verification.
It consists of checking of documents/files and is performed by human.	It consists of execution of program and is performed by computer.
Verification refers to the set of activities that ensure software correctly implements the specific function.	Validation refers to the set of activities that ensure that the software that has been built is traceable to customer requirements.
Verification is for prevention of errors.	Validation is for detection of errors.
Verification is also termed as white box testing or static testing as work product goes through reviews.	Validation can be termed as black box testing or dynamic testing as work product is executed.
Verification finds about 50 to 60% of the defects.	Validation finds about 20 to 30% of the defects.

11.5 Software Maintenance

Software maintenance is a part of the Software Development Life Cycle. Its primary goal is to modify and update software application after delivery to correct errors and to improve performance. Software is a model of the real world. When the real world changes, the software require alteration wherever possible.
Software Maintenance is an inclusive activity that includes error corrections, enhancement of capabilities, deletion of obsolete capabilities, and optimization.

11.5.1 Types of Maintenance (Corrective, Adaptive, Perfective)

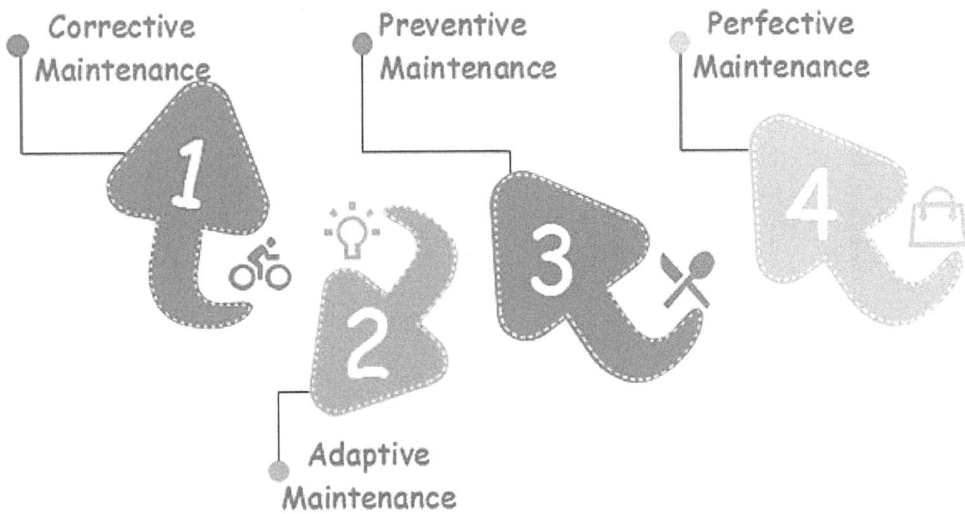

Corrective Maintenance

Corrective maintenance aims to correct any remaining errors regardless of where they may cause specifications, design, coding, testing, and documentation, etc.

Adaptive Maintenance

It contains modifying the software to match changes in the ever-changing environment.

Preventive Maintenance

It is the process by which we prevent our system from being obsolete. It involves the concept of reengineering & reverse engineering in which an old system with old technology is re-engineered using new technology. This maintenance prevents the system from dying out.

Perfective Maintenance

It defines improving processing efficiency or performance or restricting the software to enhance changeability. This may contain enhancement of existing system functionality, improvement in computational efficiency, etc.

11.5.2 Characteristics of Quality Software

Software quality product is defined in term of its fitness of purpose. That is, a quality product does precisely what the users want it to do. For software products, the fitness of use is generally explained in terms of satisfaction of the requirements laid down in the SRS document. Although "fitness of purpose" is a satisfactory interpretation of quality for many devices such as a car, a table fan, a grinding machine, etc.for software products, "fitness of purpose" is not a wholly satisfactory definition of quality.

Example: Consider a functionally correct software product. That is, it performs all tasks as specified in the SRS document. But, has an almost unusable user interface. Even though it may be functionally right, we cannot consider it to be a quality product.

The modern view of a quality associated with a software product several quality methods such as the following:

Portability: A software device is said to be portable, if it can be freely made to work in various operating system environments, in multiple machines, with other software products, etc.

Usability: A software product has better usability if various categories of users can easily invoke the functions of the product.

Reusability: A software product has excellent reusability if different modules of the product can quickly be reused to develop new products.

Correctness: A software product is correct if various requirements as specified in the SRS document have been correctly implemented.

Maintainability: A software product is maintainable if bugs can be easily corrected as and when they show up, new tasks can be easily added to the product, and the functionalities of the product can be easily modified, etc.

11.5.3 Techniques for Software Maintenance

Software maintenance is the process of modifying, enhancing, and optimizing existing software applications to ensure their continued functionality and usefulness. There are several techniques involved in software maintenance, each addressing specific aspects of the process. Here are the techniques of software maintenance in detail:

Corrective Maintenance:

Problem Identification: The first step in corrective maintenance is identifying and reporting issues, often referred to as software bugs. This can be done through user feedback, automated error reports, or manual testing.

Defect Analysis: Once a problem is identified, a thorough analysis of the defect is conducted. This involves tracing the issue back to its source and understanding the root cause of the problem.

Defect Fixing: Developers fix the identified defects by modifying the software code or configuration. The goal is to correct the issue without introducing new problems.

Adaptive Maintenance:

Environmental Changes: Adaptive maintenance deals with changes in the software environment. This could include adapting the software to work with new hardware, operating systems, or third-party components.

Regulatory Compliance: Ensuring that the software complies with new laws, regulations, or industry standards often requires adaptive maintenance.

Changing User Needs: If user requirements change, adaptive maintenance is needed to modify the software to accommodate these new needs.

Perfective Maintenance:

Enhancements: Perfective maintenance involves adding new features or enhancing existing ones to improve software functionality. These enhancements are often based on user feedback or market demands.

Optimization: Performance improvements and optimization techniques are applied to make the software run more efficiently, use fewer resources, and respond faster.

Preventive Maintenance:

Proactive Bug Fixing: Preventive maintenance aims to address issues before they become major problems. This includes fixing minor bugs and issues that might not be immediately critical but could lead to larger problems in the future.

Code Refactoring: Cleaning up and optimizing code, even when it's not directly causing issues, can help prevent future problems and make the software easier to maintain.

Risk Management:

Risk Assessment: Identifying potential risks in the software and developing strategies to mitigate them. This can include assessing security vulnerabilities, performance bottlenecks, and other potential issues.

Contingency Planning: Preparing for potential disruptions or failures in the software and having contingency plans in place to minimize downtime and data loss.

Documentation Maintenance:

Keeping Documentation Updated: Software documentation, including user manuals, technical documentation, and code comments, should be maintained and updated to reflect the current state of the software. This helps in onboarding new team members and users.

Change Logs: Maintaining detailed change logs to record modifications and improvements made to the software. This is essential for tracking changes and understanding the software's history.

Configuration Management:

Version Control: Using version control systems to manage software versions and track changes made to the codebase.

Release Management: Planning and coordinating software releases, including updates, patches, and new versions.

Legacy Software Maintenance:

Maintaining Legacy Systems: Legacy systems, which may be outdated but still essential for business operations, require ongoing maintenance to ensure their reliability.

Knowledge Transfer:

Transferring Knowledge: Ensuring that knowledge about the software's design, architecture, and functionality is passed on to new team members or support staff.

Exercise

Exercise 1 – MCQ

Q 1. What is the main objective of software validation?

A. Identifying defects in the software
B. Ensuring that the software is efficient
C. Confirming that the software meets user needs
D. Improving software maintainability

Q 2. Which of the following is a validation activity?

A. Unit testing
B. Integration testing
C. User acceptance testing
D. Static code analysis

Exercise 2 – True/ False

Q 1. Software validation ensures that the software product works correctly and is free of defects.

Q 2. Inspection is a validation technique used to evaluate software by running it and comparing the actual results with the expected results.

Exercise 3 – Fill in the blanks

Q 1. __________ is the process of evaluating a system or component during or at the end of the development process to determine whether it satisfies the specified requirements.

Question 2: Software __________ ensures that the software product works correctly and is free of defects.

Answer: Validation

Exercise 4 – Match case

1. Inspection	A. An internal team tests the software in a controlled environment before it's released to external users.
2. Alpha Testing	B. A formal review process to evaluate software documents or code.
3. White-box Testing	C. Testing the software based on its internal logic, code structure&algorithms.
4. User Acceptance Testing (UAT)	D. End-users evaluate the software in a real-world environment

Exercise 5 – One word answer

Q 1. What type of testing focuses on the software's functionality without considering its internal code structure?

Answer: Black-box

Question 5: Which testing involves end-users evaluating the software in a real-world environment to ensure it meets their requirements?

Answer: Validation

Exercise 6 – Small answer

Q 1. What are some common software verification methods?

Answer: Code reviews, static analysis, and walkthroughs.
Question 5: What are some common software validation methods?
Answer: User acceptance testing, system testing, and beta testing.

Exercise 7 – Long answer

Q 1. What is the importance of Software Verification and Validation in the software development process?
Q 2. What are some common challenges in software validation?

Answers

Exercise 1 – MCQ

Ans: 1 C, 2 C

Exercise 2 – True/ False

Ans: 1 False, 2 False

Exercise 3 – Fill in the blanks

Ans: 1 Verification, 2 Validation

Exercise 4 – Match case

Ans: 1 B, 2 A, 3 C, 4 D

Exercise 5 – One word answer

Ans: 1 Black- box, Validation

Online Resources

Online Exam Paper:
Link: https://forms.gle/982ZrnaiGxsVWBps8
QR Code:

Chapter 11 Videos Playlist:
Link: https://www.youtube.com/playlist?list=PLzlh_31VWEFqX1uizMngXNCbNQNaSZZFV
QR Code:

Previous Years Solved Questions

Q 1. Explain verification and validation. [R.T.U.2018, 2014]

Ans 1: Verification testing

Verification testing includes different activities such as business requirements, system requirements, design review, and code walkthrough while developing a product.

It is also known as static testing, where we are ensuring that "we are developing the right product or not". And it also checks that the developed application fulfilling all the requirements given by the client.

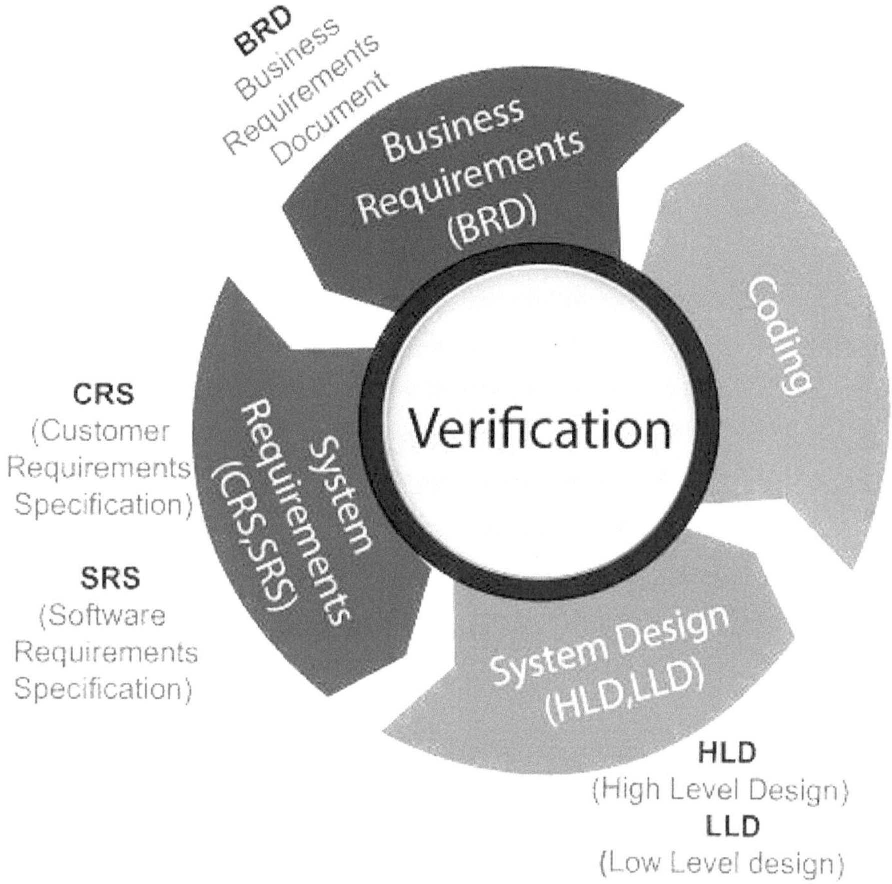

Validation testing

Validation testing is testing where tester performed functional and non-functional testing. Here functional testing includes Unit Testing (UT), Integration Testing (IT) and System Testing (ST), and non-functional testing includes User acceptance testing (UAT).

Validation testing is also known as dynamic testing, where we are ensuring that "we have developed the product right." And it also checks that the software meets the business needs of the client.

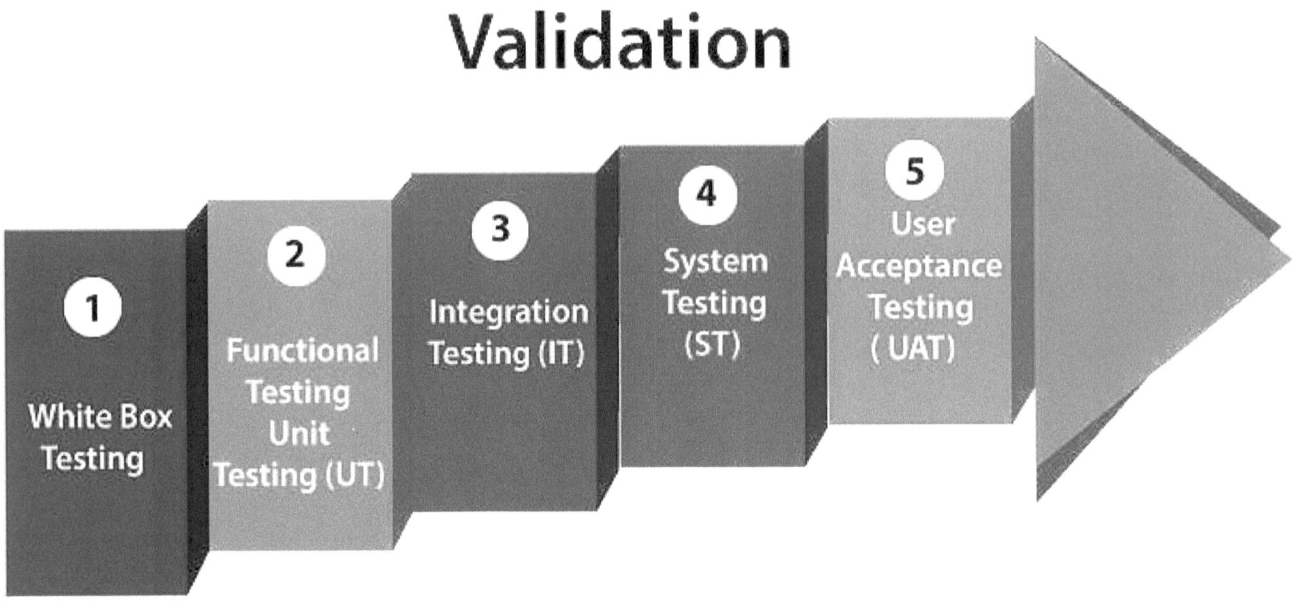

Note: Verification and Validation process are done under the V model of the software development life cycle.

Difference between verification and validation testing

Verification	Validation
We check whether we are developing the right product or not.	We check whether the developed product is right.
Verification is also known as **static testing**.	Validation is also known as **dynamic testing**.
Verification includes different methods like Inspections, Reviews, and Walkthroughs.	Validation includes testing like functional testing, system testing, integration, and User acceptance testing.
It is a process of checking the work-products (not the final product) of a development cycle to decide whether the product meets the specified requirements.	It is a process of checking the software during or at the end of the development cycle to decide whether the software follow the specified business requirements.
Quality assurance comes under verification testing.	**Quality control** comes under validation testing.
The execution of code does not happen in the verification testing.	In validation testing, the execution of code happens.
In verification testing, we can find the bugs early in the development phase of the product.	In the validation testing, we can find those bugs, which are not caught in the verification process.
Verification testing is executed by the Quality assurance team to make sure that the product is developed according to customers' requirements.	Validation testing is executed by the testing team to test the application.
Verification is done before the validation testing.	After verification testing, validation testing takes place.
In this type of testing, we can verify that the inputs follow the outputs or not.	In this type of testing, we can validate that the user accepts the product or not.

Previous Years Unsolved Questions

Q 1. State the types on software maintenance and its importance. [Anna University 2022]
Q 2. What is the test measurement process in software testing? [Anna University 2017]
Q 3. What are the different classes of defects? Discuss. [Anna University 2017]
Q 4. Provide an example for defect and explain defect repository as well as test design using it. [Anna University 2017]
Q 5. Elaborate the various components of test plan and attachments in test management. [Anna University 2017]
Q 6. Distinguish between Verification and Validation. [MCU 2019] [VTU 2022]
Q 7. What is software maintenance? [Kota University 2021]
Q 8. Demonstrate SQA activities in software development and software maintenance. [RGPV June 2020]

Chapter 12: Unified Modeling Language (UML)

12.1 Introduction to UML

The UML stands for Unified modeling language, is a standardized general-purpose visual modeling language in the field of Software Engineering. It is used for specifying, visualizing, constructing, and documenting the primary artifacts of the software system. It helps in designing and characterizing, especially those software systems that incorporate the concept of Object orientation. It describes the working of both the software and hardware systems.
The UML was developed in 1994-95 by Grady Booch, Ivar Jacobson, and James Rumbaugh at the Rational Software. In 1997, it got adopted as a standard by the Object Management Group (OMG).

12.1.1 Overview of UML

UML stands for Unified Modeling Language.
UML is different from the other common programming languages such as C++, Java, COBOL, etc.
UML is a pictorial language used to make software blueprints.
UML can be described as a general purpose visual modeling language to visualize, specify, construct, and document software system.
Although UML is generally used to model software systems, it is not limited within this boundary. It is also used to model non-software systems as well. For example, the process flow in a manufacturing unit, etc.
UML is not a programming language but tools can be used to generate code in various languages using UML diagrams.
UML has a direct relation with object oriented analysis and design. After some standardization, UML has become an OMG standard.
Goals of UML
A picture is worth a thousand words, this idiom absolutely fits describing UML. Object-oriented concepts were introduced much earlier than UML. At that point of time, there were no standard methodologies to organize and consolidate the object-oriented development. It was then that UML came into picture.
There are a number of goals for developing UML but the most important is to define some general purpose modeling language, which all modelers can use and it also needs to be made simple to understand and use.
UML diagrams are not only made for developers but also for business users, common people, and anybody interested to understand the system. The system can be a software or non-software system. Thus it must be clear that UML is not a development method rather it accompanies with processes to make it a successful system.
In conclusion, the goal of UML can be defined as a simple modeling mechanism to model all possible practical systems in today's complex environment.
A Conceptual Model of UML
To understand the conceptual model of UML, first we need to clarify what is a conceptual model? and why a conceptual model is required?
A conceptual model can be defined as a model which is made of concepts and their relationships.
A conceptual model is the first step before drawing a UML diagram. It helps to understand the entities in the real world and how they interact with each other.
As UML describes the real-time systems, it is very important to make a conceptual model and then proceed gradually.
The conceptual model of UML can be mastered by learning the following three major elements –
UML building blocks
Rules to connect the building blocks
Common mechanisms of UML
Object-Oriented Concepts
UML can be described as the successor of object-oriented (OO) analysis and design.
An object contains both data and methods that control the data. The data represents the state of the object. A class describes an object and they also form a hierarchy to model the real-world system. The hierarchy is represented as inheritance and the classes can also be associated in different ways as per the requirement.
Objects are the real-world entities that exist around us and the basic concepts such as abstraction, encapsulation, inheritance, and polymorphism all can be represented using UML.
UML is powerful enough to represent all the concepts that exist in object-oriented analysis and design. UML diagrams are representation of object-oriented concepts only. Thus, before learning UML, it becomes important to understand OO concept in detail.
Following are some fundamental concepts of the object-oriented world –
Objects – Objects represent an entity and the basic building block.
Class – Class is the blue print of an object.

Abstraction – Abstraction represents the behavior of an real world entity.
Encapsulation – Encapsulation is the mechanism of binding the data together and hiding them from the outside world.
Inheritance – Inheritance is the mechanism of making new classes from existing ones.
Polymorphism – It defines the mechanism to exists in different forms.
OO Analysis and Design
OO can be defined as an investigation and to be more specific, it is the investigation of objects. Design means collaboration of identified objects.
Thus, it is important to understand the OO analysis and design concepts. The most important purpose of OO analysis is to identify objects of a system to be designed. This analysis is also done for an existing system. Now an efficient analysis is only possible when we are able to start thinking in a way where objects can be identified. After identifying the objects, their relationships are identified and finally the design is produced.
The purpose of OO analysis and design can described as –
Identifying the objects of a system.
Identifying their relationships.
Making a design, which can be converted to executables using OO languages.
There are three basic steps where the OO concepts are applied and implemented. The steps can be defined as
OO Analysis → OO Design → OO implementation using OO languages
The above three points can be described in detail as –
During OO analysis, the most important purpose is to identify objects and describe them in a proper way. If these objects are identified efficiently, then the next job of design is easy. The objects should be identified with responsibilities. Responsibilities are the functions performed by the object. Each and every object has some type of responsibilities to be performed. When these responsibilities are collaborated, the purpose of the system is fulfilled.
The second phase is OO design. During this phase, emphasis is placed on the requirements and their fulfilment. In this stage, the objects are collaborated according to their intended association. After the association is complete, the design is also complete.
The third phase is OO implementation. In this phase, the design is implemented using OO languages such as Java, C++, etc.

12.1.2 UML Diagram Types

The UML diagrams are categorized into structural diagrams, behavioral diagrams, and also interaction overview diagrams. The diagrams are hierarchically classified in the following figure:

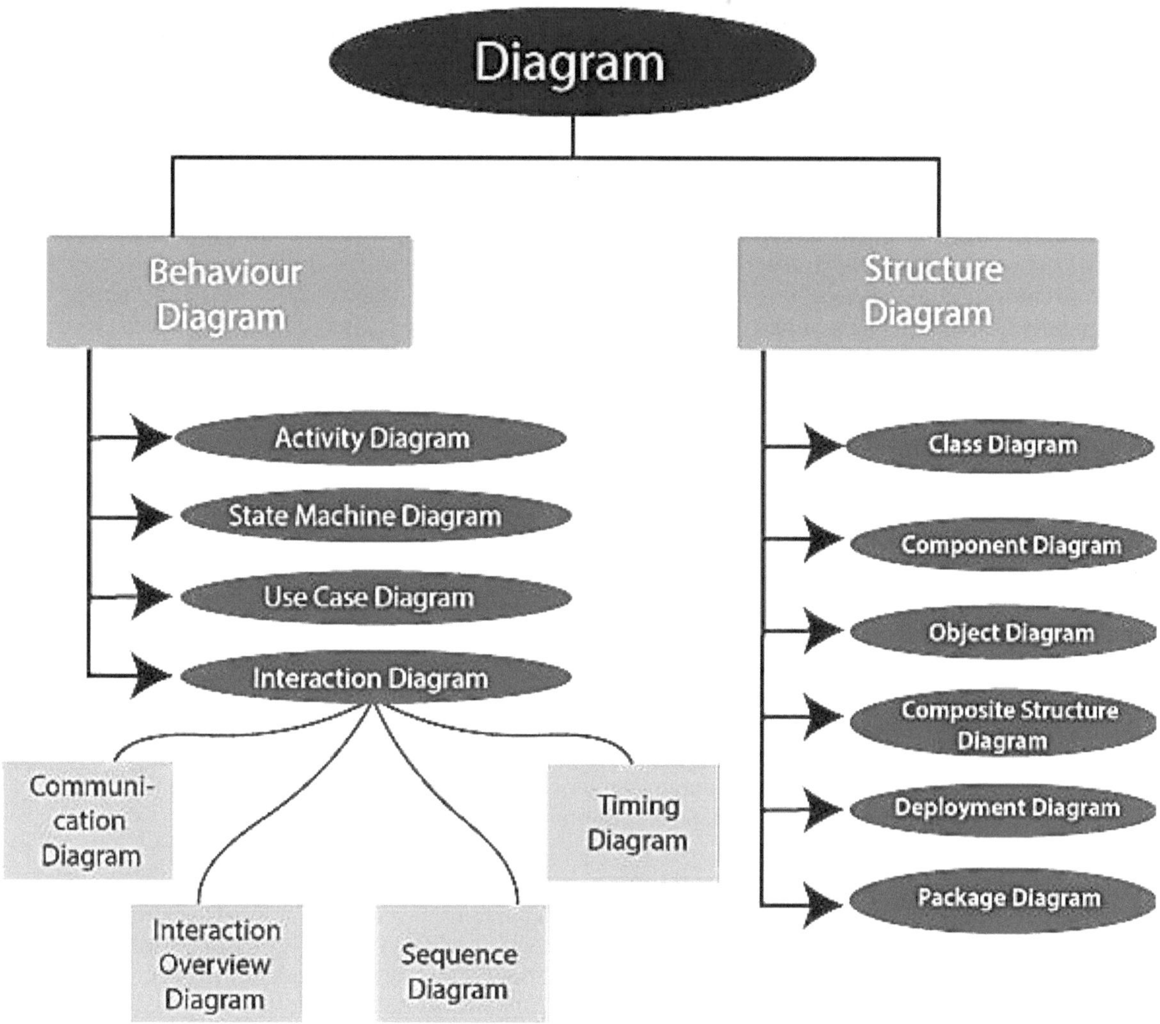

1. Structural Diagrams

Structural diagrams depict a static view or structure of a system. It is widely used in the documentation of software architecture. It embraces class diagrams, composite structure diagrams, component diagrams, deployment diagrams, object diagrams, and package diagrams. It presents an outline for the system. It stresses the elements to be present that are to be modeled.

Class Diagram: Class diagrams are one of the most widely used diagrams. It is the backbone of all the object-oriented software systems. It depicts the static structure of the system. It displays the system's class, attributes, and methods. It is helpful in recognizing the relation between different objects as well as classes.

Composite Structure Diagram: The composite structure diagrams show parts within the class. It displays the relationship between the parts and their configuration that ascertain the behavior of the class. It makes full use of ports, parts, and connectors to portray the internal structure of a structured classifier. It is similar to class diagrams, just the fact it represents individual parts in a detailed manner when compared with class diagrams.

Object Diagram: It describes the static structure of a system at a particular point in time. It can be used to test the accuracy of class diagrams. It represents distinct instances of classes and the relationship between them at a time.

Component Diagram: It portrays the organization of the physical components within the system. It is used for modeling execution details. It determines whether the desired functional requirements have been considered by the planned development or not, as it depicts the structural relationships between the elements of a software system.

Deployment Diagram: It presents the system's software and its hardware by telling what the existing physical components are and what software components are running on them. It produces information about system software. It is incorporated whenever software is used, distributed, or deployed across multiple machines with dissimilar configurations.

Package Diagram: It is used to illustrate how the packages and their elements are organized. It shows the dependencies between distinct packages. It manages UML diagrams by making it easily understandable. It is used for organizing the class and use case diagrams.

2. Behavioral Diagrams:

Behavioral diagrams portray a dynamic view of a system or the behavior of a system, which describes the functioning of the system. It includes use case diagrams, state diagrams, and activity diagrams. It defines the interaction within the system.

State Machine Diagram: It is a behavioral diagram. it portrays the system's behavior utilizing finite state transitions. It is also known as the **State-charts** diagram. It models the dynamic behavior of a class in response to external stimuli.

Activity Diagram: It models the flow of control from one activity to the other. With the help of an activity diagram, we can model sequential and concurrent activities. It visually depicts the workflow as well as what causes an event to occur.

Use Case Diagram: It represents the functionality of a system by utilizing actors and use cases. It encapsulates the functional requirement of a system and its association with actors. It portrays the use case view of a system.

3. Interaction Diagrams

Interaction diagrams are a subclass of behavioral diagrams that give emphasis to object interactions and also depicts the flow between various use case elements of a system. In simple words, it shows how objects interact with each other and how the data flows within them. It consists of communication, interaction overview, sequence, and timing diagrams.

Sequence Diagram: It shows the interactions between the objects in terms of messages exchanged over time. It delineates in what order and how the object functions are in a system.

Communication Diagram: It shows the interchange of sequence messages between the objects. It focuses on objects and their relations. It describes the static and dynamic behavior of a system.

Timing Diagram: It is a special kind of sequence diagram used to depict the object's behavior over a specific period of time. It governs the change in state and object behavior by showing the time and duration constraints.

Interaction Overview diagram: It is a mixture of activity and sequence diagram that depicts a sequence of actions to simplify the complex interactions into simple interactions.

12.2 Basic Structures and Modeling Classes

In software engineering, basic structures and modeling classes are fundamental concepts used to represent and describe software systems. These structures and classes serve as building blocks for creating software models and visualizing the software's architecture and design. Here's an overview of basic structures and modeling classes:

Classes:

Definition: In object-oriented programming (OOP), a class is a blueprint or template for creating objects. It defines the properties (attributes or fields) and behaviors (methods or functions) that objects of that class will have.

Purpose: Classes help organize and encapsulate related data and functionality within a software system. They promote code reusability, modularity, and maintainability.

Objects:

Definition: An object is an instance of a class. It represents a real-world entity or concept within the software. Objects have attributes and methods defined by their class.

Purpose: Objects are used to model and interact with specific instances of a class. They allow data to be stored and manipulated in a structured way.

Attributes:

Definition: Attributes, also known as fields or properties, are data members of a class that store information about an object's state. These can include variables, constants, or other data types.

Purpose: Attributes define the characteristics or properties of an object. They represent the data associated with the object.

Methods:

Definition: Methods are functions or procedures defined within a class that specify the behavior or operations that objects of the class can perform. They encapsulate the object's functionality.

Purpose: Methods define how objects interact with data and other objects. They encapsulate the object's behavior and logic.

Inheritance:

Definition: Inheritance is a mechanism in OOP that allows a class to inherit the attributes and methods of another class (the base or parent class). The derived class (subclass) can extend or override the inherited properties and behaviors.

Purpose: Inheritance promotes code reuse and supports the creation of class hierarchies. It allows for modeling relationships between classes, such as "is-a" relationships.

Abstraction:

Definition: Abstraction is the process of simplifying complex systems by breaking them down into smaller, more manageable parts. In OOP, classes and objects are used to abstract real-world entities.

Purpose: Abstraction helps software designers focus on essential features while hiding unnecessary details. It simplifies the modeling and design process.

Encapsulation:

Definition: Encapsulation is the bundling of data (attributes) and the methods (behaviors) that operate on that data into a single unit, which is a class. It restricts direct access to some of an object's components.

Purpose: Encapsulation ensures that the internal state and behavior of an object are not directly accessible from outside. It enforces data hiding and provides better control over the software.

Polymorphism:

Definition: Polymorphism allows objects of different classes to be treated as objects of a common superclass. It enables flexibility and extensibility in software by providing a way for objects to take on multiple forms.

Purpose: Polymorphism simplifies code design and enables dynamic binding, allowing the selection of appropriate methods at runtime based on the actual object type.

Association:

Definition: Association is a relationship between classes that describes how objects of one class are connected to objects of another class. Associations can be one-to-one, one-to-many, or many-to-many.

Purpose: Associations help model how objects interact and collaborate in a software system. They represent real-world relationships between entities.

These basic structures and modeling classes, along with object-oriented principles, are essential for designing, modeling, and developing software systems using object-oriented programming paradigms. They provide a foundation for creating well-structured and maintainable software.

12.2.1 UML Class Diagrams

UML class diagrams: Class diagrams are the main building blocks of every object-oriented method. The class diagram can be used to show the classes, relationships, interface, association, and collaboration. UML is standardized in class diagrams. Since classes are the building block of an application that is based on OOPs, so as the class diagram has an appropriate structure to represent the classes, inheritance, relationships, and everything that OOPs have in their context. It describes various kinds of objects and the static relationship between them.

The main purpose to use class diagrams are:

This is the only UML that can appropriately depict various aspects of the OOPs concept.

Proper design and analysis of applications can be faster and efficient.

It is the base for deployment and component diagram.

There are several software available that can be used online and offline to draw these diagrams Like Edraw max, lucid chart, etc. There are several points to be kept in focus while drawing the class diagram. These can be said as its syntax:

Each class is represented by a rectangle having a subdivision of three compartments name, attributes, and operation.

There are three types of modifiers that are used to decide the visibility of attributes and operations.

+ is used for public visibility(for everyone)

is used for protected visibility (for friend and derived)

– is used for private visibility (for only me)

Below is the example of Animal class (parent) having two child class as dog and cat both have object d1, c1 inheriting properties of the parent class.

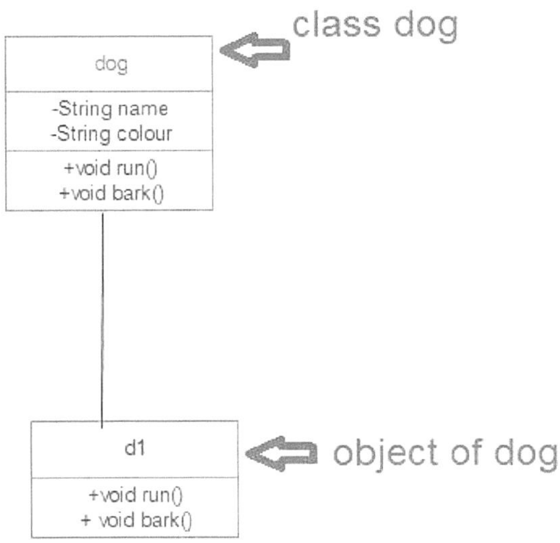

Where to Use Class Diagrams?

The class diagram is also considered as the foundation for component and deployment diagrams. Class diagrams are not only used to visualize the static view of the system but are also used to construct the executable code for forward and reverse engineering of any system.

The class diagram clearly shows the mapping with object-oriented languages such as Java, C++, etc. From practical experience, a class diagram is generally used for construction purpose.

In a nutshell, it can be said, class diagrams are used for –

Describing the static view of the system.

Showing the collaboration among the elements of the static view.

Describing the functionalities performed by the system.

Construction of software applications using object-oriented languages.

Code:

```
import java.io.*;

class GFG {
   public static void main(String[] args)
   {
      dog d1 = new dog();
      d1.bark();
      d1.run();
      cat c1 = new cat();
      c1.meww();
   }
}

class Animal {
   public void run()
   {
      String name;
      String colour;

      System.out.println("animal is running");
   }
}
class dog extends Animal {
   public void bark()
   {
```

```
            System.out.println("wooh!wooh! dog is barking");
        }
        public void run()
        {
            System.out.println("dog is running");
        }
    }

    class cat extends Animal {
        public void meww()
        {
            System.out.println("meww! meww!");
        }
    }
```

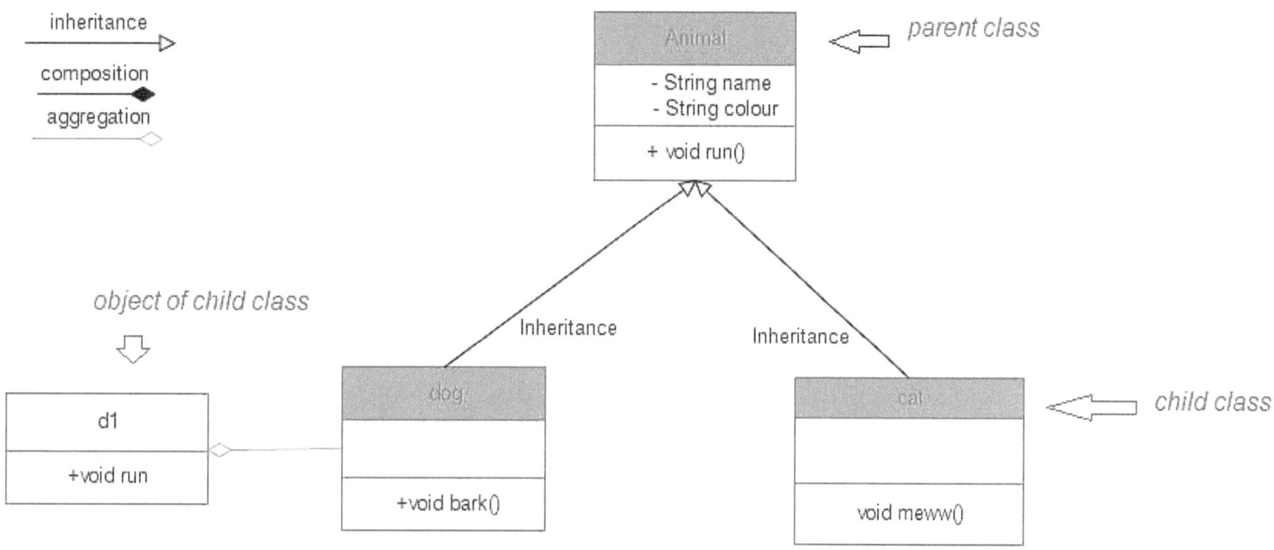

The process to design class diagram: In Edraw max (or any other platform where class diagrams can be drawn) follow the steps:
Open a blank document in the class diagram section.
From the library select the class diagram and click on create option.
Prepare the model of the class on the opened template page.
After editing according to requirement save it.
There are several diagram components that can be efficiently used while making/editing the model. These are as follows:
Class { name, attribute, method}
Objects
Interface
Relationships {inheritance, association, generalization}
Associations {bidirectional, unidirectional}
Class diagrams are one of the most widely used diagrams in the fields of software engineering as well as business modeling.
The exact meaning of the arrows :

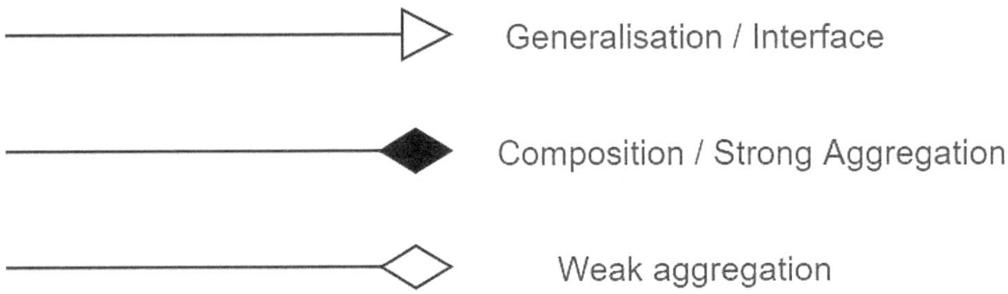

12.2.2 Object and Class Concepts

1. Class:

A class is a user-defined data type. It consists of data members and member functions, which can be accessed and used by creating an instance of that class. It represents the set of properties or methods that are common to all objects of one type. A class is like a blueprint for an object.

For Example: Consider the Class of Cars. There may be many cars with different names and brands but all of them will share some common properties like all of them will have 4 wheels, Speed Limit, Mileage range, etc. So here, Car is the class, and wheels, speed limits, mileage are their properties.

2. Object:

It is a basic unit of Object-Oriented Programming and represents the real-life entities. An Object is an instance of a Class. When a class is defined, no memory is allocated but when it is instantiated (i.e. an object is created) memory is allocated. An object has an identity, state, and behavior. Each object contains data and code to manipulate the data. Objects can interact without having to know details of each other's data or code, it is sufficient to know the type of message accepted and type of response returned by the objects.

For example "Dog" is a real-life Object, which has some characteristics like color, Breed, Bark, Sleep, and Eats.

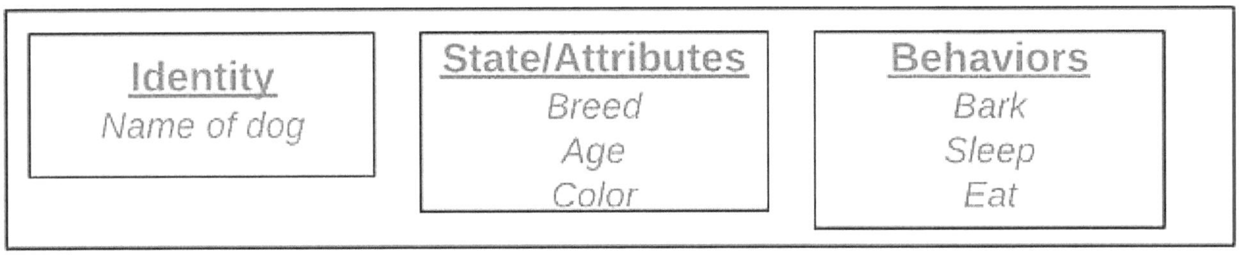

12.3 Common Modeling Techniques

Common modeling techniques in software engineering refer to methods and notations used to represent various aspects of a software system during the software development process. These techniques provide a visual and conceptual way to understand, design, and communicate software systems. Here are some common modeling techniques used in software engineering:

Unified Modeling Language (UML):

Definition: UML is a widely used modeling language that provides a standardized way to visualize and document software systems. It encompasses a variety of diagrams, including use case diagrams, class diagrams, sequence diagrams, and state diagrams.

Purpose: UML helps in specifying, visualizing, and documenting different aspects of a software system, such as its structure, behavior, and interactions. It is used for both analysis and design.

Data Flow Diagrams (DFD):

Definition: DFDs are used to represent the flow of data within a system. They consist of processes, data stores, data flows, and external entities. DFDs help in understanding how data is processed and transformed within a system.

Purpose: DFDs are valuable for analyzing and designing information systems. They provide a clear overview of data movement and processing.

Entity-Relationship Diagrams (ERD):

Definition: ERDs are used to model the entities (data objects) in a system and the relationships between them. They involve entities, attributes, and relationships.
Purpose: ERDs are primarily used in database design to define the structure and relationships of a database. They help in understanding data modeling.
Use Case Diagrams:
Definition: Use case diagrams are part of the UML and are used to represent interactions between a system and its users (actors). They consist of use cases, actors, and associations.
Purpose: Use case diagrams help in identifying and defining the functional requirements of a system by illustrating how users interact with it.
Class Diagrams:
Definition: Class diagrams are another part of the UML and are used to represent the static structure of a system. They involve classes, attributes, operations, associations, and inheritance relationships.
Purpose: Class diagrams provide a blueprint of the system's structure, showing the classes and their relationships. They are particularly useful for object-oriented design.
Sequence Diagrams:
Definition: Sequence diagrams are part of the UML and depict interactions between objects over time. They show the chronological order of messages and method calls.
Purpose: Sequence diagrams are used to model the dynamic behavior of a system and illustrate how different components interact during specific scenarios.
State Diagrams:
Definition: State diagrams, also part of the UML, describe the different states and transitions that an object or system can go through in response to events.
Purpose: State diagrams help in modeling the behavior of an entity or system and are particularly useful for systems with complex, state-based logic.
Activity Diagrams:
Definition: Activity diagrams, part of the UML, depict the flow of activities or processes within a system. They show the sequence of actions and decision points.
Purpose: Activity diagrams help in modeling business processes, workflows, and system behaviors that involve complex control flows.
Deployment Diagrams:
Definition: Deployment diagrams are used to model the physical deployment of software components on hardware nodes. They include nodes, components, and relationships.
Purpose: Deployment diagrams help in understanding the physical architecture of a system, including how software is distributed across different servers or devices.
These modeling techniques are essential tools for software engineers to plan, design, and communicate the architecture and behavior of complex software systems. The choice of technique depends on the specific aspects of the system being modeled and the intended audience for the models.

12.3.1 Use Case Diagrams

A use case diagram is used to represent the dynamic behavior of a system. It encapsulates the system's functionality by incorporating use cases, actors, and their relationships. It models the tasks, services, and functions required by a system/subsystem of an application. It depicts the high-level functionality of a system and also tells how the user handles a system.

Purpose of Use Case Diagrams

The main purpose of a use case diagram is to portray the dynamic aspect of a system. It accumulates the system's requirement, which includes both internal as well as external influences. It invokes persons, use cases, and several things that invoke the actors and elements accountable for the implementation of use case diagrams. It represents how an entity from the external environment can interact with a part of the system.

Following are the purposes of a use case diagram given below:

It gathers the system's needs.
It depicts the external view of the system.
It recognizes the internal as well as external factors that influence the system.
It represents the interaction between the actors.

How to draw a Use Case diagram?

It is essential to analyze the whole system before starting with drawing a use case diagram, and then the system's functionalities are found. And once every single functionality is identified, they are then transformed into the use cases to be used in the use case diagram.

After that, we will enlist the actors that will interact with the system. The actors are the person or a thing that invokes the functionality of a system. It may be a system or a private entity, such that it requires an entity to be pertinent to the functionalities of the system to which it is going to interact.

Once both the actors and use cases are enlisted, the relation between the actor and use case/ system is inspected. It identifies the no of times an actor communicates with the system. Basically, an actor can interact multiple times with a use case or system at a particular instance of time.

Following are some rules that must be followed while drawing a use case diagram:

A pertinent and meaningful name should be assigned to the actor or a use case of a system.

The communication of an actor with a use case must be defined in an understandable way.

Specified notations to be used as and when required.

The most significant interactions should be represented among the multiple no of interactions between the use case and actors.

Example of a Use Case Diagram

A use case diagram depicting the Online Shopping website is given below.

Here the Web Customer actor makes use of any online shopping website to purchase online. The top-level uses are as follows; View Items, Make Purchase, Checkout, Client Register. The View Items use case is utilized by the customer who searches and view products. The Client Register use case allows the customer to register itself with the website for availing gift vouchers, coupons, or getting a private sale invitation. It is to be noted that the Checkout is an included use case, which is part of Making Purchase, and it is not available by itself.

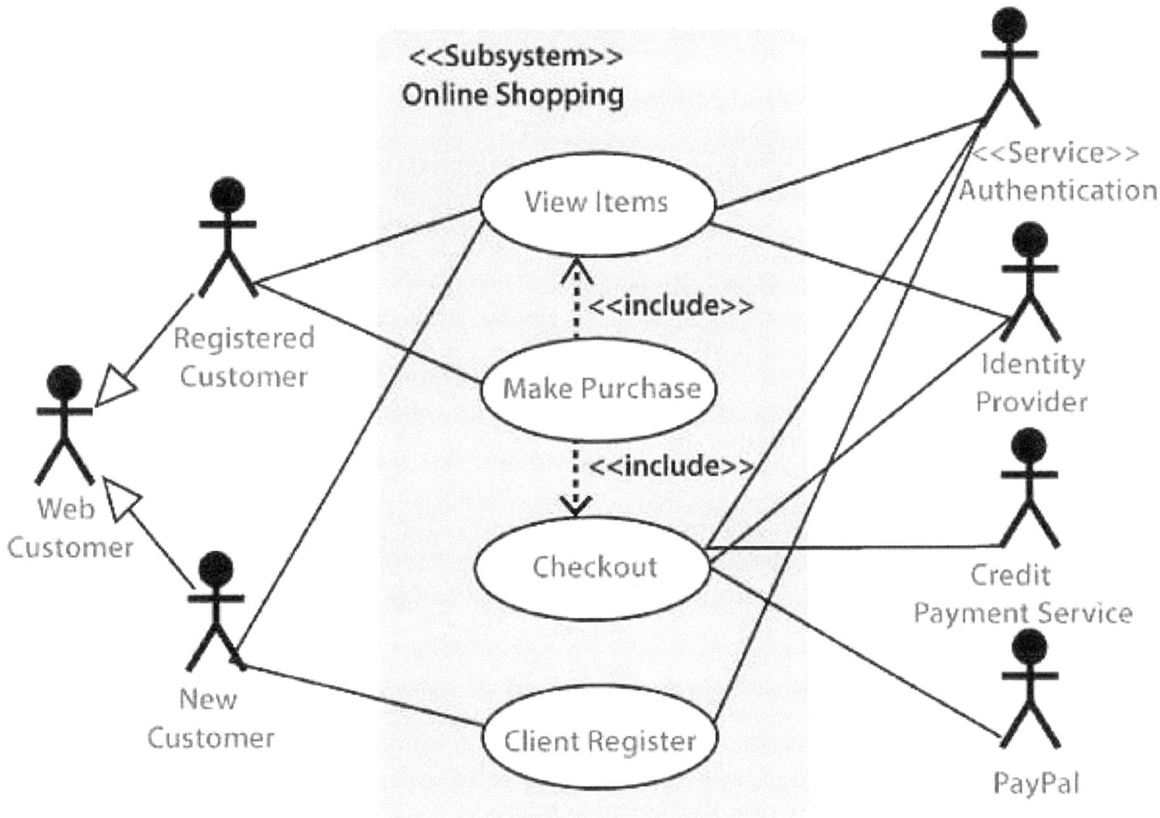

The View Items is further extended by several use cases such as; Search Items, Browse Items, View Recommended Items, Add to Shopping Cart, Add to Wish list. All of these extended use cases provide some functions to customers, which allows them to search for an item. The View Items is further extended by several use cases such as; Search Items, Browse Items, View Recommended Items, Add to Shopping Cart, Add to Wish list. All of these extended use cases provide some functions to customers, which allows them to search for an item.

Both View Recommended Item and Add to Wish List include the Customer Authentication use case, as they necessitate authenticated customers, and simultaneously item can be added to the shopping cart without any user authentication.

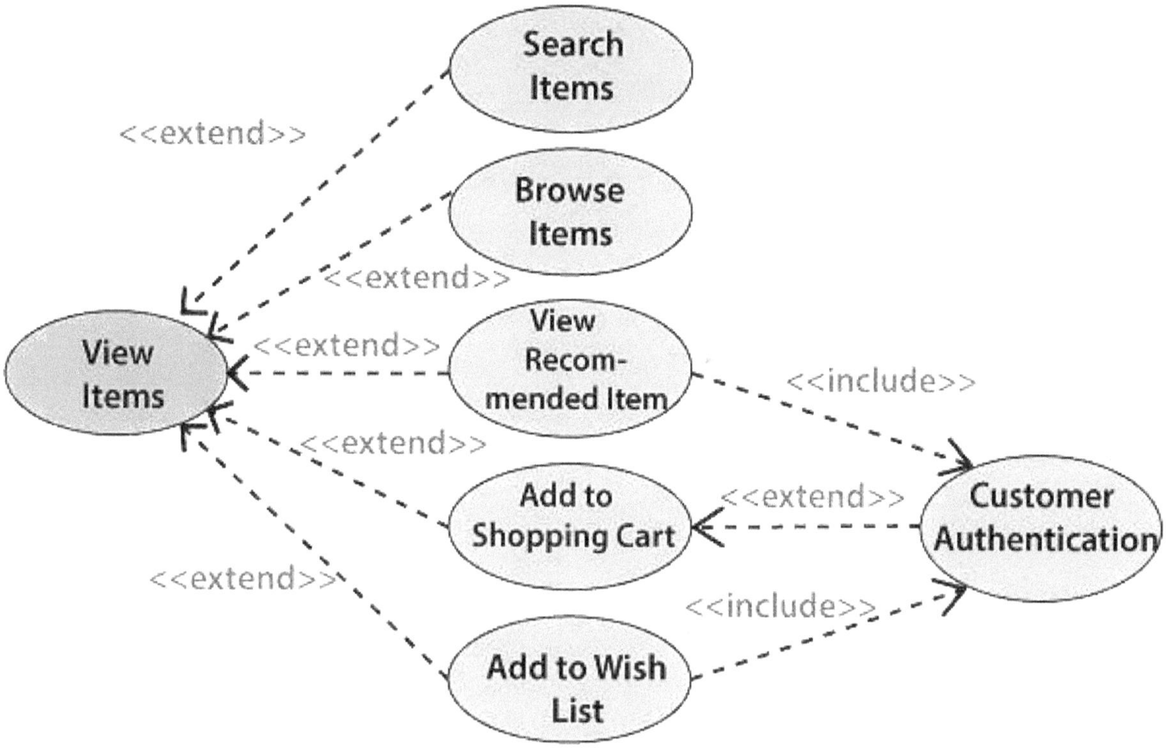

Similarly, the **Checkout** use case also includes the following use cases, as shown below. It requires an authenticated Web Customer, which can be done by login page, user authentication cookie ("Remember me"), or Single Sign-On (SSO). SSO needs an external identity provider's participation, while Web site authentication service is utilized in all these use cases.

The Checkout use case involves Payment use case that can be done either by the credit card and external credit payment services or with PayPal.

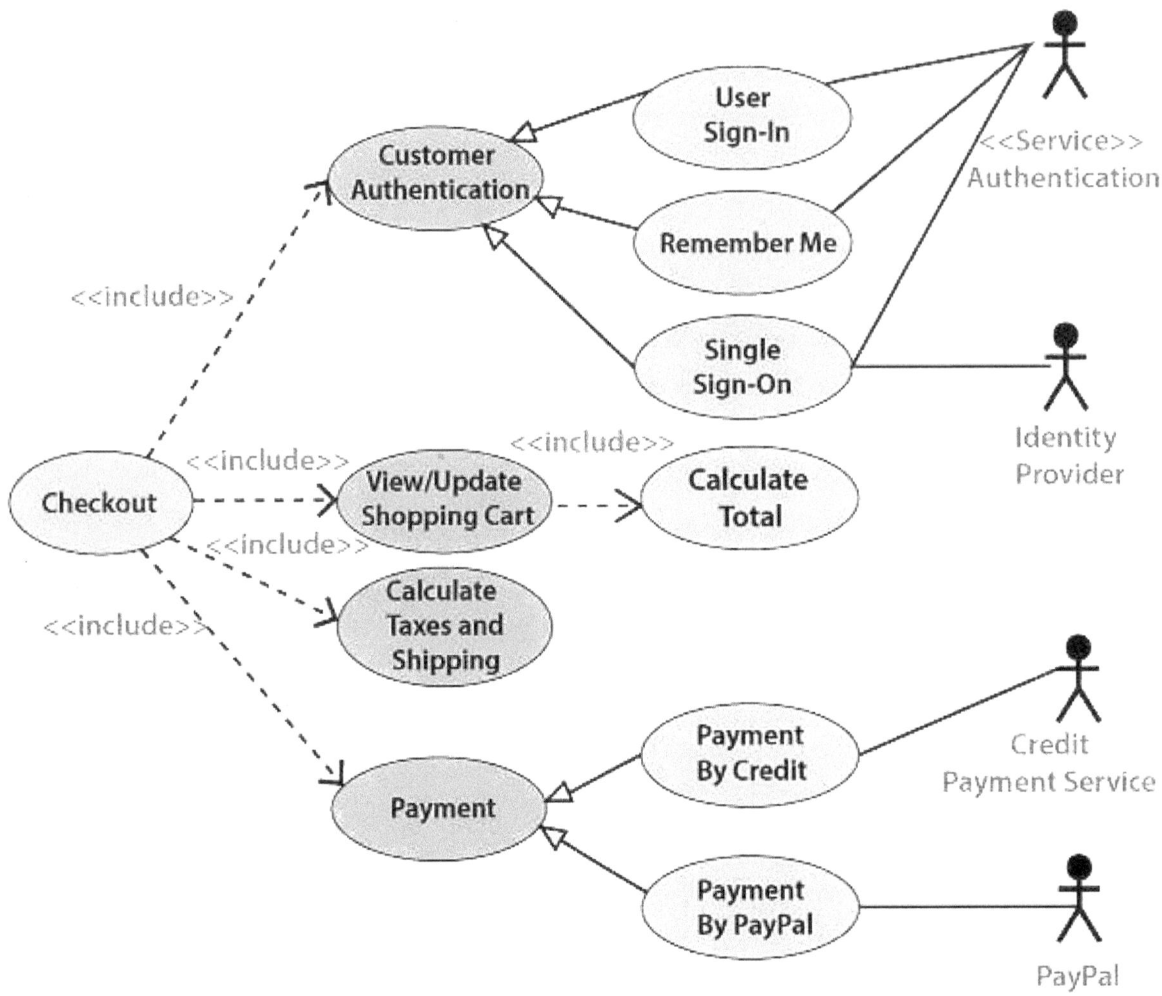

Important tips for drawing a Use Case diagram

Following are some important tips that are to be kept in mind while drawing a use case diagram:

A simple and complete use case diagram should be articulated.

A use case diagram should represent the most significant interaction among the multiple interactions.

At least one module of a system should be represented by the use case diagram.

If the use case diagram is large and more complex, then it should be drawn more generalized.

12.3.2 Activity Diagrams

In UML, the activity diagram is used to demonstrate the flow of control within the system rather than the implementation. It models the concurrent and sequential activities.

The activity diagram helps in envisioning the workflow from one activity to another. It put emphasis on the condition of flow and the order in which it occurs. The flow can be sequential, branched, or concurrent, and to deal with such kinds of flows, the activity diagram has come up with a fork, join, etc.

It is also termed as an object-oriented flowchart. It encompasses activities composed of a set of actions or operations that are applied to model the behavioral diagram.

Components of an Activity Diagram

Following are the component of an activity diagram:

Backward Skip 10sPlay VideoForward Skip 10s

Activities

The categorization of behavior into one or more actions is termed as an activity. In other words, it can be said that an activity is a network of nodes that are connected by edges. The edges depict the flow of execution. It may contain action nodes, control nodes, or object nodes.

The control flow of activity is represented by control nodes and object nodes that illustrates the objects used within an activity. The activities are initiated at the initial node and are terminated at the final node.

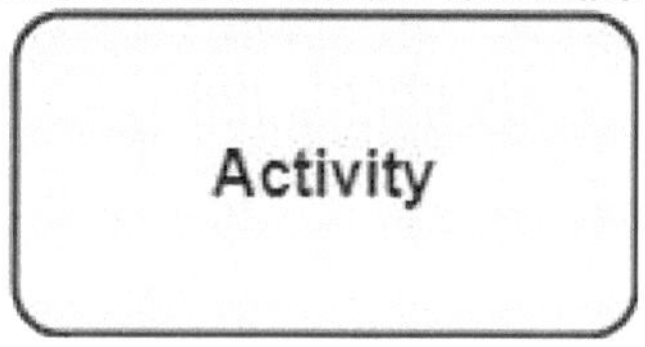

Activity partition /swimlane

The swimlane is used to cluster all the related activities in one column or one row. It can be either vertical or horizontal. It used to add modularity to the activity diagram. It is not necessary to incorporate swimlane in the activity diagram. But it is used to add more transparency to the activity diagram.

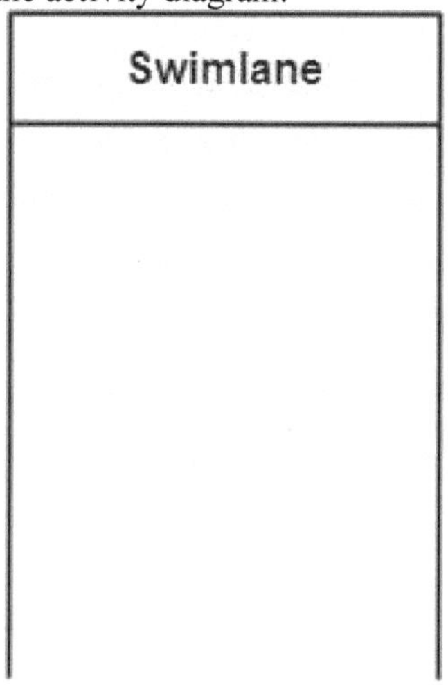

Forks

Forks and join nodes generate the concurrent flow inside the activity. A fork node consists of one inward edge and several outward edges. It is the same as that of various decision parameters. Whenever a data is received at an inward edge, it gets copied and split crossways various outward edges. It split a single inward flow into multiple parallel flows.

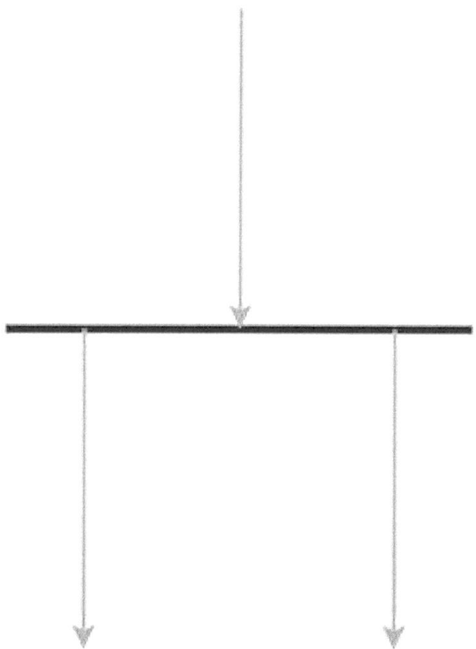

Join Nodes

Join nodes are the opposite of fork nodes. A Logical AND operation is performed on all of the inward edges as it synchronizes the flow of input across one single output (outward) edge.

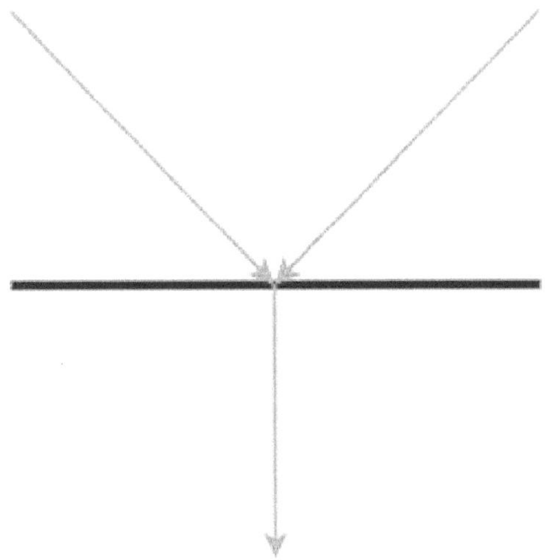

Pins

It is a small rectangle, which is attached to the action rectangle. It clears out all the messy and complicated thing to manage the execution flow of activities. It is an object node that precisely represents one input to or output from the action.

Notation of an Activity diagram

Activity diagram constitutes following notations:

Initial State: It depicts the initial stage or beginning of the set of actions.

Final State: It is the stage where all the control flows and object flows end.

Decision Box: It makes sure that the control flow or object flow will follow only one path.

Action Box: It represents the set of actions that are to be performed.

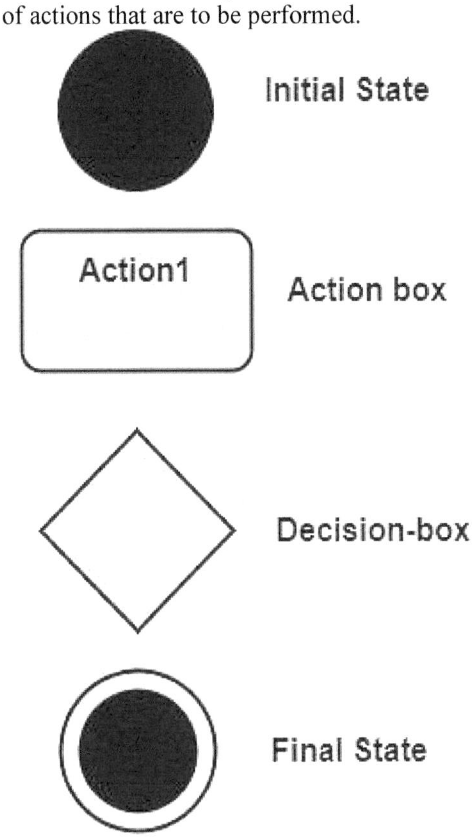

Why use Activity Diagram?

An event is created as an activity diagram encompassing a group of nodes associated with edges. To model the behavior of activities, they can be attached to any modeling element. It can model use cases, classes, interfaces, components, and collaborations.

It mainly models processes and workflows. It envisions the dynamic behavior of the system as well as constructs a runnable system that incorporates forward and reverse engineering. It does not include the message part, which means message flow is not represented in an activity diagram.

It is the same as that of a flowchart but not exactly a flowchart itself. It is used to depict the flow between several activities.

How to draw an Activity Diagram?

An activity diagram is a flowchart of activities, as it represents the workflow among various activities. They are identical to the flowcharts, but they themself are not exactly the flowchart. In other words, it can be said that an activity diagram is an enhancement of the flowchart, which encompasses several unique skills.

Since it incorporates swimlanes, branching, parallel flows, join nodes, control nodes, and forks, it supports exception handling. A system must be explored as a whole before drawing an activity diagram to provide a clearer view of the user. All of the activities are explored after they are properly analyzed for finding out the constraints applied to the activities. Each and every activity, condition, and association must be recognized.

After gathering all the essential information, an abstract or a prototype is built, which is then transformed into the actual diagram.

Following are the rules that are to be followed for drawing an activity diagram:

A meaningful name should be given to each and every activity.

Identify all of the constraints.

Acknowledge the activity associations.

Example of an Activity Diagram

An example of an activity diagram showing the business flow activity of order processing is given below.

Here the input parameter is the Requested order, and once the order is accepted, all of the required information is then filled, payment is also accepted, and then the order is shipped. It permits order shipment before an invoice is sent or payment is completed.

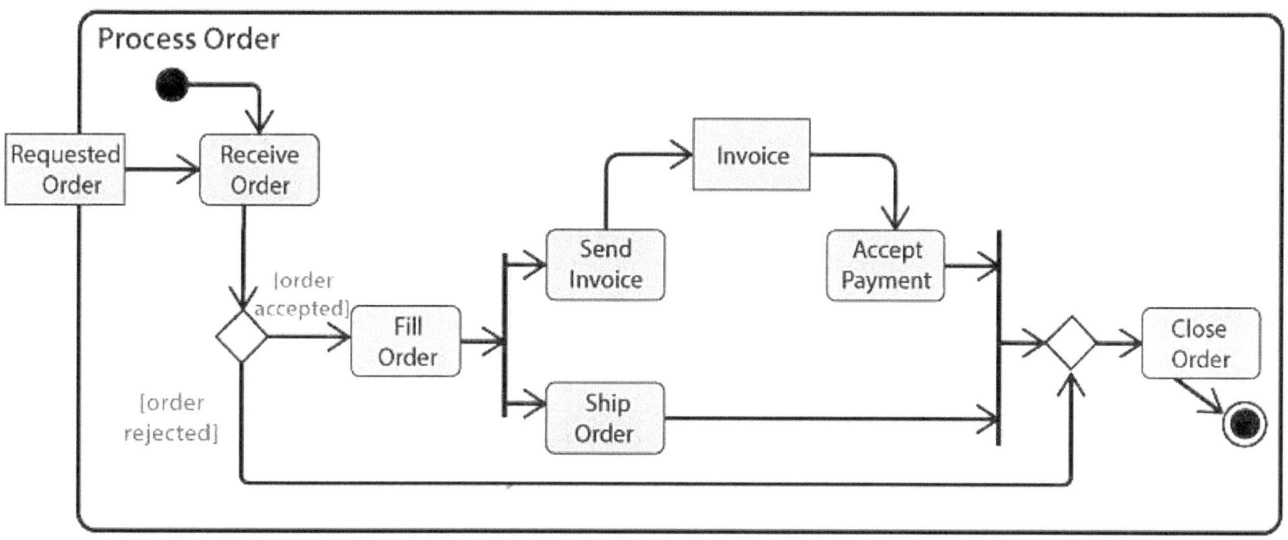

When to use an Activity Diagram?

An activity diagram can be used to portray business processes and workflows. Also, it used for modeling business as well as the software. An activity diagram is utilized for the followings:

To graphically model the workflow in an easier and understandable way.

To model the execution flow among several activities.

To model comprehensive information of a function or an algorithm employed within the system.

To model the business process and its workflow.

To envision the dynamic aspect of a system.

To generate the top-level flowcharts for representing the workflow of an application.

To represent a high-level view of a distributed or an object-oriented system.

12.3.3 Sequence Diagrams

The sequence diagram represents the flow of messages in the system and is also termed as an event diagram. It helps in envisioning several dynamic scenarios. It portrays the communication between any two lifelines as a time-ordered sequence of events, such that these lifelines took part at the run time. In UML, the lifeline is represented by a vertical bar, whereas the message flow is represented by a vertical dotted line that extends across the bottom of the page. It incorporates the iterations as well as branching.

Purpose of a Sequence Diagram

To model high-level interaction among active objects within a system.
To model interaction among objects inside a collaboration realizing a use case.
It either models generic interactions or some certain instances of interaction.

Notations of a Sequence Diagram

Lifeline

An individual participant in the sequence diagram is represented by a lifeline. It is positioned at the top of the diagram.

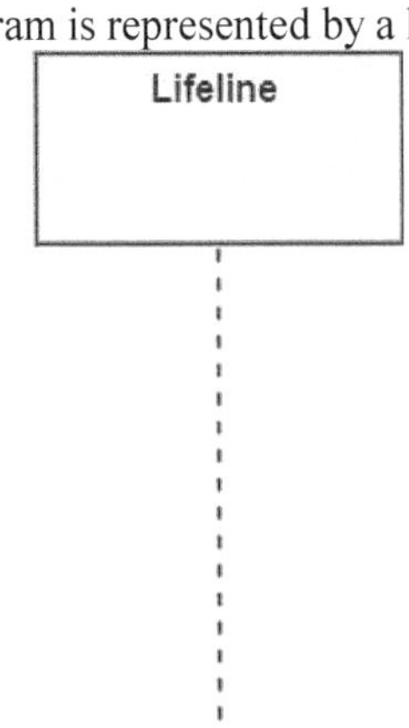

Actor

A role played by an entity that interacts with the subject is called as an actor. It is out of the scope of the system. It represents the role, which involves human users and external hardware or subjects. An actor may or may not represent a physical entity, but it purely depicts the role of an entity. Several distinct roles can be played by an actor or vice versa.

Activation

It is represented by a thin rectangle on the lifeline. It describes that time period in which an operation is performed by an element, such that the top and the bottom of the rectangle is associated with the initiation and the completion time, each respectively.

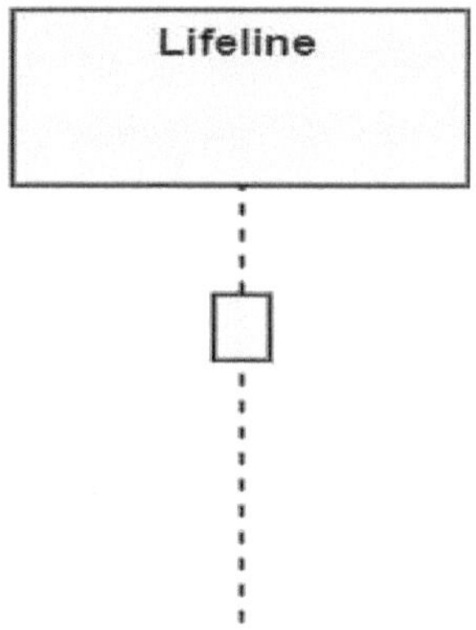

Messages
The messages depict the interaction between the objects and are represented by arrows. They are in the sequential order on the lifeline. The core of the sequence diagram is formed by messages and lifelines.
Following are types of messages enlisted below:
Call Message: It defines a particular communication between the lifelines of an interaction, which represents that the target lifeline has invoked an operation.

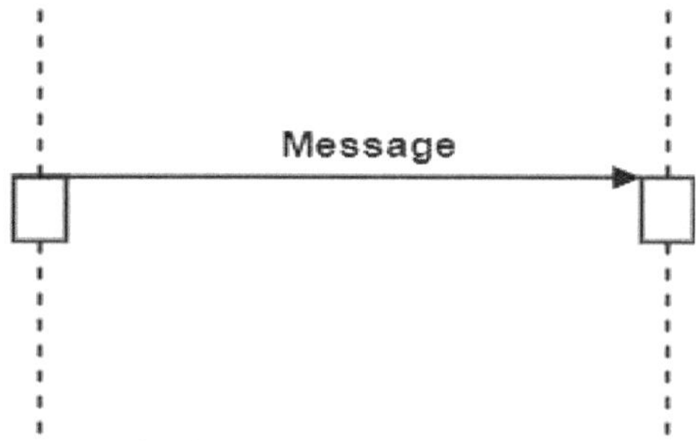

Return Message: It defines a particular communication between the lifelines of interaction that represent the flow of information from the receiver of the corresponding caller message.

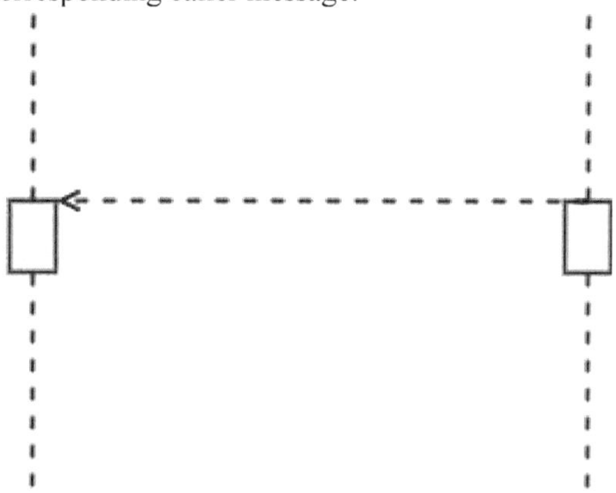

Self Message: It describes a communication, particularly between the lifelines of an interaction that represents a message of the same lifeline, has been invoked.

Recursive Message: A self message sent for recursive purpose is called a recursive message. In other words, it can be said that the recursive message is a special case of the self message as it represents the recursive calls.

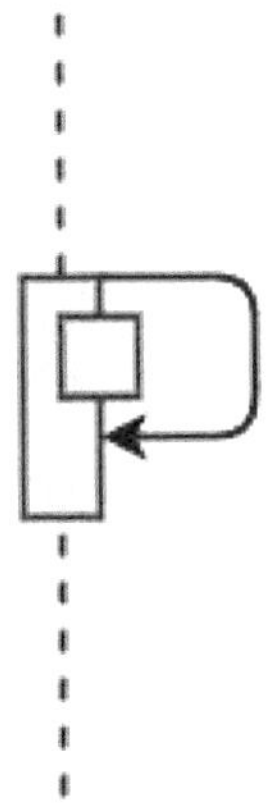

Create Message: It describes a communication, particularly between the lifelines of an interaction describing that the target (lifeline) has been instantiated.

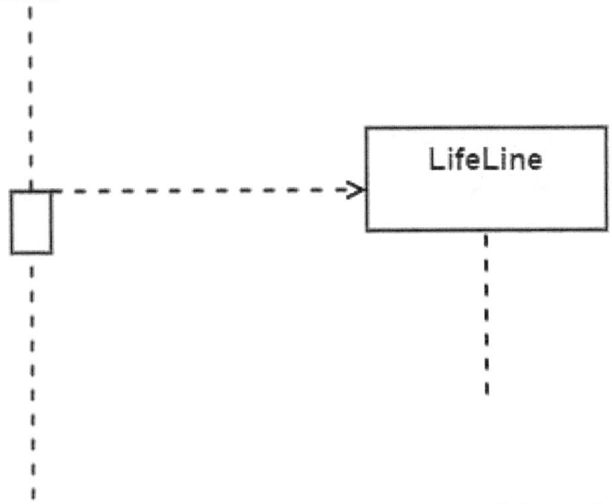

Destroy Message: It describes a communication, particularly between the lifelines of an interaction that depicts a request to destroy the lifecycle of the target.

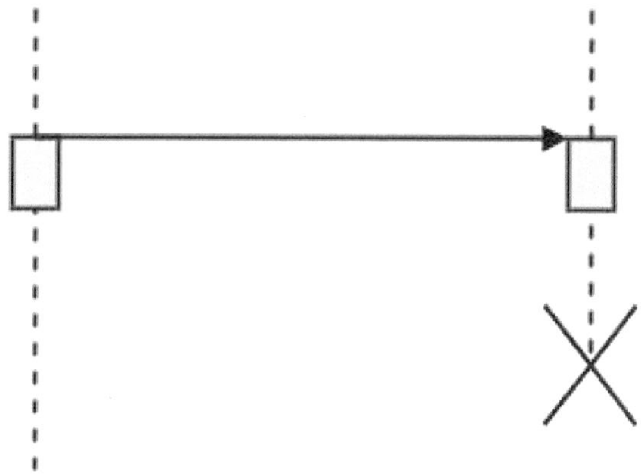

Duration Message: It describes a communication particularly between the lifelines of an interaction, which portrays the time passage of the message while modeling a system.

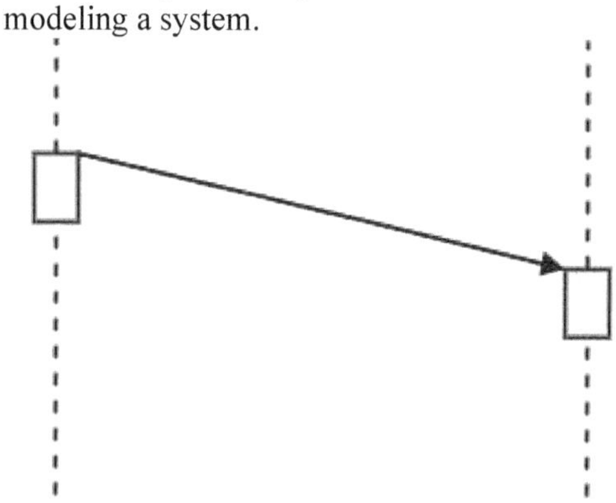

Note

A note is the capability of attaching several remarks to the element. It basically carries useful information for the modelers.

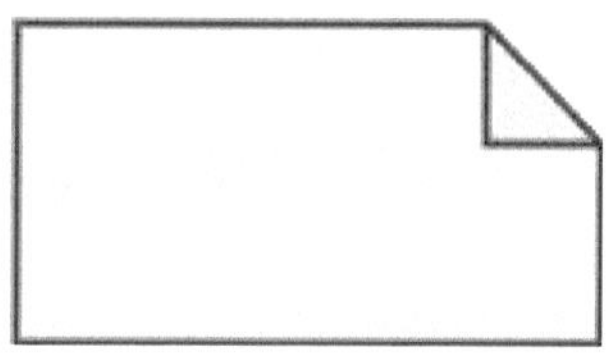

Sequence Fragments

Sequence fragments have been introduced by UML 2.0, which makes it quite easy for the creation and maintenance of an accurate sequence diagram.

It is represented by a box called a combined fragment, encloses a part of interaction inside a sequence diagram.

The type of fragment is shown by a fragment operator.

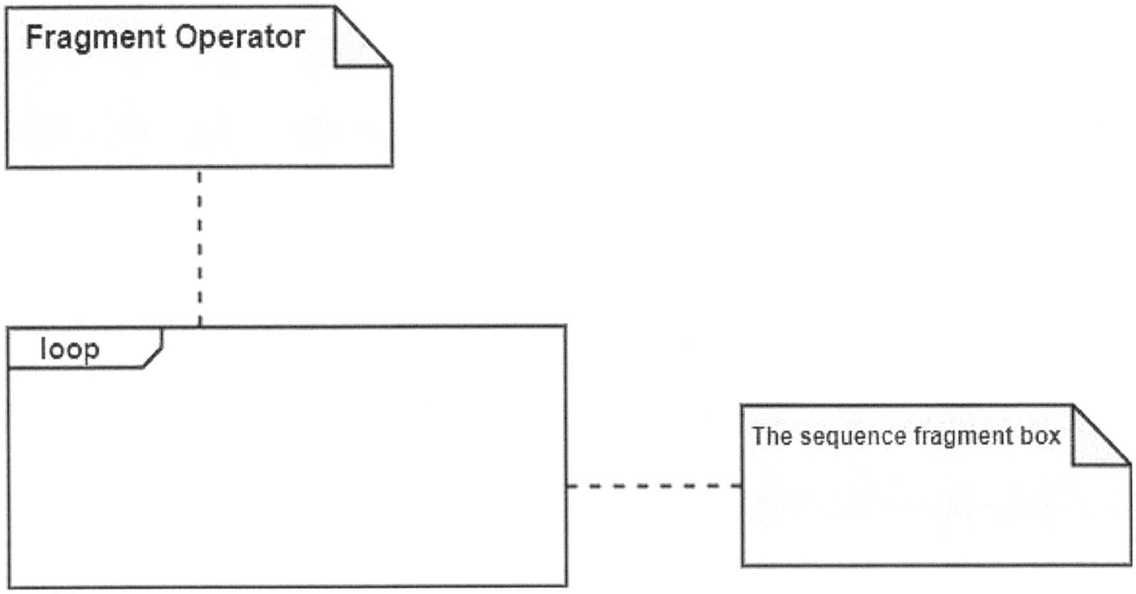

Types of fragments

Following are the types of fragments enlisted below;

Operator	Fragment Type
alt	Alternative multiple fragments: The only fragment for which the condition is true, will execute.
opt	Optional: If the supplied condition is true, only then the fragments will execute. It is similar to alt with only one trac
par	Parallel: Parallel executes fragments.
loop	Loop: Fragments are run multiple times, and the basis of interaction is shown by the guard.
region	Critical region: Only one thread can execute a fragment at once.
neg	Negative: A worthless communication is shown by the fragment.
ref	Reference: An interaction portrayed in another diagram. In this, a frame is drawn so as to cover the lifelines involv in the communication. The parameter and return value can be explained.
sd	Sequence Diagram: It is used to surround the whole sequence diagram.

Example of a Sequence Diagram

An example of a high-level sequence diagram for online bookshop is given below.

Any online customer can search for a book catalog, view a description of a particular book, add a book to its shopping cart, and do checkout.

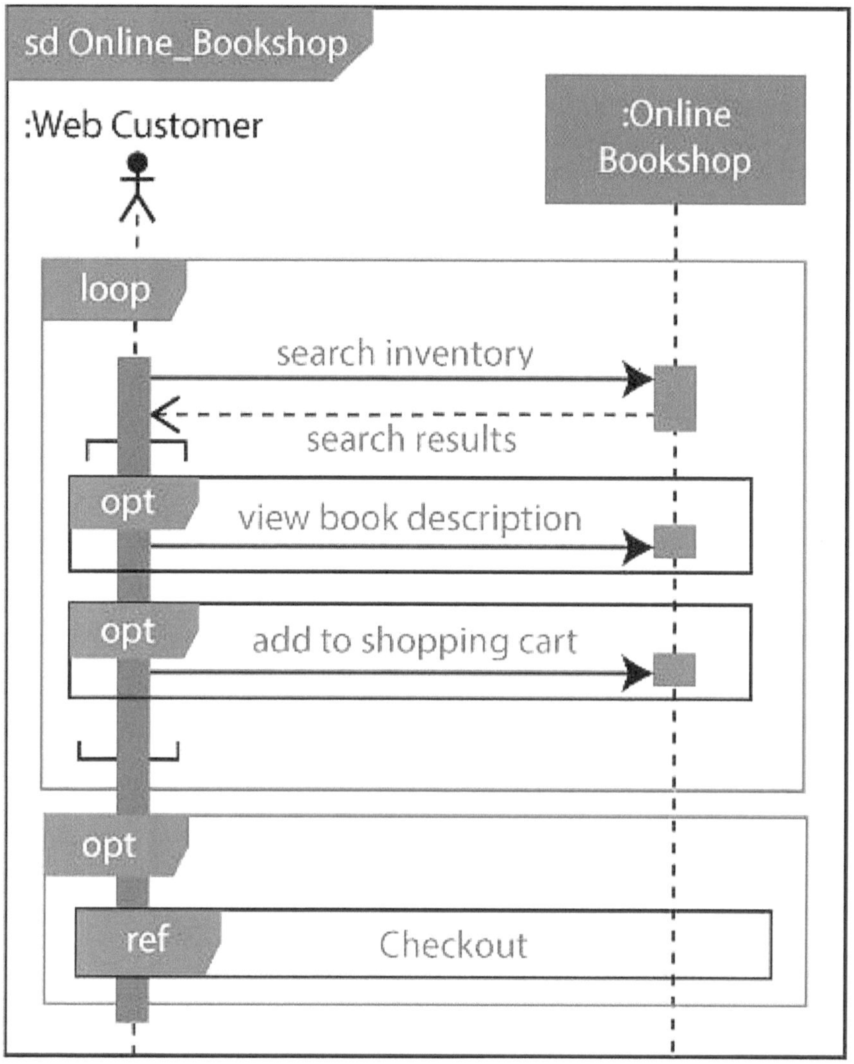

Benefits of a Sequence Diagram

It explores the real-time application.

It depicts the message flow between the different objects.

It has easy maintenance.

It is easy to generate.

Implement both forward and reverse engineering.

It can easily update as per the new change in the system.

12.4 Relationships and Mechanisms

relationships refer to associations or connections between various elements or entities within a software system. Relationships are used to depict how different components, classes, or objects interact and collaborate with each other. These relationships help in modeling and understanding the structure and behavior of the software. Here are some common types of relationships in software engineering:

Association:

Definition: An association represents a basic relationship between two or more classes or objects, indicating that they are somehow connected or related.

Purpose: Associations are used to model the links between classes and show that one class can access or use another class.

Aggregation:

Definition: Aggregation represents a "whole-part" relationship between classes, where one class (the whole) contains or is composed of other classes (the parts).
Purpose: Aggregation helps in modeling components that are part of a larger entity. For example, a car has wheels, and this relationship is an aggregation.
Composition:
Definition: Composition is a stronger form of aggregation, indicating that the whole is responsible for the creation and lifetime of its parts. If the whole is destroyed, its parts are also destroyed.
Purpose: Composition is used when one class is composed of other classes, and the lifetime of the parts is dependent on the whole. For example, a university comprises departments, and if the university ceases to exist, so do the departments.
Inheritance:
Definition: Inheritance represents an "is-a" relationship between classes, where one class (the child or subclass) inherits attributes and behaviors from another class (the parent or superclass).
Purpose: Inheritance is a fundamental concept in object-oriented programming and allows for code reuse and the creation of class hierarchies.
Dependency:
Definition: Dependency signifies that one class relies on another class, typically through method parameters or local variables, but it doesn't imply a permanent or structural relationship.
Purpose: Dependency relationships are often used when one class needs the services or information provided by another class.
Association Class:
Definition: An association class represents a class that is part of an association and plays a specific role in the association.
Purpose: Association classes help in modeling complex relationships where the association itself has attributes or methods.
Realization:
Definition: Realization is a relationship between an interface and a class, indicating that the class implements the methods defined in the interface.
Purpose: Realization is used to show how a class fulfills the contract specified by an interface. It is often used in interface-based programming.
Generalization/Specialization:
Definition: Generalization is a relationship that represents the inheritance hierarchy between classes. It shows that one class is a more general (parent) class, while another is a more specialized (child) class.
Purpose: Generalization is used to create class hierarchies and depict relationships in object-oriented design.

12.4.1 Associations, Aggregations, and Compositions

In UML diagrams, relationships are used to link several things. It is a connection between structural, behavioral, or grouping things. Following are the standard UML relationships enlisted below:
Association
Dependency
Generalization
Realization
Association
Association relationship is a structural relationship in which different objects are linked within the system. It exhibits a binary relationship between the objects representing an activity. It depicts the relationship between objects, such as a teacher, can be associated with multiple teachers.
It is represented by a line between the classes followed by an arrow that navigates the direction, and when the arrow is on both sides, it is then called a bidirectional association. We can specify the multiplicity of an association by adding the adornments on the line that will denote the association.
Example:
1) A single teacher has multiple students.

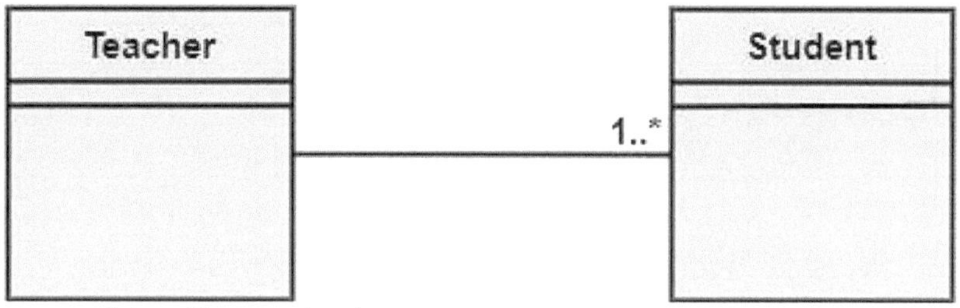

2) A single student can associate with many teachers.

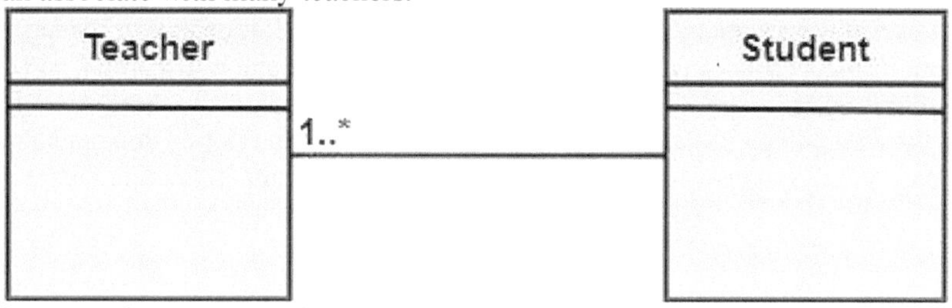

The composition and aggregation are two subsets of association. In both of the cases, the object of one class is owned by the object of another class; the only difference is that in composition, the child does not exist independently of its parent, whereas in aggregation, the child is not dependent on its parent i.e., standalone. An aggregation is a special form of association, and composition is the special form of aggregation.

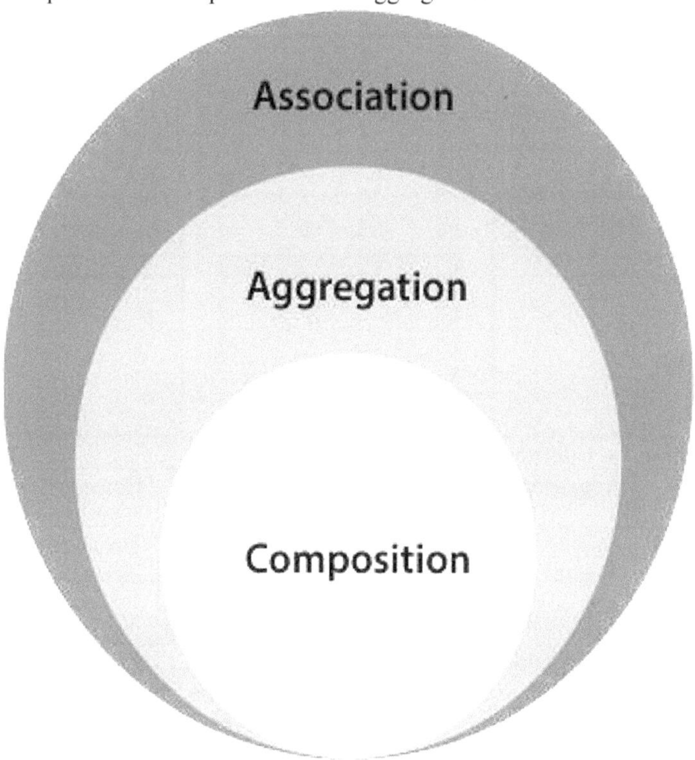

Aggregation

Aggregation is a subset of association, is a collection of different things. It represents has a relationship. It is more specific than an association. It describes a part-whole or part-of relationship. It is a binary association, i.e., it only involves two classes. It is a kind of relationship in which the child is independent of its parent.

For example:

Here we are considering a car and a wheel example. A car cannot move without a wheel. But the wheel can be independently used with the bike, scooter, cycle, or any other vehicle. The wheel object can exist without the car object, which proves to be an aggregation relationship.

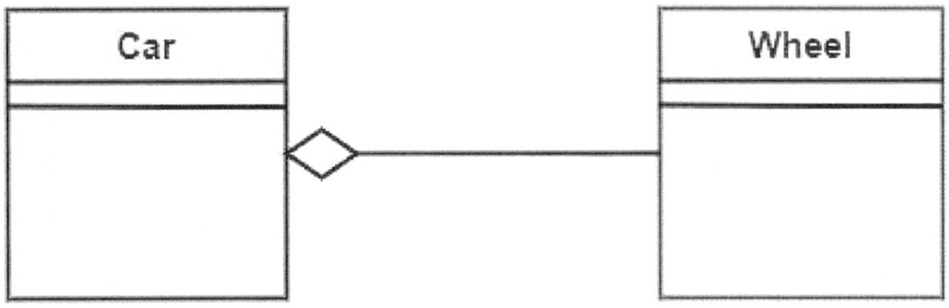

Composition

The composition is a part of aggregation, and it portrays the whole-part relationship. It depicts dependency between a composite (parent) and its parts (children), which means that if the composite is discarded, so will its parts get deleted. It exists between similar objects.

As you can see from the example given below, the composition association relationship connects the Person class with Brain class, Heart class, and Legs class. If the person is destroyed, the brain, heart, and legs will also get discarded.

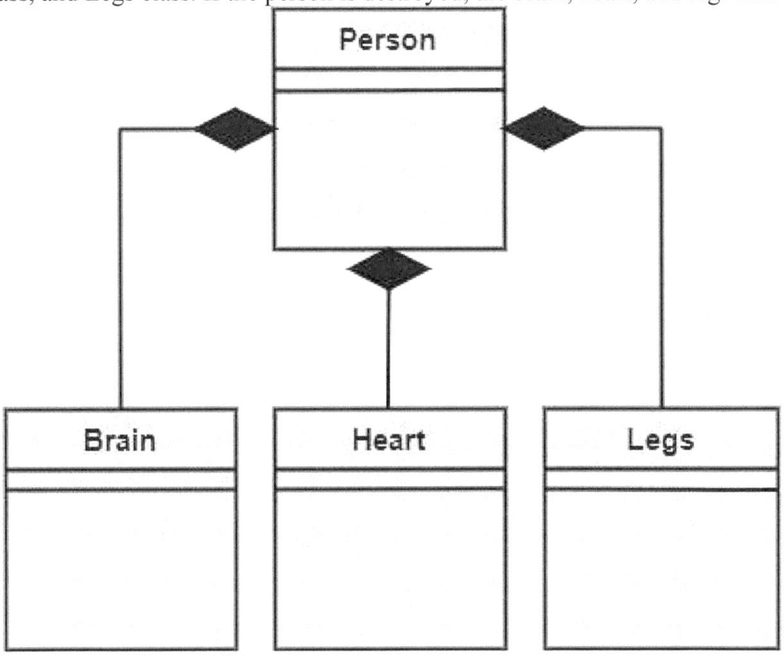

Association vs. Aggregation vs. Composition

Association	**Aggregation**	**Composition**
Association relationship is represented using an arrow.	Aggregation relationship is represented by a straight line with an empty diamond at one end.	The composition relationship is represented by a straight line with a black diamond at one end.
In UML, it can exist between two or more classes.	It is a part of the association relationship.	It is a part of the aggregation relationship.
It incorporates one-to-one, one-to-many, many-to-one, and many-to-many association between the classes.	It exhibits a kind of weak relationship.	It exhibits a strong type of relationship.

It can associate one more objects together.	In an aggregation relationship, the associated objects exist independently within the scope of the system.	In a composition relationship, the associated objects cannot exist independently within the scope of the system.
In this, objects are linked together.	In this, the linked objects are independent of each other.	Here the linked objects are dependent on each other.
It may or may not affect the other associated element if one element is deleted.	Deleting one element in the aggregation relationship does not affect other associated elements.	It affects the other element if one of its associated element is deleted.
Example: A tutor can associate with multiple students, or one student can associate with multiple teachers.	Example: A car needs a wheel for its proper functioning, but it may not require the same wheel. It may function with another wheel as well.	Example: If a file is placed in a folder and that is folder is deleted. The file residing inside that folder will also get deleted at the time of folder deletion.

12.4.2 Inheritance and Generalization

"Inheritance is defined as a mechanism where the sub or child class inherits the properties and characteristics of the super class or other derived classes. It also supports additional features of extracting properties from the child class and using it into other derived classes."

Types of Inheritance

1. Single Inheritance:

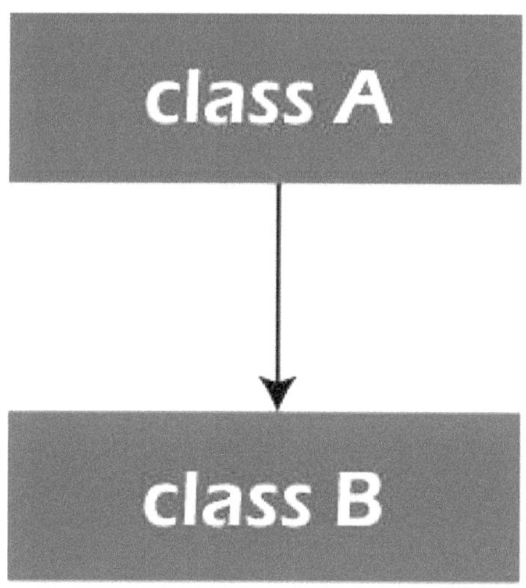

Single Inheritance

In this type, the child class inherits the properties from the superclass.

In the below example, you will notice class One is the superclass, and class Two is the base class. Therefore, class Two inherits the properties and behaviour of the base class One.

Syntax

//Super Class

class One

```
{
public void addOne()
{
//CODE TO DO:
}
}
//Child Class
class Two : One
{
public void addTwo()
{
//CODE TO DO:
}
}
```

2. Multiple Inheritance:

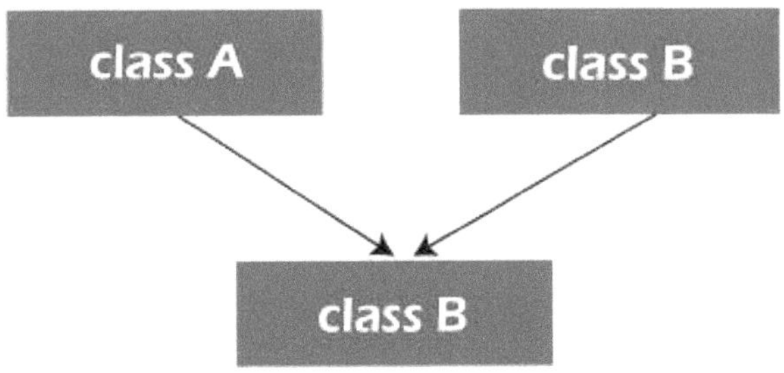

Multiple Inheritance

The child class inherits the properties and features from two or more parent classes with this type.
In the below example, you will notice class Three inherits the features and behaviour of class Two. Further, class Two inherits the properties of class One. Therefore, we can conclude that class One is the base class of class Two, whereas class Two is the base class of class Three.
Hence, class Three implicitly inherits the behaviour and properties of class One along with class Two, thereby creating a multiple inheritance.

Syntax

```
//Superclass
class One
{
public void addOne()
{
//CODE TO DO:
}
}
//child Class
class Two : One
{
public void addTwo()
{
//CODE TO DO:
}
}
//Derived Class
class Three : Two
{
//CODE TO DO:
{
```

```
//TO DO:
}
}
```

3. Multilevel Inheritance:

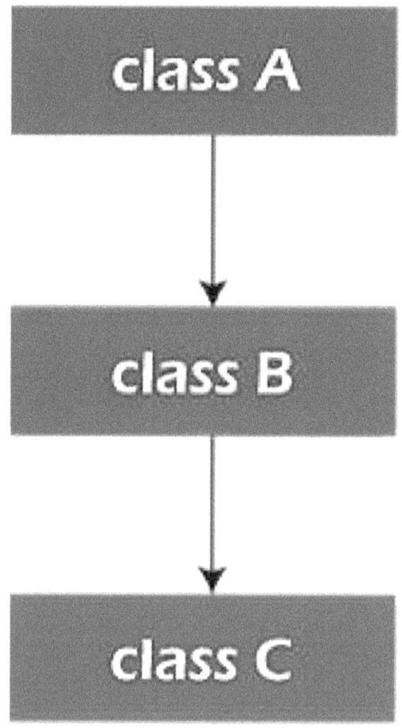

Multi - Level Inheritance

With this type, one child class inherits the properties and behavior from two or more superclasses.
In the below example, class three inherits the properties, functions and objects for both class Two and class One at the same level. Therefore, both class One and class Two are the superclasses for class Three.

Syntax

```
//Super Class
class One
{
public void addOne()
{
//CODE TO DO:
}
}
//Super Class
class Two
{
public void addTwo()
{
//CODE TO DO:
}
}
//Child Class
class Three : One, Two
{
public void addThree()
{
//CODE TO DO:
}
}
```

4. Hierarchal Inheritance:

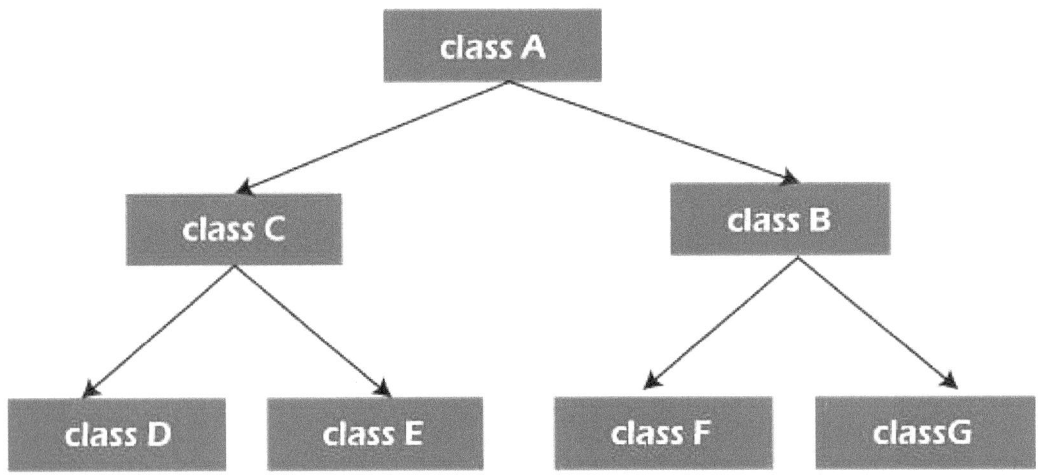

Hierarchical Inheritance

In the Hierarchical Inheritance type, two or more child classes inherit the properties and behaviors from one superclass. In the below example, the following hierarchies:

(I) The base class One has two derived classes, i.e., class Two and class Three.
(II) Next, class Two acts as a base class for two child classes named Six and Seven.
(III) Further, class three is also a base class for class Four and class Five, respectively.

Syntax

```
//Superclass
class One
{
public void addOne()
{
//CODE TO DO:
}
}
//Child Class
class Two : One
{
public void addTwo()
{
//CODE TO DO:
}
}
//Child Class
class Three : One
{
public void addThree()
{
//CODE TO DO:
}
}
//Child Class
class Four : Three
{
public void addFour()
{
//CODE TO DO:
```

```
}
}
//Child Class
class Five : Three
{
public void addFive()
{
//CODE TO DO:
}
}
//child Class
class Six : Two
{
public void addSix()
{
//CODE TO DO:
}
}
//Child Class
class Seven :Two
{
public void addSeven()
{
//CODE TO DO:
}
}
```

5. Hybrid Inheritance:

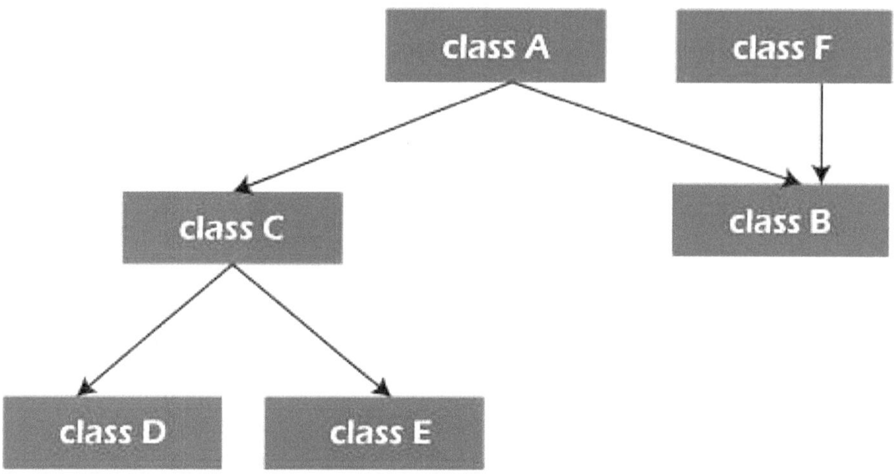

Hybrid Inheritance (a combination of Hierachical and multiple)

With this type, the programmer can call a combination of two or more types of inheritance. Therefore the code can include a combination of Multiple and Hierarchical inheritance, Multilevel and Hierarchical inheritance or Hierarchical and Multipath inheritance, or it may be a combination of three of them, i.e., Multiple, Multilevel and Multiple Hierarchical inheritance.

Generalization

It is also called a parent-child relationship. In generalization, one element is a specialization of another general component. It may be substituted for it. It is mostly used to represent inheritance.

The parent model element can have as many children, and also, the child can have one or more parents. But most commonly, it can be seen that there is one parent model element and multiple child model elements. The generalization relationship does not consist of names. The generalization relationship is represented by a solid line with a hollow arrowhead pointing towards the parent model element from the child model element.

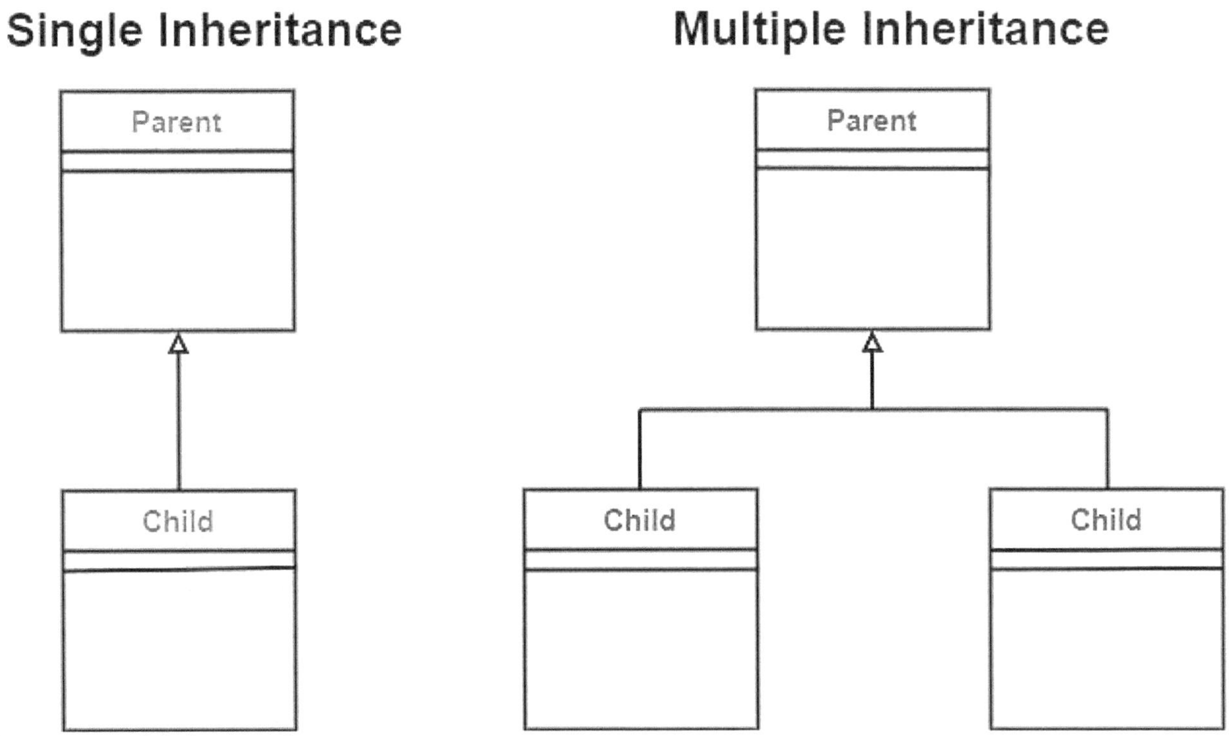

Stereotypes and their constraints
<<implementation>> - It is used to show that the child is implemented by its parent, such that the child object inherits the structure and behavior of its parent object without disobeying the rules. The implementation of stereotype is mostly used in single inheritance.
In the generalization stereotype, there are two types of constraints that are complete and incomplete to check if all the child objects are involved or not in the relationship.
Example:
As we know, the bank account can be of two types; Savings Account and Credit Card Account. Both the savings and the credit card account inherits the generalized properties from the Bank Account, which is Account Number, Account Balance, etc.

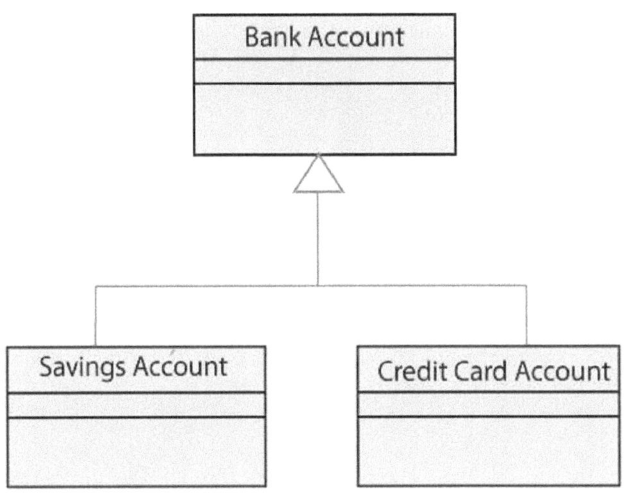

12.5 Class Diagrams

The class diagram depicts a static view of an application. It represents the types of objects residing in the system and the relationships between them. A class consists of its objects, and also it may inherit from other classes. A class diagram is used to visualize, describe, document various different aspects of the system, and also construct executable software code.

It shows the attributes, classes, functions, and relationships to give an overview of the software system. It constitutes class names, attributes, and functions in a separate compartment that helps in software development. Since it is a collection of classes, interfaces, associations, collaborations, and constraints, it is termed as a structural diagram.

Purpose of Class Diagrams

The main purpose of class diagrams is to build a static view of an application. It is the only diagram that is widely used for construction, and it can be mapped with object-oriented languages. It is one of the most popular UML diagrams. Following are the purpose of class diagrams given below:

It analyses and designs a static view of an application.

It describes the major responsibilities of a system.

It is a base for component and deployment diagrams.

It incorporates forward and reverse engineering.

Benefits of Class Diagrams

It can represent the object model for complex systems.

It reduces the maintenance time by providing an overview of how an application is structured before coding.

It provides a general schematic of an application for better understanding.

It represents a detailed chart by highlighting the desired code, which is to be programmed.

It is helpful for the stakeholders and the developers.

Vital components of a Class Diagram

The class diagram is made up of three sections:

Upper Section: The upper section encompasses the name of the class. A class is a representation of similar objects that shares the same relationships, attributes, operations, and semantics. Some of the following rules that should be taken into account while representing a class are given below:

Capitalize the initial letter of the class name.

Place the class name in the center of the upper section.

A class name must be written in bold format.

The name of the abstract class should be written in italics format.

Middle Section: The middle section constitutes the attributes, which describe the quality of the class. The attributes have the following characteristics:

The attributes are written along with its visibility factors, which are public (+), private (-), protected (#), and package (~).

The accessibility of an attribute class is illustrated by the visibility factors.

A meaningful name should be assigned to the attribute, which will explain its usage inside the class.

Lower Section: The lower section contain methods or operations. The methods are represented in the form of a list, where each method is written in a single line. It demonstrates how a class interacts with data.

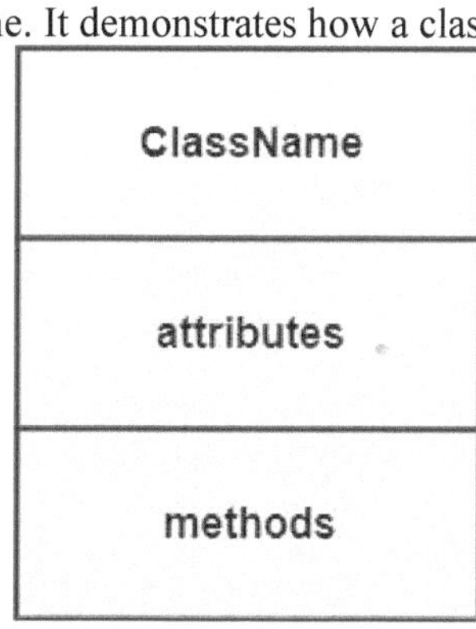

Relationships

In UML, relationships are of three types:

Dependency: A dependency is a semantic relationship between two or more classes where a change in one class cause changes in another class. It forms a weaker relationship.

In the following example, Student_Name is dependent on the Student_Id.

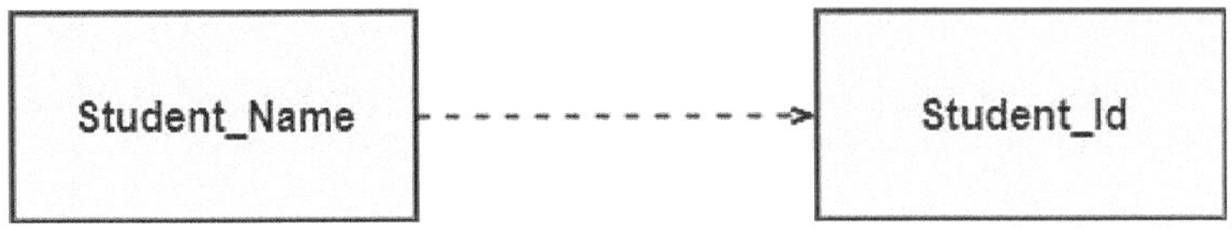

Generalization: A generalization is a relationship between a parent class (superclass) and a child class (subclass). In this, the child class is inherited from the parent class.

For example, The Current Account, Saving Account, and Credit Account are the generalized form of Bank Account.

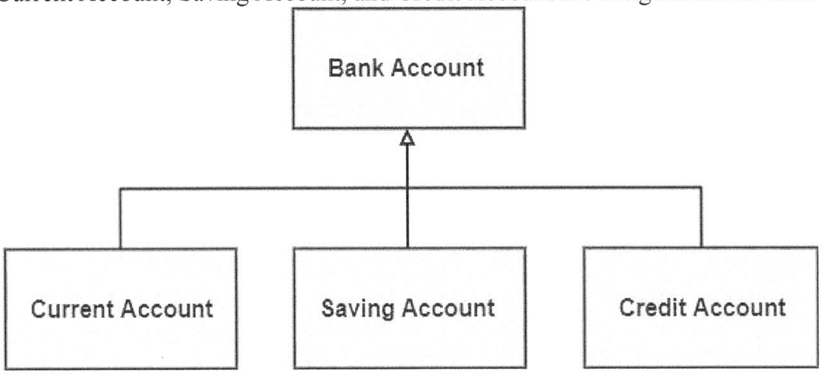

Association: It describes a static or physical connection between two or more objects. It depicts how many objects are there in the relationship.

For example, a department is associated with the college.

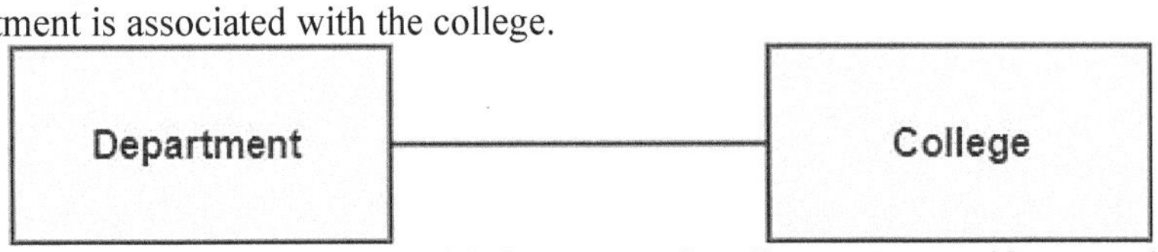

Multiplicity: It defines a specific range of allowable instances of attributes. In case if a range is not specified, one is considered as a default multiplicity.

For example, multiple patients are admitted to one hospital.

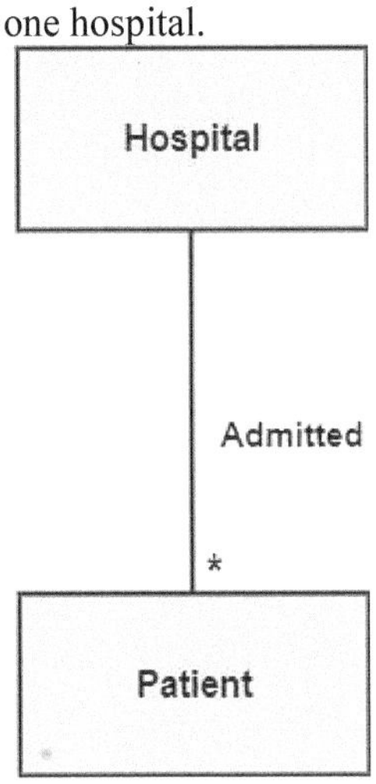

Aggregation: An aggregation is a subset of association, which represents has a relationship. It is more specific then association. It defines a part-whole or part-of relationship. In this kind of relationship, the child class can exist independently of its parent class.

The company encompasses a number of employees, and even if one employee resigns, the company still exists.

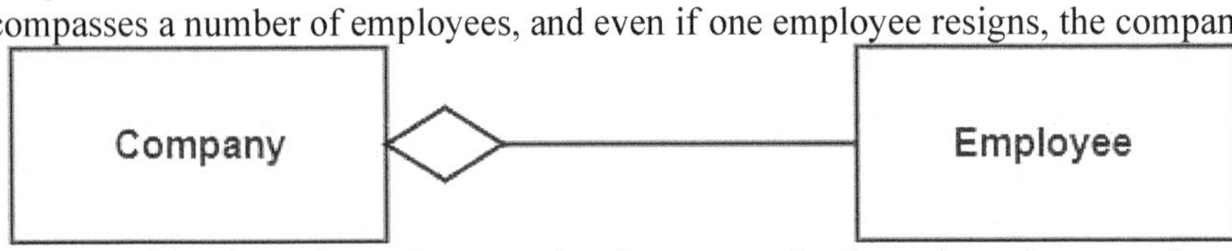

Composition: The composition is a subset of aggregation. It portrays the dependency between the parent and its child, which means if one part is deleted, then the other part also gets discarded. It represents a whole-part relationship.

A contact book consists of multiple contacts, and if you delete the contact book, all the contacts will be lost.

Abstract Classes

In the abstract class, no objects can be a direct entity of the abstract class. The abstract class can neither be declared nor be instantiated. It is used to find the functionalities across the classes. The notation of the abstract class is similar to that of class; the only difference is that the name of the class is written in italics. Since it does not involve any implementation for a given function, it is best to use the abstract class with multiple objects.

Let us assume that we have an abstract class named displacement with a method declared inside it, and that method will be called as a drive (). Now, this abstract class method can be implemented by any object, for example, car, bike, scooter, cycle, etc.

How to draw a Class Diagram?

The class diagram is used most widely to construct software applications. It not only represents a static view of the system but also all the major aspects of an application. A collection of class diagrams as a whole represents a system.

Some key points that are needed to keep in mind while drawing a class diagram are given below:

To describe a complete aspect of the system, it is suggested to give a meaningful name to the class diagram.

The objects and their relationships should be acknowledged in advance.

The attributes and methods (responsibilities) of each class must be known.

A minimum number of desired properties should be specified as more number of the unwanted property will lead to a complex diagram.

Notes can be used as and when required by the developer to describe the aspects of a diagram.

The diagrams should be redrawn and reworked as many times to make it correct before producing its final version.

Class Diagram Example

A class diagram describing the sales order system is given below.

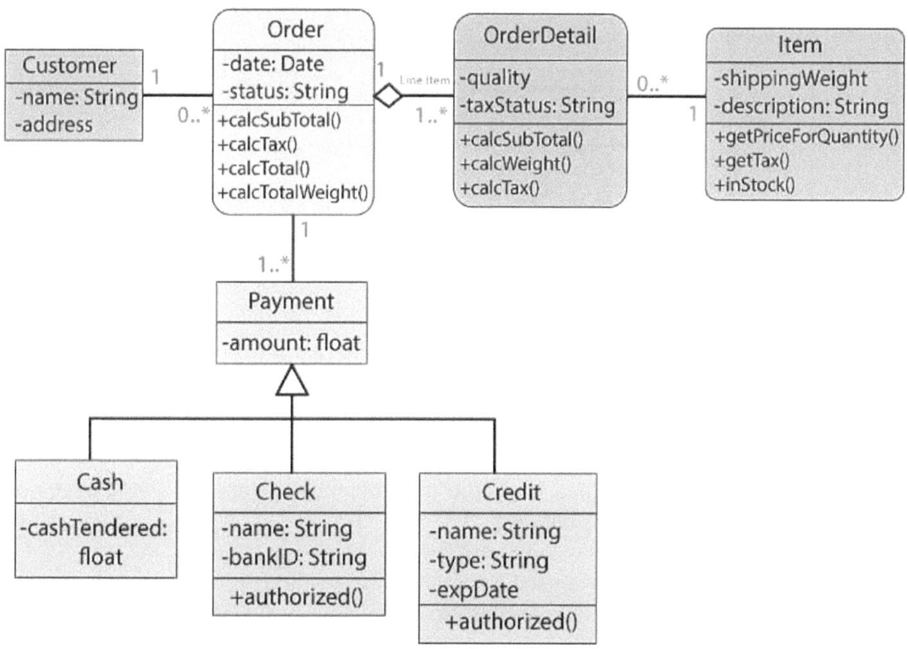

12.5.1 Modeling Classes and Attributes

In software engineering and object-oriented modeling, classes and attributes are fundamental concepts used to represent the structure and characteristics of objects in a system. Let's explore these concepts in detail:

1. Classes:

A **class** is a blueprint or template for creating objects (instances) in an object-oriented system. It defines the structure, behavior, and attributes of objects.

Each object in a system belongs to a specific class and inherits the properties and behaviors defined by that class.

Classes are the primary building blocks of object-oriented design and represent real-world entities, concepts, or components in a software system.

They encapsulate data (attributes) and methods (functions) that operate on that data.

2. Attributes (Data Members):

Attributes are the data members of a class. They represent the characteristics or properties of objects belonging to that class.

Attributes define what an object is and can store information about the object's state.

In class diagrams and UML (Unified Modeling Language), attributes are often depicted with their names and data types.

For example, let's consider a simplified class definition in Python:

pythonCopy code

class Person: def __init__(self, first_name, last_name, age): self.first_name = first_name # Attribute: first_name self.last_name = last_name # Attribute: last_name self.age = age # Attribute: age def greet(self): print(f"Hello, my name is {self.first_name} {self.last_name}. I am {self.age} years old.") # Creating an instance of the Person class person1 = Person("John", "Doe", 30) # Accessing attributes of the object print(person1.first_name) # Accessing the 'first_name' attribute print(person1.last_name) # Accessing the 'last_name' attribute print(person1.age) # Accessing the 'age' attribute # Calling a method of the object person1.greet() # Calling the 'greet' method

In this example:

Person is a class representing a person with attributes such as first_name, last_name, and age.

first_name, last_name, and age are attributes that store data specific to each instance of the Person class.

The greet method is a behavior associated with the **Person** class.

Classes and attributes are essential for modeling the structure and data of objects in software systems. They help in organizing and managing the complexity of the system by defining clear boundaries and encapsulating related data and behaviors within a class.

12.5.2 Relationships Between Classes

There are six main types of relationships between classes: inheritance , realization / implementation , composition , aggregation , association, and dependency . The arrows for the six relationships are as follows:

Then we come to understand the specific content of the class relationship.

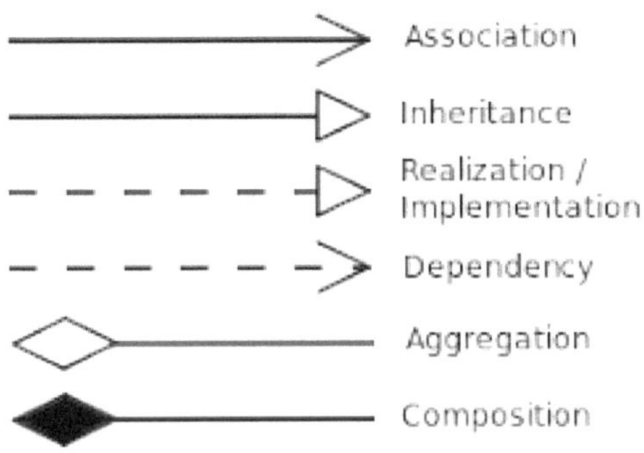

Six types of relationships

In the six types of relationships, the code structure of the three types of relationships such as composition , aggregation , and association is the same as using attributes to store the references of another class. Therefore, they must be distinguished by the relationship between the contents.

Inheritance

Inheritance is also called generalization and is used to describe the relationship between parent and child classes. A parent class is also called a base class, and a subclass is also called a derived class.

In the inheritance relationship, the subclass inherits all the functions of the parent class, and the parent class has all the attributes, methods, and subclasses. Subclasses contain additional information in addition to the same information as the parent class.
For example: buses, taxis, and cars are cars, they all have names, and they can all be on the road.

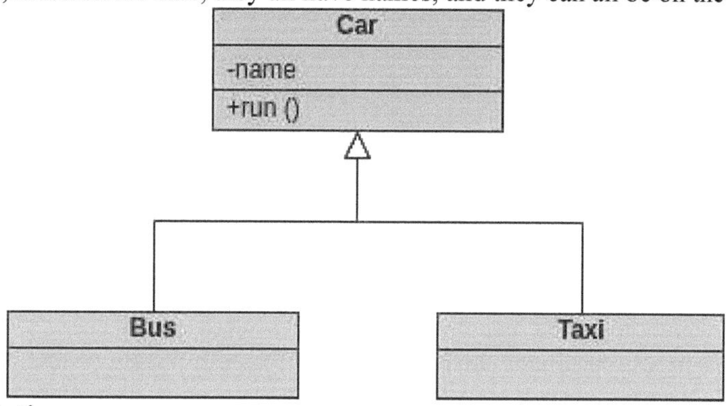

Realization / Implementation
Implementation (Implementation) is mainly used to specify the relationship between interfaces and implementation classes .
An interface (including an abstract class) is a collection of methods. In an implementation relationship, a class implements an interface, and methods in the class implement all methods of the interface declaration.
For example: cars and ships are vehicles, and the vehicle is just an abstract concept of a mobile tool, and the ship and the vehicle realize the specific mobile functions.

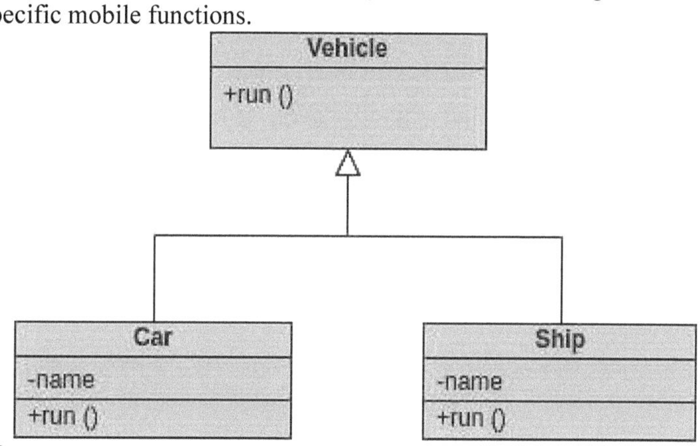

EDIT THIS TEMPLATE
Composition relationship
Composition: The relationship between the whole and the part, but the whole and the part cannot be separated .
The combination relationship represents the relationship between the whole and part of the class, and the overall and part have a consistent lifetime. Once the overall object does not exist, some of the objects will not exist, and they will all die in the same life.For example, a person is composed of a head and a body. The two are inseparable and coexist.

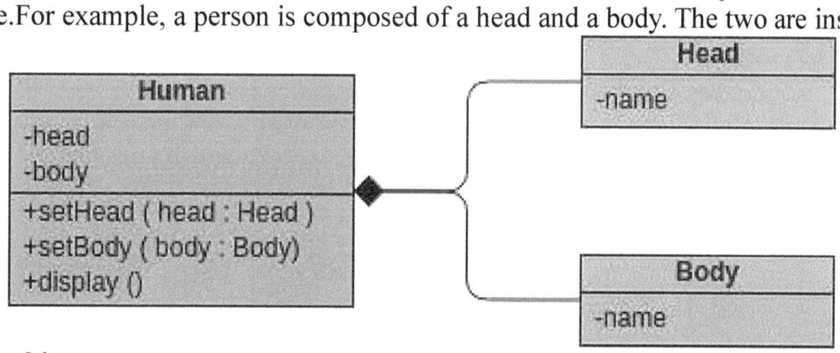

Aggregation Relationship
Aggregation: The relationship between the whole and part, and the whole and part can be separated.
Aggregate relations also represent the relationship between the whole and part of the class, member objects are part of the overall object, but the member object can exist independently from the overall object.

For example, bus drivers and work clothes and hats are part of the overall relationship, but they can be separated. Work clothes and hats can be worn on other drivers. Bus drivers can also wear other work clothes and hats.

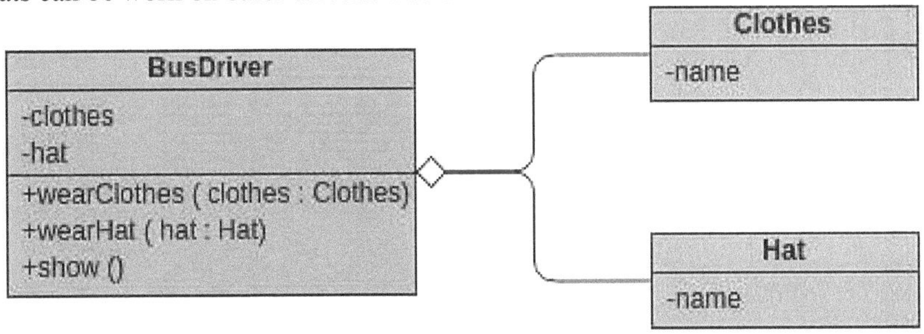

Association Relationships

Association: Indicates that a property of a class holds a reference to an instance (or instances) of another class .

Association is the most commonly used relationship between a class and a class, which means that there is a connection between one type of object and another type of object. Combinations and aggregations also belong to associative relations , but relations between classes of affiliations are weaker than the other two.

There are four kinds of associations : two-way associations , one-way associations , self-association , and multiple-number associations .

For example: cars and drivers, one car corresponds to a particular driver, and one driver can drive multiple cars.

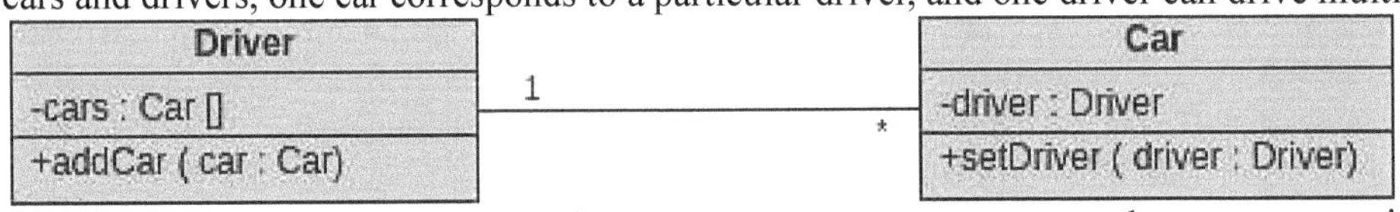

In UML diagrams, bidirectional associations can have two arrows or no arrows , and one-way associations or self-associations have an arrow .

In a multiplicity relationship, you can add a number directly to the associated line to indicate the number of objects in the corresponding class.

1..1: Only one

0..*: Zero or more

1..*:one or more

0..1: No or only one

m..n: at least m, at most n (m<=n)

Dependencies

Dependence: Assume that a change in class A causes a change in class B, then say that class B depends on class A.

In most cases, dependencies are reflected in methods of a class that use another class's object as a parameter.

A dependency relationship is a "use" relationship. A change in a particular thing may affect other things that use it, and use a dependency when it is necessary to indicate that one thing uses another.For example: The car relies on gasoline. If there is no gasoline, the car will not be able to drive.

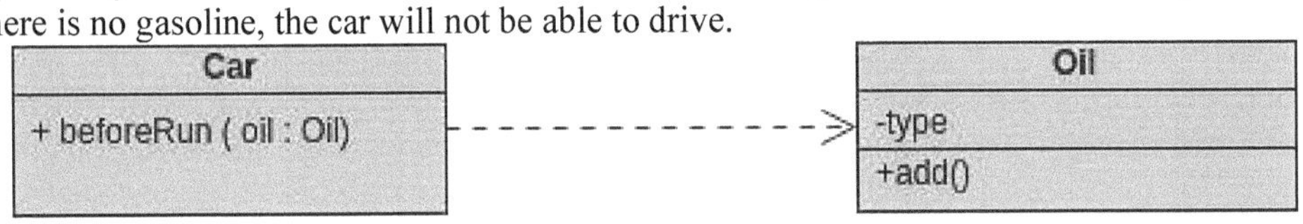

Class Diagram – Order System

The class diagram below models a customer order from a retail catalog. The central class is the Order. Associated with it are the Customer making the purchase and the Payment. A Payment is one of four kinds: Cash, Check, Credit or Wire Transfer. The order contains OrderDetails (line items), each with its associated Item.

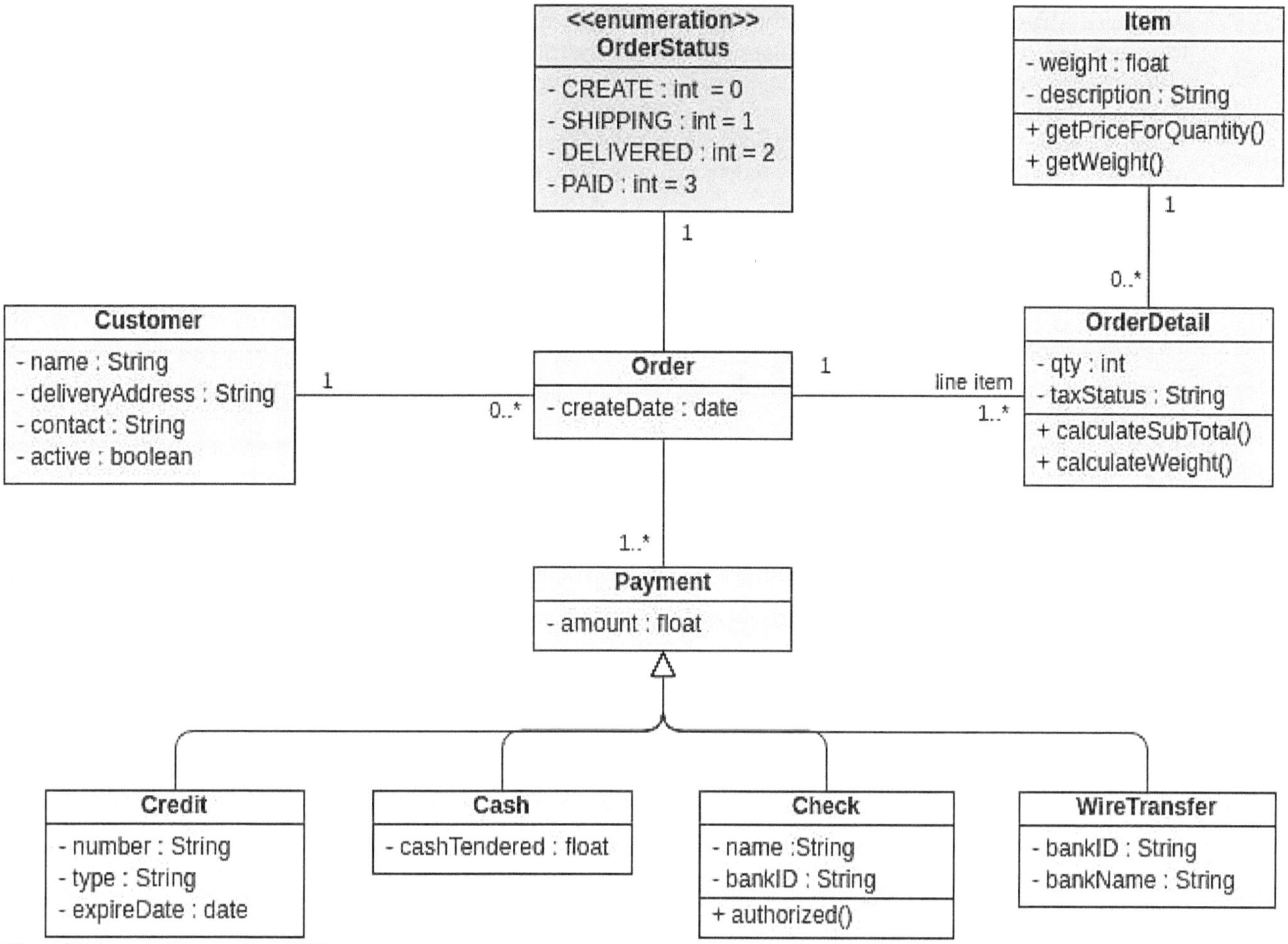

Class Diagram Example: GUI

A class diagram may also have notes attached to classes or relationships.

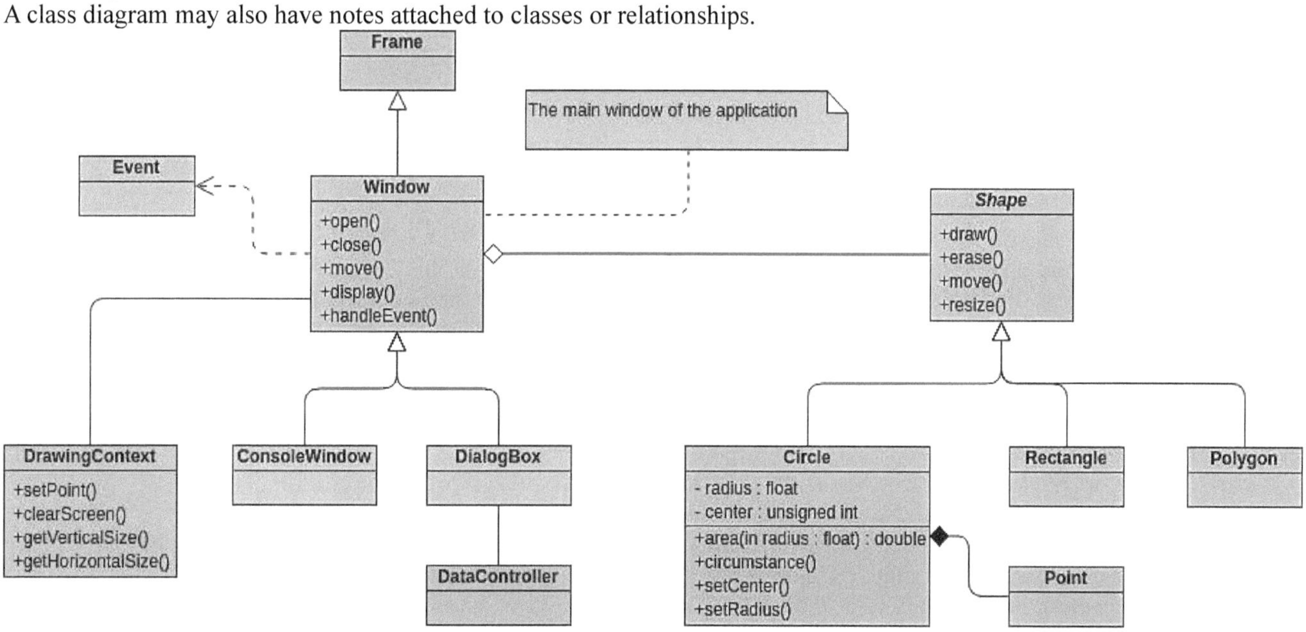

12.6 Advanced Structured Modeling

Advanced Structured Modeling, in the context of software engineering, refers to a set of techniques and tools used to create detailed, well-structured designs of software systems. These designs help developers understand how different components of the software interact and work together to achieve the desired functionality.

In simple terms, advanced structured modeling is like creating a detailed blueprint or map of a complex software program before actually building it. It involves breaking down the system into smaller parts, specifying how these parts will function, and illustrating how they connect with each other. This makes it easier to manage and develop large software projects effectively.

Some common techniques used in advanced structured modeling include data flow diagrams, structured analysis, and entity-relationship diagrams. These techniques help software engineers plan, design, and document the software system's architecture and behavior, making the development process more organized and efficient.

12.6.1 Behavioral Modeling

In software engineering, behavioral model describe the overall behavior of the system. There are two types of behavioral models that are used to describe the system behavior, one is data processing model and another is state machine models. Data processing models are also known as DFD (Data Flow Diagram) which is used to show how data is processed as it moves through the system. State machine model is also known as State diagram which is used to show how the system will react with external events.

Data Flow Diagram

Data flow diagram is used to model the system's data processing.

It is also cay as the Functional model as it is a graphical representation of an enterprise function within a defined scope. Data flow diagram shows end to end data processing.

It can be easily converted into software as they just represent flow of the data objects. DFD diagram enable Software engineer to develop a model of the information domain and Functional domain at the same time.

It provide a logical model of the system and show the flow of the data and the flow of logic involved.

Characteristics of Data Flow Diagram

It shows the process, that transforms incoming data flows into outgoing data flows.

Process that performs this transformation normally creates as well as uses data.

External entities send and receive data flow from the systems.

It is also called a bubble chart.

Data flow diagram support a top-down approach for analysis.

Guidelines for Data Flow Diagram

Level 0 DFD should depict software system as single bubble.

Primary input and output are carefully noted.

Refinement should begin by isolating candidate processes, data objects, data stores to be represented at the next level.

All arrows and bubbles should be labeled with full names.

Information flow continuity must be maintained from level to level. That means the data objects that flow into the system of any transformation at one level must be the same. Data objects that flow into transformation at the more refined level.

One bubble at a time should be refined.

Data Flow Diagram Notation

Data flow diagram consists of a series of symbols joined together by a line. Data objects are represented by circles which are also called bubble charts. Data flow diagram are represented in hierarchical order. The first level data flow model is also called as DFD 0 level or context diagram which represents the system as a whole. Second level data flow model refines the context diagram and provides more details of first-level DFD. In a similar way, third level DFD refines the second level DFD, and so on. Data flow analysis models are developed by two organizations – Yourdon incorporation and Gane and Sarson.

Notations are as follows:

Data Flow: It represents the movement of data flow from a specific origin to a destination.

Process: It represents the users, procedures, or devices that use the data.

Entity: It represents the source of data or destination data external sources or destination of data which may be users, programs, organizations or other entities that interact with the system but are outside its boundary.

Data Store: There can be a single DFD diagram or can be exploded into various levels lime level 1, level 2, level 3, etc.

Notation Name	Yourdon Incorporation	Gane and Sarson

Data Flow		
Process	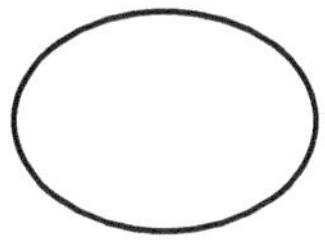	
Entity	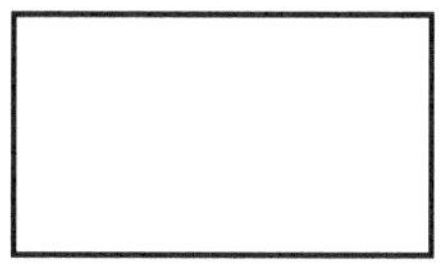	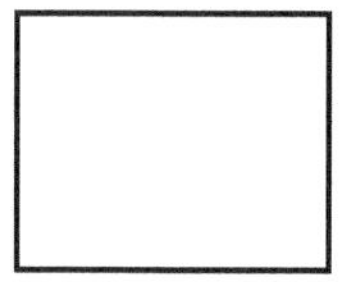
Data Store	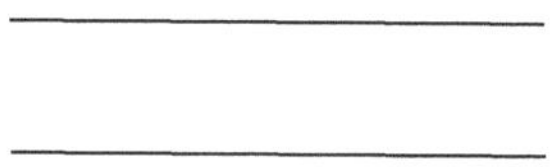	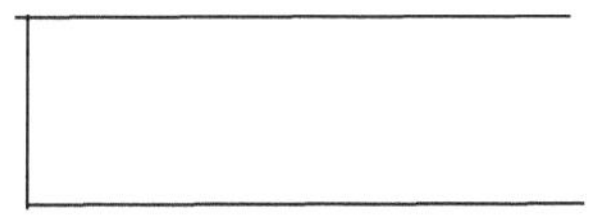

State Diagram

State diagram is a dynamic model which represents the changes of state that an object goes through during the lifetime in response to events. It is used to help the developer better understand any complex functionality of specialized areas of the system.

Notations used in state diagram:

1. Initial State

It represents the start point of the diagram. It is also called as pseudo state where state has no variables and no activities.

2. Final State

It represents the end point of the diagram. It is also pseudo state as it doesn't have any variable or activities. State diagram can have zero or more final states.

3. State

It represents the state of the object at an instant of time. State is a recognizable situation and exists over an interval of time.

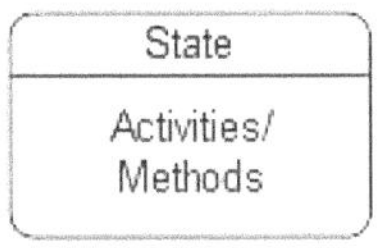

4. Transition
It represents the changes from one state to other. It is denoted by an arrow. The event or action causing the transition is written beside the arrow, separated by slash. Triggerless transition occurs when the state completed an activity.

5. Event and Action
Trigger that causes a transition to occur and changes the state is called event or action.
6. History State
A flow may require that the object go into a wait state and on the occurrence of a certain event, go back to the state it was in, in this situation this notation is used.
7. Signal
When even causes the trigger to be sent to a state that causes the transition, then that message sent by the event is called a signal.
8. Self Transition
A state that has a transition that returns to itself is called self-transition.
12.6.2 State Diagrams
A **state diagram** is used to represent the condition of the system or part of the system at finite instances of time. It's a behavioral diagram and it represents the behavior using finite state transitions. State diagrams are also referred to as State machines and State-chart Diagrams. We can say that each and every class has a state but we don't model every class using State diagrams. We prefer to model the states with three or more states.
Uses of statechart diagram –

- We use it to state the events responsible for change in state (we do not show what processes cause those events).
- We use it to model the dynamic behavior of the system .
- To understand the reaction of objects/classes to internal or external stimuli.

Basic components of a statechart diagram –
Initial state – We use a black filled circle represent the initial state of a System or a class.

Figure – initial state notation
Transition – We use a solid arrow to represent the transition or change of control from one state to another. The arrow is labelled with the event which causes the change in state.

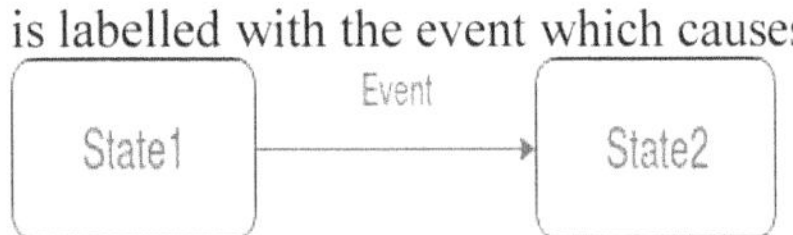

Figure – transition
State – We use a rounded rectangle to represent a state. A state represents the conditions or circumstances of an object of a class at an instant of time.

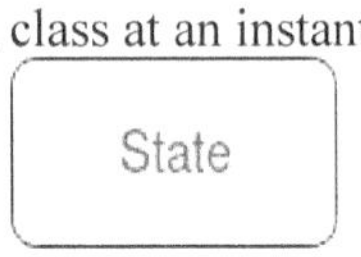

Figure – state notation

Fork – We use a rounded solid rectangular bar to represent a Fork notation with incoming arrow from the parent state and outgoing arrows towards the newly created states. We use the fork notation to represent a state splitting into two or more concurrent states.

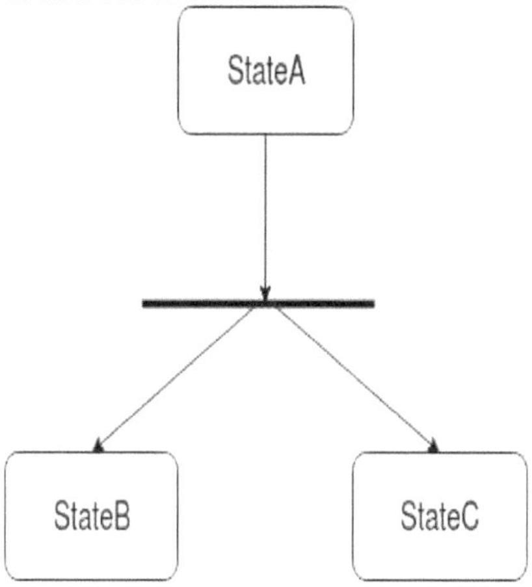

Figure – a diagram using the fork notation

Join – We use a rounded solid rectangular bar to represent a Join notation with incoming arrows from the joining states and outgoing arrow towards the common goal state. We use the join notation when two or more states concurrently converge into one on the occurrence of an event or events.

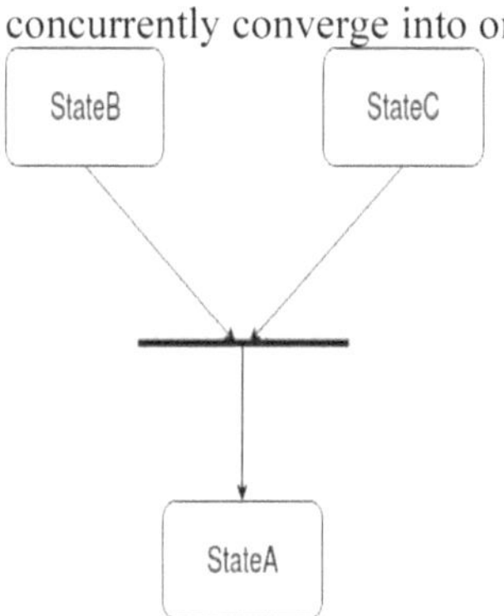

Figure – a diagram using join notation

Self transition – We use a solid arrow pointing back to the state itself to represent a self transition. There might be scenarios when the state of the object does not change upon the occurrence of an event. We use self transitions to represent such cases.

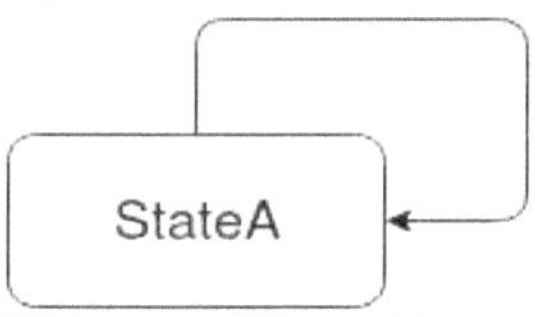

Figure – self transition notation

Composite state – We use a rounded rectangle to represent a composite state also.We represent a state with internal activities using a composite state.

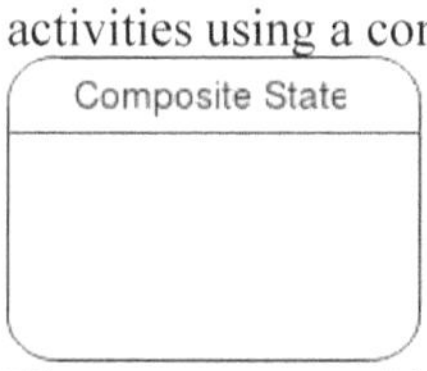

Figure – a state with internal activities

Final state – We use a filled circle within a circle notation to represent the final state in a state machine diagram.

Figure – final state notation

Steps to draw a state diagram –
Identify the initial state and the final terminating states.
Identify the possible states in which the object can exist (boundary values corresponding to different attributes guide us in identifying different states).
Label the events which trigger these transitions.
Example – state diagram for an online order –

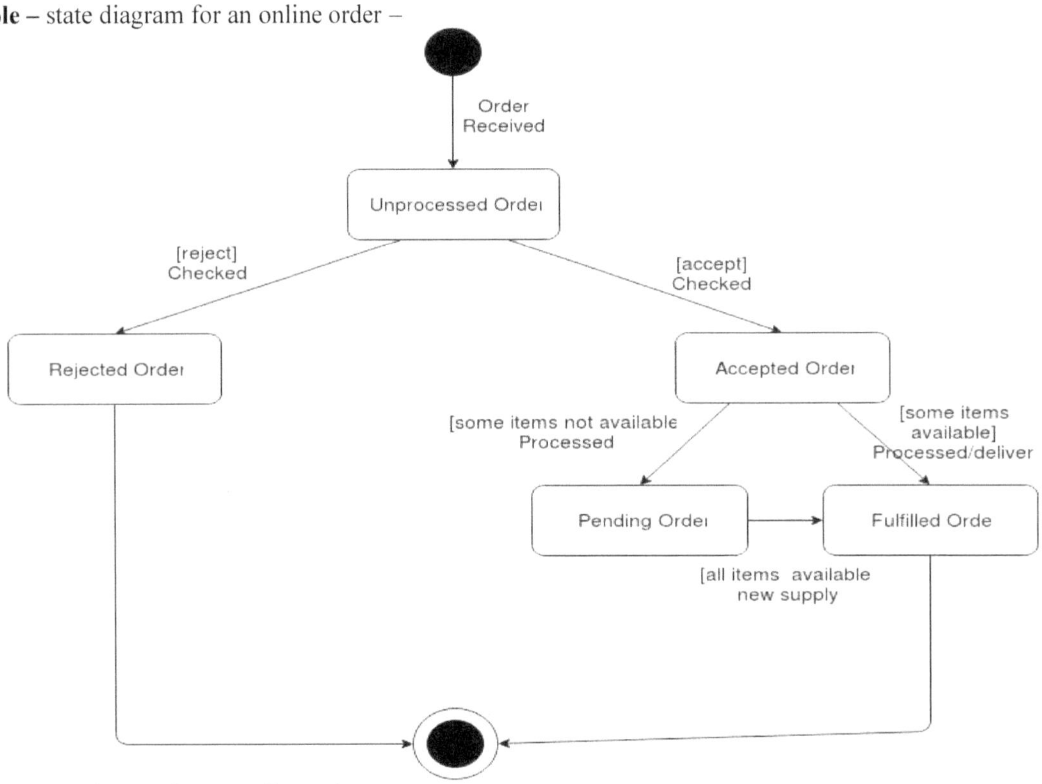

Figure – state diagram for an online order
The UMl diagrams we draw depend on the system we aim to represent. Here is just an example of how an online ordering system might look like :
On the event of an order being received, we transit from our initial state to Unprocessed order state.
The unprocessed order is then checked.
If the order is rejected, we transit to the Rejected Order state.
If the order is accepted and we have the items available we transit to the fulfilled order state.
However if the items are not available we transit to the Pending Order state.
After the order is fulfilled, we transit to the final state. In this example, we merge the two states i.e. Fulfilled order and Rejected order into one final state.

12.6.3 Interaction Diagrams (Collaboration and Sequence Diagrams)

A Sequence diagram is an interaction diagram that details about the operation that is carried out. The sequence diagram captures the interaction between the objects in the context of collaboration. Sequence diagrams are time focused and they show the order of the interaction visually by using the vertical axis of the diagram to represent time.
Example:

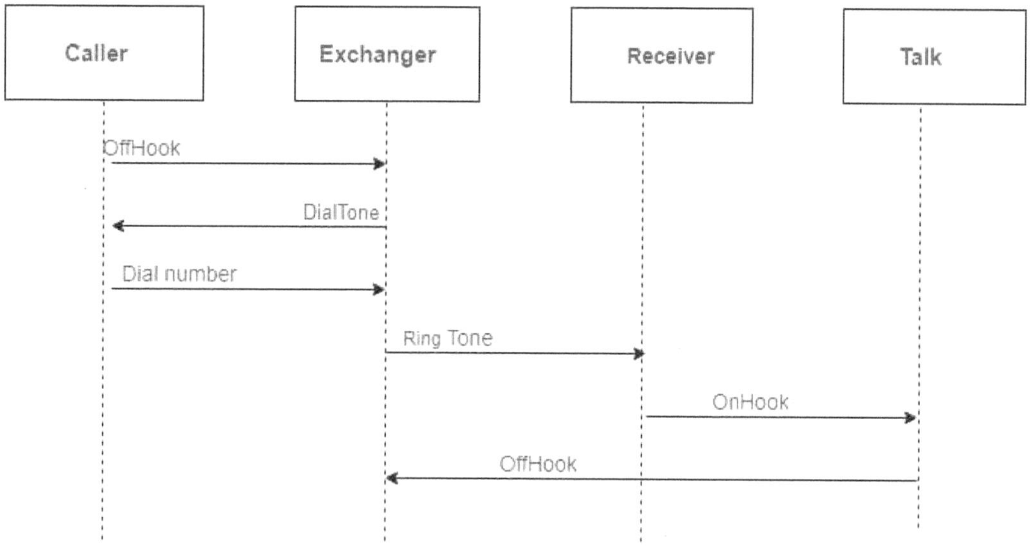

Collaboration Diagram represents the interaction of the objects to perform the behavior of a particular use case or a part of use case. The designers use the Sequence diagram and Collaboration Diagrams to define and clarify the roles of the objects that perform a particular flow of events of a use case.

Example:

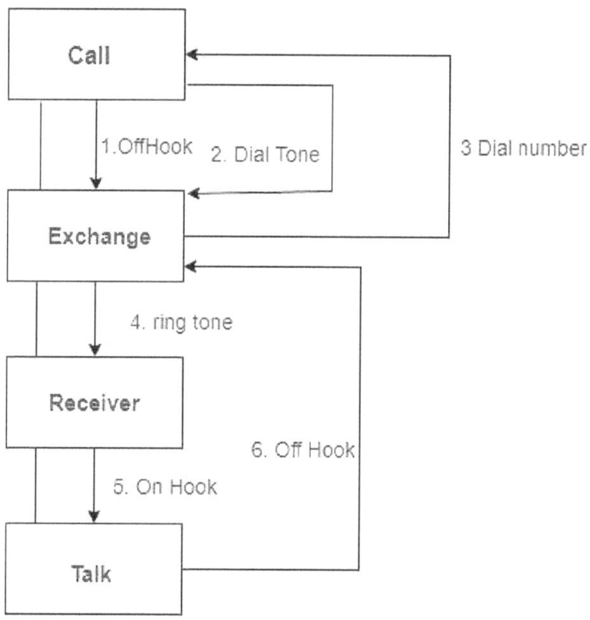

Similarities Between Sequence and Collaboration Diagram

In Unified Modelling Language both the sequence diagram and collaboration diagram are used as interaction diagrams.

Both the diagrams details about the behavioral aspects of the system.

Differences Between Sequence and Collaboration diagram:

Sequence Diagrams	Collaboration Diagrams

The sequence diagram represents the UML, which is used to visualize the sequence of calls in a system that is used to perform a specific functionality.	The collaboration diagram also comes under the UML representation which is used to visualize the organization of the objects and their interaction.
The sequence diagram are used to represent the sequence of messages that are flowing from one object to another.	The collaboration diagram are used to represent the structural organization of the system and the messages that are sent and received.
The sequence diagram is used when time sequence is main focus.	The collaboration diagram is used when object organization is main focus.
The sequence diagrams are better suited of analysis activities.	The collaboration diagrams are better suited for depicting simpler interactions of the smaller number of objects.

12.7 Use Case Diagrams

A use case diagram is used to represent the dynamic behavior of a system. It encapsulates the system's functionality by incorporating use cases, actors, and their relationships. It models the tasks, services, and functions required by a system/subsystem of an application. It depicts the high-level functionality of a system and also tells how the user handles a system.

Purpose of Use Case Diagrams

The main purpose of a use case diagram is to portray the dynamic aspect of a system. It accumulates the system's requirement, which includes both internal as well as external influences. It invokes persons, use cases, and several things that invoke the actors and elements accountable for the implementation of use case diagrams. It represents how an entity from the external environment can interact with a part of the system.

Following are the purposes of a use case diagram given below:

It gathers the system's needs.

It depicts the external view of the system.

It recognizes the internal as well as external factors that influence the system.

It represents the interaction between the actors.

12.7.1 Use Cases and Actors

In software engineering, "use cases" and "actors" are fundamental concepts used in the analysis and design of a software system, particularly in the context of requirements gathering and analysis. They help in understanding the system's functionality and its interactions with external entities. Here's an explanation of these concepts:

Use Cases:

Definition: Use cases are a way to describe the interactions or operations that a system performs to achieve a specific goal or requirement. Each use case represents a specific functionality or feature of the software from an end-user's perspective.

Purpose: They help to capture and define the system's behavior by detailing how it responds to various inputs or requests from users or external systems.

Format: A use case is typically documented using a use case diagram, which includes the use case name, a brief description, and an oval shape to represent the system boundary. It may also contain a set of actions or steps that the system takes to complete the use case.

Actors:

Definition: Actors are external entities that interact with the software system. They are not part of the system but play a role in its functioning by initiating use cases. Actors can be individuals, other software systems, or hardware devices.

Purpose: Actors help in identifying who or what interacts with the system and what kind of interactions they have. This understanding is essential for defining use cases.

Types of Actors: There are two main types of actors:

Primary Actors: These are the main users or entities that initiate a use case and achieve a specific goal through the system.

Secondary Actors: These are entities that assist or interact with the system but are not the primary users or initiators of the use case.
For example, in an online shopping application:
Use Case: "Place an Order"
Description: This use case represents the process of a user placing an order for products.
Steps:
User logs in.
User adds items to the shopping cart.
User proceeds to checkout.
User provides shipping and payment information.
User confirms the order.
Actors:
Primary Actor: Customer (initiates the "Place an Order" use case).
Secondary Actor: Payment Gateway (assists in processing payments).

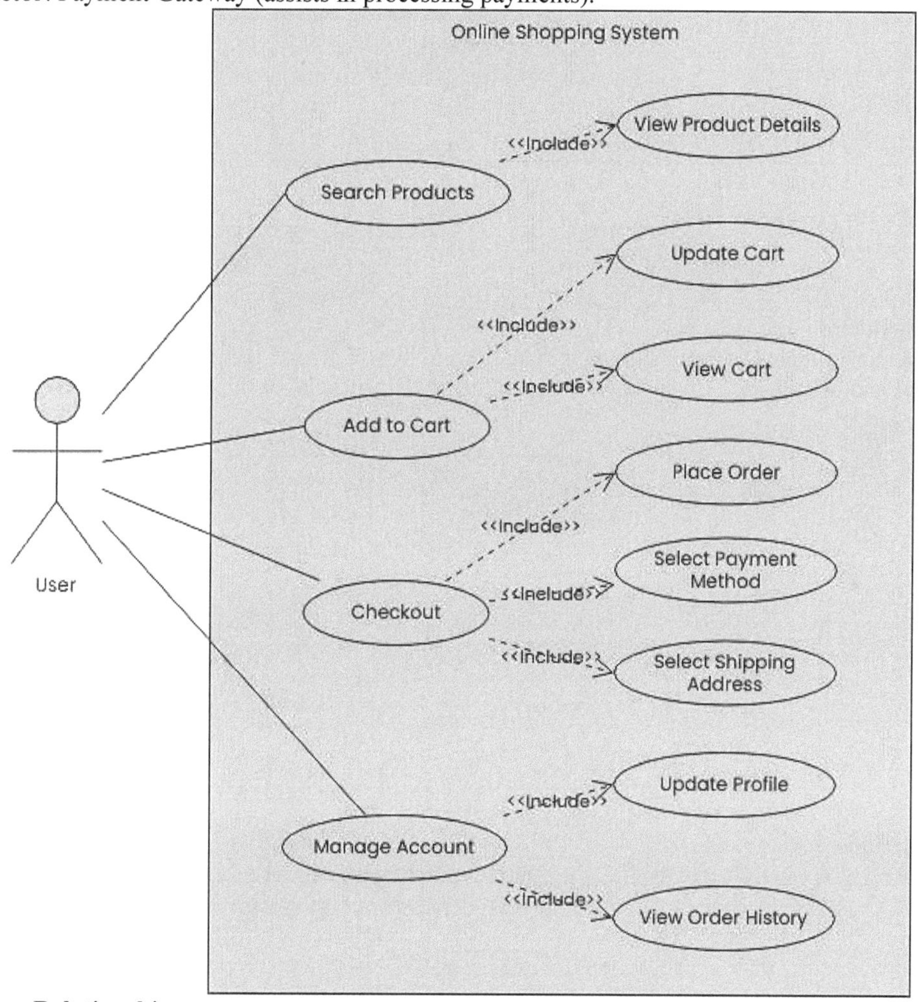

12.7.2 Use Case Relationships

In UML, relationships are connections between model elements. Use cases are also connected to each other in different kinds of relationships. The relationship between two use cases basically models the dependencies between two use cases. By reusing existing use cases using different types of relationships, the overall effort required to develop the system is reduced.

There are 4 types of Use Case Relationships are: -
1. Association Relationships
2. Generalization Relationships
3. Include Relationships
4 Extending Relationships

Association Relationships

An association is a relationship between two classifiers, such as an actor and use cases, that describes the cause of the relationship and the rules that govern it. An association is a relationship between an actor and a business use case. It indicates that an actor can use the functionality of the business system.

Generalization Relationships

A generalization relation is a relationship in which one model element (child) is based on another model element (parent). Generalization relations are used in class diagrams, component diagrams, deployment diagrams, and use case diagrams to indicate that the child element accepts all the attributes, operations, and relationships defined in the parent element.

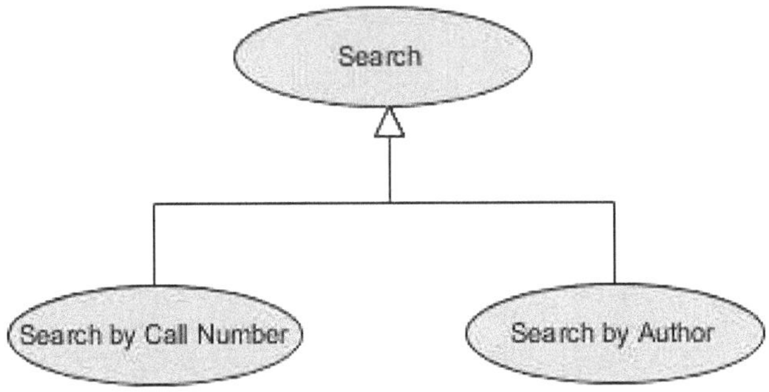

Include Relationships

In UML modeling, a Include relationship is a relationship in which one use case (base use case) contains the functionality of another use case (inclusion use case). A containment relationship supports the reuse of functionality in the use case model.

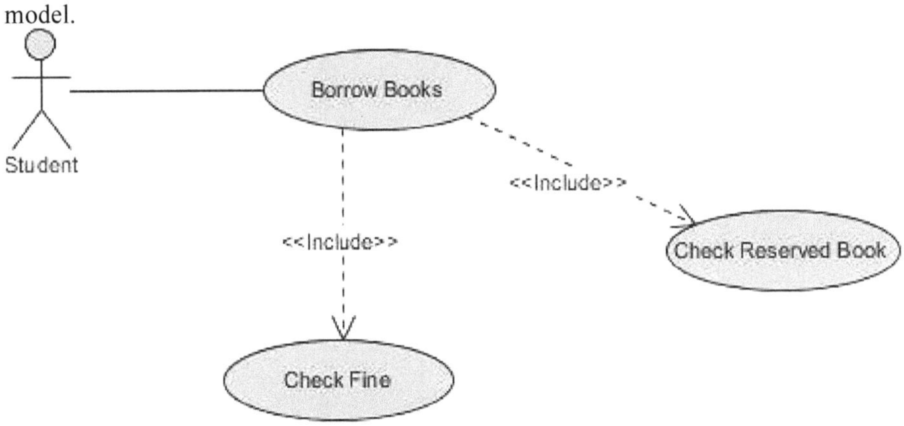

Extending relationships

In UML modeling, you can use an extend relationship to specify that one use case (extension) extends the behavior of another use case (base). This type of relationship reveals details about the system or application that are usually hidden in the use case.

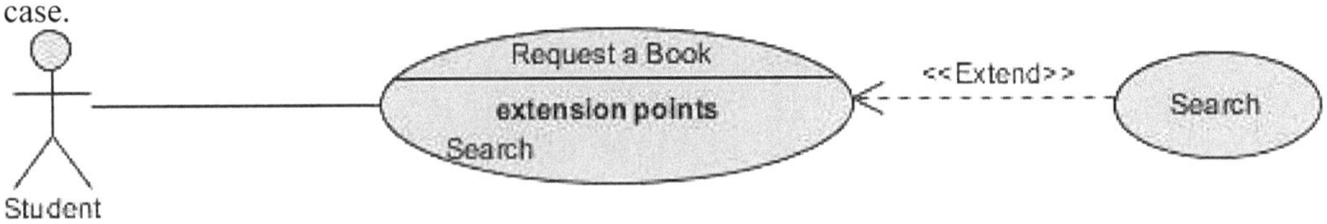

Use Case Diagram: Online Examination System

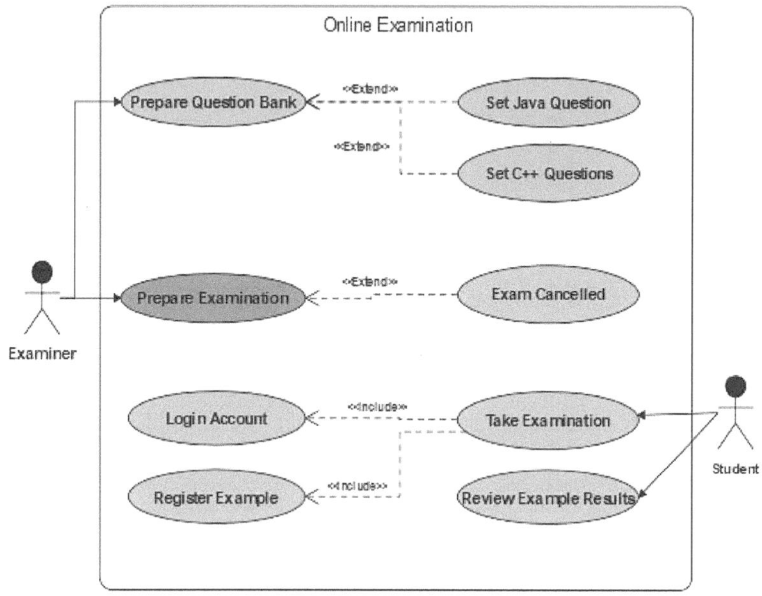

12.8 Object-Oriented Concepts and Principles

Object-oriented concepts are fundamental principles in software engineering that are used to design and develop software systems based on the object-oriented programming (OOP) paradigm. OOP focuses on modeling real-world entities and their interactions using objects and classes. Here are some key object-oriented concepts:

Objects:

An object is a self-contained unit that represents a real-world entity or a concept within the software system. It combines data (attributes) and behaviors (methods) related to that entity.

For example, in a car rental system, an "Car" object could represent a specific vehicle and include attributes like make, model, and license plate, along with methods to start the engine or calculate fuel efficiency.

Classes:

A class is a blueprint or template for creating objects. It defines the structure and behavior that its objects will have.

Using the car rental system example, the "Car" class would specify what attributes and methods each car object should have.

Encapsulation:

Encapsulation is the concept of bundling data (attributes) and the methods that operate on that data into a single unit (i.e., a class).

It enforces access control to protect the integrity of the data by specifying which parts of the program can access and modify the data.

Inheritance:

Inheritance allows a new class (subclass or derived class) to inherit attributes and methods from an existing class (superclass or base class). It promotes code reuse and the creation of specialized classes.

For instance, you can have a "Vehicle" superclass with attributes and methods common to all vehicles and then derive "Car" and "Motorcycle" subclasses with their specific features.

Polymorphism:

Polymorphism enables objects of different classes to be treated as objects of a common superclass. It allows methods to behave differently based on the object's specific class.

For example, a "calculateCost" method may perform different calculations when applied to a "Car" object compared to a "Motorcycle" object, but you can call the same method on both.

Abstraction:

Abstraction is the process of simplifying complex reality by modeling classes based on their essential attributes and behaviors while hiding unnecessary details.

It helps in managing complexity by focusing on the high-level structure and design of the software.

Association and Aggregation:

These concepts deal with relationships between classes. Association represents a simple link between classes, while aggregation represents a more complex relationship where one class is part of another class.
In the context of a university management system, "Student" class may have an association with "Course" class, and "Department" class may have an aggregation with "Professor" class.
Composition:
Composition is a stronger form of aggregation, where one class is composed of other classes, and the composed classes have no independent existence.
In a graphical user interface system, a "Window" class may be composed of "Button," "Menu," and "Text" classes.
Messages and Methods:
Objects communicate with each other by sending messages. These messages invoke methods (functions) defined in the receiving object's class.
For instance, a "sendEmail" message might invoke the "sendEmail" method in the "EmailService" object.

12.8.1 Principles of Object-Oriented Design

In the object-oriented design method, the system is viewed as a collection of objects (i.e., entities). The state is distributed among the objects, and each object handles its state data. For example, in a Library Automation Software, each library representative may be a separate object with its data and functions to operate on these data. The tasks defined for one purpose cannot refer or change data of other objects. Objects have their internal data which represent their state. Similar objects create a class. In other words, each object is a member of some class. Classes may inherit features from the superclass.
The different terms related to object design are:

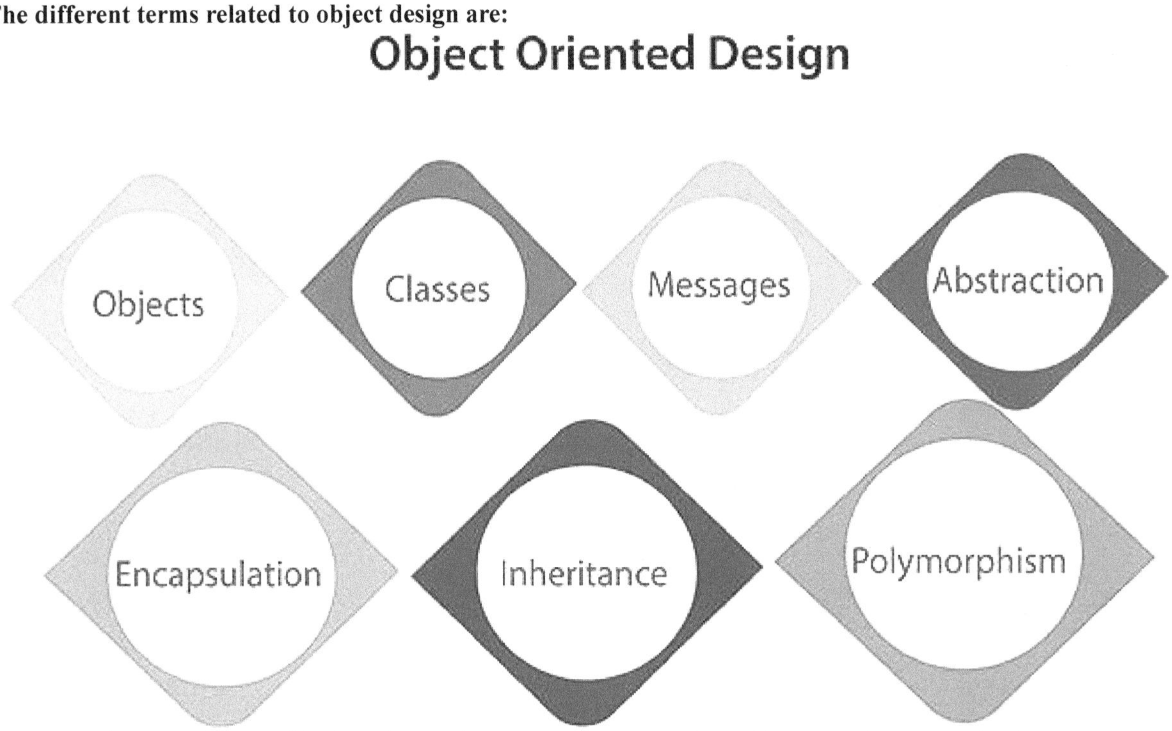

Objects: All entities involved in the solution design are known as objects. For example, person, banks, company, and users are considered as objects. Every entity has some attributes associated with it and has some methods to perform on the attributes.
Classes: A class is a generalized description of an object. An object is an instance of a class. A class defines all the attributes, which an object can have and methods, which represents the functionality of the object.
Messages: Objects communicate by message passing. Messages consist of the integrity of the target object, the name of the requested operation, and any other action needed to perform the function. Messages are often implemented as procedure or function calls.
Abstraction In object-oriented design, complexity is handled using abstraction. Abstraction is the removal of the irrelevant and the amplification of the essentials.

Encapsulation: Encapsulation is also called an information hiding concept. The data and operations are linked to a single unit. Encapsulation not only bundles essential information of an object together but also restricts access to the data and methods from the outside world.
Inheritance: OOD allows similar classes to stack up in a hierarchical manner where the lower or sub-classes can import, implement, and re-use allowed variables and functions from their immediate superclasses.This property of OOD is called an inheritance. This makes it easier to define a specific class and to create generalized classes from specific ones.
Polymorphism: OOD languages provide a mechanism where methods performing similar tasks but vary in arguments, can be assigned the same name. This is known as polymorphism, which allows a single interface is performing functions for different types. Depending upon how the service is invoked, the respective portion of the code gets executed.

12.9 Identifying Elements of an Object Model

In software engineering, an object model is a conceptual representation of a software system's structure and behavior. It is typically used in object-oriented programming and design to describe how the system's components, often represented as objects, interact with each other. Identifying elements of an object model involves understanding and defining the key components and relationships within the system. Here are the essential elements of an object model:
Classes: Classes are the blueprints for objects. They define the attributes (data) and methods (functions or behavior) that objects of that class will have. In an object model, you need to identify the classes that represent the main entities in your system.
Objects: Objects are instances of classes. They represent specific instances of entities in the system and have their own unique state (attribute values) and behavior (method implementations). Identify the objects that will exist in your system and which classes they belong to.
Attributes: Attributes are the data or properties that describe the state of an object. These can be represented as fields or properties within a class. Identify the attributes that each class should have and their data types.
Methods: Methods are the functions or behaviors associated with classes. They define what an object can do. Identify the methods that each class should have and their parameters and return types.
Relationships: In an object model, it's crucial to identify how classes and objects are related to each other. This includes associations, dependencies, and hierarchies. Common types of relationships include aggregation, composition, inheritance, and association.
Inheritance: Inheritance represents the "is-a" relationship between classes. It allows one class (the subclass or derived class) to inherit the attributes and behaviors of another class (the superclass or base class). Identify the inheritance hierarchy in your object model.
Aggregation and Composition: These represent the "has-a" relationship between classes. Aggregation implies a weaker relationship, where one class contains or is associated with another, but the contained class can exist independently. Composition implies a stronger relationship, where one class is composed of another, and the contained class cannot exist independently.
Interfaces: Interfaces define a contract for classes to adhere to. They specify a set of methods that implementing classes must provide. Identify the interfaces that classes need to implement.
Polymorphism: Polymorphism allows different classes to be treated as instances of a common superclass. It enables code to work with objects of different classes through a common interface. Identify how polymorphism is utilized in your object model.
Encapsulation: Encapsulation is the principle of bundling data (attributes) and methods that operate on that data within a class, and restricting access to the data to protect it from unauthorized manipulation. Identify how encapsulation is enforced in your object model.
Packages or Modules: In larger software systems, classes and objects are often organized into packages or modules. Identify the grouping of classes into these higher-level structures.

12.10 Object-Oriented Projects Metrics and Estimation

Metrics and estimation in object-oriented software projects play a crucial role in project management and quality assurance. Object-oriented programming (OOP) is a common paradigm in software development, and measuring and estimating the progress and quality of such projects is important for delivering successful software. Here's an overview of metrics and estimation in object-oriented projects:
Metrics in Object-Oriented Projects:
Lines of Code (LOC): This metric counts the number of lines of code in the software. However, it's a basic metric and doesn't provide a comprehensive measure of software complexity.

Cyclomatic Complexity: Cyclomatic complexity measures the complexity of a program by analyzing its control flow. It helps identify how many test cases are needed for adequate code coverage.
Number of Classes and Methods: Tracking the number of classes and methods in your project can provide insight into its complexity and maintainability.
Inheritance Metrics: You can measure the depth of the inheritance hierarchy and the number of classes inheriting from a specific class to understand the complexity and relationships in your object-oriented design.
Coupling and Cohesion: These metrics focus on how classes are interconnected. Low coupling and high cohesion are desirable for maintainable software.
Code Coverage: It measures how much of your code is executed by automated test cases. High code coverage indicates better testing.
Defect Density: This metric quantifies the number of defects per unit of code, helping you identify problematic areas in the code.
Object-Oriented Design Metrics: Metrics like the Lack of Cohesion of Methods (LCOM), Depth of Inheritance Tree (DIT), and Response for a Class (RFC) provide insights into the quality of your object-oriented design.
Estimation Techniques in Object-Oriented Projects:
Function Point Analysis (FPA): FPA is a technique for estimating the size and complexity of a software project. It's useful for estimating the effort required for development and maintenance.
Use Case Points (UCP): UCP is a method for estimating software size and complexity based on the number of use cases in the system.
Story Points: Agile development often uses story points for estimating the effort required to implement user stories. It's a relative estimation technique.
Wideband Delphi: This technique involves experts making estimations about the project's complexity, effort, and duration. It's useful for risk assessment and mitigations.
Planning Poker: Agile teams often use planning poker, a collaborative estimation technique where team members discuss and vote on the complexity of user stories or tasks.
Parametric Estimation: This approach uses historical data and statistical models to estimate effort, cost, and duration based on project parameters and past experiences.
Expert Judgment: Relying on the expertise of experienced team members can be a valuable estimation technique. Experts can provide insight into the complexity and risks of the project.
Monte Carlo Simulation: This method uses probabilistic models to estimate project outcomes, taking into account uncertainty and risk factors.
Earned Value Management (EVM): EVM is a project management technique that helps in tracking project performance and predicting future performance.
Estimation in object-oriented projects is challenging due to the inherent complexity and uncertainty. Using a combination of these metrics and estimation techniques can help in making informed decisions, managing risks, and ensuring that your project is delivered on time and within budget while maintaining high software quality. It's important to regularly update your estimates as the project progresses to adapt to changing requirements and conditions.

12.10.1 Metrics in Object-Oriented Development

Metrics in object-oriented development in software engineering are quantitative measures used to assess various aspects of object-oriented software projects and the resulting software systems. These metrics provide valuable insights into the quality, complexity, maintainability, and performance of the software, helping development teams make informed decisions and identify areas for improvement. Here are some important metrics in object-oriented development:
Lines of Code (LOC):
Definition: The total number of lines of code in the software.
Purpose: Provides a basic measure of the software's size.
Use: Helps in estimating development effort, but it doesn't capture complexity or quality.
Cyclomatic Complexity:
Definition: Measures the complexity of a program by analyzing its control flow.
Purpose: Indicates how many test cases are needed for code coverage.
Use: High cyclomatic complexity may indicate more complex and error-prone code.
Number of Classes and Methods:
Definition: The count of classes and methods in the software.
Purpose: Offers insight into software complexity and maintainability.
Use: High numbers may indicate potential issues with comprehensibility and maintenance.

Depth of Inheritance Tree (DIT):
Definition: Measures the depth of the inheritance hierarchy.
Purpose: Identifies the levels of subclassing in the code.
Use: High DIT may indicate complex inheritance structures that can be hard to maintain.
Number of Children (NOC):
Definition: The number of immediate subclasses derived from a single class.
Purpose: Measures the degree of class specialization.
Use: High NOC may indicate overuse of inheritance and decreased maintainability.
Coupling and Cohesion:
Definition: These metrics measure how classes are interconnected and how closely related elements within a class are, respectively.
Purpose: Evaluates software design quality.
Use: Low coupling and high cohesion are desirable for maintainable and understandable code.
Code Coverage:
Definition: Measures how much of the code is executed by automated test cases.
Purpose: Indicates the quality and thoroughness of testing.
Use: High code coverage suggests better testing and lower risk of undiscovered defects.
Response for a Class (RFC):
Definition: Counts the number of methods that can be executed in response to a message to an object of a class.
Purpose: Measures the complexity of a class's interface.
Use: High RFC may suggest a class with too many responsibilities, which can affect maintainability.
Lack of Cohesion of Methods (LCOM):
Definition: Measures the lack of cohesion among a class's methods.
Purpose: Identifies how well methods in a class work together to achieve a common goal.
Use: High LCOM may indicate a class with unrelated or loosely related methods.

12.10.2 Estimation Techniques for Object-Oriented Projects

Estimating the time, effort, and resources required for object-oriented software projects is a crucial aspect of software engineering. Several estimation techniques can be applied to gauge the scope and complexity of such projects. Here are some common estimation techniques used in object-oriented software engineering:
Function Point Analysis (FPA):
Description: FPA is a technique used to estimate the size and complexity of a software project based on the functionality it provides to users.
How it works: Analysts identify and categorize the functions or transactions provided by the software. Points are assigned to each function based on its complexity and influence factors. These points are then converted into an effort estimate.
Use case: FPA is particularly useful in estimating the effort required for both development and maintenance of object-oriented software.
Use Case Points (UCP):
Description: UCP is a technique that estimates software size and complexity based on the number of use cases and actors in a system.
How it works: You count the number of use cases and actors and assign complexity points to each based on various factors. The total points are then converted into an effort estimate.
Use case: UCP is commonly used in object-oriented projects, especially when use cases are well-defined.
Object Points:
Description: Object points extend the concept of function points to object-oriented software. They focus on estimating the effort required for developing and maintaining objects and classes.
How it works: Objects are counted, and complexity factors are applied to determine object points, which are then converted into an effort estimate.
Use case: Object points are useful in projects that heavily rely on object-oriented principles.
COCOMO (Constructive Cost Model):
Description: COCOMO is a model that estimates software development effort based on various project factors, including size, complexity, personnel, and experience.
How it works: It uses a set of equations and factors to estimate effort, taking into account the type of project, the development mode, and other parameters.

Use case: COCOMO can be applied to object-oriented projects by considering the size and complexity aspects specific to the project.

Wideband Delphi:

Description: Wideband Delphi is an expert judgment-based technique that involves experts making estimates about project complexity, effort, and duration.

How it works: A panel of experts is consulted, and they provide individual estimates. The estimates are discussed and iteratively refined to reach a consensus.

Use case: It's useful in projects where objective metrics are hard to define or where expert opinions are valuable.

Story Points:

Description: Commonly used in Agile development, story points estimate the effort required for user stories or features.

How it works: Teams assign relative points to user stories based on complexity, uncertainty, and other factors. Story points are used for planning and tracking progress.

Use case: Story points are beneficial in Agile-oriented, iterative development projects.

Expert Judgment:

Description: Relying on the expertise of experienced team members or domain experts to provide estimates based on their knowledge and experience.

How it works: Experts review project requirements, complexity, and risks and provide educated estimates.

Use case: This technique is valuable when you have a highly skilled team with domain knowledge.

Monte Carlo Simulation:

Description: This probabilistic technique estimates project outcomes by considering uncertainty and risk factors.

How it works: It uses statistical models to simulate various scenarios, helping to quantify project uncertainties and providing a range of possible outcomes.

Use case: Useful when there is a high degree of uncertainty or when assessing the impact of various risks.

Parametric Estimation:

Description: Parametric estimation uses historical data and statistical models to estimate effort, cost, and duration based on project parameters.

How it works: Historical data is used to develop equations that take into account project characteristics to provide estimates.

Use case: Suitable for projects with well-documented historical data.

Planning Poker:

Description: An Agile estimation technique that involves team members discussing and voting on the complexity of user stories or tasks.

How it works: Team members use a deck of cards with numbers representing story points to estimate the complexity of tasks collaboratively.

Use case: Effective for Agile teams to estimate user stories or tasks in a collaborative manner.

Exercise

Exercise 1 – MCQ

Q 1. What does a UML Class Diagram represent?

A. Object instances and their relationships
B. The flow of data in the system
C. A blueprint of classes and their relationships in the system
D. System behavior over time

Q 2. Which UML diagram is used to depict the dynamic behavior of a system during runtime?

A. Class Diagram
B. Use Case Diagram
C. Sequence Diagram
D. State Machine Diagram

Exercise 2 – True/ False

Q 1. UML stands for "Universal Modeling Language."

Q 2. A UML Class Diagram is used to represent the dynamic behavior of a system during runtime.

Exercise 3 – Fill in the blanks

Q 1. UML provides a standard set of notations for modeling software systems and __________.

Q 2. A UML Class Diagram is used to represent the _________ structure of a system, including classes, attributes, and relationships.

Exercise 4 – Match case

1. Class Diagram	A. Represents a specific interaction in a system.
2. Sequence Diagram	B. Depicts the dynamic behavior of objects.
3. Deployment Diagram	C. Models the static structure of a system.
4. State Machine Diagram	D. Illustrates the flow and sequencing of activities.
5. Activity Diagram	E. Describes the configuration of hardware or software components.
6. Collaboration Diagram	F. Emphasizes the distribution and location of components.

Exercise 5 – One word answer

Q 1. Which UML diagram is used to represent the static structure of a system?

Q 2. Which UML diagram illustrates the dynamic behavior of objects in a system?

Exercise 6 – Small answer

Q 1. How many types of UML diagrams are there?

Q 2. Which UML diagram is used to represent the static structure of a system's classes and their relationships?

Exercise 7 – Long answer

Q 1. What is Unified Modeling Language (UML), and why is it essential in software engineering?

Q 2. How many categories or types of UML diagrams are there, and can you provide examples of each?

Answers

Exercise 1 – MCQ

Ans: 1 C, 2 C

Exercise 2 – True/ False

Ans: 1 False, 2 False

Exercise 3 – Fill in the blanks

Ans: 1 Processes, 2 Static

Exercise 4 – Match case

Ans: 1 C, 2 A, 3 E, 4 B, 5 D,6 F

Exercise 5 – One word answer

Ans: 1 Class, 2 Sequence

Online Resources

Online Exam Paper:
Link: https://forms.gle/MTiM35xWJzqXaTZT7
QR Code:

Chapter 12 Videos Playlist:
Link: https://www.youtube.com/playlist?list=PLzlh_31VWEFre6AlDgvKDNNhMOL1bow0k
QR Code:

Previous Years Solved Questions

Q 1. Draw Data Flow Diagram of Traffic Control System for all 3 levels: a-level, I-level and 2-1evel. [R.T.U2018]
Q 2. Write short QFD (Quality, Function, Deployment) use-cases. [R.T.U. 2016]
Q 3. Draw a DFD for a hotel management system. Explain each part briefly. [RTU2013]
Q 4. "Can we have inheritance without polymorphism?" Comment on it. [R.T.U. 2018]
Q 5. List object-oriented design approaches. [R.T.U.2018]
Ans 5: Object Oriented Design: Object oriented design works around the entities and their characteristics instead of functions involved in the software system. This design strategies focuses on entities and its characteristics. The whole concept Of software solution revolves around the engaged entities.
Let us see the important concepts of object-oriented design:
(1) Objects:
All entities involved in the solution design are known as objects. For example, person, banks, company and customers are treated as objects. Every I entity has some attributes associated to it and has some methods to perform on the attributes.
(2) Classes:
A class is a generalized description of an object. An object is an instance of a class. Class defines all the attributes, which an Object can have and methods, which defines the functionality of the object. In the solution design, attributes are stored as variables and functionalities are defined by means of methods or procedures.
(1) Encapsulation:
In OOD, the attributes (data variables) and methods (operation on the data) are bundled together is called encapsulation. Encapsulation I not only bundle important information of an object together, but also restricts access of the data and methods from the outside world. This is called information hiding.
(2) Inheritance:
OOD allows similar classes to stack up in hierarchical manner where the lower or sub- classes can implement and re-use allowed variables and methods from their immediate super classes. This property of OOD is known as inheritance. This makes it easier to define specific class and to create generalized classes from specific ones.
(3) Polymorphism:
OOD languages provide a mechanism where methods performing similar tasks but vary in arguments, can be assigned same name. This is called polymorphism, which allows a single interface performing tasks for different types.
Depending upon how the function is invoked, respective portion Of the code gets executed.
Q 6. What is sequence diagram in context of UML? [R.T.U.2018]
Ans 6: In the context of UML (Unified Modeling Language), a sequence diagram is a type of interaction diagram that visualizes the interactions and the order of messages exchanged between various objects or components within a system. Sequence diagrams are particularly useful for modeling the dynamic behavior of a system, illustrating how objects collaborate to accomplish a specific task or use case.
Key characteristics and elements of a sequence diagram in UML include:
Lifelines: Lifelines represent objects or components participating in the interaction. Each lifeline is depicted as a vertical dashed line, typically labeled with the name of the object or component it represents.
Activation Bars: Activation bars, represented by horizontal lines extending from a lifeline, indicate the time period during which an object is actively processing or involved in the interaction.
Messages: Messages are represented by arrows and lines connecting lifelines. They indicate communication or interaction between objects. Messages can be synchronous (blocking), asynchronous (non-blocking), or self-referential (a message from an object to itself).
Return Messages: Return messages indicate the flow of control and data returning from the called object back to the calling object after a message has been processed.
Combined Fragments: Combined fragments are used to depict conditional behavior, loops, and alternatives in the sequence of interactions. They help illustrate how the sequence of interactions can change based on certain conditions or decisions.
Interaction Occurrence: Interaction occurrences are used to represent recursive interactions or recursive calls within a sequence diagram. They allow for nesting and repetition of interactions.
Sequence diagrams are commonly used to model a variety of scenarios and interactions, including:
Use cases: To illustrate how actors and system components interact to achieve a specific use case.
Collaboration: To show how objects collaborate and communicate to perform a specific function or task.
System behavior: To visualize how different system components interact in response to certain inputs or events.

Software design: To document the interactions between objects in the context of software design, especially in object-oriented programming.

Benefits of using sequence diagrams in UML include:

Clarity: Sequence diagrams provide a clear visual representation of the dynamic behavior of a system, making it easier to understand how different parts of a system work together.

Communication: They facilitate effective communication between stakeholders, including developers, designers, and business analysts, by visualizing system interactions.

Analysis: Sequence diagrams help in identifying potential issues, bottlenecks, or inefficiencies in a system's behavior.

Documentation: They serve as valuable documentation for software design, analysis, and testing.

Design Verification: Sequence diagrams can be used to verify that the system design aligns with the intended behavior and requirements.

A sequence diagram for an emotion based music player –

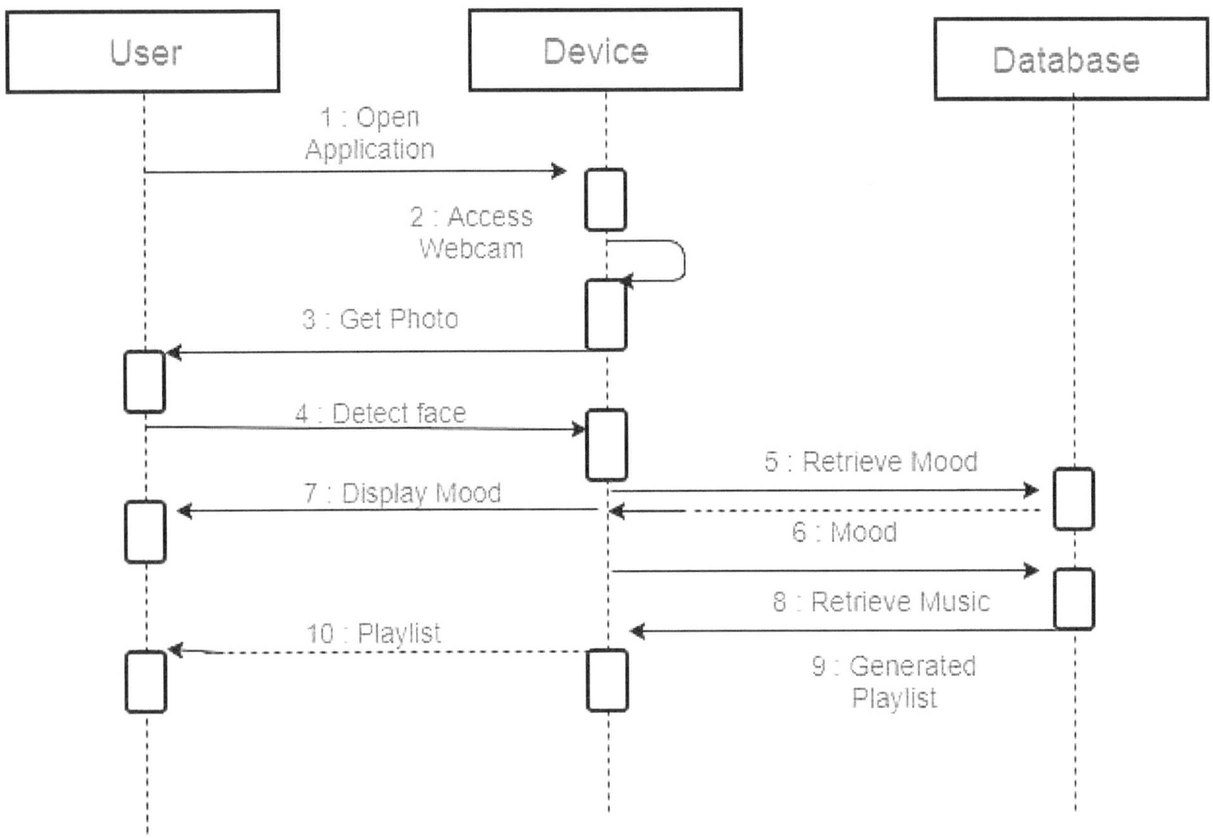

Q 7. Define class and object in context of UML. [R.T.U.2018]

Ans 7: Ans. Classes and Objects: Class is an UML representation which has basic three section.

(l) Class name

(2) Class attributes

(3) Class functions

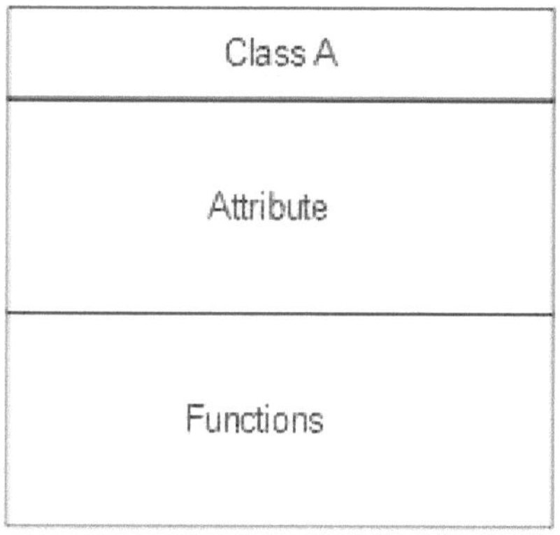

Object is an UML representation that is used to represent objects. It has two sections.
(l) Object name
(2) Class name

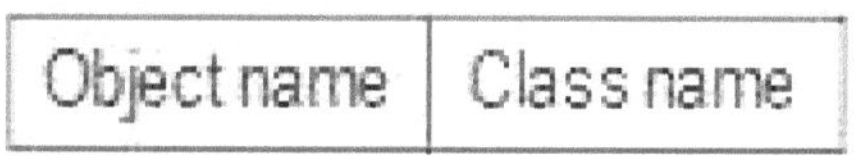

Q 8. Write short note on state diagram. [R.T.U.2018]
Ans 8: State diagram models the dynamic nature of a system. It describes the various states and the events that changes the state. so, it controls the flow of events from one state to the other.

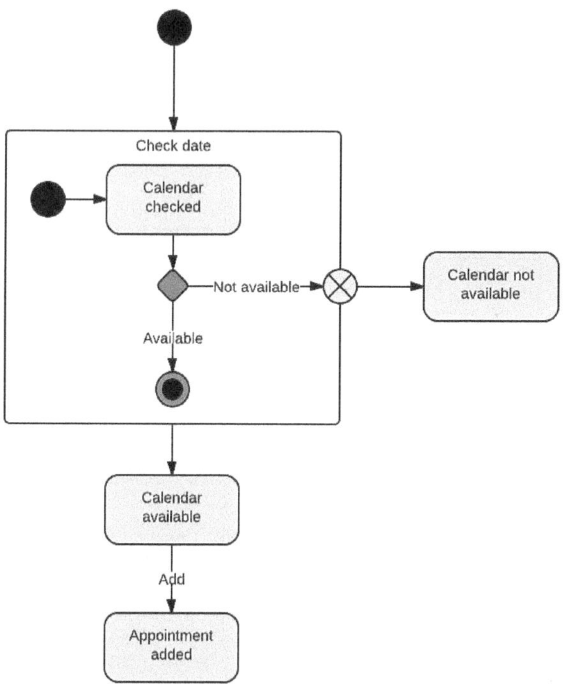

Components Of state Diagram
(I) States
(2) Events triggering to a state.
The above figure shows three states idle, place order and pay bill. Place order is the event that triggers from idle to place order state where if pay the bill event triggers then it leads to pay Bill state.

Q 9. Define unified Approach? Explain UML with all its diagram and advantages. [R.T.U.2016, 2013,2009,2008; Raj.Univ.2007]

Ans 9: A Unified Approach refers to a comprehensive and standardized methodology for software development and system design. In the context of software engineering, the Unified Approach often refers to the Unified Modeling Language (UML) and the Rational Unified Process (RUP). Let's explore UML and its diagrams, as well as its advantages:

Unified Modeling Language (UML): UML is a standardized visual language for modeling software systems and processes. It provides a common set of notations and diagrams for representing various aspects of software design, architecture, and behavior. UML is widely used in software engineering to improve communication, understanding, and documentation of software systems.

UML Diagrams: UML consists of several types of diagrams, each designed to represent specific aspects of a software system. The major UML diagram types include:

Class Diagram: Represents the static structure of a system, showing classes, attributes, methods, and relationships among them.

Use Case Diagram: Describes the interactions between external actors and the system, focusing on the system's functionality and user roles.

Sequence Diagram: Illustrates the dynamic behavior of a system by showing the interactions and messages exchanged between objects over time.

Activity Diagram: Models workflows and processes, depicting the activities, actions, and transitions within a system.

State Diagram: Represents the states and state transitions of an object, helping model its dynamic behavior.

Component Diagram: Focuses on the physical and logical organization of system components, including libraries, modules, and executables.

Deployment Diagram: Shows how software components and hardware nodes are distributed in a system, helping with deployment planning.

Package Diagram: Organizes and categorizes the elements of a system into packages, facilitating modularization and organization.

Object Diagram: Represents a snapshot of objects and their relationships at a specific moment in time.

Communication Diagram: Similar to a sequence diagram, it depicts object interactions and messages but emphasizes the relationships between objects.

Collaboration Diagram: Provides an overview of the interactions and relationships between objects in a system.

Advantages of UML:

Standardization: UML is an internationally recognized and accepted standard for software modeling, ensuring consistency and clear communication across project teams.

Visualization: UML diagrams provide visual representations of complex systems, making it easier to understand and communicate system design and behavior.

Abstraction: UML allows for different levels of abstraction, enabling both high-level system overviews and detailed design specifications.

Communication: UML fosters effective communication between stakeholders, including developers, designers, clients, and business analysts.

Documentation: UML diagrams serve as valuable documentation for software design, requirements analysis, and architectural decisions.

Analysis and Design: UML aids in system analysis, design, and verification, helping to identify potential issues and validate system behavior.

Reusability: UML models can be used to design and document components and patterns that can be reused in future projects.

Agility: UML supports iterative and incremental development processes, aligning well with agile and iterative development methodologies.

Tool Support: Various software tools and platforms support UML modeling, making it practical and efficient for software development.

Interoperability: UML diagrams can be easily integrated with other tools and technologies, promoting interoperability and collaboration.

Q 10. What is UML? Explain how it is useful in object-oriented modeling. [R.T.U. 2018, 2013, 2014]

Ans 10: UML (Unified Modeling Language) is a standardized and widely used visual language for modeling software systems and processes. It provides a common set of notations and diagrams that enable software developers, designers, and stakeholders to represent, visualize, document, and communicate various aspects of a software system. UML is particularly useful in the context of object-oriented modeling for the following reasons:

1. Standardized Representation: UML offers a standardized and universally accepted way to represent complex software systems. This common language helps ensure that everyone involved in the software development process can understand and communicate using the same notations and diagrams.
2. Visual Modeling: UML uses visual diagrams to represent different aspects of a software system. These diagrams are more intuitive and easier to understand than textual descriptions, making it simpler to convey and comprehend complex system structures and behaviors.
3. Abstraction Levels: UML supports multiple levels of abstraction, allowing modelers to create high-level system overviews or detailed design specifications. This flexibility is crucial in object-oriented modeling, where different stakeholders require varying levels of detail.
4. Structural Modeling: UML provides a range of structural diagrams such as class diagrams, object diagrams, and component diagrams. These diagrams are particularly useful for modeling the static aspects of object-oriented systems, including classes, objects, attributes, and relationships.
5. Behavioral Modeling: UML offers behavioral diagrams like sequence diagrams, activity diagrams, and state diagrams. These diagrams help model dynamic aspects of object-oriented systems, illustrating how objects interact, how processes flow, and how system states change.
6. Encapsulation: Object-oriented modeling principles, such as encapsulation and information hiding, are represented naturally in UML diagrams. For example, in a class diagram, you can define the visibility of attributes and methods to indicate public, protected, or private access.
7. Inheritance and Polymorphism: UML diagrams support modeling of inheritance and polymorphism relationships between classes. Inheritance hierarchies are visually represented in class diagrams, while polymorphic behavior can be shown in sequence and state diagrams.
8. Collaboration: Object-oriented systems often involve collaboration between objects. UML's collaboration and communication diagrams (e.g., sequence and communication diagrams) provide a clear way to represent object interactions and message exchanges.
9. Real-World Mapping: Object-oriented systems often model real-world entities. UML allows modelers to represent real-world concepts as objects, classes, and relationships, which facilitates the mapping of software systems to the problem domain.
10. Code Generation: UML tools and platforms often provide the ability to generate code directly from UML models. This seamless transition from design to implementation can significantly improve the efficiency of the software development process.
11. Documentation: UML diagrams serve as valuable documentation for software design, architecture, and requirements analysis. They can be used to communicate design decisions and system behavior to stakeholders.

Q 11. Explain unified modelling language diagrams with the help of appropriate example. [R.T.U.2017]

Ans 11: Unified Modeling Language (UML) diagrams are a set of visual representations used to model various aspects of software systems and their behaviors. UML diagrams serve as a common language for software developers, designers, and stakeholders to communicate, document, and understand system designs. There are several types of UML diagrams, each tailored to represent specific facets of a software system. Here's an overview of some common UML diagram types:

Class Diagram:

Represents the static structure of a system.
Shows classes, their attributes, operations (methods), and relationships between classes.
Useful for designing and documenting class hierarchies and data structures.

Use Case Diagram:

Focuses on the system's functionality and the interactions between external actors (users or other systems) and the system.
Helps in identifying use cases (functional requirements) and understanding system functionality from a user's perspective.

Sequence Diagram:

Illustrates the dynamic behavior of a system.
Shows the interactions and messages exchanged between objects or components over time.
Useful for understanding the order of operations and collaborations between system components.

Activity Diagram:

Models workflows, business processes, or system behaviors that involve multiple components or actors.
Depicts activities, actions, decisions, and control flows.
Useful for illustrating complex processes and business logic.

State Diagram:

Represents the states and state transitions of an object or system.
Useful for modeling the dynamic behavior of objects in response to events and changes in their state.

Component Diagram:

Focuses on the physical and logical organization of components within a system.
Shows components, interfaces, dependencies, and relationships.
Useful for system architecture and design.

Deployment Diagram:

Describes how software components are deployed on hardware nodes (servers, devices, etc.).
Shows the physical infrastructure and communication paths.
Useful for deployment planning and hardware configuration.

Package Diagram:

Organizes and categorizes elements into packages.
Helps manage and modularize the system structure, improving clarity and maintainability.

Object Diagram:

Represents a snapshot of objects and their relationships at a specific point in time.
Useful for debugging, testing, or illustrating specific system states.

Communication Diagram:

Similar to a sequence diagram but focuses on showing the relationships and interactions between objects.
Useful for understanding the flow of messages and collaborations between objects.

Collaboration Diagram:

Provides an overview of the interactions and relationships between objects in the system.
Emphasizes the organization of objects and their interactions.

Timing Diagram:

Focuses on illustrating the timing and delays in the interactions between objects.
Useful for real-time systems and timing-sensitive applications.

Q 12. Draw and explain class diagram, object diagram and process diagram. List all the diagram available in UML. [RTU2011, 2010]

Ans 12: The class diagram depicts a static view of an application. It represents the types of objects residing in the system and the relationships between them. A class consists of its objects, and also it may inherit from other classes. A class diagram is used to visualize, describe, document various different aspects of the system, and also construct executable software code.

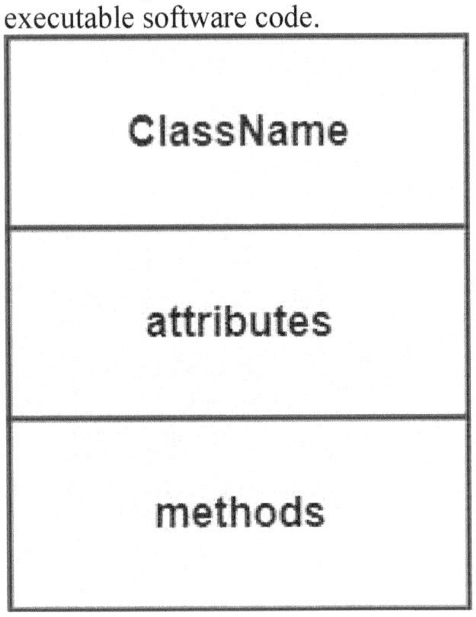

A class diagram describing the sales order system is given below.

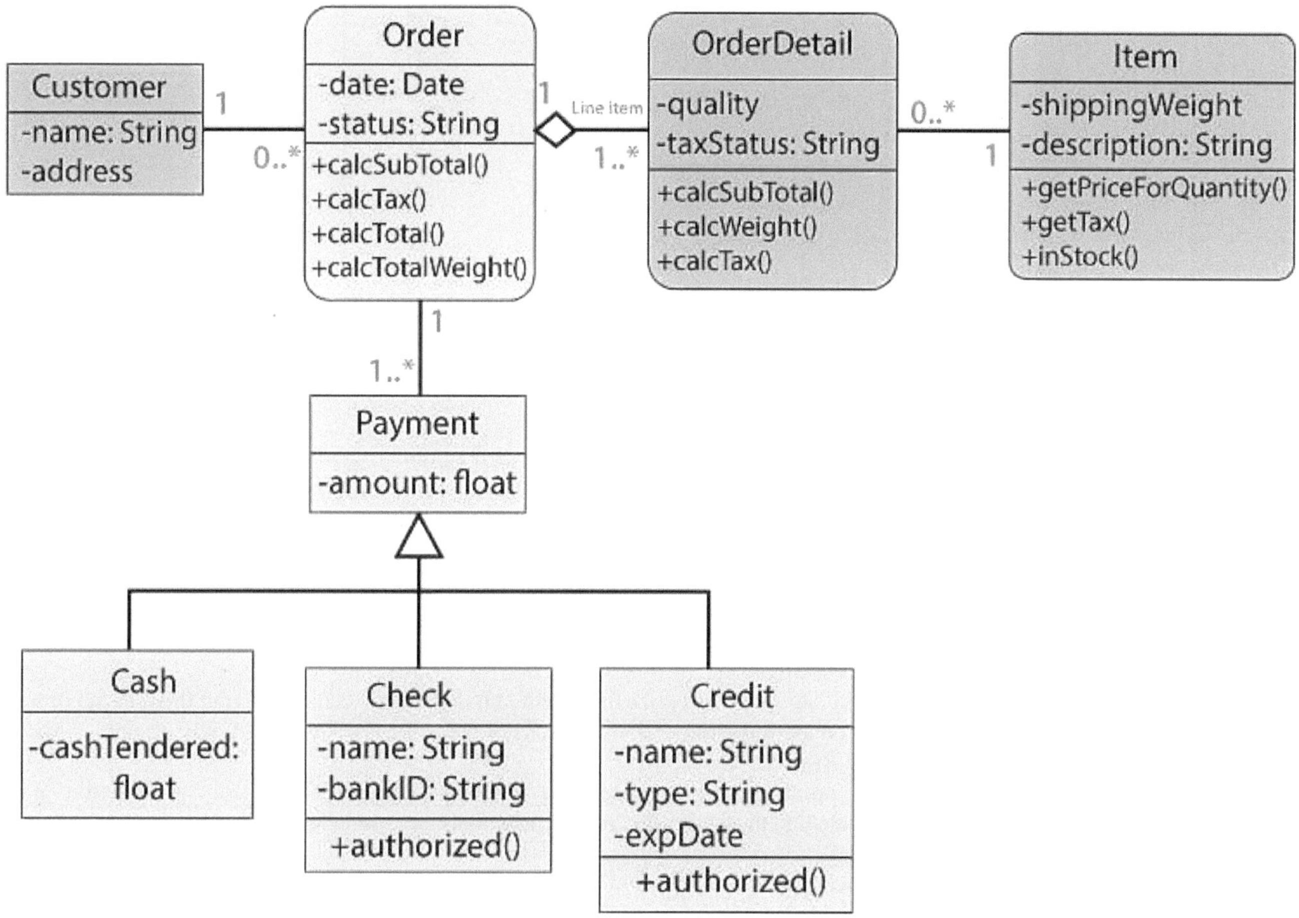

Object Diagram:-

Object diagrams are dependent on the class diagram as they are derived from the class diagram. It represents an instance of a class diagram. The objects help in portraying a static view of an object-oriented system at a specific instant.

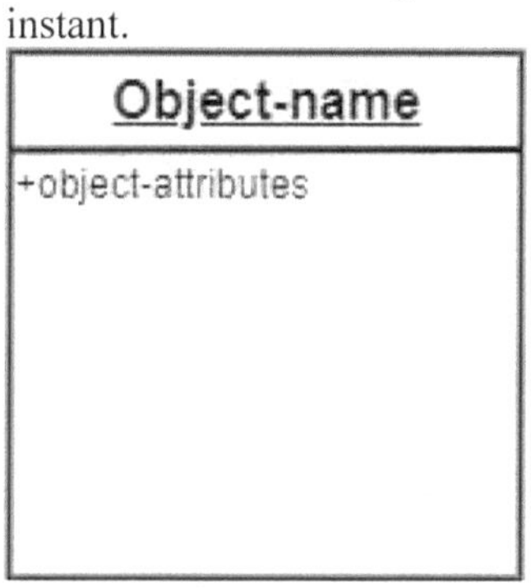

Example of Object Diagram

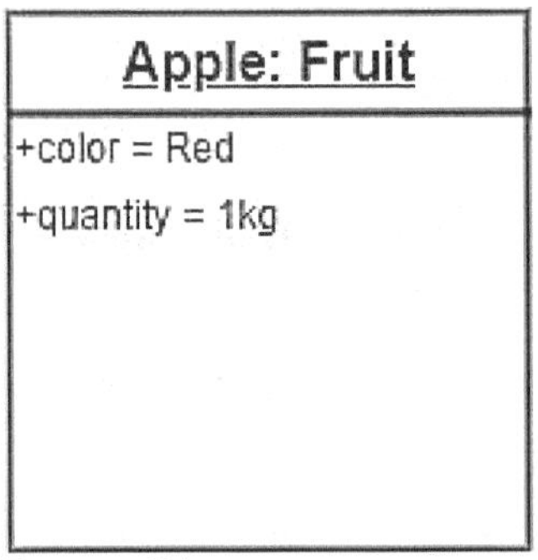

Process Diagram:

A process diagram, otherwise known as a flowchart" is a visual representation of a process or workflow. They usually consist of symbols and arrows that show the sequence of steps in a process. They guide you through a process step-by-step and help you to see the process as a whole.

Step 1: Define the Start and End Points

Start by identifying the start and endpoint of the process you want to diagram. This might be the initiation of an order or the completion of a shipment. Once you have identified these points, you can work backwards to determine the steps and activities that occur between them.

Step 2: Break Down the Process into Smaller Steps

Next, break down the process into smaller steps or tasks. This might involve speaking with process stakeholders or analyzing data to determine the necessary level of detail. It's important to be thorough in defining each step and to clearly label it within your diagram.

Step 3: Organize the Steps Sequentially

Once you have identified the individual steps, organize them sequentially. This means arranging them in the order in which they occur. This will help you identify potential bottlenecks or areas for improvement within the process.

Step 4: Add Decision Points and Branches

Often, processes involve decision points, where a choice must be made between different courses of action. When defining your diagram, be sure to include these decision points, as well as any branches that might result based on the chosen course of action.

Step 5: Connect the Steps with Arrows

Once you have defined all individual steps, decision points, and branches, connect them using arrows or lines. This will help to illustrate the flow of the process and the relationship between the individual elements. Be sure to label the arrows to indicate the direction of the workflow.

Step 6: Review and Refine the Diagram

Finally, carefully review and refine your diagram. Make sure that everything is labeled correctly, the order of the steps is accurate, and the diagram as a whole is easy to follow. This review process can help you identify areas where the process can be streamlined or improved, leading to a more efficient workflow.

The UML includes nine such diagrams:

- Class Diagrams
- Object Diagrams
- Use Case Diagrams
- Sequence Diagrams
- Collaboration Diagrams
- State Chan Diagrams
- Activity Diagrams
- Component Diagrams
- Deployment Diagrams

All these diagrams explained as follows:

1. Class Diagrams: Class diagrams show a set of classes, interfaces, and their relationships. Class diagrams are specifically to model the static design view of a system.

Consider an example of house building. During its building, we include basic building blocks such as wall, doors etc. These are inherently structural is nature as they are related with height, width etc. But they are somewhat behavioral also (different kinds of walls can support different loads). We can't consider these features independently. The process of house construction involves assembling these things.

So, with UML, we use class diagrams to visualize the static aspect of the building blocks and their relationships and to specify their details.

The various contents of a class diagram are

• Classes
• Interfaces
• Collaborations
• Relationships

The class can be better understood with the help 0 examples.

Example-a class diagram is shown for the withdrawal Of money from the account.

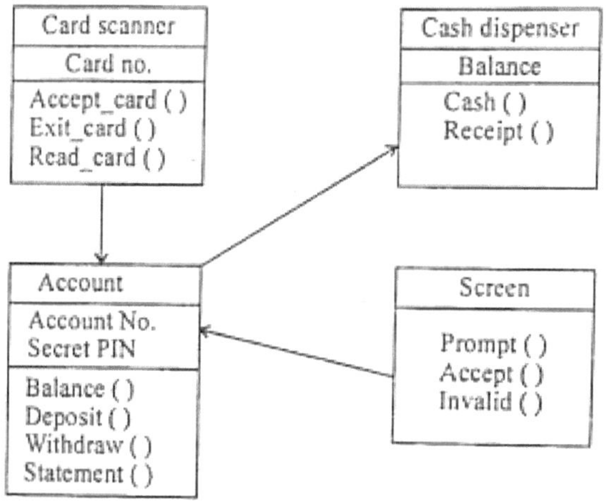

2. Object Diagrams

Object diagrams models the instances of things contained in a class diagram, shows set of objects and their relationships
at any time' and, modelling a snapshot of system at that moment in time and rendering a set of objects, their State and their relationships.

To understand how the object diagram works, we can visualize a game of soccer. Its overview looks as if it is a terribly simple spolt with a mob of people running wildly chasing a ball, there hardly seems any systematic sense in it.

Now, for a moment, freeze the motion. Classify the individual players. We are able to distinguish their particular positions like forwards, modified, left wing, full back, right back, defenders, goal keepers etc. Further insight reveals how these players collaborate following strategies for attacking and defending. Similar to this, we ought to have the snapshot of the system under concern to look at the objects present, their neighbors and their relationships to these neighbors.

Contents of Object Diagram

There are two contents Of an Object diagram. They are:

• Objects
• Links

An object diagram expresses the static part of an interaction, consisting of the objects that collaborate but without any of the messages passed among them,

Example—3 This example tells the object diagram for a company:

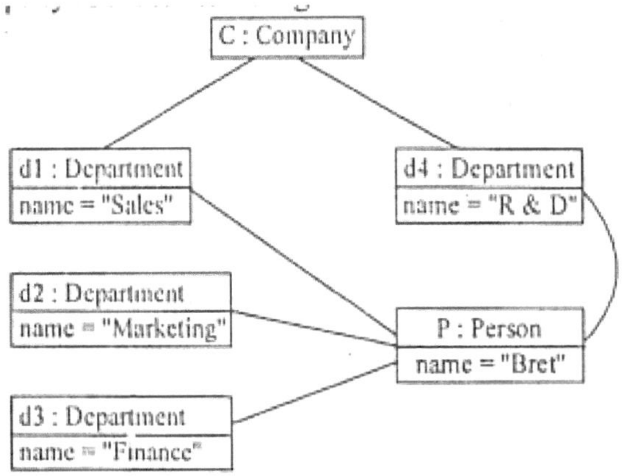

3. Case Diagrams : Various aspects related to use case diagrams are given below :

• Use case diagrams model the dynamic aspects of a system.

• A use ease diagram depicts :

I. Use cases : Use cases are the description of a set of sequences of actions, that a system performs yielding an observable result ofvalue to an actor.

2. Actors : Actors are the set of roles that users of use cases play when interacting with the use cases.

• Use case diagrams help in understanding how the elements of the system may be used in the context. This enables the user to comprehend how to use that element effectively.

• Use case diagrams are represented as shown below:

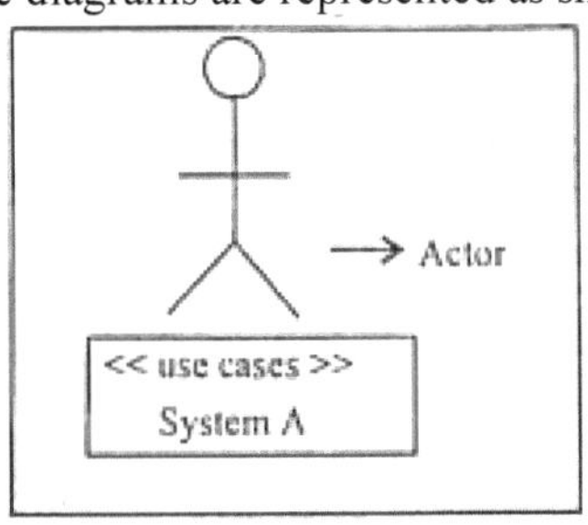

•Use cases are represented by ovals. Labels with ovals represent the functions of the system.
Representation of Use Case is shown:

•Actors are the users of a system. They represent who will access the functions of the system. An actor is shown who exercise the use cases.

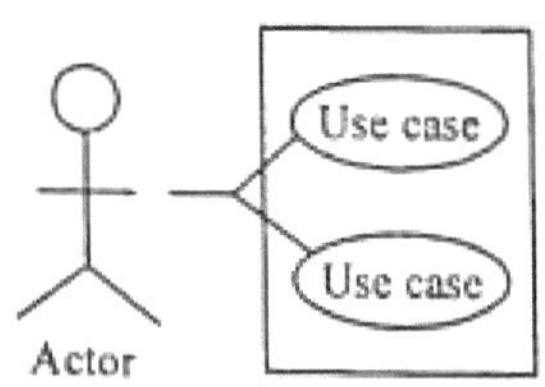

Relationship between an actor and a use case is illustrated with a signal line. Relationships between use cases are labeled either "uses" or "extends" "uses" indicates that one use case is needed by another in order to perform a task.

• Use case diagrams model the use case view of a system. This view supports the behavior of the system.
This represents the visible services that the system provides in context of its environment. Use case diagrams are applied in the following ways:

• Modelling the context of a system: It involves defining a system and asserting which actors lie outside the system and interact with it.

• Modelling the requirements of a system: It involves specifying what that system should do.

Example: Consider, to model behavior of a cellular phone we identify the elements that form the system. The actors are cellular network and user. And the use cases are making a call, sending message and capturing photos. The use case diagram Of cellular telephone is shown:

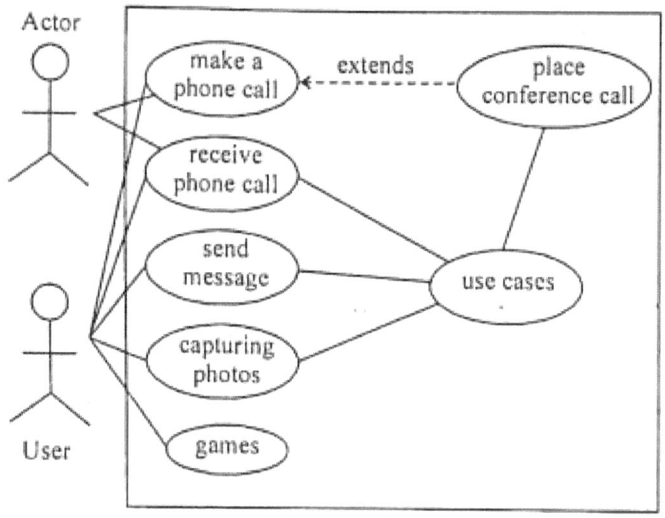

Q 13. Consider a student Information System as an Example. Explain the following UML diagrams in details, with the help of neat sketches. [R.T.U.2016, 2014]

(a) Use Case Diagram

(b) Class, Object Diagram

(c) Deployment diagram

(d) Sequence diagram

Ans 13:(a) Use Case Diagram:

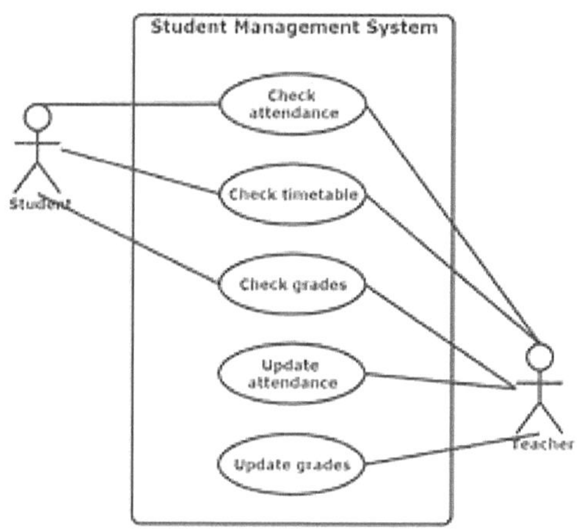

(b) Class, Object Diagram:

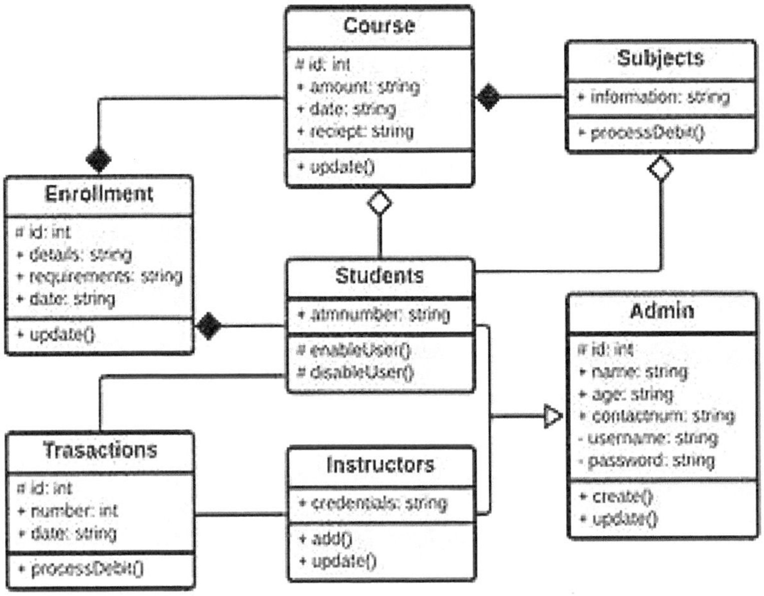

(c) Deployment Diagram:

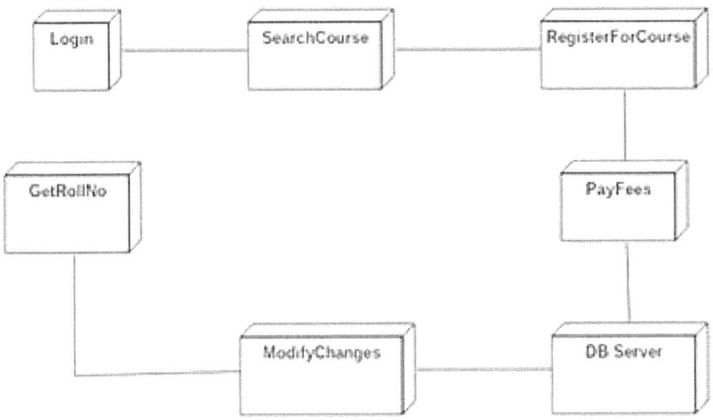

(d) Sequence diagram:

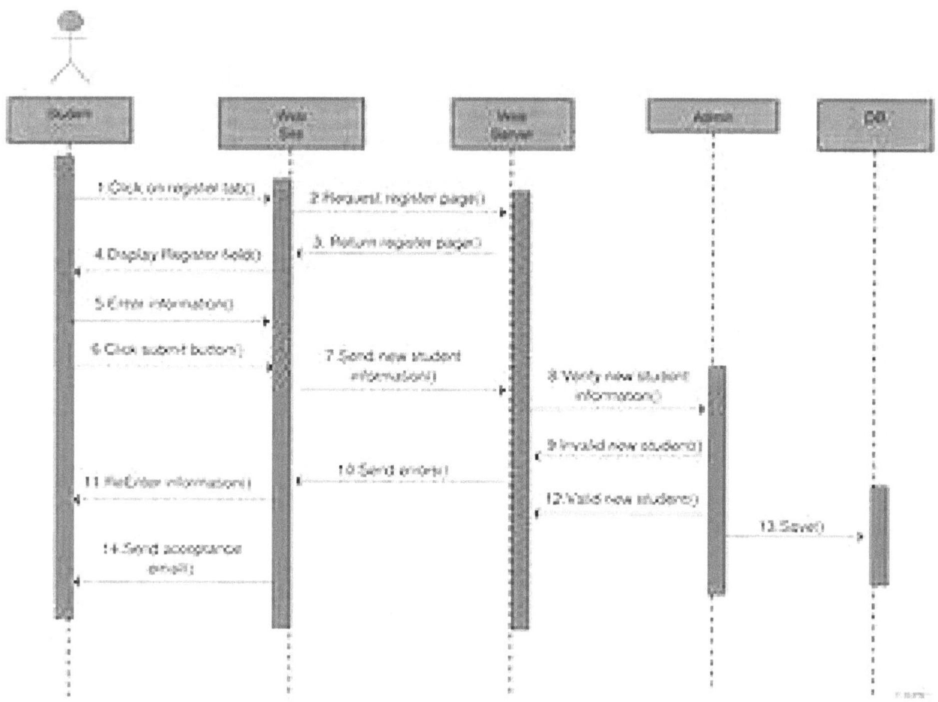

Q 14. List out the various activities that are encompassed by system design process under object-oriented design (OOD) and explain each one briefly. Explain the object modularization with example. [RTU2015]

Ans 14: In object-oriented design (OOD), the system design process encompasses various activities that focus on defining the architecture, structure, and relationships of the system's objects and components. Here are the key activities in OOD system design, along with brief explanations of each:

System Architecture Design:

This activity involves defining the high-level structure of the system, identifying the major components or subsystems, and their interconnections.

It establishes the overall framework that sets the foundation for the system's design.

Subsystem Design:

Subsystem design breaks down the system into smaller, more manageable components or subsystems, each responsible for specific functionality.

It includes defining the classes, interfaces, and relationships within each subsystem.

Class Design:

Class design focuses on designing individual classes, defining their attributes (data members) and methods (functions), and specifying their relationships with other classes.

It includes selecting appropriate attributes and methods for each class to achieve encapsulation and modularity.

Interface Design:

In OOD, interfaces represent contracts or blueprints for classes, defining the methods that must be implemented by classes that implement the interface.

Interface design specifies the methods and their signatures in the interfaces to ensure consistency and abstraction.

Object Relationships Design:

This activity involves defining relationships between objects and classes, such as associations, aggregations, compositions, and generalization/specialization (inheritance).

It determines how objects collaborate and interact with each other.

Collaboration and Interaction Design:

Collaboration and interaction design focuses on how objects interact with each other to fulfill use cases or scenarios.

It involves defining sequence diagrams, interaction diagrams, and message flows to depict object collaboration.

Data Management Design:

Data management design includes designing data structures, databases, and data access mechanisms for storing and retrieving information within the system.

It ensures that data is managed efficiently and in a structured manner.

Security and Access Control Design:

Security and access control design addresses how security features and access controls are implemented within the system to protect sensitive data and functionality.
It includes defining user roles, permissions, and encryption methods.

Error Handling and Exception Design:

This activity focuses on designing error handling and exception mechanisms to gracefully handle unexpected situations and errors.
It includes defining exception classes and handling strategies.

Testing and Verification Strategy Design:

In OOD, the design process also considers testing and verification strategies to ensure that the system's design is testable.
It includes defining test cases, unit testing, integration testing, and verification procedures.

Performance and Scalability Design:

Performance and scalability design addresses how the system will perform under various conditions and how it can be scaled to handle increased loads.
It includes optimization strategies and performance monitoring considerations.

Object Modularization with Example:

Object modularization is the process of organizing objects into modules or classes, promoting encapsulation and information hiding. Here's a simple example to illustrate object modularization:
Suppose you are designing a library management system. You can modularize the system by defining the following classes:

Book:

Attributes: Title, Author, ISBN, Genre, Availability
Methods: CheckOut(), CheckIn()

LibraryMember:

Attributes: MemberID, Name, Address, CheckedOutBooks
Methods: BorrowBook(), ReturnBook()

Library:

Attributes: BooksInCollection, Members, Librarian
Methods: AddBook(), RemoveBook(), RegisterMember(), RemoveMember()

Q 15. Write a short note on: [RTU2015, 2017]
(i) Unified modeling language (UML)
(ii) Object Oriented Analysis modelling

Ans 15: (i) **Unified Modeling Language (UML):** Unified Modeling Language, commonly known as UML, is a standardized visual language for modeling, designing, and documenting software systems. It provides a common notation and set of diagrams that enable software developers and stakeholders to communicate and understand various aspects of a system. UML is widely used in software engineering for its versatility and the clarity it brings to system design and analysis.
Key aspects of UML include:

Standardization: UML is an internationally recognized standard, ensuring that everyone involved in software development uses a common language and notation.

Visualization: UML uses diagrams to represent structural, behavioral, and functional aspects of a system, making it easier to grasp complex ideas.

Modeling: UML supports different levels of abstraction, allowing for high-level system overviews and detailed design specifications.

Adaptability: UML can be used in various software development methodologies, from traditional to agile.

Interoperability: UML models can be integrated with other tools and technologies, enhancing collaboration.

(ii) **Object-Oriented Analysis (OOA) Modeling:** Object-Oriented Analysis (OOA) is a phase in the software development process that focuses on understanding the problem domain, the system's requirements, and the conceptual model of the software system to be built. During this phase, OOA uses object-oriented modeling techniques to represent real-world entities, their relationships, and their interactions. Here's an overview of OOA modeling:

Object Modeling: OOA begins with the identification of objects, which are real-world entities or concepts relevant to the system. These objects are represented as classes in UML and have attributes and methods.

Relationship Modeling: OOA defines how objects interact with each other. This includes specifying relationships such as associations, aggregations, and generalizations in UML class diagrams.

Behavior Modeling: OOA models the dynamic aspects of the system by defining use cases, scenarios, and state machines. This helps capture how objects collaborate to achieve system functionality.

Functional Modeling: OOA identifies system functions and use cases, represented in UML as use case diagrams. It defines the functional requirements of the system and how external actors interact with it.

Data Modeling: OOA includes data modeling to describe how data is structured and organized within the system. This is typically represented using class diagrams.

Analysis of Requirements: During OOA, the analysis of user requirements is crucial. This phase helps transform high-level requirements into detailed models that can be used for system design.

Q 16. Explain object-oriented concept with an example. [RTU 2013]

Ans 16: Object-oriented programming (OOP) is a software development paradigm that organizes code into objects, which are instances of classes, and emphasizes the use of encapsulation, inheritance, and polymorphism to model real-world entities and their interactions. Here's an explanation of OOP concepts with an example:

Concept 1: Class

A class is a blueprint or template for creating objects. It defines the structure and behavior of objects. A class is a user-defined data type that can include attributes (properties) and methods (functions).

Concept 2: Object

An object is an instance of a class. It is a concrete realization of the class's blueprint and contains its own set of attribute values and can perform actions based on the methods defined in the class.

Concept 3: Encapsulation

Encapsulation is the concept of bundling data (attributes) and methods (functions) that operate on that data into a single unit (a class). It restricts access to certain components, allowing you to control how data is manipulated. Access to the internal data should be controlled through methods.

Concept 4: Inheritance

Inheritance is a mechanism that allows a new class (a subclass or derived class) to inherit properties and behaviors (attributes and methods) from an existing class (a superclass or base class). It promotes code reuse and establishes an "is-a" relationship between classes.

Concept 5: Polymorphism

Polymorphism means "many shapes" and allows objects of different classes to be treated as objects of a common superclass. It enables methods to be called on objects of various classes in a uniform way. Polymorphism can be achieved through method overriding and method overloading.

Previous Year Unsolved Questions

Q 1. The Computer Services Division of a University wants to design a software solution to automate its Complaints Management System. The system should be allowed to record all the complaints from the users/departments of the University and provide services on priority basis. It should also produce reports of daily listing of complaints (attended and unattended), pending, etc. Assumptions can be made, wherever necessary. accomplish the above mentioned tasks, perform the following: (i) Develop SRS for this system. [IGNOU, June, 2018]
(ii) Draw context-level DFD, 1st level and 2nd level DFDs.
(iii) Identify all the modules and their functionalities.
(iv) Design an ER diagram.
Q 2. Draw level-0, level-1 and level-2 DFDs for Grade Card Generation System. Make necessary assumptions. Mention the assumptions made. [IGNOU, December, 2015, 2017]
Q 3. Explain the following with examples: (i) Data Flow diagram 5 E-R diagram. [IGNOU, June, 2016]
Q 4. Draw level-0, level-1 and level-2 DFDs for an Online Railway Reservation system. [IGNOU, June, 2017] [Anna University 2022]
Q 5. Draw levels - 0, 1 and 2. DFD's for an Open 10 University Management system. Make necessary assumptions and list them all. [IGNOU, December, 2011]
Q 6. Write a detailed note on behavioral model. Also, give an example. [IGNOU, December, 2012]
Q 7. Write a sequence diagram for ATM withdrawal process. [VTU 2021]
Q 8. Explain the sequence model for the online stock broker system with a neat diagram. [VTU 2022]
Q 9. What is use case model? Write and explain the use case diagram for a vending machine. Write the guidelines for use case model. [VTU 2022]
Q 10. Draw a nest state diagram behavior for telephone line system. Write transitions with reference to state diagram behavior. [VTU 2022]
Q 11. Describe Generalization, specialization, inheritance concepts. [VTU 2022]
Q 12. What are links and associations? Write and explain UML notations for links and association. [VTU 2022]
Q 13. What is object orientation? Explain themes of object-oriented methodology. [VTU 2022]
Q 14. Describe the steps to be followed in Object Oriented development. [VTU 2022]

Miscellaneous Chapters

1. CASE Repository

In software engineering, a CASE (Computer-Aided Software Engineering) repository is a central database or storage system that is used to store and manage various artifacts and information related to the software development process. These artifacts include documents, source code, design specifications, test plans, and other elements of a software project. The CASE repository plays a crucial role in facilitating collaborative software development and maintaining the integrity of project information. Here are some key details about CASE repositories:

Artifact Storage: The primary function of a CASE repository is to store various artifacts created during the software development lifecycle. These artifacts can include requirements documents, design models, code modules, test plans, user manuals, and more.

Version Control: The CASE repository often includes version control features to track changes made to artifacts over time. This ensures that developers can access and retrieve previous versions if needed and helps in managing concurrent development by different team members.

Access Control: Access control mechanisms are implemented to regulate who can view, edit, or delete artifacts in the repository. This helps maintain security and protect sensitive project information.

Collaboration: CASE repositories promote collaboration among team members by providing a centralized location for sharing and updating project artifacts. Team members can work on different aspects of the project while having access to the latest versions of relevant documents and code.

Traceability: A CASE repository can support traceability, allowing project stakeholders to trace the relationships between different artifacts. For example, you can trace requirements to design elements, code modules to test cases, and so on.

Search and Retrieval: To enhance productivity, CASE repositories often include powerful search and retrieval capabilities, enabling team members to quickly find specific artifacts or information within the repository.

Integration with Tools: CASE repositories can be integrated with other software development tools like integrated development environments (IDEs), project management tools, and issue tracking systems to streamline the development process.

Backup and Recovery: Data stored in a CASE repository is critical to a project, so repositories typically implement robust backup and recovery mechanisms to ensure data integrity and availability.

Change Management: The repository can help manage changes to artifacts by providing change history and approval workflows. This is crucial for ensuring that only authorized changes are accepted into the project.

Reporting and Metrics: Some CASE repositories include reporting and metrics generation features, which allow project managers and stakeholders to track progress and make data-driven decisions.

Compliance and Auditing: In regulated industries, CASE repositories may include features for compliance and auditing purposes to ensure that the development process adheres to specific standards and regulations.

Security: Security features are crucial to protect sensitive project information. This includes user authentication, encryption, and access controls.

Popular CASE repository tools and platforms include IBM Rational ClearCase, Microsoft Visual SourceSafe, and more modern version control systems like Git with Git repositories, which can be considered a type of CASE repository for source code and related artifacts.

The use of CASE repositories has become increasingly important in modern software development, particularly in agile and distributed development environments where collaboration, version control, and traceability are critical to project success.

2. Software Review

In software engineering, a software review is a systematic examination of a software product, project, or process to assess its quality, identify issues, and make improvements. Software reviews are a fundamental part of the software development and maintenance life cycle and serve various purposes, including quality assurance, error detection, and knowledge sharing. Here are the key aspects of software reviews:

Objective: The primary objective of a software review is to evaluate a software product, project, or process to ensure it meets its specified requirements and is of high quality. Reviews aim to identify defects, inconsistencies, and potential improvements.

Types of Reviews: There are several types of software reviews, including:

Code Review: A detailed examination of source code to find coding errors, maintainability issues, and adherence to coding standards.

Design Review: An assessment of the software design, architecture, and system structure for correctness and efficiency.
Requirement Review: Evaluation of the software's requirements for completeness, consistency, and clarity.
Test Plan Review: A review of the test plans to ensure that testing procedures cover all aspects of the software.
Document Review: Examination of project documentation, such as user manuals, design documents, and technical specifications.
Peer Review: Collaborative reviews where team members or peers provide feedback to each other, often used in code and design reviews.
Participants: Software reviews involve various participants, including developers, testers, project managers, and other stakeholders. The goal is to have diverse perspectives to identify issues and make improvements.
Process: The review process typically follows a structured set of steps, which may include:
Planning: Defining the objectives, scope, and participants of the review.
Preparation: Reviewers study the software or documentation before the review meeting.
Meeting: A formal meeting where participants discuss findings and reach consensus on identified issues.
Follow-up: After the review meeting, action items are assigned to address the identified issues and make necessary improvements.
Benefits: Software reviews offer several benefits, such as:
Early defect detection: Identifying and fixing issues in the early stages of development is more cost-effective.
Knowledge sharing: Reviews help disseminate knowledge among team members and improve understanding of the project.
Quality assurance: Reviews contribute to the overall quality and reliability of the software.
Improved communication: They encourage effective communication among team members and stakeholders.
Challenges: Despite their advantages, software reviews can be time-consuming, and scheduling and conducting review meetings can sometimes be challenging. It's important to strike a balance between thorough reviews and project timelines.
Tools: Software review tools, such as code review tools and collaborative platforms like GitHub and GitLab, can facilitate and streamline the review process, especially for distributed and remote teams.
Continuous Improvement: Organizations often use the findings from software reviews to implement process improvements and best practices to prevent similar issues in future projects.

3. Software Reengineering

Software reengineering, also known as software reverse engineering or software renovation, is the process of reworking, restructuring, or enhancing existing software systems to improve their quality, maintainability, and functionality. It involves taking an existing software system and making significant changes to its structure, design, and sometimes even its implementation to address various issues, such as outdated technology, poor performance, and a lack of maintainability. The goal of software reengineering is to extend the useful life of existing software, reduce technical debt, and adapt it to evolving business needs. Here are some key aspects of software reengineering:
Motivations for Software Reengineering:
Technological Obsolescence: The software may be built on outdated technology or dependencies that are no longer supported.
Enhancing Functionality: Expanding or improving the functionality of the software to meet new business requirements.
Performance Improvement: Optimizing the software to enhance its speed and efficiency.
Maintainability: Enhancing the codebase to make it more understandable and easier to maintain.
Integration: Integrating the software with new systems, platforms, or services.
Regulatory Compliance: Ensuring the software complies with new industry or legal regulations.
Reengineering Phases:
Understanding the Existing System: The first phase involves analyzing and documenting the existing software system, understanding its architecture, components, and dependencies.
Assessment: Evaluating the current state of the software and identifying areas that require reengineering.
Planning: Developing a detailed plan for the reengineering effort, including defining goals, scope, resources, and timelines.
Restructuring and Refactoring: Making structural changes to the code, including modifying the architecture, improving code quality, and enhancing system design.
Reimplementation: In some cases, reengineering may involve rewriting or reimplementing parts of the software to modernize its technology stack.

Testing and Quality Assurance: Rigorous testing is essential to ensure that the reengineered software meets quality and performance standards.
Deployment: Deploying the reengineered software into the production environment and making it available for users.
Maintenance and Ongoing Improvement: Like any software project, the reengineered software requires ongoing maintenance and updates to stay relevant and effective.
Tools and Technologies: Software reengineering may involve various tools and technologies, including code analysis tools, reverse engineering tools, refactoring tools, and modernization frameworks. These tools help automate certain tasks and improve the efficiency of the reengineering process.
Challenges and Risks: Software reengineering can be complex and risky due to the potential for introducing new defects and challenges related to documentation gaps, changing requirements, and resource constraints. Thorough planning and careful execution are crucial to mitigate these challenges.
Cost-Benefit Analysis: Before undertaking a software reengineering project, organizations often conduct a cost-benefit analysis to assess whether the investment in reengineering is justified compared to building a new system from scratch.
Documentation: Reengineering efforts often emphasize improving or creating documentation for the existing software, which may have been lacking or outdated.

4. Cleanroom Software engineering

Cleanroom software engineering, also known as the Cleanroom methodology, is a rigorous software development approach focused on producing high-quality software with a strong emphasis on defect prevention and formal methods. It was developed in the 1980s by Harlan Mills and his colleagues at IBM. Cleanroom software engineering aims to create reliable and defect-free software by using a combination of formal methods, statistical quality control, and disciplined development techniques. Here are the key principles and practices of Cleanroom software engineering:
Statistical Quality Control: Cleanroom places a heavy emphasis on statistical quality control techniques to monitor and improve the software development process continuously. It involves collecting data on defects and defects' origins and using this data to identify and rectify issues systematically.
Certification of Correctness: Cleanroom advocates using formal methods, such as formal specification languages and formal proof techniques, to verify and validate software correctness. The goal is to mathematically prove the correctness of software components to the highest extent possible.
Incremental Development: Cleanroom promotes an incremental and stepwise development process where software components are developed and tested independently before integration. Each component is considered correct before moving on to the next one.
Box Structure: Cleanroom defines a box structure for the software, where each box represents a component or module. The structure specifies input and output relations for each box, and these relations are validated using formal methods.
Black-Box and Clear-Box Testing: Cleanroom uses black-box testing to validate the external functionality and clear-box testing to ensure the internal correctness of software components. Clear-box testing, also known as glass-box testing, involves testing components based on their logical structure and design.
Cleanroom Process Model: Cleanroom follows a specific process model that includes stages like specification, design, code, correctness verification, and statistical testing. These stages are performed in a structured, disciplined manner.
Use of Cleanroom Tools: Cleanroom relies on specialized tools and techniques to facilitate formal methods, including the development of mathematical specifications and correctness proofs.
Zero Defects Philosophy: Cleanroom aims for zero defects, striving for perfection in software development. It is based on the belief that reducing and eventually eliminating defects at every stage of development will result in high-quality software.
Cleanroom Teams: Cleanroom projects are typically organized into small, highly skilled teams that work collaboratively and follow defined processes and methodologies.
Documentation: Comprehensive documentation is essential in Cleanroom, including mathematical specifications, correctness proofs, and statistical quality control records.
Independent Verification: Cleanroom promotes independent verification and validation of software components to ensure that each component meets its requirements.
Iterative Improvement: The Cleanroom process emphasizes iterative improvement and learning from data and experience to continually enhance the quality of software development.
Cleanroom software engineering is known for its discipline and rigorous approach. It is most often used in critical and safety-critical systems, where software reliability and correctness are of paramount importance, such as aerospace,

medical devices, and defense applications. While Cleanroom is highly effective in producing high-quality software, it can be resource-intensive and may not be suitable for all types of projects.

5. Version Control

Version control, also known as source code management or revision control, is a fundamental aspect of software engineering. It is a system that tracks changes to source code and other files over time, allowing developers to collaborate, manage multiple versions of a project, and maintain a history of changes. Here are the key concepts and components of version control in software engineering:

Repository: A version control system (VCS) operates with a central repository that serves as a centralized location where all project files and their various versions are stored. Developers can commit changes to the repository, and it serves as the single source of truth.

Version: In a version control system, a "version" represents a snapshot of the project at a particular point in time. It includes all the files and their content at that moment. Developers can refer to specific versions to track changes and compare different states of the project.

Commit: A "commit" is an action that records changes made to the project and stores them in the repository. Each commit is accompanied by a message describing the purpose of the changes, providing context for other team members.

Branching: Version control systems allow developers to create branches, which are separate lines of development. Branches are used for tasks like feature development, bug fixing, or experimentation. Branches can be merged back into the main or parent branch when the work is complete.

Merging: Merging is the process of integrating changes from one branch, often a feature or bug-fix branch, into another branch, usually the main development branch. This ensures that new code becomes part of the main project.

Conflict Resolution: When multiple developers make conflicting changes to the same file or section of code, version control systems provide tools to resolve these conflicts. This typically involves manual intervention to decide which changes to keep.

History and Log: A VCS maintains a history or log of all changes made to the project. This history includes details about who made the changes, when they were made, and the associated commit messages. It helps in tracking changes, debugging, and understanding the evolution of the project.

Distributed Version Control: Some version control systems, like Git, are distributed, which means that each developer has a full copy of the repository, including the entire history. This allows developers to work offline and collaborate more flexibly.

Collaboration: Version control enables multiple developers to work on the same project simultaneously without overwriting each other's work. It provides mechanisms for sharing and synchronizing changes.

Tagging and Release Management: Version control systems allow for tagging specific commits to mark important milestones, releases, or versions of the software. Tags serve as reference points for stable and well-tested releases.

Rollback and Recovery: Version control systems enable the easy rollback of the project to a previous version in case of errors or issues. This rollback and recovery feature is crucial for maintaining project stability.

Popular version control systems include Git, Subversion (SVN), Mercurial, and Perforce. Git, in particular, is widely used in modern software development due to its speed, distributed nature, and strong branching and merging capabilities. It has become the de facto standard for version control in open-source and commercial projects.

Version control is a foundational tool in software engineering, helping teams manage code changes, collaborate effectively, and maintain the integrity of their projects over time. It is an essential component of modern software development workflows.

6. Auditing and reporting.

Auditing and reporting in software engineering are crucial processes that help ensure the quality, compliance, and effectiveness of software projects. Auditing involves the systematic examination of software processes, documentation, and code to identify issues, while reporting is the communication of findings and insights. Here's a closer look at these processes:

Auditing in Software Engineering:

Code Review: Code audits involve the examination of source code to identify defects, adherence to coding standards, and overall code quality. These reviews are typically performed by peers or senior developers.

Security Audits: Security audits focus on identifying vulnerabilities and security issues in software. This includes checking for common security flaws, such as SQL injection, cross-site scripting, and authentication issues.

Compliance Audits: In regulated industries, software may need to comply with specific standards and regulations, like ISO 9001, HIPAA, or PCI DSS. Compliance audits ensure that the software meets these requirements.

Documentation Audits: Auditing documentation, such as requirements, design specifications, and test plans, helps ensure that project information is accurate, complete, and up-to-date.

Performance Audits: These audits assess the performance of the software, including areas like response times, resource utilization, and scalability.

Configuration Audits: Auditing configuration files and settings is important to ensure that the software is correctly configured and can run in various environments.

Process Audits: Auditing software development processes, such as agile methodologies or DevOps practices, ensures that teams follow defined processes and best practices.

Reporting in Software Engineering:

Audit Reports: After conducting audits, reports are generated to document findings, including identified issues, their severity, and recommendations for resolution. These reports are typically shared with stakeholders and team members.

Bug Reports: When defects are found during code reviews or testing, bug reports are created to provide details on the issue, its impact, and steps to reproduce it. Bug reports are essential for tracking and prioritizing fixes.

Compliance Reports: In regulated industries, compliance reports detail how the software aligns with specific standards or regulations. These reports may be required for certification and audits.

Performance Reports: Performance testing generates reports on the software's performance metrics, helping to identify bottlenecks and areas that require optimization.

Progress Reports: Regular progress reports are shared with stakeholders to update them on the status of the project, including completed tasks, upcoming milestones, and any potential risks.

Release Notes: When a new version of the software is released, release notes provide information on new features, enhancements, bug fixes, and any known issues.

Change Logs: Change logs document all changes made to the software over time, including new features, improvements, and bug fixes. They are useful for tracking the software's evolution.

Traceability Reports: Traceability matrices and reports help establish links between requirements, design, code, and test cases, ensuring that all requirements are adequately covered and validated.

Reporting in software engineering is critical for transparency, decision-making, and accountability. It allows project stakeholders to understand the state of the project, make informed decisions, and track progress. Effective reporting is often facilitated by the use of project management and issue tracking tools, which can automate the generation and distribution of reports.

Previous Years Solved Questions

Q 1. Why is accuracy important in data dictionary? [R.T.U.2018]

Ans 1: Accuracy in the context of a data dictionary is crucial in software engineering for several reasons:

Data Consistency: Accuracy ensures that data elements are defined and described correctly. Inaccurate or inconsistent data definitions can lead to confusion and errors in data usage. When data elements are consistently defined and named, it becomes easier for developers and data users to understand and use them correctly.

Interoperability: Accurate data definitions are essential for interoperability, especially in software systems that need to exchange data with other systems. When data is accurately defined, it is more likely to be interpreted correctly by external systems or components.

Quality Assurance: Data accuracy is a fundamental aspect of quality assurance. Inaccurate data definitions can lead to defects and issues in software applications. Ensuring data accuracy through a data dictionary helps identify and prevent potential problems early in the development process.

Documentation: Accurate data definitions serve as valuable documentation for the software project. They provide a clear and consistent reference for developers, analysts, and other stakeholders. This documentation can be especially helpful during software maintenance or when new team members join the project.

Data Integrity: Data integrity is maintained when data is accurate, complete, and consistent. Inaccurate data definitions can compromise data integrity, leading to incorrect results or actions based on the data.

Data Understanding: Accurate data definitions help developers and data users understand the meaning and purpose of each data element. This understanding is essential for designing, implementing, and maintaining software systems that rely on the data.

Data Quality: Data quality is a critical aspect of software applications. Inaccurate data definitions can result in data quality issues, such as duplicate entries, missing values, or incorrect data transformations. Accurate data definitions support data quality initiatives.

Data Management: Accurate data definitions are fundamental to effective data management. They help in data classification, data governance, and data stewardship efforts, ensuring that data is handled appropriately and securely.

Change Management: In software engineering, systems evolve over time. Accurate data definitions make it easier to manage changes, such as updates to data structures, migrations, or data model enhancements, while preserving data accuracy.

Regulatory Compliance: In some industries, regulatory compliance is essential. Accurate data definitions help ensure that data handling and reporting meet regulatory requirements, reducing the risk of non-compliance.

Efficiency: Accurate data definitions contribute to the efficiency of software development and maintenance processes. When developers have clear and precise data definitions, they can work more efficiently and with fewer errors.

Q 2. Write short note on data dictionary. [R.T.U.2017, 2016, 2012]

Ans 2: A data dictionary, in the context of software engineering, is a centralized repository of metadata and information about the data structures and elements used in a software system. It serves as a reference guide for understanding and managing data within a software project. Here are key points to consider about data dictionaries in software engineering:

Data Description: Data dictionaries provide detailed descriptions of data elements, including their names, data types, length, format, and any validation rules. This information helps software engineers understand the structure and semantics of the data used in a system.

Attributes: For each data element, the data dictionary may include attributes like data source, author, creation date, modification history, and relationships with other data elements. These attributes offer insights into the data's origin and evolution.

Data Relationships: Data dictionaries often document the relationships between data elements, showing how data is related and interconnected within the software system. This is especially valuable when working on database design and data modeling.

Data Usage: The dictionary may describe how data elements are used within the software application, including where the data is input, processed, and output. Understanding data usage is crucial for designing software features and functionality.

Consistency and Standardization: Data dictionaries promote data consistency and standardization across a software project. They help ensure that data is named and structured uniformly, which simplifies data management and maintenance.

Impact Analysis: When changes or updates to data elements are needed, the data dictionary can be used to perform impact analysis, determining how changes might affect other parts of the software system.

Documentation: Data dictionaries serve as valuable documentation for developers, analysts, and database administrators. They provide a comprehensive reference for understanding the data used in a software project.

Compliance and Regulations: In software domains subject to regulatory requirements, such as healthcare or finance, data dictionaries help ensure that data is managed in accordance with industry standards and legal regulations.

Data Dictionary Tools: Software engineering teams often use specialized data dictionary tools or features within integrated development environments (IDEs) and database management systems to create and manage data dictionaries.

Data Quality: Data dictionaries can play a role in data quality management by providing information about data constraints, validation rules, and data lineage, helping to maintain data integrity.

Q 3. What do you understand by data dictionary? Where and how is used?

Ans 3: A data dictionary is a centralized repository of metadata that provides detailed information about data elements or attributes used in a database, information system, or software application. It serves as a comprehensive reference for the data structures, definitions, and characteristics used in a particular context. Data dictionaries are commonly used in database management, software engineering, and data modeling to document, manage, and understand data-related components. Here's what a data dictionary typically includes and how it is used:

Components of a Data Dictionary:

Data Element Name: The name or identifier for the data element, such as "CustomerID" or "Product Description."

Description: A clear and concise description of the data element, explaining its meaning and purpose.

Data Type: The type of data that the element can store, such as text, numeric, date, or Boolean.

Size/Length: The maximum allowable length or size of the data element.

Validation Rules: Any rules or constraints that apply to the data, like minimum and maximum values or allowed characters.

Example Values: Sample data values to illustrate what the data element contains.

Source: Information about the source or origin of the data, including data systems or external sources.

Dependencies: Indications of how the data element is related to other elements in the database or system.

Usage and Business Rules: Information about how the data element is used in the business processes and any specific rules or requirements associated with it.

Uses of a Data Dictionary:

Data Modeling: Data dictionaries are integral to data modeling, helping modelers define entities, attributes, and relationships in a structured and standardized manner.

Database Design: In the context of database management, data dictionaries facilitate the design and creation of database tables and fields by providing a detailed specification of the data to be stored.

Documentation: Data dictionaries serve as valuable documentation for data structures and definitions, making it easier for developers, analysts, and other stakeholders to understand and work with the data.

Data Integration: When integrating data from multiple sources, a data dictionary helps in mapping and transforming data elements to ensure they align correctly.

Data Governance: Data dictionaries are essential for data governance initiatives, supporting data classification, data stewardship, and data quality efforts.

Data Analysis: Data analysts and business users often reference data dictionaries to gain insights into the meaning and usage of data elements.

Compliance: Data dictionaries are crucial for ensuring that data handling and reporting practices meet regulatory requirements and compliance standards.

Data Quality Management: In data quality management, data dictionaries aid in defining data quality rules and standards.

Software Development: Data dictionaries can be used in software engineering to specify the attributes and data structures used in software applications.

Maintenance and Change Management: When modifying or maintaining a database or system, data dictionaries help in managing changes and ensuring data consistency.

Previous Years Unsolved Questions

Q 1. Explain the significance of CASE Repository. What are its contents? Comment on each one of them. Also, briefly describe the two primary segments of it, [IGNOU, June,2018]
(i) Information repository, and
(ii) Data dictionary.
Q 2. Define "Software Review". What are the various types of Software Review? Explain them. [IGNOU, December, 2015]
Q 3. What is meant by "Software Reengineering"? Explain the phases of Software Reengineering Life Cycle. [IGNOU, December, 2012, 2013, 2015, 2017]
Q 4. What are CASE Tools? List the features of any two CASE Tools. [IGNOU, December, 2015] [Kota University 2021]
Q 5. What is a software review Explain. [IGNOU, December, 2016]
Q 6. Define Cleanroom software engineering. What is its significance? Discuss the underlying principles of cleanroom-based software development. [IGNOU June 2017, December 2017, 20111]
Q 7. Explain the factors affecting the task set for a project. [IGNOU, December,2017]
Q 8. Describe the challenges for Component Based Software Engineering (CBSE). [IGNOU, December,2017]
Q 9. Define Version Control. With the help of an evolutionary graph, discuss the whole process of version control. [IGNOU, December,2017]
Q 10. Write a detailed note on auditing and reporting. [IGNOU, December,2017]
Q 11. Explain the step-by-step evolutionary view 10 of the s/w Reengineering life-cycle. [IGNOU, December,2011]
Q 12. What do you mean by data dictionary? [Anna University 2018]
Q 13. Describe architecture of CASE environment. [MCU 2019]
Q 14. Differentiate between [VTU 2021]
i) CBSE for Reduce
ii) CBSE with Reuse

Viva Voce Questions

Question 1: What is Software Engineering?
Answer: Software Engineering is the application of engineering principles to software development in a systematic method, involving the design, development, maintenance, testing, and evaluation of software.
Question 2: What are the key activities involved in Requirements Analysis and Specification?
Answer: Requirements analysis involves gathering requirements through stakeholder interviews, use cases, or user stories, and specification involves documenting these requirements in a detailed, systematic, and comprehensive manner.
Question 3: Explain the significance of software metrics.
Answer: Software metrics are important for measuring various aspects of software development, including code quality, project progress, team productivity, and to help in decision-making processes regarding project management.
Question 4: What is the Waterfall Model in software development?
Answer: The Waterfall Model is a linear sequential development approach, where progress flows through distinct phases such as conception, initiation, analysis, design, construction, testing, deployment, and maintenance.
Question 5: How does Agile Software Development differ from traditional models?
Answer: Agile software development emphasizes iterative and incremental development, where requirements and solutions evolve through collaboration between self-organizing cross-functional teams, contrasting with the more rigid and linear approaches of traditional models.
Question 6: Describe the role of a software architect in the design phase.
Answer: A software architect plays a critical role in the design phase by defining the structure of the system, choosing appropriate design patterns, and ensuring that the system will be robust, scalable, and maintainable.
Question 7: What are the principles of good software design?
Answer: Good software design should adhere to principles such as modularity, encapsulation, abstraction, separation of concerns, and should be robust, maintainable, and scalable.
Question 8: How do design patterns facilitate software development?
Answer: Design patterns provide standardized solutions to common problems in software design. They facilitate development by providing proven techniques for solving issues, which can be repeatedly applied to improve the efficiency and reliability of software applications.
Question 9: What is the purpose of Software Project Management?
Answer: The purpose of software project management is to ensure that software projects are completed on time, within budget, and meet customer requirements, through proper planning, execution, monitoring, and control of the software development process.
Question 10: Explain the importance of testing in software development.
Answer: Testing is crucial to ensure that the software meets its requirements, is free of defects, and performs as expected under specific conditions, thereby ensuring the quality and reliability of the product.
Question 11: What is software verification and validation?
Answer: Software verification checks whether the software meets specified design requirements, while validation checks whether the software meets the actual needs of the stakeholders.
Question 12: What is UML and its significance in software development?
Answer: Unified Modeling Language (UML) is a standardized modeling language used to visualize, specify, construct, and document the artifacts of a software system. UML helps in understanding the system and serves as a blueprint for the construction phase.
Question 13: What challenges do software engineers face when conducting requirement analysis?
Answer: Challenges include understanding user needs accurately, dealing with changing requirements, and ensuring clear communication between stakeholders and developers.
Question 14: What methodologies are used for measuring software quality?
Answer: Methodologies like ISO/IEC 25010, which defines a set of quality attributes, or using software metrics such as cyclomatic complexity, lines of code, and function points are common practices.
Question 15: How do Agile methodologies address changes during a software project?
Answer: Agile methodologies like Scrum or Kanban welcome changing requirements, even late in development, and employ iterative cycles (sprints) that allow for regular adjustment of the product to better fit customer needs and market demands.
Question 16: What is modular design and why is it important?

Answer: Modular design divides a system into separate components (modules) that can be independently created, modified, replaced, or exchanged. It's important because it enhances flexibility, maintainability, and scalability.

Question 17: Discuss the impact of poor software design.

Answer: Poor software design can lead to products that are difficult to maintain and extend, may cause security risks, and can result in higher costs due to the need for more frequent modifications and fixes.

Question 18: What are some common software development models?

Answer: Common models include Waterfall, Agile, V-Model, Spiral, and Iterative development models, each with its own approach to managing software development processes.

Question 19: How can software testing be automated?

Answer: Software testing can be automated using tools that execute tests without manual intervention, often used for regression testing, performance testing, and load testing.

Question 20: How do software engineers ensure that software is accessible and inclusive?

Answer: Engineers must design software with accessibility features such as screen readers compatibility, keyboard navigation, and clear visual contrast to ensure it is usable by people with a wide range of physical abilities.

YouTube Link for Viva Voce Questions:

Link: https://www.youtube.com/playlist?list=PLzlh_31VWEFrqpzLZ8DxHN9VtpC6p6GcT

QR Code:

Additional Resources

Deep Learning Whole Book Videos Playlist-
Link: https://www.youtube.com/playlist?list=PLzlh_31VWEFrBi9sg2-Z4nlhVzPDGYQ4D
QR Code:

Chapter 1 Video Playlist Link:
Link: https://www.youtube.com/playlist?list=PLzlh_31VWEFrDf4zXXgAioMA65U29k8HO
QR Code:

Chapter 2 Video Playlist Link:
Link: https://www.youtube.com/playlist?list=PLzlh_31VWEFrDf4zXXgAioMA65U29k8HO
QR Code:

Chapter 3 Video Playlist Link:
Link: https://www.youtube.com/playlist?list=PLzlh_31VWEFq6abfB2vbz8ywNTiJHYlT-
QR Code:

Chapter 4 Video Playlist Link:
Link: https://www.youtube.com/playlist?list=PLzlh_31VWEFqbzHlzjwusOUsKqmd--N_y
QR Code:

Chapter 5 Video Playlist Link:
Link: https://www.youtube.com/playlist?list=PLzlh_31VWEFrWA5FERgUE8ep4A7EozqHZ

QR Code:

Chapter 6 Video Playlist Link:
Link: https://www.youtube.com/playlist?list=PLzlh_31VWEFom6wCTWdQCnZPkydwJ2q40
QR Code:

Chapter 7 Video Playlist Link:
Link: https://www.youtube.com/playlist?list=PLzlh_31VWEFoXz4gGbaKXut7wXzat2rEU
QR Code:

Chapter 8 Video Playlist Link:
Link: https://www.youtube.com/playlist?list=PLzlh_31VWEFriJeCZcFzN9UH8yi15QlPt
QR Code:

Chapter 9 Video Playlist Link:
Link: https://www.youtube.com/playlist?list=PLzlh_31VWEFow9HYgM3oguN1hUEq3UkC4
QR Code:

Chapter 10 Video Playlist Link:
Link: https://www.youtube.com/playlist?list=PLzlh_31VWEFr0zXl2bGwqt2jwSMFGMzDD
QR Code:

Chapter 11 Video Playlist Link:
Link: https://www.youtube.com/playlist?list=PLzlh_31VWEFqX1uizMngXNCbNQNaSZZFV
QR Code:

Chapter 12 Video Playlist Link:
Link: https://www.youtube.com/playlist?list=PLzlh_31VWEFre6AlDgvKDNNhMOL1bow0k
QR Code: